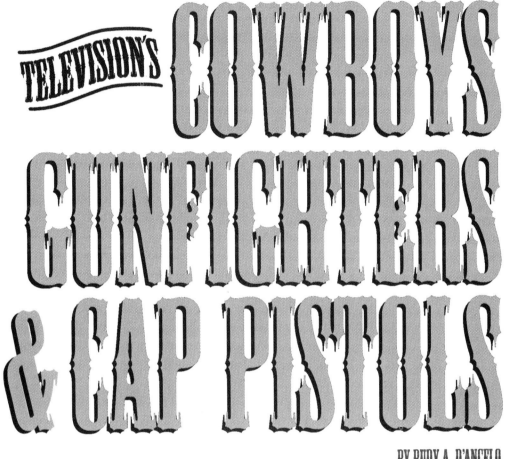

TELEVISION'S COWBOYS GUNFIGHTERS & CAP PISTOLS

BY RUDY A. D'ANGELO

D1560548

ANTIQUE TRADER BOOKS

A DIVISION OF LANDMARK SPECIALTY PUBLICATIONS

NORFOLK, VIRGINIA

September 1951 through September 1960
New Britain Avenue, Webster Street, Queen Street
New Park Avenue, and Broad Street,
Hartford, Connecticut, U.S.A.

Bang! Bang! Bang! Bang ! Bang!
Bang! Bang! Bang! Bang ! Bang!

". . .I tell you, Edna, I've had it with those boys and those
blasted cap guns!
I've had it, I tell you. . .I'm going to. . ."
Who is it now, Irwin? Calm down, they're only kids.
Who is it now?"
"I'll tell you who, it's those damn Italian boys, that's who!"
They can barely speak English, but they can sure blast
away with those damn guns!"
I've had it! Come here, you little bastards,
I'll break those cap guns over your heads!. . ."

Bang! Bang! Bang! Bang! Bang!
Bang! Bang! Bang! Bang! Bang!

Rudy: "Did we plug old man Carleton?"
Louy: "Yeah, I think so, I'm out of caps!"
Rudy: "Me too, let's reload!"
Louy: "Right, just in case!"

Old man Carleton was a cranky neighbor in Hartford in the mid-1950s. I'm willing to bet
he'd give anything to have those damn "Italian boys" shooting cap guns in his back yard today.
Some of the streets where we grew up are today dominated by gangs that sell and shoot
drugs—the scourge of America—and fire real guns at each other in drive-by shootings that
often kill young and innocent people . . . .

****

Copyright 1999 by Rudy A. D'Angelo
    All photos not credited are from the author's collection.
    All rights reserved. No part of this publication may be reproduced, stored in a retrieval system, or
transmitted in any form or by any means, electronic, mechanical, photocopying, recording, or otherwise, without
prior permission in writing from the publisher.
    Trademarks and copyright of products listed in this book are the sole property of their respective
trademark and copyright owners. Copyrights for items depicted in photographs and illustrations are reserved by
their respective owners, and the items are depicted here for the sole purpose of identification. The content of this
book is the work of the author, and is not authorized, approved, or endorsed by any manufacturer, licensee, or
trademark or copyright owner listed herein. This book is published without warranty, solely for the educational
and informational benefit of the reader. None of the information, advice, or pricing data presented is guaranteed in
any way.

ISBN: 0-930625-83-8
Library-of-Congress Catalog Card Number: 98-89185

Editor: Tony Lillis   Copy Editor: Sandra Holcombe
Graphic Designer: Cynthia Dooley   Editorial Assistant: Wendy Chia-Klesch
Art Director: Chris Decker

Printed in the United States of America

To order additional copies of this book, or to obtain a catalog, please contact:

Antique Trader Books P.O. Box 1050 Dubuque, Iowa 52004
1-800-334-7165
www.collect.com

CONTENTS

CAST OF CHARACTERS

DEDICATION

This book of happy memories from my youth is dedicated to, and in loving memory of, my younger brother.

LOU E. D'ANGELO
1946-1994

We always rode together; across the continents, up the hills and down the valleys; We fought off the Indians, outgunned the corrupt sheriff, got the girls and treated our horses right; We lived by the Code of humanity, love and compassion; We took care of Mom and Dad, protected our cowgirl sisters and gave a sense of family pride to our children, using the by-gone days of our youth as a guide. You built the old Homestead with your bare hands; We ate grub and drank the java together. We talked way into the night, with the full moon shining, as we nodded off to sleep. We laughed and cried together, as we shared life's joys and sorrows, triumphs and tragedies; We planned our next adventure together, as always. Then one warm, dark night, the Lord called— and you rode off, leaving me to ride the range—alone. You were the best sidekick any cowpoke could ever ask for. I miss you terribly, pardner. Until we can ride the happy trails of brotherly love again, I ask you to give me some cover from above.

Your loving big brother,
Rudy

FOREWORD

"Return with us now to those thrilling days of yesteryear..."

Those among us who have a smidgen of Buckaroo blood in our veins, vividly remember all those thrilling episodes during the early days of television westerns. Probably everyone of us can recite verbatim the opening epilogues of each show. Our ethics were definitely impacted by Hoppy, Roy, Gene, The Lone Ranger, Dale Evans, The Rifleman, Wild Bill Hickok, and countless others. The moral fibers that were woven into each story witnessed good defeating evil, fist fights and lassos rather than guns, peacekeeping versus violence, and a strong emphasis on religion, family values, friends, patriotism, and ethics. These western characters were not just childhood heroes. They greatly influenced our adulthood as role models with strict codes of ethics and morals.

Authoritative and accurate books dictate an uncompromising love of the subject, untold research energy, and the ability to persevere despite the lack of adequate historical records. Any book on collectible toys is especially trying due to the minimum amount of existing material. Only someone who has experienced the rewards and constant failures inherent with collectible research can fully appreciate the efforts of Rudy D'Angelo. This book is a legacy of love that will add to the appeal, significance, and respect of western characters, toy guns, holsters, and related artifacts.

Rudy's investigative background ensures that no stone was left unturned in his quest to authenticate factual information on each show, its actors, the characters, and the related items we presently own as curators. His photographic skills and diligent attention to detail add immeasurably to this important book. You will be captivated by each section of this book, just as you were by the original thrilling stories. Each infinitesimal tidbit of research will most assuredly recall less stressful childhood memories and stir your imagination once again as you ride the imaginary range. As you recall each of these western characters, I believe your heart will beat nearly as fast as the original thundering hoofbeats!

May America's love affair with western heroes and nostalgia never diminish. Thanks for the memories, Rudy.

JIM SCHLEYER
Author, historian, and recognized expert
of western toy guns and related artifacts.
Burke, Virginia

PREFACE

When I first dreamed of doing such a book, my aim was to walk down the memory lane of TV and movie western heroes that were so popular to our generation, the baby boomers, and weave into these popular shows the cap pistols that were introduced and then mushroomed into what we call the "character guns" so sought after today.

Most of us started at least with the guns we all call "generic" these days. We may have had a Kilgore Mustang, or the Nichols Stallion, maybe the simple Hubley Cowboy, or the reliable Hubley Texan, even a Schmidt Buck 'n Bronc. But the guns that we remember most are those with the name of the western character, the western show, even if it was a generic title that became a popular TV western show—male, female, horse or man's best friend. I have talked to many people who share this wonderful hobby with me for hours on end, and we can all recall, more than any other gun, those that had character names, such as Roy Rogers, Gene Autry, Hopalong Cassidy, The Lone Ranger, Paladin, Wyatt Earp, Bonanza and so many other great TV western characters that made us kids cast members of the show—no matter what company manufactured the gun.

There are hundreds of cap guns and holster sets out there—all sizes, shapes, colors, materials, and designs. Rifles, shotguns, hats, spurs, even rubber knives and a variety of western collectibles that carried the character's name. Therefore, for the collector as well as the historian, afficionados of the TV and movie westerns, would-be bandits and fearless lawmen, it is my intention to present these western characters blended in with these fabulous cap guns and holster sets.

Remember what happened the minute we strapped them on, loaded the bullet clips, tied down the leg thongs, and slapped leather? Why, we became Matt Dillon, Bat Masterson, or Wild Bill Hickok! And those cute little pig-tailed cowgirls on the block became Dale Evans or Annie Oakley! Good guy or bad guy, the toy gun companies capitalized on the popular TV western shows. Just imagine that even now, more than 35 years after the TV western frontier has just about faded away, the romantic gunfighter, the fearless lawman, the trusty sidekick, and the faithful Indian are still as sharp and clear in my mind as they were when I sat glued to my TV set with my guns strapped on! It really didn't matter whether you lived on the West Coast or the East Coast. For that half hour or hour, even mom and dad joined you to watch that favorite western.

And we learned about honor and courage. Loyalty and glory. Modesty and faithfulness. We learned right from wrong because the good guy always won in the end. Our imaginations were enough—we didn't really need to see blood gushing from horrific wounds, a body count that read like a grocery bill, or foul language in front of the ladies. Call it "hokey" or "corny" but in those wonderful days when America was plenty more gentle, the men tipped their hats, we always said grace at meals, never missed a parade, and we held our hands over our hearts when "Old Glory" came by. Our dads fought in the "the big war" and mom greeted us with cookies and milk when we got home from school.

How times have changed! I would have never dreamed of bringing a cap gun to school while today, youngsters bringing real guns and using them in school is all too common a tragedy. But let's leave the sadness aside for a moment and take a nostalgic ride through the 1950s and early 1960s, the "golden age" of TV westerns full of colorful characters that remain in our memory, complete with the cap pistols and holsters that made it "real" for all of us that grew up in those wonderful times. TV western shows of the late 1950s became such a phenomenon that at the peak of 1958, a weekly total of 31 new western shows kept us kids at home, with the family, and out of trouble as we watched them ride in and out of our lives before we "hit the hay" dreaming of our heros!

What wonderful times! What happened? I've asked myself this question a zillion times. President Kennedy, of course, launched the "space frontier" during his administration and sadly, the "old frontier" began to fade out. By 1978, the 31 western shows of the 1958 season was down to one TV western, *How The West Was Won.* There had been some spectacular TV westerns that surpassed all critic expectations, such as *Gunsmoke, Bonanza, and Death Valley Days.* Of course, the old reliables such as *Hopalong Cassidy, Roy Rogers* and *Gene Autry* maintained cult status.

But for the most part, the television became what is rightfully referred to as "the boob tube" today— with all sorts of mindless comedies, one-parent situations, and bratty kids who relish challenging authority of adults, including parents and teachers. Our nation's obsession for gun control and its feeble attempts to stem violence turned to children's toys, and the cap guns were the first to go. The "proliferation" of guns—and taking aim at the very toys we grew up with instead of focusing on the disintegration of the family unit—was the scapegoat for all the social ills. Even the old rhetoric, "poverty" was blamed. Yet, all of us kids from the early 1950s were "poor" by today's standards—just look at any of your old childhood photos! Where in our day, it was so shameful to go to school with ripped or patched trousers, today's "poor" kids actually pay a fortune for ripped jeans!

In the past, cap gun manufacturers such as Nichols and Hubley actually went out of their way to produce a cap pistol that looked real, felt real in your hands, and even sounded real! The cap pistols produced after the 1970s and 1980s swung the pendulum the opposite way—they are a combination of cheap, ugly, multi-colored plastic that make us old-timers shake our heads and cringe when compared with what we had the joy of playing with. Child psychiatrists, and the standard psychobabble added fuel to the fire, and convinced our sisters and daughters that no self-respecting mother would give her son or daughter a gun to play with! Why, you would be sending a message to the child that violence is the way to go!

As a private detective with over 30 years of experience in related law enforcement, I can tell you without hesitation, reservation, or equivocation that the prisons are not full of criminals from the 1950s and 1960s. The young criminals of today—the same ones who bring real guns to school and engage in drive-by shooting sprees and take pride in having a criminal record to show off for the girls, know nothing of the Old West and the "code" that we grew up with, for as we watched *The Lone Ranger, Bonanza,* even *Paladin,* the emphasis was NOT on handgun violence, but on resolving disputes with old-time advice from our elders, featuring compassion, understanding, and love. The truth of the matter is that the peak of the "Old West" (which today's officials like to say was the "Wild West" with a "Dodge City mentality") pales to the "Wild East, West, North and South" that permeates our country today.

Today's "gunslingers" have no conscience, no responsibility, no accountability, and no respect for anyone, beginning with themselves. And these are the kids that were denied cap guns, bows and arrows, Daisy BB guns, and a host of other "evil weapons." With mom and dad separated or divorced, idle afternoons, and single-parent homes where the parent juggled career and often ineffective child-rearing, it is alcohol, drugs, teenage pregnancy, and real violence that replaced any "evil cap gun" we played with in the 1950s and early 1960s. It's a sad and dismal commentary on today's affluent, permissive and self-centered society.

I, for one, long for the good, old days. I'll take the low wages and the old Studebaker, and willingly ditch the VCR, boom boxes, cellular phones, and answering machines—but, please give me back my Hoppy guns and holsters, Tonto rubber knife, my Lone Ranger mask, and my sheriff badge! I want to watch Wyatt Earp clean up Dodge City nestled in dad's arms, and I want mom standing by the door when I get home from school, asking

me how was my day. I want my little friends to respect my sisters, 'cause she's got a Dale Evans' cap gun of her own! And when I leave my Gene Autry .44 out in the rain, I know I made a "big mistake" and dad is going to take it away from me and mom will back him up! When I've been a good boy and done all my homework and my chores around the house, inside and out, I know mom and dad are going to reward me with the most beautiful set of guns and holsters, full of studs and fringe, for Christmas, and maybe even my birthday! And I'll put away my guns when I finish playing with them, keep them clean and oiled. And I'll say my prayers by my bed when I go to sleep, and ask that God keep mom and dad safe, and that He will let me grow up to be. . .a good COWBOY!

So, in closing this epistle of a Preface, I ask, who are we as collectors and curators of these wonderful toys and pieces of Americana? Why, we are just temporary caretakers of these mere possessions, keeping them clean, oiled, polished, and safe from destruction for future generations of would-be cowboys when we ourselves ride into the everlasting sunset.

RUDY A. D'ANGELO
Farmington, Connecticut

ACKNOWLEDGMENTS • MUCHAS GRACIAS, AMIGOS!

The foundation for this work and the thanks that I owe goes back to 1958. I can hardly believe that I started this book in longhand since I didn't have a typewriter, and finished it on a computer that took me forever to learn to work with. I guess I'm just resistant to change. Forty years is a long time and it wasn't until locating my first post-childhood cap gun at an antique show some twenty years ago, that this long dream was re-ignited. As a young teenager, I started to gather the historical data, photographs, documents, and the Hollywood connection. I kept on adding to it for nearly four decades to what this exhaustive project now contains. A newspaper article in The Hartford Times dated July 27, 1959, reads as follows: "Native of Italy, 15, is Writing Authentic Stories of Old West." There I am, in the photograph, thin, young, and good looking—the opposite of what I am today—with my "book," all in longhand, complete with photographs. I wanted *The Hartford Times* to print my book! How little did I know at age 15, having just mastered the English language, and having become very obsessed with the Old West, lawmen, outlaws, and driving my parents crazy to buy me cap guns and rifles— something that as a poor *ragazzo* in Italy, I had never seen, much less owned! And so it came to pass, that the dream became a reality, so without further adieu, I have many folks to thank, from the bottom of my heart.

As anyone who has ever done a book on any collectible knows all too well, it is a labor of love. The love is shared by all of us who lived those wonderful days and nights of our youth when these western heroes and six-gun buckaroos rode the range of our endless mind's eye. Likewise, to put this labor of love together requires the dedication, the courtesy, consideration, and the cooperation of many individuals. To all the dear friends and acquaintances I've made as I went ahead with this project, I found that these individuals shared the same love of the Old West as it came alive for us little cowpokes through the movies, television, and these wonderful toy guns as much as I did and still do. I want to say, muchas gracias, amigos, to the following hombres:

First and foremost, I'd be remiss if I didn't start with the head honcho, the Indian chief, the man who led the rebel charge, the man who gave us the *Toy Gun Purveyor Newsletter* and *Backyard Buckaroos-Collecting Western Toy Guns,* "the bible" for us collectors and present curators of these toys, my dear friend, Jim Schleyer. Jim was always ready to help—with his knowledge, photography, vast archives, and just plain encouragement. I owe him a heap of thanks! I know I speak for the whole wagon train when I say we all owe Jim a lifelong feeling of gratitude for the memories, the knowledge, and his unselfish giving of his time and talents to all of us greenhorns!

Thank you is such a redundant expression for the following list of friends and acquaintances who gave of their time, knowledge, expertise in special areas, photographs of their wonderful collections, and, in short, their enthusiasm. I want to also say how much I've appreciated being able to add pieces to my own private collection as result of these wonderful people. My gratitude is endless and I only hope that I am repaying all of you with this labor of love and memories for you to relive, share, and enjoy many times over. Thanks, Pardners!

"Roll Call—Boots and Saddles": Ralph Perlberg, Bill Longstreet, Brian Wolf, Ron Scisciani, William A. Young, Jr., Chuck Scaglione, Tom Kolomjec, John Bracken, Herb Taylor, Jack Rosenthal, Bill Hamburg, Peter Karp, Pat Connors, Dave Luellen, Ron Witman, L.H. Banks, Brian Roeder, Ron Doub, Robert Johnston, Steve Arlin, Jim Krantz, Dave Hay, Bill Adams, Tim Markley, Sam Logan, Ben Graves, Bob Williamson, Bob Lauver, Ernie Cremese, Mike Merryman, Jim Lefante, Frank McMath, Richard Thomas, George Newcomb, Jim Huskey, Chuck Quinn, Vic Lanzotti, Dusty Holickes, Fred Whittman, Fred Carlson, Mike Cherry, Doug "Cotton Eye Joe" Hamilton, Ron Wright, Joe Wishart, Jim "Mr. Daisy" Thomas, whose vast knowledge and his Daisy archives he willingly shared with me; Mr. Jack Crockett of the Unionville Museum in Connecticut; The Cromwell Public Library Historical Department who were kind enough to share data and catalogs of the Stevens Manufacturing Company which made some great guns, both cast iron and die cast. I must give a special, heartfelt thank you to fellow enthusiast, collector, and dealer Terry Graham—the only man, who when he says "if I find it, I'll call you," keeps his word! Terry and I shared information, photos, and the most important ingredient of all—friendship! I have a deep feeling of gratitude for the special assistance afforded me by Libro E. DiZinno, M.D., of San Diego, whose vast archives, photographs, books, obituaries, and era periodicals on movie and TV stars is a wealth of information, and he was kind enough to place them at my disposal. Finally, I want to say a special thank you to Bob Ball, who encouraged and pushed me to the limit, a friend who knows the meaning of the word. I tested his patience when he should've pulled out his six-gun and just plugged me!

My appreciation, and the gratitude I feel for the following organizations, institutions, historical museums, and the dedicated people who work there knows no bounds. They were more than happy to assist me in searching for and providing me with the photographs of the real western heroes and characters that caught the fancy of Hollywood and TV producers as the basis for the shows we loved. Most were thrilled that such a venture was in the works and reminisced along with me about the TV western characters that brought back so many memories. Most of these hard-working souls love the West and its history so much that it was obvious in the first five minutes of conversation! They are: Kit Carson Historic Museum, Taos, New Mexico; Roger Crowley, of the Old West Shop, Vienna, West Virginia; University of Oklahoma and the Rose Collection; Texas State Archives, Houston, Texas; State Archives of New Mexico; Kansas State Historical Society, Union Pacific Railroad; Colt's Patent Firearms, Hartford, Connecticut; Ben Traywick, City Historian, Tombstone, Arizona; Virginia State

Historical Society, Richmond, Virginia; Historical Society of Montana; *Life* magazine; Wells Fargo Bank, San Francisco; Minnesota Historical Society; Missouri Historical Society; Frank Garo and William Tell Images; Jesse L. James III, of Colorado; the late Zoe Tilghman, widow of famous lawman Bill Tilghman; Ed Bartholomew and his old Frontier Pix Collection; Chief Moses Buffalo, South Dakota; Jack Mills of New Mexico; celebrated western historians and authors Carl H. Breihan, Glenn Boyer, and William Waters, who supplied me with much data and many photos so many years ago, never thinking I'd finally get around to actually using them years later!

The western stills and photographs used to highlight this book are from my own private collection dating back to the 1950s and 1960s. For some reason, even as I grew into manhood, and girls replaced my cap guns as my number one interest, I treasured and kept these photos of my heroes in the basement of my parent's home. Even when I left for the army, I made my mother promise me not to throw out my photos, my western comics, and all those wonderful letters to the stars that I kept copies of, even then! I do wish to gratefully acknowledge, however, the following firms, companies, and studios which may hold original copyrights to these photographs, including those personally autographed to me: ABC, NBC, and CBS Television, Walt Disney Productions, Revue Productions, Universal Television, ZIV Television, Warner Brothers TV Productions, MGM Studios, Michael Landon Productions, 20th Century Fox Productions, Screen Gems Incorporated, the Estate of William Boyd, Andrew Fenady Associates, Four Star Productions, Roy Rogers Frontiers Incorporated, Flying "A" Productions, Fess Parker Productions, Desilu Productions, R. Hayden Productions, Arness and Company, Cherokee Productions, Paramount Television, Inc., Overland Productions, Lorimar Productions, Aaron Spelling Productions, Goodson-Todman Productions, Kellogg's, General Mills, Proctor & Gamble, and Mondial. If I have neglected any other company, I did so purely because of an accidental discharge of my cerebral fluid, for I have tried to give all proper credit due to those companies that gave us endless hours of fun and wide-eyed attention as our heroes rode in and out of our lives.

I'd also like to extend thanks to Dell Comics, Western Publishing Company, Gold Key Comics, DC Comics, that wonderful old *TV Western* magazine, which kept me up half the night with a Hoppy flashlight under my bed covers long after mom went to sleep; as well as *True West, Real West, Frontier Times,* and *True Western Adventures.* My sincere thanks also goes to those auctions that bring some of these wonderful toys right to our mailbox, specifically Hake's Americana, Toys & More, Smith-House Toys, and Manion's International Auction House, Inc.

I also want to express my sincere sympathies and to remember fellow cowhands Jim Moore, Ed Greene, and Tom Lockhart, who have passed on to that big prairie in the sky. We'll miss you, pardners.

There are two additional establishments which deserve both thanks and praise. I need to say *muchas gracias* to the employees of the Camera Shops and Ritz Camera Center in Farmington and West Hartford, Connecticut, for their unbelievable patience in dealing with both a collector and as one who knows what he wants another collector to view in photography, thus, I was a royal pain in the keester, for sure. This was compounded by the fact that being somewhat of a photographer of sorts myself, I kept hammering that what I wanted the eye of the camera and the eye of the collector and reader of this study to see, had to be "perfectamundo." They were a great bunch of guys and I owe them a heap of thanks!

Finally, I must say that Pam Bombara, Debbie Dondero, Alex Pagano, Terry Matava, Ann Arcari, and Sue Cartnick, along with the entire staff of the adult research department of the Farmington Public Library are "the best." They were most helpful, most gracious, and a friendly, wonderful group of cowgirls that helped me patiently and consistently. They gave their time, expertise, and "got into it" with the same gusto that I must have been showing ad nauseam during this project. Before anyone says "but that's their job"—let me say that I have dealt with a lot of libraries, research institutions, and city, state and federal agencies, and the difference in people is how they do their job when serving the public, and on that note, the staff at the Farmington Library wins, hands down! Thanks to all the "Dales" and "Annies" at that fine institution!

Those of us that can no longer starve to death standing by the mailbox waiting for the old *TGP* newsletter to arrive, bringing us photos and tidbits of information to match notes and argue about, we can still look forward to two worthwhile newsletter-format publications: they are the *Toy Gun Collectors of America* (T.G.C.A.) and *Cowboy Collector Network* (C.C.N.) both based in California. It's been a pleasure to get you in my sights on a quarterly basis! Let's keep up the good work, for in the sharing of knowledge and information is the foundation of courtesy and comradery—the difference between serious collectors versus the greed and commercialism that unfortunately often stains our hobby. *Muchas Gracias, Amigos!*

Now, let's get these doggies moving. . . .

Rudy A. D'Angelo
Farmington, Connecticut

INTRODUCTION

This book is the beginning of a wonderful ride through memory lane. A ride that will take us to our youth—childhood memories—when we all wanted to grow up to be cowboys, gunfighters, Indians, and sidekicks. It will bring us back to a more gentle America. We may not have had the affluence of today, but we had much more important values and priorities.

I wish there were even more characters and cap guns for me to identify, to connect with, to tell the story of, and to go search for. As I have tried to drive home in this very personal study, the western was not just a "cowboy." In fact, the cowboys that we grew up with were our role models. They taught us, in their own way, that crime did not pay, that mom and dad were to be honored and obeyed. They asked us to do chores, to help

lighten our parent's load as they worked and sacrificed so that we had more than they did. The smiling faces of Hoppy, Roy, Gene, and The Lone Ranger made us want to do our best, and to treat our fellow man and woman the way we wanted to be treated ourselves.

Even when the "adult westerns" came along, history came with them, albeit glamorized, because in reality, the real West was a hard life, often uncertain, and in that respect, the good had to win over the bad. As we will see, the desperadoes got what was coming to them and the brave lawman of the day stood tall in the face of adversity. Will future generations be looking up to lawmen of today? I don't know. Television is such a powerful tool to hit our senses, to let us feel like few other mediums can. Thus, I have always felt it is incumbent upon the powerful entertainment industry to be responsible, to be the beacon of morality, values, traditions, and patriotism. This is the way it should be, to ensure the survival of our country and its people.

Those of us who grew up in the 1950s will also have a few things that we can really call our own. We have the distinction of being the "original" television generation. Television was just getting its "antennas wet," and it developed into an era of sights, sounds, color, and experiment, and it sought to teach, shape our lives, and expose us to products that we thought of the minute we got to a store. Television is a shared experience that also brought us closer; on the next telephone call with family and friends, we could immediately relate to what we had just seen, how it affected us, what we enjoyed, and what we didn't like. All of us carry this wonderful God-given human element called "memory." Television, through the wonderful westerns that are the focus of this book, additionally left our generation with even more unique memories. It has been my honor and pleasure to have once again tapped into this childhood memory and with it, the nostalgia of the cap pistols, cap rifles, and western gear that, for a time, made us "one of them"—the cowboy and the gunfighter.

Now that we are "grown-up cowboys," we have the luxury of not having to wait for mom and dad to buy us the cap gun we want. We don't have to fill out the Daisy form to remind mom which gun to get us for our birthday. While *Rawhide* drove the cattle herds, we are now at the point where we can drive a hard bargain, ever searching for the elusive cap guns and rifles to complete our collections, something we did not have the luxury to afford back in the 1950s. Seventy-five cents got my brother and me into the old Webster Theater in Hartford, where with our own popped corn under our jackets, we sat down to watch two westerns, cartoons, and the news. We used to line up wearing our studded holsters and cap guns! We could hardly wait to "help" our hero out of a tight situation by blasting away at the screen. The smell of the caps filled the theater many a time, but we were all good kids and the management didn't mind a bit. They don't make these wonderful toys any more and the ones they do make, as they say, well, "they don't make them like they used to," and I guess, sadly, the same must be said for our heroes, for they, too, seem to have galloped away from the American landscape and the screen.

What do we have left of this wonderful era? Besides the countless cowboy collectibles, we old geezers have the cap guns, cap pistols, rifles, and shotguns that are shown throughout this book, and as adults we marvel at the quality, the construction, and even the intricate mechanisms of these wonderful toys. As America fell in love with the western, the world of advertising, merchaindising, and manufacturing fell right into step and produced the toys that give us so much pleasure and, more importantly, so many memories today.

It's no secret that western cap guns and rifles have literally gone to record levels on the collector markets. Antique dealers, auction houses, and western shows have all spurred up the interest, and along with it, the prices. While one can still find a bargain at a flea market or a garage sale, I dare say, from my own perspective, even that is fast disappearing. Recently, I had an old friend visit with me. He was astounded at the quality and workmanship of several of the cap guns he held in his hand. He is much younger than I, and after trying to do the "road agent's spin" and other "fast draw" antics, he came out with a number of sentences that were music to my ears and to which I have alluded to all through this book. When he reads this, he'll have to sadly nod his head because he left my home frustrated and a bit jealous.

First, he said, "mom would never let me have a toy gun." Then, twirling the guns a little longer, he said "I guess my generation missed out on some great toy guns." I felt like saying they had missed out on a lot more than just great toy guns, but I controlled myself. Then he finished up by saying, "where can I find a few of these?" As I went into each character and the reasons for each, he said "what made Walt Disney, or Hollywood for that matter, pick this character , or that one?" I knew that the interest was beginning to mushroom and with it, a look back at what we know to be the golden age of television westerns.

I believe we are better human beings for it and the heroes of my youth are just as vivid and "alive" today as they were almost fifty years ago. I know that as long as I am blessed with my family, my friends, and the comrades who share this fondness with me, my memories will remain forever young. The 1950s was truly the "golden age of television" and for us western afficionados, there was nothing like it. I hope that I have in some way entertained and informed you readers and enthusiasts for years to come. It is an honor that I have dreamed about for most of my adult life. Thanks for the memories.

Alan Ladd
PARAMOUNT

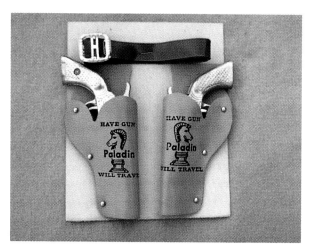

ABOUT THIS BOOK

In the compiling of this list of characters, it is important to note that there did not exist a cap gun for every TV western program or every TV western character. Some companies made only the cap pistol with the lead character's name on it. Other companies made only the holster set with the show title on them and used generic western guns. Still others spawned future shows. Some guns have a character's name on it even though that character may have been on another TV western show altogether. Some character guns didn't even have a show with the name on the gun.

On some other lesser-known character guns, I have taken the liberty to match a known cap gun title to a show's title or character even before such a show surfaced. This will all be explained in the text of each character. I even made efforts to match a popular gun with an existing show or character from the 1950 to 1960 era, even if the gun produced came on the market years before. This allows us collectors to add that certain gun to the list of character guns and holster categories that we previously would have never known about.

Thus, we enter the "Golden Age" of the TV westerns and the cap guns that immortalized them! Many newly-discovered guns and holster sets with character names on them continue to surface. At the end of this book, I list other TV western shows for which, remarkably, even with the immense popularity of the given show, no gun has been found to date. This leaves the future open to many new and exciting possibilities. "Who knows what's out there in them thar' hills?"

COLLECTING CAP PISTOLS

I have been a collector of military and western collectibles for almost 40 years. I started the addiction of collecting as a teenager and haven't stopped. I find that there are many kinds of collectors. Some are in it for the true love of the hobby, the passion, the hunt—and then the satisfaction that you've finally filled that void on the wall, or the cabinet, or display case. The time, the cost, the waiting, the negotiating, the disappointments and the frustrations can't compare to the joy, the triumph, and the jubilation that it was "all worth it." when you find that missing piece.

There are other collectors that are in it for the money, the investment, the value, the prices. That's what makes their world go around. And that's fine with me; this America, land of the free. And there are collectors who don't have a clue to what is rare, what is seldom seen, and what is common. It never fails to amaze me that some collectors will plunk down $500 for a cap gun, but won't spend $50 for a book. They don't take the time to learn about the subject, the hobby, and often, if you'll pardon the pun, they "shoot from the hip" and they usually miss.

Not a week goes by that something new, something unique, or something none of us have ever seen before surfaces among the collecting communty. We are always learning: nobody is truly an expert because we haven't seen it all—and there is still more to come. And that's the way it should be, because when you've stopped learning, you're dead and buried.

Any serious collector will tell you that there is no substitute for experience. You have to read several books. You have to attend several antique shows, toy shows, western shows, and so on to get the real flavor of what is rare and what is common. I use a very simple, common sense approach to what is rare and what is fairly common when dealing with toy cap guns and cap rifles.

What, for instance, makes a Hopalong Cassidy cap gun so expensive? Are they rare? Not in my opinion. Hoppy guns are in big demand, but they are not rare. Hoppy guns are expensive, but not rare. They are seen at every show, listed in every auction, and collectors can buy and sell them with a phone call. What makes Hoppy guns desirable is the character, the amount of people that want to add the gun to a Hoppy collection, and so between nostalgia, passion, and investment, the prices go up.

Now let's use the same logic for, say, a Gray Ghost or perhaps a Rebel cap gun. In terms of "rarity" they leave Hoppy in the dust. Few were made, few were bought, few survived. And now, most cap gun collectors looking for the really rare cap pisols, will sell the farm, throw in the wife and kids, and the dog (well, maybe not the dog!) to get one to fill the void in the collection.

So how do you put a value on a "rare" cap gun? And when we say its rare, it begs the question, "rare to whom?" In my opinion, a cap gun is worth what the buyer is willing to pay for it to add it to the collection. This means that a "tire kicker" is going to whine and moan, then walk away and miss out on adding a rare gun to his collection. A serious collector quickly adds up how many he's seen, how many shows he has attended, and how many times a certain gun has been offered to him, or comes on the market. Then he makes an educated, experienced, informed decision to buy it.

The investment-minded collector is going to try to figure out how much it will be worth "down the line" if he decides to sell it. He watches the dealers, the shows, the auctions, and then makes his own decision based on that criteria. The passionate collector, which I consider myself fist and foremost, is in it for the love of the hobby; to hang on to wonderful memories of our youth; to marvel at American-made quality and workmanship of a bygone time; to learn more about our great western heritage, and to recall the wonderful episodes of television's greatest westerns!

CONDITION GUIDE

One surely cannot expect that the toy manufacturers made these cap guns with the collector in mind. Proof of that will become apparent all through this book, as manufacturers did whatever they had to do to market and sell the products. Youngsters, as well, did what we did: We played with them! We left them outside! We used them as makeshift hammers! We carved our names into the grips! We notched them when we "shot the desperadoes!"

As far as I'm concerned, a cap gun or rifle that is complete with all original parts, is still in working condition, and has not lost its appeal due to the elements, extensive cap corrosion, or total finish loss, is a fine specimen to add to your collection. Guns that have been repaired or have had parts replaced should be labeled as such. There is nothing more important than being honest, fair, and giving an accurate description of a collectible. You'll find that most serious collectors will appreciate the honesty and buy the item anyway, again, to fill that missing gap in the collection.

A "mint in box" gun may have great investment potential and may bring "top value"—whatever that may be. But the inherent nostalgia of a toy gun; that special feeling of a loved and "played-with" toy cannot be measured by condition. It is a precious part of our youth, and as such, a played-with gun has more intrinsic value. Imagine the thrill of going to an antique show, or a flea market, or a garage sale, and finding a gun that was like one you had as a boy! You'll instantly remember when mom or dad bought it for you—your birthday, or maybe that special Christmas. You'll remember that pungent smell of cap sulphur as they were fired, the billowing smoke, and how you oiled your gun and kept it safe for years. And then one day. . .it was gone. Where did it go? That's what this book is about.

THE TOY GUN COMPANIES

Except for a few specific examples, this work deals with the die-cast cap pistols, rifles, and shotguns that for the most part, replaced the cast irons of the 1930s and 1940s. The following represents the names of the known toy companies, and specifically toy gun companies, as well as companies that made cap pistols, rifles, shotguns, holster sets and accouterments. Some are the distributors, as well as retail outlets for the purposes of filling holsters with a wide variety of guns.

The names and logos that have surfaced to date will help you identify the particular gun(s) you own, as well as those you are searching for to add to your collections. A variety of markings, labels, and stampings have been documented on various guns themselves, as well as cards, boxes, wrappings, and catalogs. This listing is by no means meant to represent all of the known manufacturing companies, outlets, and retail stores, for new information surfaces all the time. However, the most popular "character name" manufacturing companies are listed, as well as where they were located at the time.

We collectors are always looking for the "perfect" match for a holster set and a character cap gun to fill it. But we must remember these companies were making guns for kids to play with. They were "toys"to be used, abused, and discarded. The "perfect" gun for the "perfect" holster set didn't always exist, and so we have to be content with what we find. After all, the fun of collecting, in my view, is the "hunt"—the search, if you will, for that elusive gun to fill that gap, that void in your display case, your shelf, your den wall. If you could just call somebody and "order" your favorite character gun at any price, it wouldn't be near as much fun!

There is little doubt that there are more obscure companies all over this great land that certainly took advantage of the western "craze" of the 1950s and early 1960s, and no doubt that more companies that will surface from time to time on a card, box, leather holster stampings, and any number of western collectibles heretofore unknown. Collectors are encouraged to let the author know of other companies "out there" for future archival documentation. Keep an eye out there, boys! Cover me while I do more reconnaissance, lads!

Actoy—Esquire Novelty Company, Union City, New Jersey
Arrow Sales Company, Boston, Massachusetts
Balantyne Manufacturing Company, Chicago, Illinois
Barash Company, Incorporated, New York City, New York
BCM—British Cast Metals, Derby, Yorkshire 7 London, England
Buckaroo Holsters—Ellman-Whiting Company, Detroit, Michigan

Buzz-Henry, Leslie-Henry Company, Mount Vernon, New York

C. Ray Lawyer Companies, Berkeley, California

Carnell Manufacturing Company, Brooklyn, New York

Carnell Manufacturing Company Showrooms, Manhattan, New York

Carnell Manufacturing, Middlesex, New Jersey

Circle N Toys—Nichols Manufacturing Company, Pasadena, Texas

Circle N Toys—Nichols Industries, Jacksonville, Texas

Cisco Kid Leather & Metal Products Company, Los Angeles, California

Classy Products Corporation, New York, New York

Classy Products Corporation, Los Angeles, California

Classy Products Corporation, Woodside, Long Island, New York

Corkale Circle-K-Bar Manfacturing Company, California

Craighead, John Holsters Company, Denver

Crescent Toy Company, Ltd., Cwmcarn, Mon, England

Daisy Manufacturing Company, Plymouth, Michigan

Daisy Manufacturing Company, Rogers, Arkansas

Daisy Manufacturing Company, Ltd., Preston, Ontario, Canada

Danlee Company, Van Nuys, California

Deluxe Toy Creations, Inc., Newark, New Jersey

Denver Holster Company, Colorado

Duncan Sales Company, Los Angeles, California

Empire Manufacturing, Tarboro, North Carolina Eureka, France

Feinburg-Henry Company, New York City, New York

F.J. Strauss Company, Inc., New York, New York

George Schmidt Manufacturing Company, Los Angeles, California

Haig Manufacturing Company, Alhambra, California

Hamilton Line Specialties, Inc., Hamilton, Ohio

HALCO—J. Halpern Company, Pittsburgh, Pennsylvania

Hahn ManufacturingCompany, Inc., Freeport, New York

Harvell-Kilgore Sales Corporation, Bolivar, Tennessee

Herman Frederick Co., New York City

Hubley-Gabriel Manufacturing Company, Lancaster, Pennsylvania

Hubley Manufacturing Company, Lancaster, Pennsylvania

J. & E. Stevens Company, Cromwell, Connecticut

Kenton Hardware Company, Kenton, Ohio

Keyston Brothers, San Francisco, California

Kilgore, Incorporated, Westerville, Ohio

Kilgore Manufacturing Company, Waterloo, Quebec, Canada

Knox-Reese Manufacturers, Philadelphia, Pennsylvania

Kusan Manufacturing, Nashville, Tennessee

Lansing Company Incorporated, Lansing, Iowa

LATCO—Los Angeles Toy Company, Los Angeles, California

Leslie-Henry, Wilkes-Barre, Pennsylvania

Leslie-Henry (Oval LH), Mount Vernon, New York

Leslie-Henry (Diamond H Brand), Mount Vernon, New York

Lone Start Products, Ltd, Palmers Green, London, England

Lone Star—Die Cast Metal Toys—D.C.M.T.— London, England

Lone Star Products, Ltd., Welham Green, Hertshire, England

Long Island Die Casting Company, Inwood, Long Island, New York

Louis Marx & Company, Inc., New York City, New York

Louis Marx & Co., Inc., Glen Dale, West Virginia

Lincoln Industries, Ltd., New Zealand

M.A. Henry Western Company, Santa Monica, California

M.A. Henry, Ltd., Dundas, Ontario, Canada

M.A.M., Italy

Marx Toys, Erie, Pennsylvania & Florida

Mattel Incorporated, Toymakers, Los Angeles, California

Mattel Inc., Hawthorne, California

Milton A. Henry Company (Oval H), Mount Vernon, New York

Modern Toy Companies, Japan

Mondial, Italy

National Metal & Plastics Toy Company, Berkeley, California

Nicholas-Kusan, Inc., Jacksonville, Texas

Nicholas-Kusan Manufacturing, Nashville, Tennessee

Oval L-H—Leslie-Henry, Mount Vernon, New York

Oval H—Milton A. Henry Company, Mount Vernon, New York

Parris Manufacturing Company, Savannah, Tennessee

Pilen, S.A. Spain

Pilgrim Leather Company, Haverhill, Massachusetts

Product Engineering Company, Portland, Oregon

Ray Line Grand Toys, Winchendon, Massachusetts

Redondo, Spain

River Company (Halco Distributors), Memphis, Tennessee

Rodeo King Western Holsters, Los Angeles, California

Roth American, Incorporated, Wilkes-Barre, Pennsylvania

R & S Western Boy-Toy Manufacturing Company, New York, New York

Sackman Brothers Company, New York, New York

S-BAR-M—Service Manufacturing Company, Inc., New York, New York

Service Manufacturing Company, Yonkers, New York

Smart Style, Incorporated, Ridgefield, New Jersey

Tumbleweed Togs, Arcadia, California

Viril Manufacturing Company, Los Angeles,
  California
Wornova Manufacturing Company, New York,
  New York
Wyandotte—All Metal Products Company, Wyandotte, Michigan
Young Premium Company, Los Angeles, California

LOGOS, TRADEMARKS, AND SPECIAL FEATURES

Many collectors tell me that often they are unsure of various logos and trademarks. There are many confusing features found on cap pistols, rifles, and holster sets. This is because, these days, as rabid and passionate collectors, we thirst for the knowledge and detail that perhaps the companies that made them didn't make a big deal out of it themselves! When you add that to the fact that we are a bunch of old geezers trying to hang onto our youth—a time when we couldn't have cared less about company names, logos, addresses, and distinguishing marks, well, I can see how confused we can get, me included! So, get out that magnifying glass, fire up that memory bank, and let's see if we can make this a little easier:

ACTOY-ESQUIRE

The logo used on the Actoy-Esquire guns, rifles, and shotguns is a pony's head in a circle. The pony's head is bridled and has a stiff brush appearance to the mane. The pony head logos are matching in that they face the respective sides on the gun grips. However, the pony's head normally faces to the left as you look at it when it is shown as the logo for Esquire . Few of the Esquire-Actoy guns are marked "Actoy." Most are marked "Esquire." Although it is in a circle on the gun grips, the larger and more official logo of the company shows the pony's head, facing left, in a more ornate circle, with a sign hanging below it (similar to an old western bar sign) with the words "An Esquire Toy" on the sign. The guns marked "Actoy" usually have this name on the back of the cap box.

BCM—BRITISH CAST METALS

The logo on BCM guns, when shown on the grips consists of an Indian-style phoenix "sun bird" with its wings outstretched. A superbly sculptured Indian chief's head with full headdress makes the grips a one of a kind beauty in both design and workmanship. The BCM models that were made for Daisy in the "Guns of the West" series at the Canadian plant also have an identical gun that is almost an exact copy of the Hubley Cowboy but sporting an Indian warrior's head and red jewels. These are marked both "BCM" and "Made in England."

BUZZ-HENRY

The logo used on the "Buzz Henry"-marked guns is the "BH" in a circle at the top of the unusual inset plastic grips which also sport the rearing horse. The metal butt frame has "Buzz Henry" raised across the bottom. No other M.A. Henry or Leslie-Henry markings are seen on the Buzz Henry- marked guns.

CARNELL

The logo used by Carnell Manufacturing consists of a steer head, looking to the right, encircled, with the wording "Carnell Roundup." This logo is usually found on the box containing Carnell guns and those guns marketed under the Carnell name. The logo used on the gun grips is a circle "C." It appears that many of the guns marketed under Carnell's name were Lone Star guns with another special feature and that was the "notch bar" on the plastic grips, which were a simulated stag design. This way, the kid could keep a record of all the gringos he out-gunned in a hundred gunfights! Of course, he probably had a character named jack-knife to do it with! (see the Lone Star descriptions for similar features).

CLASSY

The logo documented on Classy Products boxes and catalogs is actually the word "Classy" in cursive, with a cowboy sitting on the lower portion of the "C" with his gun drawn. Since Classy marketed a lot of Roy Rogers guns and products, they utilized the Double "RR" brand on the grips and gun frames. Another logo they used on both boxes, cards, and the catalog, was a horseshoe in a circle with a lariat forming the word "Corral" from the end of the left arm of the horseshoe.

CRESCENT

The logo used by Crescent Toys consisted of a crescent moon—a half-moon—with the words "Crescent Toys" on each side of the moon. The logo was the same on the gun grips but without the wording. Ironically, a Crescent "Buntline Special" that I have in my collection has "38" in a circle on the grips where the logo would normally be located—even though the "38" assuming it is supposed to be a caliber, has nothing to do with the Buntline Special, or the size, shape, and design of the Crescent Buntline Special. Crescent guns also have a wolf's head on some grips, and many grips come in red, orange, and pearl-like white. "45" as well as "38" was used on the logo circle of the grips. Strange? You bet!

DAISY

The well-known Daisy logo consists of the "D" of the word Daisy forming a bull's-eye. Another lesser seen logo, usually seen on catalogs and boxes is another circle bull's-eye with the words "It's a Daisy toy" across it. Another yet lesser known logo, appearing in a 1956 catalog is a 5 pointed star with a circle behind and in front of the five points with the words "It's a Daisy Play Gun" inside the smaller circle in front of the star. Of course, something mothers would never look at today was the "Seal of Commendation" which accompanied the Daisy line of toy guns and rifles - the seal and blue ribbon with the words "Commended by the Consumer Service Bureau of *Parents* magazine as advertised therein." Now wouldn't the anti-violence advocates have a field day with that today! Imagine a mother buying her son or daughter a gun to play with! Horrors! But God love them, all of OUR mothers did!

HALCO

The J. Halpern Company used a variety of logos and trademarks. These include an "H" with a branding iron going through it; A circle with "Halco Superior Products" written on it; and since they copied other manufacturer's logos and markings, the circled 5 point star as well as the rearing horse can be found on Halco guns. Halco and Esquire made the most character guns.

HAMILTON

The Hamilton line of character guns amounted to four that are known—the Cheyenne, the Range Rider, Annie Oakley, and The Westerner. The Hamilton guns came in the gray metal finish. The grips are always found plain except for the Cheyenne Shooter, which carries a logo made up of a large "C" and a smaller "S" inside the "C." The same logo is found on the frame under the cylinder. The Westerner model has plain grips but has a longhorn's head on the frame along with the name under the cylinder. The full name and address is found when the gun is broke open for loading.

HUBLEY

The Hubley logo was the five pointed star in a circle on the grips. The most widely used grip design was the familiar steer head looking downward on the grips, and probably the most copied grip design! Since Hubley made the biggest of them all, the Colt .45, that gun has the rampant colt with the lance in its teeth as seen on the real Colt Firearms of Hartford, Connecticut fame. The Hubley star is encountered both in red enamel paint and in the plain nickel or metal used on the particular gun (factory black, nickel, gold finish, etc). Another logo used by Hubley, as seen in the catalogs is a circle with a label across it with the words "It's a HUBLEY toy." The other trademark usually encountered on holsters, studs, catalogs and when the Hubley word is spelled out is what appears to be a triangle, with the top of the triangle pointing up and being the left side of the "H" of Hubley. Another lesser known Hubley marking is an octagon with Hubley Pistol Line printed within the inner circle of the octagon. The longhorn classic grip, however, was certainly the most widely used and copied Hubley feature. After the merge with Gabriel, only the name "Gabriel" is found on the later guns with all plastic grips, but without the circle star logo. The late Hubley guns with the side-gate were copied by Halco and are just about identical in every way, including the star logo, but with "Halco" prominently on the frame!

KILGORE

The logo used by Kilgore was the circled "K." It is found on the grips as well as the frames, and on the gun barrels of various designs. The "catchy" phrase was "This "K" means "OK" because with the K in the Circle, it reads "OK." Another feature of the Kilgore guns was the heavy use of lettering and other western designs on the barrels. These included the Double "RR" brand for Roy Rogers, the "DE" for Dale Evans, a serpent, cactus, branding irons and other such symbols. Kilgore's other features also included a horse's head, but not to be confused with either the Leslie-Henry, Marx, Wyandotte, Lone Star and other uses of horse's heads on grips, the Kilgore horse head is facing downward on the grips, has a full mane of hair in the design and has a closed mouth. The disc mammoth caps, the "Dura-Gleam" sparkling finish, and "swing out" revolving cylinder were other Kilgore features and characteristics. After the company became Harvell-Kilgore, the letter "H" was added to the circled "K" attached to the back of the "K" to form the "HK" with the "K" still in the circle, but only half of the "H" is within the circle.

LESLIE-HENRY

The Leslie-Henry line of guns, like the Halco line, used a number of logos, trademarks and distinguishing features that set it apart to the close observer. The Diamond "H" was the official logo, seen at the top of the grips and on certain guns, on the frame itself, below and between the cylinder and the grips. They also used the oval with both "H" and "L-H" at the top of the grips. Two other important features on the Leslie-Henry guns are the rearing horse on the frame and the horses' head positioned upward on the beautiful grips. Another minute detail is to be noted. On the larger frame guns, the rearing horse has no lasso around its head, while on the smaller guns and the single shots, the rearing horse sports a lasso that forms the area where the character name is located on the frame directly under the cylinder. Leslie-Henry made a variety of grips, including the inset cameos, copper grips with the steer head, and they came in a great variety of colors. Leslie-Henry catalogs are difficult to find. I've also never seen a gun stamped or marked "Leslie-Henry." They truly made a great number of quality character guns. Leslie-Henry made both nickel finish and bronze finish guns. The most desirable are the 9-inch model character series and the large .44 model character series. Canadian made Leslie-Henry guns ae interesting. Both "LH" in a circle and the Hubley 5 point star in a circle was used. Additionally, a special "square" screw on grips was used. The box markings for the Canadian market carry the "M.A. Henry Ltd., Dundas, Ontario" address. They also used a logo that consisted of a circle with the rearing horse in the center and with "L" and "H" on each side of the horse, not used on the American market. Some of the metal grip models made in Canada resemble a Hubley and the steerhead was used instead of the usual Leslie-Henry horse head models marketed in the USA.

LONE STAR

Lone Star utilized so many different logos that one needs to carefully study a number of specimens to appreciate them all. Some of the earlier Lone Star models are just as well made and resemble the 9-inch Leslie-Henry cap guns. The nickel finish is excellent, along with the scroll work and designs. However, where Leslie-Henry used the familiar rearing horse, the early Lone Star used only the bare horse head, without any bridle, ending at the neck of the horse, with mane flowing back. These early Lone Star guns are not even marked Lone Star or Made in England which raises debate with some collectors over whether they are Leslie-Henry, Canadian made or British Lone Star. However, new data that has surfaced and the fact that they were marketed by Carnell on the Gray Ghost, Bat Masterson, Rawhide, Maverick and Buntline series, show the same features, designs, and lack of markings other than the character names on the frames. These include the above mentioned horse's head on the frame; notch bar simulated stag grips, and the Leslie-Henry "look." The Lone Star markings on the huge Range Rider Mk II, an almost identical copy of the classic Nichols Stallion has some interesting features: The name Lone Star with a small "star" between Lone and Star is raised on the frame; the grips carry a red, 5-pointed star identical to the Hubley star on the grips. A front face view of a long horn in a circle adorns both sides of the frame right behind the cylinder and it is the only known gun that sports a Pegasus—the same winged horse of Mobil gas fame, galloping across a 5-pointed star on the center of the grips! Incredible!

The Lone Star markings on the Cisco Kid series shows two other interesting details that set the Lone Star apart. The grips, which are found in various colors such as black, white, red, blue, brown, and a stunning red and black marbleized pattern, all have a gorgeous horses' head, looking downward. The teeth of the horse are prominently seen! Right under the horse's mouth and almost touching the teeth, as if the horse is going to grab it, is a small circle with a 5 pointed star within the circle. The frame is marked "Cisco Kid" in various places on the several Cisco Kid guns they made. Inside the chamber where the caps are loaded, finally, we have the correct Lone Star markings for solid identification: "DCMT—Lone*Star Product—Made In England." The same five point star is found at the top of the grips, exactly where the Hubley star would be located. You have to hand it to the Brits—rogues that they are! While the earlier Lone Star guns have the superb nickel finish, the later models have the flat black factory finish as well as the chrome and flash finishes. The holsters that I have inspected and own that come with Lone Star Products are rather thin, crude, in some cases with painted details and do not have anywhere near the quality of the American-made counterparts.

LONG ISLAND DIE CASTING

The design of the Long Island Die Casting cap guns is almost identical to the Hubley. In the place of the star logo, however, is a large "T." The steerhead, also an almost identical copy of the Hubley steerhead, is all one color, without the usual different color of the steer's mane and face on two tone grips. The full name and address of the company is raised on the inside chamber when it is broken open to load the caps.

MARX

Without a doubt, Marx made more toys, prototypes and experimented with all kinds of models and features on its many guns and rifles than anyone else. The official Marx logo consists of a circle with the "mar" and then "X" for the full name of Marx across the circle, giving it an almost bull's-eye look with a large "X" in front. Another almost identical logo has both the full name "Marx" as well as the larger "X" in the circle. Marx made some spectacular grips on both its generic and its character guns. These include a bison head in almost 3-dimension; a horse's head that is half-turned to the observer so that almost the full face of the horse is shown; sharp swooping eagles; huge longhorns and rearing cowboys on horseback. Marx also had some great character guns covered in this book with special features that no other company made or copied.

MATTEL

Mattel's logo shows a little boy wearing a crown sitting on a large "M" within a solid circle. The wording "Mattel, Inc. Toymakers" is also within the same circle. It's more famous motto "If it's Mattel, it's swell" resounded everywhere as they marketed the Fanner 50 and other guns in the mid-1950s. The African antelope head, stag grips, "shootin'shell," the Dura-Hide holsters, and the "fan it" became the best known features of the Mattel guns even though they made only a few character guns and rifles.

MONDIAL AND M.A.M.

The logos for these Italian toy gun firms are interesting. The Mondial firm used three circled "M"s design within a diamond. M.A.M. also used a pony medallion, but the pony's head is of superior design and workmanship. They also used simply the initials "M.A.M." It's also important for the collector to know some Italian words found on these guns. "Matricola" means serial number. "Modello Depositato" means "Patent Pending" and "Brevettato" means "Patented." These guns are stamped "Made in Italy" in the English language. The Italian guns are very well made with highly scrolled frames, factory black finishes and fluted grips. They are so well made that they resemble reproduction Civil War guns in both size, frames and weight. Mondial and MAMguns were made to take disc caps in series of 6, 8, and 12 "colpi" which means "shots" in Italian and the boxes are marked as such. Mondial also made non-western cap shooter guns.

NATIONAL METAL & PLASTIC TOY CO.

This company, also known as the C. Ray Lawyer Company of California, using the Dodge-Melton design has some strange features that set it apart. The gun was nickel, but has an aluminum opening latch on the left side which pushes the revolving and sliding cylinder forward for loading. The gun was very heavily engraved with beautiful raised scroll work covering almost the entire gun as well as checkered and scrolled grips with an imitation yellowed ivory look. A rather heavy and complicated gun, it has the weight, look and feel of a real gun! The psychiatrists would have a field day with a kid found playing with one of these today! This gun also carried the names of the company and the designer on the frame as well as the character up on the side of the barrel.

NICHOLS

The logo used by Nichols became widely known as the "Circle 'N Ranch" and was simply the N in a circle. This is found on the grips. Other Nichols embellishments on the superb quality of the guns they made included stag grips, a full wagon train and bison on the gun barrels, heavy scroll work and fine engraving. Another logo also used in the advertising of Nichols guns was the same Circle "N" with an additional circle in which the words "Circle 'N Ranch" is known. Another hawking advertisement was the face of a smiling little boy with the words "Oh boy, it's a Nichols toy." Nichols also carried the enviable "Seal of Commendation" by *Parents* magazine. When Nichols merged and became Nichols-Kusan, the logo changed slightly, in that the "N" was totally within the circle and with the name "Nichols" totally within and under the large "N." While the boxes are stamped Nichols-Kusan with the new logo, the guns carry only the "Kusan, Inc., Nashville, Tenn" name on the barrel. They no longer have the rugged quality, workmanship or the deep groove feel of the stag grips of the older Nichols guns. While Nichols did not make a large variety of character guns, they were certainly copied by the Lone Star Products for the character models they made!

REDONDO

This gun is included in this description for two main reasons. First, it is an almost identical copy of the Kilgore "Buck" and "Eagle" design, right down to the "silver flash finish" and swooping eagle on the one color grips. The hammer also sets this apart because it resembles the spurs on a boot. An eagle's head, similar to a bald eagle, is located on both sides of the barrel. The name "Redondo" is located under the ejection rod to the front of the cylinder. Palm looking leaves and the character name is located on the frame. There is no logo on the grips. The box I've been able to inspect in the Redondo line is that which came with "The High Chaparrel." The logo is a red oval with "Redondo" fully inside and a "O" below it in black. The Spanish word for a circle as well as "round" is "redondo." The box is also marked "Fabricado en Espana," meaning Made in Spain. The box, like the guns, are very colorful.

SCHMIDT

The logos used on Schmidt guns, even the character models are far and few in between. Other than "LB" for the "Lasso 'em Bill" and the circled "AL" for the Alan Ladd, the Schmidt guns have other more visible features such as the copper stag grips, copper flowered and scroll grips, copper checkered grips, the

Double "RR" and "DE" for the Roy Rogers-Dale Evans models, the exclusive break from the top pattern for cap loading, and heavy engraving as well a ribbed barrels. Schmidt also used a variety of colored grips for the Hopalong Cassidy and the series of Buck 'n Bronc models they made. The logo used on the Schmidt Buck 'n Bronc series shows a double "B" back to back as well as a bucking cowboy on horseback within the lasso design. Obviously the Hoppy bust on the Schmidt Hopalong Cassidy models makes them stand apart from the other companies licensed to carry the Hoppy character. The main feature of the guns themselves is that they break open from the top and are generally very fragile.The "Geo.Schmidt Mfg. Los Angeles, 21, Calif. Made in USA" is found inside the frame when opened for loading.

STEVENS

The Stevens logo was a simple "S" in a circle. However, Stevens made some special pearl-like grips, as well as all metal grip with a full standing buffalo, and metal stag grips. Other than the British Lone Star, Stevens was the only other gun manufacturer that sported an Indian chief in full headdress. Stevens was more famous in the cast iron variety of guns and relatively made only a few character guns, all of which are covered in this book.

WYANDOTTE

All Metal Products, the company name for Wyandotte came up with a cute little logo which consisted of a "Y," the symbol "&" for "and" and a "dot" all inside a circle on the grips. Wyandotte is the name of the city in Michigan where the guns were made. Wyandotte's most famous grips are the Hopalong Cassidy ones of course, showing the outline and signature of Hoppy as well as the "Hopalong Cassidy" name formed out of bullet holes on the smaller Hoppy models. Wyandotte was also the company that other than its famous Hoppy models, made only generic guns. The horse head logo used on the Wyandotte guns is totally different than the other horse head styles. The Wyandotte horse head is looking downward, is bridled, mouth open and with the design of it's mane, appears to be going at a fast rate of speed. The other side of the horse head grips utilizes a lasso and huge horseshoe design, both heavily sculptured.

The Wyandotte logo found inside the gun chamber when opened consists of a circle with the wording "Wyandotte Toys" and "Made in USA" in the center of the circle with "Reg. US Pat.Off." on the lower rim. Strangely enough, however, on the more generic "Red Ranger Jr" cap gun, the logo of the more familiar "Y&." was substituted by a 5 point star with a hole indented in the center of the star. The bridled horse head remained the same, but applied on both sides of the small model. The small Hoppy gun made by Wyandotte with the bullet holes forming the full name, however, has no logo of any kind on the grips.

This ends the descriptions and study of the logos, trademarks and other features of the major manufacturers of western character guns and also the generic western guns since many of the same features are found on both. This by no means tends to indicate that these are all the logos that exist, indeed, as we collectors have learned and which the reader will see all through this book, new, strange, and interesting logos, trademarks, and features surface all the time. So much for the better, lads! "O.K. boys, you have no excuse now wondering who the culprits are that made these thar' weapons. . .now let's go get 'em!

MOM!
CHOOSE YOUR CHILD'S NEXT GUN From These

COMMENDED BY THE CONSUMER SERVICE BUREAU OF PARENTS' MAGAZINE AS ADVERTISED THEREIN

HARMLESS DAISY TOYS!

All Daisy Toys advertised here are commended by the Parents' Magazine and guaranteed by Daisy!

Prices Subject to Change Without Notice Prices Higher in Canada

No. 1160 SUPER SCOPE SMOKE RIFLE
Gun 32' with 11' magnifying scope! $4.98

DAISY HOLSTERS
49¢ to $13.95
Daisy offers you the best values for the least cost! Styled like those worn by your TV-Western Heroes! Ask for "Daisys!"

No. 660 CHEYENNE* SINGIN' SADDLE GUN
Whines like real bullet! Smokes! 32'. Looks like rifle TV's Cheyenne shoots! $4.98

No. 960 AUTOMATIC SMOKER
Durable 32' gun; adjustable sling! $2.98

IT'S A DAISY

THIS DAISY TRADEMARK ON TOY GUNS GUARANTEES SATISFACTION!

A-2447   ©1959 Warner Bros. Pictures, Inc.   PRINTED IN U.S.

ALAN LADD · SHANE

Rare "Shane"-marked holster with several silver conchos and Schmidt Alan Ladd pistol. (Courtesy of Brian Wolf)

Alan Ladd, along with both John Wayne and Nick Adams, was the only actor whose non-character name was immortalized on a cap pistol and holster set. Alan Ladd's classic western, *Shane*, was released in 1953 by Paramount Pictures, and it brought Ladd—touted in the advertisement for the cap gun and holster set as "The All American Ladd"—everlasting fame.

The George Schmidt Manufacturing Company of Los Angeles produced the Alan Ladd Shoot'n Iron and the Alan Ladd Circle-A-Bar-L holster sets, each with a special box of its own. Alan Ladd, of course, starred in dozens of westerns, but critics agree that *Shane*—a real western classic, even in its own time—is how he will be best remembered.

Born in 1913 in Arkansas, Alan Ladd started with a bit part in Universal Picture's *Once in a Lifetime* in 1932, then progressed to bigger roles, including 1939's *Come 'on, Leathernecks*. Ladd had a certain sad, soft-spoken appeal. Blonde, green-eyed, and athletic, his break came in Paramount's *This Gun for Hire* in 1942 with Veronica Lake. The critics and the public loved him, even though he played a psychopathic killer.

Paramount seized his overnight success and cast him again with Veronica Lake in *The Glass Key* in the same year, 1942. This was followed by *The Great Gatsby*. Ladd then plunged into a series of movies that proved he had great talent, starring in romance classics, army and navy films, and of course, westerns. Some of his best westerns included *Drum Beat*, *Branded*, *Santiago*, *Red Mountain*, and *The Proud Rebel*. However, in 1953, he was cast in *Shane*, his most famous role.

In *Shane*, Ladd's style of "underplaying" the character, allowed him to portray a laconic, mysterious gunfighter who comes to the aid of a group of homesteaders in a bitter war with a local cattle baron. This movie put Ladd at the top of the charts, and although he played in more than a dozen movies after *Shane*, the movies that followed never achieved the same appeal. Ladd redeemed himself as "Nevada Smith" in his last role in *The Carpetbaggers* in 1964, shortly before his death. His son, Alan Ladd, Jr., became a leading film industry executive in his own right. Alan Ladd formed his own production company the year he died, at age 50, in 1964.

The pistol that Schmidt marketed as "the All-American Ladd" was unique because never before had a living person—an actor, no less—been "immortalized" on a cap pistol, box, and holster set. That kind of fame is usually reserved for a western hero or outlaw long deceased. The only other actors that would share that honor, were John Wayne and Nick Adams. However, while the John Wayne holsters have his name and image, the guns were generic. Thus, this strange happening makes the Alan Ladd Shoot 'n Iron a unique piece of Americana.

CAP GUN COLLECTIBLES

The Alan Ladd cap pistol was a 10-inch chromed die-cast gun with copper grips bearing the "AL" logo on the simulated stag grips and "Alan Ladd" in script on both sides of the frame under the cylinder. The high-luster chrome gun breaks open from the top, and has the release lever on the left side of the hammer. These guns came with both a dark copper and a shiny copper finish to the copper stag grips. Both have the "AL" in a circle logo on the grips.

The Alan Ladd holsters put out by the Schmidt Company also included other "go-withs," such as spurs and wrist cuffs, all of which sported the "AL" within a circle logo, prominently shown on the wrist cuffs, the sides of the spurs and on the conchos of the holster belt, which also included the full signature of Alan Ladd, the same as on the cap pistol. The rich-looking leather holster set has metal long horns, studs and jewels adorning it, as well as the monogrammed conchos and the "Alan Ladd" signature on the back of the belt.

Alan Ladd in his most famous role as "Shane," which inspired the introduction of the cap pistol bearing his name. Van Heflin co-starred.

Close-up view of the "AL" logo on the holster pocket concho. (Mike Merryman Collection)

A single holster with "SHANE" in western lettering on the front of the holster pocket also was made, possibly of Canadian manufacture, complete with conchos similar, but not identical to, the conchos worn by Ladd in the movie of the same name. The holster takes the 10-inch Alan Ladd cap pistol by Schmidt, and it was advertised in the Eaton's Canadian catalog.

In September 1966, ABC presented the TV western program *Shane* starring David Carradine, who was later to achieve fame in *Kung Fu*. The show was based rather loosely on the *Shane* film with Alan Ladd. Unfortunately, the show only lasted 17 episodes, and went off the air in December 1966. While David Carradine also played a serious, quiet, mysterious character, he lacked the appeal of Alan Ladd as "Shane."

No cap pistol with the title "SHANE" honoring either the original feature film or the TV show is known to exist. However, it was Alan Ladd who immortalized "Shane," so happily, we have the cap pistol and the holster sets to add to our collections! Schmidt was the only manufacturer of the Alan Ladd gun and holster set.

Schmidt Alan Ladd cap pistol and original box; note Alan Ladd's photo, signature, and "AL" logo on both the box and the gun. (Courtesy of Brian Wolf)

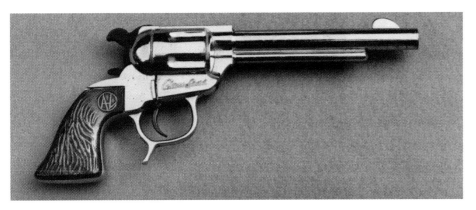

Above: Right side view of Schmidt Alan Ladd cap pistol.

David Carradine in the short-lived television series Shane. Note the several conchos on the gunbelt, similar, but not identical to, Alan Ladd's gunbelt in the movie of the same title. (Courtesy of Old West Shop)

Above: Left side view of Schmidt Alan Ladd cap pistol.

(Right) Rare Alan Ladd double holster made by Schmidt. Note the "AL" logo on the conchos as well as the unique double-buckle affair on the belt. (Mike Merryman Collection)

Note back of belt illustrating impressed "Alan Ladd" signature. (Mike Merryman Collection)

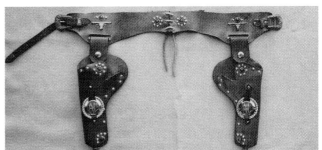

ANNIE OAKLEY

The real Annie Oakley at the height of her career, as a member of Buffalo Bill's Wild West Show. This photo was taken in England. Note her titles and chest full of medals.

Gail Davis, that beautiful, pig-tailed blonde, showed us that women were just as clever at handling law and order, and shooting and riding with the best of her male counterparts. *Annie Oakley* rode into our living rooms from April 1953, through December 1956, covering 81 episodes on ABC. Produced by Gene Autry's Flying "A" Productions, Gail Davis, a former leading lady in some 20 westerns before *Annie Oakley,* was both beautiful and a no-nonsense cowgirl sharpshooter.

Her younger brother, "Tagg," was played by actor Jimmy Hawkins. *Annie Oakley* was also the first TV western starring a female lead. Prior to that, Annie Oakley was memorialized by the dynamic and irreplaceable Ethel Merman, who played Annie in MGM's *Annie Get your Gun.* Other movie "Annie Oakley" greats were Betty Hutton and Barbara Stanwyck. However, it's Gail Davis who will best be remembered for bringing Annie Oakley into our living rooms in one of TV's earliest westerns.

The real Annie Oakley was born Phoebe Anne Oakley Mozee in Ohio in 1860. Before she turned 9 years old, she had taken her father's cap and ball rifle, and was shooting everything from small game and targets until she became proficient enough to feed the family of 8 children. She then began selling quail and turkey in the markets of Darke County, Ohio, where they lived.

Like many county areas of the time, shooting matches were held regularly. When a professional rifleman named Frank Butler put down $100 to anyone who could beat him, Little Annie took him on, beating him at shooting, and then falling in love with him. They married, and started a shooting act together. She dropped her name to simply "Annie Oakley."

In 1885, the team signed on with Buffalo Bill's "Original Wild West Show." Billing her as "Little Miss Sure Shot," and at times, simply "Little Missy" the "Greatest Wild West Show in the World" toured the United States, and then Europe. There, she dazzled royalty and commoners alike. She even out-shot the Grand Duke Michael of Russia, much to Buffalo Bill's initial embarrassment that a woman, a commoner, and a dead shot could outshoot the Duke. The Duke shot 15 out of 50 targets, while Annie shot 47 out of the same ball targets. Even Queen Victoria presented her with a special medal. The Butlers toured Germany, where Annie shot a cigarette out of Kaiser Wilhelm's mouth!

The show went on to Spain, France, and Italy. Little Miss Sure Shot was now world famous! None other than Chief Sitting Bull, also touring with the Wild West Show, had given her the name "Watanya Cicilia" meaning "Little Sure Shot." She was also called "Miss Annie" on other billings. London photographers took hundreds of photos of Annie, bedecked with medals.

In 1901, she was injured critically in a train wreck, and it took her two years to get over partial paralysis, and five major operations, before she got up to shoot again. She later went into vaudeville, and later still, gave shooting lessons in North Carolina. A woman of great humanity and compassion, she adopted 18 young girls that she put through school on her own, for the Butlers had no children themselves. Annie could shoot backwards with both rifle and shotgun with deadly accuracy. She could shoot from a bicycle and a galloping horse. Photos from the period show her with her own hand-made clothes covered with medals and ribbons.

A car accident in 1922 broke her hip. It took years of great pain and effort for her to get back on her feet, but she never lost her humility, or her compassion, for other less fortunate people. She also eulogized Buffalo Bill at his funeral in Colorado. In 1926, this wonderful all-American woman died, only to be followed by her beloved husband just three weeks later. They are both buried in their native Ohio.

Gail Davis as "Annie Oakley," TV's first western with a female lead. This is the role for which the beautiful Gail Davis will always be remembered.

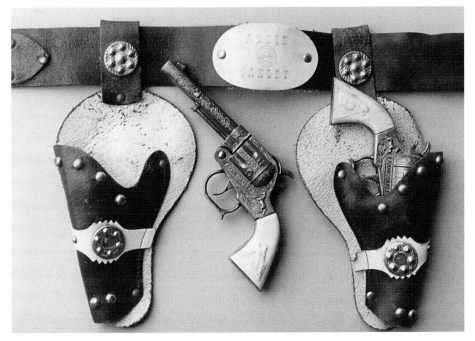

*Betty Hutton, the big screen's first "Annie Oakley" in MGM's **Annie Get Your Gun**. The movie was in technicolor. (Courtesy of A. Forman)*

Leslie-Henry Annie Oakley double holster sets. Note the "Annie Oakley" logo on the back of the belt in between her name. (Courtesy of John Bracken)

Unfortunately, Annie Oakley was just a distant memory until Gene Autry's Flying "A" Productions brought her back into the hearts of America, as Gail Davis made "Annie Oakley" a household name again, and became one of the most popular and beloved western stars in the 1950s. Certainly Hollywood added some glamour and excitement, since this was a weekly series, but one cannot set aside the fact that TV's Annie Oakley was a woman to be reckoned with, in beauty, brains, and the handling of a six-gun!

CAP GUN COLLECTIBLES

The only known cap pistols with "Annie Oakley" on the frames were made by Leslie-Henry in both the 7- and 9-inch sizes, with the nickel finish and white horsehead grips. The 7-inch gun has the name on both sides of the gun, breaks open from the top with a left side release lever, and lots of scroll work. The 9-inch pattern is the standard Leslie-Henry classic model, sporting the well-known white horse head grips, raised lettering, nickel finish, left side lever, and also breaks open from the top. Two variations have been identified. One has the name on both sides of the frame; another pattern carries "ANNIE OAKLEY" on the right side and "GENE AUTRY" on the left side, as it was a Flying "A" Production. The rearing horse logo is also raised on the frames.

A double holster set that came with the same guns, also by Leslie-Henry, in blue-and-white leather, is typical of a cowgirl's holster set. "ANNIE OAKLEY" lettering is shown on the back of the holster belt, sporting the full name, as well as the Annie Oakley logo, consisting of a bulls eye, made up of the "A" and the "O" and a rifle across the logo. It also sports red jewels and studs.

Daisy also marketed several Annie Oakley holster sets, in both single and double models. The cap pistols used in the Daisy sets were Hubley Western and Texan guns, with both the gorgeous turquoise grips as well as the purple swirl grips. The Daisy holsters are spectacular. Made of quality leather, the belt and holsters are in dark blue leather with suede lower sections of the pockets, and suede fringe. The belt has Annie's logo on the holster sections consisting of the "A," "O" and rifle target. On the back of the belt, there is another suede section with fringe which holds three bullets. The buckles came in the standard horseshoe shapes with longhorns and the more decorative hexagon model with western motifs. The belt was adjustable.

Beautiful box for the Daisy double holster set showing Gail Davis on the cover. Note "Annie" on the horse with brother "Tagg" following behind. the box advertises the set for boys and girls.

Pair of Leslie-Henry 7-1/2-inch Annie Oakley cap pistols. (Courtesy of John Bracken)

The Daisy boxes came with a great photo and graphics, showing Gail Davis on the cover, and "Annie Oakley with Tagg." The box also shows "Annie" doing some trick riding, standing on her horse as she did at the beginning of the program. All the Annie Oakley boxed sets carry the older Plymouth, Michigan, address. Interestingly enough, the box lid advertises the holster set for girls and boys. Daisy marketed the Annie Oakley sets with and without guns, the smoke and bang rifle, canteen, and even a "golden" scope for the rifle. Even *Parents* magazine commended the these outfits for "quality."

Another double holster set, perhaps the most beautiful ever made for Annie Oakley, came in white soft calf's leather, with red fringe, red jewels, lots of studs, red hearts, red lettering in the full name, and in the cross-draw style. These came sporting the turquoise gripped Hubley Texan .38s, and has also been found with Schmidt Buck'n Broncs and Latco Ruf Rider guns. This Annie set even has sterling silver conchos and mother-of-pearl studs. The hearts and fringe are red suede and the entire outfit is a superb set to behold. Even the real Annie Oakley would have been proud to strap these babies on!

Daisy also marketed the Annie Oakley smoke-noise rifle in white, blue, and gold colors, again for both "girls as well as boys." The stock and forepiece was white, with the Annie Oakley logo on the left side. They came in specially-marked cardboard boxes with and without other accoutrements, such as a white plastic canteen, and what is easily seen as a Hubley Western cap pistol, and the same blue and white-fringed buckskin holster and belt in the single style. The 1956 Daisy catalog shows this set as #1967 Annie Oakley Golden Smoke Rifle Outfit. The rifle was a strapping 32 inches long, and came with a blue sling. I'm sure a lot of little "Annie Oakley" cowgirls became good shots. My little sister, Anna, was one of those cute little cowgirls.

The same logo that made Annie Oakley famous was used on both the rifle stock and the top portion of the slide-on holster to the adjustable belt. Another Annie Oakley rifle marketed by Daisy was called the Harmless Super Smoker Rifle, and it came in its own special box showing both Annie and Tagg on the graphics. This was marketed in Daisy's Guns of the West series. A final note on other Annie Oakley guns. While we have yet to see an Annie Oakley gun by other than Leslie-Henry and Daisy, it appears that the Hamilton Line, which made the more popular Cheyenne shooter, did make an Annie Oakley and it is shown advertised as such on the box for the Cheyenne Shooter.

Here's the real Annie Oakley with her famous rifle while on tour, circa 1890.

Daisy's Annie Oakley Super Smoke Rifle complete with the carrying-case-style box marked to Annie and Tagg. Note the Annie logo on the white stock and the blue rifle sling.

Daisy's beautiful double holster set for Annie Oakley which came with Hubley's Western cap pistol with turquoise grips. Made of blue leather with suede fringe. Note the logo over each holster pocket.

THE TV STARS

Gail Davis, who was born in Little Rock, Arkansas, landed her first movie role in the 1946 *Romance at Rosy Ridge* with Van Johnson. She made a string of westerns with Allan "Rocky" Lane and Tim Holt at RKO Pictures. But it was in the 1949 movie, *The Far Frontier* with Roy Rogers that brought her to the attention of Gene Autry. He signed her right up to be his leading lady in several Autry movies. When *The Gene Autry Show* aired on television in 1950, she was a guest star on several episodes in the first three years. Autry's Flying "A" Productions then cast her as the good-looking, blonde pig-tailed, fast riding, sharp shooting, and forever memorable "Annie Oakley."

Annie Oakley began each week with Annie riding hell-bent for leather on her horse. At one point, she stands up on the saddle and shoots toward a man whose back is to the screen. As she rides by and takes her shot, the camera zooms in on the man, who is now holding a card in his right hand. As the camera gets closer to the card, you can see Annie shot a hole right through the center spade on the card, a 9 of spades. The man, of course, was actor Brad Johnson, who also starred on the show as "Deputy Sheriff Lofty Craig." In the program, Annie and younger brother Tagg are invited to move in with Lofty Craig after the death of their parents. Annie's "Uncle Luke McTavish" would also occasionally be seen on the show.

The setting for the show was Diablo County, Arizona, where Lofty tried to keep law and order. Tagg was always shown as a younger brother with a lot of love and respect for his older sister, who tries to bring him up as mom and dad would have wanted. It's obvious Lofty Craig is smitten by Annie's beauty and brains, as well as her sharpshooting, but the romance is never consummated in any way. The most "risque" line that Lofty ever said to Annie was "Annie, you're just getting prettier every day." Of course, any man with blood in his veins who recalls the fringed skirt, vested blouse with Annie's logo on the wrists and the cowboy boots, can see why Lofty was just wild about Annie. No wonder Lofty was always going to Annie for help!

After the end of the show, Gail Davis fans with a good memory may recall she appeared on *The Andy Griffith Show* as Andy's date, and true to form, she tops Andy in a shooting contest! In later years, Gail Davis continued to appear at numerous western film festivals all over the country to adoring, yet older fans, who will never forget her. Lovely Gail Davis once said "So far as I'm concerned, I'm going to be Annie Oakley for the rest of my born days." She was right, of course.

Sadly, Gail Davis recently passed away at age 71 of cancer in the spring of 1997. Brad Johnson and Jimmy Hawkins are still with us. If you really had a great eye and good memory, you may recall that a young and relatively unknown Fess Parker often appeared on the show as "Tom Courier," the editor of *The Diablo Courier* newspaper.

O.K., a final test: How many of you gringos out there remember the name of Annie Oakley's horse? It was NOT "Tagg" as some people think! It was "Target." It was certainly very appropriate, don't you think? The name of Tagg's horse was "Pixie."

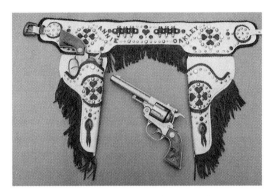

Beautiful early Annie Oakley double holster set in white leather with red details, fringe, and studs, complete with a pair of Hubley Texan .38 cap pistols with turqoise grips. Note they are in the butt-first crossdraw style ala Wild Bill Hickok.

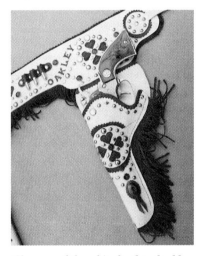

Close-up of the white leather double set showig the beautiful red heart details, red suede fringe, deeply-tooled name, mother-of-pearl studs, and the gorgeous Texan cap gun with turqoise grips.

The box for the Hamilton-Cheyenne indicates that Hamilton made an Annie Oakley and a Range Rider cap gun—both Gene Autry Flying A Production TV westerns. A Hamilton marked "Annie Oakley" has yet to surface.

Close-up of details on the Daisy holster set with Hubley Western cap pistol. Note the "AO" logo and the suede fringe against blue leather. The Western was one of the most popular cap guns that Hubley made.

The Dell comic book featuring Gail Davis as "Annie Oakley." A lot of cowgirls in the 1950s looked up to Annie Oakley, a wonderful role model. Note the same logo on the outfit that Gail Davis wore on the show. Annie's horse was named "Target."

BAT MASTERSON

This TV western program was based on the real western lawman whose full name was William Barclay Masterson. Some say he was one of the toughest lawmen that ever graced the Wild West. Some say he was one of the most clever and shrewd. "Bat" Masterson would never use his gun when he could use his brains, or his "bat" instead. In fact, he earned his nickname as he patrolled Dodge City's Front Street at night with his cane, and instead of firing bullets, he cracked heads when cowhands and malcontents tested his nerve.

The second of seven children, Bat was born November 24, 1853. It might be interesting for readers to know that Masterson was born in Henryville, in Quebec, Canada. The family lived and worked on various farms in New York, Illinois, and Kansas, and Bat learned to work hard

The real William Barclay "Bat" Masterson, one of the finest lawmen of the Old West, at the height of his career. (Courtesy Kansas State Historical Society)

Above: The Dodge City Peace Commission. Standing left to right: W.H. Harris, Luke Short, Bat Masterson. Sitting left to right: Charlie Bassett, Wyatt Earp, Frank McLain, and Neal Brown. These lawmen tamed Dodge City, Kansas, in the 1870s. (Courtesy Kansas State Historical Society)

Gene Barry, TV's "Bat Masterson." Just as slick and well dressed as the real hero, and never without his "bat." Note he wears his gun in the crossdraw fashion.

Lone Star Bat Masterson cap pistol. Nickel plated with cream colored "notch" bar grips. Early pattern.

Lone Star Bat Masterson cap pistol, second pattern with full-stag plastic grips. This model was sold both separately and in the Carnell full outfit sets.

at a young age. At the age of 17, he got a job on the railroad. He next teamed up with buffalo hunters, and at age 20, rode with Billy Dixon, a famous buffalo hunter who said of Bat that "he was like a chunk of steel."

Both men drew plenty of lead at the Battle of Adobe Walls. In June 1874, it was Bat and some 19 or 20 other buffalo hunters who stood off and held the ground against a thousand Comanche, Kiowa, and Arapaho warriors, led by Chief Quanah Parker. After the Quanah Parker Indian uprisings, Bat was made second in command of 18 scouts under Gen. Nelson Miles. They operated out of Kansas, and specifically out of Dodge City, riding and scouting in the southwest. But Bat's life would forever be changed as his scouting missions took him to Sweetwater, Texas.

Bat's first recorded killing took place at this time. On a cold night in January 1876, our man Masterson was in a saloon in the company of a lady named Molly Brennan. A jealous would-be lover by the name of Sergeant King, spurned by the cute Brennan, turned his rage to Masterson, and as was often the macho image of the day, decided he'd settle the score with his six-shooter. The courageous Molly threw herself in front of Bat as King fired his gun, taking the bullet, which passed right through the unfortunate lady and then entered Bat's pelvic bone. As he went down, Bat pulled his own gun and shot King through the heart. Although he recovered from the dramatic triangle, Bat walked with a limp the rest of his life. His reputation and his nickname was born.

In the spring of 1876, he returned to Dodge City on a call from Wyatt Earp, whom he had met back in 1872 while buffalo hunting in Arkansas. Bat's brother, Jim Masterson, was already working for Earp as a deputy and Earp appointed Bat deputy marshal. Bat was a fine officer, and his service in Dodge City's records are all well kept. Leaving the post in July, he moved on to Deadwood, South Dakota, and joined the gold seekers. He went into gambling and saloon keeping, and meeting up again with Wyatt Earp. Earp suggested Bat run for sheriff of Ford County, and on November 6, 1877, he was elected. He also bought an interest in the Lone Star Dance Hall and Saloon. Bat was just 23 years old.

In March 1878, Bat captured the notorious Dave Rudabaugh, who had been robbing trains, ala Jesse James, in the vicinity of Dodge. He did so without firing a shot. In April 1878, Bat's other brother, Ed Masterson, also a deputy, was involved in a shootout while trying to apprehend Jack Wagner and Alf Walker. Bat just came around the corner to see his brother fall in a hail of gunfire. Bat whipped out his gun and fired four shots at sixty feet—shooting Walker through the lungs and the arms, and killing Wagner with a shot in the gut. Walker got away as Ed died in his brother's arms, but the lung shot soon induced pneumonia, and Walker died shortly thereafter. Bat was very close with his two lawmen-brothers, Jim and Ed. Seeing his brother Ed get shot and die in his arms had a very profound effect on Bat Masterson.

As a member of the Dodge City Peace Commission, along with Wyatt Earp, Neal Brown, and Bill Tilghman, Bat was presented with the same "Buntline Special" by Ned Buntline, the famous dime novelist writer. Unlike Wyatt who kept his Buntline intact, Bat cut the barrel down on his to eight inches, preferring a shorter barrel. Described as handsome, rather pleas-

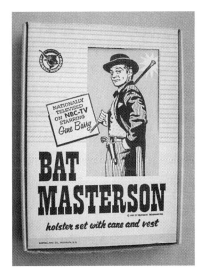

Carnell's Bat Masterson outfit box cover showing colorful box with Gene Barry as TV's "Bat Masterson."

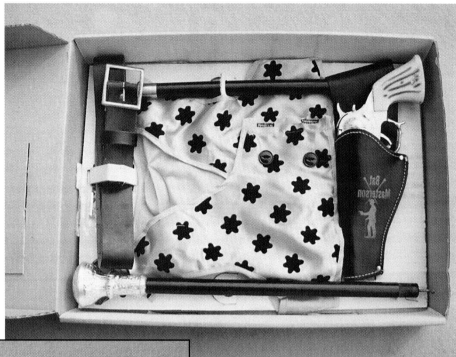

Contents of the superb Carnell Bat Masterson out-fit—cane, which comes apart, gunbelt with holster just like Bat wore on the show, fancy vest, and Lone Star second pattern stag-gripped cap pistol.

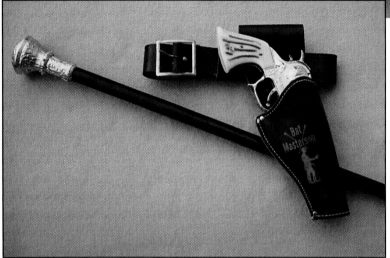

Bat Masterson's trademarks—his cane, which is also marked "Bat Masterson" on the top of the cane's holding portion, and the gunbelt with holster showing image of Bat with crossed canes and name on the sleek black leather.

ant, calm but calculating, Bat was known to carry two ivory handled Colt six-shooters. Bat was a restless sort of man, but he had a sense of humor as well. In 1881, he moved on to Tombstone and became a dealer in Wyatt Earp's Oriental Saloon, as well as serving on several posses. In 1883, he returned to Dodge City on a call from former Dodge City Peace Commission member, Luke Short. It seemed that every time a fearless lawman was needed, old friends called on Bat.

In 1891, Bat married Emma Waters, a song and dance girl he met at the Palace Theater, and began to settle down for the first time in his life. Like his friend Wyatt, he, too, got involved with prize-fighting and promotion. In 1902, Bat moved to New York City. President Teddy Roosevelt appointed him U.S. deputy marshal of New York after Bat declined to be appointed to the same post for Arizona. He told Roosevelt that he didn't want to kill any crazy kids who would want to try and kill him for his reputation. In 1905, Bat resigned the post to become a sports writer for the New York *Morning Telegraph.* He was also a writer for *Human Life* magazine. Bat had finally found his niche in life. He continued to write his sports column for 17 years. On October 27, 1921, after having typed up daily his column, Bat Masterson, hero of many gunfights, died of a heart attack at his desk.

TV's "Bat Masterson" was played with eloquence by Gene Barry. While the outfit he wore was based on the real Bat Masterson, the producers shunned the moustache and fitted Barry with a single cross draw left side holster as well as the famous "bat"—a black wooden, gold topped cane. In answer to cries of violence, it is interesting to note that TV's Bat Masterson disarmed the bad guys with a whack of the bat and lots of wit and guts. The TV show was a popular one, running from October 1959, through September 1961. It brought the popularity of the dapper flowered vest, gold topped cane, and the black cross-draw left side holster to many young "Bat Masterson" wannabees!

Carnell's own Bat Masterson model with revolving cylinder, beautiful stag grips, and window-type box with image of Gene Barry on cover.

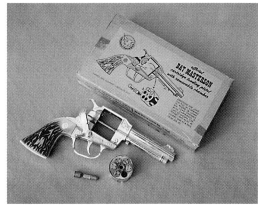

Rear of box shows how to take the gun apart for loading the bullets into the revolving cylinder. Showing the right side of the gun disassembled and the 2-piece bullet.

CAP GUN COLLECTIBLES

The Bat Masterson cap guns were made by Lone Star and marketed by Carnell Roundup of New York. Two patterns exist. The most common model is the Lone Star 9-inch, nickel-plated model with two grip variations. The earlier models have the simulated stag with the "notch bar" grips, found in both a coffee cream swirl and brown. A later pattern, and the model that came in the Bat Masterson complete set, came with a chrome finish and an all-plastic stag grip that surrounded the entire grip frame.

The more elusive, and most desirable, of the Bat Masterson cap guns is the Carnell-manufactured model, which came with a revolving cylinder that was removed by a special release of the ejection rod by pushing it forward. This gun also takes six bullets, loaded into the cylinder when the right side lever is pushed downward, much like the superb Nichols 41-40. This beautiful gun has a nickel finish and gorgeous stag grips and the "C" logo for Carnell. The left side of the frame is marked "Bat Masterson," while the right side is marked "200." It is solid and well made, and appears to have also been made with a gold finish and black grips with the same simulated stag design. This gun does not "break open" in any way other than the removal of the revolving cylinder.

The Carnell Bat Masterson, one of the finest cap guns made. Superb stag grips are deeply grooved. Note the unique sight and sliding spring catch to remove revolving cylinder.

Left: Close-up of the spectacular Carnell Bat Masterson showing raised name. Note the "C" logo on the fine stag grips.

The box for this gun has a plastic cover with Gene Barry as "Bat Masterson" on the cover, and instructions for the removal of the cylinder and bullets on the back of the box. While we know for sure the other model is a Lone Star product, it appears this model may have been USA-made, since the ejector rod housing under the barrel is stamped "Carnell Manufacturing Co., Brooklyn, NY" and the "C" logo on the grip is most apparent as is the lack of the Lone Star horse head on the frame.

Imagine the thrill of a youngster getting the boxed official Bat Masterson outfit, consisting of the black leather belt, holster, Lone Star cap gun, fancy vest and the cane, also marked "Bat Masterson on the top of the gold cap. The cane comes in two pieces and are screwed together, making it a rather long weapon. The holster has the image of Bat Masterson, the name, and two crossed canes, all in gold lettering. The vest is yellow with black six-point star design. Neat! In some stills of Gene Barry in his costume, the gun he carries is definitely the stag handled model. In fact, it almost looks like the revolving cylinder Carnell model in one photo.

A lesser known actor played Bat Masterson on *The Life and Legend of Wyatt Earp* series that starred Hugh O'Brien. That actor was also one of my favorites, and few western trivia buffs even remember him. He was Mason Allen Dinehart III. While he was not as dapper as the Gene Barry character, Dineheart was mustachioed like the real Bat and did more no-nonsense talking, and had a temper. I even wrote to the star asking for his autographed photo, which he sent me and is shown here, as well as that of Gene Barry. Gene Barry still relishes his role as TV's Bat Masterson, and he went on to several other TV series, none of which were westerns.

Classy Products put out a "copy," in a sense, of the Bat Masterson outfit marketed by Carnell, which is little known and seldom seen. In fact, none have ever surfaced that this writer has ever seen or heard about for sale or in collections in the past 15 years. Classy called it Fancy Dan Combination Set, Model #2956. Remarkably, it came in a single belt and holster similar to the Carnell outfit, but with a Classy Roy Rogers nickel-plated cap gun. The cane, which looks almost identical to the Carnell "Bat" can, was advertised as a "cap firing" cane with a die cast metal handle. The set also included a vest, sheriff's badge, a "chap-style" bow tie, and a small derringer in its own miniature holster. The set sold for $4.98. The Fancy Dan cane was also sold separately, as Model #150, for 98 cents, which was shipped in a display stand of 12 canes

Lone Star made the Bat Masterson cap pistol in two models. Carnell made the Bat Masterson cap pistol with the revolving cylinder. Carnell Roundup marketed both guns and the holster set, vest and cane outfit. Classy made a "copy" of the Carnell Bat Masterson outfit called Fancy Dan.

Dell comic featuring Gene Barry as "Bat Masterson." Notice that Carnell was able to capture the essence of the cane and cross draw holster and stag-gripped pistol that Gene Barry wore on the show.

Actor Mason Alan Dinehart, who starred as Bat Masterson on The Life and Legend of Wyatt Earp. He had the moustache, but it's Gene Barry that we remember as TV's "Bat Masterson." Dinehart played a tougher role, while Barry played a more sophisticated Bat Masterson.

BILLY THE KID

illy the Kid, a true western character, was born William H. Bonney in New York City in 1859. The family moved to Kansas when Billy was about three years old, and a short time later, his father died there. His mother moved again, with Billy and his younger brother, Eddie, to Colorado, where she remarried. They again moved, this time to Sante Fe, New Mexico, and later still to Silver City, a shoot 'em up roaring mining village.

Billy's mother, now Mrs. Jack Antrim, ran a boarding house, while her new husband worked the mines. At age 12, Billy killed his first of the 21 men he was to kill in his twenty-one years of life. He stabbed a drunken blacksmith to death with his jackknife after the man insulted his mother. The mother helped her young son get on the run and he left town, never seeing his mother again. The legend was born.

Billy became a "cowboy," working on several ranches in Arizona and the New Mexico territory. But harboring an attitude, trying to grow up fast among the tough men of his day, he had a short fuse and an even faster trigger finger, and the bodies began to mount up—3 Indians near Fort Bowie, a man in Tucson, a black soldier in a card game, a young Mexican gunman, a gambler in Chihuahua, Mexico, all before the age of 16. They say he dressed neatly, had buck teeth, and was popular with women. Before long, he made the first of several mistakes that brought relentless peace officers after him.

He killed several men in a string of disputes between cattlemen in the New Mexico area. He killed a sheriff named Jim Brady and his deputy, Hamilton. A posse of 60 men went after Billy and his companions, who hold up at what was known as the McSween House. The gun battle lasted 3 days, but the "Kid" escaped. He was out of control, and even Gov. Lew Wallace (who was writing *Ben-Hur* at the time) offered him full amnesty if he'd take off his guns and settle down—the "Kid" as he was called, refused. It is said they met and made a deal, but the governor allegedly reneged on it.

Then Pat Garrett, a six-foot-four former cowboy, was elected sheriff of Lincoln County, New Mexico, where Billy "hung out" with a rough band of killers and rustlers. At first, strangely, Sheriff Garrett befriended Billy, played cards with him, and seemed to get along just fine. In reality, Garrett was patient, methodical, and it was his aim to bring the Kid to justice alive. On Christmas Eve of 1880, Garrett made his move, ambushing the Kid's gang and killing two of his men. The Kid and his remaining four companions surrendered the next day. Taken to Mesilla, the Kid was tried, convicted of killing Sheriff Brady, and sentenced to hang.

A few days before the hanging, one of his two jailers went to lunch, while the other, Tom Bell, played cards with the Kid. When Bell went to pick up a card the Kid dropped, the Kid grabbed Bell's gun and jail keys. He killed Bell and then, as the other jailer, Bob Ollinger, came running across the street after he heard the shooting, Billy killed him instantly with two shotgun blasts, and took off after stealing a horse. Some say Billy the Kid went back to Fort

The real Billy the Kid—William H. Bonney. Not handsome, but very deadly. Taken about 1879, two years before his death. (Courtesy of Museum of New Mexico)

Robert Taylor, who played "Billy the Kid" in the 1941 MGM film. A lot older than the real Billy and certainly a more handsome one, but just as deadly! (Courtesy of A. Forman)

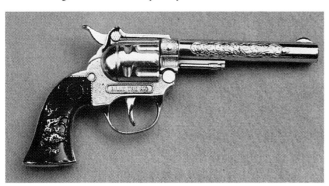

The Stevens Billy the Kid all-metal die cast cap pistol.

Audie Murphy as "Billy the Kid" in the 1951 movie The Texas Kid.

Richard Jaeckel, also played "Billy the Kid." He passed away in 1998.

TV's "Billy the Kid," played by Clu Gulager, in The Tall Man. (Courtesy of Old West Shop)

Above: The nickel pattern and the much harder-to-find gold pattern of the Stevens Billy the Kid cap pistol.

Left: Close-up of the Stevens cap pistol. Note raised "Billy the Kid," the "S" logo, and the full standing buffalo on the all-metal black painted grips.

Sumner to see his Mexican girlfriend before planning to escape into Mexico. Garrett went after him and on the night of July 14, 1881, shot him dead. Billy was 21 years old. The "legend" of Billy the Kid began almost the minute he died as Sheriff Garrett yelled out "I shot Billy the Kid!" Twenty-one men had died testing the Kid's guns, temper, patience and his own brand of loyalty to his friends.

Since his death, dozens of books and movies have been produced on Billy the Kid. Although no actual TV western was produced in his name, a TV show covering the strange friendship between Sheriff Pat Garrett and Billy the Kid did surface and is covered later on in this book. Billy the Kid, the Old West's most famous juvenile delinquent, was immortalized in several movies. Over the years, beginning with 1931, he was played by Noah Berry, Richard Jaeckel, Jack Buetel, Buster Crabbe, and Don "Red" Barry. However, the two most famous of the "Billy the Kid" movies, and the actors who played the wild kid, were Robert Taylor, in *Billy the Kid*, a 1941 movie, and Audie Murphy, who played Billy in *The Texas Kid* in 1951.

The Audie Murphy film was a typical stretch-the-truth for romance and entertainment, while the movie with Robert Taylor is considered one of the best on the life of Billy. Lately, none other than Val Kilmer played in *Billy the Kid*, a 1989 movie based on Gore Vidal's screenplay. "Pat Garrett" was played by Duncan Regher (who also starred as *Zorro*). Television's approach to *Billy the Kid* was played by Clu Gulager, who brought a different style to the portrayal of the deadly delinquent. This is covered in the *The Tall Man* section of this book.

CAP GUN COLLECTIBLES

It would only be natural that toy guns—of all types—would carry the name of such a legendary western character, perhaps second to only Jesse James in terms of life, legend, and the truly homemade American outlaw from the Wild West. And, so it was with cast iron guns, the most well known being the Billy the Kid by Stevens of Connecticut, and Kilgore of Ohio. Since we are dealing mainly with the die cast guns, it is interesting to note that as Stevens moved on from cast iron to the few die casts that it made in the 1950-1960 period, they retained the Billy the Kid cap gun.

The Stevens Billy the Kid is an all-metal die-cast metal gun, including the grips. It is 7 inches and breaks from the top for cap loading. It has the raised name "Billy the Kid" on both sides of the frame, within a rope design. The grips carry the Circle "S" and a full standing American buffalo looking downward on the grips. The gun came in both a nickel and a gold finish. The grips are painted with a factory black enamel. It is a well made and nifty little gun. Shucks, if you were going to play the "bad guy" in the afternoon gunfight, you might as well be Billy the Kid!

BLACK SADDLE

Peter Breck and his co-stars, Anna-Lisa and Russell Johnson, who played Marshal "Gib Scott" on Black Saddle.

H ere's another great TV western show that few remember. The show ran on NBC from January 1959, and lasted until September 30, 1960, after moving to ABC. I recall the show well, with actor Peter Breck playing the lead role as "Clay Culhane," a former gunfighter turned lawyer. Traveling through the southwestern territories, the character carried his law books in his black saddlebags, also mounted on a black saddle, hence the rather strange name of the show.

While Clay Culhane was a former gunfighter, in *Black Saddle*, the character did his best to avoid bloodshed, relying on his lawyer's creed to settle disputes. Another character actor, Russell Johnson (later of *Gilligan's Island* fame) played the local marshal. The setting was the town of Latigo, New Mexico. Peter Breck went on to star in *The Big Valley*, which brought him greater success in TV westerns since the *Big Valley,* unlike the year and half run of *Black Saddle*, ran for just over four years.

Peter Breck star Black Saddle, as "Clay Culhane." Note that the black saddle, which carried his law books, has his initials "CC" on it.

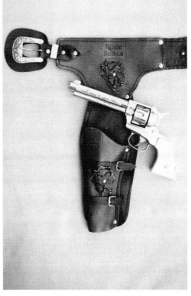

No cap guns with either "Black Saddle" or the lead character, former gunfighter-turned lawyer "Clay Culhane," are known to exist or have surfaced to date. However, a "Black Saddle" double holster set in at least two known variations exist, and both are shown here. The first is a tannish rough leather double holster set with "Black Saddle" imprinted on the top portion of the holster pockets, near the trigger guard edge. This pattern has black leather double straps with silver buckles on the pockets.

The belt itself has six bullets, a black ink border, and the buckle end and strap end of the belt are both in black leather. Both the holster pockets and the belt also sport black factory finish metal "black saddles" riveted to the belt and pockets and are very attractive. This pattern, of which two are known to be in collections, both came with Hubley "Texan Jrs."

The second variation, which is also a double holster set, appears to be better made of soft black and brown quality leather. This pattern also sports the metal "black saddles" on the belt and on the holster pockets. Interestingly enough, on this set, "Black Saddle" is printed on the belt itself, just over the metal black saddle. A couple of other subtle variations include a rather nice leather "border" around the buckle itself, and only three bullets on the back center of the belt. This set is shown with two Nichols Stallion .38s.

Another interesting note is that on the *Black Saddle* show, the character wore a single holster set. It is certainly possible that due to general design of the holsters and the fact that the same metal black saddles were used elsewhere, the J. Halpern Company (Halco) may have made the holster sets, using generic guns.

Black Saddle double holster outfit with Hubley pistols. Note the metal Black Saddle adornments on the belt and holster pockets. (Mike Merryman Collection)

Above left: Close up of the holster pocket showing details (Mike Merryman Collection)

Above right: Close up of the second pattern showing details of the Black Saddle adornment and the show title. Note the additional leather tab behind the ornate buckle.

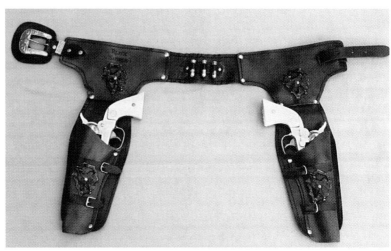

Second pattern of the Black Saddle double holster set with Nichols Stallion 38s. Note the show title is on the belt instead of the pockets on this model.

BONANZA

etween 1959, when TV westerns were still riding high across our black and white TV screens, and 1973, long after the TV western was becoming a baby boomer memory, *Bonanza* was and remains one of the longest running western series of all time, trailing only behind *Death Valley Days* and *Gunsmoke*. *Bonanza* ran for just over 14 years, made household names out of the Cartwrights, and launched a variety of *Bonanza* memorabilia that, for us cap pistol afficionados, left us a great deal to choose from and add to our western character list. First, some highlights of the program.

Actors Lorne Greene, Pernell Roberts, Dan Blocker, and Michael Landon played the Cartwright family, who owned the Ponderosa ranch in Nevada. As "Ben Cartwright," the patri-

arch of the clan and widower with three sons, Lorne Greene tried to keep his Ponderosa from being spoiled from gold-diggers and encroaching capitalists, while at the same time, trying to keep his sons, all with distinct personalities of their own, out of trouble, guns holstered, and the family intact.

"Little Joe," played by Michael Landon, was the quick-tempered one, with Dan Blocker playing the gentle giant of a man, and Pernell Roberts the more serious of the three. Roberts, who went on to *Trapper John, M.D.* eventually left the show and was replaced by "Candy" a ranch hand played by David Canary. Blocker, who played "Hoss," died in 1972. Lorne Greene died in 1987 and Michael Landon, who went on to many more years of success in *Little House on the Prairie*, died in 1991. *Bonanza* finished its 14-1/2-year

Television's most famous western family, the Cartwrights of Bonanza. Left to right: Dan Blocker ("Hoss"); Lorne Greene ("Ben") Pernell Roberts ("Adam") and Michael Landon ("Little Joe").

Leslie-Henry 9-inch Bonanza cap pistol with cameo grips.

Lelsie-Henry 10-1/2-inch long barreled Bonanza with black stag grips.

Leslie-Henry 11-inch .44 model Bonanza with revolving cylinder.

Halco-Hubley 9-1/2-inch Bonanza with brown and white stag grips.

reign in January 1973. It was also the first hour long TV western in color.

The popularity of *Bonanza* allowed the toy companies to reap a "bonanza" of their own, since the show became an internationally known western due to syndication. Visiting my cousins in Italy in 1988, I was surprised to see an episode of *Bonanza*, dubbed in Italian, 15 years after it had finished its run here in the States. That was some sight to see—Little Joe throwing a fit in Italian!

Pilen's 9-inch blued model Bonanza with revolving cylinder and colorful box with image of Lorne Greene as "Ben Cartwright" on cover. (Courtesy of Mike Cherry)

CAP GUN COLLECTIBLES

With regards to the cap guns marked "Bonanza," here is what is available: Leslie-Henry made a number of Bonanza cap guns. We begin with the popular 9-inch nickel pattern, marked "Bonanza" on both sides of the frame. This also came in a dull gray finish. Many grips were used—black stag, brown stag, white with cameo inserts, and the standard horse head plastic grips. All have the release lever on the left side and the rearing horse on the frame, and the standard scrollwork on the barrels. "Bonanza" was the raised pattern on the frame under the cylinder.

Leslie-Henry also made the very desirable "long barrel" Bonanza model, same as the above patterns, but with the length being 10 inches. These came in both nickel and dull gray finishes.

Leslie-Henry also made the large .44 model with revolving cylinder, sporting the horse head grip in various colors, and the oval logo with "L-H" and "H" on the grips. This was a late production and the finish is more of a dull gray-silver painted like finish. However, it is a very desirable model for the collectors of the .44 series of Leslie-Henry guns. The length of this gun is a big 11 inches overall.

Leslie-Henry also made the large .45 Bonanza model, complete with revolving cylinder and white stag grips, in its large .45 series. This pattern is found in both nickel and bronze finish. The logo is the Diamond "H" in a diamond on the grips. The frame carries both the rearing pony as well as the "Bonanza" title below the cylinder on both sides and "45" on both sides of the frame.

Halco also made the "Hubley" copy of the Bonanza, using the star logo and a unique variation of stag grips in dark brown and white. This model has a nickel finish and is stamped "Bonanza" on the left side, and "Halco" on the right side, under the cylinder. This model has the slide-up side gate for loading the caps and is identical to the Hubley Texan Jr. model, except that the slide gate on the "Bonanza" has a "checkered" inset area to push it up with the thumb while the Hubley Texan has the push-in button ejector release, breaking the gun open from the top. The length of this Bonanza model is 9 inches.

Halco also made a series of Bonanza single and double holsters, with and without guns. One of its series of holsters, interestingly enough, carries an oval medallion on the holster pockets of the Paladin horse head. Another version of the Bonanza holster set carries both the name as well as all four Cartwright characters on the belt. The holsters for this popular show are endless.

Marx came out with a Ponderosa Ranch set in the mid-1960s, which includes a rifle, holster, and clicker gun, and a bandoleer style belt. The gun and rifle were generic Marx models, however. Marx also came out with a Hoss Range Pistol, mounted on a card with Dan Blocker's picture on it. This was a plastic and metal clicker gun with a fanning action. The gun is not marked "Bonanza" or "Hoss."

Spain's Pilen line of guns honored *Bonanza* with a well-made Model 1917 U.S. army-style cap pistol in both nickel and blued finish, with fine checkered grips. This gun is stamped "Bonanza" on both sides of the frame and the colorful box sports Ben Cartwright's picture on it. This gun is approximately 9 inches in length, and comes with a slide forward release on the left side of the frame, and revolving cylinder.

Dell Comic book issued for Bonanza. Great color shot of the Cartwrights!

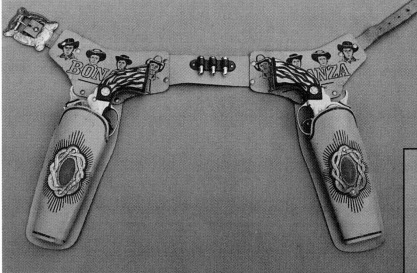

Closeup showing details of cap gun and gunbelt. Note concho and red jewel.

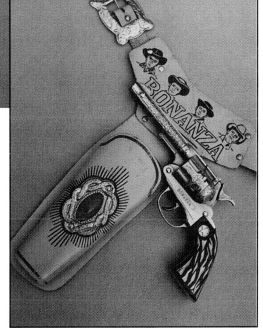

Beautiful Halco Bonanza double holster set with Hubley-Halco Bonanza cap guns with brown stag grips. Note the images of the Cartwrights on the gunbelt.

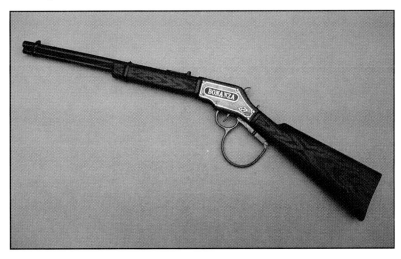

Seldom seen Bonanza cap shooting "ring lever" rifle made by Leslie-Henry/Halco.

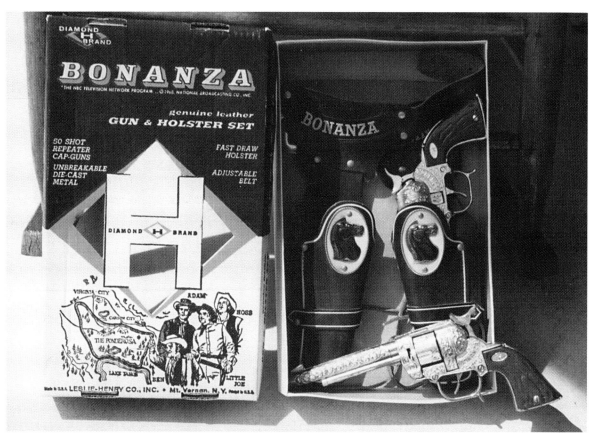

Wonderful Leslie-Henry boxed set of double holsters with 11-inch Bonanza .44 cap guns with revolving cylinders. (Courtesy of Brian Wolf)

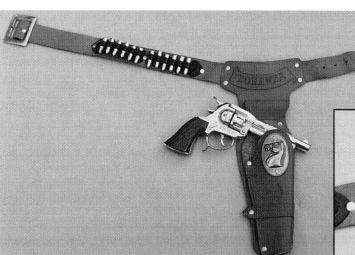

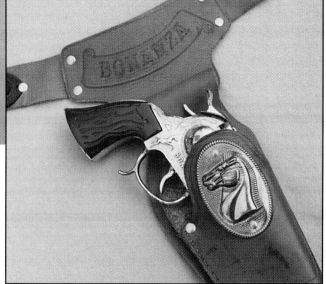

Gunfighter style single holster set with Leslie-Henry 9 inch cap gun with black stag grips. Note 12 bullets on this one!

Right: Close-up of details. Note Paladin-style horse head concho in brass on the holster pocket. This style concho was used on both single and double sets.

BRONCO

ew western buffs and cap gun collectors may recall this fine
western program, because it was initially a replacement for the
popular *Cheyenne* series on ABC, a product of the Warner
Brothers Studios. "Bronco" was actually "Bronco Layne," a former
Confederate captain who wanders westward after the Civil War and
encounters gunfighters, corrupt sheriffs, and pretty girls. He was an
adept horseman, lightning fast on the draw, and a handsome star
that, due to the popularity of the show even while under the
Cheyenne title, gathered a great many fans. It was an hour long
western adventure show.

Bronco went on the air in 1958 while Clint Walker was in a
salary dispute with Warner Bros. After Walker returned to his
"Cheyenne Bodie" role, *Bronco* was on its own as *Bronco Layne*
and lasted until August 1962, running a full four years, first as a fill
in with alternating episodes of *Sugarfoot* (with actor Will Hutchins
in the role) and then carrying a good audience on its own right.
Handsome actor Ty Hardin, who played the title role of Bronco
Layne went on to do feature films, including *Merrill's Marauders*,
Red River, and *PT 109*, of John F. Kennedy fame in World War II.

Above: Ty Hardin in his role as "Bronco Layne." (Courtesy of Old West Shop)

CAP GUN COLLECTIBLES

Although we cap gun nuts know that Kilgore made the first "Bronco" die cast in 1950,
it also came out with the second pattern in 1955. The first Bronco came with a nickel finish,
revolving cylinder, bucking "bronco" on the frame, mountain cat on the barrel, and white
grips with a saddle and boots on it in high sculptured relief.

The second model sported a longer barrel, with an overall length of 8 inches. The
mountain cat was replaced by two horse heads on the barrel and pine trees on the frame.
The black grips have a bucking bronco on them in high relief, and "BRONCO" in raised
letters at the top of the grips. The Kilgore Circle "K" logo is prominently shown on the
frame amid high floral and scrollwork. This model also has the revolving cylinder with the
"swing-open" cylinder for disc cap loading.

The much rarer Bronco cap pistol that came out in 1958-1960 was put out by Leslie-
Henry, the character-loving company that jumped on the popularity of the shows. The L-H
Bronco is a 7-inch single shot, well-made, all-nickel-plated cap gun. "Bronco" is shown on both
sides of the frame under the cylinder, along with the rearing horse. The grips are simulated stag
with the Diamond "H" logo. The gun has beautiful scrollwork and a pebbled frame design
and is a nifty little gem not easily found.

Above: Dell Comic book for **Cheyenne**
featuring Ty Hardin as "Bronco Layne"
before the show went on its own as
Bronco. *Ty Hardin was an imposing*
figure as "Bronco."

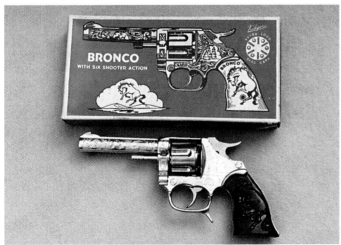

**The Kilgore Bronco with revolving cylinder and black grips with
bucking bronco. Note the very colorful box. This is the longer-bar-
reled second model.**

**Seldom-seen Leslie-Henry Bronco single-shot nickle model
that came out in 1958-1960 during the run of the show. Note
rearing horse on frame and Diamond "H" logo.**

BUFFALO BILL

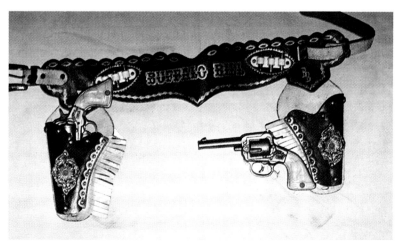

illiam Frederick Cody, born in 1846, went on to everlasting fame in the history books, our American heritage, countless books, movies, and TV appearances as Buffalo Bill. He was the renowned buffalo hunter that with deadly accuracy, gave him his nickname, but he was also a U.S. cavalry scout, frontiersman, trapper, prospector, Pony Express dispatch rider, Indian fighter, and one of the world's greatest showmen, perhaps ranking with P.T. Barnum in the western lore.

Born in Iowa, but moved to Kansas as a young boy, he helped support the family after his father died in 1857 when young Bill was only 11. Between 1857 and 1867, when he went on to the buffalo hunting that made him famous, Bill had alredy completed an incredible feat as a rider for the Pony Express—riding 320 hard miles in 24 hours. During the Civil War, he rode with the Union Cavalry as a Scout. After the war, General Philip Sheridan made him Chief of Scouts of the Fifth Cavalry. He took part in 11 Indian War campaigns, surffering a serious head wound, but killing Cheyenne Chief Tall Bull. By 1870, well into his fame as a buffalo hunter, Cody also guided prominent people of the day as well as European and Russian royalty on hunting and trapping expeditions. Then he met the man who made household word—Ned Buntline, a dime novel writer looking for western heroes to blaze his novels on the East Coast. Not only did Buntline immortalize him in novels, he also starred Cody in a very popular play in 1872 called *The Scouts of the Prairie*.

Ten years later, Buffalo Bill launched his most famous role— the Wild West Show that brought him international fame. His show included real Indians, such as Chief Sitting Bull; incredible sharpshooters such as Frank Butler and his wife—"Little Miss Sure Shot"—Annie Oakley. He added cowboys, mountain men, and buckskinned Indian scouts, as he had been himself. As his fame grew, he made millions, bought land in Wyoming, and gave his name— Cody—to a new town. For just over 30 years, Buffalo Bill's Wild West Show astonished and entertained people on two continents.

He led an adventurous life. Scout for Sheridan and Custer, friend of Wild Bill Hickock, admirer of Kit Carson (he named his son Kit Carson Cody) married to Louisa Frederici, whom he dearly loved, and a man who loved children, even more so after the death of his only son, Kit, from which he never fully recovered. A man who also had a very trusting nature, Cody made several bad investments and eventually lost his Wild West Show to creditors. In 1917, less than 4 years after losing his show, Buffalo Bill Cody died at the age of 71 in Denver. He was buried on top of Lookout Mountain in a special vault hewn out of rock. His death was mourned by millions of people, and President Teddy Roosevelt immortalized him in a special speech.

Actor Louis Calhern played "Buffalo Bill," with Betty Hutton as "Annie Oakley" and J. Carroll Naish as "Sitting Bull" in MGM's **Annie Get Your Gun.** *J. Carroll Naish, who was often cast as an Indian, also gained immortal fame as "Charlie Chan."*

Above: William F. Cody, America's beloved "Buffalo Bill" at the height of his career. Note the two guns worn butt first just like his friend, Wild Bill Hickok.

Right: Early cast-iron Buffalo Bill cap guns in a beautiful double holster set. The guns are by Stevens, which continued its Buffalo Bill into die casts. (Courtesy of Terry Graham)

Stevens gold model (above) and nickle model Buffalo Bill die-cast repeaters. Note the beautifully sculptured bust of Buffalo Bill on the grips.

His death also gave birth to the legend of this great western hero that lived on in dozens of books, plays, movies, and TV shows where the character of Buffalo Bill could never be anything but the colorful figure that he really was. Hollywood may have taken liberties with other real western heroes, but not Buffalo Bill. The huge Stetson, flowing shoulder-length hair, moustache and goatee, buckskins, high boots and his Winchester rifle remain the colorful character that we instantly see in our mind's eye when we think of William F. Cody, Buffalo Bill—the man who actually represented the Wild West that America is known for.

Not long after Cody's death, the character was soon immortalized on real guns, rifles, knives, commemoratives, and naturally, the toy guns that every kid, even before TV western heroes had to have—the Buffalo Bill toy gun, cast iron, die cast, or plastic! Stevens continued the Buffalo Bill it had already been selling in the cast irons for dozens of years. While other cast iron favorites like Kenton and Ives also immortalized Buffalo Bill, we move forward to the die cast varieties that is the main focus of this study.

CAP GUN COLLECTIBLES

The Stevens die cast Buffalo Bill is a 7-1/2-inch gun that came in both nickel and gold finishes. The gun breaks open from the top with a release lever on the left side, slightly below the hammer. "Buffalo Bill" is raised on both sides of the frame, under the cylinder. The Circle "S" logo that Stevens utilized in the 1950-1960

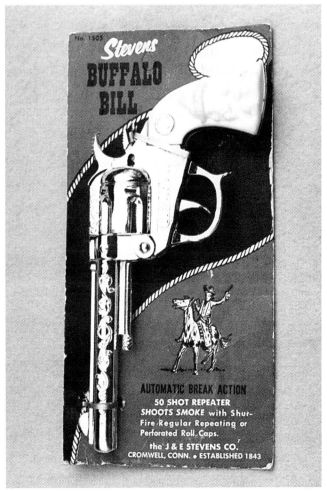

Stevens Buffalo Bill die-cast model on its original card.

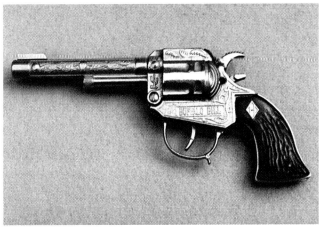

Leslie-Henry Buffalo Bill cap pistol with amber stag grips and lots of engraving. Note the Diamond "H" logo on grips.

Left: Leslie-Henry Buffalo Bill cap pistol, later model with extension barrel and white stag grips.

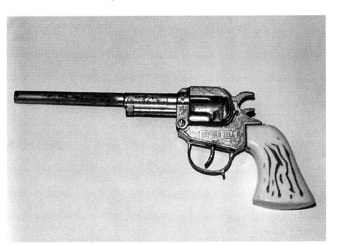

English Lone Star's tribute to Buffalo Bill is the "Cody 45" complete with a colorful box showing Buffalo Bill on the front and giving a short biography on the back. A well-made 10-inch die cast cap repeater with nice black grips.

period of die-cast manufacture is on the grips. The most important feature of this gun is the yellowed ivory-like grips which sport a beautifully-sculptured and remarkable likeness to Buffalo Bill—complete with hat, buckskins, and his well-known facial hair. It is exceptionally done, right down to the ear lobes and hair lines. This gun came on a colorful car that Stevens advertised as a "50 shot repeater" that "shoots smoke" and with "automatic break action."

Leslie-Henry, that wonderful company that loved characters, also gave us the Buffalo Bill in at least two varieties. The first model is an 8-1/4-inch nickel-plated gun that has a left side release lever below the hammer. "Buffalo Bill" is shown prominently raised on both sides of the frame under the cylinder, amidst scroll-work, cactus plant, and a longhorn on the barrel. This gun came with white simulated stag grips and the pretty amber or "root beer" colored grips, also in simulated stag. The Diamond "H" logo is on the grips. The second pattern is the identical gun, but with an extension, factory made and assembled long barrel, extending the gun to 11 inches overall. This pattern, obviously made later than the 1955 era, has an all-plastic stag grip, but without the Diamond "H" logo. It is, however, the identical gun in size, shape, design, and finish as the earlier model.

Lone Star of England came out with its own tribute to Buffalo Bill, since he was extremely popular in England, and called it the Cody 45. This is a die-cast, 10-inch gun, with a silver flash finish, lots of scrollwork, and all plastic black grips which sport a Hubley-style steerhead raised on both sides with a prominent mane and slightly longer horns than the Hubley model. "Cody 45" is raised on the left side of the frame only, under the cylinder. The other side has only the scrollwork pattern. The gun breaks open from the top strictly by hand pressure when one grabs the barrel and pushes downward. The gun is also marked "Lone Star" and "Made in England." It comes in a very colorful box adorned with the familiar figure of Buffalo Bill Cody and the reverse of the box gives a capsulized biography of Buffalo Bill, mentioning how he had come to London and amazed audiences with his showmanship. This is a nice, big, well-made cap gun considering it is out of the 1950-1960 era.

"Buffalo Bill"-marked holsters such as shown here are made of buckskin leather, and carry the "Buffalo Bill" signature bust and lettering on the pockets. Both the Stevens and the Halco fit these holsters perfectly. The other set of Buffalo Bill holsters appear to be of heavier leather, no doubt of earlier manufacture since both the cast-iron and the die-cast Buffalo Bill made by Stevens fit perfectly into the pockets. These are black and white leather, with colorful fringe, conchos, and "Buffalo Bill" in gold lettering on the back of the wider than usual belt, along with six bullets in holders of 3 on each side of the holsters. Buffalo Bill holster sets are rather scarce, with or without guns.

Above: Close-up of the neat Buffalo Bill image and name on holster pockets along with the Stevens nickel die-cast cap repeater for Buffalo Bill. Seldom seen.

Right: Colorful Buffalo Bill double holster set with Stevens die-cast cap guns in buckskin leather with black holster pockets with signature and image of our hero.

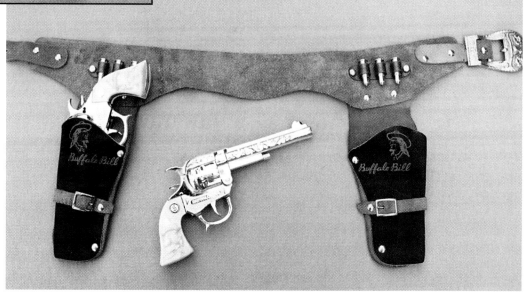

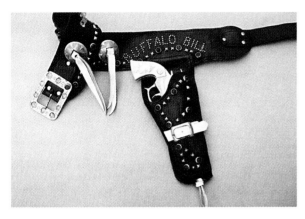

Above: Nice early black leather single holster set with lots of studs, jewels, and silver conchos for Buffalo Bill. Gun shown is Stevens Buffalo Bill, but this set takes both the cast-iron and die-cast varieties. (Courtesy of Mike Cherry)

Right: The real Buffalo Bill and the real Chief Sitting Bull, showing friendship between the white man and the red man, circa 1885.

Balantyne Manufacturing of Chicago also honored Buffalo Bill with a large 10-1/4-inch nickel-plated pressed steel die cast with a revolving cylinder and a handsome set of grips with the bust and good likeness of our hero, complete with Stetson, long hair, buckskins, the works, and that is how we will always remember Buffalo Bill Cody.

Daisy also commemorated Buffalo Bill with the Buffalo Bill Chief of Scouts BB gun, with a colorful box showing the same Buffalo Bill Chief of Scouts medallion that is inset into the brown plastic wood-grained stock. The forearm is also brown plastic. The barrel is black enamel while the lever action, bands, butt, and receiver are all gray metal. The receiver has the signature facsimile of "Buffalo Bill" and the word "Scout" below it along with scrollwork on both sides of the rifle. The Daisy logo, Arkansas address, and "Model 3030" are on the barrel, as well as the colorful box.

Leslie-Henry appears to have also marekted a Buffalo Bill die-cast cap firing rifle with a scope mounted on it (no doubt for all those buffalo roaming in the kid's room!) along with a sling, measuring 26 inches in length. "Buffalo Bill" is printed on the grip section of the stock, and the plastic stock allowed you to store extra caps in the butt. This scarcer model sold for only $1.95.

Many actors have portrayed Buffalo Bill on both the wide screen and television— Howard Keel, Louis Calhern, Keith Carradine, even Clayton Moore, better known as "The Lone Ranger." I have to admit that most people have a good image of the real Buffalo Bill, one of America's greatest Wild West showmen, Indian fighter, scout, and all-around western hero.

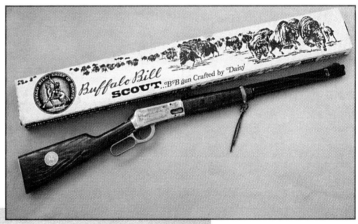

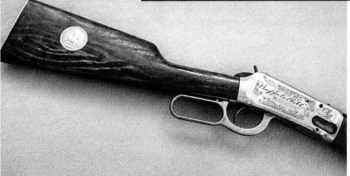

Above: Daisy's Buffalo Bill Scout rifle with original box.

Left: Close-up of Chief of Scouts medallion on stock and "Buffalo Bill" signature on the lockplate. (Courtesy of Bill Longstreet)

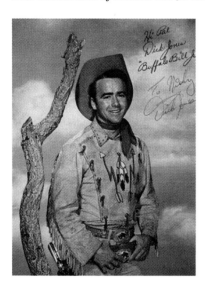

Dell Comics issue of Buffalo Bill Jr. starring Dick Jones.

Dick Jones, star of **Buffalo Bill Jr.** *with his trademark Indian buckskin shirt, one of TV's earliest westerns.*

BUFFALO BILL, JR.
YOUNG BUFFALO BILL

This section's title may be confusing, but really, it's an easy one. The TV western program, which hit the CBS airwaves, was titled *Buffalo Bill, Jr.* and starred Dick Jones. The cap guns, for some unknown reason, carried the title "Young Buffalo Bill." In real life, Buffalo Bill Cody did have a young son, Kit, but he died as a youngster. In this program, however, he carries his father's famous name and fights for law and order.

Produced by Gene Autry's Flying "A" Productions, (which had already given us the wonderful *Annie Oakley*) *Buffalo Bill, Jr.* ran in 1955-1956, and the handsome actor playing this ficticious character with an already legendary name had starred in the "Range Rider" series as "Dick West," with Jock Mahoney as "Range Rider." In "Buffalo Bill, Jr.," the character was an orphan, who along with his sister, was adopted by "Judge Ben Wiley," which was also the name of the town, Wileyville, Texas, where they lived.

Buffalo Bill, Jr., was quick with his fists, even quicker with a lasso, and he was very protective of his kid sister, "Calamity," played by Nancy Gilbert. Later, he became Marshal of Wileyville. Buffalo Bill, Jr.'s, trademark was a very colorful buckskin shirt, complete with fringe, and a beautiful Indian design consisting of arrows and three Indian warrior's feathers in the center of the shirt. The buckskins were so popular that clothing companies soon marketed the shirt. Other collectibles followed as well as the ever-popular Dell Comics that also came out with several issues of *Buffalo Bill, Jr.*

Actor Dick Jones initially started off in radio in his home state of Texas. An excellent stuntman, he starred in seven of Gene Autry's films before landing roles in *The Range Rider* as well as *Buffalo Bill, Jr.* Attesting to Dick Jones' stunt work, one must recall the beginning of each program. As the narrator goes on about the character being Buffalo Bill's son, Dick Jones is shown riding hard, trying to stop a runaway wagon. At one point, he hops off his saddle on the left side of the horse, touches the ground with the horse at full gallop, and then jumps back into the saddle, and quickly repeats the stunt on the right side of the horse. Don't try this at home, kids! The only other actor that was said to have been able to do such a stunt, himself, without the aid of a stuntman, was Jock Mahoney, Jones' co-star.

Actor Harry Cheshire, who played Judge Wiley, passed away in 1968. Nancy Gilbert retired from films and Dick Jones, alive and well, works in the banking industry. Gene Autry produced and syndicated 52 episodes of *Buffalo Bill, Jr.* in the 30-minute format, which was telecast on Saturday mornings. Besides Dell Comics, Gold Key Comics was still issuing *Buffalo Bill, Jr.* in 1965, long after the show ended its run.

CAP GUN COLLECTIBLES

The cap guns and holster sets that hit the stores carried the name "Young Buffalo Bill." Leslie-Henry made the Young Buffalo Bill in its standard 9-inch model, nickel finish, white horse head plastic grips, and with "Young Buffalo Bill" raised on both sides of the frame, under the cylinder in the usual pattern with the rearing horse logo, scrollwork on the barrel, frame, and with the left side release to break open for cap loading.

Leslie-Henry also made two variations of the smaller "Young Buffalo Bill." The first pattern was a single shot nickel framed, 7-inch gun with "Young Buffalo Bill" inside a rope frame, on both sides of the frame, under the cylinder, and with the usual rearing horse logo. The grips carry the Diamond "H" logo and are a white simulated stag design. The second pattern, while also being the same 7-inch size, nickel finish, and single shot style, distinct differences are notable. One is the fact that the grips, which came in both white and amber color, has a horse

Beautiful boxed set of Leslie-Henry double holsters with first pattern Young Buffalo Bill cap guns with stag grips. Note blue jewels and blue bullet holders. The belt adjustment instructions are partially visible in the box.

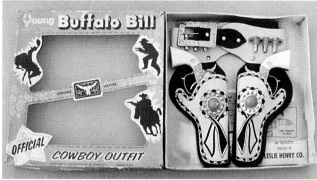

Two beautiful Leslie-Henry Young Buffalo Bill cap shooters. The top model has amber grips with horse head and checkering design, and is extensively engraved, while the lower model has stag grips, with the Diamond "H" logo. Both are single shot cap guns.

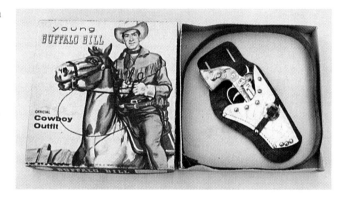

*Canadian-manufactured seldom-seen boxed set for **Buffalo Bill Jr.** made by the M.A. Henry plant in Ontario. The little single shot cap shooter is marked "Texas" and is gold plated. While the nifty little gun resembles a Hubley with its trademark steerhead, the logo has "LH" in a circle. The gun is extensively engraved and all metal.*

This photo clearly shows that the M.A. Henry's Canadian plant in Ontario made its version of the Texas for the Young Buffalo Bill, yet it also made a Hopalong Cassidy with the almost identical design, solving a long mystery and debate explained in the Hopalong Cassidy chapter.

head design, bridled, looking up, on both sides, with the top section of the grips, just above the horse's head, checkered.

A closer look at the rearing horse shows that the lasso frame within which is the "Young Buffalo Bill" has the lasso going around the neck of the rearing horse. This pattern, repeated on several of the second pattern Leslie-Henry guns, sports the horse head checkered grips without any medallion or Diamond "H" logo of any kind. Closer scrutiny of the rearing horse shows that the earlier model resembles the Colt rearing horse, with legs in a bent knee position, while the later models have the rearing horse with both legs—front and back—in the same position. These may be subtle, but very distinct changes.

Leslie-Henry marketed a boxed set of the Young Buffalo Bill cap guns and double holster set in a colorful box. The black and white leather holster set came with blue stoned conchos and a feature explaining how the youngster could adjust the belt in 3 ways—small, medium, and large—calling it an "exclusive feature of Leslie-Henry Co."

Once again, the holster sets and designs are literally endless for this very popular gun, marketed to the smaller youngster. The guns are exceptionally well made, tight, and with excellent details and nickel finish. The amber or "root beer" grips make them especially colorful. A cute little Young Buffalo Bill "Official Cowboy Outfit" was marketed in Canada under M.A. Henry, carrying the address of Dundas, Ontario, Canada. This little set has an all metal, gold-plated nifty little single shot cap gun stamped "Texas." It is a 6-1/4-inch gun, with a raised steerhead on the grips and a totally different logo, obviously used by the Canadian firm. It has "LH" totally within a circle at the top of the grips. The gun has extensive raised scrollwork as well.

The Young Buffalo Bill box has great graphics, but since the Canadian boxes are not easily found, the box is a great piece of documentation. It gives the "M.A. HENRY LTD. DUNDAS, ONT." address, of course, but it shows a round logo with the familiar rearing horse with an "L" at the lower left and an "H" at the upper right, and "Cowboy Ranch Outfit" on another red solid circle. The top of the box shows their rendition of Young Buffalo Bill, complete with buckskins on a spotted horse, gun drawn, with buffalo roaming in the background by huge cliffs. The belt and holster, for a little cowpoke, is white and brown leather with an alligator skin motif. It is exceptionally well made with a great silver concho and several half-moon studs on the holster pocket. You have to hand it to those Henrys—they sure knew how to capitalize and market those cap guns.

CHAMPION

Champion, the wonder horse, getting plenty of affection from Barry Curtis who starred in the early western as "Ricky." (Courtesy of Old West Shop)

Leave it to the TV's golden years of westerns to have a number of TV shows about the horse, one of God's most magnificent creatures. In the TV show entitled *The Adventures of Champion* it did just that. Produced by Gene Autry's Flying "A" Productions, the show featured the already famous "Wonder Horse," Champion, Gene Autry's chestnut-colored stallion. Champion, of course, was of magnificent beauty, with his white blaze and stocking hoofs and superb mane, the trademarks of a horse that kids of all ages dreamed to one day own.

In the program, this majestic horse is reprogrammed as the leader of wild horses that ends up befriending a young boy named "Ricky" who saves a foal that had slipped into a deep crevasse. The boy was played by young actor Barry Curtis. His dog, a German Shepherd, was named "Rebel." Champion became a star in his own right—as he traveled all over the country with his master, being snapped in thousands of photographs with kids of all ages.

Even presidents, other movie stars, and prominent politicians that attended western fairs, visited the local charity hospitals and rodeos wanting a photo next to Champion. Champion was featured in many magazines and news articles of the 1950-1955 period, boasting of his uncanny ability to dance, pivot, curtsy, answer questions with his gorgeous arched head, and even kneel in prayer at the master's bidding.

The Adventures of Champion ran for only one season, 1955-1956, and again was geared mainly towards youngsters. The show taught the kids of the 1950s all about love, trust, and the friendship between man and beast. Both Champion and Little Champion starred in the show. Champion, of course, is forever immortalized in statue-form at the Gene Autry Western Museum in Griffith Park, California.

CAP GUN COLLECTIBLES

Leslie-Henry made the only cap gun honoring the wonder horse, Champion. The 9-inch gun came in both nickel and gold patterns.

Leslie-Henry gave us the 9-inch standard model in the Champion cap pistols and it is found in both nickel and gold finish, both with the plastic horse head grips in both white and black. The name "Champion" is raised on both sides of the frame, along with the usual scroll-work, the rearing horse and left side top break release lever. Both the cap firing, and a dummy version of the Champion was made, as well as an earlier heavier cast frame model, and a later model with a slight variation of the spur hammer. The Champion is a sturdy and well-made cap pistol. There are also a set of double holsters with both "Champion" and "Gene Autry" printed on them most probably made by Leslie-Henry or Halco. No gun exists marked "Ricky North," the human star of the same show.

The Kilgore Champion, which was manufactured in the 1960 era, has sometimes been mistaken as another tribute to Champion. However, while it carries the same name on the frame on both sides, and is a heavily engraved, 10-inch gun with plain, black plastic grips, this Champion was hawked (by Art Linkletter, no less!) as a "fast draw" cap gun which sported a special ratchet timer in the grip that was "set" by the youngster before he did the fast draw. It is shown here only for reference purposes compared to the Leslie-Henry Champion, honoring Gene Autry's wonder horse.

Kilgore's Champion—sometimes confused with, but not made for the famous "Champion" wonder horse by Leslie-Henry. Shown for reference purposes only.

Gene Autry with his famous horse, "Champion." Note the guns on Champion's bridle. Wouldn't they be a great find!

CHEYENNE

ne of TV's greatest westerns, *Cheyenne*, starring a 6 foot, 6 inch giant named Clint Walker, ran from September 1955 through September 1963. Even when the star was having a dispute over feature films with Warner Brothers, the *Cheyenne* program continued to run, alternating with *Bronco Layne* and *Sugarfoot* until Walker resumed the *Cheyenne* role in 1959.

"Cheyenne Bodie," a lone and restless drifter after the Civil War, roamed the West, trying to make his way and find his fortune, but the lawless and the curious just couldn't help picking on Cheyenne because of his size, his quiet, unassuming ways, and his patience. Cheyenne did not resort to violence until provoked beyond patience and understanding.

The show was a big hit immediately (unlike other westerns that got off to a slow start and then picked up viewers) and kids all over the country wanted to emulate Cheyenne Bodie, the "big man." It is interesting to note that "Cheyenne," along with its one-year temporary shows *Bronco* and *Sugarfoot* were all shown at 7:30 p.m.—a one-hour, prime-time, the "kids-are-up" time slot! And since it came on Mondays, and later Tuesdays, it grabbed the older kids, teenagers, and parents that today still recall the show fondly.

Clint Walker had been a deputy sheriff in Nevada, as well as having served in the Merchant Marine. His real-life experiences almost paralleled with his restless big cowboy character, so when he was tapped to play the lead role, Walker was right at home. He was a mild-mannered man in real life and he went directly to the public to explain the nine month suspension from the *Cheyenne* show. He explained it had to do with his wanting to do more feature films as well as *Cheyenne* and he explained to happy fans that *Bronco* did not replace *Cheyenne* but was a show entirely on its own. Walker explained to his many fans that he was his own man as an actor and the fans responded with an even greater love for this gentle Goliath of a man. Walker did several movies, but he will always be remembered as Cheyenne. To his credit, Walker shunned the glitz of Hollywood and remained a very private family man.

After the full run of *Cheyenne*, Walker later starred in the short run series *Kodiak*, which ran for only a month in September 1974. The popularity of *Cheyenne* is how Clint Walker will always be remembered. Walker also starred in several western movies, as well as a war movie with Lee Marvin called *The Dirty Dozen* in which he played a similar big, but soft-spoken, "don't provoke me" kind of character.

CAP GUN COLLECTIBLES

Kilgore made the Cheyenne cap gun in one variety. It is a nickel/chrome plated 9-inch die cast repeater, which breaks from the top. It came with white simulated stag grips. *Cheyenne* is raised on the left side of the gun only. The right side carries the Circle "K" Kilgore logo. The barrel sports the usual Kilgore "branding iron" motifs; otherwise, the gun is smooth finish. As noted below, other Kilgore guns were sold to Daisy, which placed them in a variety of its "Cheyenne" holster sets.

Clint Walker as "Cheyenne Bodie." Note the little arrowheads on his cowboy hat band.

Great color photo of Clint Walker autographed and sent to author on November 17, 1959. One of television's most popular westerns, Cheyenne was a man of ethics.

Kilgore Cheyenne die-cast cap repeater in nickle finish and stag grips, along with its Cheyenne holster, which was also marketed with Daisy sets.

Close-up of the Kilgore Cheyenne showing details and raised image of "Cheyenne Bodie" in the same configuration as the show logo.

Close-up of the Hamilton Cheyenne showing details and logo on sleek white grips.

Hamilton's Cheyenne Shooter which came with both white and black and red grips, with its colorful box.

Above: Seldom-seen English BCM Cheyenne in black finish with checkered white grips, along with its original holster. Cheyenne was also very popular in England.

Right: Daisy's boxed Cheyenne came with the Nichols Stallion Mark II and a superb quality top grain leather holster and gunbelt. Daisy used a variety of guns for its Cheyenne series of holsters in several sizes for all ages of youngsters. (Courtesy of J. Schleyer)

Hamilton made the Cheyenne Shooter, a 9-inch die cast repeater with a dull gray finish, which breaks from the top. It comes with smooth white and black and red grips, which carry the logo for the gun itself—a large "C" for "Cheyenne" and a smaller "S" for "Shooter" within the large "C," on both sides of the grips. "Cheyenne Shooter" is also raised on both sides of the frame under the cylinder. The box is a colorful white, red, and yellow, with black lettering details. The side of the box also shows how to load the gun. The box indicates a number of revealing features. The gun is advertised as "it smokes!" It shows a cowboy with rearing horse, waving his six-shooter. The back of the box indicates that, in addition to the Cheyenne, the Hamilton Line also made Annie Oakley and the Range Rider, although I personally have never seen either cap gun. The only other Hamilton character gun that I have seen (and own) is the Westerner, covered later in this book.

England's BCM also made a small version of the Cheyenne. Like the BCM Buntline Special and other British guns, the Cheyenne came in a factory black finish with a set of well formed and checkered white plastic grips. This is a 7-inch well-made cap pistol with plenty of scrollwork on the frame and barrel, and it has "Cheyenne" raised on both sides of the frame. It breaks open from the top by pressure on the barrel downward. Inside the cap box area it is stamped "A BCM Product - Made in England." This is a nifty cap pistol that also comes with a small dark red leather holster with fringe and concho that slips onto any conventional belt. *Cheyenne* was also very popular in England.

Daisy also marketed a boxed Cheyenne holster set showing Clint Walker as Cheyenne, both on the box itself, and on the top portion of the holster pocket, tooled into the leather in the same image and lettering of the title *Cheyenne* as it was on the TV show itself. The gun in this "fast draw" Cheyenne set is a Nichols Stallion .45 Mark II series with the white pearlescent grips.

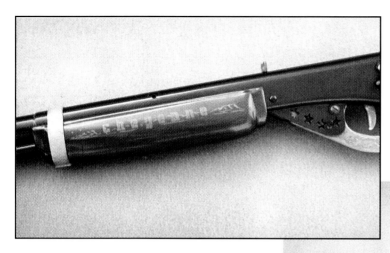

Close-up showing screened "Cheyenne" on fore-stock in the same lettering as the show title. (Courtesy of Jim Thomas)

Daisy's 1959 catalog actually features *Cheyenne* on the cover touting it as "TV's favorite western," and Daisy marketed several Cheyenne holster sets—double, single, with even the "cowboy canteen" in a suede holster of its own! The guns that Daisy sold with the Cheyenne sets were: Nichols Stallion .45 for the larger sets, both single and double; Nichols Stallion .38 for a medium sized holster set; the Hubley Marshal on its Cheyenne Little Brother set.

Daisy also marketed various sizes and designs of Cheyenne holster sets which also utilized three other Kilgore guns—the Mustang and the Laredo, as well as the Deputy, all in varying sizes for youngsters of all ages in its Cheyenne series of guns. The holsters carry a variety of Cheyenne lettering, image of Clint Walker as Cheyenne on the top portion of the slide-on holster pockets; "Cheyenne" on the leather straps across the holster pocket, similar to the holster design Walker himself wore on the show, and with the image of Cheyenne on both the belt and the holster pocket itself. No question that Daisy was the largest supplier of the Cheyenne holster sets with a variety of Kilgore and Nichols guns.

Daisy also put out the Cheyenne ricochet-sound smoke rifle, complete with the suede butt "boot" as they called it, and the saddle ring leather lanyard they called "thong" on the left side of the rifle. The left side of the forestock has "Cheyenne" screened on it with the letters in the same style as the TV show itself, along with mountain peaks in the background. Unfortunately, since this was rather lightly screened, many of these rifles are found with much of this worn off.

The Cheyenne rifle was also advertised in Dell Comics featuring "Cheyenne" as well as other TV western stars and shows of the period. *Cheyenne* was one of television's most popular westerns and it made a big star out of Clint Walker. Few western characters were as big and imposing as the "gentle-but-don't-get-me-riled Cheyenne Bodie."

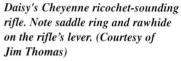

Daisy's Cheyenne ricochet-sounding rifle. Note saddle ring and rawhide on the rifle's lever. (Courtesy of Jim Thomas)

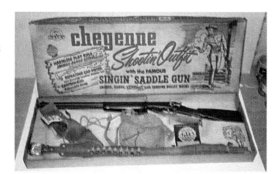

Spectacular boxed Cheyenne outfit by Daisy which included rifle, gun belt, cap shooter and canteen. (Courtesy of Mike Cherry)

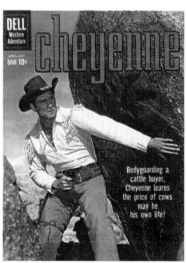

Dell Comics issue for Cheyenne *starring Clint Walker.*

$5000.00 REWARD!

"The Cisco Kid"
HOLDUP AND ROBBERY
of
POSTAL STAGE

Warner Baxter, the first "Cisco Kid," won an Oscar for his portrayal of "The Robin Hood of the West."

Latin lover Cesar Romero also played "The Cisco Kid." Ironically, he had a part in **The Return of the Cisco Kid** *with Warner Baxter, the first "Cisco Kid."*

Above: Duncan Renaldo as "The Cisco Kid," the fourth actor to play the dashing role on his horse, "Diablo." (Courtesy of Libro DiZinno)

Right: Leo Carillo as "Pancho," Cisco's loyal sidekick, on his horse, "Loco."

THE CISCO KID

The honor of being TV's first western series belongs to *The Cisco Kid*, also known as the "Robin Hood of the West." So popular was this show, that in my research, I found that while westerns of the late 1950s and early 1960s were forgotten by some people, even those of us that go back to the 1930s all remember *The Cisco Kid*. It remains one of my personal favorites, and the only show that both I and my cousins back home in Italy were both watching at the same time, since the show had international appeal and was broadcast throughout Europe, South America, and even the Orient.

The Cisco Kid was created by the writer O. Henry (the pen name of Sydney Porter) in the early part of the century and like *Zorro*, *Tarzan* and other adventure stories, it first hit the movies. Several famous actors played the "Cisco Kid" before the show came to television. Warner Baxter played the first Cisco Kid in the 1929 movie *In Old Arizona*, followed by *The Return of the Cisco Kid*. Baxter, an early matinee idol, won an Oscar for his portrayal of the Cisco Kid. Gilbert Roland, born Luis Antonio Damasco De Alonso, played a handsome Cisco Kid, but didn't wear the fancy Mexican outfit, big sombrero, and two gun holsters that Warner Baxter made famous.

The third Cisco Kid, though, was Cesar Romero, who made women swoon with his killer smile and Latin looks. He returned with a more Mexican flair to his sombrero and fancy duds with fancy borders and string ties. On the big screen, "Pancho" was played by Frank Yaconelli, who was really an Italian-American character actor with a big "bandido"-style drooping moustache and a big hearty laugh. Cisco and Pancho roamed the West, always helping the less fortunate.

In 1951, the movie *The Daring Caballero* brought us the fourth Cisco Kid, Duncan Renaldo. The same portly sidekick named "Pancho," was played by Mexican actor Leo Carillo. Together, they set out to prove that the local Padre is right about a local man named "Del Rio," who is innocent of charges leveled against him. The fourth Cisco Kid and Pancho made such a great team together that when *The Cisco Kid* came to television, the best known Cisco Kid turned out to be Duncan Renaldo, who was also the first Cisco Kid without a moustache.

Leo Carillo continued to ride with the Cisco Kid as his loyal, but fumbling sidekick who managed to mangle the language with "O.K., Cisco, let's went" as they rode off. We also learned that when Pancho was really shook up and surprised, he'd blurt out "Caramba!" Cisco's horse "Diablo" and Pancho's horse "Loco" ("Devil" and "Crazy" in Spanish) became just as famous. Cisco and Pancho always included horse tricks, talking to and "reasoning" with the horses in the acts.

The two came to fairs, rodeos, and circus acts to meet the long lines of youngsters, all of whom wanted their photos and autographs. I was one of those youngsters when Duncan Renaldo came to Hartford with the Shrine Circus in 1955. Although Duncan Renaldo was very gracious and very patient with hundreds of youngsters who fumbled with his belt and wanted photos taken by mom and dad wearing the big sombrero, Leo Carillo was not known to be patient.

Duncan Renaldo's "Cisco" outfit was one of the fanciest black outfits ever to flash across the screen. There was white accented filagree and floral designs on both shoulders and down the arms. A huge, wide belt with two silver buckles, sported the silver eagle clutching a snake in its beak, the symbol of Mexico.

He wore a single holster outfit which was adorned with large silver conchos of Cisco's own sombrero. A fancy floral string tie had the same silver sombrero as the slider. The outfit just oozed "romance" and as the two fighters for justice roamed all over the New Mexican Territory, there was always a scene involving a pretty Senorita. The romantic duo flirted with the ladies that either took a liking to Cisco or they were insulting his advances even after they had just been rescued! How's that for gratitude! But the only on-screen affection Cisco showed was for "Diablo," his horse. It was good-humored, pure romantic fun.

156 episodes were shot in color, the first for early TV westerns, but they were shown in black and white. The re-runs in syndication have been shown in color. *The Cisco Kid* had serious international "swashbuckling" appeal. It was like an updated *Zorro* who was always a popular defender of justice in foreign markets. *The Cisco Kid* was being shown dubbed for the foreign markets and in the Orient, the subtitles were shown on the right side of the screen. In 1958, it was being shown in 176 American markets, covering nearly 95 percent of all U.S. TV homes.

Every summer, both Duncan Renaldo and Leo Carillo, with their horses, would appear in a star performance in Canada's famous "Calgary Stampede." Everywhere they went, the two actors were mobbed by adults as well as youngsters. While Renaldo did not wear the more Latin-look moustache, he had a brilliant smile that endeared him to millions. *The Cisco Kid* show was big on action, adventure, good humor, and romance—the horses got kissed, not the girls!

All of the prior "Cisco Kid" actors are gone. Warner Baxter died in 1951, just after the show had come to television. He was only 58 years old. Both Gilbert Roland and Cesar Romero have passed away. Sadly, both Duncan Renaldo and Leo Carillo succumbed to lung cancer. Carillo died in 1961 and Duncan Renaldo passed away in 1980. But even in this decade of the fast nineties, *The Cisco Kid* rode again, in a movie starring Jimmy Smits (*L.A. Law, NYPD Blue*) as "Cisco" and Cheech Marin (*"Cheech & Chong"*) as "Pancho." While it was a noble attempt, I am convinced that today's producers just cannot seem to grasp the 1950-1960 television westerns.

Between the original series and syndication, *The Cisco Kid* ran for nine years, still charming the ladies, "winging" (but not killing) the bad guys, and trading barbs with each other as Cisco and Pancho sold products ranging from holster sets to Tip Top bread. However, the code of the west— honor, courage, and upholding the law— earned *The Cisco Kid* numerous awards. Among the citations were honors from the National Association of Secondary School Principals, honors and proclamations from the cities of Omaha, Washington D.C., and even the State of Michigan. The president of ZIV-TV Production, said of *The Cisco Kid*, "while we geared the show to youngsters, we also attribute this long success of *The Cisco Kid* to our adult viewers."

The Cisco Kid, as TV's first western, stuck to what the audience of the time wanted to see—action, adventure, galloping horses and trick shots as Cisco and Pancho rid the West of the lawless element. The Cisco Kid, in his fancy black outfit with its silver accoutrements, wide sombrero, and quick six-gun made him one of the best remembered TV western heroes. The show ran from 1950 through 1959.

Duncan Renaldo as he looked when he came to Hartford, Connecticut, in 1955. Note the gorgeous gunbelt with the silver sombreros and the Mexican eagle. Duncan Renaldo always had a great smile for his fans. He will always remain the best-known Cisco Kid.

Warner Baxter, the first "Cisco Kid," wore a fancy outfit with two guns, while Duncan Renaldo, the fourth "Cisco Kid," wore a single holster rig. Ironically, Baxter died in 1951 as the fourth "Cisco Kid," Duncan Renaldo, was introduced.

Cisco Kid double holster set with Kilgore Rangers. Note the conchos, as well as the unique center belt and buckle on the gunbelt. (Courtesy of Brian Wolf)

Spectacular Cisco Kid double holster set with Lone Star Cisco Kid cap guns. This variation comes with Cisco Kid wrist cuffs. Note that while this is a similar set to the one shown above, there are very distinct variations.

Close-up detail showing the spectacular and heavily sculptured concho that adorned the Cisco Kid holster sets and accoutrements.

Lone Star double holster set for the Cisco Kid on original card. Guns are die-cast repeaters with red and black swirl grips. The **Cisco Kid** was very popular in England.

Lone Star single holster Cisco Kid set. The grips on this model are a reddish brown with no marbleizing. The holster, while durable, is made of heavy cardboard.

CAP GUN COLLECTIBLES

Remarkably, even with the great success of *The Cisco Kid*, no American-made cap guns marked "Cisco Kid" are known to exist. While Duncan Renaldo was featured on the boxes of "The Cisco Kid Leather and Metal Products," made in Los Angeles, California, these were only holster sets which were outfitted with and without guns. A variety of generic guns as well as the Lone Star Cisco Kid guns are found with these holsters.

The Cisco Kid holster sets are something to behold. Made of top quality leather, they are usually found in black and white. Adorned with plenty of studs and jewels, several varieties exist, but all in the general black and white theme. The name "Cisco Kid" is usually found in white lettering on the belt as well as the pockets. However, the most spectacular feature is the Cisco Kid nickel and gold concho. It is heavy and well sculptured, featuring a bust size Cisco Kid with his gun drawn, and with "Cisco Kid" on each side of the bust. These are found on the belt, on the holster pockets, and even on the seldom-seen wrist cuffs.

The Alan Ladd, Gene Autry, Roy Rogers, and the famous Hoppy conchos do not hold a candle to the superior quality and high relief of the Cisco Kid conchos. Another unique feature was the belt itself. On some more elaborate models, the black wide belt sported a thinner white belt with two buckles, which laced through the holsters pockets and could be tightened to the youngster's waist size from the inside, thus not "crinkling" the outer belt. As Pancho would say "Eeeen-crayy-dee-bee-laaayyyy."

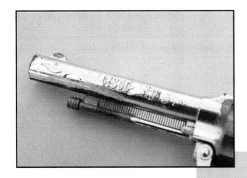

Above: Close-up of the barrel with raised "Cisco Kid" on the black gripped variation of the same model.

Right: Lone Star silver finish 8-1/2-inch gun with beautiful red and black swirl horse head grips. Note star logo and horse head looks

When it came to the cap guns themselves, Lone Star of England, jumped on the bandwagon, since The Cisco Kid was extremely popular in England. At least three variations of the Cisco Kid cap pistol was made by Lone Star. The first and most encountered is the 8-inch nickel "gleam" finish cap gun that came both on a card, in a box, and with and without holsters. This gun has a spectacular set of deep reddish, maroon marble swirl grips with the horse head looking down, almost biting the "lone star" logo of the five-pointed star found also on top of the grips. The gun has a mesh circle with "Cisco Kid" on it on both sides of the frame. With a left-side lever, it breaks from the top for cap loading. The holsters for this gun do not have the quality and workmanship of the American holsters, and yet are found both in a cardboard-style and in a thin leather-style, with painted details and the "Cisco Kid" on the pockets.

The second pattern is a black-gripped version of the same 8-inch gun, but remarkably, the barrel has the raised "Cisco Kid" on both sides, and "Lone Star" on the frame. Both guns have the same opening mechanism and sculptured grips, silver finish and a rather small hammer. As the readers will note later on in this book, the Cisco Kid Lone Star guns were used in other sets put out by Lone Star such as "The Lone Rider" (not a TV character show) and *Wells Fargo* which was, of course, another popular TV western also covered in this book.

The most beautiful of the Cisco Kid gun is the huge 10-inch cap pistol with super engraving on the entire frame, barrel, and cylinder and with "Cisco Kid" raised under the cylinder on both sides of the gun. The spectacular grips are red, with the Lone Star horse looking downward. The 5-pointed silver star logo is also on the grips. A left-side lever opens the gun from the top for cap loading. While the gun is marked "Lone*Star" on both sides of the frame, in the cap box area, it has "BCTM" Lone Star Products, Made in England" markings. This pattern is seldom seen and is the most sought after of the Cisco Kid cap pistols. It is awesome!

Close-up of the frame and grips. "Cisco Kid" is raised in the circle seen on the frame below the cylinder. Note release to break open the gun for loading.

If any collectors out there have other models or an American-made gun marked the "Cisco Kid," I'd sure like to hear about and see it. As stated, the California-made Cisco Kid Leather and Metal Products used both generic American-made guns, such as Kilgore's Ranger, Hubley's Western, Nichols' Stallion as well as the Lone Star Cisco Kid guns in holster sets.

Dell Comics did a series of *The Cisco Kid* comics for many years. Dozens of products bear the smiling faces of both Duncan Renaldo and Leo Carillo. Tip Top Bread included photos of both Cisco and Pancho for the kids to collect. And, of course, good boys also joined the "Cisco Kid Amigos" Club. My mom, brother, and I waited in line for hours to meet the Cisco Kid. As a special tribute to Duncan Renaldo, I would be totally remiss if I did not let readers know more about this wonderful "Cisco Kid." I know of no adult or youngster, Hispanic or otherwise, that would not find the following short bio remarkable, moving, and poignant.

Duncan Renaldo was orphaned at a very young age and never knew where he was born. This would come to haunt him later in life. He joined the Merchant Marine at age 13. By 1922, he was out of work and took a job as a janitor at New York's old Tec Art studio. He made his way west, landing in Hollywood in 1926 where he was cast in *Trader Horn* with Harry Carey. Just before the movie was released, Renaldo was arrested by Immigration authorities and he was charged with entering the country illegally.

In the sensational trial that followed in 1931, Renaldo was convicted of perjury for claiming that he was born in Camden, New Jersey. As stated, Renaldo never knew exactly where he was born, but he had to note a birthplace for his Marine service and his work. That got him 18 months in federal prison. Renaldo did his time, and just as he was about to be released, he was granted a pardon by President Roosevelt. Few people know that Renaldo was also an accomplished artist, and one of his works was owned by Eleanor Roosevelt, which she displayed at the White House.

Above: Photo of the 3 Lone Star Cisco Kid models made.

Left: Close-up of the large Cisco Kid Showing super details.

Right: The largest and most beautiful Cisco Kid made by Lone Star, or anyone! Note name, heavy scrollwork and red horse head grips with Lone Star logo.

After his release, Renaldo returned to Hollywood, this time working again as a janitor at Republic Pictures. Other men might have given up, but Renaldo perservered, and by 1940, was cast in movies with two new young cowboy stars—Roy Rogers and Gene Autry. In four years, Renaldo made several pictures, including *Zorro Rides Again*, *For Whom the Bell Tolls,* and *The Bridge of San Luis Rey*. But in 1944, he landed the role that made him world famous as "The Cisco Kid."

Renaldo refused to do scripts with unnecessary violence and revenge-oriented themes. Renaldo pointed out later on in his life that he and his partner, Leo Carrillo "never killed anyone on the show." He pointed out that the Cisco Kid was a happy, smiling, and cheerful soul and that "kids went to sleep smiling, never having nightmares over the Cisco Kid or Pancho." The Cisco Kid was a romantic "Robin Hood of the West"—not a "gunslinger."

When asked about the Old West and "gunplay," Renaldo quickly pointed out that the real West was settled with "hard work" and courageous people. He knew that after the 156 episodes of *The Cisco Kid* were over, many people would think that due to the modern day western, people would think that "everybody shot everybody on sight" which, of course, was never the case. Renaldo stressed that he and Pancho always captured the bad guys and then turned them over to the sheriff" before riding off to do more good deeds.

Perhaps one of Duncan Renaldo's most endearing traits was that he was a religious and humble man. He attributed his success as the Cisco Kid to the thousands of youngsters that loved him. Proof of this was revealed in 1953. During the filming of a rock slide scene, Renaldo was struck by a huge boulder that broke his neck. More than 17,000 get-well cards, along with the prayers of thousands more youngsters, convinced Renaldo that they were the reason for his miraculous recovery and he was eternally grateful. Perhaps this is one reason why Renaldo always made time for "the kids" even after the long run of the series. Duncan Renaldo appeared in over 150 pictures and stage productions, but he will always be fondly remembered as the Cisco Kid. "Hey, Cisco!" Pancho would blurt out. "Hey, Pancho" the Cisco Kid would shout back. Pancho would then give his farewell greeting,. . . "Let's went. . . ." I sure wish the Cisco Kid and Pancho would come back!

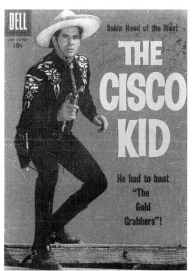

Dell Comics issued for **The Cisco Kid** *with Duncan Renaldo, January 1962.*

Left: Duncan Renaldo, as the ever-smiling "Cisco Kid," waves to his fans. This photo card came in a package of Harvest Bread. The greeting on the back reads as follows: "Si, amigo—if you want to be side by side with Cisco—you must eat Harvest Bread." (Courtesy of Libro DiZinno)

COLT .45

Wayde Preston, handsome star of Colt .45, this time with a moustache he often wore on the show for the part of "Chris Colt." Note the rampant Colt conchos on his gun belt. Preston wore a double-holster set on the show.

Samuel Colt, the designer, inventor, and producer of the firearms that bear his name. (Courtesy of Colt's Patent Firearms Company, Hartford, Connecticut)

A nother popular Warner Brothers western, telecast on ABC, *Colt .45* was centered on "Christopher Colt," played by handsome hunk Wayde Preston, a 6 foot, 4 inch former U.S. National Park Ranger. The program went on the air in October 1957. Colt was one of the descendants of Samuel Colt, the inventor of the revolver, and of course, the legendary Colt .45. The name of "Colt," and the rampant Colt with the spear in its mouth, is legendary and it has been synonymous with the "gun that won the West" for as long as anyone can remember.

Samuel Colt was born in Hartford, Connecticut, on July 19, 1814. His father gave him a gun when he was only 7 years old, an old horse pistol, and Colt became fond of guns, memorized the formula for making gunpowder and all the gun parts before he was even 8 years old. At age 11, he worked on a farm in Glastonbury, Connecticut, and after work, would go to the local general store and listen to old men talking about guns. One of them said that if a gun was ever made that could fire five or six shots without reloading, that nation would "rule the world."

Young Colt began entertaining thoughts of someday becoming an inventor. He later went to work at his father's textile plant in Ware, Massachusetts. Here he thought of experimenting with a "revolving barrel," and one day bound four barrels together. After trying to get them to revolve, he fired, but alas, they didn't revolve—all four barrels fired together. But young Sam didn't give up. In his late teens, he was sent to Amherst Academy, where he was popular with students but not with his teachers. He was always working on "something" using firecrackers, and all sorts of tricks and experiments. Leaving the Academy in a short time, he decided to run away to sea.

He became apprentice to a Captain Spaulding, commander of the ship "Corvo" which was on its way to India. Colt was eager to go, leaving from Boston, while the Captain sent a bill to Colt's father for a full sailor's uniform. On the ship's long voyage, Colt whittled and carved a full, working model of a revolving 6-cylinder handgun. He worked in secret and mentioned it to no one. By the time the ship returned to Boston, his model was ready.

Discussing it with his father, the elder Colt agreed to pay for the manufacture of two revolvers, and if they were successful, he'd pay for the patents. He completed the full details by 1832. He drew a description of the revolver and deposited it in the Patent Office. He sent for a gunsmith named John Pearson of Baltimore and made various calibers. He hired Frederick Brash as a helper and returned to Hartford for financial support. Sam wanted patents in Europe as well as America. He obtained patents by going to London personally in 1835, then went to France and Prussia, obtaining patents there as well. Back in Washington, he finally received his patents on February 25, 1836.

On March 5, 1836, the New Jersey Legislature allowed Colt to set up his corporation. It was called Patent Arms Manufacturing Company at Paterson, New Jersey. Here, along with an office in New York, he sold his "Patersons" and "ring trigger revolving rifles" that he also made. The shop went bankrupt in 1842. Disappointed, but hardly discouraged, Colt attained some fame the following year, 1843, for succesfully laying the Submarine Telegraph Cable in New York Harbor, making it the first cable laid and operating successfully.

In 1847, Colt's luck changed when he met Capt. Sam Walker of the Texas Rangers, who came to New York to inspect and buy guns for his Ranger force. Becoming good friends, he and Colt worked on drawings and designs for a more positive revolver. Finally it worked, and the new models began to sell. They were called the "Colt Walker Whitney Model" and the "Walker Models," and they were made at Whitneyville, Connecticut. Proving its accuracy and dependability, the U.S. government purchased 1,000 of these revolvers in late 1847.

Returning to Hartford in 1848, and from his office on Pearl Street, Colt designed the powerful "Colt Dragoon Model." Business got better and finally, after moving around to many locations, Colt purchased 250 acres for his company on the banks of the Connecticut River, on the east side of Hartford. In 1855, the "Colt Armory" was completed and got its world famous title, "Colt's Patent Firearms Manu-facturing Company." All the guns Colt designed were made there, except those manufactured directly in Europe, where Colt opened a factory in London in 1853, near the Thames River. Both the "Pocket Model of 1849" and the "Navy Model of 1851" were made there. Besides guns, Colt also manufactured disc engines, sewing machines, bicycles, lawn mowers, drilling machines, oil pumps, shotguns, sporting and hunting rifles, as well as the omnipotent

"Gatling Gun." Colt became rich and famous, meeting royalty, presidents and the common folk alike. The Civil War began and the Colt factory went full steam ahead.

But in 1862, just as his powerful weapons were being used by North and South with deadly accuracy and consequences, Samuel Colt died at the young age of 47. The men of Company "A" of the 12th Connecticut Regiment, which Colt himself had raised as a militia unit for the Civil War, escorted the silver mounted casket to its final resting place. Samuel Colt, the man who never himself bore arms in battle, never killed a man and was only an honorary "Colonel" was eulogized by his friends and family, while his one thousand workers lined up to view the body at Armsmear, in Hartford's South Meadows. His ingenuity, vision, and hard work remain a testament to the firearms that bear his name and known worldwide. He was one of Hartford's greatest sons. Sadly, that rich factory that adorned millions of fancy letterheads sent all over the world, with its blue "onion dome" still stands today, albeit idle, and in general need of a serious face-lift.

The idea for this TV program was not new, actually. None other than western great Randolph Scott starred in the movie *Colt .45,* released in 1951 by Warner Brothers. In this movie, Scott is the salesman who brings the newly-manufactured Colt .45 out West to promote and sell it, but at the same time has to fight off thieves and glory-seeking characters who believe that once they get their hands on such a new weapon, they hold the power for more sinister motives.

This old cowboy action movie starred other old time favorites that went on to bigger things. Besides Randolph Scott, other characters were played by Lloyd Bridges (*Sea Hunt, Joe Forrester*) Alan Hale (*Gilligan's Island*), and Walter Coy (*Frontier*). Even a real Indian, actor Chief Thundercloud, had a part in this western. In fact, if you have a sharp eye for details, faces, and old western trivia, it's great to catch these old favorites.

In this popular TV series, Chris Colt played a soft-spoken sales representative of the Colt factory going around the western frontier demonstrating, taking orders, and selling the Colt firearms. In reality, he was an undercover government agent of President Grant, tracking down and bringing to justice the lawless elements of the time. Preston's outfit was especially tailor made. He wore at times a special frock coat with slits on the sides for his two guns to prominently show. Other times, he wore a special holster with the rounded discs showing the famous "Colt" logo. Even his Stetson had a special band with little metal replicas of the Colt. 45 going all around it.

Alternating his rugged looks, with and without a moustache throughout the series, the show ran for three solid years, ending its run in late September 1960. During the course of the show, actor Donald May was brought on as his cousin, Samuel Colt, Jr., son of the original founder. Together and for a time on his own, Sam Colt and Chris Colt hit the trails together.

Above: Close-up of details showing rampant Colt logo, raised title, sleek white grips, and gold revolving cylinder.

Left: The very impressive Hubley Colt .45, one of the largest cap guns ever made for a youngster, and one of the most real.

Wayde Preston as "Chris Colt," the undercover agent and Colt firearms salesman wearing his special frock coat on the TV western Colt .45.

The Colt .45 in its beautiful Hubley single holster rig. Note the Paladin chess knight logo on the holster pocket. The design was simple, but nobody was going to mess with any kid wearing this outfit!

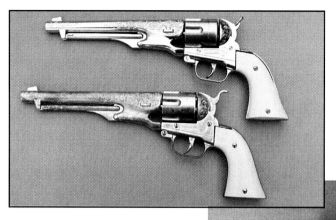

Like Clint Walker, Wayde Preston had his disagreements with Warner Brothers, but later returned to the show.

After *Colt. 45*, Preston starred in several westerns and war movies, but by his own words, hated the "Hollywood" jet set and eventually moved to Italy, where he continued to make westerns and became even more popular there. Sadly, Preston passed away in 1991. Donald May went on to star in the soap opera *All My Children*. Warner Brothers could boast that along with *Maverick*, *Cheyenne*, *Sugarfoot*, and *Bronco*, that *Colt .45* was riding the top of the western charts in 1958.

CAP GUN COLLECTIBLES

Above: The Hubley Colt. 45 and its brother, the Model 1860 .44. Besides the pattern name, the only difference is the longer hammer with a different style on the .44.

Right: The Colt. 45 in its breakdown form for loading or changing the cylinder, along with the two-piece bullets used. Sam Colt would have been proud!

This popular show spawned the "biggest of 'em all," as the toy gun giant, Hubley, came out with the Model 1860 Army Colt .45, a full 13 inches in length, and its "brother," the Model 1860 Cal. 44. Both guns came in the same design and length and with the same solid white grips. The Colt .45 came in polished nickel, but with a gold cylinder, while the Model 1840 .44 came in a dull gray finish with the same gold cylinder. Both guns are taken down simulating the "real" Colt of the period, with the ramrod taken down, swung over to the right, and then pulling out the entire cylinder to reload the "bullets," then putting it all back together and fire away.

Hubley sold these by the thousands and it is still an intimidating cap pistol to hold and aim today. Hubley also came out with a special single holster large enough, and of superior quality leather, with six bullets and the gold embossed lettering, along with the rampant colt logo over the pocket of the holster. This huge rig also has, strangely enough, the Paladin chess knight logo on the pocket, even though Hubley did not manufacture the Paladin cap pistol. Hubley also marketed a double holster set with these gorgeous guns, studs and buckles and also a "gunfighter" style model in russet leather with "Colt. 45" and the Colt logo on the strap across the pocket. Consequently, both the gun and these variation holsters became popular, housing the Colt .45, the Colt .44, Paladin, and even the Ric-O-Shay guns that were also produced by Hubley.

Only Hubley came out with the Colt .45. A special red-lined box came with the Colt .45. Hubley also did a special commemorative Texan .45 of the same gun but with the Texan .45 markings. The Army Model .44 was done in commemoration of the 100-year anniversary of the beginning of the Civil War. The only drawback to this gun is the fact that the rather long and heavy barrel tends to "droop" slightly forward and away from the cylinder-turning mechanism, which at times will not allow the cylinder to turn as you cock and fire the gun. However, tightening it and pushing it up and against the frame itself should allow the cylinder to turn when cocking the gun. The "biggest of 'em all" is an intimidating and handsome cap pistol. Old Sam Colt would have been proud that a 100 years later, the toy gun companies were churning out more of his "designs" for millions of young "Yanks" and "Rebs" all over the country.

Above: Here's a pair of Colt. 45s in a fancy double holster rig, full of studs, "Colt. 45" markings, and 12 bullets, six over each holster pocket! Note the fancy double steerheads open face buckle!

Right: Close-up of the Colt. 45 in the double holster set.

COWBOY G MEN

Whoa, there! Melvin Purvis with a cowboy hat? Eliot Ness on a horse? Undercover agents on the wild frontier? Yes, Sir! *Cowboy G Men* was one of television's earliest westerns, and yes, it did have an odd name with the "Roaring 20s" ring to it. When we think of "G-Men," naturally government agents, even *The Untouchables* comes to mind. But sure enough, in September 1954, "Cowboy G Men" came to television, and no, they were not the pilot for *The Untouchables. Cowboy G Men* was set in the 1880s—some 40-50 years before!

Cowboy G Men starred veteran western star Russell Hayden and the veteran child star Jackie Coogan. Russell Hayden had starred in plenty of action westerns in the 1940s, but he was a well known face after his role as "Lucky" in several episodes of the *Hopalong Cassidy* series. Hayden also co-produced the show. Hayden had also played opposite Jimmy Ellison in *West of the Brazos*, the 1950s action western set in Texas. He played with a sense of humor and plenty of wit and charm, but he was a two-gun man and he looked tall in the saddle.

Jackie Coogan, a child star who rose to fame with Charlie Chaplin in *The Kid*, worked in all kinds of movies until World War II service. He returned to show business and appeared in one of television's first quiz shows as a regular. He was then cast alongside Hayden for the *Cowboy G Men* when it debuted in 1954. Both stars remained on the show until its early demise, but they made plenty of appearances all over the country promoting the show, as many stars did, in the early days of television. He connected with the audiences, and especially with legions of youngsters who all wanted to be "G-Men."

Set in the 1880s, the two men played undercover government agents who arrived on the scene simultaneously, and then brought the culprits to justice before the action-packed half-hour show finished. Hayden played the part of "Pat Gallagher," a cowhand on a local ranch. Coogan played the part of "Stoney Crockett," a horse wrangler. In reality, however, they were undercover government agents who were set to maintain law and order against the lawless of the period. As he had done in film westerns, Hayden wore two guns while Coogan wore a single holster. Remarkably, even though the early westerns featuring Roy Rogers, Gene Autry, William Boyd, and others had the characters wearing fancy outfits, fringed shirts, colorful bandanas, and even fancier boots, both characters of *Cowboy G Men* wore more simple attire on the show, and concentrated on Western-style detective work. The show lasted only 39 episodes and went off the air in the summer of 1955. A syndicated show, this program was originally filmed in 1952 and sources differ on whether 26 or 39 episodes actually made it to our television screens. Still, *Cowboy G Men* was a valiant attempt to give credit to the noble and dangerous work of undercover agents in the 1880s.

Russell Hayden went on to produce and direct, as well as star in other westerns, and his TV credits included *26 Men, Judge Roy Bean,* and *Marshal of Gunfight Pass,* an impressive array of westerns even for the early days of television. Hayden passed away in 1978 at the ripe old age of 95. Jackie Coogan also went on to star in several programs, but his role as "Uncle Fester" in *The Addams Family* is what he is usually remembered for. Coogan died in 1984.

Russell Hayden, veteran western actor, producer, director, and star of Cowboy G-Men, *tall in the saddle. (Courtesy of Libro DiZinno)*

Child star and veteran character actor Jackie Coogan, who played the part of "Stoney Crockett" on Cowboy G-Men. *(Courtesy of Old West Shop)*

The Cowboy and its G-Man special holster rig. Note the "G-Man" tooling and the U.S. Capitol building on the holster pocket. (J. Schleyer Collection)

Note the fancy entwined rope work design on the holster, giving it a western look, as well as its "special agent" outline of a badge around the U.S. Capitol. Super rare holster outfit! (J. Schleyer Collection)

Seldom-seen Lone Star Cow-Boy—an almost identical copy of the Hubley Trooper, alongside the G-Man badge! It's enough to make any kid want to be an FBI man! The perfect combination—Cowboy and G-Man! (J. Schleyer Collection)

CAP GUN COLLECTIBLES

This early western came along long before the toy gun companies jumped on the capitalistic bandwagon of outfitting millions of youngsters. Yet, we did find the holster and the cap gun that we believe went with this early show. Indeed, I could find no reference to other Cowboy G Men collectibles, not even comic books, Whitman books, games, or other memorabilia. But, a six-point star badge for G Men—obviously "cowboy" G-Men.

The Cowboy G-Men holster is a western-style early holster in heavy leather, and it is a colorful, well-tooled rich brown leather holster. Both holster and belt have fine studs and different color jewels. The tooling is a combination of both western and later law-enforcement G Men topics. The border shows a braided rope pattern while the holster pocket reads "G-Man" and "Special Agent" with none other than the U.S. Capitol on the front of the pocket. The holster and belt is of superior early construction, great western styling, and color. The buckle is a nickel rectangular pattern.

The cap pistol is the very rare and early Lone Star "Cow-Boy," an exact copy of the Hubley Trooper, right down to the opening device under the barrel and in front of the trigger guard. Also evident is the red 5-pointed star logo on the grips, and its size. It is an all-metal 7-inch gun with checkered grips and simple, yet elegant, scrollwork frame and barrel. "Cow-Boy" as the Brits like to spell it, is raised on both sides of the frame under the cylinder. The lever breaks the gun from the top for cap loading. A wonderful little gem of a cap gun! The badge is a sheriff- and marshal type, six ball points, brass, and with "G" in the center and "men" below.

COWBOY IN AFRICA

This strangely named show was an "African Western" and starred Chuck Conners, after the run of *Rifleman*, and his second series, *Branded*. The show was a noble endeavor, for the *Cowboy in Africa* was a world champion rodeo star that was hired by an English ranch owner in Kenya, Africa. The character was "Jim Sinclair," played by Connors, and instead of battling it out with gunfighters transplanted in Africa or African tribal wars, Sinclair ended up fighting poachers, dealing with tropical diseases afflicting the local population, and trying to stop local corruption and pesky tourists who wouldn't have survived a day in the wild African jungle.

The British commander was played by Ron Howard, the son of famous actor Leslie Howard. A native orphan boy that ends up being adopted by Sinclair was "Samson," played by Gerald Edwards. The part of a Navaho Indian named "John Henry" was played by Tom Nardini, who assists Sinclair, "Commander Hayes," and the orphan boy. Instead of a trusty steed, Connors drove a Jeep, among other vehicles, both animal and mechanical. The program had breathtaking shots of Africa. The characters all assist Jim Sinclair in his efforts at game "ranching," trying to prove that this was Africa's best defense against the ravages caused by unrestricted cattle grazing. This, of course, doesn't sit well with Boer cattlemen who are not fond of Sinclair or his plan.

Unfortunately, the ABC show lasted only one season, from September 1967, to September 1968, already well after the death knell for westerns was ringing loudly on TV. For some reason, even the popularity of Chuck Conners, who had a huge following from his previous shows and his old baseball-playing days, couldn't save *Cowboy In Africa* from its final ride on the Serengeti plain. Syndicated, this show aired only 26 episodes.

The stars of **Cowboy in Africa***, left to right: Chuck Connors ("Jim Sinclair"), Gerald Edwards ("Samson"), Ron Howard ("Commander Hayes"), and Tom Nardini ("John Henry"). (Courtesy of Old West Shop)*

Black finish and chrome finish models of the Fanner 50 with the Cowboy in Africa holsters.

Above: Pair of Mattel Fanner 50s in the Cowboy in Africa double holster set in brown Dura-Hide. Only the holsters were marked for the show title.

Right: Mattel's Fanner 50 boxed for **Cowboy in Africa** *series. Note that the gun shown did not just come in the black finish. Note Chuck Connnors and Gerald Edwards with the giraffe in show photo on box. (Courtesy of J. Schleyer)*

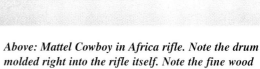

Close-up details showing the show title on the receiver, lever action, and the impressive bullet drum.

Above: Mattel Cowboy in Africa rifle. Note the drum molded right into the rifle itself. Note the fine wood graining. A seldom-seen Mattel rifle.

Above, left: Bronze finish Fanner 50 with brown African antelope on grips that were used in both Cowboy in Africa and Planet of the Apes outfits.

CAP GUN COLLECTIBLES

Mattel Toys came out with the Cowboy in Africa cap gun, utilizing its already proven bestseller in the Fanner 50 model. The Fanner used for the *Cowboy In Africa* series came in both a chrome finish and a black factory finish. It had the non-revolving cylinders, but the same cap loading gate on the left side. The grips were the most dramatic change to the model used for the Cowboy in Africa. The usual stag grips were replaced by beautifully-grained white grips, which sported a unique Antelope head with curved back, thin long horns. The same white grips were used on both the chrome and black models.

As a side note, some collectors call the horned animal an "Ibis" which it is not. An Ibis is a bird. Others call it an Ibex, which it is not, as the Ibex is an alpine mountain goat. Still others call it an "Impala" which is a 3-foot high deer family animal. Correctly, it is the African antelope of the curved (and hollow) and ribbed (or "ringed") horns, one of the fastest animals on hoof. The same grips, in brown plastic, were used on the Planet of the Apes gun, which came with a bronze finish. The Cowboy in Africa was not marked with the show title, nor were they marked with the character's name, "Jim Sinclair."

The holsters, however, made in the Mattel "Dura-Hide," developed by Mattel in 1960, came in both brown and black in a fine tooled appearance with "Cowboy In Africa" raised on the holster pockets. The box for the Cowboy in Africa guns, when sold singly, was advertised by Mattel using its "Fan it! Trigger it!" concept. The gun was the 10-inch Fanner 50 model. The colorful box also hawked "TV's famous Chuck Connors" as well as *Cowboy in Africa*, with a photo showing Connors, and his black orphan "Samson," petting a giraffe. Seems like the show was well ahead of its time!

Mattel also marketed a Cowboy in Africa rifle, seldom found. Given that the show only lasted one season, one can understand why. The rifle is an all-plastic clicker-type; originally it was Mattel's Rapid Fire model. "Cowboy in Africa" in a circle, is raised on the molded plastic receiver on both sides as is "Rapid Fire." The barrel is black while the forearm and the stock are in a finely grained brown plastic. The unique feature of the Cowboy in Africa rifle is the round drum situated directly in front of the trigger. It gives the rifle a "machine-gun" appearance with 18 molded bullets perfectly situated in the drum, with the shell part of the built in bullets stamped "Mattel .38 Spec." On this rifle, the Mattel address is shown as Hawthorne, California. The rifle is 26 inches long and rather unique. The same model was also used in the Mattel Planet of the Apes series. Only Mattel made the Cowboy in Africa guns, holsters, and Rapid Fire rifle.

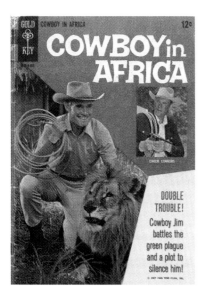

Rare Gold Key Comic issued for **Cowboy in Africa.**

DALE EVANS
THE QUEEN OF THE WEST

Along with Roy Rogers, the "King of the Cowboys," it is only fitting that we have "The Queen of the West" in his beautiful wife and talented actress, singer, and writer, Dale Evans. Born Frances Smith in 1912, Dale Evans was already an established singer and actress when she teamed up with Roy Rogers in the 1944 film, *The Cowboy and the Senorita.*

They fell in love, married in 1947, and Dale went on to become "The Queen of the West" after appearing in more than 30 movies with Roy as well as *The Roy Rogers Show*, which came to television in 1951. Dale played the owner of the cafe in "Mineral City" where Roy, his wonder horse, "Trigger," and his faithful shepherd, "Bullet," fought for law and order. Character second banana Pat Brady and his famous jeep "Nellybelle" rounded out the show.

Dale Evans soon became what every little cowgirl on the block wanted to emulate. It also began a full run of all kinds of children's products—school bags, watches, slippers, cowgirl outfits, cowboy hats, gloves, even bath products. Dale appeared on hundreds of TV magazines, books, western magazines, Dell comics, and coloring books. She also wrote two beautiful and moving books based on letters to her two sons, Tom, and Sandy, who died while in the army.

Deeply religious, Dale also recorded a number of spiritual and Christmas songs and albums. Dale has been inducted into the Cowboy Hall of Fame, and helps run the Roy Rogers-Dale Evans Museum in California, which is visited by thousands of old fans and youngsters today.

CAP GUN COLLECTIBLES

Dale Evans cap guns were made by a number of toy gun companies. The George Schmidt Co., Los Angeles, came out with the Dale Evans Queen of the West Shoot 'n Iron, complete with its colorful box showing Dale on her rearing horse. The gun is a long barrel, 10-inch polished nickel gun with copper grips. The grips are checkered copper with a red jewel and a butterfly logo with "D" and "E" cast right into the grips. "Dale Evans" is in raised script, signature-style, on both sides of the frame, under the cylinder. The ribbed barrel is plain, but there is ample design and the "rope" border on the cylinder and frame of the gun. Schmidt also made this in a dull gray finish, too.

The King of the Cowboys with Dale Evans, the Queen of the West. Trigger certainly approves!

The George Schmidt Dale Evans cap shooter. Note butterfly on grips along with red jewel. The name is in cursive lettering.

Pair of Schmidt Dale Evans cap Shoot 'n Irons with the original boxes. (Courtesy of Brian Wolf)

Pair of Buzz-Henry Dale Evans cap shooters with inset grips that came in white, black, green, and red. (Courtesy of Brian Wolf)

Above: Dale Evans and three of the Rogers children—Dusty, Dodie, and Sandy, already a growing bunch of cowhands!

Right: A super Dale Evans outfit that included Schmidt cap gun, wrist watch, pen set, derringer, bolo tie, and accessories. Note image of Dale and "Queen of the West" title. (Courtesy of Joe Saine)

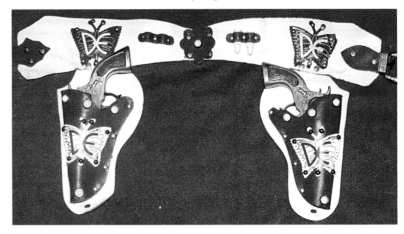

Extremely rare early Dell Comic issued for Dale Evans, Queen of the West. Yep, that's Buttermilk!

Schmidt also made a small framed model with ribbed plain barrel; "Dale Evans" on a bell curve on the frame, over the trigger area; and simulated stag copper grips with the same "DE" butterfly logo, but without the jewel. This smaller-framed gun is a polished nickel 8-inch gun. Both of the Schmidt models have the opening lever on the left side, up by the hammer, and as with all of the Schmidt guns, break from the top, and are generally fragile.

Buzz-Henry also made a Dale Evans cap gun. The gun is an 8-inch model that came in both nickel and gold finishes. It is identical to the Roy Rogers and Gene Autry models put out by Buzz-Henry. It came with colored inset plastic grips in white, black, and red. The grips have the "BH" logo and the rearing pony on both the grips and the frame, with the lasso going from the pony's neck and around the name "Dale Evans" in raised print. This is on both sides of the frame under the cylinder. The gun is 7 inches long and has lots of scrollwork on the barrel and frame, as well as western designs consisting of cactus plants and horseshoes. The gun breaks from the top for cap loading with a lever located on the right side of the hammer.

This is an early, heavy, and solid cap gun that was well made. While some of the Buzz-Henry guns also have "Buzz Henry" at the bottom of the gun butt raised on the metal frame, the Dale Evans model has a plain, unmarked butt.

Classy Products put out a series of Dale Evans holster sets, both single and double, which they marketed as Classy Model #2977, and a Model #2906-DE. The guns used in these sets were Lone Star "Apache," strangely enough. The same script signature of "Dale Evans" came on the holster's belt loops on the Model #2906. The Model #2977 was much more elaborate and typical of a cowgirl's set—white leather belt with red pockets, green and black, black and white, with and without fringe, lots of studs and jewels, and remarkably, the same "DE" butterfly logo that was cast on the Schmidt Dale Evans copper grips. These holsters take both the Schmidt 8-inch and 10-inch guns, as well as Buzz Henry 7-inch guns. The larger Classy holsters take the longer Apache cap guns. The #2906 pattern was also sold, strangely enough, marked "Dale Evans" on the belt, but came with Classy Roy Rogers guns.

O.K., who remembers the name of Dale's horse? Give up? Buttermilk. How sweet!

Only Schmidt and Buzz Henry made Dale Evans-marked cap pistols. No rifles marked "Dale Evans" have surfaced to date by any company. Classy marketed Dale Evans holsters with a variety of guns.

Colorful and ornate Dale Evans double holster set with Buzz-Henry guns with red grips. The white leather gunbelt has both red and white details. Note the "DE" initials and butterfly logo. The envy of any cowgirl! (Courtesy of J. Schleyer)

DANIEL BOONE

A color illustration of the real Daniel Boone, with his dog and his trusty rifle he nicknamed "tick licker" due to its accuracy. (William Tell Images)

One thing is for sure about handsome star Fess Parker—he just looked good in a coonskin cap, and after he had already achieved great fame and popularity as "Davy Crockett," he was cast in the title role as "Daniel Boone." Daniel Boone, like Crockett, was a real American frontiersman who also became a folk hero.

The show fictionalized the real Boone, of course, and added sidekicks and Indian friends such as "Mingo," played by singer-actor Ed Ames, and "Gabe Cooper," played by sports hero-turned actor Rosie Greer. Even sausage maker Jimmy Dean came on board the show. *The Daniel Boone Show* on NBC became a very popular program and lasted from September 1964, through August 1970, a rather lengthy run after the TV westerns were already well on the way to memory lane.

Daniel Boone had so many wonderful stars during its six-year run, from comedians to singers, from old western character actors to beautiful actresses that made your eyes bulge, including Patricia Blair, who was cast as Daniel's wife, "Rebecca." The show was initially in black and white, then went to color. Another whole generation of would-be "frontiersmen" were wearing coonskin caps and buckskins and buying all kinds of "Daniel Boone" products, from lunch boxes to pens and pencils for school. Fess Parker is one of the few stars that found immortal fame playing two real pre-western American heroes in two series.

Remarkably, there were three Daniel Boone TV programs. Walt Disney did four one-hour long episodes of *Daniel Boone* for the 1960-1961 season, starring Dewey Martin, also a Texas native, with actress Mala Powers as "Rebecca Boone." It never achieved the fame and popularity as Disney's *Davy Crockett*. Yet, five years later, with Fess Parker in the role, it did, but this time it was 20th Century-Fox Television. With the great popularity and its six-year run, 20th Century Fox tried to revive *Daniel Boone* in 1977. This time the series was titled *Young Dan'l Boone* starring Rick Moses and a whole slew of characters, but the CBS-TV show lasted only four episodes and died a fast death in October 1977.

THE REAL DANIEL BOONE

The real Daniel Boone came along even before Davy Crockett. Daniel was born in 1734, the sixth of 11 children to an English Quaker family in Pennsyl- vania. His father gave him a musket at age 12 and young Boone became a hunter, trapper, and crack shot before the age of 16, when the family decided to leave Pennsylvania and settle in the Carolinas, getting there by way of a Conestoga wagon. At 21, Boone joined the Carolina militia, and fought in the battle of Fort Duquesne, along with George Washington, as both were young men in General Braddock's expedition to drive the French from the fort.

Boone returned to hunting and trapping, as he truly loved the wilderness, and was gone for long periods of time, leaving his young wife, Rebecca, and two children, and moving the family each time he returned home from the wilderness. The family moved to Kentucky, then Ohio. By 1774, now a captain, Boone helped defend new frontier forts and new settlers from the Shawnees in Lord Dunsmore's War. Boone was entrusted to cut a trail into the Kentucky wilderness with 30 men for 300 miles, and upon completing this incredible feat, the new settlement was named Boonesboro.

At the start of the American Revolution, Boone was captured by the Shawnees. General Hamilton of the British Army offered the Shawnee chief, Blackfish, 100 pounds sterling for Boone, but the chief refused. After several months of captivity, Boone escaped, and fled towards Kentucky. In just four days, Boone, alone, on foot and by canoe, reached Boonesboro after covering 160 miles in that period of time. In 1778, Boone and 40 men held off an Indian war party of more than 400 Indians bent on destroying Boonesboro.

Fess Parker in his TV role as "Daniel Boone," the best known and most remembered Daniel Boone star.

Above: Dewey Martin as "Daniel Boone" with Randy Banks as "Squire" in TV's first series of the frontiersman. (Courtesy of Old West Shop)

Above Right: Actor Rick Moses who starred as "Young Daniel Boone," television's third series on the life of our frontier hero. (Courtesy of Old West Shop)

The siege lasted nine days and finally, the Indians gave up as the men held their ground, even fighting off Indians that had dug a tunnel to place gunpowder under the fort. When Kentucky was made part of Virginia, Boone was elected to the state legislature. During a meeting, British cavalry raided the meeting at Charlottesville and Boone was captured. He was later paroled. Boone continued to hunt, trap, even sell horses, and run a tavern. In 1791, he was elected to the Virginia legislature for the second time.

In 1799, Boone and his family moved again, this time to Missouri. In 1810, he returned to Kentucky, meeting John James Audubon (who would later gain fame as a painter of birds) and Boone taught him the ways of the wilderness. Boone returned to Missouri as he advanced in age, to enjoy his grandchildren, and finally settle down. He had achieved fame in young America, and he was a true trailblazer and Indian fighter. He also lost two brothers and three sons at the hands of Indians.

He died at age 86 in 1820, and was initially buried in Missouri. Years later, Kentucky decided to pay tribute to this fearless man and Boone's body was brought back to Kentucky, and reburied under a monument. Boone left a great family and a great legacy. In fact, actor Richard Boone (who gamed immortal fame as "Paladin") was a direct descendant of Daniel Boone.

CAP GUN COLLECTIBLES

As popular as *Daniel Boone* was, this writer was able to find only three toy guns which prominently are marked "Daniel Boone." Louis Marx put out a flintlock-style plastic and die cast cap pistol marketed as #133—the Daniel Boone Derringer, but it is actually a full size 8-inch cap pistol in black plastic with silver highlights, and die-cast hammer and trigger. Strangely, the lockplate has "derringer" on the left side where the hammer is also situated, and while it looks like a flintlock, this "repeater," as Marx labeled it, fired roll caps and is actually a percussion-type pistol with a unique design in the firing of caps. By pulling back the hammer, you then lift the cap box from the center of the gun upward to load the roll of caps, slide it back into its unseen position, cock the hammer and fire away. This came on a card showing Daniel Boone as a "Wilderness Scout," wearing coonskin cap and buckskins and firing a Kentucky rifle. The card carried the Louis Marx Company

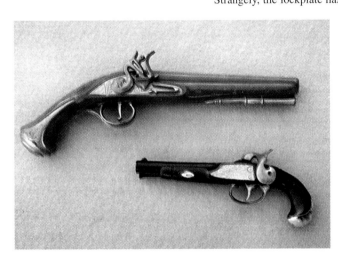

The Marx Daniel Boone flintlock and derringer models. The flintlock fired one cap at a time while the derringer was a cap repeater.

Marx Daniel Boone large flintlock on original card marked "Daniel Boone."

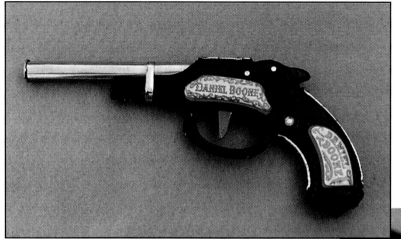

Above: Japanese-made Daniel Boone cork firing pistol. Note the beautiful graphics.

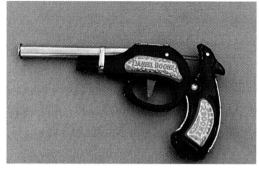

Above: The pistol in its cocked position.

Close-up of the "Japan" marking. Not to be confused with "Made in Japan" or "Made in China" markings used much later. (Courtesy of Terry Graham)

address in West Virginia as opposed to the usual New York address.

Marx also did a much larger version of a cap-firing flintlock-style pistol, which was also carded in the same series as #134. This flintlock has a different pose of Daniel Boone as well as the one on the smaller card. This gun is plastic with die-cast parts. It is 12 inches long on a six-by-thirteen-inch card. While the smaller model described above has "derringer" on the back lockplate, this gun is truly designed as a flintlock pistol with hammer, flint, and cover plate. This gun is chocolate-colored plastic with gold highlights on the lockplate, butt, ramrod and trigger, with the flintlock mechanism in grayish colored die-cast parts. While the ingenious Marx designed the smaller model as a "repeater," this larger model, in true "flintlock" style, fires only one cap at a time seated on the lockplate. Both models are stamped with the Marx logo on the plastic frame, and the card carries the Marx address in Glendale, West Virginia.

The Japanese came out with a pressed tin cork-firing pistol, prominently marked "Daniel Boone" with spectacular lithographic details. The gun is marked only "Japan." Like many tin toys made in Japan, there were two companies using only initials, K. Toy Co., and K.O. Toys (and also Cragston, a U.S. company that marketed Japanese-made toys) that put out a few guns. This Japanese-made Daniel Boone came in very colorful chrome, black, white, and red details, and it has "Daniel Boone" on both sides of the frame, as well as the grips in vibrant red lettering. This colorful gun is also 8 inches long.

Unlike Walt Disney's *Davy Crockett*, which achieved never-to-be-repeated popularity in record numbers 10 years before, no western-style guns marked "Daniel Boone" have surfaced to date.

Daniel Boone was one of the best "sharpshooters" that ever lived. He was so "dead on center" that his flintlock rifle was called "Tick Licker" because he could shoot a "tick" off a varmint in the woods.

*Gold Key Comic issued for **Daniel Boone**. Ed Ames, shown on the cover, played the part of "Mingo," his trusty, Oxford-educated Indian friend.*

DAVY CROCKETT

To do "the King of the Wild Frontier" proper justice, you'd need to do two books—one on Davy Crockett himself, and one on the popularity of Walt Disney's *Davy Crockett* starring Fess Parker. Crockett was a real American frontiersman who became a legend in his own time and a bigger one after his death at the Alamo. But it was Walt Disney, always in his efforts to give American youngsters real life heroes to imitate and emulate, that made Davy Crockett a household word in 1954. There is little debate that Davy Crockett became an American phenomenon in the mid-1950s.

Even today, as soon as I bring up the subject of Davy Crockett, the listener will almost immediately say, "Oh, yeah, I remember—the ballad went like this "Davy, Davy Crockett, King of the Wild Frontier! Born on a mountain top in Tennessee. . . ." Whoa there, I have to say, O.K., O.K., I believe you, you remember Davy Crockett!" Even those people who were not fortunate to have grown up in the 1950s, even they know about Davy Crockett, and that's wonderful. Though not a western character, we can't ignore Davy Crockett, and as we shall see, neither did the western toy gun companies.

The real David Crockett was born on August 17, 1786, at Strong's Springs, near Limestone, in eastern Tennessee. Life was hard, work was even harder. His family was a poor one. His father sent him to work with more prosperous farmers, so Davy didn't get much schooling. Historians say he may have received only about "100 hours of schooling from farmers," but Davy taught himself to be a prominent speaker, and had great oratorical skills.

During the harsh winters, the young Davy became a dead shot, expert tracker and hunter, and along the way, hunted bears and racoons. When he decided to use the hide, complete with the racoon fur and striped tail for a hat, the "coonskin cap" was born. Davy related folk stories, backwoods yarns and homespun humor and metaphors, and used a vivid storytelling mode of speaking that was well recorded in Davy's speeches and writings that were later found.

He took part in the Creek Indian wars in western Tennessee between 1813 and 1815. In 1821, he was elected to the Tennessee legislature, winning immense popularity through his campaign speeches, using old backwoods yarn-telling when he wanted to make a point. This image of a rough frontiersman wearing buckskins and the racoon skin cap soon made him popular during his lifetime.

Following a second term in the legislature in 1823, he ran for the House of Representatives, in 1825, but lost. He won in 1827, again in 1829, but lost the seat in 1831. He won again in 1833 by a narrow margin of votes, but finally lost again in 1835. He lost against "Old Hickory," Andrew Jackson. Crockett was eagerly courted and well publicized by the Whig Party. They wanted a "coonskin politician" to offset Jackson, who disagreed on treatment of land squatters in western Tennessee. The well-publicized speeches of the time tended to show Crockett as a "b'ar hunting and grinning" frontiersman who was a

The real Davy Crockett along with his famous motto and his signature. (Courtesy of Western History Collection, University of Oklahoma)

Fess Parker starring in his most famous role—"Davy Crockett, King of the Wild Frontier."

Davy Crockett as he appeared as the famous frontiersman with his famous rifle, "Betsy," and his trademark coonskin cap. (Courtesy of Texas State Library Archives)

crack shot, and—even without formal education—a shrewd politician.

In reality, Crockett engaged in several business ventures and was able to communicate, speak, and write very well in conventional English. In 1834, Crockett wrote his autobiography along with Thomas Chilton, the U.S. Representative from Kentucky. Between 1834 and 1836, shortly before his death, Davy also wrote several "Almanacs" and these continued well after his death, along the lines of old folk epics and tales about life and his own brand of philosophy. In fact, Davy's well publicized motto was "I believe this rule, for others when I am dead—Be always sure you are right, then go ahead."

After his last political defeat, Crockett headed west to Texas. He

Above: Actor Jeff York, who played the role of "Mike Fink" of the River Pirates in the Davy Crockett series.

Above, left: Fess Parker as "Davy Crockett," Buddy Ebsen as "Georgie Russell," and character actor Hans Conreid as "Thimblerig" from the series. (Courtesy of Old West Shop)

joined the beleaguered American forces in the old mission, the Alamo, and as is well known, died there in the Battle of the Alamo on March 6, 1836, in San Antonio, Texas. Since Davy Crockett came along before the development of photography, we have portraits and images of the real Davy Crockett done by prominent artists of the day. Two of the most famous are a portrait by Pierre Saint Jean, done in 1828 and an engraving by Asher B. Durand, circa 1835, being the closest to what Davy looked like a year before his death. This is one that carries his motto and his own signature. A painting of Davy in his buckskins, with his coonskin cap and trusty rifle, "Betsy," was done by William Huddle, and hangs today at the Capitol in Austin, Texas, in tribute to this Tennessee-born hero for Texas independence.

Equally interesting is the story of how Davy Crockett became an American hero worshiped by millions of youngsters in 1954—118 years after his valiant death at the Alamo. NBC and Disney Productions aired *Davy Crockett* under Disneyland's hour-long weekly productions that alternated between Fantasyland, Tomorrowland, Adventureland, and of course, Frontierland. As always, Disney introduced the shows personally, and on December 15, 1954, the first of the three *Davy Crockett* episodes took America by storm.

The trilogy that brought Davy back to life were "Davy Crockett, Indian Fighter," followed by "Davy Crockett Goes to Congress" in January 1955, and "Davy Crockett at the Alamo," run on February 23, 1955. Naturally, in this third episode, Davy went down in a blaze of glory, and youngsters—and adults, I might add—thirsted for more, and Disney decided to bring back Davy Crockett by doing episodes in Davy's life before the climax at the Alamo. This included "Davy Crockett and the River Pirates," where Davy encountered Mike Fink, the self-proclaimed "King of the River." Eventually, all of the episodes were made into an 88-minute film entitled *Davy Crockett, King of the Wild Frontier,* released in 1955. *The New York Times* hailed the movie as "the kind of adventure that nobody wants to outgrow." Boy, did they get that right!

Cast as "Davy" was Fess Parker, a 6'4" hunk of a relatively unknown actor that became an overnight sensation. With most people never having seen a photo or other details of the real Davy Crockett other than a passing notation in American history classes that Davy, Jim Bowie, and Colonel Travis died at the Alamo for Texas independence, Fess Parker became the persona of Davy Crockett reincarnated. Fess Parker was now Davy Crockett. He made thousands of appearances all over America and Europe, teaching

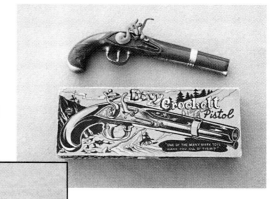

Above: Marx Davy Crockett flintlock cap pistol with original box.

Left: Close-up of details showing "Davy Crockett" on left side of the barrel.

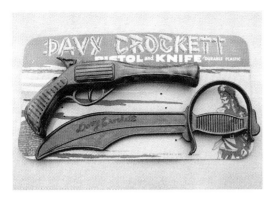

Multiple Products Company's version of the Davy Crockett pistol and Bowie knife set on its original card. Note Davy's raised signature on the blade.

youngsters to "do the right thing." He showed off his flintlock rifle and promoted safety, respect for parents and authority, and to study in school so they could speak "better than I do." After his role as Davy Crockett, as we have seen, Fess Parker was cast as the other legendary frontiersman, Daniel Boone. Davy's side-kick, "Georgie Russell," was played by Buddy Ebsen, a veteran character actor. Ebsen gained even more fame after the *Davy Crockett* series, in television's *The Beverly Hillbillies* as "Uncle Jed," and lastly as milk-drinking, gracefully aged private eye, "Barnaby Jones."

For the record, as with the character of Jim Bowie, several movies highlighting Davy Crockett, and most dealing with the Battle of the Alamo, came to the big screen before Fess Parker got the coveted role. George Montgomery (married for a time to Dinah Shore) played Davy Crockett in the 1950 production of *Davy Crockett, Indian Fighter*. A not-too-convincing Glenn Ford played Davy in Universal's 1953 movie *The Man from the Alamo*. In 1955, the same year that Disney aired the most watched of the *Davy Crockett* series, Republic Pictures released *The Last Command* starring veteran grizzled actor Arthur Hunnicut as Davy Crockett. In 1960, John Wayne played a more philosophical Davy Crockett in *The Alamo*.

All over the world, every kid wanted to be "Davy" and coonskin caps, buckskins, and just about everything imaginable was marketed under the "Davy Crockett" character. The popularity of Davy Crockett expanded to the kitchen, and it included cookie jars, coin banks, cups, saucers, tumblers, wall clocks, even sand pails and bookbags, so both boys and girls fancied themselves as the kings and queens of the wild frontier. Dell Comics did all the episodes into issues that sold by the millions. Books, usually showing Davy on the wall at the Alamo, or fighting the "b'ar," were huge sellers. As with any popular character of this magnitude, there was a whole score of unlicenced material from toy companies all over the world capitalizing on the huge success of our hero.

CAP GUN COLLECTIBLES

Several toy gun companies made Davy Crockett cap pistols. While we know that Davy Crockett came along well before the Wild West, western guns with "Davy Crockett" were huge sellers and are among some of the most well-made cap pistols of the 1950s. They are also some of the most sought after. Let's highlight the flintlocks and percussion ones first, since they truly would reflect the real life period of Davy Crockett.

Marx made the Davy Crockett Flintlock pistol in two sizes. There is the 11-inch and the 16-inch models. Both came in plastic with die-cast flintlock action, triggers, and guards. The stocks are of brown marbleized design with both solid brown and black barrels. The bands, back straps, and other fittings are painted gold. "Davy Crockett" is stamped into the left side of the barrel and painted gold. The 11-inch model was a left over of Marx's Buccaneer model.

Some of the Davy Crockett marked flintlocks also carry "Buccaneer" across the left side plate, as well as a sailing pirate ship on the left side of the grip and a pirate on the right side of the grip. The boxes, however, are prominently marked "Davy Crockett" and "authentic flintlock action." These are remarkably well made with scaled flintlock action parts. Similar models were used for "Daniel Boone" and "Zorro," also characters of the time.

Above: Hubley's beautiful Davy Crockett flintlock cap shooting rifle.

Right: Close-up of details showing name and flintlock system. The real Davy would have approved!

The Multiple Products Company of New York City made a plastic clicker percussion-style gun with a blunderbuss-style barrel. It is a brown marbleized all plastic 9-inch clicker with the works set on top of the gun itself, similar to a rimfire more than a right side plate percussion. This is a fragile gun and has none of the appeal of the Marx, and it is not even marked "Davy Crockett" anywhere. However, this was marketed with a Davy Crockett knife.

The knife is the more interesting of the two. It is also of brown marbleized plastic, but it is in the style of a Bowie knife with a knuckle bow grip, and "Davy Crockett" in cursive signature is prominently cast into the wide Bowie blade. These came on a card, highlighting Davy in buckskins, with both pistol and knife at an old frontier fort. This was one of the many unlicenced products since there is no resemblance to Fess Parker, nor is there any Walt Disney trademark. Still, it is an interesting piece of Crockett memorabilia and an interesting duo. The Ohio

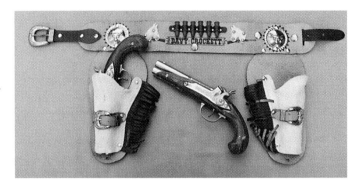

Hubley's fabulous Davy Crockett double holster set with double barreled percussion-style cap pistols. Note the beautiful caramel swirl grips.

Art Company marketed a very colorful pressed tin clicker, 8-1/2 inches long, with great details in white, red, yellow, and black, showing a full standing Davy with his rifle on the grips.

Hubley marketed an absolutely dynamite Davy Crockett double holster set of superior quality. It came in a double set with Hubley Flintlock pistols, and in a single set with a Hubley Flintlock pistol and a rubber knife on the left side. Let's examine the pistols first. While they are nickel die cast over and under double barrels, and they have "Hubley Flintlock" raised on the left side of the upper barrel, the double hammers are more percussion style, and not flintlock. They are single shot hammers, and when cocked back, the single trigger fires one at a time. The grips are a beautiful caramel in marbleized design. The lockplates and hammers are beautifully scrolled. The guns are 9-3/4 inches and well made.

These holsters have it all—tan leather belt, six bullets, conchos with steer heads, holster pockets made of fur cowhide, and horse heads on the belt also of fur cowhide. Brown fringe, nickel buckles on the pockets, nickel belt buckle, studs and "Davy Crockett" across the back of the belt in black lettering on a wooden sign design with a flintlock rifle on each side. Spectacular! The Hubley guns fit perfectly into the pockets, which even accommodate the wide percussion-style hammers.

Schmidt made three of the finest and most desirable Davy Crockett guns. The first is the 7-1/2-inch single shot Davy. It featured a polished chrome finish, with ribbed barrel, and beautifully made checkered-design copper grips. The left side of the frame has "Davy Crockett" in raised high letters. The right side of the frame has "Buck 'n Bronc." Not a "put-together" job, close scrutiny shows that this is the way these were made, just like the Buck 'n Bronc Hoppy. This is a seldom seen and rare single shot Davy. It is of superior quality and, unlike many Schmidt guns, it is tight and well fitted.

The second Schmidt Davy is the large 10-inch model, which came in both nickel and gray finish. This model has the simulated stag copper grips, similar to the Roy Rogers, Alan Ladd, and Lasso 'em Bill models. This also very rare model has "Davy Crockett" in cursive signature on the left side of the frame under the cylinder, and "Buck 'n Bronc" on the right side. The lever to break open from the top for cap loading is below and to the left of the hammer.

Seldom-seen Davy Crockett 7-1/2-inch cap shooter by Schmidt.

Schmidt Davy Crockett cap pistol with cursive signature raised on frame and copper stag grips.

The Schmidt Davy opened, showing compass in grip and cap box.

Close-up of details showing bronze checkered grips and name on frame.

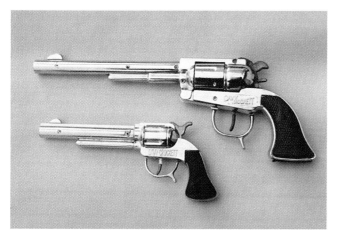

The most desirable and most elusive of the Schmidt Davy Crockett cap guns—the "daddy" and the "baby" side by side for comparison.

The third and most desirable of the Schmidt Davy Crockett is the gorgeous, 12-inch polished chrome model. This spectacular model is similar to the Schmidt "Pathfinder" model. The checkered grips have a secret compartment that comes out from under the butt, revealing a compass. It also has enough room for a roll of caps. The grips on this 12-inch model and the 7-inch model are so perfectly made and fitted, there is no room for sloppiness; they are striking. There is a thin ribbon design that runs across the grips. This long barreled beauty has a revolving cylinder, a rare feature on Schmidt guns. The lever to break this open from the top is located on the left side slightly below the hammer.

This 12-inch model is one of the largest guns Schmidt made; the barrel is half of the size—6 inches. This beautiful monster has "Davy Crockett" raised inside a frame in stamped letters in a 3-D style on the left side and "Buck 'n Bronc" on the right side of the frame. At 12 inches, this is just an inch shy of the largest of them all—Hubley's "Colt .45"—yet, it has an entirely different appeal. Its plain, but highly polished chrome finish with absolutely no scrollwork or engraving, gives it a "sleek" appearance. Stand in line, "pardners," this is one Davy they all want to get their hands on—no, no, not the kids, us adult collectors!

The third line of well-made, beautiful Davy Crockett guns are those made by Leslie-Henry. I have been able to document three variations. The first is a single shot, 7-inch nickel-plated cap gun with heavy scrollwork on the barrel and frame. This has white plastic grips, with horse head and checkering, and has "Davy Crockett" raised on both sides of the frame under the cylinder, and the rearing horse logo on the frame as well. A lasso forms the outline around the name and is then tied to the rearing horse's neck. This model has a standard trigger guard without the extra nub to rest the middle finger.

The second pattern is also a 7-inch model, which came in both nickel and gold finishes. This is a cap repeater and has a lever on the right side of the cylinder, just below the hammer, and it breaks open from the top. It comes with the same white grips, with upraised horse head and checkering details. While it is similar to the above model, there are three distinct differences. Besides the fact this is a repeater and breaks open for cap loading, it has more extensive scroll-work and design, including the addition of two horseshoes and a cactus on the cylinder and frame. This has the extra metal nub on the trigger guard, and finally, the sight on this model is an elongated triangle, while the above model has a rounded half-moon sight. The name, rope border, and rearing horse on the frame is the same. Leslie-Henry made the same guns for Wild Bill Hickok and Gene Autry. While the frames appear to have the same style and same markings as the Buzz-Henry models, they are not stamped "Buzz-Henry" on the frame butts.

The third pattern is the standard 9-inch Leslie-Henry model, made for some other characters. This is the cap repeater, has the left side lever to break open for cap loading, and has the large grips with horse head design. The frame has "Davy Crockett" raised on both sides, as well as the larger rearing horse logo on the frame after the name. Note that the larger pattern

Leslie-Henry 9-inch Davy Crockett with white horse head grips.

Leslie-Henry 7-1/2-inch cap shooter (above) and single-shot model (below) of the Davy Crockett line of guns.

does not have the lasso around the name and tied to the horse's neck. All of the models I have encountered are nickel plated, and with the white horse head grips although given the popularity of Davy Crockett in 1955, it would appear that a gold-plated model and other colored grips must have been made. The trigger guard has the extra nub section.

Given the immense popularity of Davy, the holster sets that were marketed for the Schmidt and Leslie-Henry guns are virtually endless, and I have already described and shown the beautiful Hubley ones. Leslie-Henry put out a boxed set for "Davy Crockett" that, to the contrary, shows a cowboy rearing up on his horse. The double set of holsters has "Davy Crockett" on the tan holster pockets with a young-looking Davy in buckskins holding his Betsy rifle. This tan and brown set has two beautiful metal, full-standing, horses over each holster pocket. The guns are the 9-inch models.

Another Leslie-Henry set in a beautiful box with great graphics of Davy came with a single holster, and with the 9-inch model. The holster is in rich dark tan leather, with studs and tooling. An almost identical holster for the 9-inch model made by Leslie-Henry came with a super additional feature on the belt over the holster pocket rarely found on the Davy sets—a full and finely tooled depiction of the Alamo. This set has both "Davy Crockett" and "The Alamo" on the belt as well as bullet loops and conchos. The holster pocket has both fringe and a western-style belt, with an elaborate buckle on it. Leslie-Henry sure brought Davy into the Wild West with its magnificent holsters!

Before moving to the rifles, it is safe to say that many lesser-known companies made all kinds of toy guns for Davy Crockett— among these are Ideal, Ohio Art, and even some Japanese firms. Davy guns are endless—metal, plastic, tin, clickers, and as stated at the inception of this chapter, a Davy Crockett "memorabilia" book could sure be filled with all kinds of guns and go-withs. However, I have found that the three most sought after and most important Davy guns were made by Marx, Leslie-Henry, and Schmidt.

Recently-found Leslie Henry 7-inch Davy single shot cap gun with Davy holster. Note buckle with "Betsy" title for Davy's rifle. Suede and cowhide holster has metal plate with Davy's picture embossed!

Above: Boxed Leslie-Henry double holster set with 9-inch Davy Crockett cap guns. Note that the box lid shows a cowboy, while the holster pockets show Davy as a frontiersman.

Left: This boxed Leslie-Henry 9-inch single holster set shows Davy as a frontiersman on the lid. (Courtesy of J. Schleyer)

Ohio Art colorful tin Davy Crockett clicker model with great graphics. (Courtesy of Terry Graham)

Davy Crockett rubber knife and cowhide sheath with fringe. Note molded figure of standing Davy Crockett on the red grips. (Courtesy of Pete Karp)

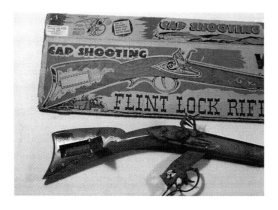

Above: Close-up of stock showing cap box storage and mechanism of rifle.

Right: Marx Davy Crockett flintlock rifle with original box marketed under "Wild Frontier" title. Note the gold details of the lock, stock, and barrel bands.

Unique Davy Crockett single holster set with 9-inch Leslie-Henry. Note that the gunbelt has a deeply-tooled image of the Alamo.

Marx marketed the Davy Crockett rifle in both a flintlock style and in the western style. Not all the flintlock models encountered are marked "Davy Crockett," but the figures and graphics on the box clearly show reference to Davy, as they are done in the same way as Marx's Davy flintlock pistols. The rifle is made of a gorgeous caramel and marbleized toffee-colored plastic, with painted details, and it comes with the patch box which opens to store caps. This rifle is as colorful and well made as any Leslie-Henry model. The style was certainly inspired by "Betsy." The rifle is 35 inches long. It's beautiful enough to hang it up over a mantle! Leave it to Marx. . . .

Marx's western-style rifle has "Davy Crockett" on the stock. The rifle is in the Winchester lever action style, with black barrel and tan stock. Besides the name, the stock indicates it is the "Official Walt Disney Davy Crockett" rifle, and it was 35 inches long. The rifle's lever action comes down for cap loading and while it has that action, the overall appearance of this Marx Davy is more of a "sporter" looking rifle than anything else. Still, it is seldom seen with the full name and Walt Disney's "official" seal of approval.

Daisy put out a Davy Crockett smoke and bang rifle in blue-black finish, with the name on the stock and the leather boot on the butt. It was 35 inches long, in the lever action style, and it came in a set with a plastic powder horn, and a 9-inch Leslie-Henry cap repeater six shooter. The name on the stock, on the right side, has additional artwork depicting Davy's rifle and powder horn.

Hubley's Davy Crockett was none other than the superbly made #205 Buffalo Rifle, which was already a flintlock pattern. One of the finest toy rifles ever made, this rifle has a swirl walnut plastic stock, blued steel barrel, and bright nickel lockplate, flintlock parts, and trigger. The right side of the stock has a "patch box" that swings open to carry caps. The forearm section of this flintlock

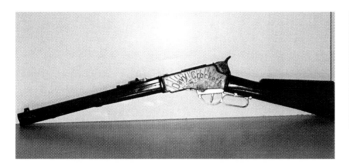

Leslie-Henry Davy Crockett Winchester-style rifle. (Courtesy of J. Schleyer)

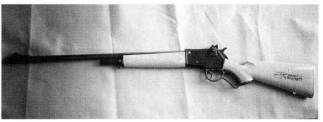

Marx's "official" Walt Disney Davy Crockett cap shooting rifle. Note the stock markings on this model. (Courtesy of Tom Kolomjec)

model was stamped "Davy Crockett" in gold letters. The rifle was 24 inches in length.

Leslie-Henry also made the Davy Crockett rifle in Winchester-lever action style. Twenty-six inches long, it came with black plastic stock and forearm, and with nickeled-metal action parts and lockplate, which has "Davy Crockett" raised on it and the Alamo in the same design as on the above described Leslie-Henry holster set. The lever action comes down for cap loading. It is one of the most attractive toy rifles, and also seldom seen.

As with the cap guns and other toy guns, Davy Crockett rifles, both the licensed and unlicenced, were manufactured in huge quantities. Parris Manufacturing, Ideal Toy Company, Ohio Art Company, and certainly Japanese-made rifles in all materials—plastic, pressed tin, clickers, cork shooters, with and without wood and plastic stocks—were made and marketed. Wyandotte made at least two Davy rifles. One was a pump action cork firing rifle of pressed tin, with "Davy Crockett" in gold lettering on the stock. The other was a slightly larger cork firing rifle that had a lever action for cocking. As with the toy guns, the most desirable, and the better made Davy rifles, were manufactured by Marx, Hubley, Leslie-Henry, and Daisy.

Seldom-seen Davy Crockett cap shooter made by Latco. Sleek nickel finish with the pewter floral grips. (Courtesy of Ron Doub)

Fess Parker as "Davy" showing two young fans in Davy Crockett outfits the importance of gun safety on a promotional tour in 1955. (William Tell Images)

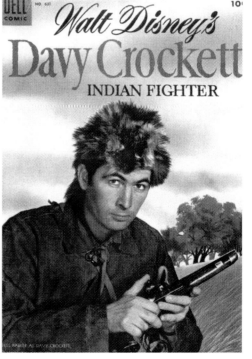

Dell Comics issue #631 for Walt Disney's **Davy Crockett** *in 1954. Note the flintlock held by Fess Parker.*

THE DEPUTY

Allen Case and Henry Fonda, the stars of **The Deputy** TV western. (Courtesy of Old West Shop)

Contents of the Hubley Deputy includes a red and silver Deputy's badge!

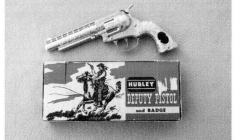

Above: Both models of the Deputy. Note release on top model is on ejector while the scarcer lower model has the release on the side of the cylinder.

Right: Hubley's all-metal, beautifully engraved Deputy with original box.

he Deputy, starring the late Henry Fonda, was also the Oscar winner's first TV role in a western series. Strangely enough, however, while Fonda was the lead actor, "The Deputy" really referred to the man that Fonda, as "Marshal Simon Fry," would occasionally deputize—"Clay McCord," played by Allen Case. The show was a fictional one, since my research does not turn up a Marshal named Fry or a deputy named McCord in the annals of the Old West. The show came on board at NBC in mid-September 1959, and ran for a solid two years.

Fonda's feature film commitments and increasing cameo roles on the show eventually led to its being dropped. However, I recall the show fondly and having always been a great fan of Henry Fonda, who was a great western star, with his drawl of a voice and steady gait, he was a much tougher character as Marshal Simon Fry. Marshal Fry was tough as nails and didn't care to give desperadoes a slap on the wrist. His deputy, Clay McCord, was more sympathetic, and preferred negotiation to annihilation. He also preferred to work as the town's storekeeper instead of pinning on the deputy's badge at Marshal Fry's orders. The old westerns did it the right way, tough only when you had to be tough.

After the show ended in September 1961, Fonda returned to feature films, but also starred in a second TV show called *The Smith Family*. Henry Fonda, who had a wonderful and strong screen presence, passed away in 1982 at age 77. Allen Case went on to play in *The Legend of Jesse James*. Sadly, he died in 1986 at the young age of 51.

CAP GUN COLLECTIBLES

The most popular Deputy cap pistol was made by Hubley, in two models. Coming in a colorful box, complete with a red deputy's badge, the Hubley Deputy has a beautiful, bright nickel finish, and is a totally engraved, all-metal gun. It sports a unique ribbed barrel with pierced sections and a grip cameo in black with a mounted deputy. The grip release on the first pattern is on the right side of the ejector rod, and you slide it forward to break the gun from the top to load. The second model is identical in every way except that the grip is black metal, while the cameo is nickel. On this model, the release is a push-button type, located on the right side behind the cylinder, and this model also breaks from the top. Both guns are 10 inches long. "Deputy" is on both sides of the frame below the cylinder.

Kilgore made the Deputy as a silvery nickel finish, all-metal, 7-inch die cast repeater, which, similar to the Esquire, breaks from the top without a release, but by pressure on the barrel. This bright cap pistol has "Deputy" on both sides of the gun stretching across the top of the grips. The grips also sport a bullet on both sides, and the Kilgore Circle "K" logo at the bottom of the grips, while "Kilgore" is raised on both sides of the scrolled barrel. This gun came on a card which also read "Deputy" in Kilgore's #2046 product line, and the card also shows a Deputy's badge.

Schmidt marketed the Deputy in its Buck 'n Bronc Shoot 'n Iron series, but this was just before the show debuted on NBC. In any case, the Schmidt Deputy that I possess came in a cellophane bagged card with a black leather holster and belt, white details, and a concho on the center of the holster pocket with a blue jewel. The card reads "Deputy Holster Set" and shows a deputy just about to draw his gun. The label also reads "Authentic Fast Draw" and "50 Shot Repeater" and "Genuine Leather." The reverse of the card shows this Schmidt Deputy being sold by the Danlee Company, Van Nuys, California, with the motto "Made in the West, where they Use 'em."

It would appear that after the TV show went on the air, the Danlee Company must have contracted with the George Schmidt Company in Los Angeles to market its "BB Deputy" to capitalize on the show. The Schmidt Deputy is an 8-inch bright polished

Kilgore's Deputy, all-metal cap shooter. Note bullet on grip design.

Schmidt's Deputy, all-metal cap shooter with copper stag grips.

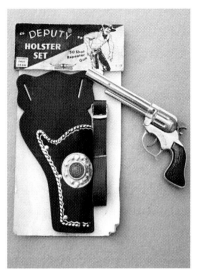

Schmidt Deputy with its original holster and card put out by Danlee of Van Nuys, California.

nickel repeater, with simulated stag copper grips. It has a ribbed barrel and "BB Deputy" on the left side of the frame on a rocker label just above the trigger. The copper grips have the "BB" logo and the gun has a lever on the left side of the hammer, and breaks from the top. A white-painted set of the same metal simulated stag grips is also found in this model Deputy.

Finally, Halco marketed the Deputy holster sets which prominently features both Henry Fonda and Allen Case on the colorful box. The guns are Halco 8-inch die cast nickel plated guns, with horse head grips and Diamond "H" logo. The black holsters have white details and "The Deputy" on the front of the holster pockets. The Halco guns are not marked "Deputy" and several generic guns were used, such as Pinto, Western, and others. The six-pointed star is the correct "deputy" star worn by the deputies of the period. The Deputy holster sets came in both single and double holsters, and they are one of the few holster sets that carry both the name of the show *The Deputy*, and the name of the character, "Chief Marshal Simon Fry," on the holster details. Double sets also came with a fancier pattern with fringe, and both black and brown holsters with white details have been found. Both the Kilgore and the Schmidt Deputy cap guns will fit these holsters.

Kilgore had previously made another Deputy but this was long before *The Deputy* TV show. While some collectors consider it a western style cap gun, close scrutiny of the earlier Kilgore Deputy shows that it is a 6-inch all-metal, nickel-plated cap pistol with a revolving cylinder. However, its appearance is more of a "police" or "detective" cap gun rather than a western six shooter. Additionally, the grips read "Deputy Sheriff," so it is not just a "deputy" gun. The frame shows a police-type whistle and a set of handcuffs on the left side of the frame, and a whistle, handcuffs, and nightstick on the right side. The area at the top of the grips just above "Deputy Sheriff" also sports a law and order-style American eagle. This gun really is not connected to the TV western show, *The Deputy*.

Deputy deluxe double holster set by Halco with Kilgore guns. Note the Henry Fonda character, "Chief Marshal Simon Fry" on the top holsters. Note fringe.

*Dell Comic issued for **The Deputy** in 1960.*

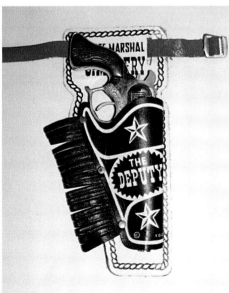

Schmidt Deputy with official "The Deputy" single holster put out by Halco.

Boxed double holster set by Halco which also came with generic guns. Note the graphics showing both stars of the show on box cover. (Courtesy of J. Schleyer)

ELFEGO BACA

The real Elfego Baca, with his signature, taken in Socorro, New Mexico, while sheriff. (Courtesy of Museum of New Mexico)

Robert Loggia, handsome star of TV's Elfego Baca.

What a name! You have to scratch your head to recall this great TV western that Walt Disney Productions put out. Besides *The Cisco Kid*, *Zorro*, and a few other sidekick notables, *Elfego Baca* was one of the few westerns that gave credit to Latins—and in this case, a Mexican lawman turned-lawyer you really loved. The show, actually called *The Nine Lives of Elfego Baca*, was run between episodes of *The Swamp Fox* and *Texas John Slaughter*.

Born in 1864 in Mexico, Elfego's life reads like exactly like the nickname he was given—"El Gatto"—meaning "the cat" in Spanish, because he "had nine lives," just like a cat. A year after he was born, Apaches raided his father's hacienda, and baby Elfego was taken hostage. For some unexplained reason, he was returned unharmed. At age 15, Elfego's father, Don Baca, was arrested, allegedly for killing a cowhand in self-defense.

Young Elfego, fearless even then, somehow sneaked into the cellar of the jail, and with a jacknife, cut away at floorboards, eventually freeing his father. An early fire-wagon, responding to a fire, struck and ran down young Elfego, but despite terrible leg and back injuries, he survived. Elfego's ambition, early in life, was to be a lawyer. He knew he would have to work and study hard to achieve this goal. He came across the border to Socorro, New Mexico, where he got a job working as a cattle-puncher on a ranch. He was just under 19 years old. Baca had nerves of steel and wasn't afraid to work hard.

In 1884, just turning 20, young Elfego was to become involved in an incredible episode that made him famous. He rode into Frisco, New Mexico, to see the sheriff on important matters for his cattle boss, but the sheriff was out of town on a posse, so Elfego decided to wait for his return. As he waited, a young cowhand from the nearby Slaughter ranch, had gotten himself wildly drunk and was shooting up the town. The endangered citizens all ran for cover, and with the sheriff out of town, nobody had the courage to grab the drunk and haul him off to the local jail. Elfego put on a spare sheriff's badge and single-handedly arrested the man for "disturbing the peace."

Trouble was inevitable as the cowboy's friends came for him, but Elfego refused to turn him loose since the sheriff hadn't returned. Soon a fight ensued and the cowmen went for their guns. Elfego drew his gun, and returned fire, killing one of them. The men left, but soon returned with their boss, Bill French, and some 80 cowboys, bent on teaching Elfego to mind his own business. Elfego, still alone, took refuge in a small, two-room jacal, a stone and mud hut. The cowboys assembled for a siege. Elfego had his two guns and a belt of ammunition. The jacal was bare, except for a bed, table, chairs, and a statue of Santa Anna, the mother of the Virgin Mary.

The siege lasted 33 hours, with the cowboys firing over 4,000 rounds of ammunition, trying to kill or get Elfego to surrender. At one point, they even used some dynamite and also tried to burn the place down. Elfego was unmoved, carefully returning fire, and in the siege, he killed 4 of the cowboys and wounded 8 more. Then the sheriff and some townspeople finally arrived to his rescue. When Elfego walked out of the jacal, he did so incredibly, without a scratch. Even more strangely, the entire place, the furniture, half of the wall, and part of the roof was riddled with bullets and burned, but only the statue of Santa Anna, along with Elfego Baca, remained unscathed. His legend was born. Tried twice and acquitted twice, Elfego decided to run for sheriff of Socorro County, New Mexico. He was soon elected.

On his very first day, he was handed a crumpled folder containing a handful of warrants that the former sheriff had not been able to serve on the well-known criminal element in the area. The new, rotund, mustachiod Mexican sheriff with a thick accent sat down and wrote the following letter to each criminal for which he held a warrant:

Dear Sir,

It has come to my attention that you are wanted by the law on criminal charges. Kindly surrender yourself at my office on or before the 15th of the month.

Failure to comply with this order will be considered resisting arrest and I shall be forced to shoot you on sight.

Best Regards,
ELFEGO BACA

Within a month, each of the wanted men turned themselves in, for Baca's reputation was well known in New Mexico. One of the wanted men, Art Ford, even apologized to Baca for being "late" because he had gotten drunk, and he hoped that Sheriff Baca was not too angry. Baca served with distinction, and soon turned to studying law under J. Henry Newman.

He rose from sheriff of Socorro, New Mexico, to attorney-at-law, and even entered New Mexico politics. Despite the hard life of the western territory, Elfego went on to live a "few more lives." He had run-ins with Pancho Villa; was stabbed by a maniac with an ice pick in Albuquerque; and was sliced up badly by a drunk in a knife fight, with Elfego doing his best not to kill the man.

In the 1920s, he bought himself a car. In three separate accidents, the car was demolished and rolled over him, but he survived. In his long career, Baca went on to become mayor of Socorro, county clerk, district attorney, and school superintendent. He also made an unsuccessful bid for governor and district judge. "El Gatto"—the man who had "nine lives" and "couldn't be killed"—outlived most of his adversaries, friends, relatives, and critics. In 1944, at the ripe old age of 80, Baca died peacefully in bed in Albuquerque, New Mexico. He had survived the lawless Old West, fought cases all the way to the Supreme Court, and was a true western hero.

TV's "Elfego Baca" was played by handsome Robert Loggia. The series started in the 1958 season and ran for several episodes, alternating with *Texas John Slaughter*, played by Tom Tryon, and *The Swamp Fox*, played by Leslie Nielsen. One thing about Walt Disney's western productions, he gave youngsters great history lessons, since all of his western programs were based on real live heroes, from the American Revolution to the western frontier. Robert Loggia, a wonderful character actor, went on to play in dozens of westerns and movies, and later starred in *Mancuso, FBI. The Nine Lives of Elfego Baca* finished its run in 1960.

CAP GUN COLLECTIBLES

Perhaps the fact that *Elfego Baca* was, in essence, a short-run show alternating with two other characters, none of the major toy gun companies capitalized on this character. However, leave it to Daisy to market an Elfego Baca Law and Order outfit in its 1959 catalog. This set was marketed as #49-06-1902, and consisted of a 31-inch double-barreled cork shotgun, a top grain leather single holster with "Elfego Baca" printed on the back, and a Kilgore Pinto cap gun. The set also included a western canteen and sling, with the whole outfit selling for $4.98. The shotgun was not marked "Elfego Baca," only the holsters.

Two other holster sets were marketed under the "Elfego Baca" title. A double holster set, also with Kilgore Pinto's, and a smaller set that was a single holster with a Kilgore Pinto, and a special carrier for a western canteen on the same belt, was handsomely stamped with "Elfego Baca" across the back of the belt. These are quite scarce, and it is unknown how many survived, as this writer has never encountered a set in 15 years of serious search and collecting. Thus, outside of the photo of the Kilgore "Pinto" which I have been able to document as the only gun that Daisy marketed in the Elfego Baca sets, I can only show the Daisy advertisement for this wonderful real life hero that Disney brought to our TV screens.

Kilgore's Pinto, used in the Daisy-marketed Elfego Baca single and double holster sets. Note Palomino horse head grip design.

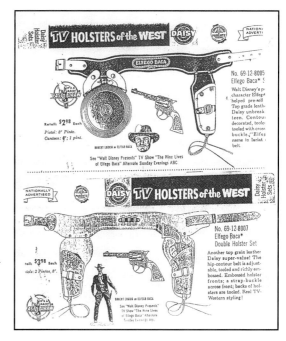

Above: Daisy advertisement for the Elfego Baca holster sets from its 1959 catalog. Note the Kilgore Pinto was used in both sets. (Courtesy of Jim Thomas)

Left: Dell Comic issued for the "Walt Disney Presents" series which featured Robert Loggia as "Sheriff Elfego Baca." Recognize the actor who played "The Swamp Fox?" It's a very young Leslie Nielsen.

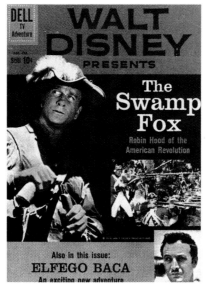

FRONTIER

A nother of television's early westerns, *Frontier* came on board in September 1955, and ended its run after 39 episodes in September 1956. The star, and also narrator of the show, was long-time character actor, Walter Coy.

Since every episode was a different story of "the way it was in the West," many great character actors of the 1950s, all of whom went on to other TV westerns or shows of their own, starred in the thrilling episodes meant to show the way things were and the way things happened in the Old West, without fanfare, fancy outfits, or sidekicks that brought laughs at the end of an episode.

Rather, it centered on the hard life that our forefathers encountered and endured on the way west. The show's realistic stories, and the hardships that were presented, brought a wonderful theme to the show, similar to *Death Valley Days* and other such narrated westerns to point out the right and the wrong, the good and the bad.

The show's time slot, unfortunately, ran up against *The Ed Sullivan Show*, and it was only a half-hour program. Some-time show star Tom Tryon, (who went on to play "Texas John Slaughter") passed away in 1991. Other character actors that went on to other shows were James Griffith, Don Kennedy, Jan Merlin, Scott Forbes *(Jim Bowie)*, and Dick Garland. Walter Coy passed away in 1976.

Walter Coy, star of **Frontier,** *blasts away at the bad guys. (Courtesy of Old West Shop)*

CAP GUN COLLECTIBLES

Kilgore was the only toy gun company that made the Frontier gun, although due to the title itself, several other Frontier theme guns hit the market after the show's demise. Kilgore's Frontier was an 8-inch nickel-plated, rotating cylinder, disc cap firing gun. It was strong, well made, and fit the general size, style, and appearance of the Kilgore Eagle. The Frontier had the early roaming buffalo on the barrel and lots of scrollwork. "Frontier" was raised on both sides of the frame, under the revolving cylinder, and the Kilgore Circle "K" logo was up by the hammer, on the left side.

The grips came in two styles—a black simulated stag, and black with the swooping American eagle. This early Kilgore model has a strange and unique lever to break open the gun. It is a lever located on the right side, at the top of the frame, and it has a little knob that you grab and pull up and over, counter-clockwise, which then releases the gun, breaking it open fully to expose the disc cap cylinder. This is the only Kilgore model, or cap gun in general, for that matter, on which I have ever seen this opening mechanism.

Although only Kilgore made the Frontier, the other companies that copied the idea of America's western Frontier were: Product Engineering's Frontier Smoker; British Cast Metals' Frontier .45 and Frontier Ace; Marx's short-barreled Frontier .44; and the late American West, which brought back the Frontier .45 as late as 1970. For the sake of the only gun actually marked and marketed as "Frontier," we leave it to the wonderful Kilgore model of the correct name.

Above: Kilgore's Frontier cap shooter, nickle plated with black stag grips.

Right: The Frontier opened for cap loading. Note the unique opening lever on the left side of the gun.

FURY

Along with the horses "Champion" and "Trigger," there was also "My Friend Flicka" and "Fury." Champion and Trigger are covered in respective sections; My Friend Flicka was never honored with a cap pistol. *Fury*, one of TV's earliest shows—and one of its most popular— was a morning TV western directed to children with animal co-stars. *Rin-Tin-Tin*, *Lassie*, and *My Friend Flicka*, were all such shows, and they taught us youngsters about family, loyalty, loving, and taking care of your pet. There was always a moral to the story and lots of reflection.

Fury came to television in September 1955, and had a healthy run of five years, leaving the air in the summer of 1960. It was a show that centered on a magnificent wild horse with the right name for it, "Fury," and only one person could ride it, young Joey, the son of Jim Newton, who lived at the Broken Wheel Ranch. It was a show that featured stories about the problems of running a ranch, dealing with everything from wild animals to con artists trying to flim-flam honest ranchers. The part of "Jim Newton" was played by Peter Graves; "Joey Newton" was played by young Bobby Diamond.

Character actor William Fawcett played a ranch hand, and the love interest for Jim Newton was Ann Robinson. That thundering stallion "Fury" saved the characters and the farm, and even captured bad guys plenty of times. Youngsters learned that honesty is the best way to go. Peter Graves, the younger brother of Jim Arness (*Gunsmoke*) went on to *Mission Impossible* after the run of *Fury*. Bobby Diamond guest-starred on other shows after *Fury*, and later left the movie and TV industry to become an attorney in California. Dell Comics also put out several issues of *Fury*.

*The stars of TV's **Fury**. Left to right, Peter Graves ("Jim Newton"), Bobby Diamond ("Joey Newton"), and William Fawcett ("Pete"). (Courtesy of Old West Shop)*

THE CAP GUNS

Remarkable as it may seem, with such a popular show at the height of the westerns and with its "action" of a name, no American toy gun companies made a Fury cap pistol. Nichols made the Fury rifle, but it was a space frontier gun. In fact, the only company that made a Fury cap gun was the Italian firm of MAM of Milano, Italy. The Italian Fury is a big 11-inch Civil War-style pistol, with "Fury" on both sides of the frame under the cylinder. The gun is factory black, with a brass frame and beautifully-carved fluted simulated wood grips. The grips have a well sculptured stallion's head for a logo. The barrel is marked with "Mod. Remington Cal. 44" and "Mat. 6876," which in Italian, stands for "Matricola" or serial number. On the brass section just at the beginning of the grips, it is marked "Brevettato" which in Italian means "Patented."

Above: Left side of the Fury in the opened cap loading position.

Below: Close-up of the Fury, showing beautiful fluted grips, name on gold frame, horse head logo, rich engraving and red disc caps visible in cylinder. (Courtesy of Bill Longstreet)

The gun frame and barrel is deeply scrolled. It is tight and very well made. The gun takes a 12 shot, special shell-styled cap firing molded ring that is fit into the holes of the cylinder. It is an exceptionally-designed die-cast cap pistol. No other Fury guns have surfaced to date. Hats off to the Italians, who kept the western spirit alive with Sergio Leone's "spaghetti westerns" years after the social climate of America turned away from our western heritage.

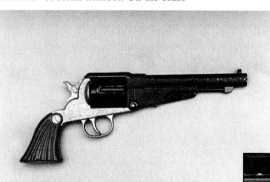

Above: Italian-made Fury—a well-made 12-shot disc cap shooter in the Civil War Remington .44 caliber-style. Note the contrasting colors and parts of the gun.

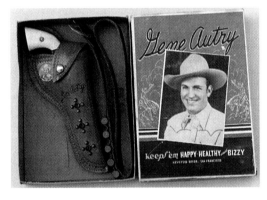

GENE AUTRY
AMERICA'S SINGING COWBOY

America's "Singing Cowboy" started off as a choir singer. Although a Texan by birth, his family moved to Oklahoma, where he grew up, and initially got billing as "Oklahoma's Yodeling Cowboy." From those humble beginnings, Gene Autry, born in 1907, went on to become one of the "Big 3 favorites," along with Hopalong Cassidy and Roy Rogers. Just about everyone I have met in this wonderful hobby started off collecting one of the "Big 3." Thus, the great and early popularity of Gene Autry goes back to cast iron guns, as does Roy Rogers, a point not shared by Hoppy, even though he, too, started his career long before the TV westerns.

Gene Autry made his first screen appearance in 1934 in *The Phantom Empire*. These were the days of Buck Jones, Hoot Gibson, Ken Maynard, and Tom Mix, already well-established western film heroes. Hitting the western film craze with a gallop, Gene was an accomplished songwriter and soft-spoken home-spun ballad singer. His acting and singing brought him eternal fame as "America's Singing Cowboy" through more than 50 films between 1936 and 1953.

Initially, he started off with Republic Pictures, moved on to Columbia Pictures—after his stint in World War II—and ended up with his own Flying "A" Productions. Gene's two sidekicks during the more than three dozen films were Smiley Burnette and Pat Buttram. They were usually in one silly predicament after another, but always managed to prove they were just as courageous when the chips were down. Pat Buttram followed Gene to his television role. Gene's "wonder horse" was, of course, "Champion," a star in his own right.

Gene came to television on July 23, 1950, and as one of the busiest actors of the time, worked in films as well as his 30-minute show, entitled *The Gene Autry Show*. Gene played himself, as did Pat Buttram. Gail Davis, who would become television's "Annie Oakley," was often on the show, as was Harry Lauter, later to star in *Tales of the Texas Rangers*. On the show, which had Gene's "Melody Ranch" as the background, Gene was the daring defender of frontier justice.

Gene also concurrently ran his "Gene Autry's Melody Ranch" on CBS Radio, which ran for 16 years. Sponsored by Wrigley's gum on both television and radio, Gene was a warm man who loved children. He and Champion appeared in countless parades, state fairs, and rodeos all over the country. Millions of youngsters had their photos taken alongside Gene and Champion, who did amazing tricks that endeared them to kids and adults.

An astute producer, Gene knew by 1953 that television was the new bonanza for westerns. Within five years, he produced some of the most popular TV western

America's "singing cowboy" Gene Autry, and Champion, the "wonder horse," enjoy a relaxing moment.

Early Keyston Gene Autry boxed set with Kenton cast-iron cap shooter in single holster boxed set. The lid bears a great photo of Gene. One of the early ones! (Courtesy of Bill Hamburg)

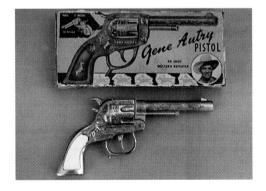

Buzz-Henry Gene Autry with inset white grips and original box. One of the first die casts made by Leslie-Henry. (Courtesy of Ron Doub)

Seldom-seen Leslie-Henry 9-inch Gene Autry bronze cap shooter with butterscotch grips with an early spectacular Gene Autry single holster with superb artwork. Note huge buckle with longhorn. (J. Schleyer Collection)

programs, including *Annie Oakley, Death Valley Days, The Range Rider, Buffalo Bill Jr.*, and *The Adventures of Champion*, starring his horse. One of America's wealthiest men, Autry ventured into many other enterprises, including ownership of the California Angels baseball team. Gene has remained one of America's most endearing cowboys, and was elected into the Cowboy Hall of Fame.

His television series continued without interruption until August 7, 1956, a strong six-year run totaling 85 episodes. Pat Buttram went on to play the irascible con man "Mr. Haney" on *Green Acres*. Smiley Burnette, Gene's chubby sidekick with the disaster of a cowboy hat, died in 1967, at the relatively young age of 60. Readers may remember that Gene's signature song "Back in the Saddle" always ran at the end of the show.

CAP GUN COLLECTIBLES

Leslie-Henry long-barreled Gene Autry cap shooter with red grips. Seldom seen and a very desirable model.

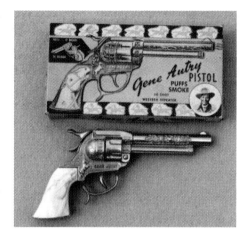

The many cap guns, both cast iron and die cast that bear Gene's name, could fill a book of its own, so I will go into the die casts that are the main subject of this study. Suffice to say that as early as 1938, Kenton started marketing the Gene Autry cast iron repeaters in varying sizes, barrel lengths, grips, and finishes. This continued up to 1950. The early, heavier, quality leather holsters of the time also carried Gene's name, face, signature, and western scenes, and were made by Keyston Brothers and Halco.

By 1950, the die casts began to come on the market and Buzz Henry made the 7-inch model in the Buzz Henry-marked model, with the inset into the butt frame grips, with the rearing horse and rider and "BH" logo. The grips came in colors of white, black, and less frequently for the Gene model, in red. Extensively engraved, there was both the nickel and gold finish, and with "Gene Autry" raised on both sides of the frame within the lasso leading back to the raised rearing horse on the frame. "Buzz Henry" is raised in metal on the bottom frame of the butt. The lever to break open for cap loading is up by the hammer on the right side.

The second 7-inch model is almost identical to the above, except that the grips are not inset, but, instead, full size, with the upraised horse head and checkered section above the horse. This model also came in nickel and gold finish, as well as a dull gray, and all models are extensively scrolled and engraved. The grips on this pattern have been found in white and a clear amber color. Some shades of the amber grips are darker, and are called "root beer" color by some collectors.

Leslie-Henry came out with the 9-inch Gene Autry in the standard design, with the full horse head grips. This has the lever for cap loading on the right side, is marked "Gene Autry" on both sides of the frame without the lasso, but the rearing horse is still present. Leslie-Henry made this model in nickel, gold, and antique bronze. The grips came in white, black, orange, butterscotch, root beer, and light tan.

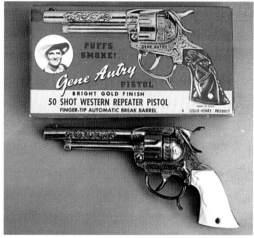

Above: Leslie-Henry 9-inch Gene Autry in gold finish with original box. (Courtesy of Ron Doub)

Above left: Leslie-Henry 9-inch Gene Autry in nickel finish with original box. (E. Cremese Collection)

Above: Seldom-seen gold-plated model of the Leslie-Henry 44 with black grips and the original box. (Courtesy of J. Schleyer)

Left: Leslie-Henry 11-inch 44 models. Seldom-seen bronze model with stag grips at top and the more common nickel finish with white horse head grips.

Gene Autry with a gold-plated gun that resembles a Texan! Gene wore some of the most colorful cowboy shirts in the early 1950s. (Courtesy of A. Forman)

This model was also made in the 5-inch long barrel model for a total length of 10 inches. The "Gene Autry" name is found in both raised and incised variations. Some collectors are very fond of the "long barrel" models, and with all the finish and grip color variations, there are plenty to choose from.

Leslie-Henry also made a 9-inch, slightly larger and more robust, with the harder to find "pop-up" cap retainer. The lever for this model is found on the frame, directly under the barrel. This model is also found in both nickel and gold, and with a variety of horse head grip colors. The scrollwork and engraving of this model brought back the double horseshoes and variation scrolling found on the smaller 7-inch early Buzz Henry models. "Gene Autry" is raised on the frame on both sides, with the "L-H" logo of the rearing horse.

The "big one" was the beautiful 11-inch Leslie-Henry Gene Autry .44. With a 5-inch barrel, this model came with the revolving cylinder, which took 6 small solid metal bullets. The lever is located so that it protrudes on both left and right side of the frame, and when lifted, opens the side-gate version on the left side, so that one can load bullets as well as a roll of caps. These Model .44s came with both the same-style horse head grips, and also in simulated stag. These grips also carry the oval logo bearing both "H" and "L-H" initials.

The many colors of all the Leslie-Henry models are found on this model, although the ones most encountered have white horse head grips, amber grips, and black stag grips. On these models, "Gene Autry" is found on a rocker panel just behind the cylinder on the frame and ".44" right next to it. This model is also heavily scrolled, and came in nickel, bronze, and gold finishes. It is a very desirable pattern.

Gene Autry holsters came in every imaginable size, shape, and variation, both single and double. The markings on Gene Autry holsters include the full name in both stamp and script, cursive and signature on the belt, holster pockets and straps on the holsters. New variations surface all the time. Some Gene Autry holsters are plain, while others are heavily adorned with studs, conchos, jewels, fringe, and scalloping. A very desirable set of double holsters for Gene guns came with gold and nickel metallic pocket fronts, with and without Gene's name on thebelt. An extra added feature is getting a Gene holster set that also carries the logo of the Flying "A" Ranch screened or tooled into the belt.

One of the most desirable holsters are those that have the Gene Autry concho in the same style and configuration as the Cisco Kid concho, with Gene's picture embossed on them as well as the signature. Of course, Gene Autry appeared on the scores of boxes for both Kenton and Leslie-Henry, in bust size photos, full regalia, on Champion, and with Champion alongside him.

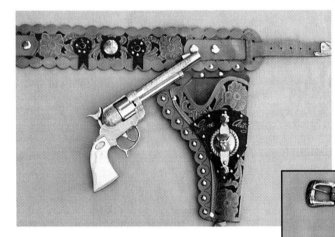

Above: Closer view showing name, details, conchos and the 44 cap shooter.

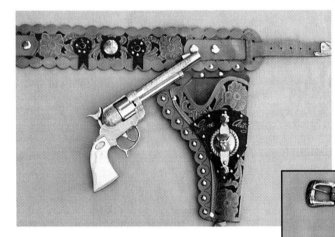

Above: Spectacular scalloped Gene Autry single holster set with a Leslie-Henry 44.

Left: Detail of the Gene Autry concho bearing Gene's image and signature.

Leslie-Henry also made two Gene Autry rifles. The first is the Gene Autry Western Ranch rifle which came out in the early 1950s. It was a metal and plastic cap shooter with engraved side plates bearing the Flying "A" Ranch logo and floral work. The box carries Gene's name and photo. It featured a brown plastic stock with metal barrels and works. The second pattern, although similar in appearance to the first pattern, is all plastic except for the cap box, trigger and lever action. The side plates have the Flying "A" Ranch logo. The rifle came in red and light tan models. The rifle is the identical model used for the Texas Rangers that came in the deluxe 11-piece boxed sets. The rifle is 26 inches long.

Leslie-Henry and Kenton were the only American toy gun companies that made Gene Autry guns and rifles. After Gene appeared at London's Empress Hall, putting on a spectacular Western Show along with his wonder horse Champion, Marx Limited of England put out a Gene Autry double barrel shotgun. This was a pop gun with black metal barrels and dark wooden stocks. The stock carries the "Gene Autry & Champion" image, and souvenir markings of the Western Show at the Empress Hall in London. Obviously, few of these were made in honor of the one show and they are seldom seen.

There is little doubt that Gene Autry, America's "Singing Cowboy," will continue to have the many legions of fans and admirers for generations. In 1941, even as Gene served his country in World War II, the little town of Berwyn, Oklahoma, officially changed its name to Gene Autry, Oklahoma. Lying between Oklahoma City and Ardmore, Gene Autry also has the Gene Autry Oklahoma Museum in the former Gene Autry High School building. In 1988, the Gene Autry Western Heritage Museum was opened in Los Angeles' Griffith Park, and it remains a popular landmark.

Sadly, America's singing cowboy, Gene Autry, passed away on October 2, 1998, three days after his 91st birthday and only three months after we lost Roy Rogers. Gene Autry remained a humble man despite his immense wealth. He was a generous man and a patriotic American. With his passing, another link with America's film and TV western heroes is gone forever. Rest in peace, Gene, and may you always be "Back in the Saddle Again."

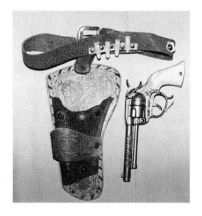

Early-style Gene Autry and Champion holster with Leslie-Henry 9-inch cap gun.

Later-style Gene Autry boxed single holster set with Flying "A" Ranch logo on gunbelt with beautiful graphics and photo of Gene and Champion on box lid. (Courtesy of Brian Wolf)

Above: Gene Autry Ranch Rifle. Note Flying "A" Ranch logo on silver side panels. The rest of the rifle is red plastic. Seldom seen. (Courtesy of Steve Arlin)

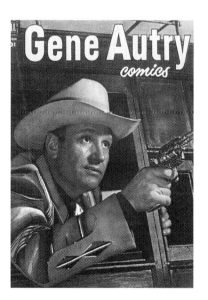

Above: One of many Dell Comics issued for Gene Autry. Check out that colorful Indian design jacket Gene's wearing!

Left: The three most popular Gene Autry cap guns made by Leslie-Henry. The 11-inch model 44 with revolving cylinder; the 9-inch model with horse head grips; and the 7-1/2-inch Buzz-Henry model with inset grips.

THE GRAY GHOST

One of my all-time favorite TV shows was *The Gray Ghost*, the true story of Mosby's Rangers, headed by Major John Singleton Mosby during the Civil War. As the show aired in September 1957, I remember the scene clearly on our Zenith black and white TV set: Yanks charge across a field, under a hail of gunfire, advancing towards the Rebs, who are holding their line; as the music rises, I see a man with a plumed cap, dressed in gray, on his horse, plumes waving against the wind.

As he is joined by more of his trusted men, the narration begins: "We took our men from Texas, Kentucky, Virginia, the mountains, and the plains. We put them under orders, guerilla fighting orders, and what we lacked in numbers, we made up in speed and brains; both Rebs and Yankee strangers, they called us 'Mosby's Rangers.' Both North and South, they knew our fame—'Gray Ghost' is what they called me; John Mosby is my name!"

It was Southern courage, wit, ingenuity, and speed every week as Mosby's Rangers met and routed Yankee superiority, and it was based on some of the actual exploits of Mosby's 43rd Battalion of the Virginia Cavalry. It was also the first Civil War "western" program, even if it was before the opening of the old Wild West. Nonetheless, *The Gray Ghost* picked up a strong following even if, initially, New York stations rejected it saying "it will start the Civil War all over again!"

Between September 1957 and May 1958, a relatively short run, this great show garnered an audience of some 20 million people, renewed Southern pride in one of its sons, and brought instant stardom to New York actor Tod Andrews, cast as the dashing Mosby. Two other show regulars were Ron Haggerty, and Phil Chambers, who played Mosby's "Lieutenant St. Clair." Tod Andrews was born in Buffalo, and acted under the name Michael Ames on stage and screen, and even replaced Henry Fonda in the 1951 stage play of *Mr. Roberts.*

The real "Gray Ghost"—John Singleton Mosby, now colonel, in full gear, at the height of his career during the Civil War. (Courtesy of Virginia Historical Society)

Above: Tod Andrews, as "Major Mosby," in TV's Gray Ghost.

Right: The stars of TV's Gray Ghost, *left to right, Phil Chambers ("Sgt. Miles") Tod Andrews ("Mosby"), and Ron Hagerty ("Lt. St. Clair").*

With his fancy plumed cap, yellow and gray uniform, double-breasted coat, gauntlet gloves and knee-high boots, Tod Andrews looked very much the part of "Major Mosby." The show was an instant hit on both sides of the terrain on which Mosby galloped. It was scooped up by 190 markets, with the number one slot in Seattle, and the third slot in Boston. The South loved it, and Tod Andrews went on dozens of personal appearances all over the country, to the delight of thousands of youngsters, including myself. Despite this huge success, CBS dropped the show after 39 episodes and "The Gray Ghost" rode back into the history books.

THE REAL "GRAY" GHOST

The real Major Mosby, later Colonel, was born in Virginia in 1833, and initially studied law until the war started. He offered his loyalty to the Confederacy on the condition that he be allowed to form and run his Cavalry of raiders his way. He raised a swift-as-lightning band of followers that began a series of raids behind Union lines; they were so elusive that he was nicknamed the "Gray Ghost" in a short time. Mosby shattered everything from supplies to communications, isolating and striking his enemy with daring hit-and-run raids that made his men willing to follow him to the end. Even after Lee surrendered to Grant, Mosby initially refused to surrender, and wanted to keep harassing Union forces in Virginia.

Mosby returned to civilian life a hero, an excellent horseman, and a man of great courage tested under fire time and again. A lot of people don't know that Mosby went into the 1st Virginia Cavalry with the rank of private and then went up the ladder to eventually muster out as a Colonel. Mosby's Rangers were disbanded on April 20, 1865. After the Civil War, Mosby returned to his beloved Virginia, became a writer, went back to law, and was later appointed U.S. Consul to Hong Kong by his former arch-enemy, none other than President Ulysses S. Grant. He died in 1916.

Remarkably, one tidbit of history that the producer of the show adopted from the real Mosby is that Mosby didn't care for the cavalry saber. He felt they were useless in battles, especially cumbersome on a horse, and instead preferred to carry two pistols on his belt, two in his boots, and two on his horse—the Colt Model 1860 .44 Army, of course. If you carefully watched and recall the TV program, Tod Andrews carried similar pistols and was never seen wielding the saber. Looks like they did their homework.

One of Major Mosby's greatest feats of daring included the capture of Union Gen. Edwin Stoughton, which was highlighted on one of the episodes. To the credit of the producers, the show also featured other Civil War personalities, giving us a good dose of history, even in entertainment form, along with the action of such a show. Episodes featured Lee, Jeb Stuart, Hooker, and many other great officers of the time. The show remained geared to both western buffs and Civil War enthusiasts. Today, the episodes of *The Gray Ghost* are among the most sought after on the video market.

The show was born out of two books, *Ranger Mosby* and *Gray Ghosts and Rebel Raiders* by a Virginian author and journalist from the *Richmond Times Dispatch* named Virgil Carrington Jones. He began the research in 1938, spent six years on the two books, interviewing what few survivors were left of Mosby's Rangers, as well as Mosby's three children. (Mosby named one of his sons Stuart, after Jeb Stuart.) Jones' book was released in 1944 and became a bestseller almost overnight.

It wasn't until 1957 that Jones was contacted by a Hollywood producer to check on the historical accuracy since *The Gray Ghost* pilot was in the works. The pilot episode centered on the famous capture of Union General Stoughton. Jones was eventually hired as the historical consultant for the show based on his voluminous research and eye for details. Jones also ended up coaching actor Tod Andrews, who became a Civil War buff himself and relished his short-lived fame as "The Gray Ghost." Tod Andrews passed away in 1972.

Box lid for the Lone Star Gray Ghost gun and holster set. The British promoted Mosby to colonel, but that's Tod Andrews there ready to blast away at the Yanks! (J. Schleyer Collection)

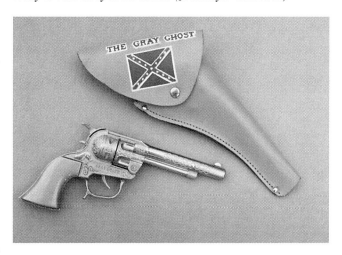

Lone Star Gray Ghost cap pistol and military-style holster with the show title and Confederate battle flag. (Courtesy of Bill Longstreet)

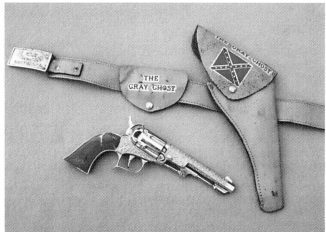

The Gray Ghost cap pistol by Lone Star, nickel finish with sleek, silver-gray grips. "Gray Ghost" is raised on both sides of the frame. Lone Star Gray Ghost belt, showing details of the CSA buckle with Gray Ghost and the bullet pouch. Imagine a youngster putting on all these accoutrements! (J. Schleyer Collection)

The Gray Ghost holster and belt outfit with its American counterpart, Hubley's fabulous Pioneer cap pistol, Civil War style, with caramel swirl grips.

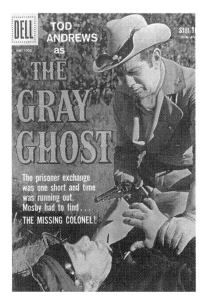

Dell Comics issued this very sought after #1000 for **The Gray Ghost.**

CAP GUN COLLECTIBLES

Remarkably, even with a program that lasted only one season, *The Gray Ghost* was an instant hit and *Gray Ghost* collectibles are extremely rare and sought after today. For some strange and unknown reason, no American toy gun manufacturers produced the Gray Ghost cap pistol, but Lone Star of England rose to the occasion in brilliant form. The Lone Star Gray Ghost remains as one of the most desired and elusive cap pistols for collectors to find and add to their collections today. Instead of designing the Gray Ghost on the line of the .44 caliber 1860 Colt, Lone Star designed it in western form.

Debate over whether the Gray Ghost cap pistol was a Leslie-Henry product, or a Lone Star, is still debated by some collectors, but the discovery of the box for the *Gray Ghost* outfit, showing Tod Andrews on his horse, his gun up in the air as he readies for a gallop, bearing the Lone Star product and England address confirms without a doubt the gun was made overseas. One of the reasons for this question is because the Gray Ghost was made of superior quality usually found on the Leslie-Henry cap guns, as opposed to some of the Lone Star guns. But to the everlasting credit of Lone Star, they made a spectacular Gray Ghost cap pistol to honor the Confederate ranger.

The Gray Ghost is all nickel, with silver-gray plastic grips which are plain. The nickel finish is superior, with deep engraving on the barrel, frame, and cylinder. Even "Gray Ghost," which is raised on both sides of the frame, is done in the style of the letters of the show itself. The frame also has the horses' head logo just above the grips. The gun is 9 inches in length and breaks open from the top for cap loading by a small lever on the right side of the gun, just below the hammer. Careful inspection of this gun confirms the identical pattern was used for the Lone Star Bat Masterson cap pistol. There are no markings on the Gray Ghost cap pistol.

Lone Star also made a spectacular holster set for *The Gray Ghost*. The belt and Cavalry-style holster is in gray leather, with the holster flap sporting both "The Gray Ghost" and the Confederate battle flag. On the leather belt is affixed a military-style bullet pouch, also with a cover flap on which "The Gray Ghost" is silk screened in red and white. The pouch holds three bullets. Finally, the buckle, of stamped and nickeled tin, is rectangular in shape, with "CSA" over a wreath and "Gray Ghost" below the wreath.

The entire holster set is well made in quality gray leather with a red felt backing. The box the outfit came in, as stated, sports great graphics of "The Gray Ghost" in show lettering, with Tod Andrews on his horse, gun drawn, and with "The Life and Legend of Colonel John S. Mosby" written across the bottom of the lid.

The stores that imported only the belt and holster outfit, outfitted them with the Hubley Pioneer, another beautiful cap pistol, which is in fact, styled like the Army .44. The Pioneer used in the Gray Ghost outfits was the nickel-plated, 10-inch gun with the orange-caramel swirled plastic grips, heavily engraved frame, and with the loading lever under the barrel functional. The holster easily takes both the Lone Star Gray Ghost and the Hubley Pioneer pistols.

The Gray Ghost remains as one of the most elusive cap guns to find—pretty much like the real Gray Ghost—sought after, but very elusive.

GRIZZLY ADAMS

There really was a "Grizzly" Adams, and I am certain it inspired both the spectacular Grizzly cap gun made by Kilgore, and the TV show, *Life and Times of Grizzly Adams,* starring Don Haggerty.

The real Grizzly Adams was born John Capen Adams in Medway, Massachusetts, in 1812. He loved the outdoors all his life, and this great love also included trapping and hunting of various animals. A shoemaker by trade, Adams eventually abandoned his wife and three children, heading west. After killing a grizzly bear, he adopted its cub and from then on, the nickname stuck.

Grizzly was a strange man. He dressed in buckskins with tails of the many Rocky Mountain animals hanging off of it. He wore a cap made out of a wolf's head, trimmed with its tail (ala Davy Crockett!). He had premature white bushy hair and a long white "grizzly" beard. He had traveled around Cape Horn, and all over the western frontier. Deciding not to kill any more animals unless it was in self-defense, Adams began to capture, collect, train, and keep animals in a "zoo" of his own making.

Among the menagerie of animals he kept were cougars, mountain lions, buffalos, several wolves, eagles, and at least twenty grizzly bears. It was said that these bears were trained to obey him and no other master. But Grizzly's body was full of scars and broken bones garnered during his strange life's calling. His favorite pet bear was "General Fremont" and it was this same bear that in a playful smack, smashed in his skull. Adams made the best of it, but with the removal of his wolf's skin cap, it was wholly apparent it would never heal properly. Adams remained in the Rocky Mountains and the Sierra Nevada area for several more years, but soon his health began to catch up with him.

In January 1860, Adams came back cast and met up with none other than P.T. Barnum, who became known as the "World's Greatest Showman." Grizzly Adams confided to Barnum that he didn't think he had a long time to live, given his body's wounds and the horrific head wound that even sent Barnum aghast. Adams was willing to join the show to show off his wild beasts.

Barnum seized the opportunity and they formed a partnership. Adams exhibited his wild animals in a tent on Broadway and 13th Street, a New York City first. A brass band led a parade in which Grizzly Adams rode his favorite "General Fremont" grizzly. Other bears rode on a float and it became a great success. Barnum sent for Adams's wife, who began to care for her husband. She was told that Adams' head wound was both inoperable and incurable and that he didn't have long to live—maybe a "few weeks."

Adams didn't pay much attention to doctors and continued to perform with his beloved bears. Finally, as Adams' health worsened, Barnum ordered him to rest before he would "die in one of his cages." The intrepid Adams made a deal with Barnum. He wagered that if Barnum would agree to pay him $500, he would work another 10 weeks on a special tour of Connecticut and Massachusetts. He would make this his "last tour" and rest. Barnum agreed. The tour was a great success. An overflow crowd in New Haven, Connecticut, swelled to more than 5,000 spectators. Too weak to ride old "General Fremont," nonetheless, Adams still performed special tricks for the crowd with his beloved bear. He pushed himself to the limit, and he finished the 10-week tour. Adams collected his $500 and went to see his wife, now living in Charlton, Massachusetts.

By October 1860, he said to his wife, as she observed all the many wounds on his body from head to foot, "I'm a used-up man."

"Grizzly Adams" in a Thomas Nast illustration. No photo of the real Grizzly Adams was found. Here he is with his pet grizzly, "Ben Franklin." Note the dead varmints on his fur hat! (Courtesy of Farmington Library)

The stars of TV's **Life and Times of Grizzly Adams.** *Left to right, Don Shanks ("Nakuma"), Dan Haggerty, ("Grizzly"), and "Ben." (Courtesy of Old West Shop)*

The Kilgore Grizzly nickel plated with revolving cylinder-fired disc caps. Superb workmanship, with its original box.

He got into bed and five days later, died, at the young age of 48. His beloved animals were added to Barnum's museum collection, and later sold to a zoo. Grizzly Adams' only sea mammal that he entrusted to Barnum was a Pacific sea lion that he named "Old Neptune." After the other animals were sold, Barnum made sure that "Old Neptune" remained in a special tank in his museum and was supplied with fresh sea water daily by Fall River steamboat workers. Grizzly Adams' show was so popular that it inspired a zoo in Central Park. This strange, but colorful character left a legacy that continues to this day. The names of two of his most famous bears were "Lady Washington" and "Ben" Franklin, no doubt the inspiration for "Ben" of the TV series on *Grizzly Adams*.

The Grizzly Adams TV western was set in the early 1800s and starred Don Haggerty, who had been an animal trainer as well as an actor. The producers stretched history, as they will always do in such shows, by having the character of Grizzly Adams seeking refuge in the wilderness for a crime he didn't commit. Another old character actor, Denver Pyle (later of the *The Dukes of Hazzard*) played "Mad Jack." Other characters included an Indian named "Nakuma" and a young boy named "Robbie Cartman," who visited the solitary Grizzly Adams, who kept a bear named "Ben" that he had raised as a cub. The show, geared mainly to youngsters, lasted only a short time, from February 1977 through July 1978.

CAP GUN COLLECTIBLES

There can be no doubt that Kilgore's famous Grizzly cap gun was inspired by Grizzly Adams because of the Grizzly bear on the grips. The Grizzly came in both nickel and gold finish, and both with superbly sculptured black plastic grips, with a snarling Grizzly looking upward. Kilgore's "authentic swing-out cylinder" also was a main feature of this large 10-3/4-inch gun, which takes Kilgore disc caps. A sturdy, well-made gun, it comes in a beautiful red, white, and blue box, with an advancing bear on it, and pine trees in the background. The same pine trees and a full standing bear is also found on the frame and barrel of the Grizzly. Whether or not the real "Grizzly" Adams was the inspiration for the gun by Kilgore and whether or not the gun preceded the show of the same name, remain topics for discussion. The beautiful Grizzly cap gun, however, is for real.

Above: Close-up showing the beautiful growling grizzly bear on the black grips of the Kilgore Grizzly.

Right: Gold-plated Kilgore Grizzly with its original box. Note the two little paper labels indicating this was a gold-plated model inside. (Courtesy of J. Schleyer)

Another short run TV "latter-day western" with a remote connection to a bear was *Kodiak* starring Clint Walker, who also had played the very popular "Cheyenne" in the late 1950s. "Kodiak" was the nickname given to an Alaskan patrol officer named "McKay," played by Walker, because of the huge Kodiak bears that roamed in Alaska. The show, shot in Alaska, lasted only a month, from September to October 1974. No cap gun has ever surfaced marked "Kodiak."

Another show that had a two-year run was *Gentle Ben,* also about an American black bear, that should not be confused with Grizzly Adams, but often is because of the same name of the bear. *Gentle Ben* starred Dennis Weaver, the former Gunsmoke deputy, "Chester."

In *Gentle Ben,* Dennis Weaver played the part of "Tom Wedloe," a wildlife officer in the Florida Everglades and "Gentle Ben" is friendly, sweet, and lovable. *Gentle Ben* lasted from September 1967, through August 1969.

So there you have it, "bear" afficionados, at least three shows featuring bears. No guns were produced for *Gentle Ben* or Tom Wedloe. We are happily stuck with the really super Kilgore Grizzly. It remains as one of the most beautiful and unique cap pistols ever manufactured. The Grizzly was made only by Kilgore of Westerville, Ohio.

GUNSMOKE
MARSHAL MATT DILLON

"Matt Dillon" (Jim Arness) and his limping deputy, "Chester" (Dennis Weaver) from an early scene from **Gunsmoke.**

Set in Dodge City, Kansas, during the 1870s, *Gunsmoke* came to television on September 10, 1955, and changed the course of TV westerns for all time. *Gunsmoke,* rarely out of the Top 10, has the unbeaten distinction of having been the longest-running, uninterrupted television show in history.

Initially it started slowly, going up against the already established *George Gobel Show* on Saturday nights, and in the first season, it didn't even make to TV's Top 15. The following season, however, it shot to No. 8. From 1957 to 1962, it was the top-rated program in all television. Even as more than 30 westerns dominated television, *Gunsmoke* continued to lead the pack. It lasted 20 years, longer than any program ever, with continuing characters and new characters.

Gunsmoke, like many other great westerns, first started on radio. The voice of radio's "Marshal Matt Dillon" was William Conrad, who later went on to fame as TV's *Cannon.* From 1952 to 1963, even after *Gunsmoke* had come to television, Conrad continued to be the voice of Matt Dillon. If the initial TV westerns such as *Hopalong Cassidy, Gene Autry, Roy Rogers,* and *The Lone Ranger* were mainly geared to the youngsters, *Gunsmoke* changed all that by being the first so-called "adult" western. The opening scene gave the viewer a hint that this western was for real.

As Marshal Matt Dillon walks slowly to that spread-legged stance and draws against his opponent, he's even a second slower. The other man misses, of course, and Dillon fires the fatal shot and then holsters his six gun. This guy, all six-foot six-inches of him meant business. *The Life and Legend of Wyatt Earp,* which aired the same week, was the other adult western that brought the same changes to prior western format.

When CBS decided to bring *Gunsmoke* to television, they initially wanted to cast John Wayne in the title role. Already a super western star, Wayne didn't want to leave the big screen and commit himself to a weekly series, and it was Wayne that suggested the young James Arness. Arness was a war hero, having been seriously wounded at Anzio, Italy. Landing with the 3rd Infantry Division (Audie Murphy's outfit) his entire company was almost wiped out. Arness took machine gun fire, in both legs, and spent a year in the hospital before he was discharged in 1945. Evidence of a slight limp can be detected if you watch *Gunsmoke* closely, and it was more apparent 20 years later.

Jim signed on with RKO after the war, later MGM. He had bit parts in *Hellgate* and *The People Against O'Hara,* but his luck soon changed when he was spotted by John Wayne. Putting Jim under his own contract, Wayne gave him parts on *Hondo, Big Jim McLain, Island in The Sky,* and even *Sea Chase.* It gave Jim the exposure he needed and he won Wayne's admiration. When *Gunsmoke* was offered, Wayne pushed for Jim Arness, who was forever grateful to John Wayne.

The cast of Gunsmoke, in the 1970s. Left to right, standing: Milburn Stone ("Doc Adams"), Jim Arness ("Matt Dillon"), Amanda Blake ("Kitty"), Ken Curtis ("Festus"). Sitting, left to right, Buck Taylor ("Deputy Newly O'Brien,") and Glenn Strange ("Sam").

Nice heavy leather Gunsmoke double holster set with Hubley Marshal guns. Note that the belt is marked to "Gunsmoke" and the holsters to "Marshal Matt Dillon." (Courtesy of J. Schleyer)

Above: Leslie-Henry 9-inch Gunsmoke with black horse head plastic grips.

Above, right: Leslie-Henry 9-inch Gunsmoke with "Marshal Matt Dillon" on copper stag and steerhead grips.

Although Wayne did not appear on *Gunsmoke,* he did film an introduction for the program, which was aired by CBS. After that, "Marshal Matt Dillon" began cleaning up Dodge City.

Gunsmoke dealt with the violent men of the day that came through Dodge City and hit the Long Branch Saloon. Matt Dillon upheld the law no matter what the cost and, during the course of the show, he was shot, beaten, framed, and went through plenty of personal mishaps himself. He got dirt on his clothes, blood on his face, and demonstrated that, unlike some earlier shows, law and order was a rough business. He was relentless when going after the bad guys. And no matter what happened, Matt Dillon never went down.

With the show lasting 20 years, there were many cast members that became equally famous; many western character actors and guest stars came and went. Dennis Weaver was cast as the limp-legged "Chester Goode," Matt's deputy. With his twang of a voice, he played the part for nine years, making Matt twitch when he made his mean pot of coffee. Although usually seen unarmed, Chester could handle a gun and rifle just fine. Old character actor Milburn Stone was cast as crusty "Doc Adams."

He made house calls, handled any emergency, had a heart of gold and rarely got paid for his services, even in the middle of the night. Amanda Blake, a pretty and fiery redhead was cast as "Kitty Russell," the owner of the Long Branch Saloon. It was obvious she had a crush on Matt, but Matt never did much more than smile at Kitty. If the old western characters had skeletons in their closets, that's where they kept them and that was just fine with the vast audience that *Gunsmoke* appealed to, both young and old, male and female. Kitty stayed on for 19 years, from 1955 to 1974.

Ken Curtis replaced Dennis Weaver as Matt's deputy, but he was his own character, "Festus Haggen," right through 1975. More of a scruffy-looking cowboy, Festus had a wonderful drawl, and you thought he was slow—but when it came to handling a gun and backing up Matt, Festus was no slouch. Burt Reynolds was cast as "Quint Asper," a half-breed who was the town blacksmith from 1962 to 1965.

"Sam," Kitty's faithful bartender, was played by character actor Glenn Strange. Fifteen additional characters came and went on the show, including Fran Ryan, who replaced Kitty for the last year, as "Miss Hannah." Other colorful characters were "Louie" the town drunk, played by James Nusser, and "Percy," Dodge City's undertaker, played by John Harper. Buck Taylor played the part of a part-time deputy named "Newly O'Brien." There was never a loss for great characters on a show of this magnitude.

By 1965, *Gunsmoke* had literally outlived nearly all the westerns, but the social issues of the 1960s, and the general decline in westerns, gave a blow to *Gunsmoke.* It suffered in the ratings for a short time, but it didn't give it a mortal wound, not by a long shot. Originally a half hour show, it had been expanded to an hour and CBS was about to drop the show, but decided to give it another chance, moving it to Monday nights in 1967.

The show returned with a stunning popularity, going back to the Top 10, where it remained well into the 1970s. When it finally left the air in September 1975, it was the last western on at the time. The show had survived 20 years of change in America's social fiber. It had survived the coming and going of hundreds of stars, and as Matt Dillon aged a bit, he

Leslie-Henry 10-inch Gunsmoke model with pop-up cap box, and "Marshal Matt Dillon" on the copper stag steerhead grips.

Seldom seen Halco-Hubley model of the Gunsmoke with white grips and black steerhead design.

was still tall in the saddle, both in size and honor as a lawman who meant business.

Dennis Weaver went on to star in *McCloud*. Milburn Stone died in 1980. Amanda Blake died in 1989. Ken Curtis died in 1991. Glenn Strange died in 1973 during the show after 12 years as Kitty's bartender. Jim Arness went on to star in *How The West Was Won* in 1978.

In 1987, *Gunsmoke* returned as a two-hour movie on TV, with Jim Arness, Amanda Blake, Ken Curtis, and Buck Taylor reprising their respective roles. Thirty-seven years had passed since *Gunsmoke* had first come to television, and it was quite an event. Even after *Gunsmoke* had gone from a half-hour to the one hour show on Saturday nights, CBS aired old half-hour reruns of *Gunsmoke* on Tuesday nights under the title *Marshal Dillon*. The re-runs ran for three years, from 1961 to 1964.

CAP GUN COLLECTIBLES

Leslie-Henry and Halco made the only known Gunsmoke guns that have surfaced to date. Hubley's Marshal series, the 9-inch stag gripped nickel cap shooter was often sold in the Gunsmoke sets. This model was extremely popular, having "Marshal" raised on both sides of the frame, deep grooved stag grips, left side slide gate for cap loading and clean scrollwork. It was the same model used in the Lawman sets.

There are five known "Gunsmoke"-marked cap guns. Leslie-Henry made two patterns of the standard 9-inch Gunsmoke. Both were the nickel-plated, extensively scrolled models, with the name raised on both sides of the frame along with the rearing horse logo on the frame. The first pattern came with the standard collection of horse head plastic grips. Specimens have been found with black, brown, white, amber, and beautiful butterscotch grips. The second model is the identical gun but with copper grips with a raised steer head and "Marshal Matt Dillon" on the grips above, and below, the steer head. These grips cannot be switched around and are well made, setting this model apart, since this carries both the title of the show and the name of the character all in one.

The third Leslie-Henry model of Gunsmoke is the 10-inch, extensively scrolled model, with the pop-up cap box with the lever under the barrel in front of the frame. This has been found with both the standard plastic grips and the copper steer head grips with "Marshal Matt Dillon" letters.

The fourth Halco Gunsmoke model is the large "Matt Dillon 45," which came with stag grips and the Diamond "H" logo on the grips. The frame is nickel and has "Matt Dillon" raised in a bordered frame and "45"

Above: Boxed Halco set for Gunsmoke with graphics showing Jim Arness as "Matt Dillon."

Left: Rich brown gunslinger-style double holsters set with Leslie-Henry guns. Note the Halco logo on the holsters just above the pockets.

Below: Unique advertisement for RC Cola on the back of the Gunsmoke double holster set by Halco. (Courtesy of John Bracken)

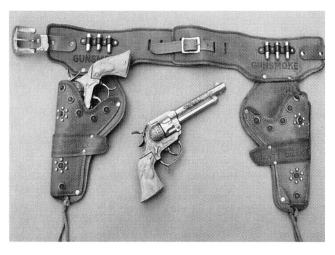

Nice heavy leather Halco set with 9-inch Leslie-Henry guns with butterscotch grips. Note show title on belt and character name on the holster pocket straps.

Nice fancy Gunsmoke holster set with Leslie-Henry 9 inch Gunsmoke with black horse head grips. Note the unique Matt Dillon concho on gunbelt and holster pockets with "Marshal Matt Dillon" on the straps. (Courtesy of John Bracken)

One of the early Dell Comics issued for **Gunsmoke.**

on both sides. This is an 11-inch gun and it accepts bullets. The same large "45" model was made for the *Bonanza, Paladin,* and *Maverick* series.

Probably the hardest to find of the Gunsmoke guns is the 9-inch Halco copy of the Hubley "Marshal." Nickel plated with stag grips and left side gate, this rare model has "Gunsmoke" raised on the left side of the frame and "Halco" on the right side. Halco made this Hubley copy for the *Bonanza* and *Paladin* series as well. It has beautiful scroll work and good looking stag grips.

Leslie-Henry and Halco made several Gunsmoke holsters, most of them double holster sets, even though Matt Dillon on the show carried a single holster. The beautiful double holster sets came in rich quality black, brown, tan, and russet leather. Some were marked only "Gunsmoke" while others are marked only "Matt Dillon." Still others have "Gunsmoke" on the belt and "Marshal Matt Dillon"on the pocket straps of the holsters. The Mother Lode would be both holsters and guns with both show title and character name.

Though not as fancy as the other cowboy characters, the "Gunsmoke" guns and holsters are more realistic in that they are more in the gunfighter styles, with just a few studs and jewels. Just like the towering Marshall Matt Dillon, these holster sets and guns mean business for the "little marshal" in all of us. No Gunsmoke rifles, carbines, or shotguns marked as such are known to exist, at least none that have surfaced to date. In this collecting experience, nothing surprises me. You never know if "Matt Dillon" will come back in some way or another.

Gunsmoke left a lasting impact on an entire generation of viewers, youngsters and adults alike. Oh, yeah, and one last thing. Have you ever wondered who the desperado was that Matt Dillon faced every week? Come on, now. Give up? I thought so. He was Arvo Ojala, the manwho taught western actors how to draw, shoot from the hip, and twirl the guns. He was also the astute designer of the "gunfighter" rigs worn by many of the western TV characters including Paladin as well as Matt Dillon. Yeah, and he let Matt Dillon "win". . . .

HAVE GUN-WILL TRAVEL · PALADIN

Richard Boone as "Paladin" in TV's **Have Gun-Will Travel** *carried a long-barreled six-gun with a factory black finish.*

Clearly, one of television's finest westerns, and one of the most popular, was *Have Gun-Will Travel* starring Richard Boone as "Paladin." It remains one of my personal favorites and, judging by the amount of collectors that are addicted to "Paladin" memorabilia, I'm not alone. Today, even the videos of the *Have Gun-Will Travel* program are on the top of the western buff's list, and anyone who remembers the show can easily understand why.

It's interesting how some TV westerns come and go, and no matter how interesting the character or the title, they are barely a distant memory. But I know of no one in my age group—the 50-something baby boomers—who doesn't almost immediately remember this western with fondness and the details of the calling card, knight's head, the all-black outfit he wore, and even that Paladin was based in San Francisco. *Have Gun-Will Travel* came to CBS Television on September 14, 1957. It was an immediate hit and stayed in the Top 10 consistently. The only two other westerns that came close to *Have Gun-Will Travel* were *Wagon Train* and *Gunsmoke*.

Adding to the mystique of this rugged, yet cultured gunfighter, was that he had only a first name (or was it a last name?). "Paladin" comes from the Italian word "Paladino," which comes from the Latin "Palatine." It means a "paragon of chivalry," a "knight errant," and a "strong defender of a cause." Well, those labels certainly described Paladin. He was a man of culture who could quote Shakespeare, Shelley, and Keats. He was college educated, and as the show went on, you learned that he had graduated from West Point and served in the Civil War.

Paladin was also suave with the ladies, and he took several of them to the finest restaurants and opera houses in San Francisco, where he lived at the Hotel Carlton. When not dressed to take care of serious business, Paladin wore fine clothes, bow ties, and high Stetsons ala beaver style. He wore jewelry, trimmed and turned up his moustache, knew good food and fine wine, and smoked expensive cigars. He was admired for his ethics, principles, and morals.

His calling card became world known—it read simply, "Have Gun-Will Travel" wire Paladin, San Francisco" with the knight's head outlined in the background. His gun was for hire, and like the private detectives of today, his clients would tell their tales of woe and pay Paladin to handle business. Settle the score. Find the runaway daughter. Go up against the corrupt sheriff, the slippery politician, or save the damsel in distress. Paladin was the "knight errant" and that's the chess piece he used for his distinct badge of chivalry in the Old West. Paladin was not a killer, he was quite the contrary. Paladin used his brain, his eloquence, and his life experiences to know when to make the right move; If he didn't believe in his client's story, he was quick to back out. But when he put on his all-black outfit, gleaming leather belt, and holster, and headed out, he was an imposing figure in or out of the saddle.

Depending on the client, or the assignment and where it would take him, Paladin wore a couple of different outfits, one of which included a printed flat-edged string tie. His black Stetson had a cap band with shiny oval discs on it. Occasionally he'd wear a black shirt with the open collar. But when the camera zoomed in on the silver "Paladin" on the holster pocket, or zeroed in on the calling card, well, you just had to know, this is one character you didn't tangle with—he meant business, and those that tested his patience, got a piece of his mind, tongue, fists, and when pushed to the limit, his six-gun.

Actor Richard Boone was born for this role. A rugged looking, direct descendant of Daniel Boone, he was not strikingly handsome, yet his craggy face, large nose, resonant voice when he growled, and that look said it all. This actor meant business in both real life and on the screen. Boone had previously acted in a TV series called *Medic*, sans moustache, in the early 1950s. He played Abe Lincoln on Broadway. At 6'2" 200 lbs., Boone was beefy and hard-

Paladin's calling card—simple, direct, and to the point!

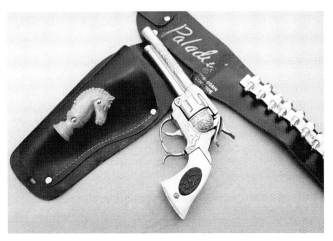

Above, left: Details of the Paladin holster set and the chess knight emblem on the pocket.

Above, right: Close-up of the Leslie-Henry 9-inch Paladin showing details.

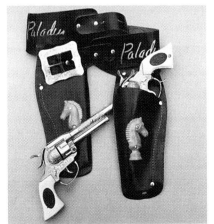

Left: Leslie-Henry double holster set marked "Paladin" with a pair of 9-inch Paladin cap shooters with cameo insert grips.

boiled, and the women loved him. Thrice-married, Boone, at age 39, went to the top of the charts, and along with six other western stars of the popular shows, made it to the cover of *Time* magazine in 1959. The magazine called him one of the few western stars "worth his whiskey" as an all-around actor.

Richard Boone, along with some heavy weight directors such as Sam Peckinpah and Andrew McLaglen (of *Gunsmoke* fame) directed some of the episodes. The show ran for a solid six years, and would have continued for more, but Boone himself had tired of the role. *Have Gun-Will Travel* finished its six year run on September 23, 1963. Guest stars by the hundreds had appeared on the 225 episodes of the show, including Angie Dickenson, June Lockhart, James Drury *(The Virginian)*, and James Coburn. In the 1961 season, Oriental actress Lisa Lu also joined the cast as "Hey Girl," while Kam Tong continued as "Hey Boy." The theme song "The Ballad of Paladin," sung by Johnny Western, also became a singles hit in 1961.

After the end of *Have Gun-Will Travel*, Boone made several movies, then returned to television as "Hec Ramsey," a sort of over-the-hill lawman who still used his wits and forensic pathology to solve crimes. Boone, now almost ten years older, looked the part of an old, grizzled lawman. *Hec Ramsey* ran for 90 minutes, alternating with *McCloud, McMillan & Wife,* and *Columbo* on the Sunday Night Mystery Movie. While *Hec Ramsey* ran for about two years, from October 1972, to August 1974, Richard Boone will always be remembered as Paladin. Richard Boone passed away in 1981 at the rather young age of 63.

Above: Halco's single shot cap shooting derringer, which came with both white and red grips, was fitted for its Paladin holsters and also on a card.

Right: Superb Paladin double holster set with pockets for guns and derringers, both of which have the chess knight on all 4 pockets. Halco set. Guns are Nichols Stallions. The derringers are Halco. (Mike Merryman Collection)

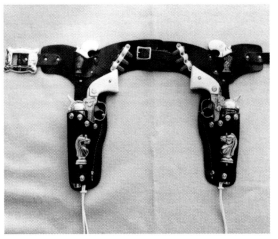

CAP GUN COLLECTIBLES

But Paladin lives on in the hundreds of toys, comic books, games, action figures, hats, the coveted business card, and, of course, the cap guns and holster sets that the gun companies couldn't turn out fast enough to capitalize on this popular show. There were costumes, fake moustaches, thermos bottles, lunch boxes, even school paper tablets. Naturally, there was also a set of Paladin checkers even though it

Halco boxed set of double holsters for Have Gun-Will Travel-Paladin. Look closely at the gun shown on the box lid in the holster pocket. (Courtesy of J. Schleyer)

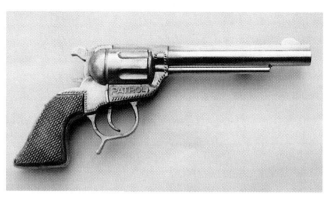

Above: Close-up of the details of the Schmidt Patrol sold in this Halco set.

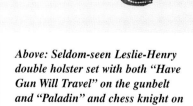

Above: Schmidt Patrol western-style cap shooters clearly is what was fitted into this Halco set!

was a chess knight that was used for his identifying symbol. For a show to run six years and garner this much popularity, which *Time* reported at 37 percent of the TV viewing public, was no small feat.

Halco made both single and double holster sets for the young "Paladins" of the late 1950s and early 1960s. All of the sets put out by Halco that I have seen and examined are of black leather, and all have the chess knight logo on the holster pockets in either print, silk screen, raised metal, or metal conchos, with the chess knight as part of the inner design. All the holsters that are found marked, carry only the name "Paladin" in both print and cursive, and usually on the belt itself, over the pockets.

Several holster sets that were obviously "Paladin"-related came with the chess knight symbol even if they were not marked "Paladin." Holster sets marked "Have Gun-Will Travel," with or without "Paladin" and the chess knight, are seldom seen. The big colorful sets in black leather with the white details, and a row of 12 bullets in white holders are exceptionally striking. Halco also marketed a double holster set that came with a set of derringer holsters mounted on the belt. Both the holster pockets, as well as the derringer holster pockets carry the chess knight symbol. Both Halco and Leslie-Henry made derringers for these sets, although the derringers are not marked "Paladin." The same derringers were used in the Maverick sets.

Before we get into the cap guns actually marked "Paladin," we can safely state, that all of the large Paladin holsters came with a variety of large guns. These are the Hubley Colt .45 as well as Hubley's large Ric-O-Shay. Some of the large holsters also take the Hubley Cowboy as well. These are the only three large guns that I have ever encountered in Paladin sets where the guns themselves were not "Paladin"-marked guns.

Leslie-Henry made the 9-inch, nickel-plated Paladin, the most widely known and most desirable. It has "Paladin" raised on both sides of the frame, which is also well scrolled. The grips are white with black insert cameos. Some of the cameos have a six-pointed star, double horseshoes, or a four leaf clover. With the lever on the left side, the gun breaks open from the top for cap loading. This model is one of the finest cap guns Leslie-Henry ever produced.

Above: Seldom-seen Leslie-Henry double holster set with both "Have Gun Will Travel" on the gunbelt and "Paladin" and chess knight on holster pockets with Halco's smaller 7-inch cap shooters.

Left: Seldom-seen Halco-Hubley Paladin in nickel finish with stag grips. Note the cursive "Paladin" on frame.

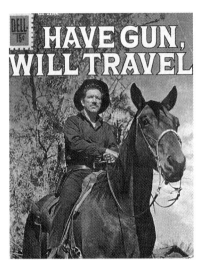

Dell Comics came out with several **Have Gun-Will Travel** *issues.*

Richard Boone as "Paladin" on his trusty steed gets ready to get his point across. Note the chess knight clearly visible on the black holster.

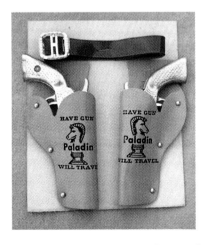

Seldom seen small double holster set for that little "Paladin" in the family. Note the holsters carry the chess knight logo, the show title and character name! The guns are all-metal, unmarked, 5-1/2 inch single shot pistols. This set was marketed by the 20th Century Novelty Casting Co. of New York. Super Graphics!

Halco also produced the huge Paladin .45 model, 11 inches long, with revolving cylinder, stag grips with Diamond "H" logos, and "Paladin .45" raised on both sides of the frame along with the rearing horse logo. This was the same design used for the Maverick .45, the Matt Dillon .45, and the Bonanza .45. The cylinder accepts bullets for side loading and has a large, fanning-type hammer. This model came in both a nickel and bronze finish.

The third and probably the most difficult to find cap pistol in the Paladin series is the Halco model copied from the Hubley Marshal series. This is a 10-inch polished nickel cap shooter with the left side loading gate that you push up with your thumb for cap loading. It has the same stag grips used on the Hubley Marshal. It has extensive scrolling on the barrel and cylinder. The great feature on this model is "Paladin" raised in cursive on the left, under the cylinder, and "Halco" under the cylinder on the right. It has the Hubley star logo on the stag grips.

Halco also made a fourth Paladin cap gun seldom seen. It is the smallest of the four known "Paladin"-marked guns. It is the identical model used for Buffalo Bill nickel-plated 8-inch cap pistol with extensive scrollwork on the frame and barrel. It has the longer sight blade, lever to release from the top on the left side of the hammer, breaking from the top for cap loading, and it came with various colored grips with, and without, the Diamond "H" logo. The frame has "Paladin" raised on both sides under the cylinder within a horizontal border. (See "Buffalo Bill" for a photo of this pattern cap pistol). It is a nifty little gun. This model came out in 1960.

A set of black double holsters with both "Have Gun Will Travel" across the back of the belt and "Paladin" on both holster pockets, along with the chess knight in white details, was made by Halco specifically for the smaller 8-inch guns. Holsters marked with both the show title and the character name are seldom seen. The show title is in white detail print while the character name is in the usual cursive style. This set has white details, and the six white bullets are also "outlined" with white details. It's a handsome set for the "little gunfighter" in the family.

The above represents the only known four models of the Paladin guns produced by American toy gun companies. I am not aware of any foreign guns made for the *Have Gun-Will Travel* western program, or any foreign guns marked "Paladin." But once again, nothing would shock me in this field. As the old cowboys would say, "Who knows what's in them 'thar hills?"

Finally, I had to see this set for myself to be able to observe and report it properly. This also proves that toy gun companies put together whatever they wanted, when they wanted, and in the way that suited them the best—economically, perhaps, as well as meeting demands. The J. Halpern Company of Pittsburgh, which also used the Halco logo, put out a full-color boxed set showing Richard Boone on the cover, and the box marked "Have Gun-Will Travel" across the box lid top.

The box also has the cellophane front in the shape of the chess knight symbol so you can look at the holster set inside. As you look to the right of the cellophane, the graphics show the black holster pocket with the same chess knight on it, naturally. But look at the gun on the graphics and what do you see upon close scrutiny? Even though Halco and Leslie-Henry made the Paladin guns, the gun in the holster appears to be a Schmidt with the checkered copper grips. That in and of itself was strange, since the set could have easily been fitted with Halco's own Paladin guns. I just had to see and inspect this myself to be sure it just wasn't a random box lid photo.

When I had the opportunity to see this holster set in hand, the guns inside indeed were the George Schmidt guns. But wait, the guns were not some generic model—they were marked "Patrol"—the gun used for the *Highway Patrol* outfit. For those that don't recall this show, it starred Broderick Crawford as Dan Matthews, and when the series first came to television, it was titled *10-4*. Halco also made the Highway Patrol set, using Schmidt guns marked "Patrol" for it. It appears for some reason, they decided to fit the Schmidt Patrol cap shooter into this Have Gun-Will Travel holster set. Since I have now had the opportunity to see three of these, I can confirm that all three came with the Schmidt Patrol—just what you see on the cover of the box. These revelations never cease to amaze me, and I am certain there will be more to come. No guns or holsters have surfaced marked "Hec Ramsey."

Dell Comics put out a whole line of *Have Gun-Will Travel* comic books, which were equally popular, then and now. Paladin, the man you want to have on your side, left a lasting impression on millions of adults and children alike. If you ever have the opportunity to catch an episode of *Have Gun-Will Travel* on video or a cable channel, don't hesitate. If you enjoyed this show as a youngster, you will love it as an adult. Wait 'til you hear the "Ballad of Paladin" again. It was a hit single in the early 1960s. *Have Gun-Will Travel,* television's first western private eye show, lives on!

HIGH CHAPARRAL

One of the "later" westerns, *The High Chaparral* came to television after the "golden" era of the 1950s, and yet, it ran a good four years on NBC, from September 1967, to September 1971. And so to its credit, *The High Chaparral* remains as an above-average TV western that even with the "anti-violence" campaigns of the time remained in the Top 20 listings in national surveys, and it remains an extremely popular western in Europe and South America today.

Filmed in Arizona, and produced by the same man who created and produced *Bonanza*—another of TV's most enduring westerns—*The High Chaparral* told the story of the Cannon family, and the challenges of living in Apache Territory, where "Cochise" wasn't all too happy about the white man's presence. The lead was veteran actor Leif Erickson, who played the part of "Big John Cannon," owner of the High Chaparral Ranch and patriarch of the Cannon family.

The family included regular stars Cameron Mitchell, Linda Cristal, Mark Slade, and Henry Darrow, all talented and veteran actors. Leif Erickson, who was much like Lorne Greene of *Bonanza,* was a wonderful, strong, and determined patriarch who was necessary for the very survival of his family and his ranch against weekly western dramas that included land swindlers, Mexican bandits, lawlessness, rampaging Apaches, and the usual elements of the hot, dusty, and often unrelenting Arizona Territory.

The huge cast of the show gave work to many character actors of the time that starred as ranch hands and distant family members. Guest stars, including old favorites such as Gilbert Roland, Ricardo Montalban, and Fernando Lamas, added much to the popularity of the show. Neil Summers, one of the great western stunt men of all time, relates in his book that the show was filmed in 100-plus degree heat in Arizona; one can't help but imagine what it must have been like a 100 years ago in the same country, with none of the conveniences we have today.

Square in the middle of some of the worst news in regards to the Vietnam War, political unrest in America, and President Nixon's unpopular last months in office, *The High Chaparral* proved to be a fine diversion. Leif Erickson passed away in 1986 at age 72. Cameron Mitchell died in 1993. All the other cast members are still alive, and many went on to play recurring roles in television. Henry Darrow, the suave Spanish speaking "Manuelito" went on to star in *Zorro and Son. The High Chaparral* is still seen in syndication on many cable stations, like many of TV's greatest westerns.

The cast of **High Chaparral,** *left to right, Cameron Mitchell ("Buck"), Linda Cristal ("Victoria Cannon"), Leif Erickson ("Big John Cannon"), Henry Darrow, ("Manuelito"), and Mark Slade ("Billy Blue").*

CAP GUN COLLECTIBLES

Even with a four-year run, remarkably, there are no American made cap guns marked "High Chaparral." However, Redondo of Spain did honor this fine TV western. The High Chaparral was very popular in Spain. The Redondo High Chaparral is an almost identi-cal copy in size and design as the Kilgore Eagle. The High Chaparral by Redondo came in both a silver flash finish and a factory black finish. It is 8 inches in length, slightly larger than the Kilgore Eagle, but there is no mistaking the Kilgore familiarities on the barrel markings and the brown plastic grips, both of which have the powerful-looking swooping eagle. The gun has "High Chaparral" raised on both sides of the frame, just above the grips.

Another interesting feature is a spur-like hammer on this gun. There is also another feature, borrowed from the Kilgore Frontier gun—a lever on the left side of the gun, up by the hammer, with another spur-like curled lever handle that, when depressed, breaks the gun open from the top, for cap loading. The left side of the ejector rod part is stamped "Redondo." The

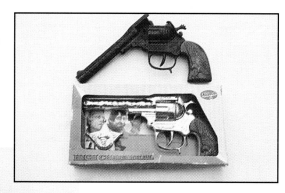

Above: Redondo's boxed High Chaparral cap shooter came in both silver finish and black factory finish. Gun breaks open from top. The grips were identical. Seldom seen.

Left: Both guns exposed. Note the Cannon family graphics and a High Chaparral star badge. Interesting collectible since the Cannons were not lawmen. Note spur hammer, the brown eagle grips, and show title on the frame.

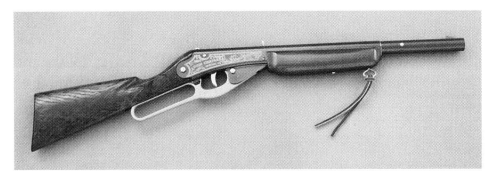

Right: Daisy's Model 966 High Chaparral Special pop rifle. Note gold lettering and lever action with a wood grained stock.

Daisy double holster High Chaparral set with Hubley Western cap guns. Top grain suede with show title on both holster pockets. Note conchos that match beautifully with the turquoise grips of the Western cap shooter. Note "High Chaparral" is printed on both sides of the cactus on the strap. Note the plastic security tab that sits around hammer to keep gun from falling out of holster. Seldom-seen double holster set.

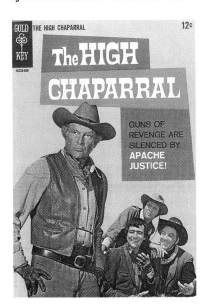

Gold Key Comic issued for **The High Chaparral.**

guns are well made and tight, considering the time frame. Even the grips are well sculptured, with the swooping eagle, and even as the American companies were skimping on the metal frames between the grips, Redondo did not. The grips are two separate plastic sections, with the metal frame in between. The Redondo box for the High Chaparral has great colorful graphics showing the show's stars and the ranch scene.

But all was not lost to the European gun maker. Fortunately, Daisy decided to honor the show with a series of High Chaparral holster sets, as well as the High Chaparral rifle. Let's identify the holster sets first. Daisy's 1968 catalog, in fact, features the High Chaparral guns and holsters, as well as the rifle. Daisy marketed at least a dozen variations, including double sets and single sets, for older and younger kids. Remarkably, while some holster sets are difficult to identify, Daisy's line of The High Chaparral holster sets are easy to spot, for the design is unique and remained the same on all of them. Made of top grain "shrunken steer" leather, as Daisy called it, the holsters have a rough look, with a strap going across the holster pockets on an angle with "High Chaparral" repeated twice on each side, as well as below a cactus plant. Two conchos adorn the top portion of the holsters that slide onto a large belt, which also has several studs and 12 bullets. The conchos have turquoise jewels in the centers.

The holsters are all fringed, and came in a variety of sizes, and the larger double sets came with what Daisy called the new "High Chaparral Armoband"—a leather armband with a row of six bullets that the little gunslinger would strap to his bicep for an easy reach to reload. No guns have been found marked "High Chaparral." Daisy used both Hubley and Nichols generic guns in the High Chaparral sets, and sets have been found with both the Hubley Western and the Nichols 250-shot repeaters. Another interesting Daisy feature on this set was a special plastic "hold down"—for lack of a better word—that you slipped over the gun's hammer, to keep the gun from falling out of the holster if the kid ran away from the bad guys. These are the only holsters on which I have seen this little feature.

The Daisy High Chaparral rifle was the Daisy Model 94, which they called the Spittin' Image of the famous carbine. The gun has a simulated gold engraving on the lockplate, with "High Chaparral" on the left side only. This rifle was 34 inches long, with a brown molded stock and brown metal for arm and barrel. The gun made a great blast, and when oiled, spouts realistic smoke.

Daisy also made a smaller rifle, the Model 966, also a "pop" gun with a great blast and-spouting smoke. This is 26 inches in length, same brown wood-grained molded stock, and metal forearm and barrel. The lockplate has gold screened lettering on the left side only, with "High Chaparral Special" with gold leaves and border all around the lettering. The forearm has a swivel ring with a leather thong. This model is smaller in size than both the Cheyenne and the Annie Oakley rifles, but has the same general appearance and Winchester 94 steel cocking lever action. The Daisy logo is on the lever. The steel barrel has the Rogers, Arkansas, address and patent numbers, as well as Model 966. These rifles are the only American-made toy guns that are marked "High Chaparral."

The rifle and the holster sets also came in the Daisy Model #8902 High Chaparral outfit, which included the rifle, double holster set, two guns, the bullet armband, and a red kerchief bandana with a metal slide—all for the "high" price of $6.49 a box. The Model 94 pop and smoker rifle sold for $9.95, and the holster sets, with guns, were yours from $1.98 for the little tyke to $7.98 for the double set for your older cowpokes. Where have those prices gone?

Redondo of Spain made the guns marked "High Chaparral." Daisy made the High Chaparral rifles and marketed the High Chaparral holster sets with a variety of Hubley and Nichols generic guns. Let's get 'em, boys, before they disappear!

HOPALONG CASSIDY

The most popular, most adored—indeed revered—as well as the most marketed cowboy that ever "lived" was America's beloved "Hopalong Cassidy." Here was, and is, a cowboy that grandfather, father, and son remember and love. That's true even if today's fourth generation never enjoyed "Hoppy" the way we did, most have heard of him from dad or grandpa. There are two excellent books on Hopalong Cassidy from the collector's perspective, so my main focus here is the background of this wonderful character, the fans that continue to idolize him, and the cap guns that we search out and collect with seemingly unabated fervor.

Hoppy was created by Clarence E. Mulford, who brought him and the "Bar 20 Ranch" to life in 1907. Mulford's short stories and novels on the Hoppy that our grandfathers remember is not the same wholesome, fancily-dressed hero that William Boyd personified. "Hop-a-long" started out as an "illiterate, tobacco-chewing, hard-drinking, able-swearing, son of a gun." He was a drifter, womanizer, two-fisted, two-gun hero who didn't have to explain himself. This first character also survived a terrible leg wound that had him going through his adventures with a "Hop-a-long" limp which got him his nickname.

In his novels, Mulford brings Hop-a-long some happiness in married life, with a young son, and then brings Hoppy despair as wife and son die by fever in 1921. His best friend, "Red Connors" (later played on the screen by Edgar Buchanan), tells how Hoppy went "loco" for a while and then becomes a loner and drifter. But Hoppy continued to survive in the harsh West, right into the 1930s.

In 1935, producer Harry "Pop" Sherman bought the screen rights to the Mulford series. Offered the chance to star in the very first Hoppy film, William Boyd accepted, but he refused to play the part of the original Hoppy, then a ranch foreman-turned drifter from the Bar-20 Ranch in Crescent City. Sherman agreed, and Boyd brought Hoppy to the screen a new and refined character. He dropped the limp, along with all the human faults that the original literary gunman possessed.

In July 1935, the same *Hop-A-Long Cassidy* entered the big screen, and by the second movie, *The Eagle's Brood* in October of the same year, Hoppy explains the leg wound had healed. Gone was the limp and the hyphenated nickname, replaced by the more endearing "Hoppy." Between 1935 and 1946, a whopping sixty-six Hopalong Cassidy films were produced and William Boyd starred in the title role in every one. In 1949, Mutual Radio aired a 30-minute series, also starring William Boyd as "Hoppy."

By 1948, the astute William Boyd, a soft spoken, handsome, former silent screen actor, knew that the "new-fangled-picture box"—television—was the way to bring Hoppy to America's homes. And so, Hopalong Cassidy became the first American cowboy hero to gallop into our hearts, minds, and memories. William Boyd proved that "good cowboys" do wear black, and his character and cowboy outfit never changed through 99 half-hour episodes that ran from June 24, 1949, to December 23, 1951.

William Boyd, born in 1898, had the foresight to acquire the television rights to the Hopalong character from both his original creator, Clarence E. Mulford, as well as Paramount and United Artists Studios. He had become his own producer in the 1940s, and by 1948, was already adapting the series for television and the 30-minute format. Silver-haired by now and already in his 50s, Boyd still cut a flamboyant figure on his magnificent white steed, "Topper." His sidekicks and regulars on the big screen ranged from George "Gabby" Hayes to Andy Clyde, but as he came to television, other character actors as well as film star favorites joined the show. These were Edgar Buchanan as "Red Connors" and Russell Hayden as "Lucky."

By the 1950-1951 season, "Hoppy" was a household word, and millions of youngsters became Hoppy's fans in look-alike outfits, cowboy hats, and double holster sets and guns. By then, 150 radio stations, and, more than 60 TV stations broadcast the show, bringing the defender of law and order on the range to those families that were fortunate enough to afford TV sets. But by the end of 1951, the Hoppy craze did not cease with the last broadcast on

William Boyd as "Hopalong Cassidy" ready to take on the bad guys! Note the trademark steerhead slider on his bandana.

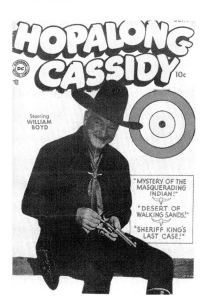

DC Comics issue for Hopalong Cassidy, *October 1954.*

MEMBERS' CREED
OF THE
HOPALONG CASSIDY
SAVINGS CLUB

All loyal members are pledged to live up to the Club Creed to the best of their ability.

- To always be thrifty
- To always be courteous
- To obey my parents
- To study well and get to school on time
- To earn, whenever possible, the money I save
- To always be truthful and fair
- To be careful when crossing streets
- To be kind to birds and animals
- To avoid bad habits

Above and right: Hoppy's Creed of the Hoppy Savings Club and special card that made me an official member and an adoring fan of Hoppy and his virtues.

The certificate that made me the "official member" of Hoppy's First Federal Savings Club. It taught me to save for a rainy day, and instilled Hoppy's Creed in me then, and now.

Topper and Hopalong Cassidy.

December 23, 1951. William Boyd had become a millionaire, but he never shed the Hoppy character, because Boyd had, in essence become Hopalong Cassidy. He spent the next several years promoting Hoppy further into the image that America had came to love, and not just as a black-dressed cowboy who sat tall in the saddle of his famous Topper.

William Boyd made Hoppy "real." By 1952, Boyd was the veteran of 15 years as Hopalong. He had starred in 66 films and 99 TV episodes of Hopalong. Everywhere he went, it was difficult to separate Boyd from Hoppy. Even some of his closest friends called him "Hoppy." Boyd married a lovely actress, Grace Bradley, but the couple never had any children. Yet a generation of millions of kids between the ages of 5, and well into the teens, were "Hoppy's kids" and he and they loved it, lived it, and remembered it.

Below is Hopalong Cassidy's "Creed for American Boys and Girls." I know of no parents today who would not embrace this creed and the children who lived by it. I dare say they would give up any of today's excesses for a youngster with these character traits and respect for authority, beginning with the parents themselves:

1. The highest badge of honor a person car wear is honesty. Be truthful at all times.
2. Your parents are the best friends you have. Listen to them and obey their instructions.
3. If you want to be respected, you must respect others. Show good manners in every way.
4. Only through hard work and study can you succeed. Don't be lazy.
5. Your good deeds always come to light. So don't boast or be a show off.
6. If you waste time or money today, you will regret it tomorrow. Practice thrift in all ways.
7. Many animals are good and loyal companions. Be friendly and kind to them.
8. A strong, healthy body is a precious gift. Be neat and clean.
9. Our country's laws are made for your protection. Observe them carefully.
10. Children in many foreign lands are less fortunate than you. Be glad and proud you are an American.

The hard-working parents of the 1950s loved Hoppy just as much as the kids—after all, he was their "partner" now, wasn't he?

William Boyd took "Hoppy" to thousands of public appearances, parades, fairs, civic events, and grand openings of department stores and restaurants. He visited thousands of crippled and hospitalized youngsters all over the country. He

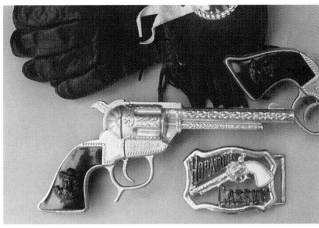

Schmidt Hoppy nickel-plated guns. White grips with black Hoppy bust (top); black grips with white Hoppy bust—Buck 'n Bronc model for the Hoppy bikes (bottom).

Spectacular Schmidt gold-plated Hoppy guns with some special accoutrements—Hoppy gloves and a super Hoppy buckle! (Courtesy of J. Schleyer)

never stopped smiling and shaking hands, even though this would have taxed a younger man. William Boyd even turned over all of his public appearance fees to charity, especially children's hospitals. He never missed a chance, when in town or large city, to visit children's wards, bringing millions of smiles, hopes, and dreams for sick and less fortunate children—true to his own creed.

Between 1952 and 1954, additional Hoppy programs were filmed, of which 26 were half-hour and 14 were one-hour programs. But by this time, new western characters and shows began to divide the interest of many youngsters. Gene Autry, Roy Rogers, the Cisco Kid, and other early western stars shared the range with Hoppy. But Hoppy remained special in a way all his own. He remained steadfast. He remained stalwart. He remained true. Note the wonderful words and contents of one of Hoppy's messages to the 1950s youngster:

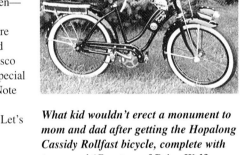

What kid wouldn't erect a monument to mom and dad after getting the Hopalong Cassidy Rollfast bicycle, complete with two guns! (Courtesy of Brian Wolf)

"Hi, little partners. Have you done anything to help mom around the house lately?. Let's do all we can to help. I'll bet you can have fun doing it and I know Mom will appreciate it. . .always mind your Daddy and Mommy. . .please remember they are the best friends you have in the world. . . ." What more could you ask a fictional hero to say? Yes, mom and dad loved Hoppy!

More than 2,500 products—just about everything in life imaginable—carried the "Hopalong Cassidy" trademark. From the moment the child got out from under his Hoppy sheets and out of his Hoppy bed, he began by brushing his teeth with Hoppy's toothbrush and combing his locks with the Hoppy comb. Hoppy's bread made the best toast. You went to school with Hoppy books, pencils, erasers, and Hoppy boots when it rained. You even drank Hoppy milk. Your bike, your wagon, your lunch box, your soap, your clothes, even the chair you sat in reminded you that Hoppy was your friend, your partner, your protector, your supporter, and your confidant. Hoppy was everywhere! People emptied their Hoppy wallets all the time.

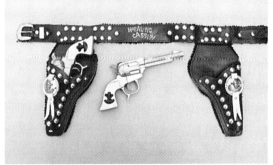

William Boyd made the cover of *Life* magazine on June 12, 1950, and *Time* magazine on November 27, 1950, both with great photos and stories of Boyd and Hoppy, all rolled into one. Foreign markets also made Hoppy a hero in Europe, Canada, and the Far East. Even the Italians added their own line to make Hoppy "Italian." When I was a youngster, people would ask "Have you heard of the Italian Hopalong Cassidy? Why, no, I'd reply. "Well, his name is Hopalong a Cassid-eech." It was sort of a play on the Italian greeting "Che si dice" meaning "what's new, what's happening, what are you saying?" Everyone would laugh!

Above: Super Hoppy double holster set with Schmidt guns.

Left: Super Hoppy single holster with Schmidt gun.

Right: The Wyandotte Hoppy guns; (top), gold plated with black grips, and (lower) nickel model with white grips with outline and Hoppy signature.

Wyandotte nickel model and its baby brother with Hoppy's signature outlined in "bullet holes."

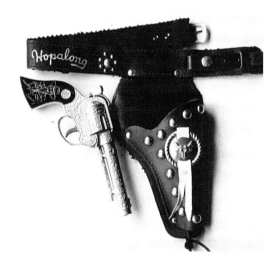

Above: Hoppy single holster set with Wyandotte gold-plated model cap gun.

Right: Boxed Hoppy double holster set with Wyandotte nickel-finish cap guns. (Courtesy of Brian Wolf)

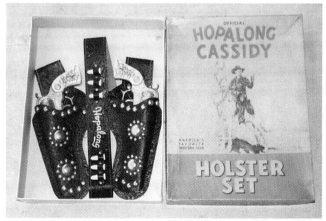

CAP GUN COLLECTIBLES

Hopalong Cassidy guns were made by two major toy gun manufacturers. These were the George Schmidt Company of Los Angeles and All Metal Products of Wyandotte, Michigan, which we call the "Wyandotte" Hoppy. We'll get to a couple of others later. Schmidt and Wyandotte contracted with Boyd to exclusively make the Hoppy guns, as well as the Schmidt Rollfast bicycle, which also came equipped with Schmidt guns. Let's identify the Schmidt guns first since there are more of these to salivate after.

The first Schmidt Hoppy guns hit the stores by 1950. This was a nickel-plated 9-1/4-inch cap repeater. The frame had "Buck 'n Bronc" in large lettering on both sides. The barrel, frame, and cylinder were fully engraved. The grips were in black plastic with a raised bust of Hoppy on both sides with "Hopalong Cassidy" under the chest area. A similar model with "Buck 'n Bronc"in smaller letters also was made. These guns also came with white grips with a black raised bust of Hoppy. Some have the lever to break the gun open from the top on the side of the hammer, while some models do not have the lever, but break open by pressure downward on the barrel.

This model also came in a gold finish with an all-black plastic grip, with the Hoppy bust also in black. Both the "Buck 'n Bronc" and "Hopalong Cassidy"-marked guns came in this pattern. Two other variants from the standard Schmidt Hoppy was an all-white plastic pattern without any bust, and a black-gripped model with a red jewel, also void of the Hoppy bust.

Schmidt also made all-plain, polished nickel and polished chrome models without engraving, but with a ribbed barrel that came with "Buck 'n Bronc" as well as "Hopalong Cassidy" markings. The grips came in both black and white, with the black and white Hoppy busts. Dummy models were also made in these varieties.

Collectors will always debate which of the Schmidt Hoppy guns are the most hard to find and the most desirable. Another controversy is which guns came with the Hoppy Rollfast bikes. The fact of the matter is that Schmidt put whatever guns it had on hand to meet the demand on the bikes. These include one black and one white gripped "Buck 'n Bronc" and the same for the "Hoppy"-marked ones. However, collectors report finding bikes with both guns black gripped and marked "Buck 'n Bronc" as well as both white gripped and marked "Hopalong Cassidy"—on two lines in the break open portion of the frame.

Some collectors really covet the black grips with the striking contrast of the white busts. Some collectors can't resist a sleek all-black single or double holster set with the white grips and the black busts for a "double contrast." At least one early Hoppy single holster set was found with a "Buck 'n Bronc" early cap shooter that had the very scarce white grips with the full bucking bronc horse and rider in red on both sides of the grips. It would certainly be safe to say that all toy gun companies were there to market and sell guns—not please collectors thirty years later! Still, there's nothing like finding something out of the ordinary to spark a new debate.

The Wyandotte set of "Hopalong Cassidy" guns, while having a totally different look than the Schmidt Hoppy guns, are generally regarded as heavier, more sturdy, and better made. Schmidt guns are certainly very pretty, but they are quite "fragile." Wyandotte made two basic models of the Hoppy guns. The first was the larger, 8-inch model, the second was the smaller, 7-inch model. Let's examine both.

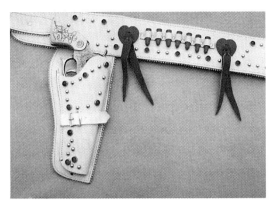

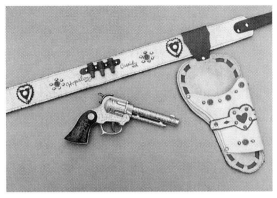

Colorful Hoppy single holster set for cowgirl with nickle Wyandotte gun. White gunbelt with red heart details and lots of jewels. Note crossdraw is on left side!

Super Hoppy cowgirl single holster set with gold Wyandotte gun. Note red hearts, lettering, and jewels.

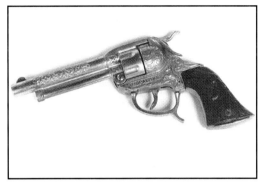

The Wyandotte larger Hoppy model came in two variations—nickel with white grips, and gold with black grips. This is an 8-inch cap repeater. The frames are extensively engraved with raised scrollwork covering, literally, the entire frame, cylinders, and barrel. The Wyandotte style of the 8-inch model is especially recognized by the attached large ejection rod under the barrel, which is also extensively engraved. The bulk frame and rather wide hammer assembly make the Wyandotte distinctive in its own right. The gun was the same pattern used for the Red Ranger. The grips for the Wyandotte "Hoppy" have its most distinctive feature. Both the "ivory" white and the black grips carry a full Hoppy figure and signature incised into the grips—black outline for the white grips and white outline for the black grips.

Our smiling hero wears his distinctive kerchief with the steerhead slider, and the signature has the end of the "g" going up to form the beginning of the "C." The grips also have the intrinsic Wyandotte logo raised in a circle bearing a "Y" the symbol "&" and a "dot." The lever to break open the gun from the top is located on the right side, just below the hammer. The outer wall of the cap box carries the round logo spelling out "Wyandotte Toys" and "Made in USA" and registered with the patent office. One final distinctive feature on the Hoppy larger gun: The left side of the frame has "Hop" beginning the name, starting to go across the frame, then "along" goes up on an angle. The right side, has "Hop" coming down vertically to "along," which then goes across the frame.

The Wyandotte 7-inch smaller model is a single shot cap pistol which also came in two patterns: The gold finish with black grips, and the nickel finish with

Seldom seen Canadian-made Leslie-Henry 9-inch Hoppy cap shooter, with black horse head grips. Note just "Hapalong" is on the left side of frame. (Courtesy of Robert Johnston)

Above: Right side of the same gun has "Cassidy."

Left: Left side of Canadian-made M.A. Henry Hoppy all-metal gun. Like the larger 9-inch model, the left side reads only "Hopalong."

Above: The Canadian Texas made by M.A. Henry (Canadian Leslie-Henry) and the Canadian Hoppy for comparison confirm both were Canadian made.

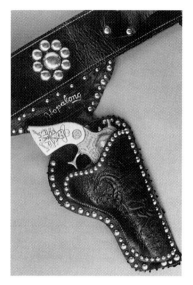

Nice early single holster with Wyandotte Hoppy gun. Note the tooling on the holster pocket and just "Hopalong" over the holster suspension. (Courtesy of J. Schleyer)

Super early double holster with Wyandotte guns. Note one holster strap reads "Hopalong" and the other reads "Cassidy." (Courtesy of J. Schleyer)

Boxed Hoppy double holster set by Wyandotte with nickel Hoppy guns. (Courtesy of J. Schleyer)

Variation double holster set that could be worn as a single or double set with a pair of Schmidt black-on-white grips. (Courtesy of Brian Wolf)

white or creamy white grips. This is a nifty little gun. Like the 8-inch model, these frames are also almost entirely engraved. The barrel, frame, and cylinder has a continuous incised and pebbled engraving of pretty scrollwork. The ejection rod is much smaller, with only the tip which is knurled. There are no markings on the frame. The grips, however, have "Hopalong Cassidy" totally spelled out in "bullet holes" and in signature form. The Wyandotte logo is also absent on the grips. As this is a single shot, it does not break open. The identical model was used for the Wyandotte Sheriff series of the same size. So we have two of each of the Wyandotte Hoppy models to go after.

One other company made the "Hopalong Cassidy" cap pistol. There are two sizes. Both were made in Canada by M.A. Henry, another Leslie-Henry division, at the Scarborough, Ontario, plant. The M.A. Henry Hoppy model is the 9-inch "standard" Leslie-Henry cap shooter with the horse head grips and the usual scrollwork. Two distinctive features are to be noted on this and the other Hoppy gun made in Canada. On the 9-inch model, "Hopalong" is on the frame on the left side, and "Cassidy" is on the right side. The second feature is the "Canadian" square hole screw feature, void on the American-made Leslie-Henry guns of this size and pattern. This gun came in both nickel and gold finish, and with black and white grips.

The smaller M.A. Henry, Canadian-made Hoppy took some time and effort to properly identify, and it required the close scrutiny, observations and personal handling of many guns. The second interesting dialogue on this little gun was the personal input of many collectors—few of which agreed on all the explanations, since it is a relatively scarce piece. At first glance, this 6-1/4-inch all metal, single shotgun appears to be a combination of a Hubley Tex, Star, Chief, Texas, and even a little Rodeo.

In essence, it has borrowed from all of these in one particular or another. In reality, the gun is the identical model of the M.A. Henry "Texas" of the exact same size and stamping, but with three distinct points to observe and note. The M.A. Henry "Texas" has "H" or "LH" in the logo on the all metal grips, whereas the Hoppy has the Hubley five-point star. The steer head and peened-simulated screw at the bottom of the grips is identical. The scrollwork on the frame, barrel, in front of and over the cylinder is identical.

The second difference is the ejector rod. It is thicker and with a knurled end on the Texas while the Hoppy is thin, fragile, and is simply an extended rod with one solder point under the barrel. The third and last feature is a small squared-off lanyard ring under the gun butt. This is "framed," but it is not pierced and thus, non-functional as a lanyard ring. The final tribute to our silver-haired hero is the name—"Hopalong" on the left side of the frame and "Cassidy" on the right. This all-metal gun has been found in both dull gray and nickel. This is one scarce and nifty little gem!

Close-up of details showing the Hoppy bust on white grips and the Hoppy concho on the holsters. Dynamite set!

Probably the most elaborate Tumbleweed Togs double holster set made, with Hoppy's trademark steerhead. The guns are Wyandotte nickel models. Count 'em—over 150 studs, 10 conchos, 12 bullets, 2 guns, and a huge buckle!

No real Hoppy rifle exists for the cap shooter, BB, pump, or smoke and bang collectors. The only rifle of sorts was the Hoppy Range Rifle—a red plastic play rifle with a Hoppy decal on the right side of the stock. The rifle has more of a military style, with a sling and is a "clicker."

No less than 60 different holster patterns and variations, both single and double exist and it would be next to impossible to saturate the readers with page after page of holster sets. Your scribe has decided to include the most colorful, most desired and those that absolutely make you want to strap them on. Therefore, it is safe to state that the majority of holsters were made by Wyandotte, which marketed them in both the single and double models in colorful Hoppy boxes, with our hero on the lid. Hoppy is shown on his faithful Topper, gun drawn, and ready to blast away!

Holsters are usually found in black with several studs, stars, and jewels. "Hopalong Cassidy" and "Hoppy" on belt, holsters, pockets, and on the pocket straps exist. Some have "Hoppy" on both belt and holsters. Others have "Hopalong" on one holster, "Cassidy" on the other. Variations are as bountiful as the holsters

Extremely rare, recently-found, British-made Hopalong Cassidy single holster gunbelt with 10 bullets.

themselves. The most desirable are those with the Hoppy conchos and steerhead conchos. Holsters with fringe and other white leather straps and details are truly decorative and harder to find. And, of course, finding them with wrist cuffs, spurs, bandanas, and badges really make it complete.

Hoppy talked to both boys and girls. Therefore, Wyandotte also made white and red-detailed holsters for our cowgirls. Usually found in creamy white leather with red hearts, jewels, studs and red lettering for Hoppy's name, the same styles with white and black cut-out hearts and details are also known to exist. The holsters take both the 8-inch Wyandotte and the 9-1/4-inch Schmidt guns. Most of the cowgirl sets that I have seen were single holsters.

Tumbleweed Togs made some of the most elaborate Hoppy holsters sets and while most came without the "Hoppy" markings, they take the Wyandotte large model perfectly, and the conchos are the identical steer head pattern used in the Wyandotte marketed holster sets. As stated, the holsters are endless, while we have four Wyandotte models to find, and at least seven Schmidt models to locate, topping the list with at least four M.A. Henry models. That should keep us busy for a while!

I have always been fascinated and often wondered what made Hoppy the most popular, the most loved, and the most enduring western character? William Boyd passed away in 1972. Yet, today, more than 40 years after Hoppy left television, and more than 25 years after Boyd's passing, Hoppy is as strong as ever to new generations, television historians, and collectors. I'd have to say that there was something magical about Hoppy. Because, when Hoppy spoke, I felt as if he was talking to "me" personally. Maybe that's it. He may have been reaching a million kids. But as far as I was concerned, he was just there, talking to me. And yes, I always helped my mom with chores around the house. I miss Hoppy and mom very much.

Color photo of Hoppy on Topper that he sent loyal fans, including me!

HOTEL DE PAREE • SUNDANCE

Earl Holliman, starred as "Sundance" on TV's **Hotel de Paree**. *Note the mirrored oval discs on his hat. (Courtesy of Old West Shop)*

Here's a TV western program that even the most astute western buffs have to scratch their heads to recall. The strange title of the show, *Hotel de Paree* sounds like a documentary about one of France's best hotels. But while the title may be forgotten, the name of the character, "Sundance" remains.

Hotel de Paree was Earl Holliman's first shot at a TV series. He played the title role of "Sundance" a former drifter, gunfighter, and ex-convict who returns to Hotel de Paree, set in George Town, Colorado—not France—after his release from prison. It's the 1870s. A number of strange particulars made this western both interesting and far-fetched, even for the western-addicted audiences of the late 1950s. *Hotel de Paree* debuted in October 1959, and ran for 33 episodes, ending its run on September 23, 1960.

Let's see who remembers some of these high points of this obscure show: Sundance was accused of killing a man, was convicted, and served 17 years in prison for it. He did the deed in Colorado, but what does he do when he gets released? He decides to redeem himself by going back to take up residence in Hotel De Paree, now run by the daughter and niece of the man he killed 17 years ago.

The ladies are gorgeous, of course, and they wear French clothes to match the name of the hotel. Well, Sundance, being the fast gun and a take-no-nonsense type of guy, soon stays on as the man who protects the women, keeps the cowhands in line, and saves the hotel from corrupt businessmen.

But wait, Sundance has not only a fast draw, but a special hat. Around the cap band of his black Stetson are a series of shiny, oval, polished silver discs, with fancy edges, no less. When he walks out to the street to meet the troublemaker, and gears up for the obligatory "Draw!"—Sundance simply twists his head a bit, or moves his head slightly up or down, and just when it's in the right place, the sun "dances" on the discs and he temporarily "blinds" his opponent. Then he blasts him away!

Even though this TV western was a bit far-fetched, it did have its following. Dell Comics put out the only comic book under the name *Sundance*.

After the show sundanced away, Earl Holliman went on to star in the long-running *Police Woman* series with Angie Dickenson. The two lovely ladies on *Hotel de Paree* were Judi Meredith and Jeanette Nolan, who went on to play in *The Virginian* with James Drury. Earl Holliman is one of Hollywood's most versatile actors, just as comfortable on a horse as well as in a cruiser. Veteran character actor Strother Martin (the warden in *Cool Hand Luke* with Paul Newman) was the only other regular on the show. Shot in black and white, it was a fun half-hour show.

The real "Sundance Kid" and the Wild Bunch. Sitting, left to right, Harry Longbaugh, the "Sundance Kid," Ben Kilpatrick, the "Tall Texan," Robert Parker, "Butch Cassidy." Standing left to right, Bill "Tod" Carver and Harvey Logan, "Kid Curry." Taken in Fort Worth, Texas in 1901. Dapper, but very deadly. (Courtesy of Union Pacific Railroad)

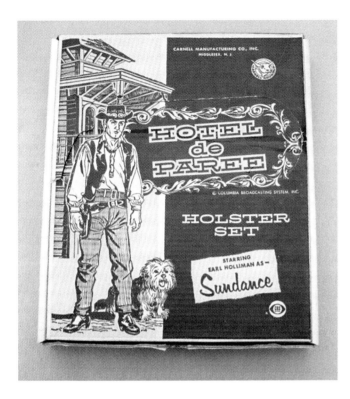

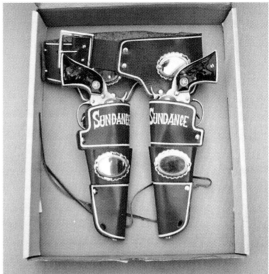

Above: Carnell's Sundance double holster set with Hubley Western cap guns.

Left: Boxed Carnell set for the Hotel de Paree Sundance double holsters. Note the little terrier standing by Sundance and the hotel in the background

THE REAL SUNDANCE

While the show was fictional, the character "Sundance" was not. The real Sundance was a deadly desperado whose real name was Harry Longbaugh. He was born in 1870 in Sundance, Wyoming. Strangely enough, the TV show begins with the 1870 date when Sundance leaves prison. Hey, they tried to be accurate, didn't they? As a young boy, the real Sundance worked on cattle farms and local ranches as a horse wrangler, soon becoming an expert rider and a dead shot. Working as a horse wrangler for the Suffolk Cattle Company, Longbaugh, now known as the "Sundance Kid," because of his age and where he came from, took a wrong turn. Stealing the horses, he was soon captured and sent to prison in Sundance, Cook County, Wyoming. When he got out, he changed some of his ways, but not the criminal streak.

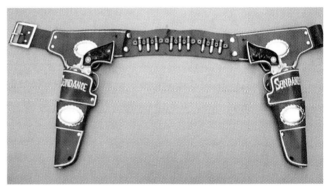

The Sundance double holster set. Note the mirrored oval discs on the gunbelt and the holster pockets. Very rare set seldom seen. The guns have the dark purple swirl steerhead grips.

He never dressed sloppily again, wearing only a black or brown full suit, complete with white shirt and tie, and black derby hat. He embroidered his initials, "H.L." on everything he owned. He wore his hair pompadour-style, and trimmed his brown, reddish-tinged moustache neatly. A handsome man, Sundance had a set of brown sad eyes, like he had lost his little dog. (Remarkably, a little white terrier was also a regular on the show.) A bowlegged character, he was calm, cool, friendly to be around, and he loved to have his picture taken with those new-fangled cameras. He also had a weakness most men suffer from—he loved women.

Between 1890 and 1902, he graduated to robbing trains and banks, with a variety of sidekicks. Even when caught, Sundance always managed to escape. The Pinkertons went after him with a vengeance, putting Italian-American agent Frank Damio on his trail. Sundance then joined the group for which he became the most known—Butch Cassidy's "Wild Bunch"—the subject of many Hollywood movies through the years, notably *Butch Cassidy and the Sundance Kid,* with Paul Newman and Robert Redford. He also fell in love with a beautiful call girl named Etta Place, whom he rescued from Fanny Porter's Sporting House in Texas, and soon had several photos taken of himself with, and without, Etta by his side.

The Wild Bunch were the last of America's Wild West outlaws. Yet each member had a distinct personality and strange characteristics of his own. But the Pinkertons were moving in, getting each of the Wild Bunch, one at a time. The 1902 "Wanted" poster, where Sundance was properly identified with the Texas photograph, offers a $4,000 reward for him and Butch Cassidy after they held up the Winnemuca Bank in Nevada. Sundance had been so good at

*Seldom-seen Dell Comics issue for **Hotel de Paree,** under the title **Sundance.***

eluding authorities, but they now had him positively identified. Cassidy and Longbaugh agreed it was time to flee the country.

In 1903, Sundance and Etta decided to have one last fling in New York City. They bought new clothes, jewelry, went to the opera, ate at fine restaurants, and had a series of six photos taken at DeYoung's Photo Studio. Then they boarded the *SS Soldier Prince* and headed for Argentina, South America, where they were joined by Cassidy.

Taking on new aliases and new clothes, learning the language, and making new acquaintances, Cassidy and Sundance continued their life of crime, robbing the new railways, banks, payroll mule trains, and silver mines that flourished in countries where law enforcement was not up to American standards and still under the control of the local cavalry. Agent Frank Damio was relentless, tracing them to Argentina, as well as Chile and Bolivia.

With the set of six photos from DeYoung, Damio made sure the Federalis now had the images as he kept up his pursuit of Cassidy and the Sundance Kid. Between 1903 and 1910, Cassidy and Sundance criss-crossed the three countries, hitting the railways and the mines, and living well. But by now, the "Yanqui Bandidos" were well known, but out of reach of the local cavalry, who hunted them wherever they did a robbery.

By 1911, both Cassidy and Sundance knew they had to give it up. They decided to make one more score, then hang up their guns and buy a ranch. They also made a pact that if one was wounded by the authorities in a shoot-out, the other would shoot him and then shoot himself. They vowed never to go back to jail and not to be taken alive. Etta Place was sent back to New York, sick with chronic appendicitis. She disappeared from history around 1908.

In 1991, they robbed the Alpoca Silver Mines mule train carrying the payroll. They headed to San Vicente, Bolivia, some 15 miles to the east and decided to bed down at a local barrio. The local peace officer, called a Corregidor, soon recognized the *Americanos,* and summoned a local cavalry detachment, only a few miles from the barrio. Galloping towards the hut where Cassidy and Sundance were holed up, they began a siege where both Sundance and Cassidy were hit, Sundance by a mortal chest wound, but Cassidy only superficially. "Bandidos Yanqui, surrender!" was met with a hail of bullets, as both Sundance and Cassidy emptied their six-guns, killing several of the *Federalis.* Cassidy tried to comfort Sundance, putting his head under his own jacket. The siege continued all night, with the hut being surrounded by the troopers, who had also called for reinforcements.

In the morning stillness at sun-up, the soldiers heard two shots. Cassidy and Sundance kept their pact. Cassidy had shot Sundance through the head, and was found sitting up with his single-action Colt .45 in his hand, his brains blown out. He had saved the last two bullets for himself and the dapper Sundance. Sundance was 41 years old. The bodies were dragged out, placed in the town square for a few hours, then buried in a small cemetery at San Vicente under makeshift wooden headboards with "Cassidy" and "Longbaugh" and "Bandido Yanqui" underneath. The Indians of the Andes say that on a very quiet night with a full moon, you can still hear "Senor Cassidy and the bow-legged one" riding their horses hellbent towards the silver mines. Leave it to Hollywood to bring Sundance back to America and make him the local hero of the hotel with the French name.

CAP GUN COLLECTIBLES

While no cap pistol has surfaced with "Sundance" on it, remarkably, even though this western had a short run of 33 episodes, Carnell Roundup did manufacture and market a spectacular set of double holsters marked "Sundance." The holsters are of a rich brown leather with white details reading "Sundance" on both holster pockets. The holsters and belt are also outlined in white details and the belt had nine bullet loops. Leave it to Carnell to add the "sun-dancing" shiny silver discs on both the belt and the center of the holsters pockets, identical to those on the cap band of Sundance's black Stetson!

The box has great black and yellow details, showing Earl Holliman as Sundance in front of the "Hotel de Paree" with the details showing the "flash" rays on the discs on his cap band. If you look closely, you'll also see a little white terrier next to Sundance. His name was "Useless" on the show. The box clearly shows "Hotel de Paree" and starring Earl Holliman as "Sundance" as well as CBS and Carnell's logo of the steerhead all over the box. The holsters take Hubley Westerns beautifully as well as Carnell's own Cowpoke perfectly. It appears that Sundance is still "sun-dancing" with us!

HOW THE WEST WAS WON

his western show has a special place in the history of TV westerns. Initially, it was a TV movie titled *The Macahans* starring Jim Arness, the big, handsome star of TV's longest-running western, *Gunsmoke*. This 1976 made-for-TV movie was well received, and ABC decided to run the series. The title was changed to *How The West Was Won* and it first aired in February 1978.

The story centered initially on "Zeb Macahan," a mountain man who had been living, hunting, and trapping in the young Dakota Territory before the Civil War. If you really know your western movies, then you'll remember that this western was also based on the 1962 movie, *How The West Was Won*, starring Henry Fonda, Gregory Peck, Jimmy Stewart, and Debbie Reynolds.

Basically a loner, Zeb didn't take much to the West opening up with new settlers spoiling the wilderness, so he decided to return to Virginia where his family lived. His brother, "Timothy Macahan," played by veteran actor Richard Kiley, had four kids. The initial episodes introduced the characters, giving us, in addition to Jim Arness and Richard Kiley, Emmy award-winning actress Eva Marie Saint as "Kate," and handsome young actor Bruce Boxleitner in the role of "Luke Macahan," the fugitive son of Tim and the nephew of Zeb.

The Macahans—"Josh" (William Kirby Cullen), "Zeb" (Jim Arness), and "Luke" (Bruce Boxleitner). (Courtesy of Old West Shop)

The other three children were played by William Kirby Cullen as "Josh," Kathryn Holcomb as "Laura," and Vicki Schreck as "Jessie." Another regular was "Aunt Molly," played by veteran actress Fionella Flanagan, who came down from Boston to help out the family when Timothy Macahan is killed, and Kate and the four kids end up under Zeb's strong care and devotion to his brother's family.

The show, which ran in a series of two-hour movies, was of epic proportions for a number of reasons. By 1978, the western's golden years were certainly long gone. Yet, with breathtaking locations, a horde of famous guest stars, the strong presence of Jim Arness, and new hunk Bruce Boxleitner, *How The West Was Won* soon had a huge following. It won critical acclaim and excellent ratings, and went into its second season.

The show was produced by Jack Mantly, who had already made his mark with *Gunsmoke*. Some of the guest stars ran the gamut of veteran actors and actresses of both movie and television, such as Vera Miles, Lloyd Bridges, Richard Baseheart, and Ricardo Montalban. The show ran for two years. With so many plots—pioneers, renegades, Indians, western con men, the usual hardships and struggles of the hard frontier life, and the complex characters and their own personalities—the series could have kept on going.

The stars of **How The West Was Won,** *left to right, Ann Doran, William Kirby Cullen, Kathryn Holcomb, Richard Kiley, Jim Arness, Eve Marie Saint, Vicky Schreck, Bruce Boxleitner. (Courtesy of Old West Shop)*

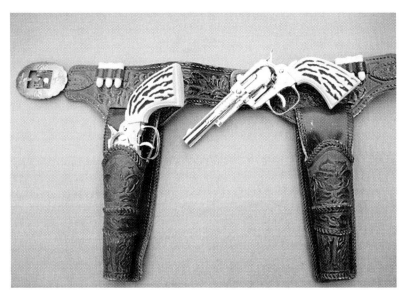

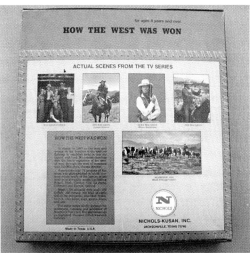

Above: Boxed set of Nichols-Kusan double holsters and guns for **How The West Was Won.**

Above, right: Double holster set with Nichols-Kusan cap shooters for **How The West Was Won** *outfit. The guns are Nichols generic cap shooters with stag grips.*

Right: Back of the box has great color photos of the show stars.

Luke Macahan, for example, was a fugitive after having killed three men in self-defense, only there were lawmen, bounty hunters, and the friends and family members of the men he killed that gave him no peace. Younger brother Josh, was aiming to prove he could fill both his late father and fugitive brother's shoes, all to prove he was capable of taking care of mom and his two sisters. Even the two sisters had special problems of their own, and there was brother Josh and Uncle Zeb to give them love, guidance, and good morals to live up to.

In the two years that this western rode across our screens, we witnessed 300 head of cattle, 1700 animals, 200 horses, oxen, mules, goats, pigs, dogs, and cats. It was breathtakingly filmed right where the action really took place—Utah, Arizona, and Colorado. It was a shame that the series did not continue. Big Jim Arness went on to play in a police show, *McCain's Law*, but he'll always be remembered as "Marshal Matt Dillon." Bruce Boxleitner moved on to *The Gambler* with Kenny Rogers, and the remake of *Red River* with Jim Arness. Eva Marie Saint still knocks 'em dead in many guest roles.

CAP GUN COLLECTIBLES

Probably the most unbelievable outcome of this latter-day western was the fact that Nichols, one of the finest cap gun makers of all time, came out with both a single and a double holster set for *How The West Was Won*. Nichols had already merged with Kusan by then, but it was still headquartered in Jacksonville, Texas. The colorful box has beautiful color graphics and actual color photos of the stars of the show. The box is bordered with printed rawhide and laced edges, with James Arness and the Macahan family on the front and back of the box. The box is also stamped "Made in Texas, USA" giving the boost to the Lone Star state. It is also marked "Nichols-Kusan" with the Jacksonville, Texas, address, the Nichols' new logo, and the 1978 MGM copyright for the name of the show.

Both the single and double holster sets are made of tooled, simulated dura-hide-style material. Two sets of three white plastic bullets fit into the holders located on the belt over each holster pocket. The tooling shows flowers and floral work on both the belt and the holsters. About the only item that is at all reminiscent of the old holster sets is the oval-shaped nickel buckle, which retains the old stamped graphics of a mounted cowboy, and horse heads. The belt is molded and comes with the studs to allow for the varying waist sizes of the youngsters.

The Nichols guns used in these sets are unmarked. They are plated with the "flash silver" finish and have plastic stag grips. The guns have the side gate that lifts up for cap-loading. The guns are 8 inches long and are stamped "Kusan-Nashville, Tenn." while the box is marked with the Nichols name and trademark. While it appears that nothing will ever bring back the cap pistols and magnificent holster sets of twenty years before, at least How The West Was Won was a good effort. Nichols even put out a *How The West Was Won* rubber knife and sheath.

JESSE JAMES

robably no other American outlaw was more widely known or feared than Jesse James. While there were plenty of desperadoes much worse than Jesse James, he still remains a legend, just as powerful now as it was in his own time. Plenty of movies have been done on Jesse and his brother, Frank James. Most show him to have been a "Robin Hood" of sorts, and he is still remembered more fondly than reviled.

Hollywood has been kind to Jesse James, portrayed more as the misunderstood ex-Confederate mercilessly hunted down by Federal troops, lawmen, and his own gang members. Even in Europe, where westerns are still extremely popular, I've never met any foreigner that didn't know about "Jesse James, the famous bad guy."

It seemed odd, then, that Jesse James didn't come to television until the mid-1960s, when the death knell for westerns had already sounded. *The Legend of Jesse James,* a half-hour program, came on the ABC Network in September 1965. Perhaps if Jesse James had hit the screen in the mid to late 1950s, the show would have been more popular, since Hollywood's remake of several of the Old West's bandits into romantic heroes was well known.

Unfortunately, TV's *Jesse James* lasted only 26 episodes, leaving the air on September 26, 1966. Cast as a young and handsome "Jesse James" was Christopher Jones, a relative newcomer to westerns. Allen Case was cast as Frank James, the older brother of Jesse. Allen Case had already made his mark alongside Henry Fonda in *The Deputy.* While writers love to make a hero out of even the worst villain, they cast veteran character actor Robert Wilke as "Marshal Sam Corbett," a fictitious character that sympathized with the James brothers and tried to convince them to "go straight."

I recall the show fondly, and Christopher Jones played a young, intense Jesse James, adding to the misunderstood mystique of the real Jesse James. Allen Case was already a favorite of mine from *The Deputy,* and Robert Wilkie appeared as a nasty, vile character in just about every TV western that ever hit the air. He had the face and voice that you just knew you'd get to hate by the middle of the program. But, here he was, cast as a "good guy" for a change.

Chris Jones had been in *East Side, West Side* with George C. Scott, and had acted in TV shows such as *Naked City,* and on Broadway in *Night of the Iguana.* He was well-known on screen for his intensity, and questioning-of-authority style. He was married to Susan Strasberg, who also appeared as a guest star on the show. Jones is still with us, having done several movies after his stint as "Jesse James."

Allen Case, a real Texan, had already appeared in several TV westerns, just like Robert Wilkie, to include *The Virginian, Have Gun-Will Travel, Wagon Train, Gunsmoke, The Rifleman, Cheyenne* and the alternative series *Sugarfoot* and *Bronco.* He later landed the role as Marshal Simon Fry's deputy in *The Deputy*. Allen Case died of a heart attack in 1986. Robert Wilkie was last seen as "General Barnaky" in a cameo role in the army spoof movie, *Stripes,* starring Bill Murray. Wilkie passed away in 1989 at the age of 74.

THE REAL JESSE JAMES

Born in Centerville, Missouri, on September 5, 1847, the real Jesse James was one of four children, and the brother of Alexander Franklin James, who was four years older. His father, Robert, was a Baptist minister and farmer, originally from Kentucky. The father eventually left the family after 10 years of marriage, and went to California looking for gold, where he died, it was said, of pneumonia.

The mother, Zerelda Cole James, was a strong woman of pioneer stock, with a quick temper and a fanatical devotion to her sons. She later remarried a man named Simms, a widower with kids, but the marriage didn't last, since he didn't take too kindly to her sons. In 1857, Mrs. James married Dr. Rueben Samuel, a doctor-farmer, who took to rearing the four children. Devoted to his new family, Dr. Samuel knew that in his new wife's eyes and heart, her "boys" came first, and he, too, remained loyal to his stepsons, even after they had become celebrated outlaws.

The real Jesse W. James, taken about 1875. While several photos of Jesse James exist, this is the only one actually confirmed as that of Jesse by his wife. (Courtesy of Jesse James III)

Above: The real Frank James with his greetings, taken about 1898. (Courtesy of Western History Collection, University of Oklahoma)

Left: The stars of **The Legend of Jesse James,** *left, Chris Jones as "Jesse James," and right, Allen Case as "Frank James."*

Chris Jones, as TV's young Jesse James in Confederate uniform, recreated the act of surrender on the TV show that started the real Jesse on his outlaw life.

Zee James, Jesse James' pretty and faithful wife, with his cache of guns after his death in 1882. What a collection that would be! (Courtesy of Western History Collection, University of Oklahoma)

Right: Bob Ford, the man who murdered Jesse James. (Courtesy of Jesse James III)

$25,000 REWARD

JESSE JAMES

DEAD OR ALIVE

$15,000 REWARD FOR FRANK JAMES

$5000 Reward for any Known Member of the James Band

SIGNED:

ST. LOUIS MIDLAND RAILROAD

"Wanted" poster for Jesse and Frank James. This is the one that Hubley decided to use for its boxed Remington 36 cap shooter.

Brought up on the Missouri farm, both Frank and Jesse were sympathetic to the Confederate cause, though the family did not own any slaves. When abolitionist John Brown fanned the flames of the bloody border wars in Kansas and Missouri, Frank James decided to join Gen. Sterling Price's command. After taking part in action at Wilson Creek, both Frank and Jesse joined a band of Confederate guerrillas under William Clarke Quantrill. Jesse's nickname was "Dingus" at the time.

He proved himself to be a fearless soldier, yet he was just a clean-shaven, blue-eyed boy of 15. Then an episode took place that made him somewhat of a martyr-rebel that some claim turned him into a notorious killer. At the end of the war, as he was surrendering under a white flag of truce, he was shot and severely wounded by Federal troops while unarmed. At the same time, Federal troops hung his father, though somehow, he survived. Jesse had tasted blood with "Quantrill's Raiders." The South lost everything. There was no turning back.

Along with brother Frank and a gang of compatriots, Jesse robbed his first bank, at Liberty, Missouri, in 1866. His cousins, the Younger brothers, soon joined the "James Gang." They robbed banks from Iowa to Alabama, Missouri to West Virginia. In 1873, they began to rob trains. They did it with lightning speed and, adding to his "Robin Hood" image, Jesse never harmed the passengers, tipped his hat to the ladies, and although it was never confirmed, was said to have given away cash to poor farmers that had been wiped out by the war and the "vile" Yankee carpetbaggers.

In 1874, both Jesse and Frank married, with Jesse marrying his cousin, Zerelda Mimms. It was said he was a good husband. He never looked at another woman, and was totally devoted to "Zee," as she was to him. She bore him two children, Jesse Jr., and Mary. It was Zerelda that had nursed Jesse from the severe wounds suffered in the "truce ambush," and her devotion and care for Jesse never once faltered, even when Dr. Samuel didn't think he'd survive. But Jesse survived with a vengeance.

Again, more tragedy struck Jesse's family, adding to his "martyr image" of a man pushed into lawlessness by the unrelenting lawmen and Pinkerton agents meant to bring him in, dead or alive. In January 1875, Pinkerton Agents surrounded the Samuel farmhouse, thinking that Frank and Jesse were there visiting their mother and half-brother. Breaking a window, the agents tossed in a "fireball," an incendiary type of flare device used at the time, to get the occupants outside where they could either shoot them down or capture them. Dr. Samuel kicked the fireball into the fireplace and unfortunately, it exploded.

When the agents stormed the house, they found Archie Samuel, Jesse's 8-year-old half brother, mortally wounded, and Jesse's mother with her right arm blown off. Dr. Samuel was also wounded. Jesse and Frank James became almost instant "heroes" as the newspapers and dime novels of the day sympathized with them, blaming the authorities for never forgiving the James boys for their allegiance to the South. To Missouri "Ozark farmers," Jesse was a hero, and they justified his bandit ways. A bill of amnesty was introduced in the Missouri legislature, but it was declared out of order and never passed.

Jesse's luck began to run out as the rewards on his head, and that of his brother, increased. Jesse killed a Pinkerton agent to avenge what happened to his mother and half-brother. He also amassed an intense hatred for Allen and William Pinkerton. On September 7, 1876,the gang suffered a terrible blow on its attempt to rob the First National Bank of Northfield, Minnesota. Of the eight men in the gang, 3 were shot dead.

The three Younger brothers, deadly outlaws in their own right, were severely wounded and captured. Only Frank and Jesse escaped, and afterward, they decided to lay low for a while. Jesse moved to Kansas City, using the name "Howard." There, he worked on a ranch, and even entered horses in the state fair. He moved with his family to Waverly, Tennessee, for a while, and returned to his life of crime, organizing a new gang of men.

Governor Crittenden of Missouri raised the reward on Jesse's head to $10,000. Jesse began to realize his men couldn't be trusted. He killed one of them, Ed Miller, when he suspected he was going to turn him in for the reward. He told Zee he had been hunted like "an animal" for 16 years and was through. He moved his family to St.

Joseph, Missouri, in November 1881, and hung up his guns and returned to farming. He was still using the alias, "Mr. Thomas Howard."

But the man Jesse didn't suspect was his own cousin, Bob Ford. Lured by the $10,000 reward, Bob and his brother, Charlie Ford, planned the murder of Jesse James. On the morning of April 3, 1882, the Fords went to visit Jesse. Zee was in the kitchen with the children. Jesse noticed one of his picture frames on the wall was crooked. He got up on a chair to straighten the picture. Bob Ford made his move, shooting Jesse in the back. Jesse died in Zee's arms. Bob and Charlie Ford ran from the house, wired the governor that the deed was done. The newspapers screamed the headlines: "Jesse, by Jehovah" at the *St. Joseph Gazette.* "Good Bye, Jesse" on the front page of the *Kansas City Journal.* Even *The New York Times* had it on the front page. America most famous outlaw, it was said, died with his boots on.

Hubley's Remington 36 short barrel model cap shooter, one the finest ever made, with sleek black grips, superb nickel finish, revolving cylinder, and bullets, marketed in the Jesse James Dead or Alive boxed set.

But there was no peace for Bob Ford. He had, after all, shot his own cousin in the back, and the song went "It was a dirty little coward, that shot Mr. Howard, and laid poor Jesse in his grave." It was a sad Mrs. Samuel who identified her beloved son's body. A funeral befitting "a banker," it was said, was conducted for Jesse James. Long lines of men, women, and children filed by Jesse's coffin, looking down at the bearded Jesse James. In the meantime, even as the funeral went on, Jesse's other half-brother, John Samuel, was shot at a dance hall, while the patient and reserved Dr. Samuel waited for word, hoping he wouldn't have to bury another son.

Jesse was buried under a coffee bean tree on the Samuel farm. The inscription on the grave reads "Jesse W. James, died April 3, 1882. Aged 34 years, six months, 28 days. Murdered by a coward whose name is not worthy to appear here." A saddened Frank James decided it was time to give himself up. Tried for murder and armed robbery in Missouri, he was found not guilty. Tried for robbery in Alabama, he was found not guilty. He retired to a quiet life and died on the Samuel farm in 1915, just four years after his devoted mother, Zerelda Samuel, died on the same farm.

Hubley's Jesse James boxed cap shooter, the Remington 36, with six bullets and the "Wanted" poster with its original box. (Courtesy of P. Connors)

Bob Ford, who went down in history as "the dirty little coward," was cursed, reviled, spit upon, and turned away. He wandered, drank heavily, and later went to Colorado, where he opened up a saloon. In 1893, he was shot to death by Ed Kelly, a local good-for-nothing who got 20 years for the killing. But nobody cried. Bob Ford, and his accomplice brother, Charlie, were soon forgotten, as was Ed Kelly. Jesse W. James, notorious bandit, killer, thief, and America's "Robin Hood" of the West, lived on.

In the late 1950s, like many other famous and prominent assassinations, a conspiracy theory went around that the real Jesse James had not been shot by Ford, that he shot an imposter instead. The western magazines of the time printed several stories, photographs, and both sides of the argument. Somehow, your scribe located Jesse W. James III, the famous outlaw's grandson, still alive and sharp as a tack, in Missouri. We kept a correspondence going for almost two years, as I got some first hand data on his famous grandfather and the James family, as well as photos and articles he had written trying to set the record straight that his grandfather had, indeed, been shot by Bob Ford in 1882.

CAP GUN COLLECTIBLES

Unlike Billy the Kid, another of America's legendary killers, no gun has surfaced marked "Jesse James." Strange that Billy the Kid would find some everlasting fame on a kid's toy gun, but not Jesse James. Perhaps by 1965, the time of *The Legend of Jesse James,* the last thing a mother would want to buy her youngster was a toy gun "honoring" or "immortalizing" such a criminal. Goodness, it might make the kid start robbing banks and trains! So, it's bad news for us cap gun enthusiasts.

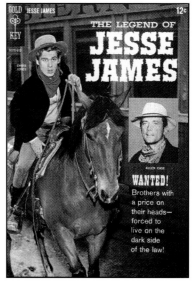

Gold Key Comic issued for **The Legend of Jesse James.**

But all was not lost. Hubley came to the rescue. Banking on the hopes that perhaps *The Legend of Jesse James* would bring a windfall to an already hurting cap gun industry, Hubley did market a boxed set of Jesse James, which included a "Wanted" poster on Jesse James and its already popular Model Remington .36 short barrel cap gun. The box has great graphics, but steers clear of really immortalizing Jesse James.

The Hubley Remington .36 with the short barrel is a well-made, nickel-plated gun with slick black grips. The revolving cylinder accepts bullets, and a spring-loaded lever on the right side of the frame near the cylinder allows you to load the bullets. The Hubley Remington has "Remington 36" raised on both sides of the frame. It is an 8-inch cap pistol with a 3-inch barrel. The Hubley "H" logo is on the grips. Interestingly enough, Jesse James carried two .45 caliber guns at the time of his death—a Colt .45 and Smith & Wesson .45. People still flock to his family farm and his grave in Missouri. Gold Key Comics put out one issue of *The Legend of Jesse James* in 1962 featuring both Chris Jones and Allen Case on the cover.

THE ADVENTURES OF JIM BOWIE

Growing up in the 1950s, the average youngster had no qualms when asked what he "wanted to be" when he grew up. Between September 1956, and for its two-year run, ending September 1958, thousands of kids wanted to be "like Jim Bowie" and carry a "big Bowie knife." *The Adventures of Jim Bowie*, starring South African-born actor Scott Forbes, was one of television's early shows, and a very popular one.

To be true, it certainly romanticized the "adventures" of this early American hero, but the man whose name went down in history as the inventor of the "Bowie" knife, was, in reality, a very courageous man. I decided to include Bowie—this "early south-mid-western hero"—because of the popular TV show that bore his name, and the "Bowie knives" that kids begged their mothers to buy them. While many people have heard of Jim Bowie, little is known of his real life except that he "died at the Alamo, along with Davy Crockett."

Historians differ on when and where James Bowie was born. Some give the date as 1790 and at Logan County, Kentucky. Other historians place his date of birth as 1796 at Burke County, Georgia. What is known is that he was the son of James Rezin Bowie and Alvina Jones. Early documents show his family migrated first to Missouri, and then settled in Louisiana around 1802. He was one of the five "Bowie boys," as they were called—James, David, John, Stephen, and Rezin.

His early years spent in Louisiana are relatively obscure, but stories are chronicled that he and his brothers were "wild boys" who enjoyed trying to snare grizzly bears and bring them home alive. Living in and around French New Orleans in those early years brought him in contact with famous rogues like Jean Lafitte, the pirate, and heroes of the Mexican Wars such as Sam Houston and Andrew "Old Hickory" Jackson. He also met Johnny Appleseed, and the man who befriended Daniel Boone, John James Audobon.

Just as mysterious as his date and place of birth is the story of how the knife that made him famous was born. Let's explore them, for between fact and legend, stories and news articles, the truth lies somewhere in between. Jim and his older brother Rezin, with whom he was very close, already had a reputation for bear fighting. The first story goes that during a fight with a grizzly bear, the standard knife that Jim carried broke off, and his hand slid down to the blade, causing a serious laceration.

The idea of designing a larger, more balanced knife with a wide blade and vicious curve—but more importantly, with a special brass hand guard—was shared by both Jim and Rezin Bowie. Knife makers of the day jumped on the "new" design and associated the name "Bowie." The design was initially carved out of wood and brought to a local knife maker named John Sowell.

The second story, better documented, has date, time, place, and names associated with it. This concerns a duel. Jim Bowie had both personal and political differences with two men—a certain Dr. Thomas Maddox and a man named Samuel Wells. The date to settle these differences was set for September 19, 1828, on a sandbar in the middle of the Mississippi River at Natchez, Louisiana. Bowie was described as "totally fearless" and a man of "immense courage" and who was not a newcomer to settling differences with "honor"—in a good, old fashioned duel.

After exchanging shots with his opponents, it appeared the injustice had been settled, but Bowie was attacked by one Norris Wright, a member of Dr. Maddox's group of attending parties—"seconds," as they were called. Wright shot Bowie, seriously wounding him, but as Bowie lay on the ground and Wright went to finish him off with a sword, Bowie pulled out his famous knife and killed Wright.

The real Jim Bowie, inventor of the Bowie knife. Note that he appears to be clutching a knuckle bow knife with his right hand. (Courtesy of Texas State Library)

A nice assortment of Bowie knives. No matter how large or small, with whatever type of grip existed, there is no mistaking the Bowie blade with its vicious width, curve, and clip point.

The duel received a lot of press and stories soon grew into legend, and men began asking for a knife "like Jim Bowie's." American and British-owned cutlery firms, blacksmiths, and frontier knife makers were soon busy trying to keep up with the demand as the legend grew. While knife making was still in its infancy, it appears that British firms in Sheffield, England, and later, in the early 1830s, the Russell Company of Massachusetts, made the majority of the Bowie knives. However, village blacksmiths made many variations, sizes, and shapes of the Bowie knife, and in Arkansas, it became known as the "Arkansas toothpick." The knife was so deadly that just the sight of a man unsheathing it could stop a disagreement. Laws were even passed to begin to regulate it.

THE REAL JIM BOWIE

By late 1828, Bowie had moved on to Texas, where he became friendly with the Mexican Vice-Governor Juan Martin de Veramendi, and eventually married his daughter, Ursula in 1831. He even assumed Mexican citizenship. However, as Mexican legislation became increasingly harsh against new settlers in Texas and other foreigners, Bowie decided to join the revolutionary movement against Mexico.

First a captain, and later a colonel in the Texas army, he took part in the battle at Nacogdoches in August 1832, later escorting prisoners to San Antonio. For the following two years, Bowie returned to his business of acquiring land grants and settlements and dealing with American-Mexican affairs. In 1835, he was chosen to lead the Committee of Safety, which was organized at Mino, Texas. As a colonel of "revolutionary forces," his daring, courage, and tenacity were tested time and again as he commanded only a mere handful of men.

By December 15, 1835, he and his men had cleared the Mexican army from most of Texas. At the beginning of 1836, Bowie joined forces with Col. William Barret Travis at San Antonio. When Mexican General Santa Ana and his army returned, the Texans, now numbering about 150 men, retreated across the river and decided to make a stand at the Alamo, an abandoned mission.

By now, Bowie was very ill and confined to a cot in one of the rooms of the mission. With the arrival of Davy Crockett and his Tennessee followers, the number of fighters increased to 188 men, who after the famous "line in the sand" by the stalwart Colonel Travis, decided to fight to the end while awaiting reenforcements. The end for Travis, Crockett, and Col. Jim Bowie came on March 6, 1836, as Santa Ana's army of some 5,000 men eventually stormed the Alamo, killing everyone except women and children. Bowie died on his bed, taking four Mexican soldiers with him—two by gunfire with his flintlocks and two with his famous knives, before he was both shot and bayoneted by additional soldiers entering his room.

Books and articles on Bowie became increasingly popular all over the country, but especially in Texas. In 1924, the book *Jas. Bowie, a Hero of the Alamo* by Evelyn Brogan, contained more facts about the man and included interviews with family members, and stories about how the famous knife got its name. Some attributed the knife as being designed by his brother, Rezin Bowie. Another story was that Bowie had injured his hand in an Indian fight when, again, his hand slipped from the hilt to the blade, and that knife maker John Sowell of Gonzalez was given the carved model by Bowie. When Sowell made the first knife, he called it a "Bowie."

Whatever the tale, the Bowie knife attained fame like no other knife in history. During the Civil War, the big and durable Bowie knife was widely adopted by Confederate troops. But on the frontier, the knife was an important weapon, for outlaw and lawman alike, and a prized member of a cowboy's few possessions. Because of the Bowie knife's size, shape, massive grip, and blade proportions, it was perfect for defensive and offensive combat, as well as camp chores such as cutting, chopping, digging, skinning, and cutting up game. And it was also good for what the Arkansas woodsmen labeled it—"picking teeth." Upon meeting Bowie and seeing the knife, Davy Crockett was said to have declared "It'll give you a stomach ache just a-lookin' at it!"

General Santa Ana, the Mexican general who gave no quarter to the defenders of the Alamo, March 6, 1836. (William Tell Images)

The Bowie knife with the knuckle-bow design. Silver fittings, often with an escutcheon with initials, ebony handle, wide and longer blade.

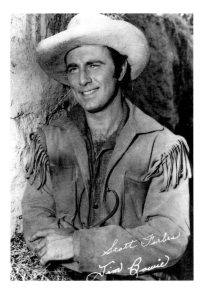

Scott Forbes, star of TV's The Adventures of Jim Bowie.

MacDonald Carey as "Jim Bowie" proves his invention is superior to the Indian tomahawk, being swung by Rick Vallin, playing an Indian brave in the 1951 Universal film Comanche Territory. (Courtesy of A. Forman)

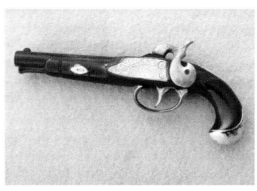

The Bowie knife has been the subject of many discussions about size, shape, width of blade, and the grip. As its reputation increased, the "Bowie" took on many shapes and sizes, including the addition of the "knuckle-bow," meaning that a "hand guard' was attached from grip pommel to the existing hand guard, much like a saber. In fact, in the only well known and documented painting of Jim Bowie (the original hangs at the Capitol building in Austin, Texas), one can see that Bowie is holding a "knuckle-bow" version of his famous knife. The "Bowie-bayonet" was also introduced later on during the Civil War, making it a vicious addition to a musket. The Bowie knife today remains famous and is still manufactured worldwide.

The Bowie knife was anywhere from 10 inches to nearly 20 inches long, with a blade spine sometimes measuring 1/4 to 1/2 inch wide. All must have the crescent curve of the blade point, which is the defining characteristic of the Bowie knife. Grips of all types of massive proportions and materials, and all with a variety of hand guards, were made and used. Wood, stag, brass, and even fancy mother-of-pearl adorn all kinds of grips. The trusty hand guard, with and without ball tips, "S" curves, and straight and oval guards, were utilized. The blade, however, with its distinct single-edged, crescent-curved point, runs anywhere from 6 inches to fourteen inches long. The sheaths came in a variety of leathers and hides, both with and without brass or other metal fittings.

The Adventures of Jim Bowie was a half-hour program, in black and white, and actor Scott Forbes became proficient in throwing his knife with deadly accuracy. Scott Forbes fit the role perfectly, right down to the well-documented sideburns of the real Jim Bowie, as well as the early New Orleans fancy outfits of the day. He always carried his namesake knife and at times, handled a flintlock pistol and flintlock musket with the same accuracy as the "Arkansas toothpick." "Rezin Bowie" was played by character actor Peter Hansen. The show left the air in 1958. Of course, after the *Jim Bowie* series, the character and his Bowie knife came back to life with Walt Disney's *Davy Crockett*. Thereafter, no TV program or movie about Texas Independence, the Alamo, or the story of Davy Crockett, was complete without including Jim Bowie.

Few people remember that Jim Bowie actually came to the big screen in an old, obscure movie. In 1951, Universal-International Pictures released *Comanche Territory* starring MacDonald Carey as "Jim Bowie". Unlike the TV program set in Louisiana and Texas, where the real Jim Bowie lived, this old movie brought him out West to fight off Indians, as well as dishonest cowboys. MacDonald Carey did, however, turn in a good performance in great "knife scenes." Cast alongside Carey was Maureen O'Hara. Other actors that played Jim Bowie were Richard Widmark, Sterling Hayden, and Kenneth Tobey.

CAP GUN COLLECTIBLES

Marx marketed the same flintlock cap firing pistol for "Jim Bowie" as it did for "Daniel Boone" and "Zorro" characters—in plastic with metal cap firing parts, hammer, and trigger. The gun was not marked "Jim Bowie," in keeping with the other characters; only the card itself was marked. I have seen only the smaller of the two models, the Derringer model, which was the 8-inch pattern. I don't doubt that the larger model, used on the Daniel Boone line, was also marketed by the intrepid Louis Marx Toys.

The knife that carried the name, however, was made by many toy companies, among which are Esquire, Arcor, Keyston Brothers, and Hubley, all of which sported the "crescent curve point" feature of the "Bowie." The most famous is the "Bowie Knife" made by the Elvin Company. Two models are known. The smaller model is 9 inches in overall length, with a 5-inch blade,which is 3/4 inches wide. The leather sheath is 6-1/4 inches long, and stamped "Bowie Knife" in gold lettering. The larger model, made by Elvin, came on a carded plastic package, showing Jim Bowie fighting a grizzly bear. This larger model is 10 inches long, with a 6-1/4-inch blade, which is one inch wide. The leather sheath measures 7-3/4 inches long, and this model is also stamped "Bowie Knife" in gold and bordered in gold trim. The vinyl belt that comes in the same package is 24 inches long and 1/2 inch wide. The brown handle and entire knife is rubber.

Strangely enough, a "Bowie knife" with a "knuckle-bow" was marketed for Davy Crockett, along with a flintlock pistol by the Multiple Products Company of New York. Dell Comics also put out two issues of The Adventures of Jim Bowie.

Above: Elvin Company's Bowie Knife on original carded bag showing Jim Bowie fighting off a grizzly bear. Note knife with all rubber parts and gold bordered sheath, also stamped with "Bowie Knife." (J. Schleyer Collection)

Above, right: Marx's standby remedy percussion cap shooting pistol, sold in Jim Bowie, Daniel Boone, Davy Crockett, Johnny Tremain, and Zorro cards.

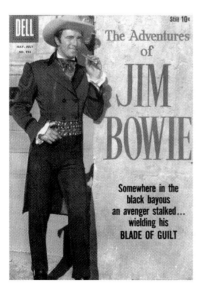

Rare Dell Comics issue for **The Adventures of Jim Bowie.**

JOHN WAYNE - THE DUKE

The "Duke" of western stars in film history was none other than John Wayne. A man of imposing size and screen presence, John Wayne seemed to embody what the American cowboy was all about. Tall, handsome, rugged, yet somewhat soft-spoken and slow to anger, he portrayed his western characters with ideals, romance, and a certain screen nobility.

Born in 1907 in Iowa, his real name was Marion Michael Morrison. Beginning as a prop man in 1928, he landed his first role in *The Big Trail* in 1930. He was just fresh out of the University of Southern California, which he had attended on a football scholarship, when John Ford recommended him to director Raoul Walsh for *The Big Trail,* a film epic being shot in 70mm. This was followed by a string of "B" westerns. It wasn't until 1938, when he was cast as "The Ringo Kid" in *Stagecoach* that John Wayne found stardom, doing his own action sequences and handling sensitive love scenes opposite Claire Trevor.

Showing his versatility as an actor, Wayne made pictures for 20th Century Fox, Republic, and Universal, playing many memorable performances in *Dark Command, The Long Voyage Home,* and *Reap the Wild Wind,* all of which were non-westerns. World War II brought him into *The Fighting Seebees* and *They Were Expendable* in 1944 and 1945, respectively. However, while the western had taken a short leave of absence during the war, it was Wayne's portrayal in 1949 as "Sergeant Stryker" in *Sands of Iwo Jima* that won his first Oscar nomination, while the picture itself was the biggest box-office hit of Republic Pictures. Wayne returned to westerns, having now risen to producer-star stature, and both *The Angel and the Badman* and *Red River* boosted him to the top of the charts in western movies.

The three films known as the "cavalry trilogy" that sent Wayne to the top of box-office stardom were *Fort Apache* in 1948, *She Wore A Yellow Ribbon* in 1949, and *Rio Grande* in 1950, all John Ford westerns. The 1950s saw the Duke in several movies, western and non-western, but *The Searchers* in 1956 and *Rio Bravo* in 1959, far outshone his non-western portrayals in such films as *The High And The Mighty,* in which he played a pilot of a doomed airplane. He directed himself in *The Alamo* in 1960 as "Davy Crockett." This was followed by *The Longest Day,* the World War II epic. He also collaborated, and had the lead role, in *The Green Berets* in 1968.

With the decline of the western in the 1960s, John Wayne kept up his pace even as his age and health began to decline. He played a cameo role in *How The West Was Won* in 1962. But it wasn't until 1969 that he finally won an Oscar for his portrayal of "Rooster Cogburn" in *True Grit.* As his career began to finally wind down, John Wayne gave his last moving performance in *The Shootist* in 1976, in which he played an aging gunfighter, dying of cancer. It was true to life, as "The Duke" himself succumbed to cancer three years later, in 1979.

John Wayne, the "Duke" in the parts he will always be remembered for—the westerns. This is from **Red River.** *(Courtesy of Bill Longstreet)*

John Wayne with moustache in **She Wore a Yellow Ribbon** *one of the "Cavalry Trilogy" films he made in 1949. (Courtesy of A. Forman)*

Right: Chancy Novelty's Boxed John Wayne double holster set. The box lid has "The Duke;" the holster pockets have his name and his image on them. (Courtesy of J. Schleyer)

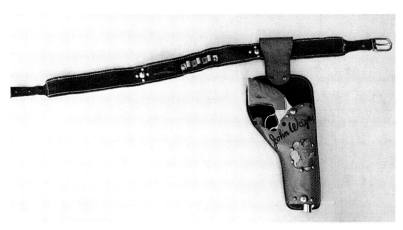

Single John Wayne holster with variation holster pocket and image of the Duke along with a Kilgore Mustang cap shooter with blue grips. (Courtesy of Brian Wolf)

Close-up of details of the holster pocket image, signature, and the Kilgore Mustang with blue grips. Kilgore Ranger has also been found in these holsters. (Courtesy of Brian Wolf)

The Kilgore Mustang with blue grips. Palomino horse head looking down, and silver finish. Same gun style used for Kilgore Kit Carson and Roy Rogers guns.

His career had spanned nearly 50 years. He starred in more than 150 films, 85 of which were westerns. John Wayne was on the cover of both *Time* in 1952, and *Life* in 1965. Dell Comics put out *El Dorado* in honor of the movie, in which Wayne starred with tough guy Bob Mitchum. Even after his death, John Wayne was immortalized on many products, collectibles, and weapons as a "Great American."

CAP GUN COLLECTIBLES

Along with Alan Ladd and Nick Adams, John Wayne also holds the distinction of having been immortalized on a set of holsters for us cap gun collectors and enthusiasts. At least two are known to exist, and both patterns were marketed by the Chancy Novelty Company of Brooklyn, New York. Both came out in the mid-1950s at the height of Wayne's "western" career.

The double holster set came in a colorful yellow and blue box, showing Wayne's image on the graphics, and galloping cowboy across the box lid, as well as "John Wayne Genuine Leather Holster Set." The holsters were tan and black with "John Wayne" across the straps of the pocket along with a tool-embossed bust of Wayne with cowboy hat at the lower sections of the pockets. The leather belt holds six bullets.

The single holster set is also tan and black leather, with "John Wayne" in signature form across the top portion of the pocket, which also had studs and a much clearer image of Wayne on the center of the holster pocket, which appears to be a two-piece studded bust picture affixed to the holster pocket as opposed to it being tooled into the leather of the large double set.

These sets are quite scarce, as few have survived. This also accounts for many varying opinions and what guns came in the sets. The guns that came in the larger holsters were black finish Daisy Western 45s. Other collectors indicate the guns were pressed steel clicker-types without the star's name on them. At least two specimens of the single holster set that are known to exist came with Kilgore Mustang guns with blue grips.

Another set has been found with the Kilgore Ranger model. Both of these guns are the die-cast 9-inch nickel models, which break open from the top, with a side lever for cap loading. The Mustang has a palomino-style horse's head, facing downward on the grips, while the Ranger has a bust size cowboy on the grips. The identical design of the Kilgore Mustang and Ranger were used on the Roy Rogers and the Kit Carson models.

JOHNNY RINGO

his is one real western badman that for some reason was fictionalized into a sheriff in the TV western *Johnny Ringo* starring Don Durant. The CBS series also starred Mark Goddard as Ringo's deputy, "Cully," and it was set in the fictitious town of Velardi, Arizona, in the 1880s. About the only accurate historical point was that in 1880, the real Johnny Ringo was in Arizona—but certainly not as a sheriff.

Not much is known about Johnny Ringo, other than his real name was John Ringgold, and he was born in Texas around 1844. He was second cousin to the Younger brothers, who rode with Jesse James. His grandfather was Col. Coleman Younger, who lived in California with Johnny's three sisters after the family moved there; Johnny decided to stay in Texas and go into the cattle "business." The business turned out to be cattle rustling.

He next showed up in 1875 in Mason County, Texas, where he was arrested for a double murder and cattle rustling. While he awaited trial, he escaped. Re-arrested a short time later, he was jailed in Austin, Texas, where he shared the calaboose with other badmen of the day such as Wes Hardin, Manning Clements, and the notorious Bill Longley. Able to prove self-defense in the double murder, Ringo was freed.

Strikingly handsome, Ringo was six feet two with piercing blue eyes, auburn hair and a sad look on his face. Although well educated and popular with the ladies, Ringo was a morose and moody man who often talked of suicide. He drank heavily, often for long periods of time, and it was said that he did so to "blank out unpleasant thoughts." He left Texas, and reappeared around 1879, in Galeyville, New Mexico, already with a deadly reputation. But, it wasn't until he traveled to Tombstone, Arizona, that Johnny Ringo really hit the big time.

The real Johnny Ringo. Handsome, intelligent, deadly. (William Tell Images)

He joined the wrong side—the Clantons—in their hatred of the Earp Brothers and Doc Holliday. Ringo was a dead shot when he wasn't drinking, and carried two ivory handled Colt .45s. It was said that he once challenged Wyatt Earp to a "handkerchief duel." Wyatt called him "drunk and crazy" and refused, not wanting to jeopardize his political position in Tombstone. But Doc Holliday took the dare and was about to duel with Ringo when Mayor Thomas stepped in and stopped it.

After the Gunfight at the O.K. Corral, Ringo continued to drink heavily, and in July 1882, went on a 10-day drinking spree with two other badmen—"Buckskin" Frank Leslie and Billy Claiborne. Drinking from ranch to ranch, somewhere along the way they split up. On July 14, 1882, Ringo was found sitting up, under a giant oak tree in Sulphur Springs Valley, with his brains blown out. His horse, coat, and boots were missing. Strips of his undershirt were found bound around his feet. His horse was later found six miles away with only one boot tied to the saddle. His mysterious death gave rise to a number of theories and accusations. His former drinking partners argued over the death with Claiborne, accusing Leslie of killing Ringo, and in return for the accusation, Leslie killed Claiborne. The local coroner decided it was a suicide, after Ringo's despondency and long bout of drinking.

Mark Goddard as "Deputy Cully" and Don Durant as "Johnny Ringo" letting the lawless element know they are in charge! Note the special holster Don Durant is wearing and the shotgun barrel on his gun. (Courtesy of Old West Shop)

Another rumor was that a gambler named John O'Rourke came upon Ringo sleeping off his drunkenness, and killed him on an old grudge, stealing his boots and horse. But that didn't sell because they found the horse and one of Ringo's boots. The last theory was that Wyatt Earp killed Ringo, as he went on the revenge manhunt for the murder of his brother Morgan Earp and the crippling of his other brother Virgil Earp. Johnny Ringo remained just another badman statistic of the Old West—until Hollywood got involved. Apparently, Johnny Ringo was too romantic a character to remain in the background in TV's attempt to come up with new westerns with the real flavor of the Old West.

Johnny Ringo was a popular western on CBS, lasting from October 1958, to October 1960. Produced by Aaron Spelling, Don Durant

Right: The Marx Johnny Ringo on its original card. The leather lanyard is tied to the youngsters belt. As you draw the gun away from the holster, the lanyard pulls and begins to fire the caps!

The Marx Johnny Ringo special cap shooter that operates by use of the lanyard ring as shown.

Esquire's Johnny Ringo nickel-plated, stag-grip cap pistol. Seldom seen.

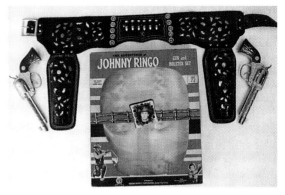

Esquire Boxed Johnny Ringo gun and holster set. The name is over the holster pockets. The guns are Esquire's 250 shot cap shooters. (Courtesy of Brian Wolf)

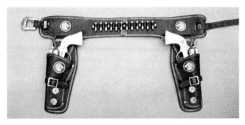

Esquire double holster set for Johnny Ringo complete with guns. Name is over the holster pockets. Super gunfighter style!

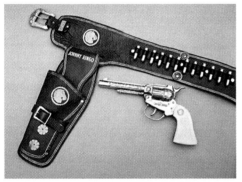

Close-up of details of the Esquire Johnny Ringo cap pistol and holster set. Note the Esquire pony medallion logo on the gunbelt.

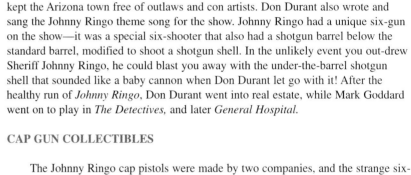

and Mark Goddard made a deadly team as sheriff and deputy who took no guff and kept the Arizona town free of outlaws and con artists. Don Durant also wrote and sang the Johnny Ringo theme song for the show. Johnny Ringo had a unique six-gun on the show—it was a special six-shooter that also had a shotgun barrel below the standard barrel, modified to shoot a shotgun shell. In the unlikely event you out-drew Sheriff Johnny Ringo, he could blast you away with the under-the-barrel shotgun shell that sounded like a baby cannon when Don Durant let go with it! After the healthy run of *Johnny Ringo,* Don Durant went into real estate, while Mark Goddard went on to play in *The Detectives,* and later *General Hospital.*

CAP GUN COLLECTIBLES

The Johnny Ringo cap pistols were made by two companies, and the strange six-shooter with the shotgun barrel, as we shall see, was just as mysterious as the real Johnny Ringo. Marx made two versions of the Johnny Ringo. There is a nickel model that came in a colorful box. The box itself is marked "Johnny Ringo," but the gun is not. The second model came on a large 12-inch-by-16-inch very colorful card showing Don Durant as "Johnny Ringo" doing a fast draw with what Marx touted as "the strangest, fastest gun in the West."

The gun came with a special holster, both of which were on the card. The gun is a 10-inch dragoon-style gun, with a strange mechanism. The gun was factory black with extensive scrollwork on the entire gun and the unique octagon barrel. There is a small lever on the left side of the gun which lifts up the cap box, which you must hold open as it is on a tight spring. In eight well-illustrated and rather complicated steps, you then load the cap roll, carefully lining up the cap with the pins of the anvil inside the cap box, advance the roll, and then carefully shut the spring lever. Then you tie a strange lanyard on a ring under the gun butt to your belt, next to the holster. As you then "fast draw" the gun from its special holster, it fires six rapid shots!

You cannot fire this gun like a standard cap shooter, since the trigger is non-functional, as is also the hammer. The gun can only be fired by the lanyard ring. The ivory-colored grips are well sculptured, with a longhorn and a lasso on the left side and an almost frontal view of a horses head on the right side, also with a lasso going around a black circle where the logo is usually located. The Marx logo is on the frame of the gun, as is a galloping stallion on both sides of the dragoon cylinder—with percussion-style design rather than a revolver-type cylinder. The holster, with "Johnny Ringo" in heavy molded relief on the belt portion of the holster, is just as strange and unique. It has three molded "holders" all of which are open on one side. The gun therefore "rests" in the holders, but once you tie the lanyard ties to the belt and you make your fast draw, you actually push and slide the gun forward as it clears the holster, firing away. What a unique design! The card is well illustrated and has the Marx, CBS, and Four Star Production markings on it with the 1960 date.

Esquire (Actoy) made both a Johnny Ringo cap pistol and holster set. The gun is an 8-inch nickel-plated die cast with barrel engravings, "Johnny Ringo" on both sides of the frame, and simulated white stag grips. The gun breaks from the top by pressure and has no release lever. Typical of the Actoy guns of this type, excessive use and opening eventually wears the "nub," and the barrel often hangs forward. The same gun design and size were used for the

Left: Halco's 6 & 7 Marshal Shooter with original box certainly resembles the gun Johnny Ringo wore on the TV show.

Far left: The Halco 6 & 7 Marshal Shooter cap pistol with a prominent view of the special shotgun barrel.

Rin-Tin-Tin and the Wyatt Earp, except that the Johnny Ringo does not have a lanyard ring on the gun butt. The Esquire pony medallion logo is on the grips. This is a seldom-seen cap pistol, and the only known cap pistol with "Johnny Ringo" raised on the frame that has surfaced to date.

Esquire made a beautiful Johnny Ringo boxed set showing Don Durant on the cover in two poses as "Johnny Ringo," and Mark Goddard as "Deputy Cully." The double holster set is a very stylish, colorful, black leather outfit with gold embossed cut-outs and silver studs. "Johnny Ringo" is on the top of the holster pockets. The guns in this set are the larger Esquire "250 Shot" models in nickel finish with black simulated stag grips, the same model and size gun Esquire used for the Restless Gun, Lone Ranger, and larger Wyatt Earp in nickel finish, without lanyard ring and in black stag, instead of the usually seen white simulated stag.

Another Esquire double holster for the Johnny Ringo came in rich brown leather with white details, Esquire pony medallions on the holster pocket and belt, and with white "Johnny Ringo" on the tops of the holster pockets with other designs. This set is not as ornate as the larger boxed set, but it is in the "gunfighter" style and will take both Esquire model guns. Esquire also issued a Johnny Ringo single holster using the same design as the Wells Fargo, but in black with white lettering for "Johnny Ringo" on the holster pocket, and white details of the Wells Fargo stagecoach on the top of the holster section where the belt was fitted. This also takes the Actoy Johnny Ringo cap pistol. It will not take the much larger Marx model, however.

Interesting variation of the Johnny Ringo small single holster which also came with the Actoy "Buckaroo," showing the six point sheriff badge and name.

Here's the strange story of the six-gun with the shotgun barrel as the "7th barrel" gun that Johnny Ringo carried on the show. Remarkably, while Halco made several TV western character guns, the gun that Johnny Ringo made famous on the TV show (which we can safely call the strange "6-7 shooter") was not marketed as the Johnny Ringo. For some reason, J. Halpern (Halco) marketed the 6-7 shooter as the Marshal 6-7 Shooter.

Yet, one look at the *Johnny Ringo* reruns or TV stills of the show where Don Durant has the gun unholstered, and you can see this was the copy. Even the Combination 6 and 7 shooter with shotgun barrel touted on the Halco box, with six illustrated steps and the image of the "marshal," resembles the Johnny Ringo character. I believe this is because Marx and Esquire must have obtained the copyright from Four Star Productions to market their Johnny Ringo guns and holster sets, while Halco made the correct gun design of the Johnny Ringo, and marketed the gun as the Marshal 6-7 Shooter. It appears that the real Johnny Ringo became more famous in death, thanks to TV, than he ever was in real life.

Above: Single holster for Johnny Ringo by Esquire that also takes the same cap gun. Note that this same style was also used for Esquire's Wells Fargo. (Courtesy of Mike Cherry)

*The stars of TV's **Johnny Ringo**, left to right, Mark Goddard ("Deputy Cully"), Karen Sharpe ("Laura Thomas"), and Don Durant ("Johnny Ringo"). The very beautiful Karen Sharpe played the love interest on the show and worked in her father's General Store. Don Durant also wrote and sang the theme song for the show.*

THE ADVENTURES OF KIT CARSON

A nother one of TV's first western shows, *The Adventures of Kit Carson* was based on the real life of Christopher "Kit" Carson. Born in 1809 in Kentucky, Kit was only three when the Carson family moved to Missouri. Kit began working as a saddler, but soon tired of it and joined a wagon train headed for New Mexico. Between 1826 and 1833, he made his mark as a hunter, trapper, and explorer on various expeditions in the Southwest, the Rockies, and California.

Taking part in an Indian battle against the Blackfeet, Carson was wounded in the shoulder. He joined another noted mountain man, Jim Bridger, on trapping expeditions. By 1841, he was also hunting buffalo, and by 1845, he became well known when he signed on as Gen. John Fremont's chief scout on western expeditions. He reached his fame in the 3-year period as General Fremont's scout, mapping and documenting the Oregon Trail, California, the Great Basin.

Soon the "dime novels" of the day highlighted his scouting exploits as "Kit Carson, The Scout." With Fremont, he took part in the Mexican War, where California was won over from Mexico. Between 1849 and 1861, Carson tried farming and sheepherding, but eventually turned to being an Indian agent for the Ute tribe. After the Civil War, holding the rank of colonel, Carson took part in several Indian campaigns, eventually attaining the rank of general.

His most famous battle was the Second Battle of Adobe Walls in Texas, where he led a band of 400 volunteers and scouts like himself in a defense against overwhelming odds of some 3,000 Indians. Kit Carson was able to get the Ute chiefs to come to Washington to form a peace treaty before he died at Fort Lyon, Colorado, in 1868.

With TV westerns still in their infancy, TV's version of "Kit Carson" put aside the historical facts of this great scout and Indian fighter and transplanted him in the Wild West. Played by former movie actor Bill Williams (who was married to Barbara Hale of *Perry Mason* fame), the series also provided Kit Carson with a Mexican sidekick, "El Toro" (*The Bull*), played by character actor Don Diamond.

Together, two-gun hero Kit Carson and his less serious sidekick, went all over the West in plenty of adventure, rather than violent gunplay. Remarkably, this popular show ran for four years, from September 1951, to October 1955. Bill Williams went on to star in another series called *Date with Angels* and Don Diamond went on to star in *F Troop* and *Zorro*. Bill Williams passed away in 1994.

CAP GUN COLLECTIBLES

Kilgore made the only known Kit Carson die-cast cap gun. Like the cast-iron Buffalo Bills and Billy the Kid, Kit Carson was already a well-known early character in cast-iron guns made by Kenton and Kilgore. But Kilgore carried the Kit Carson line into its die-cast models. Kilgore made two versions of the Kit Carson. The 8-1/4-inch die cast came in both nickel and

The real Kit Carson. Explorer, trapper, frontiersman, Indian fighter, soldier, buffalo hunter, and Scout. (Courtesy of Kit Carson Historic Museum, New Mexico)

Bill Williams as "Kit Carson."

Right: Bill Williams as "Kit Carson" and Don Diamond as "El Toro," on The Adventures of Kit Carson, *one of TV's first westerns. (Courtesy of Old West Shop)*

gold models with both white and black grips, with the raised figure of Kit Carson in buckskins.

This model has "Kit Carson" on both sides of the frame and the Circle "K" logo on the grips, along with lots of design and scrollwork on the entire gun frame and barrel. It also is one of the few guns that came with a lanyard ring at the bottom of the gun butt. The lever on this gun is on the right side, breaking it open from the top for cap loading. The colorful box was also marked "Kit Carson" and sold for a whopping 79 cents. The larger Kilgore "Kit Carson" was 9 inches, and also came in both a gold and nickel finish. A variation design of Kit Carson in buckskins was utilized on this model's grips, which also came in black and white. On this larger model, "Kit Carson" is only on the right side of the frame, under the cylinder. The frame also sports additional scrollwork and a great American bison's head on the left side, between the grips, and the raised name of "Kit Carson."

The Circle "K" logo is found on the top of the frame, on the left side, to the front of the hammer. A larger, more elaborate top breaking lever is found on the right side of the frame. Made in the style of the Bronco, Grizzly, and the large Roy Rogers, this pattern has the much larger grips with the finger groove formation, and it does not have the aforementioned lanyard ring on the gun butt.

Carnell Roundup of New York marketed at least three variations of Kit Carson holster sets. The Carnell Kit Carson holsters were sold with two generic guns as well as the most elaborate set which came with the Kilgore Kit Carson models. The two other cap pistols marketed in Kit Carson holsters were the Hubley Western with steer head grips in black, and a slightly larger double set with Nichol's Stallion 38s. All three Carnell "Kit Carson" double holster sets have "Kit Carson" on the belt and across the holster pockets. They were very elaborately tooled and came in a colorful box with actor Bill Williams as "Kit" on the cover with guns drawn.

Only Kilgore made the die-cast "Kit Carson" guns. Only Carnell Roundup marketed Kit Carson holster sets with and without Kit Carson guns.

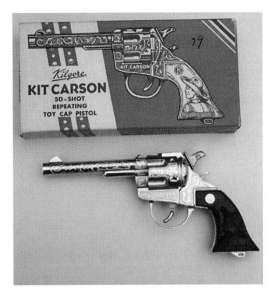

Kilgore's 8-1/4-inch Kit Carson cap pistol with its original box. Note price!

Kilgore's large Kit Carson cap pistol with its original box.

Above: All three patterns of the Kilgore 8-1/4-inch Kit Carson showing grip color along with nickel and gold plated models. Note raised image of Kit on grips.

Right: Carnell's advertisement for Kit Carson double holster set. Note this set came with Kilgore's Kit Carson cap pistols. It's apparant that Carnell used many brands of cap guns in their outfits. (Courtesy of George Newcomb)

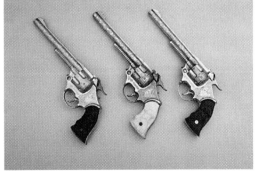

All three patterns of the large Kit Carson showing grip colors along with the nickel- and gold-plated models. Note raised image of Kit on grips.

KLONDIKE

You had to hand it to television producers in the old days. They not only tried to entertain, they also tried to inform—to base shows on real events and real people. Imagine coming up with a TV show based on the Klondike Gold Rush of the late 1890s, giving it a western flair, and adding all the adventure and excitement of turn-of-the-century Alaska! Well, I'm here to give this a quick salute as we look back at *Klondike*.

This show was based on Pierre Berton's book, called *Klondike Fever*, published in 1958. The setting for this program was Skagway, Alaska, a real city which still exists. The author had spent the first twelve years of his life in Dawson City, and he soon learned of the hardships, the luck and the tragedies of the last, colossal gold rush on the continent. He was able to put it into this wonderful book, combining both history and the telling of this tale in a most dramatic way. If you enjoy history, adventure, drama, and a damn good epic, this is one book you should read.

Back in 1724, Peter the Great, the Russian czar at the time, sent a Danish naval captain in the Russian Navy to explore land and sea east of Siberia. Braving the strait that bears his name, Capt. Vitus Bering got there in 1728, but it wasn't until 1741 that he got to the mainland itself and claimed the territory for Russia. But the freezing and risky adventure of this unsung hero came with a heavy price. His ship was wrecked and he died December 8, 1741.

Part of his crew managed to get back to Russia, and their stories of great wealth in furs sent trappers, hunters, and traders streaming into Alaska. The name "Alaska" comes from the Aluet Indian meaning "the great land" and great it is. This state has an area of 587,000 square miles and it is bigger than California, Montana, and Texas combined. The coast alone is 26,000 miles long.

Russian fur traders first set up camps on Kodiak Island in the mid-1780s. But the Spanish and the English also visited Alaska. Capt. James Cook, George Vancouver, and Alexander MacKenzie all brought the British Union Jack there between 1788 and 1794. The Russians wantonly caused a lot of destruction and slaughter of many fur animals, both sea and land. The natives of the land were cheated, abused, and at times even massacred.

When the czar got wind of these abuses, he put a stop to it by chartering the Russian-American Company to promote exploration, and commerce, as well as spreading the Russian Orthodox faith to the area. The company's director, Alexander Baranof, ran the area like a dictator for some 20 years, but he was also responsible for building churches, schools, and bringing some civilization to the area. He moved the capitol from Kodiak to Sitka, and his onion-domed steeples and churches are still standing there today, including the beautiful cathedral of St. Michael at Sitka.

Russia tried to sell Alaska to the United States in 1855, but the deal finally went through in March 1867, thanks to the efforts of then-Secretary of State William Seward. The price we paid for this territory was $7,200,000. So far from home, the Americans didn't pay much attention to this new vast possession, and so the Treasury Department, the Army and the Navy took turns in running the new land. There was no civil government until it became a "district" in 1884, governed by the laws of the state of Oregon. The discovery of the precious yellow metal—gold!—in the Klondike region in 1897 brought in armies of prospectors, and the most accessible route to the Klondike was through southeastern Alaska by way of Skagway and the very dangerous Chilkoot Pass.

It was a violent, colorful, romantic era, immortalized also by Jack London and Rex Beach. By the Act of 1912, Alaska was made a Territory. In World War II, the Japanese landed on the outermost regions of the Aleutians. American air and naval bases were established and some 100,000 men were sent to the Aleutians and Dutch Harbor. The Alaskan Command was headquartered in Anchorage. Between 1946 and 1953, several bills were introduced to grant statehood, which was finally completed in 1959.

It took many months before the Klondike "gold rush" news hit the outside world. The rush then brought the good, the bad, and the ugly to the area. There were terrible scenes at Skagway and the White Pass in 1897, followed by food panic, lawlessness, and starvation that winter of 1897. Some 3,000 clawed their way over Alaskan glaciers from the Pacific. Using several other routes, unchartered and dangerous, more than 8,000,000 inexperienced and desperate wanderers made their way down some 500 miles of unchartered waters to the new "city of gold." In the ensuing struggle, fortunes were made, desperate men lost their lives, and heroes were born.

The stars of TV's **Klondike***, left to right, Mari Blanchard, Ralph Taeger, James Coburn, Joi Lansing and "The Golden Nugget." (Courtesy of Old West Shop)*

Ralph Taeger, with his dog "Sam," starred as Mike Holliday on Klondike and later as "Hondo." (Courtesy of Old West Shop)

Almost 101 years later, the stories of these men and women came to television with the new show called *Klondike*. Set in 1897, and as with the California Gold Rush of some 45 years before, the attraction for gold and all that glitters also brings with it all kinds of characters, from men down-on-their-luck, con-artists, gamblers, men after their last hurrah and those that swear they are going to "strike it rich." It also brings all kinds of women, from struggling families to, pardon the pun—"gold diggers"—in an area where women were in short supply to begin with. Producer William Conrad—radio's "Matt Dillon" and, later, as TV's rotund private eye "Cannon"—also directed some of the episodes of this great effort. To his credit, the late William Conrad added all the elements of such an epic story, and did so in only 30 minutes. *Klondike* came to NBC television on October 10, 1960.

Ralph Taeger, an actor who had gotten his film break in the movie *The Carpetbaggers* was cast as "Mike Halliday." He came to Alaska like all the others, to search for gold, adventure and excitement. One of film and television's all-time favorites, James Coburn, was cast as "Jeff Dirain," a gambler and general all-around rogue and con artist, who is out to make a fast buck in all kinds of schemes. The character of Mike Halliday was also a ladies' man, and two gorgeous actresses of the time, Joi Lansing and Mari Blanchard were cast as the two women both after Mike Halliday. Dozens of great character actors that did the western circuit also guest starred on this fine show.

However, it failed to hold the audiences, and after only 18 episodes, it went off the air on February 13, 1961. Ralph Taeger went on to star in *Hondo*, another TV western. James Coburn, who achieved movie fame as "Our Man Flint," has acted in hundreds of movies and TV programs. Both men are still with us. Sadly, the two beauties who played "Goldie" and "Kathy O'Hara" have both died. Joi Lansing, the sweet platinum blonde that starred in many westerns of the time, was only 44 when she died of lung cancer in 1972. William Conrad, best remembered for his role as "Cannon," went on to play in *Jake and the Fatman*. He passed away in 1994.

CAP GUN COLLECTIBLES

Just as hard to find as people who remember this show is the cap pistol that none other than the giant Nichols Circle "N" Ranch made for the program. In fact, in his 1991 book about the story of the Nichols toy guns, even Talley Nichols forgot to mention the Klondike 44. It has never failed to amaze me how some short-lived TV westerns spurred the various toy gun companies to market the guns, while other more popular TV westerns that lasted much longer, and some with bigger stars, never got anywhere in the toy gun markets. Such is the case with the Nichols Klondike 44. To their credit, Nichols certainly tried to keep the interest in the show alive. The 1961 Nichols catalog features the Klondike 44, even though the program went off the air in mid-February of the same year.

The Klondike 44 was an all-blued metal cap pistol with a revolving cylinder. It was about the same size as the Stallion .38—one of Nichols' most popular guns. At 9 inches, the Klondike came in both a holster set and on a shadow box with just the gun itself. The steel-blue gun has the same finish as Nichols' Model 1861 and the Mustang. It has many features similar to both of these guns, as well as the Nichols 41-40. The revolving cylinder takes the two-piece cartridges, and the grips are a beautiful simulated walnut grain. The gun is marked Klondike 44 on the frame under the cylinder in the lettering-style used on the show title.

The holster set came in a box with great graphics in four colors, showing actor Ralph Taeger as "Mike Halliday" on the cover. The single holster was black with white details, and came with 12 dummy bullets on the belt. The Klondike 44 in the shadow box also hawks "NBC's smash hit show Klondike" and comes with six cap cartridges. This is the only known cap gun that was made for TV's Alaskan adventure show *Klondike*. It is quite scarce and seldom seen, given the short life of the program.

The Nichols Klondike 44 cap shooter, all blued, with walnut grain grips, revolving cylinder, and 2 piece bullets. Seldom seen. (Courtesy of Ben Graves)

Close-up of name and details on right side of the Nichols Klondike 44. The lettering is in the same style as the TV show of the same name. (Courtesy of Ben Graves)

Advertisement from the 1961 Nichols catalog for the Klondike 44.

LARAMIE

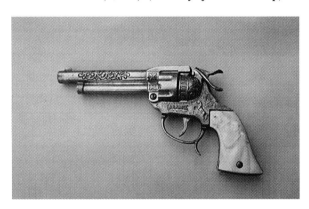

The stars of Laramie, left to right, John Smith ("Slim"), Bobby Crawford ("Andy"), Hoagy Carmichael ("Jonesy"), and Robert Fuller ("Jess"). (Courtesy of Old West Shop)

Now here's a great western program that ran a full five years, premiering in mid-September 1959, when television was "ripe" with westerns galore. The show told the story of the "Sherman" brothers, "Slim" and "Andy," whose father had been killed by a land-grabbing gunman. In the 1870s, the Sherman family owned a cattle ranch and a stagecoach station near Laramie, Wyoming, from which the name of the show was derived. After the father gets gunned down, the brothers were assisted by "Jonesy," an old friend of the father.

Soon, a young drifter named "Jess Harper," who has a fast draw, arrives in Laramie and decides to stay with the Sherman's. These wonderful characters were soon joined by sweet "Daisy Cooper," the housekeeper at the ranch and relay station. As the show grew in popularity, the cast included an orphan named "Mike Williams," whose parents had been killed in an Indian attack. With episodes bringing in many characters on the stagecoaches that arrived daily at the "Laramie relay station," there was a never-ending supply of drama that came to life on this action-packed show.

Handsome star John Smith was cast as Slim Sherman and Robert Crawford, Jr., played younger brother, "Andy Sherman." (Johnny Crawford, of *Rifleman*, was his real-life brother). Veteran singer and composer Hoagy Carmichael played "Jonesy." The good-looking drifter with the short fuse of a temper and fast draw was played by Robert Fuller. Cheerful veteran actress Spring Byington was cast as "Daisy Cooper" and young newcomer Dennis Holmes was cast as the orphan "Mike Williams." The local sheriff of Laramie was played by veteran actor Stuart Randall. The show was rich with guest stars along with a great lineup of characters played by this great array of veteran movie and television stars.

Laramie got its name from Jacques De La Ramie, a French fur trader and trapper who explored the area in the early 1800s. Laramie at the time included the new town, plains, and mountains in Wyoming that De La Ramie included on his maps. Laramie's location, on the overland trail, soon grew as countless wagon trains, cowboys, and stagecoaches stopped there for rest, repair, and new supplies.

The "Pony Express" was also cut through Laramie, sending new riders East and West with mail. The only drawback was its proximity to the hunting grounds of Sioux, Cheyenne, and Arapaho Indians. Fort Laramie was soon built to protect the area from Indian attacks between 1850 and 1880. Laramie still thrives today, and still depends on lumber and ranching, and is also the seat of the University of Wyoming, established in 1886.

The *Laramie* western program was extremely popular in Great Britain. While NBC aired it in the States, the BBC brought it to the few screens in the British Isles. The show ended its five-year run on September 17, 1963. It can still be seen in syndication today. Handsome John Smith passed away in 1995. Oscar nominee Spring Byington died in 1971, followed by Hoagy Carmichael in 1981. The others are still with us. Robert Fuller went on to play in *Emergency*, which was also a successful program. Initially shot in black and white, the hour-long program later was telecast in color. *Laramie* was a wonderful show with so many great situations given the ranch and stagecoach station setting.

Leslie-Henry 9-inch Laramie cap pistol with nickel finish and horse head grips. Note the lettering was in the same style as the show title. Seldom seen.

Leslie-Henry/Halco smaller 8-1/4-inch Laramie cap pistol with stag grips and Diamond "H" logo on the grips. Note show name lettering. Seldom-seen cap gun.

The Halco Laramie with single holster sold by Toy Shop Merchandising Corporation of New York. Note the metal black saddle concho on holster pocket.

CAP GUN COLLECTIBLES

Leslie-Henry made the 9-inch Laramie cap pistol. This was the standard, nickel-plated, engraved model with side lever, breaking it open at the top for cap loading. The grips were the standard horse head pattern. A unique feature of the "Laramie" marking was the fact that it was raised on both sides of the frame in the same lettering style as the show title itself—with the large "L" and large "E" at the end and all attached. This cap pistol is seldom seen and came out in 1959. Heavily scrolled, the frame also sports the rearing horse, which is also raised by the name, and just before the grips.

Left: Colorful BBC-sponsored boxed set of Laramie double holsters. This set took both sizes of the Leslie-Henry guns. Note sharp details. (Courtesy of J. Schleyer)

Below: Hubley's boxed Laramie double holster gun set with Hubley Marshal guns. Look who's pointing the gun on the box lid—the young boy on the show, Andy! Note the beautiful tooling on the Hubley holsters. (Courtesy of Brian Wolf)

Leslie-Henry/Halco also made the smaller version of the "Laramie" cap pistol, using the same show title design of the name, on both sides of the frame. This 8-1/4-inch model came out in 1960, along with all the smaller models that Halco made for a variety of TV westerns, as noted in the respective sections. The smaller model was also nickel plated, with the side-gate on the left side for cap loading, simulated stag grips, and the Diamond "H" logo on the grips. This cap pistol, as in all the identical models of this size and pattern, does not have the rearing horse on the frame, but is otherwise heavily scrolled with a long barrel sight.

The Japanese also made an all-metal cork firing Laramie pistol, in black pressed metal, almost identical in size and design as the Daniel Boone. The high luster black enamel gun has white painted grips with the outline of Slim Sherman and "Laramie" in black lettering below it. This is a 10-inch cork firing pistol. The exact identity of the Japanese manufacture, as with many of the lithographed tin toys made in Japan is unknown, but it was most likely Cragston or K. O. Toys.

These are the only three "Laramie"-marked guns that have surfaced to date. No Laramie rifles have surfaced to date.

R&S Toys, Lone Star, Hubley, and Toy Shop Merchandising Corporation all put out holster sets and single holsters for the *Laramie* show. The R&S double holster set came in a beautiful colored box sporting all the show stars and BBC-TV markings. The holsters are also stamped "Laramie" on the pockets, and are of black and white leather, adorned with conchos and jewels. The box has spectacular details and sharp images of the show characters. Hubley's double holster set, almost identical to the set they marketed with Overland Trail guns for that show's character, "Flip," came with Hubley Marshal guns. The holsters are well tooled, with horse head and floral patterns in tan and black details.

The only known Laramie cap pistols—the Leslie-Henry large model and the Halco smaller version. Both models are seldom seen.

The smaller Laramie gun was also marketed by Toy Shop Merchandising of New York, in a rich brown, single leather holster. This sports a metal saddle, which is identical to the logo of the Black Saddle holster series and is mounted on the pocket of the smaller holster. Well made with studs stamped "WB" with white details, sections, and white fringe, this nifty holster also came with an inch-wide leather belt and small buckle.

Laramie was so popular in Great Britain that a considerable amount of products, toys, books, and games marked with the show name were marketed there. Dell Comics also put out a *Laramie* comic book in 1962, which carried the Revue Productions markings, the company that produced the show for NBC.

DELL 15¢
LARAMIE
MAY-JULY

A half million dollars is taken from a strongbox and Slim and Jess are accused of the robbery!

Dell Comics issue for **Laramie** *in 1962.*

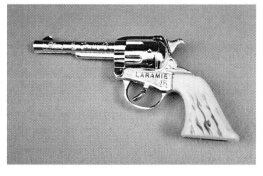

A previously unknown and very rare Laramie Jr. cap shooter made by Kilgore. This cap pistol is the same size as Kilgore's Pinto with a nickel-chrome finish and stag grip. No doubt that Kilgore tried to market this cap pistol with the success of TV's Laramie. It was believed that only Leslie-Henry previously made the Laramie cap pistols.

LAREDO

Here's another popular TV western that highlighted the adventures of the Texas Rangers. This western, however, was a combination of action, drama, adventure, and even comedy. *Laredo* premiered on NBC-TV in September 1965, and as such, was what we call a "late-comer" western. Yet, it became popular very quickly, hitting the Top 40 in its first season.

The series was set in Laredo, Texas, the headquarters of Company B of the Texas Rangers. The time period for this series (as opposed to *Tales of the Texas Rangers*) was post-Civil War, and was set away from Ranger headquarters in Austin (as in *Trackdown*). The senior officer of this company, Captain Parmalee, was played by veteran actor Philip Carey. Few people that I asked ever recalled his first TV series, *77th Bengal Lancers*. Cast as the dedicated but grim-faced Captain Parmalee, Carey remained firm, but didn't approve of the antics and lack of discipline of his Rangers, yet he knew they would never let him down.

"Reese Bennett," a former Civil War Union officer who joins the Rangers, was played by veteran actor Neville Brand. By far, he was the butt of many jokes from the younger Rangers, as he was the aging Ranger who was gruff, and rough around the edges of his poker-faced, scowling character. Brand had previously found fame when cast as gangster Al Capone in the series *The Untouchables*, with Robert Stack. The first two Rangers were later joined by a third in the second season.

The cast of **Laredo,** *left to right, Neville Brand ("Reese Bennett"), Will Smith ("Joe Riley"), sitting Philip Carey ("Captain Parmalee"), and Peter Brown ("Chad Cooper").*

Peter Brown, who starred with John Russell in "Lawman," another very popular western, was cast as Ranger "Chad Cooper." As with the real life reasons and varying backgrounds that brought men to join the Texas Rangers, Cooper's background was that of a former Border Patrol officer who joined the Rangers hoping to find the gunrunners who were responsible for the death of his comrades at the hands of warring Mexicans. Ranger "Joe Riley" was played by Will Smith, a young, handsome Errol Flynn lookalike, without a moustache, who joined the Rangers because of a questionable past as a gunfighter.

The third Ranger was "Erik Hunter," who was a dandy of a character, played by Robert Wolders, a relative newcomer to TV westerns. Between the antics and dedication to "get the job done," these Texas Rangers dispatched from Laredo were a big hit, and the show ran for a solid two years, airing 50 episodes, and leaving the network during September 1967. The show was a one-hour program cast in color. Gold Key issued one comic featuring *Laredo*.

Above: Neville Brand, the "old Ranger Bennett" and Peter Brown, the "young Ranger Cooper," lacked discipline, but were loyal to each other. Note the reclining nude on the gun butt of Peter Brown's butt first, left-side cross draw.

Right: Kilgore Laredo, silver finish with plastic stag grips.

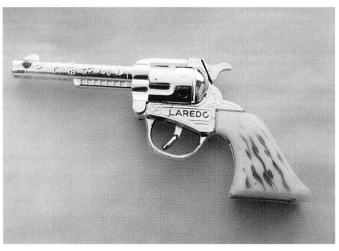

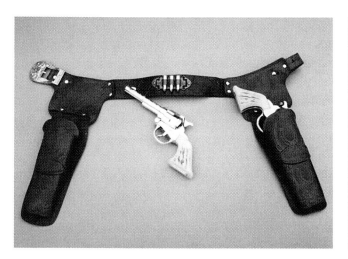

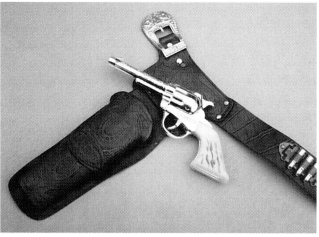

Laredo double holster set with Kilgore Laredo guns. Note that the holster pockets are designed to accept the guns in regular fashion, or butt-first cross-draw style.

Close-up of details showing the deep, rich tooling of the holster, "Laredo" across the holster pocket straps, and the alligator skin-style of the two-tone leather.

Neville Brand, who like Audie Murphy, was another of America's real heroes in World War II, was a veteran in movies, television, and Off-Broadway plays. He passed away in 1992. Philip Carey went on to play in the long-running soap opera *One Life To Live*. Peter Brown, also of *Lawman* fame, still does guest star roles on TV, and has his own Gunslinger Productions. Will Smith went on to star in another TV series, *Wildside*, and later still, on *Hawaii Five-O*. Robert Wolders joined his long time companion and screen star, the late Audrey Hepburn, and after the run of *Laredo*, moved to Switzerland. He was with Hepburn when she died.

CAP GUN COLLECTIBLES

The Laredo cap pistol was made only by Kilgore. It is a 7-inch die cast with a nickel chrome finish. It breaks open from the top, and comes with off-white colored grips, with brown stag. The barrel has the branding iron markings and the Circle "K" logo. The left side of the frame has "Laredo" in raised letters in stamp form. The right side has the Circle "K" Kilgore logo again, and scrollwork. The Laredo is similar to, but slightly larger than, the Kilgore Pinto, and has the same one piece stag grip as the Kilgore Cheyenne. These came out during the show period, from 1965 on.

The Laredo double holster set came in rich brown leather, with an alligator skin-style belt and the underlay to the holster pockets. It appears to be a Halco or Esquire-made set due to the two horse heads that are exceptionally well-tooled into the leather on the upper portion of the two holster pockets on the belt. The holster pockets are also well tooled, with two horse shoes, one above and one below the center straps, on which is the title "Laredo" in deep tooling. The belt has loops for three bullets and it has the standard steer head oval-ended nickel buckle.

It is a rich-looking set, and except for the belt, it is identical to the double holster set made for *The Texan*. The holster set takes the Laredo guns perfectly. After the end of the *Laredo* TV western show, the Laredo guns, which were also sold separately on a card, were used in a variety of other holster sets, one of them being Tombstone Territory, and some of the Daisy series of holster sets. Both Daisy and Classy bought Kilgore guns after its merge when it became Harvell-Kilgore, and those boxes are marked as such. Kilgore went from Ohio to Tennessee, where these Harvell-Kilgore guns were made.

This fast-paced action and humorous western also put Laredo, Texas, back on the map. The guns and holsters worn by the five stars of this show were just as varied as the characters they played.

Gold Key Comics issue for **Laredo** *in 1966.*

LASSO 'EM BILL

Now here's a character cap gun that has stumped many collectors for many years. Just like the other early cast iron character guns like Buffalo Bill, Billy the Kid, Kit Carson, and other well-known characters—both "real" and "reel"—the Lasso 'em Bill came out in September 1930. The early models were all made by Kenton. The variations came in many sizes, single shots, finishes and revolving cylinders, with and without jewels and fancy grips.

But just who was "Lasso 'em Bill?" If that isn't enough to make you scratch your head, the George Schmidt Company of Los Angeles continued the Lasso 'em Bill into the die-cast variety, coming out with the "Lasso 'em Bill" in the early 1950s. Bill who? And "lasso what?" And what's "'em?" Horses? Steers?

Just who this character was remains in debate among both cast-iron and die-cast collectors. The first report of this character was that he was a champion lasso artist with the Miller brothers' "101 Ranch" at the turn of the century. But Bill "who?" Another speculation was that "Bill" was a lariat expert "nonpareil" with the "Texas Jack Wild West Show," which featured none other than Will Rogers, America's most famous humorist, actor, writer, and champion roping artist. Just when we had this clinched, my research turns up the fact that Will Rogers joined the "Texas Jack Wild West Show" in 1902 and was billed as "The Cherokee Kid" (who, ironically, had been a real outlaw in the Old West). Not to be daunted, I pushed on with my exhaustive research trying to identify "Lasso 'em Bill."

The boxes and advertisements for the "Lasso 'em Bill" guns, holsters, wrist cuffs, and spurs show a youngster with chaps, bandana, a big cowboy hat—and he's roping a little dog. The hawking line reads "Keep 'em Happy, Healthy and Bizzy"—sure sounds like something the wonderful humorist Will Rogers would utter, in his common-sense approach. But, that wasn't enough. Two other characters, both real, were suggested. So the next speculation was William S. Hart, the real, old-time silent movie cowboy actor. The third character suggested was also real. He was "Broncho Billy" Anderson. But who was he? Was he a rodeo star? A mustang-taming cowboy with a circus or rodeo? Let's examine the three characters.

William S. Hart, also called "Two Gun Bill" by some admirers. One of the first silent screen cowboys. (Courtesy of Old West Shop)

WHO WAS THE REAL "LASSO 'EM BILL?"

William S. Hart, born in New York in 1870, was an actor, writer, and lastly, a director. He made his name in the stage production of *Ben-Hur* in 1900. He turned to motion pictures in 1914, and soon became a leading silent western movie star. With his gritty garb, rugged look, and his rarely smiling, but always frowning face, Hart worked in over 50 films between 1914 and 1925, when he did one of his most famous movies, *Tumbleweed.*

Hart was hard and overpowering, and with his two guns blasting away in a cloud of smoke, was lacking in grace, romance, agility, or warmth. But, he played the "good bad guy" as they say in Hollywood, the kind of guy you love or hate. The point, though, is that he was never associated with a lasso, trick roping, or lariat work in any of his films. He was not even an amateur lasso artist!

After I spent a lot of time plodding through several sources, I found that William S. Hart was in Miller's 101 Ranch, but disguised as an Indian! In fact, he relates the story in his autobiography. Offering a bet that he could get away disguised as an Indian, ride with them ("bareback" he quipped), speak their language and do all the stunts they do, the bet was on. *The Chicago Journal* in 1908 offered a fifty dollar prize to anyone who could pick out the white man among the sixty Indians.

A young boy won the prize—he figured out the man with blue eyes was the white man (our man Hart), since all Indians have dark eyes. That was the end of that deal, but in either case, Hart was never referred to as "Bill," nor did he do anything with a lasso, and none of his movies have "Bill" in the title. William S. Hart, who paved the way for the next batch of cowboy stars—Tom Mix, Buck Jones, Hoot Gibson, and others, died in 1946. Folks, I'll be glad to be hog-tied with a lasso if the Lasso 'em Bill cap pistol was made with Hart in mind. But you decide. Next. . . .

"Broncho Billy" Anderson took some time to identify. That's because he was not even a rodeo star, knew nothing about the West, and invented the name himself. His real name was Gilbert M. Anderson, born in Arkansas in 1883. He began in vaudeville, and later became a stage actor. In 1903, he starred in *The Great Train Robbery,* and by 1907, started his own production company, called Essanay Film Company. He wrote, acted and directed almost 380 one-reelers. In 1908, he invented the name and the character of "Broncho Billy," and directed himself in the first of a serial character who was a hero that never married, and never died.

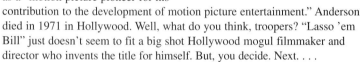

The series lacked realism, and his character was the leading role in every one-reeler. He saturated the market with these westerns, so much so that the public was tiring of them, until William S. Hart came on the scene with his own image and realistic westerns. Anderson continued to direct films, with Charlie Chaplin in *The Champion* in 1916, later with Stan Laurel (of Laurel and Hardy) in a series of two-reelers until 1920, when he retired after disagreements with studios. By 1950, he was still in Hollywood (he was also known as "Max Aaronson") running Progressive Pictures, and, in 1951, he was presented with an honorary Oscar as a "motion picture pioneer for his contribution to the development of motion picture entertainment." Anderson died in 1971 in Hollywood. Well, what do you think, troopers? "Lasso 'em Bill" just doesn't seem to fit a big shot Hollywood mogul filmmaker and director who invents the title for himself. But, you decide. Next. . . .

Above: Boxed Keyston Lasso 'em Bill double holsters and guns.

Left: Boxed Keyston Lasso 'em Bill wrist cuffs.

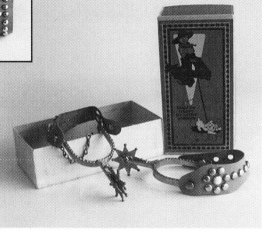

Boxed Keyston Lasso 'em Bill spurs. Note the saying, "Keep them Healthy, Happy and Bizzy" with the boy lassoing his dog. (Courtesy of Bill Longstreet)

So, I got to thinking that many characters took on stage names. We know that actors, old vaudeville acts, Wild West shows, circuses, and exhibits had a lot of men, women, even Indians that used various names. None used the real name of the real person, male or female. Annie Oakley is a perfect example as we have seen—"Little Miss Sure Shot" and "Little Missy." And "Colonel" Ned Buntline was not a colonel at all, and Ned Buntline wasn't even his real name.

In those days, long before movies, television, and instant communication, pretty much anything went, and the key was to sell tickets and get the public in to see the acts and the performers. So real cowboys, fake Indians, honorary "colonels" and even freaks were in vogue. But what kept bringing me back to Will Rogers? There had to be something to inspire the early, heavy, bulky cast-iron cap pistols.

Born William Penn Adair Rogers November 4, 1879, near Oologah, Indian Territory, Will grew up on his father's ranch in Oklahoma, where he taught himself rope twirling and lassoing. He took part as a rope-throwing cowboy in steer-roping contests and soon, his incredible feats with the lasso convinced him to hit the road with the Wild West shows that were the popular entertainment of the time.

While Will Rogers did his lariat acts in Australia, he was billed as "the Mexican Rope Artist," complete with fancy red velvet outfits. When Will Rogers debuted at New York's Madison Square Garden in 1905, he was referred to in *The Herald* as "The Indian Will Rogers." Will continued his unbelievable lasso, lariat and roping tricks even as he went into vaudeville acts and then the movies. Rogers would get up early and practice his rope tricks, which he invented and perfected himself; he wasn't taught by anyone.

In his first silent movie, *The Roping Fool,* Will did 53 roping tricks that some said defied the imagination. Billed as "The Greatest Catch in Vaudeville," Will Rogers was called the "Lariat Expert" using ropes from 7 feet to 90 feet! Roping horse and rider! Figure eights! Three Rope catch! Throwing two ropes at once, and then a finale, where he even ropes a mouse with a "string lasso." Rogers even named his rope tricks, which he used constantly to keep himself in shape. Ever the humorist, Will would say "Swinging a rope is all right when your neck ain't in it; then it's hell." He absolutely dazzled his audiences from South Africa to

Europe, and all over the United States. He also performed in Canada and South America. When he married his great love, Betty Blake, he quipped "The day I roped Betty, I did the star performance of my life."

As "The Cherokee Kid" in the Texas Jack Show, Will didn't just do rope tricks, he also rode bucking broncos and did scenes in various acts where he portrayed himself as an Indian, and a Negro, and he danced and sang songs of the time. On the program, he was billed as "The Man Who Can Lasso the Tail off a Blowfly." His calling card read "Fancy Lasso Artist and Rough Rider." When he left the Texas Jack Wild West Circus to head to Australia on his own, Jack gave Will the following recommendation, that read, in part, "I consider him (Mr. W.P. Rogers, The Cherokee Kid) to be the champion trick rough rider and lasso thrower of the world."

A few more tidbits of the suggestion of Will Rogers as the idea for the "Lasso 'em Bill." One of his first talking movie roles was *Laughing Bill Hyde,* which came out in 1918 to great reviews by *The New York Times.* When his wife was about to give birth to their first child, in a letter to Will's father, she states that "Billy wants a boy," and that if it is a boy, she will "name it after Billy." Will Rogers, Jr., was born October 20, 1911. Ironically, cast iron, long-barreled cap pistols exist in models called Texas Jack, 101 Ranch, and remarkably, Little Billy. I may be all wet, as Will Rogers would have said, but I think I'm on to something.

Will Rogers went on to make several movies, write a column (with his indomitable humor and wit), and write several books. He was a man of common sense, great faith, and intelligence. The country went into deep mourning when on August 15, 1935, Will Rogers and pilot Wiley Post, two great Oklahoma natives, died in a plane crash in Alaska. Some twenty years later, his son, Will Rogers, Jr., starred in the Warner Brothers movie *The Story of Will Rogers,* along with Jane Wyman (the first Mrs. Ronald Reagan). It was an outstanding cinema biography of one of the most popular Americans of this century—the immortal homespun humorist and philosopher—Will Rogers. Today, the Will Rogers Memorial at Claremore, Oklahoma, greets thousands of admirers from all over the country.

Well, what do you think, pardners? Is it "Bronco Billy" Anderson? William "Two Gun" Hart? Another Buffalo "Bill" perhaps? Oh, no, not another "Billy the Kid?" And how do we explain "101 Ranch, Texas Jack and Little Bill?" Shucks, I'm laying all my damn gambling chips on the lasso champion of the world—then and now—Will Rogers, known to us cap pistol buckaroos as none other than "Lasso 'em Bill."

Now that all the "evidence" is before you, let the readers decide!

Will Rogers, one of America's greatest humorists, the world's champion lasso artist in his "Cherokee Bill" costume. Was he "Lasso 'em Bill"? Note his butt-first cross-draw gun on his left side. (C.W. Campbell, Dillon Press)

CAP GUN COLLECTIBLES

The Schmidt "Lasso 'em Bill" die-cast cap gun is a 10-inch, all-metal cap repeater. It is made of polished nickel, with white painted simulated-stag metal grips. The lever to break open the gun for cap loading is on the left side, below the hammer, and the gun breaks from the top. There is also a chrome-finish and a dull gray-finish model. "Lasso 'em Bill" is raised on both sides of the frame in cursive, and the initials "LB" are prominently located on the grips on both sides. This gun is riveted, and the grips are riveted and peened, thus it is not an easy gun to take apart and interchange parts. Several varieties of "Lasso 'em Bill" holster sets were made by Keystone Brothers, some complete with wrist cuffs and spurs. The colorful red boxes show fine details of the little cowboy lassoing a little dog. Only Schmidt made the die cast "Lasso 'em Bill." The prior cast iron models were made by Kenton. The holster sets used a variety of generic guns.

Schmidt Lasso 'em Bill" cap shooter with white painted stag grips. Note "LB" on the grips. Grips are die-cast metal. Also note the "Lasso 'em Bill" signature raised on the gun frame and details of the stag grips and logo.

JUDGE ROY BEAN
LAW WEST OF THE PECOS

Here was another wonderful and early TV western that few people remember. *The Law West of the Pecos*—that being west of the Pecos River in Texas—chronicled the life of Judge Roy Bean, a self-proclaimed stalwart judge who reigned supreme in the town of Langtry, Texas, from the 1870s to the early 1900s. Named by Judge Bean, Langtry, Texas, remains to this day.

Judge Roy Bean came to television in September 1955 and ran for 39 half-hour, black & white episodes. It ran until September 1956. Cast as the stoical judge was the great character actor Edgar Buchanan, who starred in hundreds of westerns in the 1930s and 1940s, and in his own series in 1955 as "Judge Roy Bean." Buchanan, a grizzly, bearded, and raspy-voiced actor, had also co-starred in the first few *Hopalong Cassidy* episodes with William Boyd, in the role of "Red Connors." Buchanan was chosen to play Judge Roy Bean by the already well-known western star Russell Hayden, who had also starred in the *Hopalong Cassidy* series as "Lucky."

By the time *Judge Roy Bean* came to television, Russell Hayden had starred in two of his own TV western series, *Marshal of Gunsight Pass* and *Cowboy G-Men,* both of which were short lived and relatively forgotten. As executive producer of *Judge Roy Bean,* Hayden decided to give the role to Buchanan. Edgar Buchanan not only resembled the real Judge Bean, he played the part with great eloquence. Rounding out the series was another well-known film star, Jack Beutel, who played the Judge's deputy. Jackie Loughery, a former beauty queen, also starred as Judge Roy Bean's niece on the show.

Character actor Edgar Buchanan starred in dozens of westerns and literally hundreds of TV shows after the demise of *Judge Roy Bean.* Like many western character actors such as Slim Pickens, Jack Elam, Denver Pyle, and others, he had an instantly-recognizable face. Whether he played an ornery character or a non-nonsense judge, he was just great. After *Judge Roy Bean*, he went on to star in *Petticoat Junction,* a set-in-the-South comedy series which did quite well.

Edgar Buchanan passed away in 1981. Russell Hayden and Jack Beutel have also passed on. *Judge Roy Bean* was a wonderful effort that related the adventures of a no-nonsense, tough judge in the real Old West. Perhaps it came to TV too soon, for one can only imagine the endless run of great courtroom drama with His Honor holding court on the porch of his saloon!

THE REAL ROY BEAN

The real "Judge" Roy Bean, who was not really a "judge," was born in Mason County, Kentucky, in 1825. He initially went to Mexico as a goods trader, stayed a spell, and by 1848, moved to San Diego, where his brother, Josh Bean, was living at the time. It was said he had shot a Mexican between the eyes, so when he opened a saloon in San Gabriel, his reputation followed him. Arrested in 1852 for fighting a duel and killing his opponent, he was found not guilty. He got a taste of the courtroom real soon.

He and his brother served as California Rangers for a time, and when Josh Bean was killed, the future judge left for New Mexico, where another brother, Sam Bean, lived. It was said that he joined the Confederates in New Mexico as an irregular, and after the war, moved on to San Antonio, Texas. For the next 15 years, Bean worked as a butcher, dairy farm operator, freight operator, railroad worker, goods trader, and saloon keeper. He built up quite a business, and a reputation to match, and his section of San Antonio became known as "Beanville," and he was proud of it.

When the railroads began to push towards the Pecos River, Bean, always scheming for a quick way to make money, started a freight business in the town of Vinegaroon, Texas, on the west side of the Pecos River. He did well, and in 1872, he opened the Eagle's Nest Saloon. In 1882, a captain in the Texas Rangers requested that Bean be appointed Justice of the Peace, which the County Commissioner did on August 2, 1882. From then on, the rotund, bearded man with a pair of guns on his hips, became not only the Justice of the Peace, but also Postmaster, Notary Public, Coroner, Mayor, and "Judge"—and still, he was always a saloon keeper.

The real Judge Roy Bean, the "Law West of The Pecos," as he usually looked and dressed. No robes, no nonsense, little mercy, plenty of justice. (Courtesy of Western History Collection, University of Oklahoma)

Edgar Buchanan, who starred as TV's "Judge Roy Bean." Not a bad choice for the role of the good judge. (Courtesy of Old West Shop)

Left: Judge Roy Bean, center, wearing holstered six-gun and sombrero, holding court in Langtry, Texas, trying a horse thief. The building was his courthouse and saloon. Note the sign "Law West of The Pecos." (Courtesy of Western History Collection, University of Oklahoma)

The Law West of The Pecos six-gun, left side, issued to commemorate the 100-year anniversary of the statehood of Texas.

Close-up of the details on the right side of the gun frame commemorating the Texas Centennial, 1936. (Courtesy of Bob Williamson)

The Law West of The Pecos Texas Centennial all-metal gun in its originally issued holster, also ink stamped "Texas Centennial 1st '36." (Courtesy of Terry Graham and Bob Williamson)

It was said that when a railroad crew rode up to his saloon, Bean greeted them by saying "cold beer is a dollar a bottle." The men replied, "we just want to get some water"—to which the shrewd Bean replied, "That's a dollar a bottle as well, and only in cash!" They paid up. Bean sold everything to the railroads—lumber, tents, horses, nails, lard, bacon, hams, tobacco, flour, even shoes and dress goods. He soon made deals—you bought his merchandise, you got the water for free. Beer was still a buck a bottle, and that was over 100 years ago!

Roy Bean wasn't afraid to use his six-guns and he dropped a few rowdies who tried to rob him. A lot of crooks, desperadoes, murderers, horse thieves and other assorted malcontents hit Texas after the Civil War. They could make a fast living if they wanted to—hunting, trapping, robbing Mexicans, cattle-rustling, and playing hide-and-seek with sheriffs and other lawmen of the time. But when they got to Vinegaroon, which Roy Bean literally "ran," they ran into a formidable opponent. Judge Roy Bean had a sense of humor, but he also dispensed his "Law West of the Pecos" with a crude gavel, his six-guns, and a posse of men. He kept a pet bear and a huge log outside his saloon and a petty criminal who was sentenced to "jail time" would be chained to the log, in the open air, to the elements, for as long as 30 days.

Stealing horses and cattle was the major crime in the area and Judge Roy Bean took it upon himself to hand out justice at his Court—arraignment, trial, sentence, and execution, usually within two hours. His deputies did the hanging and if things got out of hand, the judge himself would pull out his own six guns and blast the hapless soul into eternity. Judge Roy Bean WAS the "Law West of the Pecos," and nobody challenged him. People were either happy that he cleaned up the area, or they were afraid to go up against him. A candidate that once ran against him was hauled into "Bean's Justice Court," where the judge promptly charged him with a felony, tried him, convicted him, and sentenced him to exile in Mexico; the man left quickly!

Roy Bean saw a photograph of the beautiful British actress Lillie Langtry and fell in love, some say madly in love. He renamed his saloon "The Jersey Lily," but His Honor didn't let it go at that; he wrote a letter to the postmaster general in Washington, advising him that he was now going to rename the town of Vinegaroon as "Langtry," and the government and the rest of the country better take notice. Langtry, Texas, with its "Judge" Roy Bean became famous. Judge Roy Bean even wrote love letters to the famous actress, who was touring back East.

The Judge kept holding court on his saloon porch and posed for many photos. He married a Mexican lady named Virginia Chavez who bore him several children, but it was said that the woman who stole his heart was Lillie Langtry. Judge Roy Bean died at his saloon in Langtry, Texas, on March 16, 1903. It was the passing of an era, for even the powers at the capitol in Austin didn't mess with "His Honor," for his reputation for fast justice became legendary even then.

CAP GUN COLLECTIBLES

I gave a lot of thought as to whether I should include the gun that bears witness to the legacy of both Judge Roy Bean, and "Law West of the Pecos," because it was a cast iron rather than a die cast toy gun—and because it came out before the TV show that bears his name. The gun is quite rare and sought after by several categories of collectors, so I decided to include this unique piece.

The great state of Texas did not forget Judge Roy Bean and his "Law West of the Pecos," and in 1936, on the 100th anniversary of statehood, made a big deal out of "His Honor." One of the toy gun companies of the time issued a cast-iron, but hollow, riveted toy gun in Judge Roy Bean's honor and labeled it "The Law West of the Pecos." The gun is 11-inches overall, with a 4-inch barrel. The all-metal, nickel-plated gun has the star logo on the grips, which are cross-hatch checkered. The gun is an excellent copy of the Colt Peacemaker .45. The barrel is hollow, as are the cylinders. Being hollow, the gun is relatively light for a cast iron piece. The gun cannot be fired; it is totally non-functional with regards to the hammer, trigger, or cylinder. The left side of the frame has "The Law West of the Pecos" in raised lettering. The right side of the frame has "Texas Centennial 1936," also raised, under the cylinder. No other markings appear on this unique, large toy gun.

A brown, well-tooled heavy leather holster with six studs instead of stitching and a herringbone pattern, came with this gun. The holster has two slits at the top which allows this holster simply to slide onto an existing belt. As with many hand-lettered and hand-marked pieces of the time, this holster is hand lettered with "Texas Centennial—1st '36'." Both pieces are quite rare and seldom seen. It has a great appeal to several categories of collectors—cast iron, die cast, western aficionados, and TV western characters—it's all there!

LAWMAN

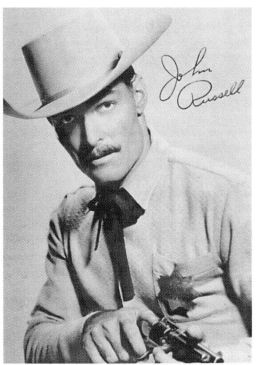

John Russell as "Marshal Dan Troop" of Lawman. *Just his rock-hard jaw and steel-eyed look was enough!*

O f all the western programs, *Lawman* was the one that was the absolute no-nonsense, straight forward series that took its title seriously. "Lawman" meant this man was there to uphold the law and Marshal "Dan Troop," played with iron-will intensity by John Russell, did just that. This character was not about cracking jokes around a bunch of people at the end of the show, ending with everybody laughing. This show was not about the lawman making a speech. This show was not about showing leniency or helping out the bad guy down on his luck and needing a bit of tender loving care to help his "self-esteem." *Lawman* was a show about serious business—enforcing the law.

Lawman came to TV on October 5, 1958, and ran for four solid years. It was an action-packed half-hour. The setting for Marshal Troop and his deputy, "Johnny McKay," played by handsome Peter Brown, was Laramie, Wyoming. If you made the costly mistake of breaking the law in Laramie, Marshal Troop was going to hunt you down, give you no quarter, and you were going to get justice—dead or alive. Marshal Troop—even the name is strong, tenacious, and bold—rarely smiled. He calculated every move and did his job—upheld the law. No nonsense and no second chances. Deputy McKay might hesitate, Marshal Troop didn't even flinch.

Clean cut and in top physical shape, with a neatly trimmed moustache and a silvertip across the hair, veteran actor John Russell was so tough, even four years of some of the most beautiful women didn't break him down. Peter Brown, as his trusted "Deputy McKay" had the eye for the ladies and a short fuse, but not Russell. When beautiful actress Peggie Castle was brought into the series as "Lilly Merrill," the owner of the Birdcage Saloon, even she didn't shake up the Marshal. I dont know about you readers, but in my mind's eye and ear memory bank, I can still hear Marshal Troop when he is brought to Laramie after the previous Marshal is killed. This was the first episode that introduced both Dan Troop as the new marshal and his eventually hiring McKay as his trusted deputy. It went like this:

He'd made his reputation in Abilene, Kansas, and the town fathers convinced him to come up to tame Laramie, where "our wives and kids can't walk the streets." After Troop takes the job, he is on the hunt for a deputy at $50 a month to help him out. There are no takers. In the local saloon, the local tough guy says to the new Marshal, "Hey, wait a minute, mister. I'm not finished talking to you. Do you know who I am?"

The new marshal replies in a crunch-of-nails-dead-serious, "Yep, I know who you are. I've never walked into a town where I didn't have to whip somebody who thought he was real tough, and you're him!" With that, Troop throws him a fast hook to the jaw that quickly rearranges the man's face and his attitude. By the end of that first episode, the young man who takes the new deputy's job is "Johnny McKay," played with initial naivety by Peter Brown. Soon, however, he learns from the master of temperament and experience.

In one scene where the young McKay questions the guilt or innocence of the man they just arrested, Marshal Troop shouts back, "You and I are the arresting officers, not a thing more! What we think about a man's guilt or innocence has nothing to do with it! We help gather evidence for or against, then we are out of it! We don't play judge, jury, or executioner! And, if you ever forget it, you get yourself another job!" Deputy McKay smartened up real quick!

Above: Peter Brown as "Deputy Johnny McKay." He learned from the disciplined Marshal Dan Troop and became a "Lawman" himself!

Left: Leslie-Henry/Halco's Marshal was the 10-1/2-inch model with revolving cylinder and cameo grips. This will also fit the Lawman holster sets. The same model was used for the Marshal 6-7 Shooter.

Hubley's Marshal nickel-plated cap pistol with stag grips which came in the Lawman holster sets.

The Lawman double holster set with Hubley Marshal guns. Note the unusually larger nickel rectangular buckle on this set.

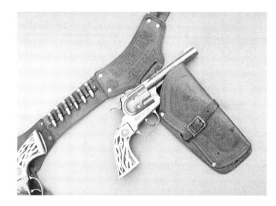

Close-up of details on the holster show both "Lawman" and "Marshal Dan Troop," the charac-ter on the show. The gun is the Hubley model.

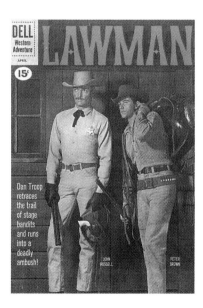

One of several Dell Comics issued for **Lawman.** *Note the great physique of* **John Russell.**

Marshal Troop was calm, mature, experienced, just what a lawman should be. He didn't hesitate when it came time to draw his six gun, empty his double barreled shotgun, or re-arrange the criminal's looks who challenged his authority. Troop's job was to make sure they didn't make "more trouble" once they tested his interpretation of the law. The audience loved it and the show garnered a lot of respect in western programming. Along with the top seven—*Cheyenne, Maverick, Wagon Train, Have Gun-Will Travel, Gunsmoke, Wyatt Earp*, and *The Rifleman*—the *Lawman* series won great reviews and had a strong following from 1958, to October 1962, when it left ABC Television.

In its four-year run, the show added the above-mentioned Peggie Castle, followed by character actor Dan Sheridan in the role of "Jake," her handyman at the saloon. Bek Nelson was brought on as "Dru Lemp," the owner of the Blue Bonnet Cafe. *The Laramie Weekly* was added for the free speech phase of the show, and Barbara Lang, a pretty character actress was cast as "Julie Tate," the firebrand editor of the paper. These great characters rounded out an already fine show.

John Russell went on to acting in several films and guest starring on other television shows after the run of *Lawman*. John Russell, the steel-jawed actor, sadly, passed away in 1991 at the age of 70. Dan Sheridan passed away at the young age of 46 in 1963. Peggie Castle also passed away at the young age of 46 in 1973. Peter Brown went on to star in *Laredo*, and he is still with us, having his own production company.

CAP GUN COLLECTIBLES

No cap pistols marked "Lawman" or "Dan Troop" or even "Johnny McKay" have ever surfaced, even though this program had a healthy four-year run. It's one of those unexplainable facts on what cap guns were made and why. However, Hubley did make the *Marshal* series and a set of double holsters were made for Lawman, which came with the Marshal cap pistols. The Marshal was a 9-inch repeater, with the side gate for cap loading on the left side of the cylinder. Nickel plated, it came with both white and brown stag grips, and also with the steerhead grips. The star logo of Hubley is on the grips and "Hubley" and Made in USA" can be found on the ejection rod under the barrel. "Marshal" is raised on both sides of the frame, which also has extensive scrollwork. This earlier model is the Hubley, and is not to be confused with the Halco model, which resembled this Hubley.

The Lawman holster rig is a double set, in rich brown quality leather. It is in the gunfighter style and it is well tooled. On the belt portion, above both sides of the holster pockets, is both the show title, "Lawman," and below is "Marshal Dan Troop." The holsters are well tooled, with floral work and the buckled straps across the front of the pockets. The belt has six bullets and a very wide scrolled nickel buckle. Although other variations were no doubt manufactured, it is a rather scarce double holster set with both the show title and character name markings on the Lawman. Complete with two Hubley Marshal cap pistols, I'll guarantee no sidewinder is going to give you any lip!

Daisy came out with the Lawman lever gun in 1960 as part of its Spittin' Image series of "famous Winchester." The rifle was a noise and smoke shooter only. It had two-way cocking action, simulated wood stock and heavy gauge, blued, metal barrel. The rifle was 34 inches long and cost a whopping $5.95. On the advertisement was a photo of both Marshal Troop and his Deputy McKay, along with "as seen on *Lawman* on ABC-TV."

Lawman holster sets and the Lawman lever gun are seldom seen. The Hubley Marshal was used on other generic holsters sets, of course. Other products that were marketed under *Lawman* were boots and chaps, the usual lunch boxes and thermos bottles, Hartland figures and many promotional photos of both stars. The show was highlighted on *TV Guide, TV Western* magazine, and of course, Dell Comics. Dell Comics put out several issues of *Lawman* featuring great color graphic shots of both stars. The comics also included great pin-up photos of both Marshal Troop and Deputy McKay so that young lawmen could adorn their rooms. Much to my mother's dismay, I must confess that I didn't just tack up my photos of the two lawmen, I glued them to the wallpaper so I wouldn't make a hole in the photos. My father was not amused. *Lawman* was a great western!

THE LONE RANGER AND TONTO

"Who was that masked man?" The Lone Ranger, of course! One of America's most beloved fictional western heroes, "The Lone Ranger" came to life, ironically, after cheating death, in 1933. Working with a young writer named Fran Striker, Detroit radio station owner George Trendle created the new "champion of justice," based loosely, it was said at the time, on some real life exploits of the Texas Rangers in the 1870s. Hoping to appeal to adults as well as children, this strange character, wearing a mask—the main tool of bandits and thieves to hide their identity—was first broadcast from Radio Station WXYZ in Detroit on February 2, 1933. *The Lone Ranger* has never left our hearts, our imaginations, or our memories.

It so happened that as I was setting aside work and photos for this book, one of my nieces, a cute and inquisitive 6-year-old, seeing the "Lone Ranger's" photo, asked me why the man was wearing a mask. Before I could answer in a story-telling mode, she said, "Bad guys wear a mask! Is he a bad man?" Her mother, my kid sister, born in 1958, just as TV westerns were at the peak of popularity, said she "remembered" the Lone Ranger, but she too, asked, "Why did he wear a mask if he was a good cowboy?" It occurred to me that while many of us recall the Lone Ranger without hesitation, that we remember his faithful Indian companion, "Tonto," and "Silver," his white horse, few people remember or know the story of why the Lone Ranger is "the masked man."

His name was John Reid and he was one of the best—a Texas Ranger. It's the late 1870s. He and his brother, Dan Reid, a captain, and four other Rangers, are on the trail of the notorious "Butch Cavendish" and his "Hole-In-The-Wall Gang." As the six Rangers approach Bryant's Gap, the scout rides ahead to the canyon to make sure it is all clear. Since the scout is secretly working for Butch Cavendish, he rides back and informs Capt. Dan Reid that the area is all clear and safe. As the Rangers ride in, they are ambushed by Butch's gang, who shoots them all to "pieces." Thinking they are all dead, the gang rides off. None of the six Rangers are even moving, as the gunfire was deadly.

Later that day, Tonto, a Potawatomie Indian, is riding through the same valley, on his way to hunting grounds. He comes upon the six men and discovers that one of them is not dead, but seriously wounded. He turns out to be Ranger John Reid, the captain's younger brother. Tonto tends to Reid's wounds and nurses him back to health. As he regains consciousness, Reid seems to recall Tonto, an Indian he had befriended as a child. While a young warrior, Tonto's village was raided by renegade Indians who killed his family and left young Tonto for dead. It was none other than a young John Reid that finds Tonto and nurses him back to health. After Reid is well enough to speak and then ride, Tonto turns to Reid and calls him "Kemo Sabe," meaning "faithful friend" in his language, and they become friends for life.

Clayton Moore as "The Lone Ranger" and Jay Silverheels as "Tonto." The horses were "Silver" and "Scout."

Chief Thundercloud, the other "Tonto," and Lee Powell, the first screen "Lone Ranger," from the 1938 serial from Republic Pictures. Note his mask has a "screen" veil to the lower portion. Powell was killed in World War II in 1944. (Courtesy of A. Foreman)

Who are those masked men? The serial Lone Rangers, that's who! Lee Powell, Bruce Bennett, Layne Chandler, Hal Tagliaferro (also known as Wally Wales), and George Montgomery, circa 1938. Note the mask is more of a sinister black veil. (Courtesy of Old West Shop)

For millions of fans, young and old, Clayton Moore will always be "The Lone Ranger."

The task of burying the five Rangers and the brother that John Reid loved and looked up to is a sad task, indeed. In Bryant's Gap, on the western side of the wide canyon, is a small patch of grass. Reid and Tonto bury the five Rangers, putting up a cross for each one—Capt. John Reid, "Jim Bates," "Ben Cooper," "Jack Stacey," and "Joe Brent." John Reid then puts up a sixth cross. It bears his name. Reid then fashions a mask from his brother's black vest. Now he hides his identity, and with Tonto convincing Cavendish that all the Rangers are indeed dead, they conceal the fact that one Texas Ranger, John Reid, is alive and will avenge the death of the others. He is "The Lone Ranger."

Posing as an outlaw and taking on various disguises from time to time, The Lone Ranger eventually hunts down the entire Cavendish Gang, one by one until all are imprisoned or hanged. The various disguises that Reid uses to avoid suspicion are the Old Timer; Professor Horatio Tucker; Jose, the Mexican Bandit; and Don Pedro O'Sullivan, the "Swede." The Lone Ranger had now buried his past along with his brother and his companions. He had avenged them all and brought the killers to justice.

But his identity also died that day, and from then on, with only Tonto knowing his real identity, he was "The Lone Ranger" to us, and "Kemo Sabe" to Tonto. Bearing the trademark of a silver bullet, he constantly reminds himself that this precious metal must be used sparingly, and that the cost of human life is very high. And so The Lone Ranger and Tonto begin the lifelong devotion to law and order, cutting a path all across the West, "forcing the powers of darkness into the blinding light of justice."

The announcer begins: "A fiery horse with the speed of light, a cloud of dust and a hearty Hi-Yo Silver! The Lone Ranger! With his faithful Indian companion, Tonto, the daring and resourceful masked rider of the plains led the fight for law and order in the early West. Return with us now, to those thrilling days of yesteryear—The Lone Ranger Rides Again!" "Silver," the magnificent horse with the thundering hoofs, was found in "Wild Horse

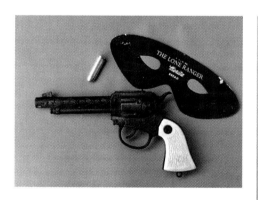

Above: Esquire's bronze model of the Lone Ranger cap shooter. This pattern has white simulated stag grips, lanyard ring, and lots of engraving. Note the mask put out by Merita Bread, and the silver bullet. (Courtesy of J. Schleyer)

Right: Here's a rare and early Lone Ranger and Tonto combination gun and knife set. The cap gun is by Kilgore; the knife is by Keyston; the long "silver bullets" are pens with graphics of the Lone Ranger, Tonto, and Silver; the holster, with colorful artwork of both Tonto and the Lone Ranger is by Feinburg-Henry. What a set! (Courtesy of John Bracken)

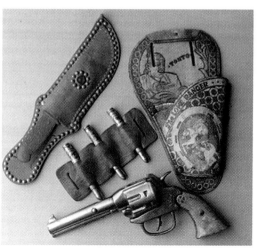

The Esquire Lone Ranger .32 nickle plated with copper floral grips, is not as common as its big brother. Note the Esquire pony logo on the grips.

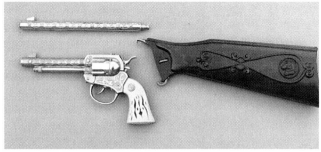

The Esquire Lone Ranger 4-in-1 rifle-gun combo. Seldom seen complete.

Esquire's three large models of the Lone Ranger cap pistol. Top is nickel plated large frame model with lanyard ring; center left is its bronze companion; bottom is the seldom-seen nickel model with stag grips for the 4-in-1 rifle. Note it has no lanyard ring on butt.

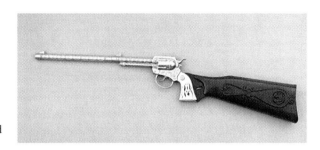

The Lone Ranger rifle-gun assembled which came to 30 inches in length!

Canyon," and the Lone Ranger made him almost human. Tonto's horse was named "Scout." Before long, the Lone Ranger, Silver, Tonto and Scout were household words. Rossini's *William Tell Overture* was picked for the unforgettable background.

And so the Lone Ranger and Tonto kept our imaginations going from 1933 to 1954, even as it came to television. The first radio "Lone Rangers" were Jack Deeds, George Seaton, Eric Graser, and finally Brace Beemer the best known of the radio Lone Rangers. Radio's "Tonto" was John Todd. This radio program ran for 21 years.

In 1938, a 15-chapter movie serial on the Lone Ranger was produced by Republic Pictures. The first screen *Lone Ranger* was Lee Powell, followed by Robert Livingston. "Chief Thundercloud" starred as "Tonto." Robert Livingston, the only "Lone Ranger" who was allowed to take off his mask (in the 1939 movie *The Lone Ranger Rides Again*) was eventually replaced by Clayton Moore in 1949, and briefly replaced by John Hart in 1952. Then the role went back to Clayton Moore, who went on to become the most famous and best-remembered Lone Ranger.

It is also interesting to note that the early Lone Ranger mask was more of a face mask, a face veil, if you will, giving actor Lee Powell an almost sinister look. By the 1940s, it had been cut down to expose the nose, and with Clayton Moore, it took on the final mask that sits in our memory bank—high on the cheeks, nose exposed, and at times, actually accenting Clayton Moore's wonderful smile. By the way, "Chief Thundercloud" was the screen name of actors Victor Daniels and Scott Williams, neither of which was a real Native American.

The Lone Ranger came to television on September 15, 1949, and along with Hoppy, Gene, and Roy, soon won over millions of youngsters across the country. The one thing that seemed to set *The Lone Ranger* apart, and the one gimmick that Trendle kept using to test

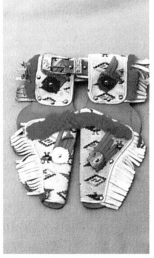

Above: This unique Tonto double holster set has an "RR" buckle! Note the brass Indian head conchos on the belt and holster pockets, as well as fringe and beadwork. (Courtesy of E. Cremese)

Left: Esquire's superb "Tonto" Indian Outfit which came in several styles with a number of accoutrements. (Courtesy of Bill Longstreet)

Tonto gunbelt with gold plated Stevens Big Chief cap shooter with Indian head grips. The Tonto quiver comes with rubber tipped arrows.

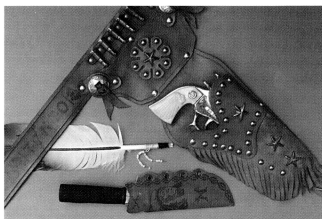

Variation Tonto gunbelt with knife and warrior's feather. The gun is a nickel-plated Stevens Big Chief. Super early set of top grain leather. (J. Schleyer Collection)

Esquire double holster Lone Ranger set with original box. Note the box has an illustration of the Lone Ranger and not a photo of any of the actors who played the part.

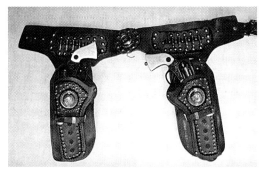

Close-up of the boxed Esquire set. What makes this unique is the light brown leather since most Lone Ranger sets came in black leather as he wore himself. The guns are Actoy bronze pattern cap shooters. (Courtesy of Brian Wolf)

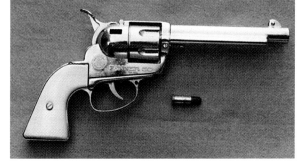

Mattel's Fanner 50 Model cap shooter with revolving cylinder and sleek white grips used for its Lone Ranger set, complete with the silver bullet.

the popularity of his audience, were the constant contents, premiums, and prizes being awarded to youngsters. If there was ever any question of how fast and strong *The Lone Ranger* caught on, Trendle's first award was to offer a free program to the first 300 kids who applied to the radio station. By May 1933, 25,000 letters poured into the station and Trendle knew his hero had won the hearts and minds of the kids. In July, Trendle announced that "The Lone Ranger" would visit the school grounds at Belle Isle. The result of that innocent announcement was the arrival of 70,000 youngsters, some with homemade masks, cowboy hats, and cast-iron cap pistols! Extra police had to be brought in to keep traffic moving and keep the crowds from going out of control.

Contests and premiums, coupons and give-away silver bullets helped spread the image and popularity of *The Lone Ranger.* One contest called for naming the Lone Ranger's new colt, for which more then 220,500 responses came in. Between 1941 and 1952, seven Lone Ranger contests were held, and even a contest about "Know Your America" in April 1952, garnered 132,250 responses.

Clayton Moore, who was to become the "Lone Ranger" in much the same way that William Boyd became "Hopalong Cassidy," was born in 1914. He played character parts in the 1930s and early 1940s, but a part in the 1942 Republic Pictures *Perils of Nyoka* gave him his stepping stone to western movies with Gene Autry, Roy Rogers, and Charles Starrett (*The Durango Kid*). When George Trendle saw Moore as "Zorro" in the 1949 *The Ghost of Zorro,* he found the man he wanted to cast as the Lone Ranger. It was the best choice the astute man ever made.

Clayton Moore fit the role like a glove. He was an honest, sincere, and soft-spoken man who just oozed trust and faithfulness. While other stars may have felt type cast, Clayton Moore still relishes his role as the Lone Ranger and the positive influence he had on millions of youngsters. Initially, Moore's contract forbid him to appear in public without the mask and Moore couldn't have been happier. In 1954, the Wrather Corporation bought the rights to the "Lone Ranger" character from Trendle, and Moore continued in the role. As the Lone Ranger, Clayton Moore was actually loved, and just as William Boyd became Hoppy, so Clayton Moore became the Lone Ranger.

The best-known and equally-loved "Tonto" was played with great appeal by Jay Silverheels, who was a full-blooded Mohawk. Born in 1919 on the Six Nations Reservation in Ontario, Canada, Jay was a former wrestling and boxing champion and a member of the Canadian lacrosse team, when he came to the United States in 1938. A handsome man with a rich voice, his famous line was, "Um, what you do now, Kemo Sabe?" Silverheels first did several supporting roles, but he gained wide acclaim for his role as "Geronimo" in *Broken Arrow* in 1950, and reprising the same role in *Walk the Proud Land* in 1956. In the spring of 1949, he too, was picked to play Tonto personally by George Trendle. Moore and Silverheels had incredible chemistry together as the Lone Ranger and Tonto. In real life, they remained close and loyal friends.

Two Lone Ranger movies were produced starring Clayton Moore and Jay Silverheels, first in 1956, and again in 1958. The syndicated TV series of *The Lone Ranger* continued its run until September 12, 1957—a total of 221 thrilling episodes. *The Lone Ranger* was shown all over the world, and nowhere was it more popular than in Italy.

The Lone Ranger came back to TV as a cartoon series in 1966 and ran three years. The voice of the Lone Ranger was Michael Rye; for Tonto it was Sheperd Menkin. It returned in 1980 in another cartoon series, running alongside another old time favorite, "Tarzan," which ran to 1982. In 1981, Wrather Productions released the movie *The Legend of The Lone Ranger*, starring Klinton Spilsbury as the masked man and Michael Horse as Tonto. I took my 10-year-old son to see the movie. He loved it, but I didn't care for it, and from all that I read about it at the time, it was a "bomb."

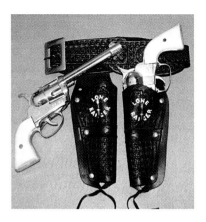

Mattel Lone Ranger double holster set in Dura-Hide. Note the silver bullet in the special loop on the holster pockets. (Courtesy of Terry Graham)

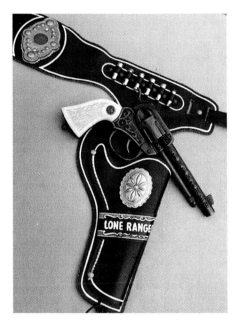

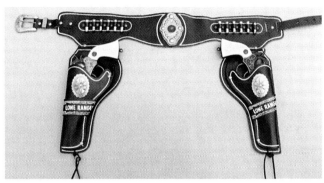

Above: Superb Esquire Lone Ranger double holster set with bronze guns.

Left: Close-up of this exquisite Lone Ranger outfit showing details.

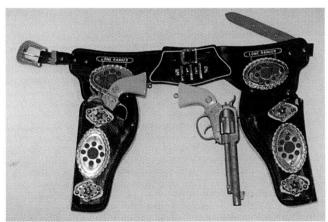

Esquire Lone Ranger double holster set with nickel-plated Actoy guns.

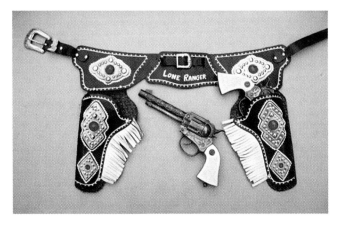

Esquire Deluxe Lone Ranger double holster set with bronze finish Actoy guns. Note the fringe, details, and basket weave underlay of the holster pockets.

The Marx Lone Ranger Thundergun model 12-inch prototype (above) and the Marx Lone Ranger Peacemaker model 9-inch plastic model with die-cast parts. Both guns are seldom seen. The lettering is in silver. Note superb grips on both.

Marx Lone Ranger rifle 26-inch Carbine cap shooter. Name on stock.

Marx Lone Ranger Winchester model cap-shooting rifle without scope. (Courtesy of J. Schleyer)

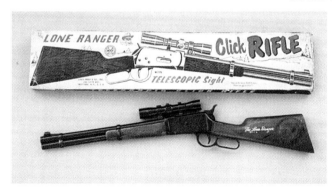

Above: Marx Lone Ranger Deluxe Winchester model with original box and scope. Note the Indian chief and name on left side of stock.

Right: Close-up of right side of stock showing Grizzly bear details and box.

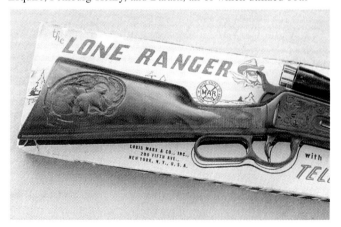

I followed the unsavory way the news reported that Wrather Corporation had issued a restraining order on Clayton Moore not to appear in public in the Lone Ranger mask and character, and I was distressed. I didn't think anyone could ever replace Clayton Moore as "the masked man." Clayton was the Lone Ranger in 221 episodes on TV and in two films and that's a tough record for anyone to surpass. The public responded along with me, and in 1985, Wrather Corporation lifted its restraining order, which allowed Moore to once again wear the Lone Ranger mask. Clayton Moore, to his credit, adopted The Lone Ranger creed, and as far as I and millions of fans are concerned, he will always be "that masked man."

For those mothers and fathers of today who decry violence, gunplay, blood, and gore, it might be interesting for them to know that the Lone Ranger never "killed" anyone on the episodes. The "bad guys" killed each other or themselves. At Trendle's strict insistence, the Lone Ranger had to be really special. Trendle made the following statement about his creation: "The Lone Ranger should be the embodiment of granted prayer. The Lone Ranger must not shoot to kill. He must be fair to all racial and religious groups. And good grammar, when the Lone Ranger speaks." Boy, would I like to see a psychiatrist analyze that. But, to those that are not convinced, and for those poor souls that don't know or don't remember what the essence of this character was all about, please allow me to relate:

THE LONE RANGER CREED

I believe that to have a friend, a man must be one. That all men are created equal and that everyone has within himself the power to make this a better world. That God put the firewood there, but that every man must gather and light it himself. In being prepared physically, mentally, and morally to fight when necessary for that which is right. That a man should make the most of what equipment he has. That 'this government, of the people, by the people, and for the people' shall live always. That men should live by the rule of what is best for the greatest number. That sooner or later. . .somewhere. . .somehow . . .we must settle with the world and make payment for what we have taken. That all things change, but the truth, and the truth alone lives on forever. I believe in my Creator, my country, my fellow man.

—*The Lone Ranger*

CAP GUN COLLECTIBLES

Just like Hoppy, Roy, and Gene, "The Lone Ranger" adorned hundreds of products. Strangely enough, however, few die-cast Lone Ranger guns exist. In the 1930-1950 period, the cast iron Lone Ranger guns were very popular, and it appears that Kilgore and Hubley made most of them. Marx also made pressed steel and pressed tin clicker guns with *The Lone Ranger* decals and artwork on them. Some were given out as premiums and gifts at movie theaters. Far more Lone Ranger holsters were made by a variety of holster makers for the cast iron guns, and among them were Esquire, Feinburg-Henry, and Barash, all of which utilized both

Mattel Lone Ranger cap shooting Winchester-style rifle. Note silver side plate.

Close-up of the silver side plate with Lone Ranger name and scrollwork.

generic guns and The Lone Ranger cast irons and some die-cast varieties. No holster boxes exist with the image of either Clayton Moore or Jay Silverheels as Tonto. All of the boxes show Lone Ranger artwork and more of the 1940s-style hero than the TV image of Clayton Moore.

Esquire of New Jersey (Actoy) made the most popular Lone Ranger die cast cap guns. They came in two sizes and three distinct models. The first is the 8-inch Lone Ranger .32. This came in both nickel and antique bronze finish. It came with copper grips, with a flower and leaf design, and the grips have the silver Esquire pony logo medallions. The name is on both sides of the frame on a raised bar. There is minor floral engraving on the frame, cylinder, and beginning of the barrel. A cap repeater, you must cock it all the way back for it to break open, from the top, for cap loading. Unlike some other Esquire guns, this is well made and tight.

Esquire made the 9-inch cap shooter in both antique bronze, the common model, and also in nickel, which is not as common. Both have off-white simulated grips, with the Esquire pony logo, and a lanyard ring on the butt. Extensively scrolled, this model has a rather thick ejector rod under the barrel, which has a unique design, and not the usual scrollwork or western floral scenes for engravings on barrels. The gun has a lever on the left side of the hammer and breaks open from the top for cap loading.

The third Esquire model is the very rare "Lone Ranger 4-in-1" 9-inch cap shooter that comes with a stock and extension barrel similar to the Restless Gun outfit. The gun is the nickel-plated 9-inch model described above, but the distinct differences are the grips, which are of a deeper stag design. It does not have the lanyard Ringo, but comes with a hole under the gun butt onto which the stock is attached, to both butt and back of the gun frame, below the hammer. The extension barrel is fitted and turned into the standard barrel, making it nearly 30 inches long as a pistol-rifle 4-in-1 carbine. The stock is plastic, with a turning geared wheel to bring the locking pins to the gun butt frame. The stock is dark brown, with a great design that encompasses the Esquire pony design logo and scalloping. This carbine model has only been found in nickel, both the gun itself and the 8-inch extension barrel. The release lever is identical on all 9-inch models.

Esquire put out the Lone Ranger bronze and nickel cap shooters in a variety of double holsters. While some early single holsters do exist, almost all Lone Ranger outfits are double holsters. The markings and tooling include "The Lone Ranger," "Lone Ranger," "Hi-Yo Silver," "The Lone Ranger, Silver and Tonto," and just "Tonto."

Confirming the popularity of Tonto, Esquire put out a colorful Tonto deluxe Indian Outfit. This outfit, in a large colorful box with Indian markings, came with several variations of items, including Indian headdress, drum, gun and holster,

Mattel Lone Ranger Winchester cap rifle in original shadow box. Note this reads "Lone Ranger" without "The" as on the Marx copyright models.

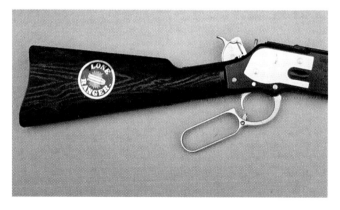

Close-up showing Lone Ranger and Silver Bullet decal on stock and special trigger for "Secret Rapid Fire."

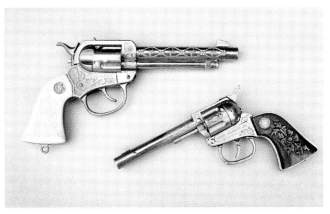

The British Lone Star's Lone Ranger cap pistol with swirl grips. *The American Esquire large and small Lone Ranger cap pistols.*
(Courtesy of Jim Krantz)

One of several issues of **The Lone Ranger** *put out by Dell Comics. Note this was a 52-page big comic and the Lone Ranger is an illustration rather than a photograph of any of the actors that played the part.*

knife and sheath, and tomahawk. Although no known Tonto cap gun has ever surfaced, a variety of generic guns were used with Tonto holsters. "Tonto" is on the belts and holster pockets, and even Indian quivers with arrows.

The guns that have surfaced with these Tonto outfits include the Stevens Big Chief, and Hubley Chief, both of which are a half-inch and inch smaller than the Esquire Lone Ranger .32, and Esquire's own Special and Buckaroo. Unfortunately, The Lone Star "Apache" is too big and the Nichols Brave is too small. However, it's a simple fact that while we, as today's collectors, like matching guns and matching holsters, the reality is that this is not always so. The best thing to do is have whatever gun came with the set, or if you have a loose holster, depending on how the gun "sits" in it, you can use any of the above.

Mattel honored *The Lone Ranger* with the double holster set in black dura-hide, which came with and without a silver bullet on the pockets of the holster in a circle with "Lone Ranger" molded into it. The guns that Mattel used are the 10-inch Fanner 50 models. These were the high polish chrome frames, non-revolving cylinder, side-gate on the left for cap load, and slick, vinyl covered all-metal grips with the retaining screw in the center of the grip. The guns were not marked "Lone Ranger," but rather "Fanner 50," along with the Mattel logo. With the special white grips with center screw, these guns are the closest to the guns the Lone Ranger wore on the program.

Marx, which had made a couple of pressed tin models in the 1935-1940 period, came back with two Lone Ranger guns, all plastic with metal part patterns. The 9-inch model has a shiny black frame with "The Lone Ranger" and the "TLR" trademark on the left side of the barrel in script in silver. This is not "painted" on, but molded perfectly into the barrel plastic. This model comes with simply beautiful and highly sculptured golden yellow grips with a steerhead on the left side and a horse head on the right side. The trigger and hammer are gray die-cast metal. The gun has the scaled down appearance of the Colt Peacemaker. A larger smoker-clicker, in silver finish, at 10 inches overall, has "The Lone Ranger" in blue lettering, also on the left side of the gun barrel. The grips are identical to the 9-inch model.

Marx also made a large 12-inch plastic-with-die-cast metal trigger and hammer model with "The Lone Ranger" painted in silver on the right side of the frame. All black, this model has creamy white grips with marvelous sculptured grips, a cowboy on a rearing horse on the left side, and a superbly detailed swooping eagle on the right side. This gun, initially a prototype from Marx's Erie, Pennsylvania, plant is the identical model of the Marx "Thundergun" in every detail, right down to the screws. Both of the Marx plastic Lone Ranger guns are very rare, but the 12-inch Thundergun pattern with "The Lone Ranger" in silver script on the right side of the frame is especially rare. The Marx logo is on the right side of the frame.

Marx made three Lone Ranger rifles. The first is the all-silver plastic-with-die-cast metal parts and lever action Carbine rifle. This is a 26-inch cap shooter. The cap box comes down by the lever action. The stock is stamped "The Lone Ranger" and the "TLR" trademark is on the left side of the stock. This was Marx's Wild West series of cap shooting rifles. This rifle has deluxe checkering, engraving, pistol grip, and octagon barrel. The boxes carried *The Lone Ranger* graphics and a large mask.

The second rifle was the smaller, 23-inch rifle carbine with Winchester-lever action. This was a clicker-style rifle with die-cast metal hammer. Its most prominent feature was the walnut-type plastic stock with a deeply molded, finely sculptured Indian chief's head and "The Lone Ranger" in gold lettering on the left side of the stock. The right side of the stock has a grizzly bear, also finely molded into the stock. It came with regular rifle barrels, and checkering and engraving on the lock and forestock. This came in two patterns—metallic silver barrels, and factory black barrels—with and without a scope.

The rifle by Marx was the Lone Ranger Deluxe Repeating Cap Rifle. This is the largest of the three, at 33-inches long, with Winchester lever action, metal barrels, walnut plastic stock with name in gold, cap shooting die-cast mechanism, and a realistic rear peep sight. This came in a carrying case-type box with graphics showing both the Lone Ranger and Tonto, as well as our hero rearing up on Silver.

Mattel also marketed one Lone Ranger rifle. This was the Lone Ranger "Winchester" model with plastic grained brown stock and black barrels. The right side of the receiver came with both an early model silver foil decal with "Lone Ranger" and scrollwork design. This was later replaced with a silver plastic engraved lock with "Lone Ranger" and scrollwork when the rifle proved to be a good seller. The second issue of this rifle was all black and the silver plate, with "Lone Ranger," was on both sides of the receiver, and you could load a "shootin shell" from the top of the receiver as well as a roll of caps on the left side. This came in both 26- and 33-inch lengths. Note these Mattel rifles were marked "Lone Ranger" and not the full "The Lone Ranger" title.

In 1958, Clayton Moore went on a tour to Great Britain promoting the movie *The Lone Ranger and the Lost City of Gold*. He was mobbed with screaming fans everywhere he went. Children lined up everywhere with guns and masks, waiting in line for hours for Moore's autograph and a photograph with the masked man. The tour was a big hit as the Lone Ranger became even more popular than he already was. The Lone Ranger

The "Lone Ranger" on his rearing horse, "Silver." Who was that masked man? Clayton Moore, that's who. The best!

program had already been airing on BBC for over a year. Lone Star eventually put out the only foreign-made Lone Ranger cap shooter. It is a 9-inch chrome-plated cap repeater, with reddish swirl grips and "Lone Ranger" raised on both sides of the frame. The lever for top breaking the gun for cap loading is larger than most, and located on the left side of the hammer. The gun has extensive engraving and scrollwork on the frame and the barrel.

Finally, Gabriel came out with the Lone Ranger rifle, also a cap shooter, perhaps trying to capitalize on a new generation of fans that had been exposed to the animated Lone Ranger cartoon program that ran between 1966 and 1969. Once more it was an 1873 Winchester-style carbine, with plastic and die cast parts, and "Lone Ranger" and scrollwork on the receiver. The plastic stock is tan, with black barrels and gray metal parts. This also confirms that the Lone Ranger's popularity had not diminished even ten years after *The Lone Ranger* series had completed its run.

Jay Silverheels, the proud Mohawk who will always be remembered fondly as "Tonto," the Indian who found, saved, and remained the faithful companion to the Lone Ranger, suffered a stroke in 1974. As he lay dying in 1980, one of his last visitors was Clayton Moore, telling him how much he was loved, and that the special bond they shared was as strong as ever. It remains that way also with his fans. Tonto was not the Lone Ranger's servant, but his equal.

Clayton Moore is the only actor that has both his name and the character—"The Lone Ranger"—on the Hollywood Walk of Fame. Jay Silverheels was also honored with his own star on the Walk of Fame a few months before he died. In 1971, Moore was honored by being made a special officer by the City of Fresno for "recognition for your outstanding contribution to law enforcement." Moore has been honored by the Newhall Walk of Fame, the Stuntman's Hall of Fame, the Gene Autry Western Heritage Award, the Western Heritage Award from the Cowboy Hall of Fame, as well as the Golden Boot Award—all for his selfless contributions to westerns, children, and entertainment. One of the greatest honors he received was being made a real "blood brother" at the Six Nations Indian Reservation, where the ashes of Jay Silverheels were scattered after his passing in 1980. Now in his 80s, Clayton Moore has never tired of being the man behind the mask of "The Lone Ranger," a real American icon. Hi-Yo, Silver, Awaaaay!

MAVERICK

James Garner, who starred as "Bret Maverick," one of television's most lovable western characters.

ew would disagree that *Maverick* was one of television's most popular and endearing westerns. Indeed, it was a "maverick" western show in its own right. Here was, first of all, a western, and a good-natured one. It was a western with a sarcastic sense of humor. It satirized the western. Here was a program about two self-centered, untrustworthy, almost cowardly brothers who were. . .gamblers! . . .cardsharks! . . .con men! Seeking rich "dudes and dudettes," they roamed the West for the "perfect poker game!" The Maverick brothers were two dapper, well-dressed, well-heeled, yet lovable characters—not your standard western heroes!

Maverick joined the western card game on September 22, 1957, and became an almost instant hit. It came to ABC on Sunday evenings, prime time, when the kiddies would be "influenced" by such a show. It was up against *The Jack Benny Show, The Ed Sullivan Show*, and *The Steve Allen Show*, all popular and steadfast programs in the mid-1950s.

But you couldn't help not liking and falling in love with the Maverick brothers. They were rogues, yes, but in the most important message of life, they, too, had a conscience. They became unwilling heroes because there is a hero in all of us when the chips are down for the lady in distress, or a fellow human being in trouble against overwhelming odds. And this is what made *Maverick* such a great western.

The adventures of the Maverick brothers—"Bret," played by James Garner, and "Bart," played by Jack Kelly, brought them all over the West, to towns that didn't exist, such as Oblivion, Hound Dog, and Apocalypse. Looking for the perfect game, getting rich quick, and breaking a pretty girl's heart as they left town, the Mavericks ended up on riverboats, old army forts, the railroad, and, of course, the local jail. No matter how much they tried to stay out of trouble, trouble just followed them everywhere they went!

James Garner soon became one of television's most popular actors, with his portrayal of Bret Maverick, the handsome, sweet-talking, wise-cracking ladies' man. Jack Kelly portrayed the more straight-laced brother, Bart Maverick, himself a ladies' man and often the unwitting hero trying to get out of a mess of trouble the brothers got themselves into. *Maverick* also did what no other western had ever done—it took satirical shots at other westerns and TV shows. One of the highlights of *Maverick* was its spoof of *Gunsmoke, Bonanza*, and even *Dragnet*.

Not even "Joe Friday" was safe, as Bret Maverick deadpanned an entire episode with intoned narration in Jack Webb's famous style. In the *Bonanza* spoof, Bart Maverick encounters a cattle baron with three moronic sons, all living on the "Subrosa Ranch." Veteran actor Jim Backus (*Gilligan's Island, Mr. Magoo*) played "Joe Wheelwright," the rancher baron. In the hilarious episode, he tries to marry off his three sons—Moose, Henry, and Small Paul, obviously spoofing the Cartwrights of the Ponderosa Ranch. It was all great fun and the audience loved it.

On another episode, the Mavericks ran into "Cheyenne" (Clint Walker), "Marshal Dan Troop" (John Russell of *Lawman*) "Chris Colt" (Wayde Preston), and even "Bronco Layne" (Ty Hardin). All in one glorious episode—a fun-filled western buff's heaven! *Maverick* also alternated between the two brothers as the lead in each week's program. Clearly, however, Bret Maverick had a higher profile, and was a more visible character.

Jack Kelly, who starred as "Bart Maverick," the more serious of the two lovable rogues on the western program.

Jack Kelly as "Bart" and Roger Moore as "Beauregard Maverick," the more refined brother, who returned from England.

Robert Colbert played the fourth brother, introduced as "Brent Maverick" in 1961.

While *Maverick* had a humorous profile, the Mavericks proved that when the going got rough, they could swing fists and blast their way out of trouble. They helped the local sheriff, and they even helped the Cavalry at times. The outfits were always fancy, with laced shirts, printed vests, three-quarter length frock coats, and string ties. Bret didn't like handling a gun and often appeared inept with it, but that was part of the humor. Neither brother liked getting punched in the face, but both did, plenty of times. Then they'd look at each other with a painful frown, and take off, after the hapless attacker. It was great humor.

At the card table, when the chips were down and they had just about lost everything, the Mavericks always, at the last second, would look inside the vest's inner pocket and unpin a one thousand dollar bill and they were back in the game! Bret Maverick would also offer advice that he got from his "Pappy," who said "son, in the face of overwhelming odds, run!" And run the two brothers would—away from furious lawmen, other con men whose games they ruined, and the pretty ladies at the end of the show.

One pretty lady proved she was more than a match for the Mavericks and had a recurring role in the series. She was "Samantha Crawford," played by Diane Brewster. Samantha was also a scheming beauty, and a phoney "Southern lady" that often got Maverick into trouble, as she used her charms to lure him into various schemes where one tried to out-con the other. Also appearing on various episodes was "Dandy Jim Buckley," another con man, played by Efrem Zimbalist, Jr.

Rounding out the series was another character named "Gentleman Jack Darby" played by actor Richard Long. These interesting and humorous characters added to the show's continuing popularity. James Garner appeared as his own "Pappy" Maverick in one episode. In 1960, after a three-year run, Garner had a dispute with Warner Brothers Studios, and not getting the better contract he requested, left the show and never went back.

The studio introduced Roger Moore as cousin "Beauregard Maverick." This was an interesting twist, since this Maverick did have honor, for he—a Texas soldier—had fought valiantly in the Civil War, but as he had been on the losing side, he moved to England. There, he acquired manners, culture, even an English accent. Soon though, he decided to return to America to look up his family and hopefully, make a fortune. With Bret Maverick out of the show, Bart and Beau alternated for two seasons. In the spring of 1961, another Maverick brother, "Brent Maverick," was introduced, played by character actor Robert Colbert. But the public couldn't forget the antics and easy smile of Bret Maverick, and the show suffered in the ratings. In the last season, Jack Kelly continued to play Bart Maverick alone.

After 124 hour-long episodes, *Maverick* dealt its last hand on July 8, 1962. In its five-year run, *Maverick* was one of TV's highest rated shows, winning an Emmy in 1959 as "Best Western Program," eventually climbing to number one in the ratings. What happened to all the many wonderful stars of *Maverick*? For some reason, neither *Maverick* as show title, or as the character would die a fast death. Few people know there were "three" Maverick shows.

James Garner went on to star in a short-lived western comedy spoof that few people remember, *Nichols,* in the 1971-1972 season. But he then gained immortal fame as Jim Rockford in *The Rockford Files* from 1974 to 1980. In 1979, still trying to capitalize on the success of *Maverick,* another TV series called *Young Maverick* came to TV with Charles Frank (*All My Children*) starring as yet another Maverick cousin, "Ben Maverick." This series, in which both Bret and Bart appeared on the first show, lasted only 13 episodes, but it was clear that no other actor could quite relay the sardonic wit and deadpan line delivery like Jim Garner. In 1981, 20 years after the original *Maverick,* James Garner returned as "Bret Maverick" on NBC. It ran only 18 episodes with re-runs in 1990. Gone was Bart, Beau, Brent, and Ben. Bret had settled down and it just wasn't the same. It proved, however, how much the studios wanted to revive *Maverick.*

In 1987, Garner did a five-part, 13-hour series called *Space.* In 1991, he returned to TV in another similar gambler-lovable-con-man spoof called *Man of The People.* The time was not ripe, however, for this type of character in 1991, and the show lasted only one season. This lovable con man was a politician, no less! James Garner today is still one of Hollywood's favorite actors on both the large and small screen, having made some memorable movies such as *The Great Escape, Up Periscope,* and *Murphy's Romance.* He was also cast as "Wyatt Earp" in *Sunset* with Bruce Willis playing another real life cowboy star, Tom Mix. James Garner is still going strong.

Richard Long, who had starred with Efram Zimbalist in *77 Sunset Strip* and later, *Bourbon Street Beat,* went on to star in *The Big Valley,* another long running western, with Barbara Stanwyck. His last TV series was *Nanny and The Professor* in 1971. Richard Long passed away in 1974.

Efram Zimbalist, Jr., who also starred in *77 Sunset Strip,* went on to play in the much-acclaimed *The FBI Story* from 1965 to 1974. A sharp eye and good memory can recall that the sweet, conniving "Samantha" on Maverick, was actress Diane Brewster, who played "Miss Confield" on *Leave it to Beaver.* Both are still with us.

(Top), Leslie-Henry 9-inch with amber grips with white cameo; (center), Halco's 8-inch Maverick; and (bottom), Lone Star's Maverick with notch bar grips.

The Leslie-Henry Maverick 45, the largest of them all!

Leslie-Henry's long barreled Maverick with cameo grips. Seldom seen.

Leslie-Henry's 10-inch, large-frame Maverick with pop-up cap box and front lever. Nickel plated, with extensive engraving and cameo grips. Seldom seen.

Right: British Lone Star Mavericks—(top), the seldom-seen long-barrel model, and the more common 9-inch Maverick, both nickel plated with caramel notch bar grips.

Lone Star's long-barreled Maverick in nickel with caramel notch bar grips. Note the horse head logo on the frame.

Schmidt's nickel-plated Maverick with copper steer head grips and extensive raised scroll-work. Seldom seen.

The Marx Maverick Saddle Rifle with original box showing images of the Maverick brothers. Note name on stock. Seldom seen.

The Leslie-Henry and Halco derringers used in the Maverick Hide-A-Way sets. These derringers were not character marked, only the cards were marked. These three varieties were used on Maverick, Paladin, and Wagon Train sets.

Roger Moore, the suave British actor who played Beauregard Maverick, went on to star as "James Bond, Agent 007" in several movies. He also starred in another TV series called *The Alaskans* with Jeff York, and is still with us. Robert Colbert, who played Brent Maverick, and later starred in several soap operas and television episodes, is also still with us.

Jack Kelly, the very gifted actor who played Bart Maverick, continued to star on both the large and small screen. Some of his memorable movies were *To Hell and Back*, *She-Devil*, *Forbidden Planet*, *Where Danger Lives*, and *Drive a Crooked Road*. In the 1980s, he was elected to city council and then became mayor of Huntington Beach, California. Jack Kelly died in 1992 at the age of 65.

CAP GUN COLLECTIBLES

Whenever I have brought up or talked about *Maverick*, everyone, male and female alike, all fondly remember this humorous western. And so it was only natural that the cap guns of choice among all those "little gamblers" and "cardsharks" that fell in love with this show and its lovable characters were sold by the thousands. Maverick is one of the most popular and most produced cap guns of the 1957-1962 period. No less than eight Maverick cap guns exist, with Leslie-Henry having made five of them.

Leslie-Henry made the Maverick .45 in bronze with stag grips. This is the big, 11-inch model with revolving cylinder. Like the Bonanza, Matt Dillon, and Paladin .45, it has "Maverick 45" and the rearing horse, raised on both sides of the frame, and the Diamond "H" logo on the grips. This model was also used on the Maverick western lamps. It is a big, beautiful cap shooter.

Leslie-Henry made the Maverick in both the standard 9-inch model and the 10-inch model with the long barrels. Both are nickel plated, with extensive scrollwork on the frames and the barrels, with horse head grips. Grips on these models come in various styles and colors, including amber with cameo inserts, white with black cameo inserts, as well as black and brown simulated stag. Leslie-Henry also made a seldom seen gold-plated model with butterscotch horse head grips in the 9-inch pattern. The release for cap loading on both models is on the left side of the hammer.

Leslie-Henry also made the 10-inch, wider framed, nickel-plated model with the pop-up cap box, with front-frame release. This model is the most extensively engraved pattern, with larger print in the raised lettering of "Maverick" on both sides of the frame. This model came with both a white grip with black cameo inserts. Also, a model is found with the copper steerhead Marshal grips that were used on the Gunsmoke and Wild Bill Hickok series. This is a beautiful and well-made cap shooter.

Leslie-Henry/Halco made the 1960 small model with simulated stag grips found in both white and black with the Diamond "H" logo in the Buzz-Henry style. This is the 8-inch, nickel-plated model with the side gate for cap loading on the left side. It has extensive scroll work and raised "Maverick" on both sides.

Lone Star made two Maverick models. Both were marketed through Carnell Manufacturing in its Carnell Roundup offerings. Identical to the 9-inch Bat Masterson and Cowpoke, the Lone Star Maverick was a nickel-plated, well-made, and extensively engraved cap shooter. The frame has Maverick and the horse head logo raised on both sides of the frame. The release, which breaks open the gun for cap loading, is located on the right side, just below the hammer. One of the significant features of the Lone Star Maverick is the "notch bar" on the grips. Imagine a toy gun being sold today where the kid can record his "kills" with a special "notch" bar on the gun! The grips came with a simulated stag pattern, in a beautifully-marbleized caramel cream swirl.

Lone Star, taking a tip from Leslie-Henry, also made a long-barreled model for its Maverick series. The long barrel model is 10 inches, beautifully nickeled, and came with the same notch bar grips, frame engraving and Maverick markings on the frame. The same pattern was used for the Lone Star Buntline Special.

The most sought-after and most difficult to find Maverick was made by the George Schmidt Company. The Schmidt Maverick is extensively scrolled and was 10 inches in length. It has a ribbed barrel, breaks open from the top with a left side lever, and has "Maverick" raised in a 3-D fashion, from small "M" to large "K" on both sides of the frame under the scrolled cylinder. Interestingly enough, the grips on this gun are copper with simulated wood grain and raised steer head with "Marshal" on the bottom, identical to the Leslie-Henry grips. These grips are peened this way and not easily removed or interchanged.

The same Schmidt model was made for the Wyatt Earp, covered later on in this study. It has a high-polish nickel finish and is a beauty. Two rifles for the *Maverick* series exist. The first came in a special Maverick cowboy outfit marketed by Carnell. The rifle was the identical model used in the Rawhide cowboy outfits. The outfit included a double holster set with Hubley "Westerns," wrist cuffs, and spurs. Note that only the box was marked with Maverick details and graphics. Louis Marx came out with the Maverick "saddle rifle" in a beautifully-colored red box with great graphics, showing Jim Garner and Jack Kelly as Bret and Bart Maverick. The rifle is 27-inches long with Winchester lever action, checkered forestock, and "Maverick" in gold on the stock with the Warner Brothers trademark. The Maverick brothers rarely used a rifle on the show, so this was a great marketing step for Marx to capitalize on the show's popularity. The Maverick rifle is seldom seen.

Leslie-Henry also marketed its "hide-a-way" derringer, which came on a card marked "Maverick" with Bret Maverick graphics. The derringer was its 3-inch nickel-plated model that was also used in the *Have Gun-Will Travel* series. It was a single-shot derringer with red plastic grips and the four leaf clover raised on the frame. The derringer was not marked "Maverick," but as with the *Have Gun-Will Travel* series, only the card is marked with Maverick graphics.

With a show this popular and with so many cap guns to choose from, it is obvious that Maverick holsters are found in dozens of styles, both single and double sets, and in a variety of leathers, designs, embellishments, and markings. Both Leslie-Henry and Carnell marketed holsters in "Maverick"-marked boxes and on the holsters themselves. One of the most elaborate Maverick sets is the Carnell double holster set which came in black leather with white details. This set, which came with the Lone Star 9-inch notch bar cap guns, has a huge 3-piece silver concho that almost covers the entire holster pocket, and "Maverick" is stamped on the back on the belt on each side of a large round concho. The set came with six red bullets.

An equally interesting double holster set was made by Leslie-Henry in a rich tan leather with horse head details on the belt and the holster pockets. This set came with a great graphic that pictures Bret Maverick on the center of the back of the belt. It is also adorned with 12 bullets. The smaller Halco Maverick guns also came in both single and double holster sets adorned with lots of conchos and studs.

Maverick spurred many collectibles. Dell Comics issued several years of *Maverick. TV Guide,* with the Mavericks on the cover, are hot collectibles. And, of course, the Mavericks also taught you how to play poker the right way, in a Dell paperback called *Poker According to Maverick.*

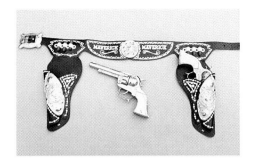

Colorful Maverick double holster set marketed by Carnell Roundup with Lone Star Maverick cap shooters. Note huge concho on holster pockets.

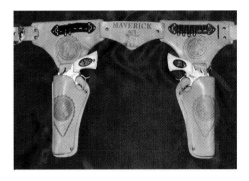

Unique Maverick double holster set with Leslie-Henry guns. Note the image of Bret Maverick on the holster gunbelt. (Courtesy of J. Schleyer)

Dell Comics January 1959 issue for Maverick. Check out the fancy duds that Bret and Bart are wearing! Dell Comics made several Maverick issues, including covers that featured both Roger Moore and Robert Colbert as "Beau" and "Brent Maverick."

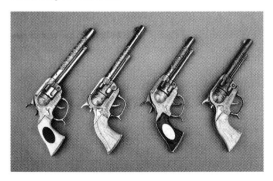

A great collection of Maverick cap guns. Left to right, Leslie-Henry long barrel; Lone Star long barrel; Leslie-Henry 9-inch; and Lone Star 9-inch.

Seldom-seen Maverick single holster set with Lone Star Maverick with stag grips. Note unique oval buckle on this set. (Courtesy of Terry Graham)

McCLOUD

Dennis Weaver in the role of "Deputy Sam McCloud," a transplated cowboy in the "Big Apple." (Courtesy of Old West Shop)

Deputy "Sam McCloud," with his cowboy hat, fancy jackets, string ties and boots cut one hell of a figure as a lawman. At 6'2", he was lean, handsome, with a good moustache to round out his looks. He carried a nice Colt .45 with a gunfighter's holster. He talked with a great southwestern accent. He had great manners with the ladies, tipped his hat, and excused himself. He was full of old-fashioned wisdom. He was comfortable riding a horse or a vehicle.

Wait a minute, a vehicle? You mean 4 wheels, metal body, flashing lights? What's wrong with this picture? Nothing. Deputy Sam McCloud was temporarily transplanted from Taos, New Mexico, where he was a no-nonsense, dedicated lawman. The problem was that he was now in New York City—the Big Apple. Blue uniforms. Nightsicks. Frustrated high-ranking officers. Traffic. Nasty people at times. Pretty ladies. Sam McCloud went there to search and re-capture a prisoner that had taken off on him, but he ended up staying seven years!

McCloud was an excellent contemporary western that was part of the first set of mini-series aired along with *The Psychiatrist, Night Gallery,* and *San Francisco Airport* under NBC's "Four-in-One" series. *McCloud* premiered on September 16, 1970, and became an instant hit, by far the most entertaining of the four series. The following year, it became one of the three NBC Mystery Movie trio, sharing the two hour program along with *Columbo* and *MacMillan and Wife.* The star of McCloud pretty much said it all. He was the very popular Dennis Weaver.

Dennis Weaver, a Missouri native born in 1934, had shot to fame playing the stiff-legged and limping Deputy "Chester Goode" on *Gunsmoke,* TV's longest-running western. Weaver had a kind personality that people liked, and they related to the character well. Prior to being instantly recognized as "Chester," Weaver had started off doing Broadway plays, which led him to Hollywood. He starred in a string of westerns which included *Chief Crazy Horse* and *Horizons West.* These led to major roles in *Dragnet, Seven Angry Men, The Bridges at Toko-Ri,* and *Ten Wanted Men.* He was a versatile actor, at home on any entertainment stage and in various roles.

When he got the part of "Chester Goode," however, he found instant stardom on a weekly series. Let's face it, you have to go see a major film to get to know an actor. Television brings the actor and character to your living room and it's not difficult to see the appeal of wonderful characters that you get to know, almost like a good friend or relative. To his credit, Dennis Weaver was exactly that kind of character on *Gunsmoke* and he brought back that warm, slightly "slow" persona—but he was not slow at all, and he proved this in his role as Deputy Sam McCloud.

McCloud featured character actor J.D. Cannon as his frustrated superior, "Peter Clifford," at the 27th Precinct in Manhattan. Rounding out the cast was "Sgt. Broadhurst," played by Terry Carter, and "Sgt. Grover," played by Ken Lynch. But Deputy McCloud was irresistible. So they gave him a love interest, "Chris Coughlin," played by Diana Muldaur. Coughlin was a writer who was doing a book on the fugitive that McCloud had come to New York to recapture. After capturing the fugitive, McCloud ends up being temporarily assigned in Clifford's precinct.

Out of his element, McCloud studies metropolitan police methods, investigation, and tactics in the Big Apple, and he's not too happy about the way they coddle criminals. He reverts to some good, old-fashioned western strong-arm tactics, which further infuriates an already teetering-on-the-edge superior, Lt. Clifford. But McCloud, who gets along well with the friendlier Sgt. Broadhurst, is neither slow nor out of touch with the reality of seamy, seedy, big city criminals.

This wonderful semi-western series brought many first-rate established stars to the small screen because of the endless scenarios in New York and the crime-related subjects. Actors and actresses ran the famous gamut from Milton Berle, Danny Thomas, Lee J. Cobb and others, to Susan Saint James, Britt Eklund, and Jane Seymour. Even New York City's most famous real-life detective, Eddie "Popeye" Egan, appeared on the show. The wonderful plots also took the show to London and Australia. The show ran full tilt to August 28, 1977, ending a seven-year run where it had been ranked 6th in the Top 10 at the time.

Dennis Weaver is still with us and still active in film projects. In 1989, he starred in an update of sorts on a McCloud film shot overseas, but by then, Deputy McCloud had progressed to becoming a U.S. Senator. After the run of *McCloud,* Dennis Weaver went on to star in another series, *Buck James*, a medical drama that ran from 1987 to 1988. Of the original cast of *McCloud*, only Ken Lynch, who played Sgt. Grover, has passed away (1990).

Few people remember that Dennis Weaver also starred in *Gentle Ben,* a wonderful television show after his *Gunsmoke* days. *Gentle Ben* was not about a nice and gentle guy named "Ben." "Gentle Ben," in fact, weighed 650 pounds, and was an American alright, but he was a grizzly bear! Weaver played the part of "Tom Wedloe," a dedicated wildlife officer, who, with his wife and eight-year old son, lived in the Florida Everglades.

They had sort of adopted Gentle Ben because he was so friendly, cute, huggable, and lovable. Young star Clint Howard played "Mark Wedloe," Tom's son. "Ellen Wedloe" was played by Beth Brickell. Young Howard's real father, Rance Howard, played the part of "Henry Boomhaieur," a sort of backwoodsman character who was a friend and advisor to Tom Wedloe. *Gentle Ben,* which was Dennis Weaver's second shot at a series, ran from September 1, 1967, until August 31, 1968.

CAP GUN COLLECTIBLES

Dennis Weaver achieved additional fame in *McCloud.* Even if there are no cap pistols named after "Tom Wedloe" or "Gentle Ben" or even "Chester Goode," we have him immortalized as "McCloud." Once again, the lack of cap pistols made in America for a show this popular, with a seven-year run, never ceases to amaze me. Shown all over Europe and other foreign markets, *McCloud* must have caught the fancy of Spain's Pilen, S.A. Manufacturers because they honored *McCloud* with a fine cap-firing, revolving-cylinder, die-cast repeater.

The 9-inch cap pistol is identical to the style and design of the Pilen Bonanza. The gun came in both a dark nickel and factory black finish with brown checkered grips. "McCloud" is on both sides of the frame under the revolving cylinder. The very colorful box gives the show name and has a great color shot of Dennis Weaver as "McCloud." We have the Spaniards to thank for allowing us collectors to remember this very fine contemporary western show.

The Pilen Company's McCloud cap shooter, complete with original box with great graphics of our hero. The same pattern was used for Pilen's Bonanza. (Courtesy of J. Schleyer)

THE OVERLAND TRAIL

The original Overland Stage Line, started by Ben Holladay back in 1846, was the inspiration for this short-lived western. Holladay started the Overland Stage Line with a small government contract and soon expanded his operations from the Atlantic to the Pacific. The original Overland Stage Line was the first complete coach line to also do the full run from Missouri to early California and back again. It was dangerous work. *The Overland Trail* puts the action in the latter part of the 19th century. It was said that "when a man takes this job, he hires on to die. It goes with the territory." So goes a line from *Stagecoach*.

The Overland Trail came to television on NBC, on February 7, 1960, and ran an hour in length. Set in the late 1860s, the ornery superintendent of the Overland Trail was "Frederick Thomas Kelly," who was known as "Kelly" on the show. This lead part was played by veteran actor William Bendix, who had starred in dozens of war movies and westerns, as well as gaining immortal fame as "Chester Riley" in *The Life of Riley*. His assistant on the stage line was "Frank Flippen," who carried the nickname of "Flip," played with young enthusiasm by Doug McClure. There were several guest stars, given the adventures that running a stagecoach line presented itself, but in the short run of this show, these were the only two main characters.

Kelly's character was as a former Union army guerrilla fighter, who later turned to civilian land engineering after the war. His efforts to establish a stage line from Mississippi to California on a route that would span two thousand miles was a challenge that he undertook with great pride and determination, no matter what the odds. His assistant, Flip, had been raised by Indians, and was an all-around scout, stage guard, and sidekick to Kelly. Together, they encountered all sorts of mayhem, Indian attacks, mail and stage holdups, and everything from tornadoes to real-life outlaws such as Cole Younger and Calamity Jane.

Throw in the personal problems and individual personalities of the passengers making the run to California and one could see where a western with these ingredients could be a hit. Unfortunately, this show lasted only 17 episodes. Perhaps this was due to the chemistry of putting a young, good looking but temperamental character alongside an older, crusty, former comedy star. In either case, *The Overland Trail* rode off into the sunset the same year it came on board, on September 11, 1960. Fortunately for us collectors and cap shooter enthusiasts, the characters live on.

CAP GUN COLLECTIBLES

Here was a show that lasted only 17 episodes, and yet, the toy giant Hubley came out with rifle and gun to immortalize both Kelly and Flip.

Kelly carried only a Winchester rifle on the show. Flip wore a single holster six-gun. Hubley which had already marketed the popular Rifleman Flip Special modified the same rifle, and came out with Kelly's Rifle. Kelley's rifle was 32 inches long, with gray metal barrel, nickel sight, barrel ends, and barrel bands.

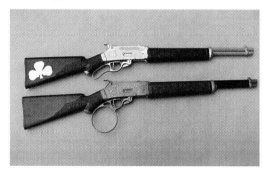

William Bendix as "Kelly" and Doug McClure as "Flip" ready to take on all comers who want to sabotage the Overland Trail. (Courtesy of Old West Shop)

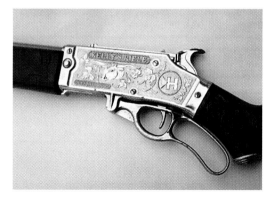

Above: Hubley made the fine-quality "Kelly's Rifle" in the Winchester style. Note the comparison between the Hubley Rifleman below Kelly's Rifle.

Right: Close-up of the receiver showing "Kelly's Rifle" and "Overland Trail" titles.

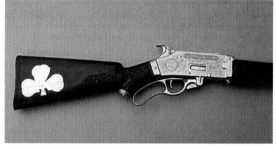

Close-up showing the shamrock and "K" decal on the right side of the stock.

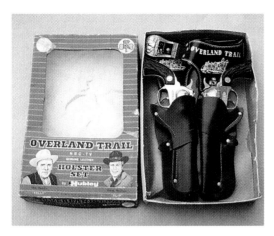

The Hubley Overland Trail double holster set with Flip guns. Note the graphics showing the stagecoach and the shamrock logo on the gunbelt. A beauty!

Hubley's boxed Overland Trail double holster set with Flip cap guns. Note the "K" and shamrock as well as images of both stars on the cover.

The receiver was all nickel and gold plated. The plastic stock and forearm was solid black plastic, but highly sculptured, with the same designs and scroll-work as the Rifleman Flip Special. Obviously, Hubley dropped the large flip special ring.The receiver is exceptionally engraved, with "Kelly's Rifle" raised on both sides as well as the the Circle "H" Hubley logo. The left side of the receiver has "Overland Trail" also raised on the receiver and the same steer head found on the Rifleman. A push button release on the left side drops the cap box for cap loading.

The Hubley Flip nickel-plated cap pistol with black stag grips. The character name of Flip is raised within an elongated oval frame on both sides.

One final detail is the presence of a silver decal in the shape of a shamrock with a large "K" in the center and is found on the right side of the black stock. Kelly was proud of his Irish lineage! This same shamrock secondary logo is found on all *Overland Trail* items.

The lever action works independently to fire one shot at a time, whereas the Rifleman's "flip special," of course, has the "rapid-fire" cocking mechanism not present on Kelley's Rifle. The rifle is a beautifully made, attractive piece with the contrast of the black plastic and gold plating of the receiver and die-cast parts.

Kelley's Rifle came in a great box with William Bendix on the cover, as well as the shamrock and "Overland Trail" and "Kelly's Rifle" all as part of the graphics. It's obvious that Revue Productions, NBC, and Hubley were betting this would be a popular western.

Hubley did not leave out Kelly's sidekick, Flip. At least two patterns of the Overland Trail holster sets were marketed. They are slick black leather holsters with white details on the belt, showing a stagecoach and "Overland Trail" in white graphics over the holster pockets, as well as a shamrock over the top of the holster pocket. There are no markings on the sleek, plain pockets themselves. A pattern with three bullets and a deluxe model with six bullets were made. The box is a colorful green box, with a shamrock, "Overland Trail," and images of both William Bendix and Doug McClure as Kelly and Flip. The shamrock also has the large "K" superimposed on it.

Hubley made a 9-3/4-inch cap shooter for Flip. The gun is nickel plated, with lots of scrollwork on the barrel and frame. It has a lift-up side gate on the left side for cap loading. The frame is marked with "Flip," which is raised from a pebbled oval bar on both sides of the frame under the cylinder. The gun comes with sleek, all-black simulated stag grips. The same gun was later copied by Halco for several other characters also covered in this book. This is the only known cap shooter marked "Flip." The "Flip" came with the "Overland Trail" double holster sets. No guns marked "Kelly" are known to exist and no rifle marked "Flip" is known to exist. This double holster set in black leather with white details, and Flip nickel guns are very handsome, indeed.

William Bendix died in 1964, just four years after the show ended. Doug McClure went on to star as "Trampas" in the long-running western *The Virginian*, with James Drury. He also starred as "Cash Conover" in another short-run TV western, *The Barbary Coast*, with Willam Shatner (*Star Trek*). He died in 1995. Given the short, but noble run of *The Overland Trail*, both Kelly's Rifle and the Overland Trail double holsters with Flip cap pistols are quite scarce. As stated, both are top quality Hubley-made guns.

PECOS BILL

Pecos Bill, riding his mountain lion and using his pet snake as a whip. (Courtesy of N. McElvey, Real West)

The Italian-made Pecos Bill 12 by Mondial, disc cap shooter.

Right side of the Pecos Bill. Note the full color cowboy on the grips!

"Pecos Bill" was not a real character, nor was he a TV western character, but Pecos Bill was one of America's greatest legends. I first heard the story of Pecos Bill at Times Farm Camp when I was a youngster. My kid brother and I were immigrant boys from Italy who were wild about American westerns, probably even more than our American pals. I never forgot the story of Pecos Bill, and over the years, I've heard and read about Pecos Bill with slight variations here and there, but the thrust of the story of American folklore's "greatest cowboy" remains the same.

Our Camp counselor at Times Farm Camp in Andover, Connecticut, was an athletic young man from Texas, who would tell us a story about folk heroes every night after "Vespers." Every night it was a different story, a different legend, a different character, but the ones I recall most vividly was "Paul Bunyon" who had a blue ox, and Pecos Bill, the greatest cowboy that ever lived! In fact, Pecos Bill was recently honored by the U.S. Postal Service, along with other American folk heroes and legends, with a special commemorative stamp.

The story goes that Pecos Bill hailed from eastern Texas—west of the Pecos—the area (as in Judge Roy Bean, who was a real western character) which was wild, lawless, untamed, where only the hardiest survived. If Judge Roy Bean was "the Law West of the Pecos," then surely Pecos Bill was the man who tamed the area with his bare hands! Pecos Bill was one of 14 children, and his folks were pioneers and loners who didn't care much for people, and kept to themselves. After all, with 14 kids running around, they had a wild brood of their own! The story continues that when another pioneer family moved to the area, even though the spot where they set up their homestead was some fifty miles away from where Pecos Bill lived, his father wasn't too happy. So he packed up the family and decided to head even further west.

As they were crossing the Pecos River, baby Bill fell out of the wagon and into the water. With so many kids, nobody really noticed and by the time the family did, it was too late to go back. They assumed he had drowned in the Pecos River. But, baby Bill didn't drown. . .nope!. . .somehow, a big turtle helped him to shore, where coyotes found him, nursed him, and brought him up. So tough was young Bill, now nicknamed "Pecos Bill" because of the Pecos River experience, he would even "teethe" on iron horseshoes and rawhide. Growing up among coyotes, Bill became strong, lightning fast, and untamable.

The story continues that when a real cowboy met up with Bill in the wild, he told him to stop living like a wild man and become a "real cowboy"—drive cattle across the country, ride fast on beautiful horses, carry six guns and win the ladies! Bill was only too happy to try to change the course of his life and straighten out. He turned out to be the best and the wildest cowboy that ever lived. He could go days without eating or sleeping, driving herds of cattle by himself. He was struck by lightning, which turned his jet black hair to golden blonde, curled his moustache, and his black piercing eyes turned a sky-blue.

He could drink boiling coffee, eat raw meat, and clean his teeth sparkling white with pine cones. He could walk a hundred miles a day, and word soon came back east that Pecos Bill had dug the Grand Canyon with his pick-axe! He was able to swing a lariat like a showman and once lassoed a lightning bolt, and water for drinking. He once rode a cyclone across Kansas, trying to get back to Texas to see his ailing Daddy. Who do you think invented the lariat and the blazing six-gun? It was none other than Pecos Bill!

Bill had a sense of humor as well. He would play practical jokes on his cowboy friends, like putting a scorpion on their pillow and a tarantula in the saddlebags. He was the one who even taught cowboys how to ride a "Bucking Bronc." He would fight bulls two at a time, and if he landed a punch with his mighty fist on the bull's forehead, the bull would drop instantly. But like a true cowboy, Pecos Bill had a lot of patience and compassion. After a rattlesnake bit him three times and gave up, Bill picked it up and decided he'd wear the snake around his neck as a bandana since he felt the snake was unable to feed itself. Bill was kind to animals. He'd walk miles carrying a lame horse to a doctor, and he raised a mountain lion cub when it got lost from its mother. (The mountain lion became his pet and he'd even ride it around at times.)

Close-up of grips showing the beautiful artwork of Pecos Bill, Italian style!

But Pecos Bill was getting older and he had to settle down. He met a cute Southern Belle named "Slue Foot Sue." Sue was Bill's match in life. Why, didn't you know that Sue could ride as hard as Bill and while Bill could ride lightning, Sue could ride catfish up and down the Rio Grande! Bill was smitten and fell in love. He had found the girl of his dreams, and he taught her how to lasso and fire the six guns—and soon she could stop a bullet with her teeth! But, there was one thing that was "off limits" and that was Bill's horse, a jet-black midnight rider stallion named "Widow Maker." Only Bill could ride the horse, with or without a saddle. Anybody else that even tried was quickly thrown off, as Widow Maker would buck and kick and off the man went.

The Pecos Bill opened for disc cap loading. Check out the 12-shot drum!

Sue begged Bill to let her ride Widow Maker. She said this would be her "wedding gift" and she'd be happy forever. Bill tried and tried to convince Sue that this was not a good idea, and besides, Widow Maker was not fond of women anyway. Sue was not to be pushed aside and it looked "rocky" there for a spell, so Bill gave in, and Sue got on Widow Maker. Snorting and bucking, the mighty stallion sent Sue bouncing off, and as she was wearing a steel and coiled spring bustle, she began to bounce all over the place, and she kept on bouncing and even Bill couldn't stop her! Sue was last seen bouncing up to the moon! Pecos Bill was devastated.

Some say he never, ever rode Widow Maker again. Others say he drank nitroglycerine, mixed with barbed wire, sarsparilla, and hot Mexican peppers, and the result was that he shot up into the sky like a space rocket, going over the moon, trying to find Sue. Pecos Bill never returned to the Old West, but on a cool, clear, and starless night, you can see Slue Foot Sue and Pecos Bill together, holding hands and flying around the moon! O.K., get to bed, there, you young whipper-snappers!

The U.S. Postal Service honored Pecos Bill in its folklore series with a stamp designed by David LaFluer. Note Bill's snake is also his bandana! (Courtesy of U.S. Postal Service)

CAP GUN COLLECTIBLES

The only Pecos Bill marked cap gun, remarkably, was made in Italy. It was made by Mondial S.P.A. Company. There were two models, both factory black. There was the Pecos Bill 8 and the Pecos Bill 12, firing 8 and 12 caps, respectively. This very well-made gun breaks from the top with a left-side lever, exposing the full cylinder, which takes disc caps. The most striking feature of the Italian Pecos Bill are the grips. They are hard enamel painted over metal, almost porcelain paint, featuring a full-color cowboy with two holstered six-guns, ready to draw! The cowboy wears a black Stetson and a black vest with a red bandana and high boots. This Italian version of America's folk hero Pecos Bill even shows him wearing a special set of double holsters! The gun is 8 inches long. "Pecos Bill" is on the left side of the frame. The right side carries "Made in Italy" and "Modello Depositato," meaning patent pending.

The gun has the logo of Mondial, a diamond with three circled "M's" on both sides of the frame and the top of the grips. The grips are peened into place at the bottom of the butt and cannot be removed or switched around. Remarkably, even with excessive wear, scratches, and laying the gun around surfaces, the colorful and extremely well-designed grips remain vibrant.

It is no coincidence that Italians have always loved, and continue to love, American westerns, for this is where many of America's old western stars moved to and continued to make what are now referred to as "spaghetti westerns," after the American TV westerns rode off into the sunset.

Again, it is remarkable that a cap gun honoring one of America's folk heroes was made overseas in the 1950s. In fact, not even the American cast irons, before the die casts, made the Pecos Bill. The Lone-Star Products of England put out a Pecos Kid, but it's not the "Pecos Bill"—that was made only by Mondial of Italy—honoring the "greatest cowboy that ever lived!"

THE PLAINSMAN

Here was a cut-above western that should have never been retired. It was ahead of its time, and I dare say *The Law of The Plainsman* would be a big hit today. This great series lasted three years. The pilot was first introduced on an episode of *The Rifleman* in the spring of 1959. Responding to a strong showing, NBC decided to order the series. It's unfortunate that few people recall this magnificent program. It wasn't until I found the superior quality and very well made cap shooter, The Plainsman, that it brought back the show to my mind immediately.

The original title was *Tales of The Plainsman* but was later changed to *The Law of The Plainsman*. It came to NBC on October 1, 1959. Set in the 1870s in New Mexico, the character, played by Michael Ansara, is "Buckhart," an Apache Indian. In a fierce battle between Apaches and U.S. Cavalry, the 14-year-old warrior comes across a severely wounded captain.

As he is about the scalp the officer, the officer shows no fear and awaits his fate with dignity. The warrior stops and thinks about what he is doing to an already helpless man. He decides to help him and nurse him back to health, thus promoting an understanding, and forming a bond with the white man. The captain returns to cavalry duty, but names the boy "Sam Buckhart."

Two years later, the captain dies in an Indian ambush. Buckhart learns that the captain did not forget his act of mercy and ensuing friendship. He left Buckhart a considerable sum of money for him to get a good education at private schools and Harvard College, where the captain himself had attended. Stunned by the white man's generosity, Buckhart decides to get the education, and develops an enormous respect for the white man's law and the U.S. Constitution.

Buckhart finishes his education and decides to return to his troubled territory as a U.S. Marshal to help his people and maintain law and order. Ten years have passed and now it's the lawless era of the 1880s. But, the now Harvard-educated Apache Indian soon learns that he has two enemies to deal with: one is maintaining law and order in the white man's way, and the other is dealing with the prejudices of his own people.

U.S. Marshal Sam Buckhart spends three years trying to establish the long-sought peace between the white man and his people. He is headquartered in Santa Fe, working under "Marshal Andy Morrison," played by character actor Dayton Lummis. Buckhart resides in a rooming house, run by "Martha Commager," who was played by Nora Marlowe. But, Buckhart soon learns that life deals him additional responsibilities. During a runaway stagecoach scene, he rescues a young orphan, "Tess Logan," an 8-year-old girl played by Gina Gillespie. She becomes Sam's "sort of" adopted ward, and Martha Commager, the rooming house matron, takes on a kind of surrogate-mother role for young Tess and, at times, Sam Buckhart himself.

This intelligent, adult western ran for three years, going off the air on September 24, 1962. Afterwards, reruns were taken over by ABC. With a three-year run of such a good show, many guest stars appeared. But, Ansara was always the standout with his wonderful, authoritative, compassionate, strong, and dignified portrayal of Buckhart. Ansara, though Lebanese, seems to have been made for Indian roles. He had already achieved fame as the honorable "Cochise" on his previous series, *Broken Arrow,* with John Lupton as his "bloodbother," also trying to foster understanding between the two races. Ironically, Michael Ansara's first role on the screen was also an Indian, as "Tuscos," in *Only The Valiant,* with Gregory Peck. In fact, many viewers actually thought Michael Ansara was a Native American. Michael Ansara, Gina Gillespie and Nora Marlowe are still with us. Dayton Lummis, the old-time character actor who played "Marshal Morrison," died in 1988 at age 84.

Michael Ansara as U.S. Marshal Sam Buckhart, from **The Law of The Plainsman.**

Michael Ansara in his most dignified role as "Cochise" on his prior TV series, the long-running **Broken Arrow.**

The Plainsman revolving cylinder cap shooter made by National Metal and Products Company. Note the unique lever on the left side to move cylinder forward.

Right side of the Plainsman has the designer's name on the frame. Note the beautiful scrolling and fine checkered grips. Gold models also exist, but are seldom seen.

CAP GUN COLLECTIBLES

The gun that I picked up at a show that brought The Plainsman to mind was made by National Metal and Plastics Company. This strange, but well made cap shooter is a 10-inch, solid, nickel gun with a revolving cylinder and creamy white grips that are handsomely checkered and scrolled in true a Old Western design. Plain white grips also came on this gun. The frame and the barrel are beautifully scrolled with an all-raised design. The revolving cylinder is plain. The gun has a very unique loading mechanism. On the left side of the frame is an aluminum sliding lever that you push forward until it clicks into place, holding the cylinder forward, towards the barrel. This will leave a space open to load disc caps. You then slide the lever back and the nice, tight cylinder action goes back into place and you're ready to go.

The right side of the frame has "A National Metal and Plastics Co. Toy" raised under the cylinder, as well as "Made in U.S.A." and "Pat. Pend." Beautifully scrolled on a banner in high relief on the right side of the barrel you will find "The Plainsman." The left side of the frame carries an additional statement: "Design by Dodge-Melton." These were made along with a similar model stamped "C.Ray Lawyer" in California.

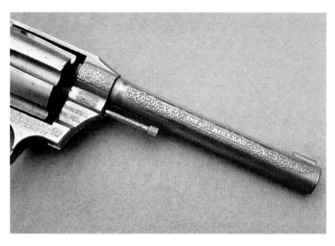

Close-up of the barrel showing "The Plainsman" raised among beautiful scrollwork of the National Dodge-Melton disc cap shooter. Top quality made cap gun!

Pardners, don't even think of waving this gun in a bank or at a cop; this cap shooter is so real, in every way, that I am told one was turned in a few years ago on that "trade your guns in for dollars" gimmick and it had the officials baffled. Meanwhile, the fellow that turned it in walked a way with $100. In any case, this a great cap shooter—unusual, unique, and not easily found.

It's so unfortunate that Hollywood and television producers cannot seem to air shows like *The Law of The Plainsman* today. What a wonderful example for children and minorities to look up to—it has everything our social climate begs for—helping a wounded man not of your race or creed; the generosity of the dying man; getting a strong education; overcoming the odds and going back to help your people as a Marshal; and the responsibility of raising an orphan while at the same time fostering understanding and peace between diverse races and groups. To its credit, *The Plainsman* was ahead of its time, and for us collectors, so was the cap shooter.

THE RANGE RIDER

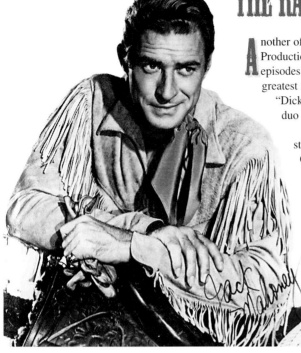

Another of television's first westerns, produced by Gene Autry's Flying "A" Productions, *The Range Rider* premiered on April 26, 1951, and ran for 78 episodes. Cast as the "Ranger Rider" was Jock Mahoney, one of Hollywood's greatest stunt men and a wonderful actor in his own right. Cast as his sidekick, "Dick West," was another early stuntman, Dick Jones. Together, this dynamic duo brought lots of action to early television and wide-eyed youngsters.

Jock Mahoney had already achieved fame stunting for such well-known stars of the 1940s as Errol Flynn, Randolph Scott, Gregory Peck, and Charles Starrett, better known as the "Durango Kid." Mahoney certainly did his own stunts on The Range Rider, as did Dick Jones. They were a great team, fighting for range justice, flirting with the ladies, but always using good manners—never drinking or smoking. And foul language was unheard of on the air, of course.

At six-foot-four, Mahoney took no guff, and he won a healthy audience of both youngsters and adults. *The Range Rider* soon made youngsters pester parents for his famous fringed buckskins, front, back, and arms! The Range Rider helped everyone—Indians, Royal Canadian Mounties, U.S. Cavalry, and of course, damsels in distress, with a smile, wink, and tip of his hat. Both he and partner Dick West flirted harmlessly on the show, but always rode off into the sunset, ready for the next adventure.

His horse, "Rawhide," and Dick West's horse, "Lucky," also became popular with youngsters. But another important note is that this defender of justice in the Old West was a nameless man, known only as the "Ranger Rider." The show was in syndication from 1951 to 1954. Reruns were also run on Saturday afternoons until 1965, 11 years after the show completed its run. Dell Comics issued several *Range Rider* issues and merchandise tie-ins were very popular, and sold through Flying "A" Productions. Many kids went to school with "Range Rider" paper tablets, and ate Langendorf Bread and ButterKrust Bread that both the Ranger Rider and Dick West also enjoyed! The show's theme song was "Home on the Range."

Dick Jones went on to star in *Buffalo Bill Jr.* and eventually retired from acting. He is still with us. Jock Mahoney went on to star in *Yancy Derringer,* which was also very popular. It was a fancy western where Yancy Derringer was an ex-Confederate officer who later owns a riverboat. He is also an undercover agent for New Orleans authorities. He carried hidden derringers

Above: Jock Mahoney, handsome star of **The Range Rider.**

Right: Dick Jones, who starred as the Range Rider's sidekick, "Dick West."

Boxed Range Rider outfit which included the Schmidt Ranger Rider cap gun, and the Halco derringer. Note graphics showing both Range Rider and Dick West on box.

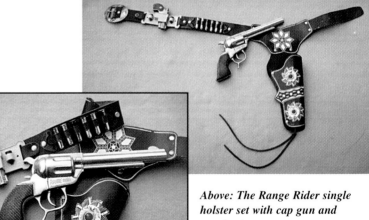

Above: The Range Rider single holster set with cap gun and cap derringer.

Left: Close-up of details of the holster, gun, and derringer.

and had a faithful mute Indian sidekick named "Pahoo." The Indian, played by X. Brands, carried a sawed off shotgun under a blanket. That show ran in the 1958-1959 season.

Jock Mahoney went on to star in films such as *Tarzan*, a role he was perfect for with his great stunts. It is well known that Jock Mahoney could do a running jump onto a horse from the side, landing perfectly into the saddle and stirrups. Jock Mahoney was also honored with the Golden Boot Award for his contribution to western films and entertainment in 1986. He guest-starred in several TV shows, as well as reprising his "Range Rider" role in an episode of *The Fall Guy*. Jock Mahoney, a great actor and stuntman, passed away in 1989.

CAP GUN COLLECTIBLES

Two wonderful Range Rider cap guns exist, one American, one English. The George Schmidt Company made the Range Rider in a 10-inch polished nickel model, with a fluted barrel. The gun breaks open from the top with a left side lever by the hammer. It came in only one pattern, with checkered copper grips. The frame has a "rope" border, and "Range Rider" is raised on both sides of the frame under the cylinder. It is a sleek-looking cap shooter with beautiful grips.

The gun was marketed separately, and also in single holster sets put out by Leslie-Henry. The brown holster with white details also sports a Halco derringer which is clipped on the belt. The box has great colorful graphics of Jock Mahoney as the "Range Rider" and Dick Jones as "Dick West." The derringer is unmarked and is nickel plated with red grips and the Diamond "H" logo. Several other generic guns were also sold in the Range Rider holster sets by Leslie-Henry/Halco, such as the Kilgore Ranger and the Buzz Henry Lone Rider. However, the only known American-made Range Rider cap pistol was made by Schmidt.

The English put us to shame with their version of the Range Rider. Lone Star made the Range Rider MK II and it is a beautiful monster of a gun. At 11 inches, it came in both a gold and nickel finish, and is extensively engraved and scrolled on the frame, the barrel, and ejector rod. The gun is an almost identical copy of the Nichols Stallion MK II, but the similarity stops there.

The gun has a right side push down lever, revealing the cylinder, which loads two-piece aluminum and lead bullets with perforated holes on the shells for smoke action. The ejection rod houses a lever and spring to eject the bullets, one by one, from the cylinder as the cylinder rotates, just like the real thing. "Range Rider MK II" is raised on both sides of the frame under the cylinder. A circle with a longhorn adorns the back part of the cylinder housing on both sides.

The grips will send a collector into orbit. They came in both black and white plastic, with the red star logo at the top. The bottom of the grip has four red jewels, one large and 3 small. In the center of the grip is a beautifully molded Pegasus, the winged horse, in super details, and it is galloping across the 5-pointed star logo in high relief and with a fifth red jewel in the center of the center. The top of the frame has "Lone Star" raised on both sides in between scrolls. This gun is seldom seen and very much in demand.

The box has a great picture of the gun itself and it briefly highlights the details and particulars of the cap shooter, especially noting the "jeweled butts" and "realistic cap-loading cartridges." It's a beautiful piece! These are the only two known Range Rider cap shooters that have surfaced to date. It is believed that Lone Star may have also produced a Range Rider rifle with plastic and die cast works. No American-made Range Rifle is known to exist. No guns marked "Yancy Derringer" have surfaced to date.

British Lone Star Range Rider and its American cousin, the Schmidt Range Rider, shown together for comparison. Note resemblance of the Lone Star model to the Nichols Stallion MK II, and even some resemblance to the Hubley Cowboy.

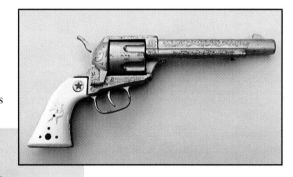

Above: Right side of the Lone Star Range Rider. Note lever for loading. Note that the location of the ejector rod clearly leads to the cylinder chambers.

Close-up of the details showing the loading of the Lone Star model along with the two-piece bullets. Note the spectacular grips with red jewels and Pegasus over the star.

*Dell Comics issue for **Range Rider** for June 1957.*

RANGO

The stars of **Rango,** *left to right, Norman Alden ("Captain Horton"), Guy Marks ("Pink Cloud"), and Tim Conway ("Rango"). (Courtesy of Old West Shop)*

Mattel's Rango boxed single holster set with its famous Fanner 50. Double holster sets were also made for **Rango.**

*R*ango has the dubious distinction of being the only western that few people remember, and one that Hollywood would rather forget. Not even one of television's most popular comedians, Tim Conway, was able to save this farce of a "western comedy." ABC bet on the huge popularity of Tim Conway so much that this program went on the air without a pilot.

Rango was first telecast on January 13, 1967, and lasted just 13 episodes, going immediately into reruns for the summer of 1967, and then going off the air September 1, 1967. Well, it was good for a few laughs, but even the word "few" is used carefully. But Rango was a Texas Ranger, so let's give him a break.

Actually, the plot was decent. Conway played the part of "Rango," a bumbling, clumsy, inept, silly, and befuddled Texas Ranger. To keep him from causing total chaos, his father, who happened to be the head of the Texas Rangers, assigned him to the Ranger Station at Deep Wells. This town's claim to fame was that nothing significant of any kind happened in Deep Wells—that is, until Ranger Rango arrived.

The Post Commander, Captain Horton, would have liked nothing better than to ship Rango out of the country, never mind his station, but Rango just slugged on, causing one problem after another. As soon as outlaws, varmints, and all-around bullies found out where Rango had been posted, they, too, followed, knowing Rango was incapable of doing much to stop them. A 20-year lull in crime and mayhem soon comes to an end.

Captain Horton assigns Rango to the Post's supply depot, where his assistant is a "former" Indian named "Pink Cloud." He's a "former" Indian because he likes the white man's way of life, a warm cot, decent food, beautiful women, and a steady job. Pink Cloud preferred this to hunting for his food, sleeping in a cold teepee, and having to make his own clothes. Additionally, he didn't fancy getting shot by the white man, so he joined them. Rango's nemesis, of course, was Captain Horton. No matter what he assigned Rango to do, it turned into a crisis.

But the producers added many beautiful female guests to the show, and they added to Rango's tongue-tied confusion, what with flirting and all, because Rango was so harmless. Even with this scenario of a harried post captain, a former Indian, and a nincompoop Ranger who could shoot himself in the foot before he got his gun out of his holster, Rango somehow manages to shine in the end, thereby saving the honor and glory of the elite Texas Rangers. Good plot, horrible acting, stale jokes, small brains, and an even smaller audience soon spelled out the demise of *Rango.*

Tim Conway had risen to top-notch comedy fame fresh from *The Carol Burnett Show.* Character actor Norman Alden was cast as "Captain Horton" and comedian Guy Marks played the part of the silly "Pink Cloud." The theme song "Rango" for the show was sung by Frankie Laine. All the stars of this show are still with us. The show was not syndicated and never seen again after it went off the air.

CAP GUN COLLECTIBLES

Mattel Toys marketed two Rango holster sets. One model is a single-holster set and the second is a double-holster set. Both came in the Dura-hide material, developed only by Mattel, in 1960. The holsters are black with lots of sculptured scrollwork, and are quite fancy. The belts were adjustable and came with a simple, square, nickel buckle. All the Rango sets came with Mattel's most famous cap pistol, the Fanner 50. The pattern used was nickle chrome with white antelope grips. The guns are not marked "Rango" and neither is the belt, although both carry the famous Mattel logo and "Fanner 50" markings. The box is bright yellow prominently marked "Rango," with instructions on the back of the box for firing and fanning the gun, loading caps, cleaning, gun safety, and holster pointers. The Rango sets were made in Hawthorne, California, and the Rango was marketed as style #9017. Actually, the Rango sets proved to be more popular than the show. The popularity of Mattel's Fanner 50 cannot be denied. As we know, the same gun was used for the *Cowboy in Africa* as well as *Planet of the Apes* holster sets. These guns came in nickel, chrome, black, and bronze finish, and with white and brown antelope grips. Complete Rango sets in the original "Rango"-marked boxes are seldom seen. The last Rango sets with the antelope-gripped Fanner 50 were produced in 1975.

RAWHIDE

Set in the 1860s, *Rawhide* followed the saga of large cattle drives from San Antonio, Texas, to the Kansas territory. Often remembered as the TV western that launched Clint Eastwood into stardom, this cut-above western was much more than that. *Rawhide* premiered on CBS on January 9, 1959, and ran for seven straight years. During its broadcast, this gritty western became very popular and was awarded the prestigious Western Heritage Award for its authenticity and western drama.

As the program started, over music and the sprawling cattle drive scene, the announcer begins: "This is the landscape of *Rawhide:* desert, forest, mountain, and plains; it is intense heat, bitter cold, torrential rain, blinding dust; men risking their lives, earning a small reward—a life of challenge—Rawhide! It is men like trail scout "Pete Nolan," the cantankerous "Wishbone," "Ramrod Rowdy Yates," good-natured "Mushy," and trail boss "Gil Favor." These men are Rawhide. . . ."

With our lives today more relaxed, comfortable, and luxurious, with plenty of food in a great land, only such a program could bring viewers back to what real hardships were, and *Rawhide* did just that. Several ranchers in Texas would entrust their herds to the men of *Rawhide,* who would then conduct one massive drive of these huge beasts, mooing and banging horns and hoofs as the rough men kept them moving, eventually to Kansas City.

But real cowboys on such drives encounter a host of problems, and there was no shortage of problems on *Rawhide.* From the comfort of our living rooms, eyes glued to the screen, we can only imagine the cost in human sweat, aching bodies, and often blood and tears, as the cowboys encounter stampedes, Indians, flash floods, rustlers, the unpredictable weather, prairie fires, and even deadly disease along the rough, and seemingly never-ending trail.

We are talking about moving cattle without the benefit of lights, weather forecasts, telephones, medical facilities, or even any resemblance of the comforts of a ranch house along the way. The program brought these struggles and hardships to the screen so that we could appreciate our western heritage all the more. Throw into this scenario the unpredictable human elements. It is obvious men are going to get irritated, tired, and will want to give up and pull out. Personalities being what they are, this added a great human touch to this wonderful show. Working as a team meant something. The trail boss didn't have to be your friend, and you didn't have to like him; you just had to do your job. A man's word was his bond.

Cast as Gil Favor, the trail boss and supervisor of this immense venture, Eric Fleming played the role with no-nonsense seriousness and command. His orders were supreme and you did your job or you got out—minus your pay! Cast as his ramrod, Rowdy Yates, was the handsome young star Clint Eastwood. Rowdy was the trail scout and while he often disagreed with the trail boss, he carried out his orders, settled disputes, and was Favor's right-hand man, a man he could trust. Both men interacted well and both were soon very popular with audiences.

A show of this size and magnitude, much like *Wagon Train,* soon introduced many regulars that became part of the family. These included a host of wonderful character actors. Sheb Wooley was cast as "Pete Nolan." The cantankerous cook the announcer talks about was "Wishbone," an old coot but lovably played by Paul Brinegar. Cast as his helper "Mushy," was character actor Jim Murdock. Other regulars included "Jim

Clint Eastwood ("Rowdy Yates," the Ramrod), and Eric Fleming, ("Gil Favor," the Trail Boss), the two lead stars of **Rawhide.**

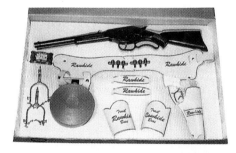

Contents of the Carnell Rawhide Cowboy Outfit. The cap gun is the Cowpoke by Lone Star. Note the show title on the gunbelt and holster pocket. (Courtesy of F. Carlson)

Above: Lone Star Cowpoke with caramel swirl notch bar grips used in the Carnell Rawhide sets. This is a well-made solid, nickel-finish cap shooter.

Left: Cowpoke Jr., also put out by Lone Star, is an all-metal gun with metal notch bar grips. The frame is heavily engraved. Seldom seen, compared to its big brother.

Above: Lone Star Cowpoke with brown stag grips and notch bar.

Right: Close-up of details, showing notch bar grips and horse head logo on frame.

Quince," played by Steve Raines; "Joe Scarlett," played by Rocky Shahan; and "Hey Soos Patines," the horsekeeper, played by Robert Cabal.

Later in the series, veteran actor John Ireland starred as "Jed Colby." Raymond St. Jacques joined the cast as "Solomon King." Midway through its seven-year run, character actors Charles Gray and David Watson also signed on as "Clay Forrester" and "Ian Cabot," respectively. Given such a setting, *Rawhide* featured dozens of guest stars along the way, including singer Dean Martin, Neville Brand (*Laredo*), Sammy Davis, Jr., Barbara Eden (*I Dream of Jeannie*), Mercedes McCambridge (*One Man's Family, Wire Services*) Julie Harris, Ed Begley, James Whitmore, Linda Cristal (*High Chaparral*), and so many others.

Sheb Wooley, the character actor, writer, and singing cowboy, also found fame with his hit song "Purple People Eater" in the mid-1960s which sold 2 million copies in just 12 weeks. He had starred in more than 30 westerns, including *High Noon* and *Little Big Horn* before being cast in Rawhide.

Eric Fleming, the rugged trail boss, was a veteran of Broadway plays, including *Portrait of a Lady, No Time for Sergeants* and *Plain & Fancy.* Considered a he-man of the time, he was a former Navy Seabee who was working as a stagehand when asked to audition. Acting lessons in both Hollywood and New York ensured his future that eventually led to *Rawhide.*

Clint Eastwood was an athletic young man when drafted into the army in 1951. A movie director for United International saw him and suggested he try acting after his army service. Ten months later, Eastwood was a newly married man, and after coming to Hollywood, landed a film contract with UI. He did a series of movies, among which were *Lafayette Escadrille, Tarantula, Never Say Goodbye, First Traveling Saleslady,* and *Francis* (the talking mule). A CBS TV producer named Bob Sparks took one look at Eastwood and decided he had the man to play "Rowdy Yates" on *Rawhide.* The rest is history.

In the last year of the show, Eastwood became the trail boss himself. The theme song for *Rawhide* was sung by Frankie Laine, which also became a well-known hit. This great western finally ended its long seven-year cattle drive on January 4, 1966. After 144 episodes of saddle sores and swallowing dust, *Rawhide* went into retirement. Today, it still can be seen in syndication, and remains very popular to us aging "cowpokes."

Carnell boxed set for Rawhide, double holsters with Cowpoke cap guns. Note this set has the same metal saddle concho used for Black Saddle but in white! (Courtesy of F. Carlson)

Clint Eastwood saw the future for westerns was dim in 1966 and headed to Italy where he made a string of "spaghetti westerns," with such memorable movies as *High Plains Drifter, The Good, The Bad and The Ugly; The Outlaw Josie Wales; A Fistful of Dollars;* and so many others. He went on to everlasting fame as "Dirty Harry" and won an Oscar for his role as the aging gunfighter in *The Unforgiven.* Clint Eastwood remains one of Hollywood's most popular actors, and is now a seasoned director with many excellent films to his credit. Sadly, Eric Fleming drowned in September 1966, just a few months after the run of *Rawhide,* while filming a movie in South America. Veteran actor John Ireland died in 1992. The other cast members are still with us.

CAP GUN COLLECTIBLES

Remarkably, as I have stated throughout this study, even a program as popular, and with seven years under its rawhide belt, no American companies made a cap pistol marked "Rawhide." No guns marked for Gil Favor or Rowdy Yates are known to exist. Carnell Roundup and Classy both marketed Rawhide gun and holster sets, and Daisy came out with the Trail Boss rifle. Several guns were used in these great toy sets. Let's examine them closely.

Carnell's Rawhide gun and holster sets came in both single and double models. The holster pockets came both plain and fancy. One double set pattern came in black leather with white details, with the holster pocket sporting the same saddle as used on the Black Saddle and other generic holsters. The guns used in the Carnell sets were Lone Star Cowpoke, referring to the cowpoke on the cattle drives while at the same time being a standard cowboy title. The fact

Classy boxed Rawhide double holster set with Hubley cap guns. Note the photo of Eric Fleming, the Rawhide *trail boss on the box. (Courtesy of F. Carlson)*

that Carnell used only the Cowpoke in its sets, including identifying it as "Carnell's own Cowpoke cap pistol" ensures it was made for the Rawhide sets.

Carnell also marketed a spectacular Rawhide cowboy outfit which featured Eric Fleming as trail boss Gil Favor on the box. This great set included a light tan single holster set with "Rawhide" on both the belt and holster pocket center. It came with a Lone Star Cowpoke 50 shot repeating cap pistol, canteen, spurs, and wrist cuffs. The spur straps have "Rawhide" on them while the wrist cuffs have both "Rawhide" and "Trail Boss" on them. The set also included a 50 shot repeating cap rifle with lever action. The rifle has dark brown plastic stock and die cast works. The box carries both the Carnell Roundup logo of the longhorn and the CBS "eye" logo. Marketed in the Carnell catalog as #4740, it sold for an "astronomical" price of $6.98.

The Cowpoke cap pistol is a 9-inch nickel cap shooter. It came with cream colored swirl grips identical to the Lone Star Maverick series. The grips are also found in white and brown. The grips have the "notch

Above: Hubley Cowpokes with rawhide leather double holster set.

Left: Hubley's Cowpoke gold-plated cap pistol with brown wood grain grips. Note the "C" in the word "Cowpoke" is a horseshoe.

bar" on them and are a simulated stag design. The nickel frames have extensive scrollwork and the horse head logo along with "Cowpoke" is raised on both sides. The lever, which breaks the gun open from the top, is located on the right side of the hammer. These guns are not marked "Lone Star" or "Carnell."

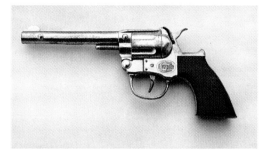

As we now know, the same design was used by Lone Star and Carnell Roundup for Maverick, Bat Masterson, Gray Ghost, and the Buntline series. It is a pretty, well-made cap gun. Lone Star also made an all-metal Cowpoke Jr which it used in the smaller holster sets of the Rawhide series marketed by Carnell Roundup. Only one inch smaller at 8 inches, even this all-metal, nickel-plated gun has the "notch bar" stag grips.

The Classy Rawhide set came in the same style box as used in the Classy Harvell-Kilgore model for Tombstone Territory. A small TV screen photo on the bottom left shows actor Eric Fleming as "Gil Favor." The heavily-tooled tan and brown holsters are marked "Rawhide" on the belt. The guns are the late Hubley-Halco models with white grips and the steer head logo on them. Halco copied this Hubley model for its Bonanza, Paladin, and Gunsmoke models.

Hubley also made the Cowpoke in both nickel- and gold-plated models. It came with white and brown simulated wood grain grips. This is also an 8-inch cap shooter, and it is has "Hubley" on the right side of the frame and "Cowpoke" on the left side of the frame raised in an oval frame with the "C" of Cowpoke being a horseshoe. This gun breaks from the top by hand pressure. A nifty cap shooter, this gun is rarely seen. It was used in the smaller Rawhide sets marketed by Classy Products and Hubley. No Hubley guns marked "Rawhide" exist.

While Hubley made several, shall we say "cowboy" titles such as the celebrated Cowboy, the Cowboy Jr., Cowtyke, and Li'l Cowtyke, only the Cowpoke model is rarely encountered and used for the smaller Rawhide sets. The smaller holsters come in the tan rough "rawhide" style. It appears that the same smaller holsters were made identical for both Rawhide, which was spelled "Raw-Hide," and Wagon Train sets—and some are found with both markings!

Leave it to Lone Star to come out with a gun to honor Rowdy Yates, the "ramrod" of the cattle drive! There is no question that this was the point and meaning for the Lone Star

Lone Star Ramrod cap gun with nickel finish and red grips. Seldom seen. (Courtesy of Steve Arlin)

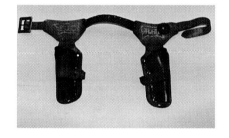

Large heavy leather Rawhide double holster set with silver details.

Leslie-Henry Longhorn cap pistol with pop-up cap box which came in some large Rawhide double holster sets and also on its own card.

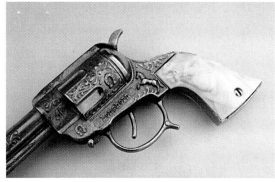

Left: Close-up of the Longhorn showing details and pearl-like translucent grips.

Right: Close-up of details on the Daisy Trail Boss rifle. (Courtesy of Jim Thomas)

Daisy's Trail Boss Winchester-style smoke and bang rifle.

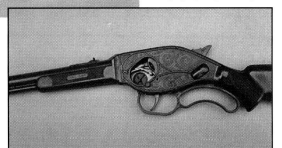

Above: Carnell Roundup unique rifle sold in Rawhide sets with Lone Star Cowpoke cap pistol.

Right: Close-up of detail showing strange and unique sliding door compartment of left side of Rawhide rifle to load caps.

Dell Comics issue of Rawhide , 1961.

Ramrod cap shooter. The Ramrod was an 8-inch cap shooter that came with a nickel finish. Engraving was on the frame, but with a plain barrel. The gun breaks open from the top with a side lever. This gun is marked "Ramrod" on the frame and comes with orange-reddish slick plastic grips, with a silver star on the upper section of the grips, similar to the five-point star used on other Lone Star models such as Apache and Rebel. This gun sports a nice western hammer. The more of an "oval" shaped trigger guard is similar, but not identical to the Lone Star Cisco Kid. For the British to come out with a gun to honor an American Wild West icon like the ramrod of a big cattle drive, the main theme of *Rawhide*, is almost a slap in the face of the American toy gun companies at the time! This Lone Star model is seldom seen.

A large, dark brown, double holster set with "Rawhide" on the belt in silver details was recently found with two Leslie-Henry Longhorn cap shooters. While the maker of this holster set is not entirely clear, it would also make some sense that Longhorn guns came with it and fit perfectly into the pockets. Perhaps, like Carnell, Classy, Hubley, and Daisy, the actual show title of *Rawhide* could not be used due to trademarks. The Leslie-Henry Longhorn is one of the most beautiful and well-made guns. At 10 inches, it is a wider than usual, sturdy cap shooter with extensive scrollwork, and the pop-up cap magazine with the lever located in front of the frame.

It has "Longhorn" raised on both sides of the frame, and comes with white, translucent horse head grips. The rearing Leslie-Henry horse is also raised on the frame. This gun was also marketed by Halco on a card showing longhorn steers on a cattle drive, with a cowboy on his horse moving along the herd. Halco called the pop-up cap box "quick snap-up opening." The same pattern gun was used for Leslie-Henry's Wild Bill Hickok and Maverick models of this design. The holsters are unique and have a "sawmill style" leather concho on the belt. A double holster set for smaller cowpokes in the family came in rawhide-style leather with Halco generic guns. The holsters and belt are silk-screened "Rawhide" in black lettering.

Daisy marketed the Trail Boss smoke and bang rifle. It was a 30-inch long rifle with a brown metal barrel and walnut plastic stock. It has the Winchester lever action, which is gold tone and marked with "Daisy" on both sides. The right side of the receiver has "Trail Boss" in gold lettering, along with a cowboy on his horse looking back, presumably, at his cattle herd. There is an open prairie scene around the cowboy. This is an attractive looking rifle in great colors.

As we know, Nichols made a series of cowboy-related cap guns, all of which were generic titles, even if one would associate them to cattle drives and cowboys. These are the Nichols Cowman, Cowhand, Cowpuncher, Cowtyke, and Tophand, but none were associated with the *Rawhide* series. Even the holsters sold with these guns are generic in style and none have "Rawhide" markings, thus leaving the Rawhide connections, shall we say, to the Lone Star-made Cowpoke, and Ramrod, Hubley Cowpoke, Daisy Trail Boss, Leslie-Henry Longhorn, and the Carnell and Classy products actually marked as "Rawhide."

No rifles marked or stamped "Rawhide" are known to exist. No guns marked "Rawhide" are known to exist and none with any of the show character names have ever surfaced. Only the holsters, accoutrements, and boxes are marked "Rawhide." All of the "Rawhide"-marked sets that are known to exist came with the guns and rifles as described above.

THE REBEL · JOHNNY YUMA

"Johnny Yuma" was a bitter, battle-hardened ex-Confederate soldier, hence, the title *The Rebel*. Set in the late 1860s, following his Civil War service, Yuma heads west, trying to carve out a new life for himself, knowing that the South he loved, for the most part, was gone. He was a young man of strong ethics and principles. As he searches for his own identity and a renewed sense of self-worth after losing everything in the war, he brings his anger, intensity, and rebel attitude along with him as he goes from town to town further westward.

Refusing to discard his Confederate kepi, as well as other parts of his uniform, Yuma soon encounters hatred and slurs against him, his uniform, and the South. Yuma carried two guns in the series—a Civil War-style dragoon pistol in a cut-off Cavalry flapped holster and what he called his "scattergun," a sawed-off double barrel shotgun altered at both ends. Yuma keeps a journal as he drifts along and records his adventures. He gets involved not only in criminal matters where the downtrodden are at the short end of the stick, but a lot of moral issues as well. The show caught on right away and became very popular.

The Rebel came to the ABC Network on October 4, 1959. It was a half-hour show, and it was placed in the only open spot, on Sunday nights at 9:00 p.m. It was one of 28 westerns when *The Rebel* premiered. Opposite *The Rebel* was *The Chevy Show* on NBC and *The General Electric Theater* on CBS, both established and popular shows. But *The Rebel* held its own in the initial ratings, caught a large audience, and received favorable reviews by the critics.

Cast as the young "Rebel" was handsome young actor Nick Adams. Adams had acted in several movies in the 1950s, among them *Rebel Without a Cause*, with James Dean in 1955. Some of his other movies that were well known are *Mister Roberts*, *No Time for Sergeants*, and *The FBI Story*. He also did other teen-oriented movies before landing the role of Johnny Yuma. Nick Adams, along with Andy Fenady, helped create the character and the show. Adams, along with Fenady and Irvin Kershner, formed the Fen-Ker-Ada Productions and got Bill Todman and Mark Goodson to put up the money for the pilot.

He brought a serious intensity to the role of Johnny Yuma and he garnered thousands of fans. Adams was hard on himself, and he not only played the role perfectly, but he studied all he could about the Civil War to also capture the essence of the Rebs that returned to ruined farms, broken lives, and shattered dreams. In the pilot,

Nick Adams—"The Rebel"—with a good shot of his holster and gunbelt. Note the brass plate at the cut off cavalry-style holster that he wore on the series.

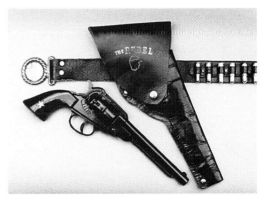

Above: Lone Star Rebel single cavalry holster outfit. Note the show title and logo of the Rebel on the holster flap. Note the buckle was similar to the one on the show. (Courtesy of Bill Longstreet)

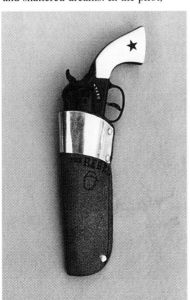

Above: Lone Star Rebel with white grips and black inset star, along with rough leather holster with metal plate, show title, and Rebel logo on the holster pocket. This was meant to resemble the one Johnny Yuma wore on the show.

Left: The Rebel in the same holster. Note how it sits high in the holster with the entire trigger guard exposed for a fast draw.

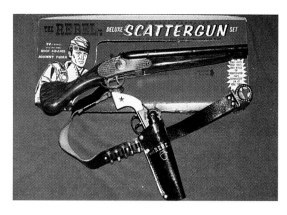

Classy Rebel scattergun with original box, and the Lone Star Rebel cap shooter with black leather gunbelt and holster. Note the metal plate and logo on holster pocket. (Courtesy of J. Schleyer)

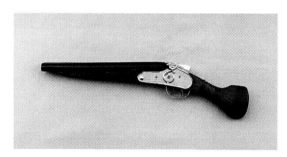

Above: Classy's Rebel cap-firing double-barreled scattergun. The scattergun itself was not marked to the show, only the box.

Right: Close-up view of the details showing percussion-style hammers and lockplate.

The Classy scattergun opened to show details of the double row of cap mounts. The scattergun breaks open like a real shotgun. (Courtesy of R. Wright)

which initially was called *Johnny Yuma*, we see "the Rebel" return home to Mason City only to find that a gang of murderers have not only taken over the town he grew up in, but have also killed his father.

Cast as the scheming outlaw gang leader was Dan Blocker, who was to gain immortal fame as "Hoss" on *Bonanza*. Jeanette Nolan was cast as Johnny Yuma's aunt. Character actor Strother Martin played a boozing deputy when the stress of what the town has become gets to him. Veteran actor John Carradine was cast as "Elmer Dodson," editor of the *Mason City Bulletin*.

"The Ballad of Johnny Yuma," the show's theme song, sung by then-struggling Johnny Cash, became a hit in its own right. Written by Andy Fenady and Dick Markowitz, "The Ballad of Johnny Yuma" has its own saga. ABC wanted the Ames Brothers to sing it, but Fenady later recalled that he preferred one man to sing it, since the character of *The Rebel* was a lone drifter.

A personal friend of Elvis Presley, Adams wanted him to sing the theme song, but the producers of the show, Goodson-Todman Productions, preferred Johnny Cash. Another serious contender was Tex Ritter, who had sung in *High Noon*, but that was also discarded in favor of Johnny Cash, which gave him instant recognition.

Nick Adams was a slender, 5'8" man, and this made him perfect for this particular role. Dwarfed by the already-established western giants such as Clint Walker (*Cheyenne*), James Arness ("Matt Dillon" of *Gunsmoke*), Wayde Preston (*Colt .45*) and others, his size also made him a "rebel" of sorts, and he brought his brand of "justice" by using the scattergun, his attitude, and his refusal to be the "vanquished rebel" to the role. He wore his single holster slung very low on the show.

The Rebel ended up as one of the most popular and respected westerns, and ran for a total of 76 episodes, ending a healthy run on September 12, 1962. Although Adams was the main character, several character and veteran actors appeared in roles related to Civil War personalities, such as "Gen. Robert E. Lee," played by George MacCready, and "Gen. Ulysses S. Grant," played by William Bryant. Veteran cowboy stars Bob Steele and Tex Ritter also appeared on the show.

After the series ended, Nick Adams returned to the big screen, acting in *Hell is for Heroes*, a great war epic that starred a number of other western heroes such as Steve McQueen, Fess Parker, and James Coburn. He also starred in *Young Dillinger* and *Twilight of Honor* for which he was nominated for an Oscar as "Best Supporting Actor" in 1963. Adams also appeared briefly on the TV series *Saints and Sinners* as a crusading reporter in late 1962-1963 season.

CAP GUN COLLECTIBLES

Lone Star, Classy, Kilgore, Hubley and Marx all honored *The Rebel* with a variety of cap guns and sawed-off "scatterguns" and holsters. It was obvious the show was a popular one, and lots of "young Rebs" were sure going to imitate their new TV western hero.

Lone Star made two models of the Rebel cap shooter. Identical to its popular Apache, it was a 10-inch cap pistol with "Rebel" raised on both sides of the frame on a rocker panel, on the frame just behind the cylinder. The Lone Star Rebel came in both nickel and black finishes. The grips came in both white and black, with the inset five-point star in the lower section of the grips. The sleek grips have a black star in the white grips and a gold star in the black grips. Both guns have a revolving cylinder and the dragoon-style pistol breaks open with a lever on the right side of the cylinder area. The cap shooter is tight and well made. Rebel holster sets marketed with the Lone Star have also been found with the Apache model.

Classy marketed the Rebel Lone Star guns in at least three holster styles. These include a black leather holster and belt with a Civil War-style round buckle. This first holster came in the cavalry style, but without the flap cover. Instead, across the top portion of the holster pocket, copying from Johnny Yuma's own holster pattern, there is a brass plate riveted to the leather. This is also found in a nickeled tin metal plate. Below the plate, in silver details, is "The Rebel" in the same lettering used on the show title, and an outline of Johnny Yuma with his bummer cap on.

As result of the way this holster was cut, the gun sits very high up on the holster pocket, since the gun's trigger guard is fully exposed and rests on the top of the holster pocket. Classy also marketed a black cavalry-style holster with a flap pocket, and on this pattern, the same markings, in silver details, and the character outline, are on the flap of the holster. Classy, as we know, marketed the Harvell-Kilgore Products after they merged and moved to Bolivar, Tennessee, and the boxes are marked as such, carrying both the Classy name and the Harvell-Kilgore name and logo.

The third holster was a rough tan "rawhide" style, with a nickeled metal plate across the top of the holster pocket, and "The Rebel" and the character outline in black details on the holster just below the metal plate.

The Scattergun was made by Classy. It was a scaled down, 21-inch long double-barrel shotgun with a brown plastic stock, nickel receiver, and double hammers and triggers. The lockplate has a circular pattern overall design. The shotgun breaks open from the top, exposing a double row of cap mounts. The hammers are the percussion style. The barrels are black. The Scattergun came in a box with graphics showing "The Rebel" on it. This was marketed with both holster and the Rebel cap gun as a set, and also as the Scattergun separately. It is not marked "The Rebel" or "Johnny Yuma." Classy marked only the holsters and the boxes.

Classy marketed and sold through Sears and other outlets a Rebel Scattergun Holster Set, and the gray felt Rebel bummer's cap that Yuma wore on the show. This set also came with the eagle's claw necklace that Yuma wore for good luck. The outstanding feature of this set was the special belt that had the holster for the Rebel cap gun, and a special leather, hand-laced holster carrier for the Scattergun that also was marked "the Rebel" with the character outline.

Kilgore came out with a Rebel cap gun that was re-introduced by modifying the Champion fast-draw model that Kilgore marketed in 1960. This is a scarce Rebel cap gun made before the move with Harvell. This is a 10-inch, nickel-plated, well-engraved cap shooter. It has scrollwork engraving on the barrel and cylinder, and has a left side gate for cap loading. It has "Rebel" raised on both sides of the frame under the cylinder, along with the Kilgore Circle "K" logo on both sides. The grips are a beautiful brown and black swirl with checkered sections, and with the Circle "K" logo on both sides. By careful observation of the gun butt and design, one can distinguish how Kilgore used the Champion pattern for the Rebel. The area where the fast draw timer is located on the

Kilgore Rebel 10-inch cap shooter in silver finish with checkered grips. Note beautiful checkered swirl grips, and show title on frame. A very seldom-seen cap shooter.

Above: Harvell-Kilgore The Southerner double holster set marketed for the Civil War Centennial in 1961 came with two gray leather Rebel holsters with title and logo on the flap, cap shooters, belt, and Confederate money! (Courtesy of Mike Cherry)

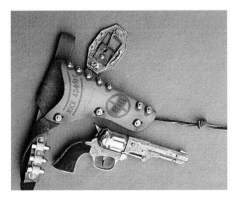

Hubley gunbelt and holster marked to both actor Nick Adams and show title "Rebel" in gray leather with burnt orange details. Hubley Coyote dragoon-style, all-metal gun came with this set.

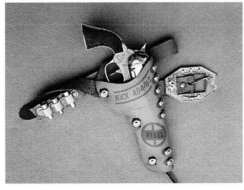

Hubley Rebel gunbelt with Hubley Coyote holstered. The rivets also have the Hubley logo. Very seldom seen set, marked to both actor and show title.

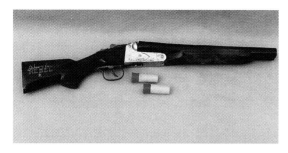

Above: Marx Johnny Yuma-Rebel double barreled shotgun with its shells.

Right: Close-up of the details of character name and show title on stock, also showing compartment in butt to hold shells. Extremely rare Rebel toy gun.

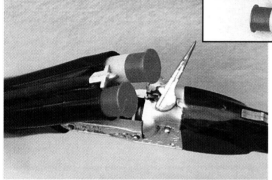

Close-up of the shells in the barrels and opening lever action of shotgun. This prototype was made at the Marx plant in Erie, Pennsylvania.

Dell Comic issued for The Rebel starring Nick Adams, for November 1962. Note the Scattergun details and Johnny Yuma's gunbelt.

Champion was expertly filled in for the Rebel. This is an extremely rare gun.

In 1961, in a "Civil War Centennial," Harvell-Kilgore marketed the Southerner gun and holster set for the "little Rebel" in your home. This set came with gray leather flap holsters and two Kilgore Pal all-metal guns. The guns are 4-inch single shot cap pistols. The holsters came with a thin adjustable belt. Both holster flaps have "The Rebel" and "Johnny Yuma" outline on them. The set came on a blister card. It is interesting that Harvell-Kilgore used the Rebel holsters and markings to market the Southerner, and for this reason it is included in this study.

Hubley paid tribute to *The Rebel* in a special way. They came out with a gray leather holster, in the western style, with a gray leather belt and 3 bullets. The typical Hubley studs and "Hubley"-marked rivets adorn the holster and belt and bullet loops. What makes this set remarkable is that both the name of the show and the name of the actor—Nick Adams—and not the name of the character—"Johnny Yuma"—are detailed in orange on the gray holster, along with "Rebel" in black lettering across what resembles the crossed-hair sights of a telescope, on the holster front.

"Nick Adams" also in orange lettering is across the top portion of the holster pocket. Hubley's all metal, dragoon-style, 8-inch Coyote came with this set. This set was made in very limited numbers, perhaps even as a prototype, and is quite rare. Both the holster, belt, and buckle are western style, as opposed to the more cavalry style of the Classy holster patterns.

Finally, Louis Marx, in its Erie, Pennsylvania, plant designed and prototyped the extremely rare Johnny Yuma double-barreled version of the Scattergun. The stock is a beautiful brown marbleized swirl. The two barrels are black plastic with the same brown swirl forestock. The lockplate is in silver, and die-cast parts with a sliding section bring down the trigger and cap loading box. A die cast lever opens and locks the double barrels similar to a real double barrel shotgun. The shotgun came with two red and yellow dummy shotgun shells. The barrels are 12 inches long and, overall, the Marx version of the Scattergun is slightly longer, at 22 inches, than the Classy model.

On the shortened stock, which also has a checkered pistol grip section, the right side of the stock sports a signature of "Johnny Yuma" in silver, and "The Rebel" in dark red lettering with a silver five-point star below. The lettering is in the same style as used on the show title. The spectacular toy was designed by Roy Atglen. Another model on which Marx was going to add double hammers was never produced. This is an extremely rare Rebel cap firing "scattergun" style, double barreled shotgun that carries both the name of the show and the name of the character. By contrast, the Classy Scattergun is not character-marked.

The Japanese made a tin toy pop rifle marked "The Rebel." It was a 21-inch blued tin rifle with a red wooden stock on which is a graphic outline of Johnny Yuma, and "The Rebel" in black, all on the left side. The tin lockplate has graphics-shown bullets chambered, and there was also a fabric style sling. The locking mechanism caused the rifle to make the "pop" sound.

Nick Adams, the brash and restive actor, always loved the South and the Confederacy. He even named his son Jeb Stuart and his daughter Allyson Lee after two of the South's greatest generals. Sadly, on February 7, 1968, he was found dead in his home. The death was ruled a suicide. But to this day, his associates, friends, and family still believe the death was accidental, since he had everything to live for, was happy with his life and his work. His promising career was cut short at the very young age of 36 years. Perhaps Nick Adams was a "rebel" in his own right.

RED RYDER AND LITTLE BEAVER

No book on western characters and cap guns and rifles would be complete without including *Red Ryder*—the most popular and most successful of comic strips—as well as scores of actors that played the part of the carrot-topped cowboy and his Indian sidekick, "Little Beaver." He was also the character that made the Daisy Red Ryder BB rifle a household word. Few people know the story of Red Ryder and Little Beaver, and even fewer people today have ever heard of him. But to us cowhands, western character enthusiasts, comic page lovers, and the nostalgic "good old days" genre, who can forget *Red Ryder*? Or Little Beaver?

Red Ryder was born out of the genius of Fred Harman, a young illustrator and western subjects painter. He dreamed up the character and initially named him "Bronc Peeler," and gave him a faithful Indian sidekick named "Little Beaver." He went from Kansas City to Hollywood, where he started his own syndication. He was also doing western books, where Little Beaver first appeared. He sold the strip to the *San Francisco Chronicle* and about 20 other initial newspapers.

Thinking that the name "Bronc Peeler" (a cowboy term for "bronc buster") was not commonly known, he changed the character's name to "Red Ryder." It was an overnight success as some 750 newspapers and foreign distributors picked up the strip. It was November 6, 1938, when *Red Ryder*, newly renamed, hit the streets as a Sunday strip. It went to a daily strip in 1939, and the following year, the movies picked up the character.

In 1942, *Red Ryder* came to radio. It was announced by Ben Alexander, who was the first of Jack Webb's partners in *Dragnet* on television. The radio show was 30 minutes and opened up with the announcement "From out of the West comes America's famous fighting cowboy—Red Ryder!" Reed Hadley was radio's "Red Ryder," with Tommy Cook, (and later, Henry Blair) as the voices of "Little Beaver." The radio series was extremely popular, but the Red Ryder movies were even more popular as several actors put a face to the voice of the roving cowboy trying to maintain law and order. The radio show ran for ten years.

Above: Fred Harman's Red Ryder and Little Beaver hell bent for leather! (Courtesy of Jim Thomas)

Above: Wild Bill Elliott as "Red Ryder" along with Bobby Blake as "Little Beaver," and George "Gabby" Hayes. Note the double holsters on Bill Elliott with gun butt-first. (Courtesy of Old West Shop)

Left: Don "Red" Barry as "Red Ryder" and Bobby Blake as "Little Beaver" in the Red Ryder serials for Republic Pictures. (Courtesy of Old West Shop)

Allen "Rocky" Lane, who played the last "Red Ryder," and was cast to be "Red Ryder" on television in 1956.

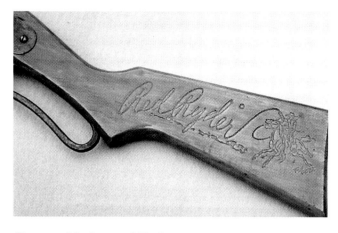

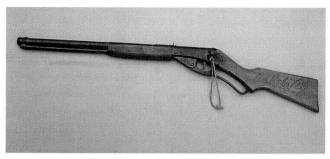

The Daisy Red Ryder carbine, probably the world's most popular rifle for a young boy. Ask dad, he had one. (Courtesy of Bill Longstreet)

Close-up of the immortal "Red Ryder" on the stock of the Daisy #111 carbine.

Between 1940 and 1956, there were four western actors that played "Red Ryder" in the movies. These included "Wild Bill" Elliott, Don "Red" Barry, Jim Bannon, and Allen "Rocky" Lane. Don Barry played Red Ryder for Republic serials, *The Adventures of Red Ryder,* in 12 chapters. The role of Little Beaver went to Bobby Blake (real name Mike Gubitosi), who had played in the children's serials T*he Little Rascals.* Robert Blake, as he became known in later life, went on to play "Baretta" on TV. When he appeared on *The Tonight Show* with Johnny Carson, the subject of his playing "Little Beaver" came up and it appears that he will certainly be remembered for that role as a youngster.

In the 1951 movie, *The Cowboy and the Prize Fighter,* Red Ryder was played by the relatively unknown actor Jim Bannon. The movie was not very popular. Another movie with Jim Bannon as "Red" was titled Ride, Ryder, Ride, but this one also quickly rode into the sunset. The most popular movie actors remembered as Red Ryder are Wild Bill Elliott and Don "Red" Barry. Although not red-haired, but wiry and of short stature, Don Barry was soon nicknamed "Red" for playing the role. He went on to play tough characters in dozens of western movies and TV western programs long after his "Red Ryder" role ended. Two more well-known Red Ryder movies with Wild Bill Elliott and Bobby Blake as "Little Beaver" were *Lone Texas Ranger* and *The Conquest of Cheyenne.*

The last "Red Ryder" was none other than western hero Allen "Rocky" Lane, who along with Wild Bill Elliott, was the best-known of the Red Ryder characters. This took some research, but apparently in 1956, 39 episodes of *Red Ryder* were filmed and syndicated for television. Exhaustive research into this program explains that the show was based on "the radio program that chronicled the 19th century exploits of 'Red Ryder' and his Indian friend, 'Little Beaver,' as they struggle to maintain law and order throughout the West." Allen Lane was cast as "Red Ryder" and Louis Letteri was cast as "Little Beaver." For whatever reason, the 30 minute show never aired.

The Daisy Little Beaver buffalo gun, a cork-firing pop rifle-gun.

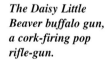

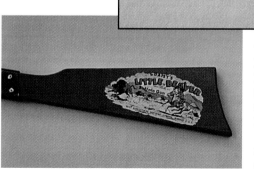

All the actors that played Red Ryder have died— "Wild Bill" Elliott in 1965, Allen "Rocky" Lane in 1973, and Don "Red" Barry in 1980. Robert "Little Beaver" Blake is still with us.

Fred Harman himself visited the offices of Daisy Manufacturing in Plymouth, Michigan, hoping to sell them the idea of putting out a Red Ryder cap pistol based on a six-shooter that Harman himself had whittled, based on his own single action frontier shooter. Meeting up with Cass Hough and other executives, they were more interested in putting this new character out as "the Red Ryder BB air rifle." They patterned it after Harman's own 30-30 carbine saddle gun and thus, in 1939, the Red Ryder BB air rifle was born. Production actually started in 1940.

Close-up of colorful decal on the red wooden stock. Seldom seen complete.

Fred Harman, a true-to-life cowboy and western artist with a great vision for the red-headed upholder of the law, hosted several celebrations for the winners of Daisy's "Red Ryder Shooting Contests" on his own "Red Ryder Ranch" in Colorado. A truly caring and dedicated illustrator who loved the open spaces and young children, Harman traveled all over the world promoting gun safety and "Red Ryder," even touring with a real Indian boy as "Little Beaver." Harman finally retired the "Red Ryder & Little Beaver" strip in 1962, and returned to devoting the rest of his life to painting western scenes on canvas.

Both Red Ryder and Little Beaver were propelled to everlasting fame via the comic strip, radio, movies, millions of comics, Whitman books, and a whole variety of products. There were also "Little Beaver" archery sets, knives, flashlights, gloves, games, and jigsaw puzzles. However, the bonanza came in the form of the Daisy Red Ryder BB air rifles and the Littler Beaver Buffalo Gun. These wonderful products, which hawked "Ask Dad, he had one" and "every boy wants a Daisy" would require a book of its own. Therefore, your scribe is only includ-ing the main Red Ryder and Little Beaver guns closer to our 1950-1960 interest.

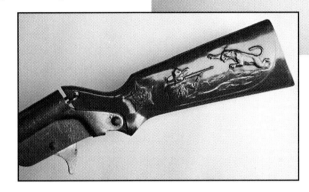

The #111 Red Ryder carbine came out in 1940, with "Red Ryder" on the wooden stock and a rawhide thong on the left side of the carbine. It was a 1000 shot repeater on "one load," and had "Red Ryder" in signature form on the stock. At 36 inches long, it sold for $2.95. This is considered the all-time favorite Red Ryder rifle. It is also known as the Number 111 Model 40. The entire Red Ryder series, from 1940 to 1962, when they were discontinued, went through as many as 15 variations, seven of which were before the Model 94 was introduced in 1954. By 1962, interest had leveled off and the Red Ryder was discontinued.

Above: Daisy's Red Ryder Cork rifle, made at Arkansas plant.

Left: Close-up of molded stock showing Red shoot-ing mountain cat. (Cour-tesy of Jim Thomas)

But in 1972, Red Ryder was again introduced, coming out with what they called the Model 1938. These new models also went through various changes in 1978, 1979, and in 1983, they came out with "The Christmas Story" model, with a compass and sundial on the left side of the stock. In 1988, Daisy came out with the 50th Anniversary Commemorative of the Red Ryder, which it manufactured in well over 100,000 units. So, while we have a generation of youngsters who never heard of Red Ryder, to Daisy's credit and as a lasting testament to Fred Harman, we'll keep him "alive" for the next generation of youngsters, hoping they, too, will want to imitate "America's Favorite Cowboy."

The Little Beaver Buffalo Gun was marketed as Model #99, which came out in 1951. This is a 19-inch "rifle" with a blued metal barrel and a red wooden stock. It came with feathers attached to the barrel and 10 corks to shoot. The stock comes with a very colorful decal with great graphics showing "Little Beaver" on his horse, with upraised rifle, riding towards buffalo. This is a seldom seen cork rifle and it has great cocking action. The gun carries the Plymouth, Michigan, address on the parts and on the Little Beaver decal.

The #950 Red Ryder's Double Barrel Training Shotgun came out in 1956, and was touted by Red Ryder himself, telling mom and dad that this was a harmless cork-shooting shotgun just like the one that was carried by "Red Ryder himself." Red Ryder, in comic strip illustra-tion, tells the youngster to "Learn Safe Shooting on a Daisy, Pardner!" It was 31 inches long with a high impact shock resistant stock, with Red Ryder's picture on the stock. With gun-blue metal double barrels, the break action cocks both triggers, and six corks were included in the set. Alluding to the 1956 TV show that was withdrawn, the advertisement also read "Number 950 was designed from the shotgun carried by Red Ryder, America's favorite cowboy of comic strip, radio, and TV fame." This is not often seen and it is a scarce shotgun of our red-haired hero. In 1958, Daisy moved from Michigan to Arkansas.

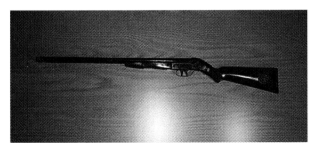

Daisy's Red Ryder Double Barrel Training Shotgun. Note two triggers.

Close-up of the details of stock, Red Ryder on horseback with name in circle. (Courtesy of Jim Thomas)

Daisy's Red Ryder double holster set Model #1540 basket weave design.

Close-up of details and "Red Ryder" tooling on holster pocket. Seldom seen. (Courtesy of J. Schleyer)

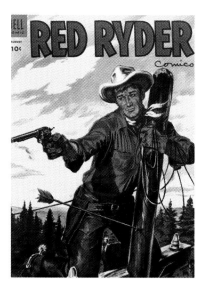

*One of several **Red Ryder** issues put out by Dell Comics for October 1954. Note this issue has a Red Ryder that was not illustrated by Fred Harman.*

The Red Ryder dart and cork rifles came out between 1955 and 1960, and similar to the Model 65, it has the Red Ryder logo on the plastic stock. The molded stock shows him shooting at a mountain cat. The stocks came in red and brown plastic with barrels in black metal. The cork shooter was only 13 inches long and came on a blister package. The dart gun was slightly longer at 17 inches, and had a trigger guard. Most of these were made in Arkansas.

There are no "Red Ryder"-marked cap pistols that are known, or that have surfaced to date. There are Red Ryder holsters and holster sets which are also quite scarce. In 1955, Daisy did market the #1537-X—the Daisy Red Ryder Black Beauty holster set. The holster set consisted of a top quality black leather holster, white leather trim, nickel studs, conchos, and came with a Hubley Texan Jr.

Daisy also put out several other Red Ryder holster sets of varying sizes and colors, which came, respectively with the Hubley Western, Hubley Rodeo, and the Hubley Trooper cap pistols. Remarkably, few holster sets themselves are stamped "Red Ryder." An early tan leather and basket-weave design holster set with "Red Ryder" tooled across the holster pockets is known, which also had conchos and metal horse heads on the belt. It is unknown what guns may have come with the set. Most probably they were a generic set of cap pistols, since even the 1950's Daisy Red Ryder sets were marketed with Hubley's classic line of guns. The holsters all take medium-sized guns.

Finally, how can I not state that all these Red Ryder products carried the blue ribbon seal with the statement "Commended by the Consumer Service Bureau of *Parents* magazine." Nice picture of Mom there, complete with her apron, smiling as she holds up the seal. The 1950s mom gave us her time, good food, old-fashioned discipline, and plenty of love, along with the "Daisy Red Ryder" rifle. In fact, in case she forgot, being so busy and all, Daisy put out a reminder that read, "Make Christmas come true—give your youngster a 'Red Ryder' from Daisy—the world's most famous BB gun, available at a store near you."

In 1983, MGM/UA Pictures produced a movie called *A Christmas Story* starring veteran actor Darren McGavin, Melinda Dillon, and Peter Billingsley, in which a young boy does all he can to get his parents to buy him a Daisy "Red Ryder" rifle. It is full of wonderful family entertainment and definitely worth seeing for anyone who ever wanted a Daisy Red Ryder rifle. In 1998, Red Ryder afficionados were happy to know that Daisy produced the 1938-1998 "Diamond Anniversary" Red Ryder rifle for the 60th anniversary of the world's most loved cowboy, and the most popular Daisy BB rifle ever made. This special commemorative model was produced in limited numbers of 3,898, which recognizes the year the Red Ryder was introduced, 1938, and the 60th anniversary, 1998.

Who knows? Perhaps a whole new generation of youngsters will get to know who Red Ryder was! Wouldn't that be great?

THE RESTLESS GUN

he Restless Gun was truly an "adult western." It starred veteran big screen actor John Payne, who had twenty years as a leading man in movies, including westerns. With more than 30 movies to his credit—with *Stardust, The Great Profile,* and the musical *Tin Pan Alley* among them—*The Restless Gun* was Payne's first and only TV series. Payne also served as the executive producer of the program. *The Restless Gun* debuted on NBC in late September 1957.

Like the character in *The Rebel,* the character in *The Restless Gun* is also a Civil War veteran who heads west. Payne starred as "Vint Bonner," a man proficient with his six shooter, a real gunfighter. The theme song for *The Restless Gun*—"I Ride With the Wind"—pretty much summed up the character. The song went "I ride with the wind, my eyes on the sun, and my hand on my restless gun." Payne also narrated the show.

His lifestyle after the war was that of a restless drifter, a restless gunfighter, one who had a well-known and feared reputation. But he was also a man who tired of gunplay, violence, and drifting. He moved from town to town, trying to settle down, but trouble followed him everywhere he went. It seemed that each new gunslinger he met was out to beat him to the draw. Whenever and wherever he could, Vint Bonner would try to reason with his opponent. The last thing he wanted to do was shoot the man and further add to his already fearsome reputation, knowing that soon after, another would-be gunfighter would try to take his place.

In one episode, Bonner, played with a serious, tired-looking appeal, is challenged again. It's another town and it's another menacing gunfighter out to add a notch to his gun. "Look," Bonner calmly says to the man itching to fill him full of lead, "we're both too old for this kind of foolishness, especially on such a nice summer day." He repeated similar lines in many episodes. Once in a while, cooler heads prevailed; other times, Bonner sent the man to

John Payne starred as "Vint Bonner" on **Restless Gun.**

Above: Esquire's second model Restless Gun, which came in both nickel and the seldom-seen gold-plated varieties. Note the gold and brown swirl grips.

Right: Close-up of the second model's special grip with secret compartment.

Esquire Restless Gun large-framed model in nickel finish with stag grips, and (below), the Esquire second model Restless Gun, nickel finish with special grips.

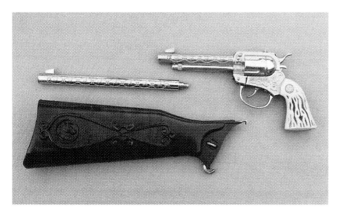

Restless Gun 4-in-1 rifle-gun with extension barrel and special stock.

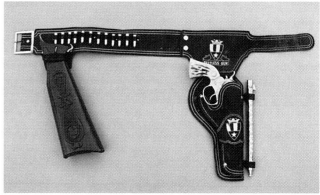

The 4-in-1 Restless Gun set with its special holster outfit. Seldom seen all complete. Note Esquire pony head logo on stock.

meet his maker. It seemed that each week, his "restless gun" was tested time and again, in town after town, and Bonner had only one true friend, his horse, named "Scar."

Bonner's character was a calm, practical, idealistic man who had seen his share of death—in the war and as he headed west to carve out a new life for himself. Each week, he kept moving. He often ended up helping others who had been wronged by the outlaw breed of the time. He moved on, so he really never made a friend, and Bonner remained the only character of the program. The show was a half-hour, filmed in black and white, and ran for two years, airing 77 episodes, and produced by John Payne's own company, Window Glen Productions.

Other veteran western stars that guest starred on *The Restless Gun*, and all as opponents of Vint Bonner's six shooter, were Chuck Conners (*The Rifleman*), Dan Blocker (*Bonanza*), Clu Gulager (*The Tall Man*), Vic Morrow (*Combat*), and veteran star James Coburn, who appeared in many westerns and war movies. Bonner holstered his gun for the last time on September 14, 1959, after a steady two-year run.

After the end of the series, John Payne never returned to television. He was a very private man who shunned the Hollywood glitz. He was married to the former Alexandra Crowell and had three children. Payne was a 6'3" former Virginia native who loved scuba diving and riding, as well as cooking exotic foods. He invested his earnings wisely in real estate and stayed out of the limelight and scandals—and never looked back at Hollywood. John Payne passed away in 1989.

Esquire single holster Restless Gun set with 1st pattern cap pistol and special "fast draw" designed holster rig. Note the 18 bullets on the gun belt!

Details showing how you can "fast draw" the swivel-style holster without taking the gun out! Ingenious design for such a toy holster set.

CAP GUN COLLECTIBLES

Esquire Novelty Corporation, also known as Actoy, was the only company that made cap guns for *The Restless Gun*. Even though this was an adult western with its share of gunfights, toy companies came out with board games and coloring books. Dell Comics issued several issues of *The Restless Gun* as did Whitman Books. "Vint Bonner" was also made by Hartland Plastics and John Payne did grace the cover of *TV Guide* in his role as Vint Bonner.

Esquire made two models of the Restless Gun, and both are remarkably different. The first model was the 9-inch, nickel-plated cap shooter with the large engraved frame, heavily designed barrel and stag grips, featuring the Esquire pony's head medallion logo on the grips. The gun breaks open from the top with a left side lever, and the frame has "Restless Gun" raised on both sides under the cylinder. As we know, this same pattern was also used for the "Lone Ranger" and "Wyatt Earp" models and is one of the few Esquire guns actually marked "Actoy" on the back of the cap box when opened.

The second pattern underwent a major change in every way. At almost 10 inches in length, this second model is stamped "Restless Gun" on both sides of the frame, along with "38" in a circle below the name. While the first model has the large frame and lots of engraving, this pattern has a plain frame, plain barrel,

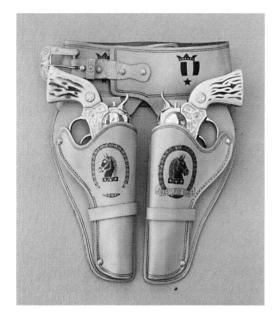

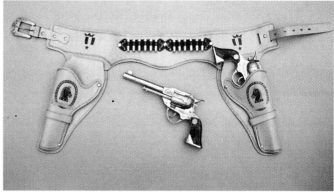

Above: Esquire Restless Gun double holster set in seldom seen tan leather with first model cap pistols. Note the difference between the black holster sets.

Left: Esquire Restless Gun tan double holster set with second model cap guns. Both models will fit this style holster set.

but, interestingly, came with a heavily-scrolled cylinder and ejector rod. A second interesting feature was the method to open this gun for cap loading. With a left side lever up by the hammer, the entire left side of the cylinder and the attached ejector rod both swing open and downward, giving plenty of room to load the cap roll.

The third remarkable feature of this pattern are beautifully-molded brown and metallic swirl grips, which are totally different than any others, and which fit almost inset onto the metal frame. The rounded section of the grips have ribbed lines into the design. The fourth feature of this remarkable gun had to be a youngster's dream. The butt of the gun had a "secret" compartment that was opened by pushing down and snapping open the "trap compartment door" under the gun butt. Well, you know any kid would store caps, coins, even "hidden" messages if captured! This model came with the amber swirl grips, solid brown grips, and white grips. It is also found in both nickel and gold-plated models. What a great cap pistol!

The first pattern, with the large frame, came in two distinct patterns. The standard pattern has already been described. The "special pattern" came with the 8-inch extension barrel and a molded plastic stock that quickly converted the gun into the "4-in-1" rifle-gun! This pattern, identical to the 4-in-1 Lone Ranger rifle gun, has a special fitting inside the barrel to twist in the extension barrel into place and it has the special hole grip section to attach the stock. If it does not have the slotted barrel and hole in the butt and grip, it is not the 4-in-1 model. With the extension barrel and stock, the rifle-gun is 30 inches long. The butt of the stock opens and can be used for cap storage.

As a great selling gimmick, Esquire used the character "Vint Bonner" to explain why the youngster would want the "4-in-1 Convertible rifle." Holding the Actoy rifle gun Vint explains, "When things become so drastic that I have to use my gun to change the course of events, it sure does feel good to know that I have a unique weapon in my holster. With it, I have double insurance, for my pistol has interchangeable parts, a stock and barrel, which convert it into a rifle for long range accuracy. It could be said that I have a gun with a reason, for it has seen me through more scrapes than you care to imagine."

Esquire made several holsters for *The Restless Gun*, and while all appear to be identical at first glance, there are several differences. It appears that all the models have a variant horse head design in an oval frame with "Restless Gun" on a banner under the horse head graphics.

While most of the patterns found are large, black single holsters for both models, there is a much scarcer double holster set in tan leather with brown details and gold lettering on the graphics. A monogram consisting of two wide bars on a shield, and a crown, appear on the belts

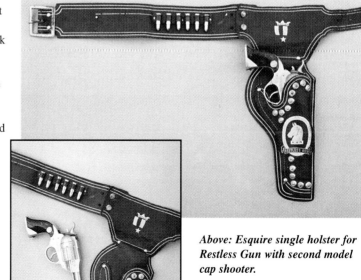

Above: Esquire single holster for Restless Gun with second model cap shooter.

Left: Details of holster and cap shooter. Note all variations of the holsters.

Esquire Restless Gun Complete Western Outfit for the 4-in-1 rifle gun. Box lid shows graphics of the show character and what the box contains.

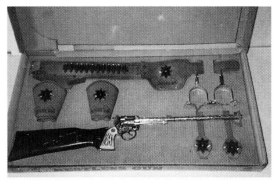

The Complete Western Outfit for the Restless Gun included the special belt and holster set, wrist cuffs, spurs, and this spectacular gold plated first model cap gun. (Courtesy of Mike Cherry)

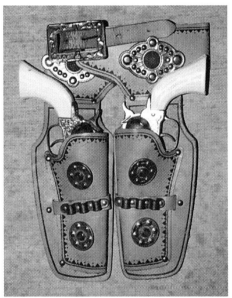

Late pattern Restless Gun double holster set with Hubley cap guns. Note the bullet loops on the holster pockets. Totally different design than the others.

***Dell Comics issue for** The Restless Gun.*

or holsters which was the trademark of the program's production company. The black holsters are large and very striking, with white details and several studs, and with as many as 12 silver bullets and tie downs. "Restless Gun" appears on the belt or the pocket fronts. A unique swivel holster exists enabling you to fire the gun without removing it from the holster! The buckles are all a plain, nickel, square garrison-belt style.

A special holster set was made to carry the gun, extension barrel, and detachable stock. On the front portion of the holster pocket are two leather loops into which you fit the extension barrel, which is secured once the sight reaches the top loop. On the left side of the belt was a special leather section with snap button leather straps that secure the detachable stock.

Esquire marketed the Restless Gun outfits in boxes as well as the guns alone on a card that also featured John Payne as "Vint Bonner." Esquire marketed The Restless Gun "complete western outfit" in a special box with Vint Bonner on the lid and this set featured a gold plated 4-in-1 rifle-gun, single holster set with the special carrier for the stock, wrist cuffs and spurs. This magnificent set came in tan leather, and the wrist cuffs were also marked "Restless Gun."

A late double holster set surfaced that is totally different than the "official" Restless Gun rigs that Esquire marketed. This pattern does not have the Esquire horse head, nor does it have the shield and crown monogram. This late variation has "Restless Gun" and "Vint Bonner" on the back of the belt. The holsters are tan with black details and lettering, conchos, and red jewels and mounted on the holster pockets are three bullet loops. The buckle is a typical generic western style rectangular buckle found on late holster patterns. The guns are generic Hubley. It is possible this is an unauthorized holster set, but it is unique in the sense that it carries both the show title and the name of the character on the belt.

While *The Restless Gun* lasted two solid years, it was responsible for Esquire coming out with several variations of two guns and holster sets that reluctant gunfighter Vint Bonner preferred not to use. These days, we collectors treasure these remarkable cap guns and unique holster sets that are no longer strapped on by today's youngsters.

Above: Details showing the back of the gunbelt which carries both the show title and the character's name, "Vint Bonner." Seldom seen. (Courtesy of Peter Karp)

RIC-O-SHAY

So, who was Rick-O-Shay? Was this just a play on words, as in "Ricochet," meaning the oblique rebound of a bullet after striking a surface on an angle? "Ricochet" is a French word, which first surfaced hundreds of years ago in fable du ricochet, a story in which the narrator consistently evaded the questions set forth. Goodness, I've known a lot of people who engage in "fable du ricochet." But this one is not so easy as that.

Initially, I had always thought that the Hubley Ric-O-Shay and its off-spring, the Ric-O-Shay Jr., was just that, a play on the word "ricochet," since the connection is the bullet, and we are cap gun enthusiasts. Deeper investigation, however, soon revealed that there was a cartoon strip character named "Rick O'Shay." Notice the difference in the spelling. We'll get back to that in a moment.

Rick O'Shay was the creation of western novelist Stan Lynde. Now in his 60s, Stan Lynde has been a cowboy and western storyteller and yarn-puller since the 1950s with his comic strip, "Ric-O'Shay." A novelist from Montana, Lynde started the "Ric-O'Shay" character in 1958 and it ran until 1977. It was carried in the *Chicago Tribune* and like the "Red Ryder" cartoon strip, was syndicated all over the country.

Born in Billings, Montana, Lynde grew up on his father's ranch, which was located near a Crow Indian reservation. Lynde grew up with a deep appreciation and sense of humor with all things western, and soon put it all together in a satirical slant on the western. Other similar cartoon strip characters with the western genre were "Redeye" by Gordon Bess, "Catfish" by Rog Bollen, and "Tumbleweeds" by Tom Ryan. Stan Lynde spoofed the traditional western, but he did so with his Ric O'Shay character using vivid and correct descriptions of the gunslinger, cowboy, the fast draw, the rustler, the prospector, all interjected with a sense of humor.

Lynde's Rick O'Shay was a slender character who wore a single holster gunfighter-style rig, dark pants, dark bandana, a black hat, black string tie, and vest with his badge on it. He wore spurs on his boots. In one strip, Rick O'Shay's friend, the gunslinger Hipshot, is shown in the first frame all set to draw at his opponent as he says "Three of 'ye, eh?" The second frame suddenly has him drawing his six-shooter, and at the same time, lightning fast, he is "fanning" the gun, firing off three quick shots—Blam! Pow! Blooy! In the third frame, as he is about to put his smoking gun away, while dust is billowing all around him as he says "Dead center, all three!" The fourth and last frame has Hipshot holding up one of three empty cans, and there is a bullet hole through all three of them. As he holds up one of the cans, still smoking from the bullet hole, it's obvious he had set up all three, one in front of the other, and he says "'course, I was standing a mite close. . . ." It was that kind of humor.

Stan Lynde also did a strip called "Latigo" and has written several books on Ric O'Shay, all of which are tongue-in-cheek western humor. He recently put out a book called *The Bodacious Kid* which is along the same lines of the characters encountered on the "Ric O'Shay" strip.

CAP GUN COLLECTIBLES

Hubley came out with the Ric-O-Shay in 1960. It is one of the largest toy cap guns ever made, coming in at 13 inches long. Nickel-chrome plated, it comes with a revolving cylinder, six brass bullets, and sleek all-black plastic grips. The barrel and frame are heavily scrolled and the name "Ric-O-Shay" on the large model is located on the barrel amid the scrolling. The Hubley Ric-O-Shay also has its special "ricochet" sound, like a "whi-i-ne" as you fire the trigger and let it go. This came in a special window box which allowed "counter demonstration of the bullet whine." This gun has a left side gate that opens when you push on the lever located on the underside of the barrel by the ejector rod.

The 1960 Hubley catalog lists the Ric-O-Shay as "new" and it was Number 279 for ordering. An important point on this advertisement shows an asterisk (*) right up by the name "Ric-O-Shay." The asterisk calls attention to the fact that this is a "Trademark of the Hubley

Stan Lynde's humorous, yet "right-on-target-about life" character, "Rick O'Shay." (Courtesy of Stan Lynde, his creator; Copyright TMS)

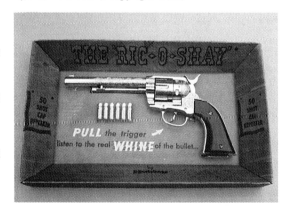

Hubley's large Ric-O-Shay cap gun repeater, in its original compartment framed box, complete six bullets, advertising its "whine" sound. One of the largest cap guns ever made and one of the finest quality.

Hubley single holster for the Ric-O-Shay Jr. in brown leather. Note the Hubley pony medallion on the gunbelt. "Ric-O-Shay" is tooled on the holster pocket. (Courtesy of Terry Graham)

Above: Hubley Ric-O-Shay big daddy (top), and the Ric-O-Shay Jr. (bottom), two well-made cap pistols for 1960 and 1965. The Ric-O-Shay Jr. is less common.

Right: Hubley's 1960 catalog listing the #279 large model Ric-O-Shay. Note asterisk explaining this was Hubley's trademark. (Courtesy of George Newcomb)

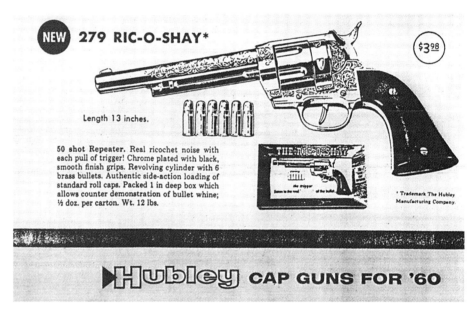

NEW 279 RIC-O-SHAY*

$3.98

Length 13 inches.

50 shot Repeater. Real ricochet noise with each pull of trigger! Chrome plated with black, smooth finish grips. Revolving cylinder with 6 brass bullets. Authentic side-action loading of standard roll caps. Packed 1 in deep box which allows counter demonstration of bullet whine; ½ doz. per carton. Wt. 12 lbs.

THE RIC-O-SHAY

* Trademark The Hubley Manufacturing Company.

►Hubley CAP GUNS FOR '60

Manufacturing Company." There is no doubt this was done so as not to confuse it with Stan Lynde's copyright on his character "Rick O'Shay," which of course, is spelled differently. Did Hubley seize on the popularity of the cartoon strip at the time and come up with another name that was also a play on the word "ricochet." It certainly appears so.

The "Ric-O-Shay Jr." is the 1965 model Hubley that Halco also copied. The Ric-O-Shay Jr. is 9 inches long, and also came nickel plated, with scrolling on the barrel and the cylinder, but not on the frame itself. It came with a side gate, with a thumb depression to push up the side gate for cap loading. "Ric-O-Shay Jr" is raised in a pebbled area on both sides of the frame under the cylinder, in much the same elongated oval frame as the "Flip" cap gun for Hubley's "Overland Trail" series. The grips came in both black and white with the raised steer head and the Hubley star logo. The large "Ric-O-Shay" does not show the Hubley star logo on the all plain black grips. The "Ric-O-Shay Jr" also has the "whi-i-ine" sound when the trigger is fired, but it is not as loud and pronounced as the larger cap gun model.

Hubley also made a single holster for the "Ric-O-Shay Jr." in brown leather with its horse head medallion on the belt and "Ric-O-Shay" on the strap across the holster pocket. We already know that the Ric-O-Shay large gun came in "Paladin" holster sets and "Colt .45" holster sets. Actually, the Ric-O-Shay Jr. is a much scarcer cap gun to find than its big daddy model.

So what do you think, gringos? Is the Ric-O-Shay a take-off on the cartoon character, "Rick O'Shay," or a play on words for "ricochet," that being the "whine" it's meant to sound like when fired? You decide. In the meantime, both the Papa and the Junior Ric-O-Shay cap guns are two of the finest quality cap guns that Hubley produced.

THE RIFLEMAN

One of TV's most popular westerns, *The Rifleman,* brought us a number of wonderful memories. *The Rifleman* was the saga of "Lucas McCain," a homesteader, and a struggling one at that. The series was set in North Forks, New Mexico, in the 1880s. McCain was a widower. His young son was 12-year-old Mark McCain. McCain was out to make his small cattle spread work, no matter what hardships came along, and at the same time, he was determined to bring up his young son honorably and make a man out of him.

The series was as much about young Mark McCain as it was about Lucas McCain and his constant efforts to lead a good life, working hard and raising his son. The one spectacular item that gave the show its name was a rifle, but it was a specially adapted Winchester rifle. In enters "The Rifleman". . . .

McCain's rifle, which he carried with him at all times instead of a six gun, was a Winchester .44-40, modified with a large trigger guard and lever ring that cocked automatically as he drew it downward. It had a hair-trigger action and McCain did a number of fancy twirls and flips with it. One twirl was a special flipping forward of the rifle, while at the same time it twirled backward, cocked, and then fired as McCain brought it back into both hands. He was able to do this on foot, as well as mounted on a horse.

The rifle could fire the first round in three-tenths of a second, so there was plenty of firing action to be seen. McCain was able to get off six shots in four-tenths of a second after that because of a special screw mounted on the guard that tripped the trigger. He really only needed to cock the rifle once, then do his "twirling action," and after that, stay out of his way! In fact, McCain goes right into this action at the beginning of each episode, firing off eleven shots. He then twirls the rifle back and walks forward with his rifle in both hands.

Lucas and his expertise with his special rifle came in handy with the Marshal of North Forks, "Micah Torrance," who was a serious, dedicated lawman, but a bit beyond his prime. He often called on

Chuck Connors, takes aim as Lucas McCain on **The Rifleman** *with his specially-adapted rifle. Note the ring lever and the protruding screw on the trigger guard.*

"Mark McCain," played by Johnny Crawford, is taught about life as his father, "Lucas," played by Chuck Connors, tried to give him a sense of values in a harsh land.

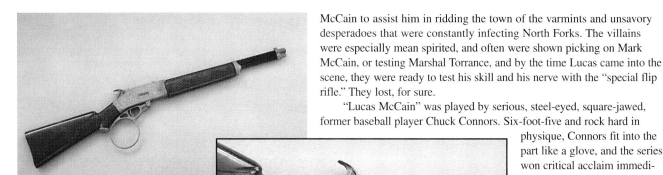

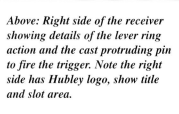

Above: Hubley's Flip Special Rifleman rifle with it's large ring lever action with a special protruding cast pin to fire the trigger repetitiously.

Above: Right side of the receiver showing details of the lever ring action and the cast protruding pin to fire the trigger. Note the right side has Hubley logo, show title and slot area.

Above: Left side of the Hubley Rifleman carries the show title and "Flip Special" as well as the Hubley logo and longhorn, beautifully raised. Note the push button at the far end of the receiver which drops down the cap box for loading.

The Marx flip rifle copied the Hubley in subtle ways, including the large ring, a second protruding lever, and dropped cap box for loading. Seldom-seen rifle.

McCain to assist him in ridding the town of the varmints and unsavory desperadoes that were constantly infecting North Forks. The villains were especially mean spirited, and often were shown picking on Mark McCain, or testing Marshal Torrance, and by the time Lucas came into the scene, they were ready to test his skill and his nerve with the "special flip rifle." They lost, for sure.

"Lucas McCain" was played by serious, steel-eyed, square-jawed, former baseball player Chuck Connors. Six-foot-five and rock hard in physique, Connors fit into the part like a glove, and the series won critical acclaim immediately. Young "Mark McCain" was played by Johnny Crawford, a young newcomer to the small screen. Old character actor Paul Fix, who had starred in dozens of big and small screen westerns, played "Marshal Torrance." *The Rifleman* came to television on September 30, 1958, and ran for five years, ending its run on July 1, 1963, after 168 episodes. Syndicated, the program is still seen all over the country and overseas.

A series that lasted this long soon added other characters to keep the scripts fresh and interesting. A handsome widower, noble and true, struggling to bring up his young son the right way, was soon given a "love interest," Miss "Lou Mallory," played by Patricia Blair, was also the owner of the Mallory Hotel. This relationship was handled with great taste, and with respect for his young son, so there was never anything immoral, nor was any sexual innuendo ever displayed on the show.

"Miss Millie Scott," who owned the town's general store, was played by Joan Taylor. Two other show regulars were "Hattie Denton," played by Hope Summers, and "Sweeney," the local bartender, played by Bill Quinn. Cast as the town blacksmith, "Nils Svenson," was Joe Higgins. "Jay Burrage," the town doctor, was played by great character actor Edgar Buchanan, already well known from the "Hopalong Cassidy" series, and his role as "Judge Roy Bean" in *Law West of The Pecos*. Other characters seen on various episodes were waitresses, the town banker, the town gunsmith, and others. It was a great "family" show in spite of the gunplay because you got to know and truly like the characters and their distinct personalities.

Numerous big name guest stars graced *The Rifleman*. Among these were Charlton Heston, Michael Ansara, Ed Ames, Kevin McCarthy, Richard Anderson, and even Sammy Davis, Jr. Many of these stars went on to their own TV series. Chuck Connors went on to star in two other westerns, *Cowboy in Africa* and *Branded*. While both were well acted and interesting westerns, they never had the appeal of *The Rifleman*.

In 1991, Chuck Connors, and a now grown up Johnny Crawford, both reprised their roles from *The Rifleman,* and came back to the screen in *The Gambler Returns: The Luck of the Draw* with Kenny Rogers. The appeal of popular characters from the golden age of westerns is obvious.

Character actor Paul Fix died in 1983 at age 82. Patricia Blair went on to play in *Daniel Boone* as Fess Parker's wife. Johnny Crawford continued to appear on several shows and is also an accomplished musician. Chuck Conners passed away in November 1992.

CAP GUN COLLECTIBLES

One can easily see why the show won critical acclaim. Both stars graced the covers and pages of many magazines and comic books, all devoted to The Rifleman. Father and son were always shown together, and of course, there was the famous flip action Winchester right along with them! In 1958, just as soon as the show became popular, Hubley came out with the Rifleman rifle. It has been called the Flip Special and the Ring Rifle.

The Hubley Flip Special, as it is prominently marked on the left side of the receiver, is a well-made and beautiful toy rifle. It was 32 inches long, and came with black metal barrel, nickel barrel ends, sight, and band. It had a brown plastic forearm and stock, both of which are highly sculptured as well as handsomely "marbleized." A scarcer stock in black plastic was also made. The receiver is highly engraved with "The Rifleman" on both sides, along with the Circle "H" Hubley logo and "Flip Special."

As with the original from the show, the trigger guard has a cast extended interior pin that acts as the "cocking action" so that as you pull down the large "ring" lever, the rifle cocks and then fires as you return the lever to the grip stock.

The Hubley Flip Special Rifleman and (below), the Marx Flip Rifle, for comparison purposes. Two great cap-shooting rifles to remember this show.

A push-button release on the left side of the receiver drops down the cap box for loading. No doubt many youngsters from 1958 to 1963 broke a bunch of stocks and rings, all trying to imitate McCain's twirling action! Casting the pin instead of mounting a screw, as can be seen on the original, was a great idea from Hubley.

Remarkably, even with a show this popular, running for five years, no other "Rifleman"-marked toy named as such and no six-guns are known to exist other than the Hubley. No guns marked "Lucas McCain" are known to exist. Marx, however, did market a large ring "flip" special rifle that was a copy from the Rifleman.

The Marx flip rifle was none other than the very popular 26-inch plastic and die-cast rifle that was used for the Roy Rogers and Lone Ranger models. The distinct differences, however, came in the special large "ring" lever, which also had a double-cocking action. Pulling it downward, in the same way as the Hubley, the ring drops down an extra lever which cocks and then fires the rifle in two distinct metal cock and firing sounds. Pressing against a metal tab on the right side of the trigger ring drops down the cap box for loading. This model is not marked "The Rifleman," but instead is marked "Wild West" on the right side of the receiver, which also has fine sculpturing and raised images of an American buffalo and a cowboy on his horse galloping to the right. The left side of the receiver has another cowboy, and the Marx logo. Another smaller, stamped Marx logo can be found on the octagon barrel. While the Roy Rogers and Lone Ranger models are silver plastic, this "flip rifle" comes with black barrel, black receiver, and a chocolate brown stock with the butt outline of the stock painted black. This Marx ring rifle is seldom seen in any condition. The use of the two solid colors, and butt border in black, make it especially colorful.

The use of identical molds was certainly not just a Marx idea. After all, Hubley brought back the Rifleman in Kelly's Rifle with some modifications, for *The Overland Trail* show. When you have a neat, popular rifle, I guess you stick with it!

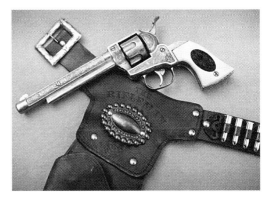

Left: An exceptionally rare, never seen, previously unknown double holster set marked to "The Rifleman" Made by Leslie-Henry. The guns are L-H/Halco Marshals with cameo grips and revolving cylinders which fit perfectly into the holsters and carry the same Diamond "H" logo as branded into the leather gunbelt at the top of the holster pockets. (Courtesy of Dave Luellen)

Above: Closeup of the details on the gunbelt showing the tooled show title "The Rifleman" along with the Diamond H brand logo and a beautiful oval brass concho. Since Lucas McCain did not wear guns and neither did his son, is it possible these were meant for Marshall Micah Torrance? The new revelations never cease!

Above, left: Dell Comics issue for **The Rifleman**. *Note the father's protective hand on his son's shoulder and the famous rifle.*

RIN TIN TIN

Just about every youngster growing up in the 1950s remembers *Lassie* and *Rin Tin Tin*. For us Old West afficionados, Rin Tin Tin, also called "Rinty" and "Rinny," was "the best." While both shows featured courageous canines with a young male companion, there were considerable and very important differences between the two four-footed heroes.

Lassie was set in a much more relaxed and domesticated atmosphere, but *Rin Tin Tin* was set in the Arizona Territory in the 1880s. As such, Rin Tin Tin, like his human counterparts, had to deal with Indians, gunfights, Cavalry troopers, the blazing desert, and other such hair-rasing situations for a dog. The story of Rin Tin Tin goes much further back than the popular TV western, which was officially called *The Adventures of Rin Tin Tin*.

The first Rin Tin Tin was found by the man who eventually trained him for the movies. Lee Duncan found Rinty as just a five-day-old puppy in an abandoned German dugout in 1918. He was just another dough boy at Chateau-Thierry, on the Marne in France, when the puppy yelped catching Duncan's attention. He became Duncan's pet, and he brought him back to the States after the war. Rin Tin Tin got into the movies under Duncan's expert training and direction, and it was said Rinty was the "only dog in Los Angeles to be listed in the phone book."

He made his first movie in 1922. He was labeled as "The Wonder Dog of the Screen" and played in a series called *The Defender,* and alongside early western star Monte Blue. Rin-Tin-Tin continued to star in films until he died in 1932 at the ripe old age of 16. By then, he had already set his paw mark on many Rin Tin Tin's to follow. Initially, *Rin-Tin-Tin* was written up with the hyphen between the three titles. This was later dropped to simply "Rin Tin Tin" for television.

Rin Tin Tin came to television on October 15, 1954, one of TV's early westerns. The story of TV's "Rinty" was born out of a great plot. Rin Tin Tin and his young master, "Rusty," were orphaned during an Apache Indian raid. Members of a wagon train, they were the only survivors when found by troopers of the 101st Cavalry, also known as the "Fighting Blue Devils." The troopers cared for the boy and his dog and brought them back to Fort Apache, Arizona, where they were headquartered. They were made honorary troopers and became the unofficial wards of "Lt. Ripley 'Rip' Masters." Lt. Masters had no children, so he adopted Rusty as his own.

Rusty and Rinty were inseparable. The dog would prick up his ears and leap to attention at Rusty's command, "Yo Ho Rinty!" Lt. Masters soon became the boy's father figure and the man Rusty looked up to for guidance and discipline. He loved, obeyed, and respected Lt. Masters. Helping out with the boy's welfare and training to be a young trooper was "Sgt. Biff O'Hara." But it was obvious Rinty and Rusty had won the hearts of all the troopers in the 101st Cavalry and all the characters interacted well.

The job of the 101st Cavalry was a big one. The Apaches were constantly on the warpath. The nearest place was Mesa Verde, a young town that still lacked law and order, and this task also fell on the cavalry. In one of the first episodes, the command is to be inspected by a tough colonel, obviously sent from Washington. Fearing that the colonel will spot the youngster and the dog and banish them from Fort Apache, Lt. Masters puts them in the care of Sgt. O'Hara to hide them from the colonel as he makes his rounds.

During this charade, young Rusty learns of a plot to assassinate the colonel. With the help of Rinty and Sgt. O'Hara, he foils the plot, and at the same time alerts the fort about an Indian attack. The fast action saves the colonel's life. In gratitude, he makes Rusty a corporal and ensures that he and his faithful, big-pawed friend will remain on the post according to "official regulations."

For the next five years, Rusty and Rinty helped maintain law and order in Mesa Verde. Rin Tin Tin was a great hit with youngsters, adults and dog lovers all over the country. The popularity and sales of German Shepherds quadrupled. Today, it may be Dalmatians, but then it was a dog like Rinty.

THE ACTORS

Cast as "Corporal Rusty" was young Lee Aaker. An actor since the age of seven, he had already graced the screen alongside John Wayne in *Hondo,* with Audie Murphy in *Destry*, and in *Arena* with Gig Young. The blonde young star acted on several other programs, but Lee Aaker will always be remembered as young Corporal Rusty. He had the pleasure of working with three Rintys on the show, as different dogs were used for various scenes, and got along

*Lee Aaker, as "Corporal Rusty" and his faithful "Rinty" along with a pretty cowgirl, on the set of **Rin Rin Tin***. *Note the scaled-down cavalry trooper's uniform that Rusty wore on the show. But look out for the cowgirl; she's wearing a set of double holsters with real-looking six-shooters.*

Jim Brown as "Lt. Rip Masters" and Rin Tin Tin.

with all of them. He made famous his upturned cavalry slouched cap and his button-down cavalry shirt, and all the kids flocked to stores, egging their moms to buy them a hat and shirt like "Rusty wears on Rin Tin Tin." Lee Aaker is still with us, and when last interviewed, indicated he kept his uniform from the program, still gets fan mail, and still meets people that recall his work on *Rin Tin Tin* fondly. Lee Aaker still stays in touch with his old show co-stars.

The role of "Lt. Rip Masters" went to big Jim Brown, a former Texas tennis champion who was to star in several films in the 1940s before being cast in *Rin Tin Tin*. He also had a fine singing voice, and at least three songs were sung on various episodes of the show. Jim Brown never regrets his casting as the young cavalry officer in *Rin Tin Tin* and, in fact, in the 1976 revival of the old "Rin Tin Tin" show, he came out of retirement to reprise his role as Lt. Masters, albeit slightly older, to do the introductions for the reruns. He went on to star as "J.R.'s" detective in the long running *Dallas* TV series.

"Sgt. Biff O'Hara" was played by Joe Sawyer, a character actor with more than 30 films to his credit before being cast in *Rin Tin Tin*. A Canadian native, Sawyer acted in several great war movies and westerns, and although he had that "oh, yeah, what's his name" face, he gained instant stardom as the lovable Sergeant O'Hara character of the show.

Other characters with recurring roles were "Corporal Randy Boone," played by Rand Brooks, "Corporal Carson," played by Tommy Farrell, and "Corporal Clark," played by Hal Hopper. "Major Swanson" of the 101st Cavalry was played by William Forrest. The part of "the colonel" was played by old character actor John Hoyt, who would occasionally guest star on the show. Of these character actors, Rand Brooks had been previously cast in *Gone With The Wind*, as well as several *Hopalong Cassidy* films before becoming Corporal Boone on *Rin Tin Tin*. William Forrest passed away in 1989. Joe Sawyer died in 1980 at the age of 82. John Hoyt died in 1991 at the age of 86. All the others are still with us.

The star of the show, Rin Tin Tin, was the grandson of the original Rin-Tin-Tin, the little pup brought over by Lee Duncan, who was also the trainer for all the Rin Tin Tins that followed. Rinty really led a "dog's life." Not only did he have the best of care, and the best food, he was also driven to and from locations in his own station wagon. He was also heavily insured against injury and theft. Of course, he also had his two "stand ins" for special stunts. His champion grandfather was slightly darker in appearance. TV's first Rin Tin Tin has also gone to that big dog pound in the sky. But Rinty didn't just "pass away" quietly.

The Adventures of Rin Tin Tin ran until August 28, 1959, a total of 164 episodes covering five years. Reruns began almost right away, from September 1959, through September 1964. In 1976, Jim Brown starred in the introduction of the reruns by bringing youngsters to visit the "old Fort Apache," and began each show with narrating the adventures of the wonder dog who had won the hearts of the old cavalrymen. The programs were on the Saturday lineup of shows, first on ABC and then on CBS, continuing the long lines of fans well past the golden age of TV westerns.

In 1988, Rin Tin Tin was again resurrected, this time in TV's *Rin Tin Tin K-9 Cop* where the Old West was replaced by the big city. The intrepid canine kept taking the bite out of crime in an urban setting. But outlaws are outlaws, whether it's the Wild West or the Wild East. This Rinty was also a descendant of the original Rin-Tin-Tin. This crime adventure show with our K-9 hero ran from 1988 to 1993, a total of 106 episodes. None of the western stars from the 1954-1959 show starred on this program.

CAP GUN COLLECTIBLES

A show involving man's best friend and his young companion, a boy in a U.S. Cavalry uniform, was just bound to become popular to the youngsters of the 1950s, and *Rin Tin Tin* spurred all kinds of collectibles. And it would also be inevitable that dog food as well as food for young

Esquire's Rin Tin Tin cap pistol, in antique bronze with white simulated stag grips. Note name on frame and lanyard ring under butt.

Esquire Rin Tin Tin cap pistol in nickel finish with checkered federal grips in off-white color. This model is harder to find than the more common bronze model.

Esquire's unique Rin Tin Tin and Rusty cavalry outfit with bronze cap gun. The outfit also included a telescope with a compass and a bullet pouch. Note the very colorful buckle with Rinty and Rusty on it. Seldom found complete.

The Esquire Rin Tin Tin and Rusty outfit showing all the parts. Note the 3-bullet pouch is also the flap cavalry-style like the holster. Note extension telescope.

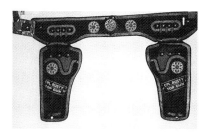

Esquire's western-style double holster set for "Cpl. Rusty." Note "Top Gun" under the name on the holster pockets. (Courtesy of J. Schleyer)

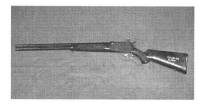

Marx Rin Tin Tin and Rusty cap-shooting rifle in the Winchester style. Note the rich walnut stock. Seldom seen. (Courtesy of J. Schleyer)

Dell Comic issued for **Rin Tin Tin and Rusty.**

bodies would embrace and welcome the selling features of both Rinty and Rusty. In his dog life-time, Rinty graced advertisements for dog food, cigars, all the Nabisco cereals, all sorts of books, magazines, and board games. Rinty and Rusty sold thousands of U.S. cavalry shirts and costumes. The "Fighting Blue Devils" of the 101st Cavalry with their wonder mascot-emblazoned flags, canteens, belts, buckles, and thousands of photo-graphs, Dell Comic books, and of course, this brings us to our cap guns and cap rifles.

"Lassie" never made it to a cap gun. Neither did "Bullet," unfortunately, that other most wonderful Alsatian that was Roy Roger's canine sidekick. Sergeant Preston's Alaskan Husky, "Yukon King," never made it to a cap gun, either. Thus, Rin Tin Tin was the only dog that was ever immortalized on a cap gun and cap rifle. Only Rin Tin Tin and Corporal Rusty's names are found on cap guns and cap rifles.

The only Rin Tin Tin cap guns were made by Esquire of New Jersey. The Rin Tin Tin cap gun came in two variations. The most common model is the antique bronze finish, 9-inch die cast with white simulated stag grips with the lanyard ring under the gun butt. The frame of this gun has scrollwork on the barrel, cylinder, and front area of the frame. "Rin Tin Tin" is raised on both sides of the frame. The gun breaks open from the top with hand pressure on the barrel. The other pattern of the Esquire Rin Tin Tin is the much harder-to-find nickel pattern of the same gun.

The nickel pattern of the Rin Tin Tin has been found with two variation grips. The first is the same white simulated stag found on the bronze model. A second variation set of grips which is sometimes called "federal grips" by collectors, are also found on the nickel model. These grips are more of an off-white color and are finely checkered. In addition to the Actoy pony medallion logo found on both patterns, the federal grip has an entire border going all around the grips made up of five-point stars. In the center of the grip is a shield with 5 stars across the top of the shield. The shield is plain but does have a federal look, hence the nick-name for these grips. The same grips are found on some Wyatt Earp models also made by Esquire. Both patterns have the lanyard ring under the gun butt. Both patterns break open the same way.

A truly unique and wonderful belt and holster set was made for the Esquire cap gun. It was an all-black soft leather cavalry trooper's outfit which consisted of a cavalry-style flap holster, flap-style bullet pouch with three silver bullets, and a special carrier for a telescope with a built-in compass. The holster flap has yellow and blue graphics showing Rinty and the 101st Cavalry motto on a banner, "Fighting Blue Devils." The rectangular nickel buckle has yellow and blue graphics showing both Rinty and Rusty. The nickel telescope expands and has a compass built into the side of the scope itself. The bullet pouch, telescope carrier, and flap of the holster all have a nickel snap to secure each item. This is a great rig! It's obvious that with lots of hard playing, locating a totally complete Rinty and Rusty cavalry outfit would be a great find!

These sets were sold with the antique bronze model, with the entire rig selling for $2.98! But with just $2.00 and one Nabisco shredded wheat box top, you could send away for the Actoy bronze cap gun, flap holster, bullets, and belt with the Rinty and Rusty buckle! Fill out the coupon and send for your "Official Rin Tin Tin Cavalry Gun & Holster Set." One can only imagine how popular a youngster on the block was that had his own "Rinty" pet and his "official" cavalry outfit!

Esquire also made a double holster set in the more traditional western style for the "Rin Tin Tin" series, but this pattern carries the character name "Cpl. Rusty" and "Top Gun" on the holster pockets in white details. The double holster set came in black leather with six bullets, conchos, and a standard western-style rectangular buckle. This set came with the Actoy "Rin Tin Tin" guns. Although Hubley made the "Top Gun" cap shooter, this came out in the mid-1960s, long after "Rin Tin Tin" had completed its five-year run. No guns marked "Rusty" or "Cpl. Rusty" have ever surfaced. No guns marked "Lt. Rip Masters" or "Sgt. Biff O'Hara" are known to exist.

Marx made the only known Rin Tin Tin cap shooting rifle. The Marx rifle used for the Rin Tin Tin was the same Winchester model used for the 33-inch-long Lone Ranger series. This rifle is a deluxe model with black barrel and brown walnut stock. The left side of the stock has "Rin Tin Tin and Rusty" in gold lettering. Both the forestock and grip section of the stock are finely checkered. This rifle is quite scarce.

Rin Tin Tin proved to be a more affectionate look at what most people in the 1940s knew of the German Shepherd, a strong, often vicious, and powerful military guard dog. Rin Tin Tin became instantly loved, and remains the most memorable of all wonder dogs of TV shows.

Rin Tin Tin didn't complain much about his contract. He was happy with a pat on the head, a nice dog bone, and he was such a ham for photographs. But when it came to proving he had what it took to be an outlaw's worst nightmare, he was "the best." After all, he was taking a bite out of the bad guys long before the word "K-9" was ever invented. . .in the Wild West, of course. "Yo Ho, Rinty!"

THE ROUGH RIDERS

Similar in theory to *The Rebel*, *The Rough Riders* revolved around the saga of three men, all former soldiers during the Civil War. The series was set in the late 1860s following our nation's great conflict. The setting was westward—from the Great Smokies to California, from the Dakota Badlands to the Nevada Territory. *The Rough Riders* rode into television October 2, 1958. Produced by ZIV Productions, it was a 30-minute program on ABC.

Three great characters, each with a distinct personality of his own highlighted this great show. "Capt. Jim Flagg" had been a Union Army officer. "Sgt. Buck Sinclair" had been a Union Army NCO. Lt. Colin Kirby had served the Confederacy. After the surrender at Appomattox, these three men decided to join forces and head westward to the new frontier to start a new life. Along the way, the three men, who formed a strong bond of friendship and loyalty to each other, encountered numerous bands of outlaws, Indians trying to stop the white man's expansion, and even deserters from both armies, some full of revenge, others desperate in search of new identities and new causes for which to fight.

"Captain Flagg" was portrayed by handsome, rough-hewn Kent Taylor, a wonderful actor who had played the lead in the "Boston Blackie" series. In the part of Captain Flagg, he was an officer with unquestionable ethics and courage, tempered with compassion and understanding. He did not flaunt the fact that his former Union Army had won the Civil War. "Lt. Colin Kirby," played by Jan Merlin, however, refused to discard his Confederate uniform. He ran into plenty of Northerners who didn't care for his attitude or his uniform. Often, Lieutenant Kirby had to be held back from losing his temper by Captain Flagg. Sergeant Sinclair was played with both a rough exterior and gentle interior by Peter Whitney, a character actor who often played the outlaw in several westerns before being cast in *The Rough Riders*.

The Rough Riders brought lots of action, adventure, and drama to the screen. Many attractive female guest stars were cast to play on the affections of our heroes, including Joyce Meadows, Kathleen Crowley, and Dorothy Provine (*The Alaskans*). Mike Connors, who later went on to gain immense popularity as "Mannix," also guest starred on *The Rough Riders*, as well as many other great western character actors of the time.

The Rough Riders ran for 39 episodes, and went off the air on September 24, 1959. The three stars of the show all went on to other big and small screen roles. Kent Taylor, the level-headed Captain Flagg, died at the age of 80 in 1987. Gruff Peter Whitney died in 1972. Jan Merlin is still with us.

All three characters on *The Rough Riders* wore parts or all of their respective Army uniforms on the show. This gave it an interesting western and military flavor. Captain Flagg and Lieutenant Kirby both wore cavalry-style double holsters and carried Remingtons. Sgt. Sinclair wore a single cavalry holster and also carried a Remington. Lt. Kirby cut away the top flaps of his holsters and wore the guns butt first. He also carried a knife in his boot. Few of us can imagine the hatred and the feelings of despair that many Confederate veterans were subjected to after the Civil War. One can see the appeal of a character such as Lieutenant Kirby.

THE REAL ROUGH RIDERS

It's difficult not to think of Teddy Roosevelt leading the "Rough Riders" during the Spanish-American War. Since the TV western *The Rough Riders* and the Latco cap shooter Ruf Rider both bring up this image, and in my efforts to give the readers a good dose of history—I felt it prudent to include some history of the "Rough Riders." What better way to honor some of America's finest cowboy-soldiers?

The Rough Riders were members of the 1st Volunteer Cavalry in the Spanish-American War. It was one group of cavalry volunteers personally recruited by

Colonel Teddy Roosevelt, in his Rough Riders uniform in 1898, as second in command of the 1st Volunteer Cavalry. (Courtesy of Museum of New Mexico)

Above: Kent Taylor, who starred as "Captain Flagg," a former Union Army cavalry officer, in TV's **The Rough Riders.**

Left: The "Rough Riders," left to right, Peter Whitney as "Sgt. Sinclair," Kent Taylor as "Captain Flagg," and Jan Merlin as "Lt. Kirby." A western-military show: What could be any better? Note the two guns butt first on Lt. Kirby in Confederate uniform.

Latco Ruf Rider cap shooter in polished nickel with floral grips. One of the finest cap guns ever made.

Close-up showing details of title on frame and gorgeous floral grips. The grips came in both nickel and copper.

Teddy Roosevelt himself. It was composed of real-life cowboys, miners, former lawmen, and even some college athletes, all were looking for adventure, as well as wanting to "Remember the Maine," which brought our country into this conflict with Spain. It was a time of great patriotism.

The flamboyant exploits and colorful hodge-podge of "personal flair" uniforms received a lot of publicity in the press at the time. Many people think Roosevelt commanded the entire group, but he was second in command. The commander was Col. Leonard Wood, who had resigned his position as the White House physician to command the regiment. Teddy Roosevelt, at the time, was Assistant Secretary of the Navy, and he, too, resigned to become second-in-command of the Rough Riders.

The unit became immortal for its uphill charge in the Battle of Santiago, in Cuba, on July 1, 1898, when the Rough Riders joined in the capture of Kettle Hill, then charged across the valley to assist in the seizure of San Juan Ridge, which was the highest point of San Juan Hill. What a glorious time for our country, here and abroad. Teddy Roosevelt went on to become one of this nation's bravest and most popular presidents. Like him or hate him, you didn't ignore Teddy Roosevelt. The real Rough Riders came along some 30 years after TV's *Rough Riders*, which was set in the late 1860s. It was a great title for a great western.

CAP GUN COLLECTIBLES

Latco, the Los Angeles Toy Company, came out with the Ruf Rider cap pistol in 1959. Not to confuse the "Rough Riders" of Teddy Roosevelt fame, the gun was marked "Ruf Rider" so that it appealed to the youngster afficionados of both groups. The cap shooter is one of the most beautiful cap guns ever made. Sleek, in high polished nickel, it is a 10-1/4-inch cap shooter, and is identical to the Classy patterns.

It came with both nickel and copper floral and scrolled grips, among one of the most beautiful grips ever put on cap guns. The

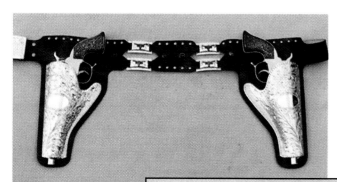

Spectacular Latco black leather and polished nickel double holster set for Ruf Riders. Note the upper and lower double steerhead belt adornments.

Close-up of details showing the Latco Ruf Rider with copper grips and the polished nickel metal holster pocket fronts and buckles. (Courtesy of E. Cremese)

grips are peened at the center, but two halves are used. Unlike many plastic grips that may warp with heat or crack from the elements and lots of use, these grips are fitted perfectly within the butt frame. It is a beautiful gun to hold, and to marvel at the quality and workmanship.

The gun also has a large, half-moon sight. The lever to break open the gun from the top is located on the left side of the hammer, and you push it forward, strangely enough, to break open the gun for cap loading. Around the rod to place the roll cap, one can see the markings of "Latco Inc" and "L.A. Calif." On both sides of the frame, in raised "bullet holes" within a rectangular frame, "Ruf Rider" between two stars is prominently marked.

These guns have been found in double holster sets with metal pockets, as well as cavalry-style black holsters with "US" on the flap. Since the Ruf Rider proved to be a popular gun, it also was marketed in other generic holster sets. Latco used the same model for both the Roy Rogers, and the rather scarce Davy Crockett.

ROY ROGERS
THE KING OF THE COWBOYS

He was, and is "The King of the Cowboys." His wife, on and off screen, was and is "The Queen of The West." With the soft and warm theme song "Happy Trails To You," Roy Rogers, one of America's most beloved and respected western stars, came to our television screens on December 30, 1951. Along with "Hopalong Cassidy," Gene Autry, and "The Lone Ranger," Roy was among this foursome to win his own place in the hearts and minds of millions of youngsters and adults in the early 1950s, and he continues to be there today.

Born Leonard Slye in 1911, this Cincinnati, Ohio, singing cowboy became "Roy Rogers" in 1938. His previous stage name had been "Dick Weston." Starting off with the 1938 Republic Pictures film *Under Western Stars,* Roy Rogers rode, sang, and entertained millions of youngsters in over 100 films and radio and television programs that continue unabated to this day. A man of great spiritual strength and family values, Roy and Dale have also suffered through the tragic loss of three children, and the passing of many wonderful co-stars and friends in Roy's career that has spanned 60 years.

Roy also introduced us to his famous horse, "Trigger," a golden Palomino, billed as "The Smartest Horse in The Movies." Roy's "best friend" was "Bullet," the "wonder dog," who could lick your face and wag his tail, but who struck fear in the hearts of the bad guys. Two of his most famous sidekicks were George "Gabby" Hayes, and Pat Brady.

Roy Rogers, "King of the Cowboys" on his golden Palomino, "Trigger."

Gabby Hayes, an old character actor that hit the movie industry in the 1920s was a popular star in his own right. Starting off as "Windy Halliday" and later settling on "Gabby," the bearded and sometimes cantankerous old geezer that he portrayed started off as the sidekick to many cowboy stars including Wild Bill Elliott and William Boyd. Hayes was a great storyteller and had a way with children that endeared him to thousands of kids with a kindly "old man" persona. Appearing in *The Lost Command* with a young Roy Rogers, they developed a special bond and friendship lasting for decades. He became Roy's sidekick on radio, film, and television as well as having his own *Gabby Hayes Show* from 1950 to 1956 on NBC. Gabby Hayes died in 1969 at the age of 84.

Pat Brady, Roy's last sidekick, along with his temperamental jeep, "Nellybelle" came on board on both of Roy's TV shows. On *The Roy Rogers Show,* the announcer began with "The Roy Rogers Show, starring Roy Rogers, king of the cowboys; Trigger, his golden Palomino; and Dale Evans, Queen of the West; With Pat Brady, his comical sidekick; and Roy's wonder dog, Bullet." Pat Brady laughed, frowned, mugged, and worried through all kinds of mishaps, but he was one sidekick that Roy trusted through thick and thin. It was lighthearted comedy, and sometimes it was "corny," but the kids loved it. His jeep "Nellybelle" had a mind of its own and was just as funny as Brady himself. Brady appeared on the show for its entire run. Brady passed away in 1972 after his retirement to Colorado. Pat Brady had appeared in more than 80 films.

Above: Roy Rogers, his wife, Dale Evans, and sidekick George "Gabby" Hayes. I can see why Dale is called "Queen of the West."

Left: Kilgore Roy Rogers cap guns: (top), the 10-1/4-inch model with revolving cylinder; (bottom), the 8-1/2-inch model. Both have the looking downward "palomino" grips.

Leslie-Henry Roy Rogers cap guns: (top), gold-plated 9-inch Roy Rogers with black horse head grips; (bottom), the Buzz-Henry Roy Rogers nickel finish with inset grips.

Schmidt Roy Rogers cap shooter in polished nickel with copper checkered grips with "RR" and "Trigger" logos.

A fine assortment of Roy Rogers cap shooters: (top), Schmidt with engraved cylinder and copper-checkered grips with logo; (top left), Classy in polished nickel with pewter floral grips; (lower right), Schmidt in polished nickel with copper grips; and (lower left), Classy with copper grips with Roy on rearing Trigger and "RR" logo.

THE TV SHOWS

The Roy Rogers Show was set in the Double R Bar Ranch in Mineral City. Roy and wife, Dale, who played themselves, were ranchers and also ran a diner. Roy strived to maintain law and order, and his wife and Brady, who played the diner's cook, helped out. The town's mayor, "His Honor Ralph Cotton," was played by Harry Lauter, who later went on to play in *Tales of the Texas Rangers.* The local lawman, "Sheriff Potter," was played by Harry Harvey, Sr. Sheriff Potter was constantly grateful to Roy and Dale for helping catch the bad guys and bringing them to justice.

Roy's backup singers were "The Sons of The Pioneers" which included Bob Nolan, Hugh Farr, Karl Farr, and Lloyd Perryman, and a good ballad was always part of the show. Roy was also one of the four producers of the show, which was sponsored by General Foods. The 30-minute show ran through almost six wonderful years, ending its run on June 23, 1957. The reruns of the show carried on in the Saturday morning lineup of shows from 1961 through 1964.

The Roy Rogers and Dale Evans Show, a western musical variety show, premiered September 29, 1962, and unfortunately, ended its short run at the end of December of the same year. Pat Brady, The Sons of The Pioneers, Kirby Buchanan, Kathy Taylor, and fuzzy Cliff Arquette as "Charley Weaver" were show regulars, in addition to guests, and circus- and horse-show acts. It was a wholesome family show, but it was obvious that the "adult" western was more popular.

As Dale Evans and Roy Rogers sang "Happy Trails To You," the duo remained in our hearts and memories through thousands of personal appearances and performing acts. Today, even in their advanced age, they are gracious hosts at the Roy Rogers-Dale Evans Museum in Victorville, California, where they greet, shake hands, and pose for photos for thousands of fans of all ages. Roy went on to establish the Roy Rogers Restaurant chain nationwide, and Dale Evans has written many inspirational books and songs. Both have been inducted into the Cowboy Hall of Fame and have been honored with the Golden Boot Awards for Western Entertainment. The couple has been married for over 50 years and remains one of the most respected couples in the show business industry, an astonishing feat that few couples in Hollywood achieve.

Roy Rogers became another successful marketing "king" as did the early four All-American western heroes. Dozens of fan clubs sprang up everywhere. Roy ran a successful "Back to School Contest," co-sponsored by Sears, that taught children going back to school these four important safety rules: (1) Cross the street only where there is Patrol (2) Go straight to and from school (3) Operate your bike according to law (4) Obey instructions of Parents, Teachers, and School Patrol. The contest, which made headlines, was won by a Texas elementary school in 1955.

British Lone Star-BCM Roy Rogers with revolving cylinder and Indian chief grips spectacular 10-1/2-inch model. Note the lever on left side of barrel for gate opening.

Close-up of details on the Lone Star-BCM Roy Rogers. Note the full headdress on the Indian chief and the BCM logo on grips. Note extensive engraving.

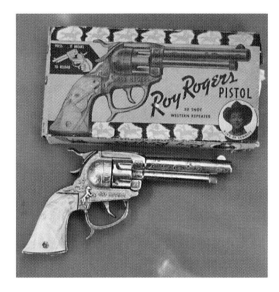

Above: Stevens 8-1/2-inch early die cast cap shooter marked to "Trigger," with extensive scrolling and horse head checkered grips. The only Trigger gun known.

Left: Leslie-Henry Roy Rogers 9-inch cap repeater with original box. Graphics on box show Roy as "King of the Cowboys." (Courtesy of Ron Doub)

Roy appeared on the cover of *Life* on July 12, 1943, one of the first western stars to do so. This was followed by literally dozens of wonderful and worthwhile family-oriented magazines that dealt with everything from raising pets to singing songs. Even Gabby Hayes and Pat Brady were honored on and in coloring books, short stories for kids, toys, and figures. One magazine that needs to be mentioned was *Jet* magazine, geared to black Americans. Roy Rogers was featured on the February 19, 1953, cover alongside a black youngster in a cute cowboy outfit with a cap pistol in his hand. Roy was color blind when it came to gun safety, and in being a role model for all youngsters, regardless of race, color, or creed. That particular issue is a rare and sought-after collectible.

CAP GUN COLLECTIBLES

While just a handful of companies made the Hoppy, Gene, and Lone Ranger cap pistols, the King of the Cowboys is also the King of the Cap Pistols! Kilgore and Hubley were producing the cast iron models in the 1940s. As the die casts came on the market, no less than 9 toy gun companies, both in the USA and England, made Roy Rogers cap guns and rifles, and who knows how many other gun-related toys are out there. Let's deal with the cap shooters first:

Kilgore made two Roy Rogers model guns. The most common is the 8-inch die-cast nickel cap shooter which came with white, swirl, tan, and chocolate brown grips, with the palomino-style horse head facing downward, and "RR" on the grips at the top. These came with short and long ejector rods. The lever, which breaks the gun from the top, is an elaborate affair on the right side. The gun has "Roy Rogers" on the left side of the frame and the Circle "K" logo on the right side. Minor engraving is on the frame, with a series of branding iron logos on the barrel, including "RR" and "DE" among others. These guns came in a variety of holster sets, both single and double, plain and very elaborate.

Kilgore also made the harder-to-find large Roy Rogers 10-1/4-inch nickel cap shooter with the revolving cylinder. This opens with a side gate latch located on the left side of the frame. This large frame gun has elaborate engraving, "Roy Rogers" on the left side of the frame, and a larger Circle "K" logo on the right side. The large grips have the horse head looking downward, and the grip itself has the extra "finger groove" design, similar to the "Grizzly" and "Bronco" models. The grips are found in white and a creamy marbleized pattern and have "RR" at the top. Again, a variety of holsters were made to accept these large Kilgore guns.

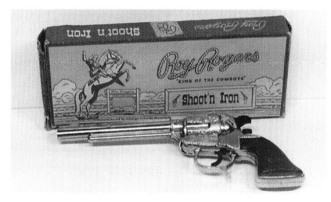

Schmidt's Roy Rogers Shoot 'n Iron with original box. This nickle model has the engraved cylinder and logo on grips. (Courtesy of J. Schleyer)

Classy Roy Rogers in gold finish with Roy on Trigger grips. Note this model does not have "RR" on grips but has signature on the frame. (Courtesy of J. Schleyer)

Back of the Tuck-A-Way model showing places to wear it.

Classy's Roy Rogers Tuck-A-Way gun and holster on original card. Touted as the "smallest cap gun made."

Classy Roy Rogers Shoot 'n Iron carded 50 shot cap repeater.

Back of Classy model card indicating the gun specifics. (Courtesy of Mike Cherry)

Leslie-Henry made its always popular 9-inch, nickel-plated and gold-plated Roy Rogers guns with the usual white and black grips, with the upraised horse head design. "Roy Rogers" is on both sides of the frame, along with extensive scrollwork on the barrel, cylinder, and frame. The frame as always, has the rearing horse logo next to the name. The lever is on the left side, below the hammer, and both dummy models and a smoker model, with anvil holes, exist. These guns also came in a variety of holsters—single, double, plain, elaborate, and of various leathers and colors, with all types of studs, conchos, buckles, and jewels.

Buzz-Henry also made the smaller 7-inch model, with the solid frame and inset grips which are found in white, red, and black. Models are found with and without "Buzz-Henry" on the gun butt. The "BH" logo is on the inset grips along with the rearing cowboy on horseback. The guns are extensively scrolled and engraved, with "Roy Rogers" on both sides of the frame, along with the rearing horse logo. This model came in both nickel and gold. A rather scarce Buzz Henry model has been identified with red grips and "Roy Rogers" and "Dale Evans" on the frames. As we know, Buzz Henry made this pattern for Dale Evans, Gene Autry, and *Lone Rider* series.

Schmidt made three sizes of the Roy Rogers guns, all with several characteristics. The small frame model is 9 inches, with "Roy Rogers" on a rocker panel over the trigger. Nickel plated with copper stag grips, it has the "RR" logo on the center of the grips. It was made of polished nickel with ribbed barrel, and breaks open from the top with lever on side of hammer. The same model was also made for Dale Evans. The gun grips have a more "rounded" appearance on the forms.

Schmidt made the medium-sized Roy Rogers with engraved barrel, rope bordered frame, and engraved cylinder. The grips are checkered copper with "RR" on the grips as well as those colorful "jewel" models, which came in red, green, blue, and yellow. These earlier models break open from the top with a side lever for cap loading. These guns are 9 inches in size.

The third Schmidt pattern, and the most common, is the 10-inch polished nickel model with ribbed barrel, with and without frame engraving. These came with: copper stag grips;

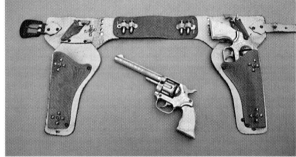

Above: Super Kilgore double holster set with Kilgore large guns and "RR" derringers up on the gunbelt just over the holster pockets. Seldom seen.

Left: Kilgore double holster set with Roy Rogers 9-inch cap guns. Note the "RR" tooling on floral holster pockets. (Courtesy of R. Cremese)

the checkered copper grips; "RR" logo on the grips; "RR" and "Trigger" logo on the grips; raised and incised "Roy Rogers" on the frames; with and without the opening lever for cap loading; and much harder to find white painted stag grips. Schmidt marketed these in boxes marked "Roy Rogers Shoot'n Iron" with a variety of holsters of both single and double styles.

Balantyne Manufacturing of Chicago made a Roy Rogers pressed steel 10-inch Roy Rogers cap shooter with a revolving cylinder and white grips with Roy and Trigger on them. They made the same model gun for the Buffalo Bill series. This is a Colt .45-style gun and is seldom seen.

Lone Star-British Cast Metals made a spectacular Roy Rogers 10-inch cap shooter that has collectors salivating to find one. Very much like the Hubley "Cowboy" in overall appearance, that's where the similarity stops. This beautiful gun came in both nickel and gold finishes. It has a left side gate that pops up, with a lever up on the frame near the barrel. It has a revolving cylinder and accepts two-piece bullets. There is extensive engraving overall on this gun with "Roy Rogers" on both sides of the frame. The most spectacular detail on this gun is the highly sculptured Indian Chief with full headdress on both sides of the grip. The detail is superb. The "BCM" logo is also on the grips. These were marketed separately by Classy in its several holster sets.

Lone Star also made the smaller model revolving cylinder cap shooter. This model was 9 inches and nickel plated, with white steerhead grips similar to the Hubley steerhead. The roundel, where the company logo is usually found, has "RR" instead on the grips. This cap shooter breaks open with a side lever, is extensively engraved on the frame only, and was Canadian-made and imported. It has a long, thin, and unadorned ejector rod. It also has a lanyard ring under the gun butt. This is a seldom-seen model.

By far, the largest number of variations were made by Classy Products of Los Angeles and New York showrooms and factories. Although not "Roy Rogers"-marked, research and catalogs confirm that Classy imported the Lone Star Apache model and marketed it with both Roy and Dale holsters. This was

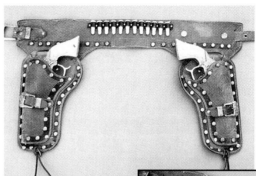

Left: Beautiful Leslie-Henry Roy Rogers double holster set with lots of studs!

Close-up of details showing 9-inch Leslie-Henry guns, "RR" studs, and name on belt.

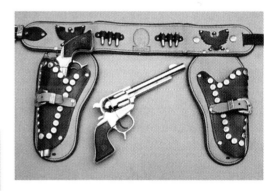

Schmidt double holster set with polished nickel model with copper grips. Note thunderbirds on belt and center logo and "RR" studs on the holster pockets.

Kilgore Roy Rogers cap gun with single holster showing graphics of both Roy and Trigger on colorful holster. Note beatiful swirl grips on gun. (Courtesy of Mike Cherry)

Kilgore large Roy Rogers revolving cylinder model in single holster showing details of tooling of name on holster and "RR" on buckle. (Courtesy of Terry Graham)

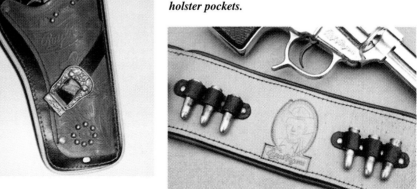

Above: Close-up of details showing tooled image of Roy and signature on gunbelt.

Boxed Roy Rogers Flash Draw double holster set with Schmidt stag grip guns which allowed youngsters to "fast draw" guns still in holsters. (Courtesy of Brian Wolf)

Boxed Roy Rogers double holster set with Schmidt checkered grip guns. (Courtesy of Brian Wolf)

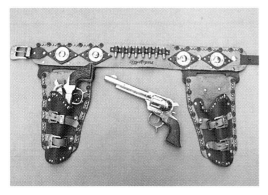

Super colorful Schmidt double holster set with Schmidt guns with copper stag grips. Note the assortment of conchos, studs, and double straps on holsters.

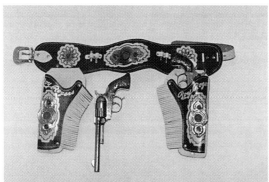

Colorful fringed double holster set with Schmidt Roy Rogers guns with copper floral grips. (Courtesy of Terry Graham)

the Civil War-style gun that came in both nickel and black factory finishes, and with white and black "star" logo grips.

Classy made the smallest Roy guns in the Tuck-A-Way models—2 inches overall. There is the 2 barrel over and under derringer, the C-31 model, all metal with checkered grips. The other is the percussion-style single shot derringer, also all metal with engraving on the frame. These came on a card showing Roy's picture and the "Tuck-A-Way" designation. The non-derringer "Model R-20" was also an all-metal, 2 inch, tiny single shot with a spur trigger and checkered grips with "RR" logo on the grips. It came in a dull gray metal finish, but also was found in bronze and gold finishes.

Classy made the next size up in the 5-inch Model R-30 Pee-Wee. It is an all-metal, nickel-plated single shot with checkered grips, and "Roy Rogers" on the side of the barrel. The next size up was the Model R-50, an 8-inch, all-metal single shot with full engraving and "RR" on the metal stag grips. The Model R-60, one of the most popular Classy models, was an 8 inch break-from-the-top model with the Roy on Trigger well sculptured on the grips. This model came in both nickel and gold finish with "Roy Rogers" on the frame.

Classy made another very popular Roy Rogers known as the Model R-90. This was a 9-inch gun, with polished nickel, as well as gold finish. The name

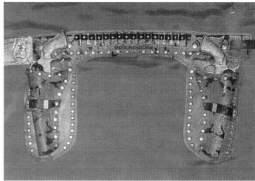

Spectacular RR double holster set with Classy guns in the style similar to what Roy himself wore with extra-wide holster pocket underlays. (Courtesy of J. Schleyer)

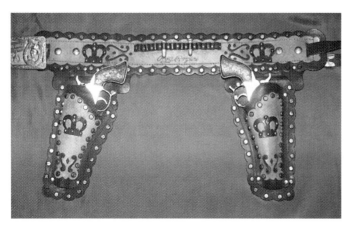

Left: Super Roy Rogers double holster set with Classy Roy Rogers guns with copper floral grips. Note crowns on belt and holsters and RR buckle with Roy and horse shoe.

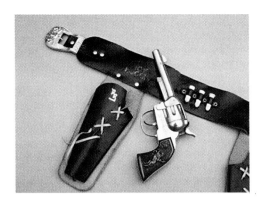

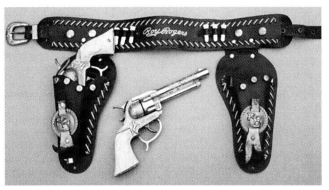

Seldom-seen Classy Roy Rogers double holster set with black and silver details. Classy cap shooter has "RR" logo and Roy on Trigger copper grips.

Rugged-looking Leslie-Henry double holster set with Leslie-Henry 9-inch guns, and "RR" conchos on holster pockets, with lacing and studs on belt.

is on the frame, and the grips were the beautifully made copper pattern with Roy and Trigger and the "RR" logo. This model is also found with dark bronze grips and a model with hard enamel, full color, hand-painted "Roy and Trigger" on the grips. This gun also breaks from the top with hand pressure.

The most popular of all the Classy models was the largest of all, the 10-inch polished nickel models. Similar but certainly not identical to the Schmidt guns, these came with copper stag grips; gold finish scrolled grips; pewter gray scrolled grips; and a model with an all gold finish on the frame, cylinder, and stag grips. This was a promotional prize awarded by Quaker Oats in the mid-1950s, while Roy's TV show was very popular. The back of the cap box on these large models gives Classy's Los Angeles address, and some are found marked "LATCO," also with the Los Angeles address. The "Roy Rogers" signature as well as the "RR" logo is found on both sides of the frame on the large Classy models. The scrolled-grips design is spectacular.

Roy Rogers' horse, Trigger, has the distinction, along with Gene Autry's horse, Champion, of also having a cap shooter honoring him. The Trigger cap shooter was put out by Stevens of Cromwell, Connecticut. It was an 8-inch solid and well-made cap shooter, one of the first die-cast models they made. It has white grips with Trigger's head on it, as well as checkering details. The frame has "Trigger" raised on both sides of the frame just behind the cylinder, and is also extensively engraved with lots of scrollwork. It has been

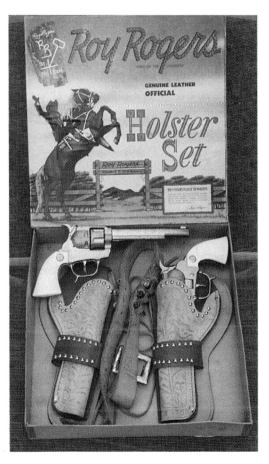

Above: Classy Roy Rogers in nickel with "RR" and Roy on Trigger copper grips (top). Classy Roy Rogers in polished nickel with pewter floral grips (below).

Fabulous Lone Star-BCM set of gold-plated Roy Rogers cap guns with plain but very elegant double holster and colorful box details. Indian head grips. (Courtesy of Brian Wolf)

Left: Here's a unique but correct Roy Rogers single holster set which came from Woolworth's with a Hubley Cowboy in gold with black grips. The name is in brass stamped letters on the gunbelt and "RR" on holster pocket, and with official "RR" buckle. (Courtesy of Brian Wolf)

Seldom-seen boxed Roy Rogers double holster set with 9-inch small frame Schmidt Roy Rogers gun with copper stag grips. Note graphics on box of young Roy. (Courtesy of Mike Cherry)

Right: Superb Roy Rogers double holster set in rich russet brown leather with Classy floral grip cap guns. Note "RR" studs, and "RR" buckle. This set is nearly identical to Roy's personal set he wore on the show. (Courtesy of J. Schleyer)

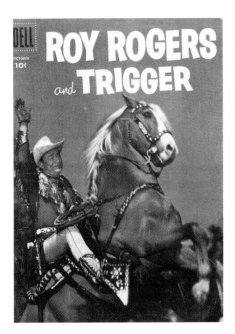

Above: One of the millions Dell Comics issued and sold for Roy Rogers and Trigger. Note the holster style.

Right: The Marx Roy Rogers rifle in gray plastic with signature on stock.

found in both a dull gray and a nickel finish. The gun breaks from the top for cap loading by hand pressure.

Marx made three rifles honoring Roy. They made the popular 26-inch cap shooter in silver all-plastic, with octagon barrel and die-cast works. This is the same Winchester-style model they made for "The Lone Ranger" and other characters. "Roy Rogers" is molded into the left side of the stock. The lockplates are extensively engraved with the usual Marx western scenes.

Marx also made a 24-inch plastic clicker Roy with black and brown plastic parts. The finest of the three Marx Roy Rogers rifles is the Deluxe Winchester 71 series, which came with black barrels, rich walnut brown stock with Roy's name on the left side of the stock in gold. The grip portion of the stock is checkered. This also came with a sling, and was the identical model also used by Marx for its Rin-Tin-Tin series.

To try and even attempt to list and describe the literally hundreds of Roy Rogers holsters would easily fill a book of its own. Therefore, I have tried to illustrate the guns I have listed and described in some of the most popular holsters. It's safe to state that no other western star had such an enormous number of holsters made and marketed under his name. Roy was certainly a two-gun cowboy star and he wore the flashiest clothes, shirts with fringe, all kinds of prints and patterns, bandanas of every color and hue, and perhaps the wildest pair of cowboy boots that ever adorned a pair of feet. Even his belt buckles were eye-popping.

Thus, it is no coincidence that an endless number of designs that range from the Classy leather gunfighter, a rather plain style, to the studded, jeweled, fringed, buckled, and even gaudy styles that exist. Roy's name is found everywhere and anywhere—on the belts, buckles, the holster pockets, holster straps, with and without Trigger! There

are the "King of the Cowboys" conchos, "RR" conchos, steer-heads, horse heads and horse-shoes, and of course, "RR" studs! Roy's name and his initials and the "RR" logo is screened, painted, raised, tooled, and found every which way on belts, holster pockets, and pocket straps. Stamped, script, cursive, Roy's signature, his initials, and even the "crown" is found on hundreds of styles. There is also a set of holsters that was an almost identical copy, as in the case of "Hoppy," that Roy himself wore on the show.

Buckaroos over 50 were saddened to learn that Roy Rogers passed away on July 6, 1998. His beloved wife, Dale Evans, said it best in exactly what the 1950s morals and values were all about: "What a blessing to have shared my life with him for 51 years. . . he was truly the king of the cowboys in my life. . . ." I'd like to add that Roy was the king of the cowboys for millions of fans all over the world and always will be. Happy trails to you, Roy, until we meet again.

SHOTGUN SLADE

H ere was a two-fisted, double-barreled western program that was set in the Old West with the special blend of a private eye in the saddle. "Shotgun Slade" was named for the character, who was only known by the name "Slade" and "Shotgun" for the special two-in-one shotgun that he preferred to carry instead of a six-gun.

Shotgun Slade was full of action as it hit the airwaves in November 1959. Initially it had been a pilot on an episode of the Schlitz Playhouse in March of the same year. Cast as "Shotgun Slade" was handsome character actor Scott Brady, already a well-known western star from the 1940s and early fifties.

Shotgun Slade was pure action and gunplay, and some stations claimed it was too violent. Even the jazz score was a pulsating crescendo that rushed through the action. The show was not at all squeamish. The critics be damned, *Shotgun Slade* had plenty of gunfire, a mine explosion, ambushes, saloon fights, hangings, and Slade blasting away with his unique shotgun.

Slade was a detective, after all, Old West or not, and his clients ran the gamut, from Wells Fargo to insurance companies to private characters who didn't always trust the local authorities; so Slade was hired to look into it, and look into it he did. He also provided protection for special clients. Not as glamorous or philosophical as "Paladin," both were "hired guns" for law and order.

Slade's love interest was played by Monica Lewis. The local saloon proprietor and Slade's friend was "Alice Barton," played by Marie Windsor. Slade strategized his assignment, loaded his deadly shotgun, and then hit the trail on his palomino horse. Scott Brady cut a handsome figure in the saddle. The show was unique in another way. It featured many real life heroes and well-known entertainers as guest stars.

Over its three-year run, some of the entertainers on the show were Ernie Kovacs, Jimmy Wakely, Johnny Cash, and Tex Ritter. Some of the real life heroes were Gregory "Pappy" Boyington of World War II fame; football star Elroy "Crazylegs" Hirsch; heavyweight boxer Lou Nova; golfer Lou Hahn; and baseball greats Chuck Essegian and Wally Moon.

The show ran a half-hour, but it was full-throttle action. *Shotgun Slade* aired 78 episodes and went off the air in 1961. Scott Brady went on to play in guest roles on many TV western and police drama shows, including the part of the bartender in *Hill Street Blues*. Scott Brady died in 1985 at the age of 60.

CAP GUN COLLECTIBLES

One of the rarest of all TV western character guns is the Shotgun Slade. As I have repeated a few times in this study, it's interesting to look back now and wonder why certain toy guns were made for some shows while other popular shows have nary a cap shooter for us addicted souls.

I'm thrilled to say that the Shotgun Slade is one of the most unique toy guns ever made. It is one of the most sought after of all the western character rifle/shotguns because, as a combination of both, it also represents an almost forgotten TV western show.

The Shotgun Slade was manufactured only by Esquire of New Jersey. It is a 30-inch long combo that is intricately made. With a special rotating lever on the left side of the lockplate, the rifle-shotgun breaks open, and you can slide out the barrels, turning them over to use whichever you prefer to blast away the varmint—rifle or shotgun!

There is a second lever on the top of the receiver that works forward and backward to break open the gun to load it with both a cap or a shotgun shell. The stock is a beautiful simulated brown wood grain. The barrels and receiver are black. "Shotgun Slade" is raised on the left side of the gun while the right side has the raised and well-molded logo of the Esquire pony head in a circle and with a sign underneath stating "An Esquire Toy." A third lever drops the two triggers and the cap box assembly, very much like the Marx Wanted Dead or Alive "Mare's Laig."

Scott Brady, in the role of "Shotgun Slade" with his specially-made and unique 2-in-1 shotgun.

Esquire's Shotgun Slade equally unique toy 2-in-1 shotgun named for the character and TV show of the same name. Seldom seen.

Close-up of the details of the raised "Shotgun Slade" on left side of shotgun, the double triggers, and the rotating lever for opening.

 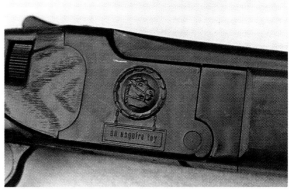

Close-up of details showing the shotgun opened. Note the upper rifle chamber and lower shotgun shell chamber. Note lever to break open and the knurled wheel on right side to line up chambers.

Close-up of right side of receiver showing the Esquire pony logo, and knurled wheel on right side to rotate chambers.

The Shotgun Slade taken apart. Barrels removed entirely from stock, and the trigger assembly comes down to show intricate mechanism. Rare and unique.

This is marvelous toy to observe and ponder over the design and intricate workings of such a kid's toy gun. The gun is certainly fragile, and between the relatively short run of the show, the fact that perhaps few were made and sold, it is safe to assume that not many of these rifle-shotguns have survived. Another factor would be that the critics blasting the show for containing too much violence may have also curtailed the new wave of mothers of the early 1960s from buying such a toy gun for the youngsters. But there is no denying that the Shotgun Slade is impressive.

Esquire made a special holster for the Shotgun Slade and it is also very scarce. It is made of black leather with gold details, and allows you to sling the shotgun into the holster rig-scabbard affair, secured with the holster strap, which is also stamped "Shotgun Slade." The belt has six bullet loops. The belt also sports an octagon concho. This is the only known holster rig for the Shotgun Slade two-in-one rifle-shotgun.

Dell Comics put out one issue of *Shotgun Slade,* in July-September 1960, as the show was on the CBS Network. The comic is also quite rare, showing a great color shot of Scott Brady in his "Slade" character duds holding his deadly shotgun. The show has never been rerun or shown after it left the air in 1961. It would be safe to say the show, the comic book, and this prized shotgun cap shooter are all pretty rare today.

Esquire "Shotgun Slade" special holster outfit for the rifle-shotgun. Note the typical Esquire belt, six bullets, and special strap with show title. Seldom seen. (Courtesy of J. Schleyer)

The only Dell Comic issued for **Shotgun Slade,** *July 1960.*

SMOKY JOE

"Smoky Joe," like "Pecos Bill," was neither a real western character, or a TV western, but he was made a popular character that spawned several Smoky Joe guns. For this reason I felt he should be properly identified and included in this study. After pouring through dozens of books, old western articles, and folktales, I did find a character named "Old Smokey Joe"—but there wasn't enough information or concrete evidence that this was the real character that the guns were named after. More on that Old Smokey Joe later.

It appears that "Smoky Joe" was "on loan" to the "Glendale Riders," also a fictitious western cattlemen riders group. Glendale Provision Company of Detroit, Michigan, produced hot dogs called "Glendale Hot Dogs" and "Glendale Weenie Weenies," which were made for what they called the "small fry" of the family. They also made luncheon meats, "zestees" sausages, and skinless hot dogs they called a "royal treat."

In 1949, it appears that the J. Halpern Company (Halco) of Pittsburgh, Pennsylvania, was already producing the "Smoky Joe" cast iron cap pistol, and the character was incorporated into the story of the "Glendale Riders." Each week, the Glendale Provision Company would put out a little book with each package of Glendale Hot Dogs and Weenie Weenies involving "Smoky Joe" and his adventures with the "Glendale Riders."

Smoky Joe was apparently a Texas Ranger, who must have traveled up to Michigan to help capture some rustlers, who must have been stealing from the Glendale Riders. After Smoky Joe helped catch the rustlers, he returned to his position with the Texas Rangers. Glendale Provision Company hired writer Ben Bolt to do the adventure stories, and the booklets were illustrated by Richard Osborne, and published by the Samuel Lowe Company of Kenosha, Wisconsin. The booklet's cover credits the use of the Smoky Joe character to the J. Halpern Company, which it also states was making Smoky Joe holster sets, chaps, and Smoky Joe caps. The booklet has a 1949 copyright date.

Now let's see about that "Old Smokey Joe" character. First off, note that the "Smoky" in this man's name has an "e" in it—"Smokey"—and it's "Old Smokey Joe" and not just "Smoky Joe." I'm not not trying to be picky; I take my western yarns seriously! According to an old article by A. M. Hartung, who I was not able to identify, he refers to this "Old Smokey Joe" in

Old Smokey Joe, mountain man, trapper, plainsman, Indian Scout—but was he the "Smoky Joe" of cap guns fame? (Courtesy of A.M. Hartung, True West, *1958)*

Above: Hubley Smokey Joe 8-inch cap repeater in nickel finish with steerhead grips.

Left: Cover of the lid for the Halco Smoky Joe holster sets shows a two-gun cowboy blasting away. (Courtesy of J. Schleyer)

Above: Close-up of details of the gunbelt and 9-inch Leslie-Henry cap gun. (Courtesy of Terry Graham)

Left: Beautifully-tooled Leslie-Henry double holster set with 9 inch guns with white horse head grips. Note character and name on both holsters and back of gunbelt.

Two patterns of the Leslie-Henry 9-inch Smoky Joe; top has root beer horse head grips, lower has the copper grips with "Texas Longhorn" on the grips.

a 1958 article for the old *True West* magazine. The article was written as if Mr. Hartung went and interviewed this old character, and after the first couple of paragraphs, he turns the story over to Old Smokey Joe himself, who then writes as if he's relating his own adventures.

The article had a photo of Old Smokey Joe, which was attributed to the author, so perhaps whoever this old character was, he may have been interviewed and photographed by Mr. Hartung himself. Since the author does not give a last name, it was next to impossible to confirm who this character was, where he lived or much more about him other than what he was actually relating himself in that article. But it was interesting enough and the name so close that it's possible the cap gun companies—certainly the cast iron ones—may have heard of this old geezer and adopted the name. It's as wild and interesting a story as the "Smoky Joe" of the Glendale Riders, so sit back and enjoy it!

According to the article, Old Smokey Joe was already in his mid-80s at the time of the 1958 article. Old Smokey Joe had seen service as a mountain man, plainsman, trapper, Indian scout, and guide. He did the guiding of the Overland Stages from Missouri to the Pacific Coast. He wore buckskins, a bandoleer belt full of ammo, carried a Winchester 94, wore a big, wide-brimmed Stetson and flowered bandana. He wore his hair long and scraggly, and had a thick handlebar moustache that had gone salt and pepper.

Old Smokey Joe was never seen without his well-worn briar pipe. Once he filled the bowl and lit it up, he'd lay back on his old chair, curl the smoke up in the air, and it was as if his memory opened up with each puff from the old bowl full of tobacco. Old Smokey Joe would relate stories of sidekicks, Indian fights, panning for gold, stagecoaches being attacked by robbers, and then with the same vivid descriptions, he'd talk about horses, baby colts, and nature.

He had a missing finger from his right hand, and if you asked him about it, he'd tell you how he had two rings on that finger, but during an Indian fight, a Crow warrior shot him, with the bullet passing through his cap and burrowing a furrow right through his scalp. Old Joe went down, knocked out cold. As the warrior went over to scalp him, he saw the rings, but couldn't get them off. With his knife, the Indian started to cut through Old Smokey's finger, determined to get the rings. Finally, he cut the finger off at the joint, and took the rings and the finger! Just as he was about to scalp Old Smokey Joe, his old trapping partner, known as "Totem Tom" shot the Indian dead. He then tied rawhide around the stub of what was left of Old Smokey's finger, and after a while it "just dried up and healed." So that's the story of "Old Smokey Joe."

One question remains: Hubley put out a cast iron Smoky Joe cap pistol towards the end of the cast iron era. We must then assume that Hubley first came up with the character of "Smoky Joe." Smoky Joe then re-appears as a die-cast cap shooter made by Hubley, Leslie-Henry, and Stevens. Did Hubley sell Leslie-Henry and Stevens the name or the idea to continue the "Smoky Joe" character into the die cast era? Obviously, J. Halpern was making the Smoky Joe line as early as 1949 if we go by the adventures of Smoky Joe and the Glendale Riders. Either way, the character of Smoky Joe was extremely popular, so much so that the line continued to the die casts. Several specimens exist.

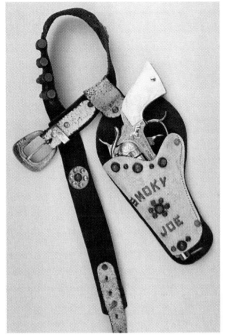

Above: Stevens Smoky Joe cap shooter in antique bronze with sleek black grips. Note "S" logo on grips and branding iron letters on barrel. Seldom-seen model.

Right: Leslie-Henry Smoky Joe single holster set with letters on holster pocket in brass. Gun is 9-inch Leslie-Henry cap pistol with white horse head grips.

CAP GUN COLLECTIBLES

Hubley's Smoky Joe is an 8-inch die-cast repeater that came in both nickel and gold finishes, the nickel with white steerhead grips and the gold with black steerhead grips. Hubley made the identical gun in its Tex series. It features a beautiful, extensively-scrolled and engraved gun, with a solid left side lever for top breaking to load caps—and white grips with black steerhead grips and Hubley star logo. "Smoky Joe" is on both sides of frame in an oval, roped design frame. Both early die casts, the nickel and gold finishes, are quality workmanship. A dull gray pattern also exists. This is the only Smoky Joe model that Hubley made as a die-cast cap pistol.

Leslie-Henry/Halco made the 9-inch Smoky Joe die-cast repeater in nickel finish with a wide variety of grips. There is the standard white horse head grip, black horse head grips, root beer grips, and it also made a Smoky Joe model with copper grips, with "Texas Longhorn" on the grips with a steerhead in between. The cap pistols have the rearing horse logo on the frame, extensive scrollwork and "Smoky Joe" on both sides. The opening lever is

The complete series of the Smoky Joe cap guns—a collection itself!

on the left side and the gun breaks from the top. The gold finish models found with black horse head grips, and the only other difference noted is the size of the rearing horse, as it is larger and more pronounced on the copper gripped model, with "Texas Longhorn" designation.

The Stevens company's Smoky Joe is much harder to find. It is 8 inches in length and at first glance, it looks like the Stevens "Cowboy King." However, while it has the identical size grips, in plain black plastic, and the same barrel markings of branding iron lettering and scrollwork, the frames and hammers are totally different. The release lever on the Stevens Smoky Joe is on the right side and the gun breaks from the top. "Smoky Joe" is on both sides of the frame and the Stevens Circle "S" logo is on the grips. The gun came in a beautiful antique copper-like finish, slightly more brilliant than the Actoy or Leslie-Henry bronze finishes. It is a tight, solid, and well-made cap gun.

Halco/Leslie-Henry made several Smoky Joe holster sets for its guns. A single and double set came with lots of studs, matching cuffs, and "Smoky Joe" in brass letters on the holster pockets. Leslie-Henry made a double holster set in exceptionally-tooled leather with a character image of Smoky Joe on the pockets and "Smoky Joe" well tooled on the back of the belt, which is extensively tooled with beautiful floral work in black and rustic brown. This set takes the 9-inch models made by Leslie-Henry, but will take the Stevens models just as nicely, thank you.

J. Halpern Company also made "Smoky Joe"-marked caps with the character on the boxes of the caps themselves, which in of itself is quite scarce. Smoky Joe may have been a fictitious character, but he had wide appeal in the late 40s and 50s. While some popular western cap guns of some of the most popular TV shows were made by only one American company, or only by an overseas maker, here a totally fictitious character was marketed by no less than three U.S. companies. All the more for us collectors today!

SUGARFOOT

Will Hutchins, starring as "Tom Brewster" on **Sugarfoot.**

Daisy Bullseye 50-shot cap pistol in metallic bronze with gold hammer and trigger, and walnut grain grips. Note logo on grips and barrel markings.

Right side of gun showing the upward lifted side gate for cap loading, a rather unique feature not usually encountered on the right side of a cap pistol.

ugarfoot was a strange name for a western, even in the 1950s. Hell, shoot, ain't nothing worse than a "Tenderfoot" in the old, Wild West. . .unless, of course, you're one step below a Tenderfoot—in which case, you're a "Sugarfoot."

As such, you just know some cowboy is going to size you up and then try to bring you down. He's going to make you "dance" to the tune of his six-gun's bullets as they shoot the floor all around you. He's going to try to re-arrange your looks. Hell, he may even hog-tie you across your horse and give the old mare a slap on the behind and send you juggling out of town until your guts come out. . .no sireee, "Sugarfoot" was not the thing to be in the Old West!

Along comes Tom Brewster. He's calm, well mannered, a little naive, trusts everybody, has that all-American "aw shucks" look and he really means well. He doesn't want to bother anybody and he doesn't want anybody to bother him. He's studying to be a lawyer, you see, but he's already getting a dose of some of the varmints he may have to defend someday. He goes from town to town, meeting rough characters and pretty girls. Both are "attracted" to Tom Brewster for different reasons, of course. The girls can't resist that "real gentleman" way about him, and the desperadoes hate that "real gentleman" way about him.

Cast as the soft-spoken, handsome and trusting "Tom Brewster" was Will Hutchins, a young actor who had worked on Matinee Theater and just about every other kind of job after getting out of the army in 1954. *Sugarfoot* came to television on September 17, 1957, and it ran on alternating weeks with both *Cheyenne* and *Bronco,* the Warner Brothers television bonanza of great westerns.

Sugarfoot was a great western that had it all: comedy, action, morals, values, knowing right from wrong, triumph of the little guy over the bad guy—but never killing for violence's sake. There was also another interesting twist to *Sugarfoot.* Tom Brewster had to also keep defending himself against a man who was the "spittin' image" of him—a notorious character, gunslinger, desperado, con artist, and all-around guy you want to stay away from—"The Canary Kid." Trouble was, Tom Brewster and the Canary Kid looked like identical twins. This added a lot of humor to the show, in an almost *Maverick* style, and it was quite enjoyable. *Sugarfoot* ran for an hour, racked up 69 episodes, and it eventually left the air on July 3, 1961, after a healthy 3-1/2 year run.

Will Hutchins went on to star in *Hey Landford,* a comedy series after *Sugarfoot.* Hutchins continued to appear on other western series and also did movies, and he is still with us. Many great stars appeared on *Sugarfoot* during its run, including Don "Red Ryder" Barry, Adam "Batman" West, Dan "Hoss Cartwright" Blocker, tough guy Charles Bronson, and sweet and perky Connie Stevens. It was a wonderful, clean, and entertaining program, and is sorely missed. It didn't need a silly laughtrack to get a laugh along with it.

My kid brother and I were great fans of *Sugarfoot,* and I'd call him "Sugarfoot" when we'd play out imaginary episodes on the railroad tracks and fields alongside the *Hartford Courant,* which bordered our backyard on Queen Street. My brother was not into writing to movie stars, but he was called "Sugarfoot" so many times and by so many of our neighborhood youngsters that he sent away for an autographed photo of Will Hutchins after explaining he was the "local Connecticut Sugarfoot." Hutchins responded by sending him the autographed photo shown here and he added a bunny rabbit to his signature.

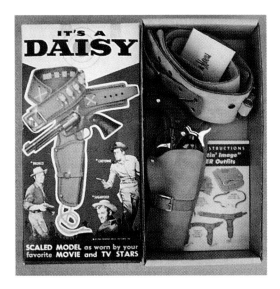

Daisy boxed single holster set for the Sugarfoot-Cheyenne-Bronco "Spittin' Image" series of scaled model guns. Note instructions and Neiman-Marcus card.

CAP GUN COLLECTIBLES

Daisy marketed its Bullseye 50 shot cap shooter in its "Spittin' Image" series. This neat cap shooter came in a dark metallic bronze finish with wood-grained walnut-like grips. At 7-1/2 inches, this cap pistol had the side gate that opened upward and on the right side marking it unique in its own way. "Bullseye 50 shot" is raised on the right side of the barrel, and it carries the circle "Daisy" logo on the grips. Another unique feature is that both the hammer and the trigger of this gun are gold plated. It came with brass bullets that are also marked to "Daisy."

The boxed sets of the Spittin' Image guns are the only known guns that carry the photo image of Will Hutchins as "Sugarfoot" on the lid. The box also has photo images of Clint Walker as *"Cheyenne"* and Ty Hardin as *"Bronco,"* which were the alternating shows with Sugarfoot from 1957 to 1961. The holster sets featuring Sugarfoot were put out by Daisy in 1960. They were sold at several department stores, including Neiman-Marcus, which inserted a business card in the box with the contents.

The boxed sets came in two styles—a double holster set and a single holster set. Both are of top grain tan leather, thick, heavy, and solid. With top quality construction and stitching, both are in the gunfighter style. Both sets came with a row of four Daisy brass bullets, and the belt had adjustable buckle and tongue strap ends on the belt. The holsters, while plain, are simply in the "don't mess with me 'cause I'm not really a Sugarfoot.

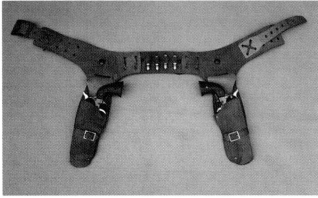

Daisy double holster set for the Daisy Sugarfoot series with the Bullseye 50-shot cap repeaters. The buckle is also brass and has the Daisy bullseye logo on it. (Courtesy and special thanks to Ron Scisciani and Terry Graham)

Close-up of box lid showing Will Huthcins as "Tom Brewster" of **Sugarfoot.** *The other characters are Cheyenne and Bronco. Rare and seldom seen complete set.*

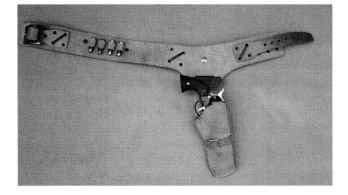

Daisy single holster set with its Bullseye 50-shot cap repeater. Note bullets.

The real Sheriff Pat F. Garrett, the lawman who shot and killed Billy the Kid. (Courtesy of Museum of New Mexico)

William H. Bonney, the notorious "Billy the Kid," poses in more respectable duds than what he was usually seen wearing. (William Tell Images)

THE TALL MAN

No, this western was not about a "tall" gunfighter. "The Tall Man" was a title used to describe of a man with character, with ethics, and with principles, such as a man "standing tall" in the face of adversity, or "walking tall," as in the movie about real-life sheriff Buford Pusser of Tennessee, who was so incorruptible that it cost him his life.

The Tall Man told the story of a strange relationship. It was more of a fictionalized account of the relationship between two real-life American legends, one a lawman, the other, a young and deadly gunfighter. *The Tall Man* was about real-life Sheriff Pat Garrett of Lincoln County, New Mexico, and real life killer, William H. Bonney, known as "Billy the Kid." Hollywood often takes great liberty with history and fact, and it certainly did so with *The Tall Man*. This western correctly portrayed Sheriff Garrett for the "tall man" that he was, but it portrayed Billy the Kid as a sort of misguided young delinquent rather than the cold-blooded killer of 21 men that he really was.

With a twist of real-life irony, the real Sheriff Pat Garrett had befriended Billy the Kid, but the showdown was inevitable. In this series, which came to television on September 10, 1960, the Tall Man, Pat Garrett, is sheriff of Lincoln County, New Mexico, and young Billy the Kid roams in and sets himself up there. He had a knack for getting into trouble, of course. Sheriff Garrett and Billy soon meet and establish a sort of big-brother relationship, with Garrett trying to steer Billy in the right direction and away from his destiny.

Sheriff Garrett had a personal creed and it was "My business is the law and I aim to mind it." This set the stage for the showdown that, although never shown on the TV show, would cost Billy his young, sadistic life, and bring eternal fame to real life Pat Garrett, who killed Billy the Kid on the night of July 14, 1881. But this sad tale of young man gone terribly wrong has already been told in the "Billy The Kid" section of this book. Since "The Tall Man" refers to Sheriff Garrett, let's tell his story, which has often been overshadowed by Billy the Kid.

THE REAL TALL MAN

Patrick Floyd Garrett was born in Alabama in 1854, but grew up in Louisiana. He was tall and gangly, it was said. He quit school in his teens and headed towards the western plains. He first worked as a cowboy in Texas, later hunted buffalo in the Panhandle area, and eventually ended up in New Mexico territory. Settling in Fort Sumter, New Mexico, he worked as a horse wrangler for the Maxwell ranch. Garrett came to know a young man who would eventually change his life. The young man was William H. Bonney, already known as "Billy the Kid," with a reputation for a hot temper and an even faster will to settle disputes with his six gun. It was around 1878.

Garrett was 24 years old, 6'4", good looking, charming, and wore knee-high boots, a sombrero, and a big moustache. He carried a Colt "peacemaker" that had formerly been owned by Wild Bill Hickok, given to Garrett by Wild Bill's surviving sister, Lydia Barnes of Oberlin, Kansas. Billy was a mere 19 years old when he met Garrett, and had already killed several men. In either case, the two men did develop a strange relationship, and did some gambling and drinking together. Both were popular with Mexican women.

Garrett eventually married Polinaria Guiterrez, and she bore him seven children. Garrett went into the grocery business for a time, and ran for sheriff of Lincoln County and was elected in 1880. Garrett was nicknamed "Big Casino," and Billy was nicknamed "Little Casino," for the gambling they did. The Mexicans also nicknamed Garrett "Juan Largo," meaning "Long John," because of his big frame and his imposing stature with boots and sombrero. He could easily pass for a Mexican.

Lincoln County in the late 1870s covered some 27,000 square miles of rich land untouched by the railroad, fenced-in farms, or an established police force. Citizens took it upon themselves to handle the honest settler and rancher, and the gunslingers that followed the exodus from Texas westward. Probably the biggest rancher was John Tunstall, a cultured Brit that befriended Billy the Kid and gave him a job. When Tunstall was killed in an ambush, Billy swore revenge, and what were called the Lincon County "wars" went full speed and many men died with their boots on from both sides. For a time, Billy and Garrett went separate ways, on different sides of the law, of course.

Gov. Lew Wallace gave Garrett the job of bringing in Billy the Kid. Two men recently added to the Kid's victims list were literally killed in cold blood, one named Grant and a man named Carlyle. Garrett then brought the Kid in alive after convincing the Kid to surrender at Stinking Springs. Billy the Kid, while in jail, managed to shoot both of his jailers, Tom Bell and Bob Ollinger, and make good his escape. He killed both of them in a daring escape only two weeks before his scheduled hanging. Garrett knew the showdown was getting closer. Garrett, aided by deputies John Poe and Tip McKinney, went after Billy.

Garrett, the tall man, physically and literally, had lost two jailers and part of his reputation by his former drinking and gambling companion. For three months, they searched for Billy and were eluded at every turn. Garrett assumed, finally, that Billy might be hiding at Maxwell's ranch, where both had worked at one time, when they first met. On the night of July 14, 1881, Garrett posted Poe and McKinney near the porch of Maxwell's ranch by a bedroom window, and around midnight, Garrett went in.

Billy the Kid, barefoot and half-dressed, had a knife in his hand and was out to cut himself some beef jerky. In the pitch black darkness, his last words were "Quien es?" (Who is it? in Spanish) as he encountered Deputy Poe outside on the porch. Garrett, from inside and in total darkness, blasted away as Billy walked backwards back into the house. Within moments Billy the Kid was dead as a doornail. But the saga of Pat Garrett was only beginning.

He wrote a book with writer Ash Upton, *The Authentic Life of Billy the Kid.* Deputy Poe, who later became a banker, also wrote his version of *The Death of Billy the Kid.* What happened to Pat Garrett after he killed Billy the Kid, ironically, with Wild Bill Hickok's Colt? First, he lost his badge. The Democratic political powers in Lincoln County denied his renomination. Billy the Kid, was, well "just a kid," and they were not happy that Garrett had ambushed him.

John Poe, who had hunted Billy with Garrett, was elected in his place. The $500 reward that Governor Wallace had offered as bounty to "any person or person(s) who will capture William Bonney, alias "The Kid" and who shall deliver him to any sheriff of New Mexico" was initially denied to Garrett. Since he brought Billy in dead, he had to hire a lawyer, and lobby at Santa Fe to have the legislature pass a special act so he could collect the reward.

Garrett went in the cattle business at Fort Stanton for a while, but law and order was in his blood. At the request of Sheriff Jim East of Tascosa, New Mexico, he hired Garrett out to lead a group of Rangers to hunt down rustlers in the Canadian River territory, which Garrett did for a year and half. Garrett performed this dangerous assignment with courage and resolve and won great praise for it.

Pat Garrett was a misunderstood man. He did not care for gunplay. In fact, he had a distaste for it. Returning back to the cattle business and working for Capt. Brandon Kirby as a cattle trail boss, Garrett would not allow his cowhands to carry guns, figuring they would get tanked up in towns and use them. The cowhands resented this, arguing that perhaps this was Garrett's personal problem, that he was afraid some young gunslinger would want to take him down for shooting Billy the Kid. After all, earning reputations was part of the Wild West genre. Garrett worked for Captain Kirby until 1886, and then went into his own business of ranching in Roswell, New Mexico.

The ranching venture failed. Garrett next tried a land irrigation project in the Pecos Valley, but that too, failed. He next ran for sheriff of Chaves County, but lost. He next decided to try his hand at breeding horses in Uvalde, Texas. Here he became friends with John H. Garner, who would later be vice-president for the first two terms under Franklin Delano Roosevelt. Garner was in his 30s then and was nicknamed "Cactus Jack." With Garner's help, Garrett was elected county commissioner and settled down in Uvalde until 1897, when friends from Dona Ana County in New Mexico convinced him to run for sheriff. He won this time and served a full term. Then President Teddy Roosevelt, who was very fond of the law-and-order types, appointed him collector of customs at El Paso, Texas, a position he held for four years.

He then turned back to raising and breeding horses in New Mexico. Garrett got into a dispute with a rancher named Wayne Brazil, who leased land from Garrett in the Organ

Barry Sullivan as "Sheriff Pat Garrett," and Clu Gulager as "Billy the Kid," on the TV western **The Tall Man,** *shared an ambivalent friendship.*

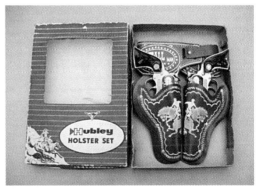

Hubley boxed set of double holsters for **The Tall Man.** *Seldom seen.*

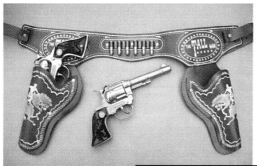

Above: Hubley's The Tall Man double holster set with Hubley Western cap guns with purple swirl grips. Made of top grain leather in rich colors and details.

Close-up showing details of The Tall Man double holster set.

One of several "Wanted" posters issued for Billy the Kid. This one was signed by Gov. Lew Wallace of New Mexico. Note that Bonney, the Kid's last name, was spelled incorrectly as "Bonny."

Mountains. Garrett tried to get Brazil to vacate the land, but Brazil refused. On the road to Las Cruces, the two met to try and resolve this impasse. It was February 29, 1908. A fierce argument ensued. As Garrett was starting to get out of his wagon, Brazil opened fire and shot Garrett in the head. Garrett's partner, Carl Adamson, pleaded with Brazil "Don't shoot, don't shoot him again" but Brazil fired another shot into Garrett's stomach and he died on the spot. Garrett was only 54 years old.

Garrett's legacy didn't end there. Brazil was acquitted. His defense was that Garrett was going to come after him with a shotgun and he was merely protecting himself. Garrett was buried at Las Cruces. Celebrated eulogies were read at the funeral, including a religious reading written by William Jennings Bryan. But today, this famous sheriff's grave lies unmarked, unfenced, and unkept. There is not even a tombstone or monument. By contrast, Billy the Kid's grave, also in New Mexico, has a granite tombstone. Two of his gang members are buried with him, Tom O'Folliard and Charlie Bowdre, under the heading "Pals." They had to put a fence around it to keep the away the souvenir hunters who were chipping away at it. Sheriff Pat Garrett deserved better than to die like a dog.

In the TV western of *The Tall Man,* some of the real life values of Sheriff Pat Garrett were copied. He didn't like using his gun, except as a last resort. Billy was shown on the show just the opposite—he wanted to settle every argument with his gun. Garrett regarded it as a tool to use only as a last resort, but to Billy it was a way to compensate for his inferiorities—his size, his buck teeth, his young age, lack of judgment, his borderline intelligence, his troubled past, perhaps.

That was the plain message of this western for the audiences of 1960-1962. It was a great show, even if the two real-life legends of the West were shown as ambivalent friends; it was clear that sooner or later, the showdown between Garrett and Bonney was inevitable.

Cast as "Sheriff Pat Garrett" was long time character actor Barry Sullivan, who had starred in all kinds of roles for some twenty years. He had also starred in a prior television series long forgotten, called *The Harbourmaster,* in the 1950s, which was an adventure program, not a western. Cast as "Billy the Kid" was actor Clu Gulager, a character actor best known for many off-beat, quirky, sadistic roles. He brought his macho, wiseguy, wacky kind of style to the character of Billy the Kid perfectly. *The Tall Man* ended its two-year run on September 1, 1962.

Barry Sullivan went on to star in *The Road West*, also a western in the 1966-1967 season. Barry Sullivan passed away in 1997. Clu Gulager went on to play Ernie Ryker in the long-running *The Virginian* with James Drury. He also acted in *North and South* as well as *The Gambler,* and is still with us.

CAP GUN COLLECTIBLES

Hubley, that wonderful giant, came out with a boxed double holster set for *The Tall Man.* The guns were the always reliable Western with purple swirl grips. The holsters are a rich russett brown color, with yellow-gold and white details showing a cowboy on a bucking bronco and a rope design border on the pockets. The belt has white details with "The Tall Man" within a large oval of stars and lines on both sides of the belt over the pockets. The belt holds six silver bullets across the back. Note that the "Tall" part of "The Tall Man" is enlarged for emphasis of the character strength. A second set, with identical holsters, came with the also reliable Hubley Coyote, nickle with metal checkered grips.

A close scrutiny of the overall design of the Tall Man double holsters by Hubley shows that they used a similar pattern for one of the many Wyatt Earp holster sets Hubley marketed. The Hubley standard size "Wyatt Earp," with purple swirl grips was also the identical model used for this Western cap shooter. This will be shown in the "Wyatt Earp" section.

I sure hope that this writer has given Sheriff Patrick Floyd Garrett a few steps back up to his tall man character. This TV western may have done a bit of stretching with the relationship between the two men, but the message that you don't use a gun to settle differences when cooler heads should prevail was not lost or unused in the golden age of westerns in the 1950s.

THE TEXAN

The real William Preston Longley, taken in 1878, shortly before he swung into eternity for his horrible crimes. (Courtesy of Western History Collection, University of Oklahoma)

Just like the TV western *Johnny Ringo,* television took great liberty with *The Texan.* The main character in *The Texan* was Bill Longley, who in real life, was one of the Lone Star state's most notorious and sadistic killers. The real Bill Longley made Billy the Kid and Jesse James look like choir boys.

It would be interesting to know why the producers of *The Texan* decided to name the character after such a killer when any good ole' Texan name could have been used, but they did. It certainly didn't affect the two-year popularity of this show. It was safe to say that most Americans, save real west historians, had never heard of the real Bill Longley, and like the audience that enjoyed "Johnny Ringo," they enjoyed the exploits of "Bill Longley," an ex-gunfighter who devotes his life to helping less fortunate people.

Naming a TV western *The Texan,* is almost synonymous with the Old West. Texas just stands for all you want to see, hear, and believe about the American western. Let's face it, to name a western show "The Delawarian" or "The Connecticut Nutmegger" just doesn't bring up memories of a fast action gunfighter blasting the bad guys or tipping his 10 gallon hat to the ladies! Besides, as we cap pistol collectors know, the Texan was also the most popular, and the most marketed American cap gun in history. More on that later. But now, let's see the real side of Bill Longley, whose name and dubious fame was called "The Texan."

THE REAL "TEXAN"

Born on October 6, 1851, in Austin County, Texas, William P. Longley was the son of Campbell Longley, a veteran of Sam Houston's army. In 1853, the family moved to Evergreen, in Washington County, Texas, where in 1866, at the age of 15, Bill Longley, who had been given the nickname "Wild Bill," killed his first man.

The hapless victim was a drunken Negro who had cursed Bill's father. From then on, he harbored an intense hatred for Negroes. He called them "upstarts" and the fact they were now free infuriated him even more. The Longley family, however, were not rich plantation owners by any stretch, and never owned any slaves. Wild Bill, already six feet tall and 200 pounds at age 15, soon joined a gang of hoodlums bent on causing trouble and mayhem in town. But Bill Longley was an equal opportunity young criminal.

Wild Bill also hated federal soldiers, Indian police, Mexicans, and well, just about anyone who decided to challenge him in any way. Wild Bill Longley, often called "the bad son of Texas" was tall, tough, mean, very proficient with a gun at an early age, and was known to show no mercy. Anyone who crossed him never lived to brag about it. Some criminals like to use a psychological crutch to justify their crimes and Bill Longley was no exception. The fact of the matter remains that he was a cold-blooded killer, period.

The same year, he and a companion named Johnson McKowen formed a partnership racing horses and fast ponies. One night, they charged their horses into a group of partying Negroes at Lexington, Texas, killing two and wounding another six. The same year, with another companion, they shot another Negro that was alleged to have insulted Bill's mother. It was unclear who fired the fatal shot. People got the message and most stayed clear of Wild Bill Longley.

In 1868, an Army sergeant, made a costly mistake. Thinking Bill Longley was another man who had wronged him, he began pursuing him and wouldn't give it up. Longley shot him right out of his saddle. Chasing another group of Negroes out of Lexington, he shot and killed one of them, and for the first time, a posse went after Bill Longley. Heading for Arkansas, Bill teamed up with a horse thief named Johnson. Vigilantes caught up with both of them. Tying them up with their hands behind them, they strung them up, with Johnson's kid brother watching.

The vigilantes took the usual liberty of firing congratulatory shots at the bodies and then rode off. One bullet frayed the rope around Bill's neck and his heavy frame broke the

Rory Calhoun starred as Bill Longley in **The Texan,** *but he had none of the real Bill Longley's murderous traits.*

Gold-plated Hubley Texan with revolving cylinder and white steer-head grips.

Gold-plated Hubley Texan with revolving cylinder and turquoise swirl grips.

Above: A nice assortment of Hubley Texan Jrs. with a variety of colorful grips.

Right: (Top) gold-plated Hubley Texan with turquoise grips; (bottom), nickel-plated Texan Jr. with white steerhead grips. Note levers for opening guns to load caps.

remaining strands and he dropped to the ground, wounded, but very much alive and in a murderous rage. Johnson's kid brother cut down the elder Johnson, who was already dead, and helped free Longley, who swore revenge. Instead of riding away, Longley went to town, figuring whoever was part of the vigilante group would brag about stringing up "Wild Bill" Longley and Johnson. He was right on the money.

In the local saloon, one of the vigilantes made the mistake of bragging about the hanging and shooting at the bodies. Even though Longley was only sixteen, he took the unfortunate man to the same tree, strung him up, and re-enacted the entire incident, complete with shooting a few rounds into the twitching braggart. The same year, still in 1868, he joined the Cullen Baker gang. Longley was now a hunted man with federal rewards on him and Baker, and he was just a teenager, albeit a mean and ruthless one. In one year, along with his brother-in-law, John Wilson, he killed "seven or eight" more Negroes in his own home town of Evergreen, in total defiance of authorities, and then took off for Salt Lake.

Along the way, he came upon a cattle drive heading for Kansas and joined it. But everywhere Bill went, trouble followed him. Quarreling with the trail boss, a man named Rector, they agreed to settle the argument with a duel with a Colt six-shooter. Bill shot Rector six times before he hit the ground, emptying the revolver. Leaving the cattle herd, one of the cowboys decided to ride with Longley. They came across two horse thieves. Bill killed one of them, and brought the other one in alive, delivering him to authorities in Abilene, Kansas, collecting a reward. It was puzzling, to say the least.

Now in Leavenworth, Kansas, a federal soldier got up and uttered his last words. Describing his army service in Texas: "Every man's a thief and every woman's a whore!" Bill Longley shot him dead like a bolt of lightning and then spit on his body. Riding away, he got as far as St. Joseph, but he was captured and returned to Leavenworth for trial. In jail, he bribed a guard and was on the loose again, this time, heading for Wyoming.

In Cheyenne, he joined up with an army quartermaster named Gregory who was robbing from the government. Soon, Bill himself was stealing from the quartermaster. When found out, he shot the soldier dead. The cavalry went after him, captured him, held him for nine months, tried, convicted, and sentenced him to 30 years at hard labor. On the way to prison, he escaped in a daring moment, took off for the mountains, and ended up living with the Snake Indians for a year. By now it was 1872, and he decided to head back to his home town of Evergreen. On the way, he stopped in Parkersburg, Kansas, and sat down for a card game. A man named Stuart managed to get Bill angry enough so that Bill fired two shots at him, one in the head and one in the stomach.

Stuart's father offered $1,500 reward for Longley's head. Longley arranged for two men to turn him in and collect the reward. The three of them then robbed the sheriff, and all three took off, splitting up the reward money. Going to the local hardware store to buy himself a pair of Colt .45s, he suddenly turned, and fired them both at a Negro man standing in the store, killing the man instantly. Turning back to the owner, he said "these are fine pistols, I'll take them."

He paid for them and left. A five-man posse went after him. Near the Santa Ana Mountains, Bill shot one of the men right off his horse. The others abandoned the quest, returning to town and wiring another sheriff near Fredericksburg, Texas, warning him that Longley was headed back home to Texas. The sheriff, named Finley, decided to take up the quest himself.

It was now early 1873, and Sheriff Finley, ever so cautious, single-handedly captured Longley when Longley arrived in Fredericksburg. The government refused to pay Sheriff Finley the federal reward still on Longley's head. Longley's relatives then agreed to pay Sheriff Finley

$500 and he let Longley go free. Still celebrating his freedom a year later, in 1874, Bill killed a Mexican in an argument.

The following year, in 1875, in Waco, he killed a man named George Thomas. The same year, getting into an argument with a man named Briggs, Bill saw that he was not armed. In a strange display of "fairness," Bill removed his guns and beat the man with his fists. The man decided to return the following day, this time armed to avenge his beating. Before the man even called out to Bill, Bill shot him dead in what was called "the wink of an eye."

Near San Antonio, Bill's horse was stolen. He tracked the man on foot, found him with his horse, and killed the man on the spot, reclaiming his horse. A man named Sawyer tried to capture Bill and turn him in for the federal reward. He never knew what hit him as Bill shot him dead before he even got off his horse to approach Bill.

Bill's next antagonist was a large, burly, extremely tough man named Wilson Anderson, who went after Bill with a pistol and a double-barreled shotgun. Before Anderson finally stopped trying to get up and keep coming at Bill, he had taken in 12 bullets from Bill's twin Colts. It was said that Anderson had killed one of Bill's cousins and Bill was settling the score, since his family had stood by him through thick and thin. That killing took place in April 1875, and it would come to haunt Longley three years later.

The same year, a young 16-year-old Lavinia Jack fell in love with the tall Texan. By now, Longley, with a full head of hair, a handlebar moustache and goatee, began to dress neatly and tried to behave himself. He even posed for the famous photographer of western lawmen and outlaws, N.H. Rose. He got a job in Delta County, but he and his employer, Parson Lay, soon got into an argument, and Bill killed him with a double-barreled shotgun.

Above: Hubley's Texan family, left to right, gold Texan Jr. with black steerhead grips; center, gold-plated Texan with turquoise grips; right, nickel-plated Texan 38 with revolving cylinder and turquoise swirl grips. Some of the finest and most popular cap guns ever made.

Left: Three super Hubley cap guns with turquose grips; left to right; nickel Texan Jr. with cylinder opening button; center, gold-plated Texan with left side lever by hammer; and Texan 38 with top lever break and revolving cylinder.

It was now 1877, and it was said that some "30 cadavers" were attributed to Wild Bill Longley. Taking off again and leaving Lavinia, he headed back to Indian territory. It was said that he was wounded in an Indian fight, and that he had been nursed back to health by a Cherokee girl. Both state and federal authorities were on the manhunt for Longley, determined this time not to let him get away.

In Louisiana, they caught up with Bill Longley. Texas Sheriff Milton Mast, Deputy Bill Burrows, and Constable Courtney captured Bill, handcuffed him, loaded him onto the back of a wagon, and rushed back to Texas without the formality of extradition. The trial for the murder of Wilson Anderson, witnessed by several people, started on September 3, 1878. Longley was convicted and sentenced to hang.

While sitting it out in jail under extra heavy guard, Bill wrote a letter to the governor, saying he had been "railroaded" and that it was "unfair" that fellow Texas outlaw John Wesley Hardin had gotten "only 25 years for his misdeeds, and why are you going to hang Bill Longley?" There wasn't much sympathy for Bill Longley. The gallows went up at Giddings, Texas.

On October 11, 1878, twenty-seven years old, smoking a black cigar, Bill Longley mounted the scaffold flanked by two deputies. Asked if he had any last words, Longley met his destiny quite bravely with the statement: "I deserved this fate. It is a debt I owe for my wild, reckless life. Goodbye, everybody." The trap was sprung, but the rope slipped and Bill landed on his feet. Two deputies quickly held him up while the rope was tightened more securely this time, and Longley then swung into oblivion. It took him 13 minutes to die, considerably longer than many of his victims. Some western historians still argue as to whether Wild Bill Longley killed 30 or 32 hapless souls in frontier Texas. Here was a man that needed "hangin," as they used to say.

THE TELEVISION SHOW

The character of Bill Longley was transformed into a good and decent man, one who went out of his way to help people in trouble in the TV western, *The Texan,* quite the opposite of the real Bill Longley. I wonder if the producers would have gotten away with this character today, but on September 29, 1958, westerns were popular and *The Texan* soon joined the weekly lineup. The

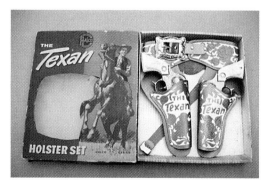

Halco boxed set for The Texan double holster outfit with Texan Jr. cap guns. This is the smaller of three Halco double holster sets.

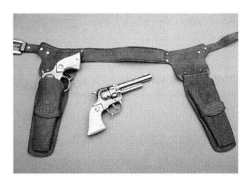

Above: Halco medium-sized double holster set for The Texan with heavy tooling on holsters and with Texan Jr. cap guns. Note guns can be worn either way on this set.

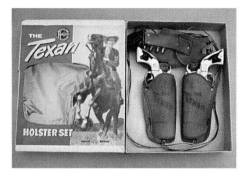

Halco's largest Texan double holster set with Texan 38 cap pistols.

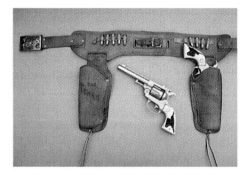

Halco double holster large set with Texan 38 cap pistols. Note name on holster pockets; large Texas buckle; gunbelt slots for waist size, and 10 bullet slots.

audience wanted adventure, and they wanted good to triumph over evil, and *The Texan* delivered that, because TV's Bill Longley brought in the desperadoes in a short half-hour every week!

Cast as "Wild Bill Longley" was handsome, rugged, big screen western star Rory Calhoun. At 6'3" Calhoun looked good in the saddle as the "The Texan," as he was an expert rider, having worked as a cowpuncher, lumberjack, miner, and forester. Meeting movie star Alan Ladd ("Shane") by accident, while in the Hollywood Hills on horseback, Ladd introduced Calhoun to his agent wife, and was soon transformed into one of Hollywood's leading western stars. Remarkably, the pinto horse that Calhoun rode on *The Texan* looked very similar to the "Cisco Kid's" horse, "Diablo."

His first movie role was the 1947 film *Adventure Island.* Between 1947 and 1969, Calhoun starred in 50 films. Among his many westerns are *Return of the Frontiersman, Four Guns to the Border, Powder River, The Yellow Tomahawk, Treasure of Pancho Villa, The Hired Gun, Apache Territory, Black Spurs,* and *Apache Uprising.* Rory Calhoun also produced many of his films, which included several war movies as well as dramas. Setting aside his impressive film roles, he was asked why he would want to do a weekly series, and he is said to have replied "where else can 28 million viewers see me in one night?"

Rory Calhoun was a co-producer, the main star, and the narrator of *The Texan* through 80 episodes, which was also set in the 1870s. In the series, he was an ex-gunfighter who had made a name for himself in his home state of Texas. He was a loyal friend and advocate of the downtrodden, and he was a mortal enemy to those who had been law breakers, especially against those friends he was close to. On the show, there was plenty of danger, action, and even occasional romance for Bill Longley. *The Texan* rode back into history on September 12, 1960, after a full two-year run. Originally a 30-minute show on CBS, it continued with reruns on ABC on Saturday mornings through May 1962.

Rory Calhoun returned to major films, as well as constant guest appearances on many westerns, including *Gunsmoke, Bonanza,* and as one the hosts of *Death Valley Days* when it was broadcast as *Western Star Adventure.* He later starred in the long-running soap opera *Capital.* Calhoun was also cast in the mini-series, *The Blue and the Gray* and *The Rebels.* He was also cast as an aging cowboy in *The Avenging Angel.* Rory Calhoun, now in his seventies, is still with us.

CAP GUN COLLECTIBLES

There is no question that the Hubley Texan and its brothers, the Texan Jr., and the Texan .38 were the most popular guns of the 1950s and 1960s. The Texan actually first came out as a cast iron in 1940 and continued, unabated, through several sizes, patterns, and variations into the die-cast era. By the early 1950s, Hubley started the die-cast Texan production, which came with a revolving cylinder, heavy engraving and scrollwork on the entire gun, and with the star logo on the grips. The grips all carried the familiar steer head and they were all white, all black, and white with the black steerhead.

The Texan was made also in the dummy variety. The Texan cap shooters came in nickel, gold-plated, and dark-finish models. The early models had the opening lever on the left side; the later models were friction, opening by hand pressure on the barrels. All break from the top for cap loading. The Texan is 9 inches long. Some of the last models, the 1960, were made with a non-revolving cylinder.

The Texan Jr., the Texan's "baby brother" also started out as a cast iron gun in 1940 and followed the same route as the Texan. It featured nickel finish, dark finish and gold-plated models, with and without levers, dummy models, models with the rampant Colt logo, as well as the same variety of grips as the Texan. By 1950, the "Texan Jr" went from 8 inches to 9 inches in length, actually surpassing its big brother in size. The star medallion replaced the rampant Colt, and more colorful grips were introduced, to include caramel, turquoise, and marbleized red swirl. The cap loading mechanism included front lever, push-button on the left side of the frame, the friction, of course, and the push button squared off lever on the left side of the cylinder on the last model that came out between 1960 and 1965. Other notable particulars are long, short, and the absence of ejector rods, as well as the longer and more pronounced sights on the gun barrel. The last patterns are also found with stag grips, and one-piece, all plastic grips without any logo, medallions or even facsimile screws on the grips.

The largest of the Texan series is the Texan .38, which came out in 1955, and continued well into the early 1960s. This gorgeous cap shooter came with a revolving cylinder and six bullets. At 10 inches, it has extensive engraving and beautiful scrollwork on the entire frame and barrel. This handsome piece breaks from the top by lifting the end of the top of the frame over the cylinder, thus exposing the revolving cylinder and six bullets for cap loading. This came in both nickel and gold plating. The grips have the Hubley star logo and came in white with black steerhead, all white, turquoise, and reddish stag. This gun is overall larger than its two brothers, thus the grips are not interchangeable. This is clearly one of the finest guns that Hubley ever made. Just about every other toy gun company fitted out many holsters, both generic, character, and TV western-related, with their Texan lines of quality cap guns.

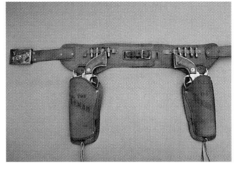

Same Halco large set but with Texan 38 cap pistols with turquoise grips.

The purpose of these descriptions are not meant to cover every gun with the word "Texas" or "Texan" on it. We know that Hubley also made the commemorative Texan 45. Hubley also made the Tex and we have the Leslie-Henry Texas Smoker, as well as the Texas Longhorn. However, with regards to the TV western *The Texan*, at least three double holster sets, each of which were marketed for the show, were made by Halco of Pittsburgh, Pennsylvania.

Close-up showing details on holsters, grips, and Texas buckle. Neat!

There are small, medium-sized, and very large-sized double holster sets, and all the guns in these sets were made by Hubley. These should not be confused with the Texan and Texan Jr., guns that came in boxes marked specifically for "A Texan" and "A Texan Jr.," or "Hubley Texan Golden Jubileers," none of which were associated with the TV western. As stated, Hubley was making these guns, long before *The Texan* came to television. Obviously, Halco produced the boxed holster sets with the graphics of *The Texan* and used Hubley's line of Texan guns.

The smaller of the three sets came in a box showing "The Texan" riding on his horse, wearing the same-style vest that Rory Calhoun wore on the show. The box has beautiful red and dark blue graphics, with "The Texan" in yellow. The holsters have "The Texan" on the holster pockets and the entire outfit is heavily tooled with lots of floral styling. The rectangular buckle is made of nickel with western motifs. This set has been found with the Texans and Texan Jr's.

The medium-sized Halco holster set is identical to the Laredo already profiled in this study. It features rich brown leather, heavy tooling with a horse head, horse shoes and "Texan" across the straps on the holster pockets. This set came with both Texans and Texan Jr's. The buckle is a generic western style with a longhorn across the horse-shoe-shaped outer edge.

Dell Comic issued for **The Texan,** *September 1959.*

The largest set of all The Texan series put out by Halco is one of the finest quality leather double holsters ever encountered. Rich, top grain leather in a plain but distinctive style has "The Texan" tooled and bordered in dark brown against the lighter tan holster pockets. The set carries the more unusual eight bullets in leather holders. Even the two-piece bullets are larger than usual. The belt carries an extra buckled strap and sectioned affair on the center of the belt for adjustment to the youngster's waist. The buckle of this large set is magnificent! In burnished brass, the rectangular buckle has "Texas" across the buckle on an angle in large letters, and between a steerhead and a five-point star.

This set came with the large Texan .38, which is the only gun of the three that sits perfectly in the holster. The other two smaller ones would be dwarfed inside the pockets and would hide the trigger guard. The Texan .38s are the nickel-plated models with the white grips and black steerhead. An identical boxed set has also been found with a pair of gold-plated, black-gripped Hubley Cowboy cap guns, another of the most popular guns ever made by Hubley. These guns also fit perfectly in this very large set.

The box has the same graphics as the smaller boxed set, except that the colors are reversed and the blue is a lighter color. All the Halco boxes for The Texan have the Halco "Superior Quality" round logo and the Halco "H" with the branding iron across it on an angle. The holsters have heavy rawhide tie-downs. The holsters are also marked with the same Halco logo deeply tooled into the leather at the top of the pockets.

The real Bill Longley far surpassed Billy the Kid's record for piling up bodies. Had he not been strung up in his native Texas in 1878, this 27-year-old sadistic killer would have certainly carried on with his own, self-described "wild, reckless life." Fortunately for the large audience of The Texan in 1958 to 1960, television's Bill Longley was a more humane and law-abiding hero, and we now have the cap guns and holsters to bring him back to life.

TEXAS JOHN SLAUGHTER

One thing about Walt Disney—he didn't want to just entertain youngsters, he wanted them to learn about some of America's great western characters who were real heroes. He did so with the "Walt Disney Presents" series in the 1958-1959 season, bringing both *Elfego Baca* and *Texas John Slaughter* to the screen. Before those golden years of TV westerns, what youngster would have learned about such heroes? I can say without hesitation that it was television's westerns that spurred the interest in me about America's Wild West and the characters that it bred, both good and bad.

Texas John Slaughter starred big and handsome actor Tom Tryon, who hailed from Wethersfield, Connecticut. His family owned a clothing business for more than a hundred years. Running an hour long, shot in color, and alternating between *Elfego Baca*, starring Robert Loggia, and *The Swamp Fox*, starring Leslie Nielsen, "Texas John Slaughter" was based on the life and adventures of real lawman, Indian scout, cattleman, and Confederate soldier John Slaughter.

The TV program highlighted some real events in Slaughter's life as well as the usual lawman-versus-outlaw episodes. Tom Tryon was picked for the lead after he starred in *Three Violent People* with Charlton Heston. Tryon guest-starred on some of TV's best western shows, such as *Wagon Train,* and also in movies such as the much-acclaimed *The Cardinal*, and the WW II epic, *The Longest Day.*

While TV's "Texas John Slaughter" didn't look a bit like the real lawman, the show had a strong following, ran two solid years, and even Dell Comics did a series of comics on the three real-life American heroes of the series by Walt Disney. In the program, Tom Tryon wore his Stetson with the front brim turned up, ala cavalry style, and he wore his guns butt-first and did cross-drawing. The guns appear to be almost identical to the Mattel "Fanner 50s" models used on the Lone Ranger sets they marketed.

THE REAL TEXAS JOHN SLAUGHTER

John Horton Slaughter was born in Louisiana in 1841, but grew up in Texas He served in the Confederate army during the Civil War, returned to Texas, and worked as a Texas Ranger for a while. Turning to the cattle business, he ran cattle into Kansas, and then ran herds into Arizona. He married and decided to settle in Arizona, building his ranch in the San Pedro Valley. His herds grew, as did his ranch, and soon he established the "Slaughter Trail." The problem was that this was also Apache Territory, and soon Slaughter's problems grew just as big as his herds. Detesting the rustlers that plagued his herds, both white man and Indian, Slaughter ran for sheriff of Cochise County, and was elected in 1886, and took up office in Tombstone, Arizona.

John was a small man, only 5'6" tall, with a short beard, steel eyes, and a ten-gauge shotgun. He believed in giving the rustlers, stagecoach bandits and cowboys looking for trouble fair warning and he did it once: "Get out or get shot—and become a permanent resident of Arizona soil." He gave each trouble-maker he encountered 24 hours. Those that tested the wiry little sheriff's warning were brought back strapped to a saddle, head-downward. During his three years as the Sheriff of Cochise County, twelve men died trying to test Sheriff Slaughter's warning to see if he was bluffing. Slaughter proved he was no man to tangle with.

Two rowdies of the time, Cap Stilwell and Ed Lyle, once tried to ambush Slaughter. Losing their nerve at the last minute, they backed out when they saw Slaughter with his shotgun. Instead of shooting them down, he allowed them to escape, following them to Charleston, Arizona. Facing them separately, the little man of steel issued each one the same ultimatum—each man had 24 hours to leave Arizona, or become permanent residents. That Slaughter didn't kill each man added to his resolve and reputation. Not even the Clantons, who faced Wyatt Earp and Doc Holliday at the O.K. Corral, tangled with Sheriff Slaughter.

The real Texas John Slaughter, one of the West's finest lawmen ever. (Courtesy of Western History Collection, University of Oklahoma)

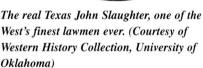

Tom Tryon starred as "Texas John Slaughter" for **Walt Disney Presents,** *alternating with episodes on* **Elfego Baca** *and* **The Swamp Fox.**

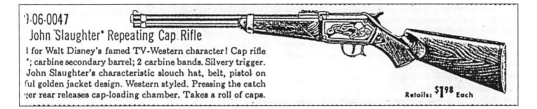

1959 Daisy advertisement for the Texas John Slaughter repeating cap rifle. Seldom-seen cap shooting rifle. Note lockplate graphics. (Courtesy of Jim Thomas)

After cleaning up the area, Slaughter retired from the office and returned to his ranch and herds. But he still faced the Indians, and so he went after such notorious figures as The Apache Kid and Geronimo. Slaughter also was present when Geronimo finally surrendered in Skeleton Canyon in 1890. Retiring to his ranch, he was given a deputy's commission in 1895, which he held until his death on February 15, 1922. Texas John Slaughter embodied the image of the real western sheriff—tough, resourceful, courageous, a man who was fair, but deadly if you crossed him. He was incorruptible. He was a man of his word. One can see why Walt Disney wanted America's youngsters to look up to Texas John Slaughter in the late 1950s.

TV's "Texas John Slaughter," in the persona of Tom Tryon, was rugged, handsome, 6'4" tall, clean shaven, and had a sidekick, played by veteran character actor Harry Carey, Jr. A host of wonderful old characters actors, from Jay Silverheels ("Tonto") to Dan Duryea, and so many more, graced the show. I'm sad to say that Tom Tryon passed away in 1991 at age 65.

Daisy 1959 catalog advertisement for the Texas John Slaughter single holster gunbelt with Kilgore Pinto cap pistol and canteen. Seldom-seen holster outfit. (Courtesy of Jim Thomas)

CAP GUN COLLECTIBLES

While no guns marked "Texas John Slaughter" have surfaced, Daisy did give us the Texas John Slaughter Repeating Cap Rifle that came out in the 1959 catalog. It sported the carbine-style rifle with the lockplate showing "Texas John Slaughter" and his famous slouch hat, belt, and the cross-draw gun and holster in the design. The carbine had the forearm and stock in simulated wood with two barrel bands and a silver trigger. Pressing the catch-release button near the trigger guard released the cap-loading chamber. The rifle, 32 inches long, sold for a whopping $1.98!

Daisy also marketed one Texas John Slaughter single holster set in the same group shown in the Law and Order series for *Elfego Baca*. The Texas John Slaughter holster set came with a canteen on the left and holster on the right with "Texas John Slaughter" printed into the top of holster pocket. The slouched, turned-up Cavalry-style hat that Tom Tryon wore on the show was also printed on the strap across the front of the holster pocket. The set came with the Kilgore Pinto, the same 8-inch cap pistol that was marketed in the Elfego Baca holster sets. The belt holds six bullets, and was made of top grain leather. Like the Elfego Baca series, it was hawked as a Daisy Fast Draw set. Both are shown in Daisy's 1959 catalog.

Dell Comics issue for Walt Disney's **Texas John Slaughter** *starring Tom Tryon as the famous lawmen. Note he wore his pearl handled six-gun in cross-draw style.*

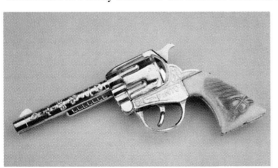

Kilgore's Pinto silver-plated 8-inch cap pistol with Palomino horse head grips looking downward on grips. The same gun was used for the Elfego Baca sets.

TALES OF THE TEXAS RANGERS

The Texas Rangers were so respected, feared, and well-known to even the most casual person that it seemed inevitable that a TV program would be devoted to this fine law enforcement group. So important were the Texas Rangers to the history of Texas, and so popular were the adventures of the Texas Rangers, that even today, *Walker, Texas Ranger,* starring Chuck Norris, can be seen on television.

But let's go back some 40-odd years. Still in its early years, with many households sharing TV sets with relatives and neighbors, *Tales of the Texas Rangers* galloped across the screens on September 23, 1955. A love affair with these fearless men and the American public, both young and old, continued for three years.

Just like *The Lone Ranger* and *Gunsmoke,* this program initially started on radio, with seasoned western actor Joel McCrea playing the role of "Jace Pearson," one of the two Rangers that the series would feature for television. When the program came to television in 1955, motion picture actor Willard Parker was cast as "Jace Pearson."

His partner, "Ranger Clay Morgan," was played by another veteran character actor, Harry Lauter. Both actors had already played in dozens of western movies such as *Apache Drums, Renegades, The Lone Texan,* and several Gene Autry and Rex Allen movies. Both characters wore black double holsters, five-pointed star badges, and "Ranger" uniforms consisting of neat shirts, black ties, and Stetsons.

What made this particular western unique was that, from week to week, the episodes placed the Texas Rangers in various time periods of their long history, from the 1870s to the then-1950s. This meant that the uniforms changed somewhat, and the horses were replaced by patrol vehicles. Rough-and-tough fists and six-guns of the early Lone Star state's Rangers also gave way to twentieth-century crime detection, sophisticated equipment, fingerprinting, and photographing of suspects. Here is the history of the Texas Rangers from the early days that the show tried to convey.

THE REAL TEXAS RANGERS

The real Texas Rangers began as a group of "Rangers" by order of Stephen Austin, the man who colonized Texas in 1823. Their purpose was to deal with local Comanche Indians and

Willard Parker as "Jace Pearson" and Harry Lauter as "Clay Morgan," stars of **Tales of the Texas Rangers** *get ready to battle the bad guys, right by their 1950s patrol car.*

The real Texas Rangers. This is a group known as Company F, Frontier Battalion of the Texas Rangers, June 1887. They look like they mean business! (Courtesy of Western History Collection, University of Oklahoma)

COMPANY "F" FRONTIER BATTALION, TEXAS RANGERS, June 27, 1887. Left to right, standing: Frank Carmichael; J.H.Rogers; Capt. Wm. Scott; J. A. Brooks; Bob Crowder; Jim Harry. -- Sitting: Ed. Randall; Billy Bridwell; Kid Rogers; Allen Newton, and Hinds.

Leslie-Henry nickel-plated early die-cast Texas Ranger cap pistol with white checkered horse head grips.

Leslie-Henry Texas Ranger with original box. Nickel finish with white grips. (Courtesy of J. Schleyer)

Mexican bandits that plagued the open country. By 1826, there were only 20 to 30 Texas Rangers in this service. They were irregulars and not all of these hardy men were scrutinized closely. Just like the Foreign Legions of other countries, when these men joined the Rangers, their past was "wiped clean" and they started with a "new slate" to uphold the law. Each man provided his own horse, saddle, clothing, six shooter, and knife. In return, he got full amnesty within the state of Texas, $25 a month in cash for as long as he lived to collect it, and a rifle. He wore no uniform. The badge, a round, pierced circle-star, came much later

The Texas Rangers took part in the war of Texas independence between 1835 and 1836, but they were not subject to military regulation. During this time period, the Rangers helped to keep and maintain order, and at certain times, to restore order. They handled Indian uprisings, went after Mexican desperadoes, monitored railroad strikes, and took care of general frontier defense. Three companies of 25 men each were organized during the Texas war for independence from Mexico.

Three of the early Texas Rangers were Jim Bowie, Ben Milam, and Erastus "Deaf" Smith. John "Rip" Ford, one of the most celebrated Texas Rangers, expected his men to "ride like a Mexican, trail like an Indian, shoot like a Tennessean, and fight like the devil." And they did, instilling pride, discipline, and respect that was the embodiment of what being a Texas Ranger was all about.

During the Mexican Wars, between 1846 and 1848, the Texas Rangers again saw service, under Captain Ben McCulloch, who came from Tennessee in 1835. During the Civil War, McCulloch volunteered his Rangers to the cause of the Confederacy. He rose to the rank of brigadier general, and was later killed in the Battle of Elk Horn in March 1862.

Leslie-Henry Texas Ranger with original box. Gold-plated model with black checkered horse head grips. (Courtesy of Terry Graham)

Temporarily disbanded after the Civil War, they were called back into service in 1874, since the Reconstruction Period following the Civil War brought feuds, thieves, murderers, cattle rustlers, and general mayhem to the big state of Texas. Six companies of 25 men each were then organized as a permanent state force. It was during this time period, the 1870s, that the Texas Rangers' fame became a legend. You could deal with the local sheriff or peace officer to some extent, but when the Rangers were called in to help, you were in for the fight of your life.

The story goes that a young man rode hell-bent into town and galloped up to the mayor's office to report that a riot was brewing just outside town on a dispute

Leslie-Henry Texas Ranger with early-style "Texas Ranger"-marked holster.

Leslie-Henry Texas Ranger Civil War-style in antique bronze, with stag grips, and revolving cylinder. Note logo on grips. Seldom-seen model.

Leslie-Henry Texas Ranger nickel-plated model with simulated stag grips.

Leslie-Henry boxed set of Texas Ranger double holsters with Texas Ranger cap pistols marked on both box, holsters and guns.

Above: Leslie-Henry Texas 9-inch cap pistol with cameo grips bearing 6-point star insert. The "Texas" was used in some Texas Ranger holster sets.

between feuding neighbors. The town council and local peace officer knew they would not be able to handle a riot so they sent out a call for the Texas Rangers, hoping to stem the riot before it got out of hand. Within a few hours, one Ranger, dressed in sloppy clothes, carrying a six-gun and a rifle, showed up at the mayor's office. In disbelief, the mayor cried out "they only sent one Ranger?" The young Ranger shrugged his shoulders and shot back "You've only got one riot, don't you?"

The Rangers were not required to perform military drills, or salute officers, although they did have a rank system. They remained an extraordinarily mobile force. Morale and discipline were high. They continued to wear the usual cowboy-on-the-range attire—Stetson, bandanas, chaps, vests, six-guns and rifle, and of course, the coveted badge. They became ever more expert trackers, sharpshooters and investigators, and outlaws feared them more than any other lawmen. As the great state of Texas became less wild and more civilized, the Ranger's responsibilities were decreased. In 1935, they were finally merged with the Texas State Highway Patrol by an act of the Texas legislature. We can see how this force appealed to the wide-eyed audiences of the early years of television.

The *Tales of the Texas Rangers* finished its healthy run on May 25, 1959. Since the show was seen on CBS as an afternoon show, the youngsters of the time lined up in cowboy duds to watch the show and dream of being a "Texas Ranger." Both characters were well liked by audiences, and Willard Parker and Harry Lauter appeared around the country, promoting safety and respect for the law. Even though show after show, photo after photo, and book after book shows these men with guns out, up and down, and blazing away, here is what the Tales of the Texas Rangers official "Deputy" membership card taught your child as soon as they got the card in the mail and signed it, and took the oath:

TEXAS RANGERS "DEPUTY RANGER" OATH
* Be Alert * Be Obedient * Defend the Weak
* Never Desert a Friend * Never Take Unfair Advantage * Be Neat
* Be Truthful *Uphold Justice * Live Cleanly * Have Faith in God

Leslie-Henry Texas (top), and the Texas made by Long Island Die Casting (bottom). Note "T" logo on the brown grips of the Long Island model.

This oath came with the star just like the one that the Rangers wore on the show, and a "Ranger" ring. Imagine the thrill of a youngster as Willard Parker or Harry Lauter, dressed in Ranger duds handed one of these cards personally! Other TV westerns were also based on the Texas Rangers. Of course, "The Lone Ranger" was a Texas Ranger. "Hoby Gilman" of *Trackdown* was a Texas Ranger. *Laredo,* a latecomer to television westerns, was also about the Texas Ranger force based at Laredo, Texas. Western great Joel McCrea, radio's original "Texas Ranger" died in 1990. Harry Lauter, TV's Ranger "Clay McCord," also passed away in 1990 at age 76. Willard Parker, who played "Jace Pearson," is still with us.

Several toy gun companies made the Texas Ranger cap pistol. Given the popularity of these shows and the Texas Rangers themselves, it was inevitable. Every kid wanted to be a "Ranger." Let's start with the earliest one that leads the line of die casts. Strangely enough, while many cap pistols began life in cast iron, Kilgore—which made a cast iron Texas Ranger—did not produce a die-cast model that I have been able to document.

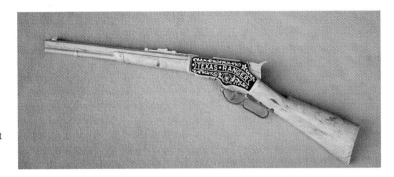

Leslie-Henry Texas Ranger rifle in caramel swirl color. The side panels on the receiver are applied. This is a cap-repeating rifle in the Winchester style. Seldom seen.

Leslie-Henry made the first pattern die-cast Texas Ranger in 1955, the year the program came on the air. It was a heavy, sturdy, 9-inch gun. Made of polished nickel, it has a large hammer, and came with both a plain barrel and a scrolled barrel. The opening lever was located in front of the frame, where the gun breaks open from the top itself. It came in both amber and white grips with a horse head design and checkered upper half of the grips. The frame has "Texas Ranger" raised under the cylinder and a five-pointed star, also raised, with "TR" in the center, also on the frame just above the grips. This cap shooter also came in a dark bronze finish with white grips, and a gold-finish model with black grips. The colorful box for this gun has blue and yellow graphics, and given the time frame of over 40 years ago, is seldom seen.

Leslie-Henry also made the large .44 model with revolving cylinder marked "Texas Ranger" behind the cylinder, with bronze finish, and stag grips, and fully engraved on frame and barrel. This is the same model for all the large 11-inch revolving cylinder models that have the side gate that open on the left side, with the lever up by the barrel. The oval logo for "L-H" or "H" is on the stag grips.

Leslie-Henry also made the desirable "Civil War" pattern for the Texas Ranger, which came in antique bronze finish, with stag grips, Oval "H" logo, and revolving cylinder with "Texas Ranger" raised on both sides of the frame. This model was copied by the Lone Star of England and is almost identical to the Apache and the Rebel. Leslie-Henry also made the identical model stamped "Cavalry." This model is 11 inches long.

Leslie-Henry made a third model for the Texas Ranger, and is usually found in single and double holster sets. This is an 8-inch model, nickel finish, stag grips, fine engraving on the entire gun, with raised "Texas Ranger" on both sides of the frame and with the grips sporting the Diamond "H" logo. This model breaks from the top with a lever on the right side of the hammer and it is the same model that Leslie-Henry made for the Buffalo Bill and the Paladin guns. The

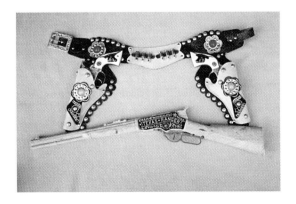

Texas Ranger Cowboy Outfit consisting of 11 pieces, marketed by Deluxe Toys of New Jersey. Note graphics on box lid.

Contents of Texas Ranger deluxe outfit. Guns are Texans. Note spurs and wrist cuffs. Holsters and cap shooting rifle marked to Texas Rangers. Seldom seen.

double holster set is also marked "Texas Ranger" on both pockets of the holsters, along with a steer head and the Ranger star, all in white details. The colorful box carries the Leslie-Henry address in Mount Vernon, New York.

The last Texas Ranger cap pistol documented was also made by Leslie-Henry. This last model came out in 1960. It is also nickel plated, with simulated inset stag grips similar, but not like, the Buzz-Henry models. "Texas Ranger" is much larger on the frame on both sides, even though this gun is slightly smaller than the above model, at 8-1/4 inches. The engraving is not the same pattern as the above model. However, the main difference besides the inset grips is the side gate which you push upward on the left side of the gun for cap loading. This model usually came on a card, which is also marked "Texas Ranger". This last pattern carries the Leslie-Henry address of Wilkes-Barre, Pennsylvania.

Leslie-Henry also made three models of a Texas Ranger rifle. The first was the Model #251, called the Texas Ranger Saddle Gun, with die-cast lockplate, barrel, and working parts. It featured a slightly large lever ring than the standard "Winchester" lookalikes, and had simulated wood-grained plastic

Texas Ranger double holster set along with Texas Ranger rifle.

Seldom seen Leslie-Henry long barrel "Texas" with cameo grips which also came in several "Texas Ranger" sets. The insert has the six point star logo instead of the crossed horseshoes. Super cap shooter!

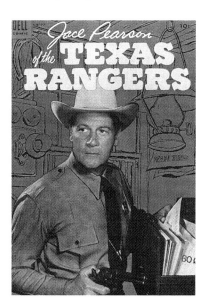

Dell Comics issue for August 1954 featured Joel McCrea as Jace Pearson of the Texas Rangers.

Seldom seen "Texas Ranger" made by Lone Star with original box. This is a beautiful, large, 10-1/2 inch cap gun with revolving cylinder, heavily engraved frame, and has some of the finest sculptured grips ever seen on a foreign cap pistol. Note box graphics.

stock. The lockplate has raised "Texas Ranger," star, and floral work. At 27 inches long, it is a 50-shot cap repeater. This rifle was also marketed in the Leslie-Henry Texas Ranger Scout Set, which included the big 11-inch Texas Ranger .44, with revolving cylinder, and single holster in brown leather with white details. The belt has the Hide-A-Way Leslie-Henry derringer which was affixed to it on the left side, but was also removable, with its own plastic holster and slide with two bullets. This spectacular set came in its own box showing a Texas Ranger. The .44 model in this set had the "zing" ricochet mechanism and was advertised as such. The same Model .44 with the "zing" was used on the Wagon Train.

The second model rifle was the Model #261. Basically the same as the above model, but 32 inches long and with a forearm and barrel band. It has the same lever action, metal parts, and plastic stock as the above model. Both can be fired single shot or as a cap repeater. This Model #261 was also used in the largest outfit that Leslie-Henry marketed, called the "Texas Ranger Complete Western Outfit." This set consisted of the cap-repeating rifle, double holster set in black and white details, with "blue desert stones" and conchos, three bullets, two Leslie-Henry six-guns, wrist cuffs, and spurs. It came in a gorgeous display box with great graphics showing three Texas Rangers on horseback. This was called the Model #CSR 2402.

The last and finest Texas Ranger set of all put out by Leslie-Henry was the Model #6/5 Texas Ranger Rifle Gun and Holster Set. This consisted of the large 450 Model "5-in-1" rifle-gun. It was none other than the same 11-inch revolving cylinder "Texas Ranger" which came with an extension barrel fitted into the barrel of the six-gun, plastic stock fitted into the backstrap of the six-gun, and the telescopic sight and forearm that slid onto the barrel of the six gun. This was a similar design to the Esquire Restless Gun 4-in-1 rifle-gun. This is also the same model used on the Leslie-Henry "Wagon Train" of the same 5-in-1 rifle gun. The only difference is the "Texas Ranger" on the six-gun. The telescopic sight fits into the stock when not being used.

The Model #6/5 outfit meant the entire set came with a special holster on which you fitted and carried the six-gun in what Leslie-Henry called a "California harness-hide holster" on the right, and the left side had a special holster for the stock and accessories, in much the same general style as the above mentioned "Restless Gun" 4-in-1 set. This outfit also came in a display-type box with great details. All of the Leslie-Henry rifles and the 5-in-1 rifle-gun are very seldom seen, and all four known models of the die cast "Texas Ranger" cap pistols are Leslie-Henry products. All are excellent, well-made toy guns.

Finally, many toy gun companies and toy gun distributors capitalized on the popularity of the *Texas Rangers*. Deluxe Toy Creations of Newark, New Jersey, put out a wonderful 11-piece Deluxe Cowboy Outfit. This particular outfit was dedicated to the Texas Rangers, even though it did not state that on the box lid itself. However, as one can see, this is a marvelous set which consisted of a beautifully-studded black and tan double holster set with red and yellow jewels, and "Texas Ranger" on the holster pockets. It came with six bullets.

The holsters also have the Leslie-Henry star logo used on the Texas Ranger model cap pistol. The set includes a caramel-toffee marbleized plastic rifle with "Texas Ranger" in silver on black floral decals. The rifle is a cap shooter with the lever action works. Wrist cuffs, spurs, clip, and bandana rounded out this great set! You could have a rather sizable and quality collection of Texas Ranger guns and rifles just made by Leslie-Henry.

Dell Comics put out the *Texas Ranger* comic books. One issue has Joel McCrea on the cover—radio's "Jace Pearson"—while the ones that came after have Willard Parker and Harry Lauter featured. While *Walker, Texas Ranger* is a fine show, it's got a long way to go before it can fill the boots of *Tales of the Texas Rangers* from the 1955-1959 season.

TOMBSTONE TERRITORY

This western program was a no-nonsense adult western, and the way the program opened each week gave a hint of what was to come. Harris Claibourne was the editor of *The Tombstone Epitaph* and he spoke the following at the beginning of the show: "An actual account from the pages of my newspaper, *The Tombstone Epitaph*. This is the way it happened, in the town too tough to die!" *Tombstone Territory* came to television on October 16, 1957, on ABC. It was an action-packed western with three main characters.

"Sheriff Clay Hollister" was a two-gun, hard as nails, rarely smiling sheriff that was tough enough to handle the town too tough to die. The outlaws that tested his strong arm of the law soon ended up in Boot Hill Cemetery. With a chiseled look, rock hard physique, black hat, black string tie against a white shirt with a six-point sheriff's badge, Hollister strapped on his double holsters, tied down the thongs against his black trousers tucked into his knee high boots, and walked with a hard and steady gait. Helping Sheriff Hollister and watching his back from deadly gunslingers was his deputy, Charlie Riggs.

Editor Harris Claibourne nobly attempted each week to show the power of the press, by not giving in to threats, and he was the only man in Tombstone that backed up Sheriff Hollister's policies in trying to maintain law and order in a town that is synonymous with gunfights, outlaws, thieves, and murderers. Boot Hill certainly proved that every week. Harris Claibourne was actually the announcer, host, and narrator of the show each week, and he "ran the story" during the program that was sure to cause a confrontation with the lawless element.

Cast as "Sheriff Hollister" was actor Pat Conway, a six-foot-two-inch native Californian, son of famous director Jack Conway, and grandson to silent film star Francis X. Bushman. Since he grew up on his father's ranch, Conway was already an expert rider and roper, and soon was cast in many of his father's films. A former Marine, he first starred in *Westward the Women,* with Robert Taylor.

Claibourne was played by character actor Richard Eastham, who just looked the part of an editor. Eastham starred in dozens of westerns and was always cast as a judge, lawyer, businessman, senator—he just had that kind of face that you saw on many programs, but could never recall the name. Cast as "Deputy Riggs" was another character actor, Gil Rankin. Conway's strong presence made the show the adult western that it was.

Several guest stars made memorable appearances on *Tombstone Territory*, which was directed by the late William Conrad—radio's Matt Dillon, and later remembered for his role as "Cannon" and in *Jake and the Fatman;* Jan Merlin of *The Rough Riders;* famous bad guy Lee Van Cleef; James Best; and lovely ladies Lisa Gaye and Carol Kelly all graced the show as guest stars.

Although Sheriff Hollister was a fictionalized lawman, Conway gave him great credibility because of *The Tombstone Epitaph* and Editor Claibourne were the only backing he really had in such a lawless town. The businessmen and merchants wanted law and order, of course, but they also wanted the business from the rowdy cowhands, drifters, and gold-digging ladies who went after the cowhands on pay day. Hollister was not afraid to use his fists or his two guns. Either way, you lost!

Initially, this western ran from October 16, 1957, to September 1958, on ABC on Wednesday nights. In an unusual move, new episodes of *Tombstone Territory* continued to be produced for another year even after the show left the air. It returned in March

Pat Conway, starring in the role of "Sheriff Clay Hollister" in **Tombstone Territory.**

"Sheriff Clay Hollister" (Pat Conway) and **Tombstone Epitaph** *Editor "Harris Claibourne" (Richard Eastham), the main stars of* **Tombstone Territory.** *Eastham also narrated the program from the official pages of the* **Tombstone Epitaph.**

Classy boxed double holster deluxe set for **Tombstone Territory.** *The guns are Stevens Cowboy King cap shooters with pearl grips. Note star Pat Conway on the box lid. Seldom seen. (Courtesy of J. Schleyer)*

1959, and ran to its final episode on October 9, 1959, for a total of 91 action-packed episodes. Pat Conway died in 1981. Richard Eastham and Gil Rankin are still with us.

CAP GUN COLLECTIBLES

Classy marketed the Tombstone Territory double and single holster sets. No guns have surfaced marked "Tombstone Territory" or "Clay Hollister." The boxed sets of Tombstone Territory guns came in a colorful blue box with Pat Conway's picture as "Sheriff Clay Hollister" shown in a TV screen frame. "Classy" markings and the Classy logo are on the box lid, but the side of the box is marked Harvell-Kilgore, Bolivar, Tennessee, and as such, many generic guns were fitted into Classy-Harvell-Kilgore sets by 1958. This was already noted in the "Rawhide" section.

The double holster model came in black leather with white holster pockets and white lettering. "Tombstone Territory" is marked around oval turquoise jewels. The white holster pockets have unique details consisting of two small straps and buckles that are placed on an angle at the top portion of the holster pockets. Silver conchos and studs also adorn this unique set. This set came fitted with Stevens Cowboy King cap shooters with the trademark mother-of-pearl style swirl "translucent" grips. Two identical sets have been found: one with Hubley Texans with white steer head grips, and the other came with chrome plated Kilgore Mustangs with blue grips, beautifully matching the turquoise oval jewels on the belt.

The Tombstone Territory single holster set also came in a unique design. The black leather belt has white details showing wood grain lines. Over the holster pocket is an outline of the state of Arizona, "Tombstone Territory," and an outline of Sheriff Clay Hollister with gun drawn, all in white details. The holster pocket, in white leather, has black "X" stitching which support the cut-away-style of the holster pocket, thus giving some good support to the holstered gun. The same holster design by Classy was used for one of its Roy Rogers models, as shown in that section. The belt extensions for the buckle and tightening end are also in white leather. Both the Kilgore Pinto and the Kilgore Laredo came with this set.

Tombstone Territory sets are quite scarce, especially in the original boxes. It may be that due to the adult nature of this western, few parents bought these sets for the kids. It would make for a great addition to any western character collection.

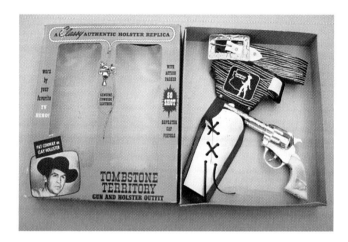

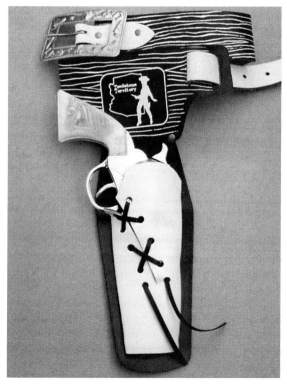

Above: Classy single holster set for **Tombstone Territory.** *The gun is a Kilgore Pinto. Note the white details showing outline of Arizona and Sheriff Hollister. Seldom seen.*

Right: Classy-Harvell-Kilgore single holster set for **Tombstone Territory** *with Kilgore Mustang cap repeater. Note unique Classy holster design also used on Roy Roger set. Note gunbelt has "wood grain" white details. Seldom seen sets.*

TRACKDOWN · HOBY GILMAN

The only show that had the "official approval" of the state of Texas and the Texas Rangers was *Trackdown,* one of television's finest westerns. *Trackdown* was originally a spin-off from Dick Powell's Zane Gray Theatre. The stories were based on actual files of the Texas Rangers. It was set in the 1870s and centered around the main character of the program, Texas Ranger "Hoby Gilman."

Trackdown premiered on October 4, 1957. The plot was simple and straight forward. Gilman set out to track down and apprehend outlaws and fugitives and bring them to justice, alive or strapped across the saddle of a horse. The character of "Hoby Gilman" was a fictional one. Cast as the intense, no nonsense Ranger Gilman was actor Robert Culp, a handsome 26-year-old who was a stickler for details, riding, handling a gun, and carefully researching the stories. Shot in black and white, it was a half-hour western that moved along as Gilman did the tracking, using both age old methods and good old common sense.

Two other show regulars assisted him in his quest for justice. One was "Henrietta Porter," played by Ellen Corby, as the Porter, Texas, newspaper editor. "Tenner Smith," the saloon keeper and show's chief gambler, was played by Peter Leeds. The local handyman, known only as "Ralph," was played by character actor Norman Leavitt.

Headquartered in Austin, Ranger Gilman was dispatched all over the great state of Texas to do his tracking and he carried a six-gun as well as a rifle. The coveted Texas Ranger badge was always prominently displayed. The Ranger always got their man. The show ran a total of 71 episodes and was last telecast on September 23, 1959. It is still in syndication in many parts of the country today.

Robert Culp went on to star in the successful television adventure *I Spy,* with Bill Cosby. Culp has played in hundreds of movies and television shows and still gets roles today, still rugged and good looking with a full head of white hair. Ellen Corby, a wonderful female character actress who starred in dozens of westerns on TV, later went on to star in the TV comedy, *Please Don't Eat the Daisies,* and later still as "Grandma" in the

Robert Culp as Texas Ranger "Hoby Gilman" of **Trackdown.**

Ranger "Hoby Gilman" (Robert Culp) has completed a successful "trackdown," and is bringing in his prisoner. Do you recognize the bad guy? Why, it's none other than a young Nick Adams, who later starred as "The Rebel."

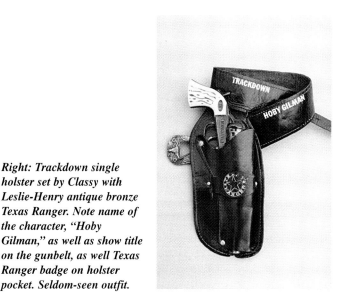

Right: Trackdown single holster set by Classy with Leslie-Henry antique bronze Texas Ranger. Note name of the character, "Hoby Gilman," as well as show title on the gunbelt, as well Texas Ranger badge on holster pocket. Seldom-seen outfit.

Close-up of details showing gunbelt with "Hoby Gilman" lettering and the Leslie-Henry Texas Ranger cap shooter in antique bronze. Note 6 bullets on belt.

Leslie-Henry Texas Ranger cap pistol with revolving cylinder and stag grips in the Civil War-style used on the Classy Trackdown single holster outfit.

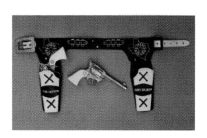

Never before seen Trackdown-Hoby Gilman double holster set by Classy, made for the "little Hoby". The guns are Actoy "Buckaroo" cap shooters. Classy also used Kilgore "Pinto" in the small sets. Attractive set with the classic cross-stitch details used by Classy. Note bullets, badge and state of Texas are graphics.

long running *The Waltons.* She suffered a terrible stroke a few years ago. Peter Leeds went on to star in "Bob Hope Specials." Norman Leavitt passed away in 1983.

CAP GUN COLLECTIBLES

Classy Products marketed the only known Trackdown double and single holster sets, nearly identical to the one worn by Robert Culp on the program. Made of top grade black leather, the single holster has both the name of the show and the character, "Hoby Gilman," in white lettering on the belt. It also has a larger-than-usual holster pocket underlay, similar to the Roy Rogers pattern. The holster pocket also has the white outline of a Texas Ranger's badge, with "Texas Ranger" on the outer circle. The belt has six bullets. The gun is the Leslie-Henry Texas Ranger in the dragoon style. It is the 11-inch antique bronze pattern with stag grips and the Oval "H" logo on the grips. It has the revolving cylinder and "Texas Ranger" raised on both sides of the frame under the cylinder. It fits into the holster as if it was molded for it. A spectacular outfit!

The double holster sets, advertised in the 1959-1960 Classy catalogs, came with the show title and the character name across the straps on the holster pockets, and the Texas Ranger badge up on both sides of the belt. Both a six- and a twelve-bullet model were available. Classy's generic 10- and 11-inch, nickel-plated guns, identical to the Classy Roy Rogers and the Latco Ruf Rider were also fitted into these sets. The sets sold for a whopping $4.98 and $5.98 for the 10-inch and 11-inch guns, respectively.

Robert Culp wore the single holster model on the show. He was so concerned with authenticity that he complained that his holster was "too soft" and thus made it difficult to do a "fast draw." He also wanted the hammer and trigger guard adequately exposed for easy reach into his hand. The show producers complied with Culp's requests. With that kind of authenticity and the official approval of the Texas Rangers, it's no wonder this was a great holster set for the young Ranger in the family! The sets were still being sold in 1960 after the show ended its two year run.

The Trackdown-Hoby Gilman sets are very difficult to find, especially complete with the Texas Ranger model cap shooter by Leslie-Henry in the antique bronze.

U.S. MARSHAL

This was not just a generic title on one of Leslie-Henry's most popular and well-made guns. This was one great TV western that underwent a number of changes that finally gave it the title that brought it to No. 1 on many American and Canadian syndicated charts. This was the only TV western that changed the title name of the show, but not the character. It's only one of this show's interesting particulars, but more will surface as we go along.

In the fall of 1956, this western show came to television under the title *Sheriff of Cochise.* This was a strange western, because it was also set in the 1950s. "Cochise" referred to Cochise County, Arizona. The lawman was "Sheriff Frank Morgan." He had two means of transportation. He went after the modern-day breed of criminals in his Dodge station wagon. When the action and the fugitive took to the hills, Sheriff Morgan mounted his trusty horse and brought the fugitive to justice the old-fashioned way.

Sheriff Morgan wore a tan uniform of sorts, with his current badge of "Sheriff of Cochise" in plain view, and other than a nice Stetson and boots under his straight-legged trousers, he was just as tough as the bad guys he was chasing on horseback in the Arizona hills. Cast as "Sheriff Frank Morgan" was handsome actor John Bromfield. Cast as his deputy, "Rafe Patterson," was actor and songwriter Stan Jones. Ironically, it was Stan Jones that had actually created the show. He played Deputy Patterson for two years, then left the show. He was replaced by actor Robert Brubaker, cast as "Deputy Blake" for the 1958 season. The show was big on team-work, and like the Mounties, they always got their man.

John Bromfield was a native Californian who had won the Golden Gloves as a light-heavyweight boxer in high school, and then got a football scholarship to college. After navy service in World War II, he returned to California and after a series of jobs, went into Summer Stock theater. This led to both film and TV roles. Director Hal Wallis first cast him in the 1948 film, *Harpoon.* Desi Arnaz, Lucille Ball's Latin husband and the head of Desilu Enterprises, was so impressed by Bromfield's easy going, but no-nonsense style, that Bromfield was cast as the relentless "Sheriff Frank Morgan," in this contemporary western

Sheriff Morgan was big on high-speed chases and rugged fistfights rather than actual gunplay. Many of the episodes of the first two years of *Sheriff of Cochise* were very similar to other law enforcement shows of the period, such as *State Trooper,* with Rod Cameron and *Highway Patrol,* with Broderick Crawford. The sponsor for the show was Anheuser-Busch, who did have a say in the

John Bromfield in the initial role of "Sheriff of Cochise" before he became "U.S. Marshal." He was always character "Frank Morgan." (Courtesy of Old West Shop)

Above: George Schmidt Buck 'n Bronc Marshal in gleeming chrome finish with copper stag grips, in very rare original box.

Left: Leslie-Henry U.S. Marshal 44 in nickel plate with seldom-seen original box. (Courtesy of J. Schleyer)

Above: Pair of Leslie-Henry U.S. Marshal 44 models in both antique bronze with black stag grips and nickel with white stag grips.

Right: Close-up of detail of the Leslie-Henry U.S. Marshal 44 with stag grips.

show, and it was this "say" that led to the title change. Sheriff Morgan was well known and the show was very popular. So how did they change the show title, and at the same time, not only retain the actor, but also the name of the character and the show setting?

Remember that Morgan was the sheriff of Cochise County. He played this part in 78 episodes from 1956 to 1958. In 1958, the program was popular enough to send it on to 86 top markets. Anheuser-Busch wanted the title changed to an easier title to remember. Desilu Productions came up with a pilot in which Sheriff Morgan transports the state's most-wanted federal prisonerto the U.S. Marshal for the state of Arizona, played by Sidney Blackmer. Three machine gun toting hit men are following Sheriff Morgan to get at the prisoner.

As they step down from the train to meet the U.S. Marshal to take custody, the three hit men open fire on the group, mortally wounding the U.S. Marshal even though in return fire, one of the hit men is killed. As the U.S. Marshal is dying in the local hospital, he asks Morgan to take over in his place as the new "U.S. Marshal." The widow also agrees to her husband's dying wish, and she wants the new marshal to get the killers that did her husband in. Thus, Sheriff Morgan of Cochise County becomes U.S. Marshal Frank Morgan for the whole state of Arizona.

The new deputy that joins Marshal Morgan is "Deputy Tom Ferguson," played by veteran bad guy and "film heavy" James Griffith. A well-known character actor who almost always played the man you loved to hate on scores of westerns, Griffith played the part of Deputy Ferguson with the same zeal and no-nonsense law and order fashion as Marshal Morgan. He wore his modern Colt revolver on the left, in a cross-draw fashion, butt first. Together in the Dodge cruiser or on faithful horses, the two lawmen closed every case each week by bringing the criminals to justice. The show was exciting and while modern methods of apprehension played down the gunfights, the highlight of the show was Marshal Morgan's relentless pursuit of lawbreakers, fugitives, and escaping prisoners in the wide open Arizona Territory.

John Bromfield insisted on doing his own stunts in the series. The character was based loosely on real life Sheriff Jack Howard of Bisbee, Arizona. As sheriff of Cochise, he wore a single holster gunbelt and the six-point sheriff's star badge. As the new U.S. Marshal, he went to a shield badge and an exposed shoulder holster with a stag-gripped Colt .45. The program was not only popular here, but even more popular in Europe, as well as South America and Canada.

U.S. Marshal ran for another two years, from 1958 to 1960, for syndicated television, racking up a hefty history of 156 episodes in four years, two years as *Sheriff of Cochise* and two years as *U.S. Marshal*. Several guest stars who moved on to shows of their own as well as big screen actors, graced *U.S. Marshal*. Among these were Jack Lord *(Stony Burke, Hawaii 5-0),* Michael Landon *(Bonanza, Little House on The Prairie)* David Janssen *(The Fugitive, Harry O),* Ross Martin *(The Wild, Wild West),* Martin Milner *(Adam 12),* and tough guys Charles Bronson and Stacy Keach. Both John Bromfield and James Griffith are still with us. Sidney Blackmer, the original "U.S. Marshal" character, died in 1973.

Above: Leslie-Henry-Halco very rare 6-7 shooter Marshal variety with extra barrel for shotgun shell. Revolving cylinder with bullets. Note amber grips with white cameo insert. Seldom seen.

Right: Handsome trio of "Marshal"-marked cap pistols, left to right, Leslie-Henry 44, Marshal 6-7 Shooter, and Hubley Marshal with stag grips.

CAP GUN COLLECTIBLES

The title of "Marshal" certainly graces many guns. Hubley and Halco both made the Marshal, as seen in the "Lawman" section. Halco, of course, also made the Marshal 6-7 Shooter as well as the smaller version of the Marshal in the Buzz-Henry style. Schmidt also made the Marshal in its "BB Marshal" series. However, the "official" gun for this western show, in the title name of "U.S. Marshal," was made only by Leslie-Henry in its 44 series. The same pattern was used for the Wild Bill Hickok 44, Gene Autry 44, Wagon Train .44, and the Bonanza .44.

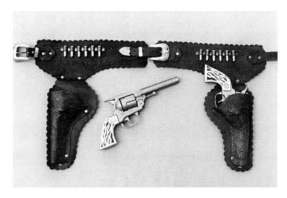

Early-style russet brown double holster set with complete foliage tooling, with Hubley Marshal cap guns. Note senter buckle and strap for waist tightening. Note that gunbelt is also stamped "Colt 38" with rampant pony logo. Seldom seen. (Courtesy of E. Cremese)

The Leslie-Henry U.S. Marshal came in antique bronze as well as a nickel finish. The nickel- finish model is usually found with the standard horse head grips. The antique bronze came with the off-white stag grips, and both carried the Oval "H" logo on the grips. The gun has a revolving cylinder, came with six copper bullets, and opened with a left side gate, with the lever on the frame. Extensively scrolled everywhere but the revolving cylinder, "U.S. Marshal" is raised and located on a rocker panel behind the cylinder on the upper frame. This is a beautiful cap shooter, and it is an impressive 11-1/4 inches long. The box for the nickel plated Leslie-Henry model with the horse head grips is also marked "U.S. Marshal .44," but has the Halco logo. The Leslie-Henry catalog for 1958 and 1960 show a TV screen photo of John Bromfield as "U.S. Marshal" and again in graphics for its smaller "Marshal" series in 1960.

British Crescent Toys cap pistol marked "US Marshal 45" came with nickel finish and red grips with rider. Also came in black painted finish. Seldom seen. (Courtesy of J. Schleyer)

The Leslie-Henry Marshal with the cameo grips, revolving cylinder, and with the push-down right side lever to load the bullets, was also advertised as the "Marshal" but without the "U.S." designation. This gun has the Diamond "H" on the frame and is also shown in the Leslie-Henry catalog with John Bromfield in character as "Marshal Frank Morgan." This Marshal cap shooter is 10 inches long, and came with both white grips with black cameo, and amber grips with the white cameo.

The small Halco Marshal came with white, black, and amber simulated grips, the Diamond "H" logo on the grips, and with the left side gate for cap loading. As previously described in the prior sections, this model was also made for *Wagon Train, Paladin, Buffalo Bill, Laramie, Maverick,* and others. Some models came with the checkered section and horse head grips. Note that this did not have the "U.S." and has only "Marshal" raised on the frame.

Very rare never before seen western shoulder holster rig made for "U.S. Marshall" with Leslie-Henry 7 inch "Marshal" cap pistol. This rig was almost identical to the one worn by Marshal Frank Morgan on the series, which he wore through a speical opening in his shirt! The gun came in both nickel and the harder to find bronze finish.

All types of holsters, both single and double, were made for the Leslie-Henry line of Marshal guns under both the Leslie-Henry and Halco designations. The same catalog shows nearly identical holsters for its series of Maverick, Bonanza, and Wagon Train series of guns that were the same pattern as the U.S. Marshal series. The rarest is the shoulder holster.

While "Sheriff," just like "Marshal," is a generic title and used on many guns, no guns marked "Sheriff of Cochise" or "Frank Morgan" are known to exist. With the show's title changing to the more recognizable *U.S. Marshal,* and with the show having already proved itself for two years, the toy gun companies devoted more Marshal guns to the character.

No cap shooting or smoke and bang rifles or shotguns marked "Marshal" or "U.S. Marshal" have surfaced to date. It appears that only Hubley, Leslie-Henry, and Halco made the U.S. Marshal and Marshal guns. Crescent Toy Company of Great Britain made a U.S. Marshal .45 in the late 1960s and early 1970s similar to its Rustler Ace and Frontier Ace patterns, but this was long after the *U.S. Marshal* show finished its four-year syndicated run. The Crescent U.S. Marshal .45 had a chrome flash finish, horse and rider grips found in both white and red, and was a 9-inch gun.

John Bromfield, now as "US Marshal Frank Morgan" and James Griffith as his deputy after the show went from Sheriff of Cochise to U.S. Marshal. Note that he then wore a shoulder holster. (Courtesy of Old West Shop)

While it is a late, fine looking cap shooter, it should not be confused with the U.S. Marshal 44 series made by Leslie-Henry for the TV contemporary western show starring John Bromfield. These are some of the finest cap guns made.

PANCHO VILLA

The real Francisco "Pancho" Villa, Mexican revolutionary, general, soldier, bandit, and all around dangerous hombre. (Courtesy of Western History Collection, University of Oklahoma)

I couldn't resist including Pancho Villa in this study. Once again, the Italians made the only known cap-shooting toy rifle honoring this Mexican revolutionary. To some, Pancho Villa was, and still, is a hero. To others, he was a bloody bandit who was hunted down by both Mexicans and Americans alike. I'd say the truth lies somewhere in between.

"Pancho Villa" was the by-name of Francisco Villa, whose correct original name was Doroteo Arango. He was born in San Juan del Rio, Mexico, on June 20, 1878. Villa was the son of a poor laborer, and was orphaned at a young age. He went to work on a rich Mexican estate, but when his sister was assaulted, Villa killed the attacker in revenge and was forced to flee to the mountains, where he spent his teen years as a fugitive.

While he lacked a formal education, he taught himself to read and write, ride and shoot. He became an expert horseman and crack pistoleer. He was cunning, courageous, and he came to know the northern Mexico territory and its poor people intimately. It was said that he started with a band of eight men which grew to several thousand, with the exact number never really known.

In 1909, Villa joined Francisco Madero's uprising again Mexico's dictator, Porfirio Diaz. Villa soon displayed his skills as both soldier and organizer. Madero soon trusted him enough to give him command of a division of trained soldiers, both infantry and cavalry. The revolution ousted Diaz, who had been a benevolent despot for 34 years. Villa decided to remain in the irregular army. Madero became president in November 1911.

In 1912, Villa took part in the Pascual Orozco Rebellion, arousing the wrath and condemnation of Gen. Victoriano Huerta, who sentenced him to death. Madero went to his defense, giving him a stay of execution, and sent Villa to prison instead. In November of 1912, Villa escaped, going across the border into the United States. The following year, Madero was assassinated, and Villa returned to Mexico and formed his own division of men. They numbered several thousand and took the name "Division 'del Norte" (The Northern Division). General Huerta, who had President Madero shot, had now become dictator. Pancho Villa joined forces with another revolutionary, Venustiano Carranza.

Villa revolted against the inefficient and repressive dictatorship of Huerta, winning several victories. By December of 1913, Villa had become governor of Chihuahua, and along with Carranza, finally won full victory over Huerta by June 1914. They entered Mexico City together as "victorious leaders of the Revolution." But rivalry soon developed between Villa and Carranza, and Villa fled Mexico City, joining up with the famous revolutionary leader, Emiliano Zapata. Carranza pursued them relentlessly, badly defeating both Villa and Zapata, who fled to the mountains in northern Mexico. It was at this point that Villa's charisma began to fail.

In an effort to show Carranza that he, and not Carranza, was in control of northern Mexico, Villa executed 16 American citizens at San Isabel in early 1916 and he attacked the town of Columbus, New Mexico, in a brash show of force. President Woodrow Wilson responded by sending an Expeditionary Force under Gen. John J. Pershing to capture Villa. This was a futile undertaking since Villa was popular in northern Mexico. Pancho Villa knew the terrain like the back of his hand, and the expedition failed to find and capture him, much less bring him to justice for his crimes. The local population resented General Pershing being on Mexican soil, and nobody cooperated with him in any way.

Villa's hatred was against Carranza, not really the Americans, but to prove his point, he was not above murder, no matter who it was. He continued his attacks against Carranza as long as Carranza remained in power. In one single incident, Zapata and Villa executed 150 men in two weeks. Both men lived by the sword. Zapata once said, "If I have a gun and I steal your watch, and then later we meet again and you have a gun, would you not have the right to demand it back?" In the bloody wars for Mexican control, the population of 15 million was reduced to 12 million. Between 1910 and 1920, three million died. Villa fought in the North and Zapata in the South. Zapata's men were called "Zapatistas" and Villa's men were called "Villistas."

But fighting among revolutionaries always carries suspicion, spies, betrayal, murder, and betrayal. Mexican Gen. Pablo Gonzalez wanted Zapata dead at all costs, and he devised an intricate plot that succeeded; Zapata and ten of his men were ambushed and shot dead. Like Villa, he, too,was regarded as both a revolutionary hero and a bloody murderer. To the peasants of Mexico, he became their new "martyr."

Six months after Zapata's death, it was Carranza's turn to die. The "new rebels" were loyal followers of Alvaro Obregon, another revolutionary. In 1920, Carranza's government was overthrown and Carranza was also ambushed and killed. Obregon still had to deal with Pancho Villa. Villa was offered amnesty and a ranch in Parral, Chihuahua, in return for his agreement to retire from politics and anti-government activity. But enemies stand in line in such "wars for independence." Villa had his share. Even though Obregon gave him a security force of 50 bodyguards, Villa himself was ambushed and assassinated in July 1923, on his own ranch. Obregon survived as president for four years, from 1920 to 1924, and then he, too, was gunned down in a restaurant. He was the last of the revolutionaries to be gunned down in the phase to eliminate the "old rebels" and begin reconstruction.

As with Zapata, Villa soon became a martyr to some of his people. And, the legends grew. Villa had been a real cowboy and he preferred horses to the new open touring cars. Zapata was the same, and in the ruse that cost him his life, he had been presented with a sorrel named "Golden Ace" just before he was shot dead. Legends among the poor peasants of Mexico even stated that neither Zapata nor Villa were actually dead, but that imposters had been murdered instead. Heroes and villains are not easy to erase from memory.

HOLLYWOOD'S PORTRAYAL

This kind of immortal fame soon spread to Hollywood, and movies about both Emiliano Zapata and Pancho Villa were made. In *Viva Zapata,* a young Marlon Brando portrayed the revolutionary on the big screen. But Pancho Villa, who had defied the American government and led General Pershing on a wild goose chase, appeared to be more popular, and several movies were made about him. Here are just a few of the more popular ones:

In 1934, just over ten years after Villa's assassination, the movie *Viva Villa* was released, starring Wallace Beery and Mexican actor Leo Carillo ("Pancho" of *The Cisco Kid* series). This was a romanticized tale of the "rowdy rebel," as it was advertised, in the fight for his life, and it was claimed to be one of Wallace Beery's best roles.

In 1955, *The Treasure of Pancho Villa* starring Gilbert Roland *(The Cisco Kid* and dozens of great westerns) was released by RKO Pictures. The movie was filmed in Mexico and centered on the Mexican cavalry closing in on Villa and his band of rebels in the Mexican mountains. It was Gilbert Roland that cut a great figure of Pancho Villa, right down to his bandoleer and single-holster gunbelt. Rory Calhoun *(The Texan)* and Shelley Winters co-starred in this great action color film. Gilbert Roland was the best of all the "Villa" portrayals that I have seen.

But Pancho Villa "didn't die." In 1968, *Villa Rides* came to the screen, starring Yul Brynner in the role of Villa, in a rare movie where Brynner is not shown with his usual shaved head. This was another remake of the Mexican revolution. Co-starring were great character actors of both the big screen and the little screen, including Robert Mitchum, Charles Bronson, Herbert Lom, John Ireland, and Fernando Rey.

In 1972, Pancho Villa came back to life again in *Pancho Villa,* starring Telly Savalas *(Kojak)* in the title role. An older, but just as imposing Clint Walker *(Cheyenne)* plays a gunrunner on Pancho's payroll. And

Gilbert Roland in the title role as "Pancho Villa" in the 1955 movie **The Treasure of Pancho Villa** *cut a daring and romantic figure as Villa, complete with bandoleer.*

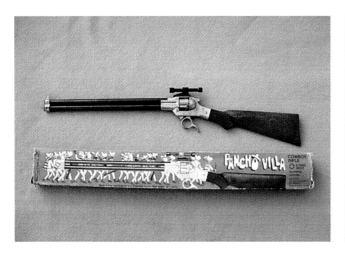

Italian-made Pancho Villa Cowboy Rifle for F. J. Strauss Company of New York, came in a very colorful box.

Close-up showing detail of receiver engraving, name, unusual ring trigger, and detachable telescope. Lever in front of trigger ring breaks rifle open for disc cap loading on the revolving cylinder.

even Chuck Connors *(The Rifleman)* co-stars as a polo-playing military officer. Anne Francis *(My Three Sons, Honey West, Dallas)* also starred. This movie has lots of action, with an incredible, thundering climax of two trains colliding together head-on.

Finally, in the recent TV series, *The Young Indiana Jones Chronicles,* produced by George Lucas for television, an old, retired, "Indiana Jones" relates stories of his life's adventures at age 93, played by George Hall. In so doing, he tells of his adventures running across several historical figures, such as Teddy Roosevelt, Lawrence of Arabia, and, of course, Pancho Villa. This TV program lacked the big-screen brawling, non-stop action—even though it was filmed in 11 countries. The TV show ran from March 1992, to July 1993. It seems that there was a "Pancho Villa" movie just about every decade after his death. All of the actors who portrayed Pancho Villa have passed away.

CAP GUN COLLECTIBLES

The portrayals of "Mexican bandidos" and Mexican "Federalis" has long roots in both films and TV westerns, and perhaps this is why the Italians produced the Pancho Villa rifle. The same firm that made the "Fury" cap gun—the Ditta MAM—produced this interesting cowboy rifle. The rifle is 23 inches long, with over and under black metal barrels. It sports a great revolving cylinder which fires eight shot disc caps. The cylinder resembles the Kilgore-style revolving cylinders. The frame is all die-cast metal with a wonderful engraving and "Pancho Villa" raised on the left side, and the "MAM" logo on the right side. It is stamped "Made in Italy" under the name, as well as "Patent" on the right side. The brown simulated wood stock has a checkered forestock. A knurled lever that is located in front of the ring trigger pushes upward, and this breaks open the rifle, similar to a shotgun, for cap loading onto the cylinder. The hammer is typical of the Italian and Spanish spur style. This rifle also comes with a black plastic scope that is fitted onto the rifle by sliding it onto the top of the receiver. A great design. It is tight and well made.

The box is a very colorful orange with a picture of the rifle with the mounted scope. It is pictured in front of a line of Mexican guerrillas all marching with a variety of rifles, guns, and swords. They are shown wearing the usual white peasant attire with colorful sombreros and shouldered blankets. The box is stamped with "Made in Italy especially for F.J. Strauss Co., Inc., New York, NY." The back of the box gives directions for mounting the scope and loading the disc caps in Italian, French, German, and English. Under "remarks," the Italians have used some common sense advice: "Though [this] gun is absolutely harmless, make a habit of not to aim it at people, or fire it close to your face."

Geez, makes sense to me. Villa Rides again!

WAGON TRAIN
MAJOR ADAMS & FLINT McCULLOUGH

Almost identical in scope as the *Rawhide* series, *Wagon Train* became a blockbuster western TV series that surpassed *Rawhide*. It was also an epic western that saw changes in two of its main characters, and still survived a second four years. Additionally, this was the only TV western that went from 60 minutes to 90 minutes, and from black and white to color. It lasted eight years and racked up a whopping 442 episodes, through two wagonmasters and two trail scouts. It was an immediate hit, and later was re-broadcast under another title. After trailing *Gunsmoke* as a close second for three years, *Wagon Train* became the No.1 program on television in the 1961-1962 season.

This sprawling series vividly portrayed the seemingly unending perils, adventures, triumphs, and failures of the pioneer stock that braved the unknown to book passage on the all-American "covered wagons" that formed a caravan en route from Missouri to California. Each episode focused on the lives and personalities of the individuals who braved this pursuit of both dreams and hopes for their families that would await them at the end of the journey. Some made it, and became better people. Some never made it. The episodes had drama, humor, warmth, and the all-American spirit to survive, often against overwhelming odds. It brought together all kinds of people, even immigrants, in the quest for the pot at the end of the rainbow. Former gunfighters, army deserters, lovable con men, broken men going for the last hurrah, widows with children, and all types of characters signed up for the journey. Big screen and small screen giants in each episode added to this western's success right from the beginning. The characters, just like the many wonderful cowboys in *Rawhide*, interacted well, and you really came to "know" them. In fact, you looked forward to each week's new adventure. *Wagon Train* was a giant among TV westerns.

Wagon Train came to television on September 18, 1957. Ironically, in the 1950 super-western *Wagonmaster* directed by John Ford, one of the stars was Ward Bond. It was Ward Bond who was cast as wagonmaster "Major Seth Adams." Major Adams was played with great humanity, compassion, and lots of mature advice by Bond, a veteran actor who had starred in dozens of westerns, and had become a personal friend of John Wayne. As wagonmaster, Major Adams had immense responsibility, much like the trail boss in a cattle drive. Adams had to get his team of scouts, cooks, and assistants to make the whole journey run as smoothly as possible and get the wagon train and its unpredictable characters to their destination, hopefully, unscathed.

Helping Major Adams on this epic journey from "St. Joe" to "Californ-eye-aye" was his trusty frontier scout, "Flint McCullough," played by relatively unknown actor Robert Horton. Flint would ride ahead to make sure that each leg of the trip was as free and clear of problems as possible. It wasn't always that way, however. As the wagon train pushed through the vast, Indian-controlled great plains, the majestic Rockies, endless desert areas, and the post-Civil War era of unbridled lawlessness, the men of wagon train were constantly trying to ensure that its baggage of human lives would make it. Throw in unpredictable weather and all the things we take for granted today, and you've got yourself one hell of an adventure. You could make it, only to face the hardships of starting a new life in California. Or, you didn't make it at all. This western was also a great study in the lives and happenings of the characters and personalities that faced the camera in each week's episode.

Rounding out Major Adams and Flint McCullough were several regular and semi-regular cast members. These included Frank McGrath, an old veteran character actor that played "Charlie Wooster," the cook. "Bill Hawks," called a "trail

Veteran actor Ward Bond starred as "Major Adams" on the TV series **Wagon Train.**

Robert Horton, who starred as "Flint McCullough," the scout, on **Wagon Train.**

Above: John McIntire, (center), the second wagonmaster, along with Frank McGrath (left), the cook, and Terry Wilson, trail scout, Wagon Train cast members. (Courtesy of Old West Shop)

Right: Box lid for Leslie-Henry Wagon Train holster set has probably the most beautiful color photo of Ward Bond and Robert Horton ever seen. (Courtesy of Brian Wolf)

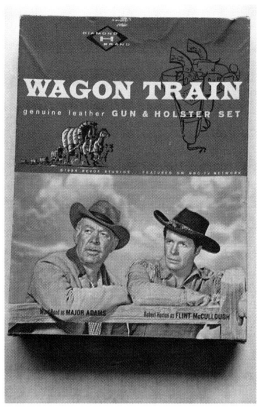

Right: Leslie-Henry Wagon Train in the Buzz-Henry style, with black simulated stag grips. Note Diamond "H" logo on grips.

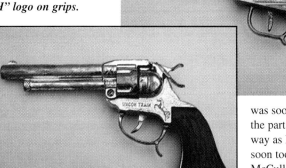

Leslie-Henry's 9-inch Wagon Train in nickel with black stag grips. Also came with standard horse head grips in many colors.

scout" and assistant to Flint McCullough, was played by Terry Wilson. These two characters remained with the show the entire eight years. "Duke Shannon," another trail scout, played by Denny Miller, joined the cast in 1961.

On November 5, 1960, Ward Bond passed away. It was a very sad day for millions of fans of Ward Bond. The loss of Ward Bond could have easily doomed the series. But the show and its content was soon pushed onward with another veteran actor, John McIntire, who played the part of the older and mature wagonmaster, "Chris Hale," in much the same way as Major Adams. McIntire had a great old face full of character, and the fans soon took to him as they had to Ward Bond. Robert Horton stayed on as Flint McCullough until 1962, when he decided to leave the series to do more films and other roles.

Replacing Robert Horton as the scout was Robert Fuller, who signed on as Cooper Smith. Fuller and McIntire remained with the series to the end. Terry Wilson, as trail scout "Bill Hawks" went on to be assistant wagonmaster. In the last two seasons of the show, "Barnaby West," played by 13-year-old Michael Burns, joined the cast. He was a young orphan found trudging along the trail

Leslie-Henry long barrel Wagon Train cap shooter with beautiful amber horse head grips and hard nickel finish. Seldom-seen model.

Leslie-Henry Wagon Train 44 model in antique bronze with revolving cylinder and stag grips. When fired, the gun made the ricochet "zing" sound.

westward on his own. Wagonmaster Hale took a fatherly interest in the boy and he soon became part of the wagon train staff.

Wagon Train ended its long trek through our living rooms on September 5, 1965. Rebroadcasts of *Wagon Train* for the Saturday and Sunday lineup of shows were re-titled *Major Adams, Trailmaster*. This great western remains in syndication. Even after 30 years, this show is still very popular in Europe and Latin America.

A western program of this magnitude certainly had big name screen and TV stars that added to the show's success and made it the No. 1 program on TV. Among these great stars, many of whom went on to their own shows, were: Lee Marvin, Ernest Borgnine, Rhonda Fleming, Mickey Rooney, comedian Lou Costello, Joseph Cotton, Gilbert Roland *(The Cisco Kid)*, Jack Lord *(Stony Burke, Hawaii 5-0)*, Jock Mahoney *(Range Rider, Yancy Derringer)*, Barbara Stanwyck *(The Big Valley)*, Michael Ansara *(Broken Arrow, The Plainsman)*, and even Italian actress Anna Maria Alberghetti. It was a wonderful way to see so many great stars, each in a special guest role every week.

When Bond passed away in 1960, veteran actor John McIntire had some big boots to fill replacing Bond as "Major Adams," but he did a great job. He had starred as "Detective Muldoon" in *The Naked City* when brought to *Wagon Train*. After the run of *Wagon Train*, he went on to star as one of the characters in *The Virginian*, the long running western with James Drury. McIntire passed on at the age of 83 in 1991. Frank McGrath, who played the grizzled cook, Charlie Wooster, always trading barbs with Major Adams, died in 1967.

Robert Horton, who played "Flint McCullough," went on to star in another western, *A Man Called Shenandoah*, in 1965-1966. Few people remember that Robert Horton had previously starred in one of TV's early drama series, *King's Row*, in 1955 alongside Jack Kelly, who went on to star as "Bart Maverick." Some of Robert Horton's motion pictures include *Tanks Are Coming, Apache War Smoke, Return of The Texan, Pony Soldier,* and *Prisoner of War*. Robert Horton is still with us. Robert Fuller, who replaced Horton, went on to star in *Laramie*. He is also still with us. Terry Wilson, Flint's trail scout Bill Hawks, is also still with us and manages a movie lot in California. Denny Miller, who played trail scout "Duke Shannon," went on to star in the TV comedy *Mary McCluskey,* and later also starred as "Tarzan" on the big screen. Michael Burns, who played the young orphan "Barnaby West," adopted by wagonmaster Hale in the 1962 to 1965 season, went on to star in *It's a Man's World,* also a TV situation comedy. Both Denny Miller and Mike Burns are still with us.

Leslie-Henry Wagon Train 44 model in original shadow frame box sold separately with bullets for the revolving cylinder. Note description of "zing" feature.

Leslie-Henry separately boxed cap shooter for **Wagon Train,** *also with bullets and revolving cylinder. While box is marked to show, the gun is a Marshal. (Courtesy of J. Schleyer)*

Leslie-Henry double holster Wagon Train set with small sized Buzz-Henry-style cap shooters in nickel finish with white simulated stag grips. (Courtesy of Mike Cherry)

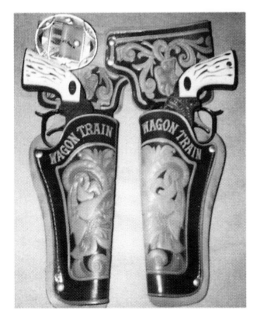

Left: Leslie-Henry double holster set for **Wagon Train** *with bronze 44 model cap guns. Gunbelt and holsters extensively tooled. (Courtesy of Tom Kolomjec)*

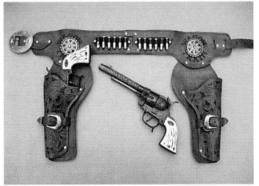

Left: Leslie-Henry double holster set for **Wagon Train** *with bronze 44 models. Note the "wagon wheel" design and show title on the belt.*

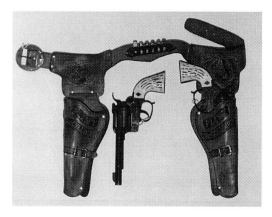

Leslie-Henry double holster set marked to "Flint McCullough" with a pair of large Halco 45 cap shooters with stag grips. Seldom-seen marked to character.

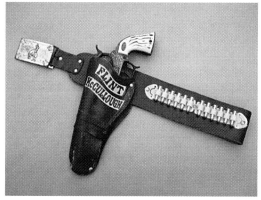

Leslie-Henry single holster set marked to "Flint McCullough" with bronze 44 model. Gunfighter style with 12 bullets. Note this is a left-handed rig. Note the unique large rectangular brass buckle. Note that the character name is tooled and raised right on the holster pocket. Seldom seen.

Above: Leslie-Henry Wagon Train 5-in-1 rifle with original box. Note graphics showing both show characters. Rifle in complete assembly with telescope. Very rare.

Middle: The Wagon Train 5-in-1 rifle disassembled. Note the telescope storage in the rifle stock. The gun is the 44 bronze model with extension barrel.

Right: Close-up of details of the Wagon Train 5-in-1 rifle gun. Note the Diamond "H" logo on stock. Note "Wagon Train" on telescope. Seldom-seen complete.

CAP GUN COLLECTIBLES

Leslie-Henry-Halco was the only company that made guns and rifles in honor of *Wagon Train*. They also marketed boxed sets for *Wagon Train* and holsters marked to the show title and both the two main characters—Major Adams and Flint McCullough.

Leslie-Henry made the 9-inch, nickel-plated Wagon Train with horse head grips and stag grips. Later models have a silver flash finish. The frames are typically engraved with "Wagon Train" raised on both sides. Left side lever is for cap loading, and the gun breaks from the top.

Leslie-Henry made the 10-inch long barrel model of the Wagon Train, identical to the 9 inch, and with the usual variety of grips—white with black cameo, and the horse head in a variety of colors. Beautifully engraved, the long barrels are very desirable models.

Leslie-Henry made the 9-inch larger frame model with the pop-up cap box, with the lever release in the front of the frame. This model came in both nickel and gold, and has some of the most extensive engraving of all the Leslie-Henry models. The same model was also used for Wild Bill Hickok, Maverick, and others.

Leslie-Henry made the beautiful antique bronze Wagon Train 44 model, extensively engraved with the left side gate and revolving cylinder which took bullets. "Wagon Train" is raised on the rocker panel on the frame just behind the cylinder. This 11-1/4-inch gun came with off-white stag grips and the Oval "H" logo. A great feature of the Wagon Train 44 model was the "richochet" sound, or the "zing" as Leslie-Henry called it, when fired. This comes from an intricate spring and sheet metal mechanism in the grips. The same pattern was used in the Bonanza, Gene Autry, U.S. Marshal, and Wild Bill Hickok series. This model came boxed separately, as well as with double and single holster sets, all marked "Wagon Train."

Leslie-Henry/Halco made the big "Wagon Train .45," which came in both bronze and nickel finish, with stag grips and the Diamond "H" logo on the grips. This model has the revolving cylinder and carries the rearing horse on the frame, as well as "Wagon Train" and "45" on both sides of the frame. This breaks open from the top for cap loading, and while it is impressive in size at 11 inches, it does not have the extensive engraving of the "44" model.

Leslie-Henry also made the late-model smaller Wagon Train. This was nickel plated, and came with white checker and horse head grips as well as all black stag grips, with the Diamond

"H" logo on the grips. This is also called the "Buzz Henry" style. It has the left side gate to push upward for cap loading. This model, 8 inches long, has barrel engraving, and was also used for the Maverick, Laramie, and other 8-inch late model Leslie-Henry series.

Leslie-Henry also marketed, for reasons unknown, their large Marshal with the revolving cylinder model, in a special brown, black, and red detailed window box. The Marshal in this boxed series of Wagon Train came in both nickel and bronze finish. The box carries the name "Wagon Train" and has good clear images of both Major Adams and Flint McCullough. The box also shows graphics of a covered wagon train, and it is unclear as to whether they would have sold the Wagon Train 44 model in this box or simply sold this box with the Marshal cap pistol to push them out. Obviously, there is no connection between Wagon Train and Marshal, since Leslie-Henry made both guns as two separate and distinct patterns.

The Wagon Train holster sets, both single and double, are some of the most colorful and highest quality leather products. Several patterns were marketed in Leslie-Henry boxes that show spectacular color graphics of both Ward Bond and Robert Horton in character. Although several holster patterns exist for Wagon Train, with "Wagon Train" on the belt as well as on the holster pockets, two patterns must be highlighted for the serious collector of this western character series.

A double holster set in tan leather with beautiful tooling came with "Wagon Train" around what appears to be a blue-tinted wagon wheel, in black old-western lettering. The highly-tooled, fancy holster pockets have "Major Adams" on the straps across the holster pockets. This is a large set that takes both the Leslie-Henry long-barrel 10-inch and the 11-1/4-inch 44 models.

A single holster made especially for Flint McCullough came in dark brown leather with the holster pocket having "Flint McCullough" actually tooled and raised against a white background section on the holster pocket itself. The belt carries 12 bullets in white holders. This extra-wide belt comes with a rectangular brass buckle with a bucking bronc rider and horseshoes on each corner. This truly spectacular holster was made only for Flint McCullough and it takes the bronze Wagon Train 44 model. A Flint McCullough double holster set was also marketed.

Leslie-Henry made two cap shooting rifles for its Wagon Train series. The first model is in the Winchester style, with lever action. It came with a black octagon barrel, walnut plastic stock, and a larger than usual lever section. This plastic and metal die-cast works rifle also came in a tan marbleized stock similar to the Leslie-Henry Texas Ranger. The receiver has applied fancy details that read "Wagon Train," and to the right of the wording is a round framed graphic photo of Robert Horton as "Flint McCullough." Under the picture of Flint is a banner that reads "Scout Gun." Two versions of this rifle were made—one for cap shooting with die-cast works and also a clicker model. This rifle is 26 inches long.

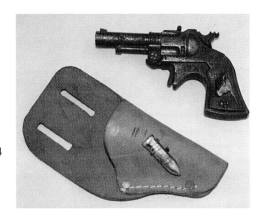

Leslie-Henry-Halco derringer with special holster to attach to Wagon Train gunbelts. The bronze derringer is marked "Tex." Seldom seen compared to the nickel model with colored plastic grips.

Above: Leslie-Henry Scout Gun marked to "Flint McCullough" with side plates showing Robert Horton as "Scout Flint McCullough." Plastic and die cast. (Courtesy of J. Schleyer)

Close-up of details of the Flint McCullough Scout Gun showing graphics and lever action. (Courtesy of J. Schleyer)

Leslie-Henry made one of the rarest and most sought-after cap shooting rifles for Wagon Train. This was the 5-in-1 Wagon Train Rifle. This spectacular set far surpasses the Esquire 4-in-1 models made for *The Lone Ranger* and *Restless Gun.* The Wagon Train 5-in-1 rifle came with the 11-inch antique bronze Wagon Train 44 model with revolving cylinder cap shooter, a 7-inch extension barrel fitted into the barrel of the cap shooter, a rich, heavily-grained walnut stock that was mounted onto the backstrap and butt of the gun, similar to the Esquire models, and it came with a telescope sight that was fitted onto the barrel.

It also came with six metal bullets. The telescope is brown plastic with "Wagon Train" raised on both sides. The rifle stock has the Diamond "H" logo near the section with the ratchet wheel to mount the stock to the gun butt. It is 29 inches long and came in a beautiful box with images of both Major Adams and Flint McCullough. The box explains how you can use the gun in 5 ways, even as a Buntline Special with just the gun and extension barrel. This extremely rare outfit is seldom seen and would be a great find complete with all the components. Both gun and extension barrel came in the antique bronze finish.

No other known toy gun companies made the Wagon Train series of cap guns and cap rifles other than the Leslie-Henry and Halco models.

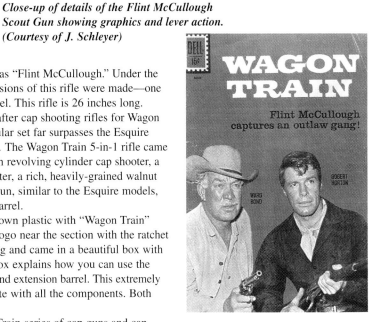

Dell Comics issued for Wagon Train showing Ward Bond and Robert Horton in 1959.

WANTED: DEAD OR ALIVE

The title alone of this great western show told you right away this was an adult western. It was not going to be about a singing cowboy, or even about a gunfighter with fancy clothes. No sir, this title and the character meant business. Serious business. He was after you because you were already a criminal, a fugitive, and thus "wanted" by the authorities. When he caught up with you, you had two choices—you went with him "alive" or he'd bring you in "dead."

Wanted: Dead or Alive came to television on September 6, 1958. Set in the Wild West in the 1880s, the character, "Josh Randall," was a bounty hunter. Bounty hunters went after fugitives and other wanted men (and women) when the system failed, lawmen were too trusting, the courts too lenient, or when the basic instinct of men, desperate men, was one of survival, guilty or not.

Josh Randall, the bounty hunter tracked the fugitives for one main reason—he was after the reward money. Bounty hunters were tough, hardy men in the Old West, and they had to be, because they could just as easily become the "dead" part of the title just for having the courage, albeit a "financial" courage, to go after desperate men. Josh Randall, however, did have a sense of compassion at times, and philosophically, on the show, he explained why he had become a bounty hunter.

In those days, bounty hunters didn't care much about whether you went peacefully or whether he had to gun you down. He was going to get the reward anyway, and less scrupulous bounty hunters had no qualms about bringing you in dead. They were not bound by the constraints of lawmen, even in those days. They pretty much did it the way they pleased, whatever was easier for them. As such, sometimes they worked in pairs, and they carried a personal arsenal of weapons to do the job.

Enter our "hero" of sorts, Josh Randall. Here was a laconic bounty hunter. A man of few words. He'd ride into town, check out the wanted posters in front of the sheriff's office, map out his strategy, and then begin his search. Josh Randall had his own special sidearm. It was a sawed-off .30-40 rifle. He called it his "Mare's Laig." It was a custom-made Winchester carbine, which he wore in a custom-made holster on his right side. Randall was an expert at using it, and use it he did. He used it with amazing speed and deadly accuracy.

While other bounty hunters carried one or a pair of six-guns, Randall preferred the "Mare's Laig," which also had a custom lever. The holster had a wider than usual belt for the shells, and he wore it strapped to his leg. If you cooperated with Josh Randall, the sullen bounty hunter might share a drink with you out of his canteen as he brought you in from Texas to California, or from Montana to New Mexico. If you didn't, he'd provide frontier justice: re-strap the Mare's Laig to his own leg, and then strap you over your mare and bring you in that way.

The pilot for *Wanted: Dead or Alive,* ironically, first aired in an episode of *Trackdown,* with Robert Culp. While the content of *Trackdown* was similar, Hoby Gilman was a Texas Ranger, while Josh Randall was a bounty hunter. Cast as the intense Randall was a very intense actor named Steve McQueen. He went from a relatively unknown actor with a string of forgettable films to an almost-overnight major star. It was Steve McQueen that brought the character, Josh Randall, to life, and in many ways, it was said that the character chronicled his own life.

McQueen was short, slender, and wiry. He personified the non-conformist, the underdog, and he battled to survive in a hostile world that didn't understand him or his motives. His strangely innocent look covered his troubled youth and the fact he had served a term in reform school. He was deliberately vague about his past, shunned publicity, and was intensely private. Moving to California as a 9-year-old with mother and a stepfather, young McQueen hit the streets early, and getting himself into trouble and becoming incorrigible, his mother placed him in a reform school in Chino, California.

Above: Steve McQueen as "Josh Randall," the bounty hunter in television's Wanted: Dead or Alive. *Note the Mare's Laig and special gunbelt.*

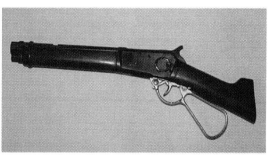

The Mare's Laig by Marx was almost identical to the one carried by Josh Randall except for a slightly smaller lever. This is the 17-inch model.

Close-up of the receiver showing "Official Wanted: Dead or Alive Mare's Laig" logo and saddle ring. Marx Mare's Laig in the largest model of the 3 made—19 inches. Note stock is a lighter brown color. Plastic and die-cast cap firing parts.

Boxed set for the Marx Wanted: Dead or Alive Mare's Laig complete with special holster. This cover has photo of Steve McQueen. (Courtesy of J. Schleyer)

After an 18-month term there, he quit school in the 9th grade and held a series of jobs that added to his persona of a cynical, but at the same time, a sympathetic loner. Oil rigger, lumberjack, traveling circus man, deckhand on a Greek oil tanker—McQueen did it all—and then went into the Marines. In his three-year hitch, he spent time in the stockade and was busted in rank "several times," he once said, for going AWOL.

In New York after his discharge, McQueen again had a series of jobs and lived for a time in Greenwich Village. He was a salesman, bartender, mechanic, TV repairman, and then one day, at the suggestion of a friend, he enrolled to study acting at the Neighborhood Playhouse. He made his stage debut in 1952. His Broadway role in *A Hatful of Rain* saw his career begin to rise. This led to a role in the science fiction thriller, *The Blob,* now considered a cult favorite.

Cast as "Josh Randall," McQueen also brought the "misunderstood" bounty hunter character to the screen that audiences immediately responded to. The show was a hit even with its adult content. In 1960, a young sidekick, "Jason Nichols," played by Wright King, was added to the show. Audiences didn't respond to this as well, and by the next season, Josh Randall was back to going after the bad guys on his own. Two well-known stars repeatedly appeared on the show. These were Gloria Talbot and Warren Oates *(The Wild Bunch).* Those of us with sharp memories may recall that a mongrel of a mutt also would follow Josh Randall on various episodes. He didn't really have a name, and was always called "Hey, Dog!" by Josh Randall.

Wanted: Dead or Alive lasted three years. It racked up 94 episodes. Josh Randall brought in his last desperado on March 29, 1961. Steve McQueen's big screen career took off like a bullet. The exposure he had received as Josh Randall made him a major star and the roles poured in.Many great stars that went on to have series of their own guest-starred on the three-year run of this adult western.

Among them were Mary Tyler Moore, Jay Silverheels ("Tonto" on *The Lone Ranger),* Clu Gulager *(The Tall Man),* Wayne Rogers *(M.A.S.H.),* Michael Landon *(Bonanza, Little House On The Prairie),* Nick Adams *(The Rebel),* John McIntire *(Wagon Train, The Virginian)* Noah Berry, Jr., *(Rockford Files),* Edgar Buchanan *(Judge Roy Bean, Petticoat Junction),* Lon Chaney *(Last Of The Mohicans),* and interestingly, old character actor Victor Jory, who later starred with Steve McQueen in the epic film *Papillon* about the brutal French penal colony on Devil's Island.

Steve McQueen loved motorcycles and car racing. He also had a large gun collection. He didn't care for the Hollywood glitz, and was quick to tell a reporter that he didn't like to be "capped" a certain way, and he didn't think reporters should try and "cap someone else." Not only was he a casual dresser, he was known to rip off the labels from his jeans. The shy, almost reclusive McQueen became one of the highest-paid actors and was a box office star all over the world.

Among his impressive movie credits are *The Great Escape, The Cincinnati Kid, The Sand Pebbles, Love With the Proper Stranger, Bullitt, Papillon, The Towering Inferno, The Thomas Crown Affair, Tom Horn,* and *The Getaway* in which he co-starred with his then-wife, Ali McGraw. His last film was *The Hunter,* in which, ironically, he played a current-day bounty hunter. Steve McQueen, the intense, volatile and yet charismatic actor died in 1980, following heart surgery in Mexico. He was only 50 years old.

CAP GUN COLLECTIBLES

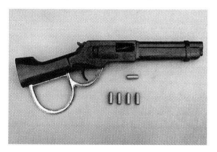

Marx Official Mare's Laig mounted on large poster card with special holster with graphics of Steve McQueen. The gun could be fired by using the lever action or single shot, and could be swung out of the holster in a fast draw.

Esquire called its Mare's Laig the "Riflegun" and it also came with a special leather gunbelt and fast draw clip and with long metal bullets, resembling the one Steve McQueen wore on the show.

Rayline Toys called its Mare's Laig "The Pursuer," but it had a ring lever closely resembling the show specimen. Built in works fired rubber bullets and made a ratchet sound when firing. Seldom seen complete and functional.

Dell Comics issue for **Wanted: Dead or Alive,** *May 1960.*

Three companies made cap shooters for the *Wanted: Dead or Alive series.* With the show being such a hit the first year, the "Mare's Laig" hit the stores in 1959. Louis Marx made the "official" and copyrighted "Mare's Laig." They made three models in three sizes for the "little bounty hunter" in your home. The first pattern was 14 inches in length; the second pattern was 17 inches. Both of these two patterns fired roll caps and were advertised as "rapid fire" lever action cap shooters. The short model came on the card. The second pattern, also carded, came with a special "fast-draw" holster in tan vinyl. Marx called it a "rifle-pistol." The graphics show Steve McQueen as "Josh Randall" on both card models. The gun could be fired manually by "both lever or trigger." The bullets on the holster are molded on, and non-functional.

Marx's third model was the largest of the three, at 19 inches. This model, as with all the others, was plastic with die-cast works. The barrel is black; the stock was usually dark brown, but some models came in a more chocolate brown simulated wood stock. The receiver was black. The left side of the receiver has a saddle ring, and also has "Official Wanted: Dead or Alive Mare's Laig."

The special vinyl "fast draw" holster came in both tan and black. The larger of these three models came with plastic bullets that could be loaded and ejected. The lever action on all of the Marx models came with the larger lever ring, just like the model used by Josh Randall. The holster for this third model holds the larger than usual bullets just like the real holster on the show. This model came in a large box with great colorful graphics showing Steve McQueen as "Josh Randall" in several poses with his Mare's Laig.

Esquire also made the Mare's Laig, but lacking the Four Star Productions copyright, called its model "The Riflegun." This was also a 19-inch gun, which was cap-firing, and could load and eject plastic bullets. With plastic and die-cast works, the frame carries the Esquire pony logo on the right side of the receiver. This came with a black leather holster, in a similar "fast draw" model, and also carried the Esquire pony logo on the larger gun belt. The box has colorful black and yellow graphics but no images of Steve McQueen, or the "official Mare's Laig" markings.

Rayline Grand Toys of Winchendon, Massachusetts, came out with an unofficial Mare's Laig outfit and called it "The Pursuer." This toy gun is 16 inches long. It is all brown plastic, but it has a number of interesting features that make it very desirable to a Mare's Laig collector. This gun actually fires soft rubber-like bullets. Built inside the receiver is a revolving cylinder. Also built into the receiver is a knurled "wheel" of sorts that allows you to revolve the cylinder to load the rubber bullets. Once loaded, you can fire them with the trigger, which also works the hammer (unlike the Marx Mare's Laig), which is spring loaded.

The lever action ring is much larger than the Marx or the Esquire models and practically resembles the Rifleman flip special ring found on the Hubley. This lever ring, however, has a ratchet sound when pushed downward as if one was using the lever action. Interestingly, it works just the opposite of the Marx, which has a non-functioning hammer but a working lever action. The Rayline has a functional trigger, hammer, and built-in revolving cylinder which actually fires rubber bullets, yet the lever ring with a ratchet sound is non-functional otherwise.

The Rayline is marked "Rayline 12" within an oval on the right side of the receiver, which is extensively engraved, while the Marx models are plain. The left side of the receiver has a round, extended spool-like rod to fit onto the black leather holster that came with this model. The wide belt has belt loops and white plastic bullets. The box is the frame-type and they were marked "The Pursuer" with instructions on loading and firing the gun, which touted the rubber-like bullets as "safe," and gave you 25 of them. This is an interesting, yet fragile and seldom-seen toy gun with a great functioning revolving cylinder system.

Wanted: Dead or Alive was a half-hour western, and it can still be seen in syndication on many cable channels all over the country. It is also on video for collector's editions. Even a western with such a serious title and content spurred collectibles such as board games, Hartland figures of "Josh Randall," and Dell Comics.

TALES OF WELLS FARGO

The official name of this popular western series was *Tales of Wells Fargo*. For five years, beginning on March 18, 1957, viewers tuned in, turning typically boring Monday nights into an exciting time watching a western detective on horseback. Wells Fargo was a stage line that transported passengers, gold shipments, cash, and a host of characters all across the western frontier during the gold rush period of the 1860s.

But such an easy target as a lumbering stagecoach in the wide open West carrying a strongbox and protected by a single guard with a shotgun proved too much of a temptation. Thus, Wells Fargo & Express Company, its official name, was plagued by holdups, robberies of passengers, even the horses themselves. The guards riding "shotgun" rarely survived and soon the holdups graduated to company shipments and even U.S. Mail robberies.

The overland delivery of parcels, packages, and other valuables started in the 1830s by "express companies" on the Eastern seaboard. The gold rush of 1849 changed all that, and business, trading, and mail order rapidly spread to the West Coast. California's largest express company was called Adams Express, and for a good number of years, it pretty much dominated the Pacific coast business. But there was room for competition and two men seized the opportunity.

Henry Wells and William G. Fargo started the Wells Fargo & Company, a bank and express company, in 1852 in San Francisco, California. It met its first crisis in the "bank panic" of 1855, which crippled its leading competitor, Adams Express. With Adams going under, Wells Fargo soon became the leading bank and express company in California. In 1857, it merged with the Overland Mail Company, initially as its banker. By 1860, Wells Fargo was in total control of the Overland Mail even as the government awarded Overland a Pony Express mail route. Wells Fargo controlled the western end of the Pony Express, but this was short lived.

In 1861, with the completion of the transcontinental telegraph, the Pony Express was forced out of business, but Wells Fargo struggled to keep the western division of the Pony Express going, running it from Virginia City, Nevada, to San Francisco. It did so until 1865, and even in its short life span, the Pony Express became a part of America's history forever. Wells Fargo was also aware that once the new railroad was completed, their days as a stagecoach line was soon to be a memory. In 1869, Wells Fargo, ever vigilant to change, developed a contract with the railroad and it continued its prosperity. In 1906, Wells Fargo divided its express company from its banking division and from then on, Wells Fargo became

Dale Robertson, who starred as "Jim Hardie," agent for Wells Fargo. One of the few western stars that was left-handed. Dale's horse was "Jubilee."

Above: Esquire Wells Fargo nickel-plated long barrel cap pistols, with stag grips and lanyard ring (top); with simulated stag grips and no lanyard ring (bottom).

Left: The real Wells and Fargo. The two men who started the Wells Fargo & Company in San Francisco were Henry Wells (left), and William G. Fargo (right). (Wells Fargo Bank 1958 History Booklet, Author's Collection)

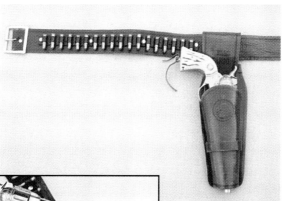

Esquire single holster gunfighter style with Wells Fargo cap pistol with stag grips. Note the show title and Esquire pony logo tooled right into the holster pocket with black details. Note this rig has 18 bullets!

Close-up of details on the holster pocket, gunbelt, and cap shooter.

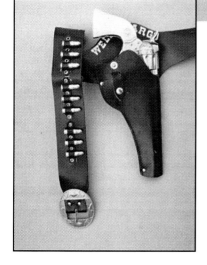

Close-up showing cap pistol positioned on special metal stud inside holster allowing gun to sit high for fast draw. Gun can also be snapped securely with snap belt.

Esquire black single holster set with unique feature which allowed gun to sit high for fast draw, or sit in holster normally. Wells Fargo gun with simulated stag grips.

one of the largest banks in the state. Wells Fargo survives to this day, in banking, as well as security services.

Tales of Wells Fargo was set in that turbulent time, following the Civil War and into the late 1860s and 1870s. Still a stagecoach line, the investigation of company shipment robberies, and mail and passenger holdups were assigned to Agent Jim Hardie, the sort of "unofficial" lawman and Western detective who worked for Wells Fargo. Such a broad range of episodic adventure soon caught on with audiences and *Tales of Wells Fargo* became a very popular western show. Each week, Agent "Jim Hardie" solved the cases and brought the criminals to justice, and Wells Fargo ran smoothly again, until the following week's adventures.

Cast as Jim Hardie was a very personable, handsome young actor named Dale Robertson. Born in Oklahoma, Robertson was an experienced horseman, and later became a horse breeder on his own ranch in his native state. He worked as a cowboy on his family's ranch and eventually went on to Oklahoma Military College, where he was voted the college's "outstanding athlete," with letters in football, baseball, boxing, tennis, swimming, golf, and polo. Robertson also studied law, but World War II rolled in, and by 1942, he was an army private first class in Patton's Third Army. Back in California, he had his photograph taken to send to his mother. When the photo studio displayed it in the window, an agent noticed his rugged good looks on his 6-foot frame and soon movie agents were after him. But the former private, who had risen to the rank of lieutenant, was still in the service.

After his discharge, he went to Hollywood, enrolled in UCLA to study film editing, design, and scriptwriting, and in 1949, landed a role in *The Fighting Man of the West,* produced by Nat Holt. A screen test at 20th Century Fox landed Robertson a seven year contract. His film credits included *Two Flags West, The Farmer Takes a Wife, Call Me Mister, Take Care of My Little Girl,* and *Caribou Trail.* Robertson also made guest appearances on many early TV shows.

In the 1950 western *The Triggerman,* starring Johnny Mack Brown, he plays a Wells Fargo Western detective hired to find a stolen payroll shipment meant for a ranch. There were many westerns that used the theme of Wells Fargo in the plot. It was somewhat inevitable, that with so many tales arising from such a setting, that a TV western bearing this famous name would soon be created and director Nat Holt rose to that occasion. Nat Holt created the series of *Tales of Wells Fargo,* and he was certain the man for the role of "Jim Hardie" was Dale Robertson, the young actor he had cast in Robertson's first screen role.

The pilot for *Tales of Wells Fargo* was initially aired as an episode on The Schlitz Playhouse in 1956. It was one of the most watched episodes, but Robertson felt TV was already saturated with westerns, and reports had it that he was considering an aviation series as well as a major part on the *Perry Mason* show. Robertson also felt initially skeptical of a TV series about a stage coach company's "tales" of the holdups and robberies, but at his old director's persistence decided to give the role a chance. The very first night the show was aired, the Nielsen ratings reported that the popular and long-established *Arthur Godfrey* Show was trailing *Wells Fargo,* and the five-year run of *Wells Fargo* began with applause. A natural rider and one of the few left-handed western stars, Robertson carried the show well.

The half-hour, black-and-white show went to a full hour and color by 1961. In its new format, additional cast members joined the show. By now, Agent Jim Hardie also had his own ranch and was often called to take on special and dangerous assignments. His ranch foreman, "Jeb Gaine," was played by veteran actor William Demarest. Hardie's young assistant was

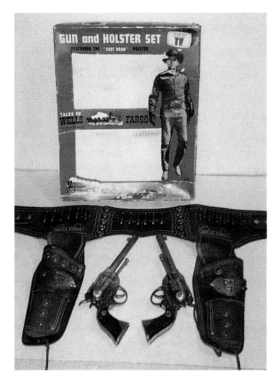

Above: Esquire boxed double holster set in light tan with name on belt. Stag-gripped Wells Fargo guns. Note great graphics of Dale Robertson and the stagecoach as well as the locomotive. Note the original price tag of $2.98! (Courtesy of Brian Wolf)

Left: Boxed Wells Fargo set of double holsters by Esquire. This deluxe set sports exceptional studs, conchos, and escutcheons with a rampant lion on them on the holster pockets. The guns are the Actoy Restless Gun models but marked to "Wells Fargo." (Courtesy of Mike Cherry)

played by another character actor, Jack Ging, in the role of "Beau McCloud." Adding the female touch to the show was the ranch next door, run by "Ovie," a widow played by Virginia Christine. Ovie's two very attractive daughters, "Tina and Mary Gee," were played by Lory Patrick and Mary Jane Saunders, respectively. These cast members remained with the show to its conclusion.

Wells Fargo was a hit that climbed to No. 2 in the ratings, at one point just behind the king of westerns, *Gunsmoke*. Dale Robertson's winning smile, amiable personality, and the slow-to-anger portrayal of Jim Hardie is what made the show so popular. The show was also well received in Europe, especially in Great Britain. *Wells Fargo* ran its last stagecoach run on September 8, 1962, for a total of 167 episodes.

Dale Robertson went on to star in another western, *The Iron Horse,* in the 1966-1968 season for a total of 47 episodes. Between 1968 and 1972, Robertson hosted *Death Valley Days,* which had been re-titled *Frontier Adventure.* Fans of the long-running *Dynasty* will recall that Dale Robertson, with a full head of white hair and a moustache, was cast as "Walter Lankershim" in the 1981 season. In the 1988-1989 season, Dale Robertson was cast in *J.J. Starbuck,* an adventure series about a Texas billionaire who moonlighted solving crimes. However, no other show that Robertson starred in had the popularity enjoyed by *Tales of Wells Fargo.* Dale Robertson is still with us.

Veteran character actor William Demarest went on to play crusty "Uncle Charley" on *My Three Sons* in the 1965-1972 season. He passed away in 1983 at the age of 91. Jack Ging went on to star in *The A Team.* He and the female characters of *Wells Fargo* are still with us.

Esquire small single holster set with Dale Robertson on the wrapper card sports an Actoy Special in the "Wells Fargo"-marked holster. Nifty set!

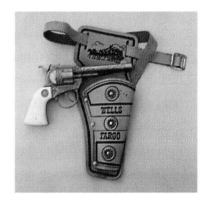

Small Esquire single holster set for the little cowpoke sports an Actoy Buckaroo cap pistol. Note the same-style holster was also used for Johnny Ringo.

Left: Both Wells Fargo small-sized single holsters with medium-sized Special and smaller-sized Buckaroo, which came in cellophane bags with show star graphics.

Esquire of New Jersey was the only American company that made the Wells Fargo cap pistol. Remarkably, however, several Wells Fargo holsters, in both large and small sizes, in both single and double sets, were made for this popular western. Given the show's healthy five-year run, many collectibles were made for *Wells Fargo*—board games, guitars, at least three Hartland Jim Hardie figures, cowboy hats, jackets, even dishes and cups. Dale Robertson graced the covers of *TV Guide,* Whitman books, Dell Comics, even advertisements for the 1958 and 1959 Buick. Yet, only one main model cap gun was made for Wells Fargo.

Esquire made the Wells Fargo cap shooter using the Buntline Special design. This made the Wells Fargo an automatic Buntline just by its sheer size and design, at 11 inches long. This came in two patterns, the polished nickel and bronze finish. Two grip patterns were also used: off white stag grips and ivory-white simulated stag grips. Both patterns have the Actoy pony medallion logo on the grips. Both have "Wells Fargo" raised on both sides of the plain frame and both have a fancy scrolled barrel. While the barrel is the Buntline pattern, the Buntline markings were changed to simple scrollwork. The gun breaks open from the top with hand pressure downward on the long barrel. The two grips are found both with and without the lanyard rings used on many Actoy guns.

Several beautiful large single and double holsters were made for the long-barreled Wells Fargo guns by Esquire. A simple, but elegant gunfighter-style single holster in rich russet leather with 18 bullets has "Wells Fargo" in black lettering and the Esquire pony on the holster pocket. The buckle is a nickel garrison-belt-square style. The holster can take the gun for a right- or left-handed youngster.

Above: British Lone Star Wells Fargo set on very colorful poster card with great graphics of Jim Hardie. Guns were Lone Star Gunfighter and Cisco Kid.

Right: Lone Star Wells Fargo shown with Gunfighter cap shooter with red and black swirl grips alongside the Lone Star variation Cisco Kid also found in these sets.

A strange but very unique single holster in sleek black leather has two positions for the gun. The lower position allows it to rest on a metal stud, and you can snap the gun securely in place with a button-down strap. The second position, over and above the stud, allows the gun to sit "high" on the holster for a fast draw fashion. This model has "Wells Fargo" arched across the top of the pocket of the holster area in silver lettering. It comes with an oval nickel buckle with crossed guns, rope, and diamond designs on it. The belt carries nine bullets.

Esquire made several double holster sets in tan, black, and brown leather with both black and white details that carry the show title, "Wells Fargo" and a stagecoach with the driver wielding a long bullwhip. Other details found on Wells Fargo holster sets are the stage's strongbox, the Esquire Pony medallions, silver conchos, exceptionally-styled and tooled holster pockets, and a variety of buckles.

Several smaller single holster sets with plain 3/4-inch leather belts and simple buckles were made for the small fry in the house, so that he, too, could solve the latest robbery. These smaller holsters came in cellophane clear plastic bags with a stapled securing card that had Dale Robertson's picture and autograph on them. At least three versions were made. Two are in tan leather with "Wells Fargo" within a roped design in black details on the top of the holster pocket. The front of the pocket has a large concho and a red ribbon design. The thin leather belt slides through the slots at the top of the holster. This set came with the Esquire "Special," which was a nickel-plated, standard-sized Actoy cap shooter with white simulated stag grips and lanyard ring. The same model was used for the Actoy Rin Tin Tin, Wyatt Earp, and Johnny Ringo. The Actoy Special inserted into the Wells Fargo smaller, single holster is an 8-inch cap shooter.

The third pattern is slightly smaller and comes with black details showing the rumbling stage-coach with driver and his bullwhip and a team of 4 horses at the top of the holster. The front of the holster pocket has "Wells Fargo" in black details and three silver conchos. An almost identical holster was made for the Johnny Ringo, also by Esquire, in black leather with white details. The cap gun found in this smaller set is the 7-inch Actoy Buckaroo, which is a beautifully-engraved gun on both frame and barrel, and has a plain white plastic grip, Esquire pony logo on the grips, and does not have the lanyard ring on the gun butt. This is a rather scarce smaller gun and single holster by Esquire. Both the Special and the Buckaroo break open from the top with hand pressure, for cap loading, and both are repeaters.

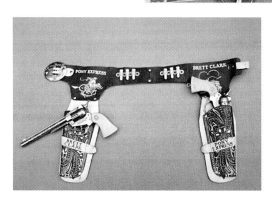

Never before seen Esquire Pony Express holster set with "Wells Fargo" guns. Who was "Brett Clark?"

All the boxed and carded Wells Fargo holsters and guns, both large and small, single and double came in "Wells Fargo"-marked boxes that also show Dale Robertson as "Jim Hardie." As the lengthy research for this chapter was nearing completion, a double holster set surfaced in rich brown leather, with 18 bullets, and "Wells Fargo" details on the belt. This remarkable set has holster pockets with seven round Esquire conchos and a strange shield with a rearing lion on it. The most remarkable feature that surfaced along with this Wells Fargo boxed set are the guns. Instead of having the only known, previously marked "Wells Fargo" long-barreled models, these guns are none other than the identical model used for the Restless Gun pattern with the secret compartment grips. The guns are identical, except that this set has Wells Fargo on the same frames where the previously described Restless Gun is located. Amazing features never cease to surface!

Marx Wells Fargo double barrel shotgun with original box showing great photo of Dale Robertson with shotgun. Note colorful shells. (Courtesy of J. Schleyer)

Lone Star of England marketed a large single holster set on a large card with one of the most colorful graphics ever encountered. The holster is soft pebbled leather with a white strap across the holster pocket, which carries white details of a standing cowboy with gun drawn. "Wells Fargo" is in white lettering across the top of the holster pocket. The belt is also a thin black leather affair with a small nickel buckle. This set, so typical of British market specimens, has been found with at least two, large-frame Lone Star guns, neither of which is marked "Wells Fargo."

Strangely enough, the colorful graphics on the card show "Wells Fargo," graphics of "Jim Hardie, Wells Fargo Agent," a stagecoach scene, a steam locomotive, a burning and smoking train wreck, and the "Overland Productions" copyright symbol. Can you guess which guns came with this set? One is the Lone Star Cisco Kid with black horse head grips and the other is the Lone Star Gunfighter, with gorgeous red and black marbleized grips, with the same Lone Star horse head design, star logo, heavily scrolled frames, and top-break action. Even the "Jim Hardie" graphics character is holding one the of the Lone Star guns, easily distinguished by the left side opening lever and very small hammer that Lone Star used on both the Cisco Kid and the Gunfighter models. Both guns are 8 inches long. No Lone Star guns marked specifically "Wells Fargo" are known to have surfaced to date.

Finally, two Wells Fargo shotguns are known to exist. The first is a French-made dart-firing shotgun with black metal barrels and wooden stock. While this 27-inch toy gun is not marked specifically to "Wells Fargo," research indicates that it was imported by Esquire and a paper label style decal was affixed to the left side of the stock, showing the four-horse-team drawn stagecoach, and "Wells Fargo Guard's Gun" in black lettering on the white decal. The company that made these was called Eureka. This is a dart-firing gun, not a cap shooter or smoke-and-bang shotgun.

Marx made a beautiful Wells Fargo Deluxe Double Barrel Shotgun that came in a colorful box with a photo of Dale Robertson holding a shotgun. This double barrel shotgun come with a reddish and black swirled plastic stock, silver receiver, die-cast works, black barrels, and the same yellow and red plastic shotgun shells that Marx made for its limited Rebel scattergun model. The box carries the 1959 date and "Overland Productions, Inc." copyright. This shotgun fired rolled caps. The right side of the stock has a yellow and red colorful decal with black letter-ring with "Tales of Wells Fargo" on it. This Marx shotgun is a seldom seen, unique toy.

No "Wells Fargo"-marked cap shooting rifles are known to exist. No cap guns marked "Jim Hardie" are known to exist. The personally-autographed photograph of Dale Robertson as "Jim Hardie," alongside his chestnut horse, Jubilee, was sent to me by Dale Robertson upon my request in 1960. Wells Fargo was an above-average western that earned respect among its many western companion shows from 1957 to 1962.

Close-up of stock decal of the Marx Wells Fargo shotgun. An intricately made and seldom-seen deluxe toy shotgun. (Courtesy of J. Schleyer)

Agent "Jim Hardie" (Dale Robertson) investigating a Wells Fargo overland stage and mail coach. Can you recognize the stage driver? It was another left-handed western star named Michael Landon, later of **Bonanza** *fame. (Courtesy of Old West Shop)*

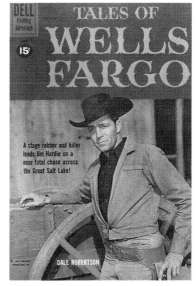

Dell Comics issue for **Wells Fargo.**

THE WESTERNER

The Westerner became one of television's shortest-run westerns. It wasn't just an "adult" western, it was one of the toughest in terms of gritty action. It was "punch" and "shoot first"—ask questions later. After all, it was created, produced, and directed by Sam Peckinpah, the same director who gave us *The Wild Bunch* and *Ride the High Country*. Peckinpah cast actor Brian Keith in the role of "Dave Blassingame." Brian Keith had starred in *The Deadly Companions,* one of Peckinpah's first feature films. The show was just as unforgiving as its shoot 'em up director.

Most people, even the most die-hard western buffs, do not recall *The Westerner*. That's because it lasted only 13 episodes, from September 30 to December 30, 1960. It aired on Friday nights on NBC as a half-hour saga. It was deadly, unglamorized, and character actor Brian Keith fit the role perfectly. The character, "Dave Blassingame," was a roving drifter. His constant companion was "Brown," a large mongrel. Brown had also achieved fame, for he had been cast as "Old Yeller" in the Walt Disney movie of the same name.

Blassingame was neither friendly or charming. He was not outgoing or chatty. All he wanted to do was settle down on his own ranch, for he was a "real" cowboy. He wanted to breed his own horses, preferably quarter horses, and mind his own business. And he really didn't trust anyone but Brown. As he roamed the southwest, along the Mexican border, trying to find his dream ranch, he kept coming across nothing but thieves, con men, unscrupulous settlers, and killers. But Blassingame also had his own ethics and principles. He didn't like people getting "fleeced" and he especially didn't like the con men that did the fleecing. In comes the second character of the show, "Burgundy Smith," played by old character actor John Dehner, who must have appeared in every western in the 1950s and early 1960s.

This character added some humor to the rough show, and he kept appearing, it seemed, in every new town that Blassingame roamed into. There were the poor pioneers and settlers that were victims of Burgundy Smith, and there was Smith, trying to weasel out of his own con work. It was his explanation that he was really an "enterprising agent." The two did form, even in only 13 episodes, a love/hate "bond." Smith was a delightful rascal and Blassingame was a no-nonsense cowboy who really had just about had enough of life's rough blows and just wanted to settle down. But since he had a heart as big as a mountain under that rough exterior, he just couldn't ignore people in distress. And so he got involved and he helped them out. Nice guy.

His loyal canine companion, Brown, was often left to fend for himself, yet he kept coming back for that pat and growl—not his, but from his master. A couple of rough characters made the big mistake of showing cruelty to Brown and they received the unparalleled wrath of Blassingame in one episode. On another episode, Brown went after a cat in a general store, causing a lot of damage, and neither Blassingame or Smith had any money to pay for the damage. As far as he was concerned, Brown had just as much of a right to be left alone as he did.

Brian Keith as "Dave Blessingame" of **The Westerner,** *along with his dog, "Brown." (Courtesy of Old West Shop)*

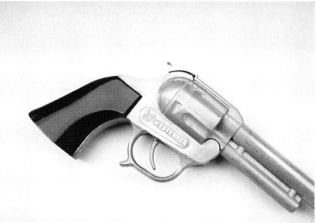

Westerner cap shooter in grey metal die cast by Hamilton Specialties. This cap pistol is the identical pattern used by Hamilton for its Cheyenne model.

Close-up of frame details showing name, longhorn and sleek black grips.

After the show went off the air, character actor John Dehner continued to make non-stop guest appearances on countless westerns. He passed away in 1992. Brian Keith was one of Hollywood's most versatile and underrated actors. His acting career was both sad and triumphant. Since *The Westerner* is the only TV western that Keith starred in, I wanted to remember this versatile actor's long career in television in a special way.

He started out on television back in 1954, starring in several *Studio 57* shows. That lead to parts in *Best in Mystery* during the same time period. Next came *The Crusader,* a short-lived series and *Undercurrent,* another short-lived show. He found his biggest audience in the hit *A Family Affair* from 1966 to 1971. This was followed by *Archer,* another quickly canceled show. He found another hit in *The Little People* between 1972 and 1974, with the name of the show being changed to *The Brian Keith Show,* about two doctors, a father, and daughter. He was cast in James Michener's *Centennial* in the 1978-1980 TV epic. He again found another hit in *Hardcastle and McCormick* which had a three-year run. His next series was another ill-fated show, *Pursuit of Happiness,* in the 1987-1988 season, followed by *Heartland* in the 1989 season, which was quickly canceled for lack of an audience. It seemed that Brian Keith never gave up, returning in *Walter & Emily* in the 1991-1992 season, but this too, was short-lived. Few of us recall that he was also cast as "Davy Crockett" in the mini-series *The Alamo.*

Personally, I was fond of this gruff exterior, but soft interior, this growling and smiling actor who played in show after show—western, detective, mystery, comedy, drama—you name it, Brian Keith did it. Sadly, he died in June 1997, as this study was in its stages of completion. His death was a sad and tragic one. Perhaps Brian Keith gave up in the end. I wanted to pay my own little tribute to this wonderful actor who, while not being remembered as "The Westerner," will certainly always be remembered for *A Family Affair* and *Hardcastle and McCormick.*

CAP GUN COLLECTIBLES

The Westerner cap pistol was only made by Hamilton Specialties of Hamilton, Ohio. It was a 9-inch gray metal cap repeater. It came with slick and plain black grips. It is identical to Hamilton's Cheyenne in size and design. Both sides of the frame have an elongated oval panel with "Westerner" raised, with a longhorn also raised next to the name. The gun breaks open from the top for cap loading. Breaking open the gun reveals "The Hamilton Line" and the company name and address. It is a well-made repeater. This cap pistol should not be confused with Hubley, Stevens, Kenton, Haig, or Roth, all of whom made the Western, Western Boy, and Western Man." The only Westerner was made by Hamilton, shown here.

WILD BILL HICKOK

I f there is one thing I've learned about the Old West, it's that there is no other area of general historical interest that has had more than its share of romantic and controversial characters. Few would question that Wild Bill Hickok was a legend, even in his own time. Historians by the dozens in the 1940s and 1950s added to this legend, with articles, books, interviews, additional evidence, and photos on this feared lawman-gunfighter. Certainly, Hollywood took notice, since movies and television programs that featured Wild Bill Hickok and his "legend" abound, just as they did about Wyatt Earp, Hickok's closest match.

One of television's earliest westerns, *Wild Bill Hickok* began production in 1951. Begun in syndication, it was first shown in April 1951 and it continued until 1958. Hollywood also took some expected liberties. For one, they cut his locks and shaved off his huge moustache. They tuned him down to largely a program geared to youngsters. They gave him a portly sidekick named "Jingles," and added some humor to the action.

The Adventures of Wild Bill Hickok, the official name of this popular western, ran for seven years. First on CBS, it then went to ABC, and it also ran concurrently in the radio version from 1951 to 1956, with the same stars. To understand the man behind the program, let's investigate the legend of the real Wild Bill Hickok and try to give him a more honest place in our western history.

THE REAL WILD BILL HICKOK

The real James Butler "Wild Bill" Hickok, as Marshal of Abilene, Kansas. (Courtesy of Kansas State Historical Society)

He was born James Butler Hickok in LaSalle County, Illinois, on May 27, 1837. His father ran a a general store in Troy Grove. As a youngster, he worked on neighboring farms, and it was said that he helped his father in assisting escaped slaves. He learned to ride and shoot, much like any other youngster growing up on a farm in those days. The young farm boy left home around 1855 and traveled to Kansas, where he became involved in the Free State activities as a political bodyguard. He was also appointed constable of Monticello Township.

By his own account, Hickok told that his first killing took place when a gang of ruffians attacked him in Leavenworth, Kansas, in 1858, and in the ensuing gun battle, Bill killed at least five of the hoodlums. Beginning with this episode, Hickok has engendered more dispute than any other western character of his time. Was he a hero? A two-gun marshal? A man of his word, worthy of the legend that soon grew? Or was he a rogue? A glory-seeking gunfighter? Just a western Romeo? A raconteur of tales that added to his own legend?

After studying this colorful western character for some 30 years, I'd say he was a bit of both. He was certainly a ladies' man. He had a reputation that begged to be tested by every young gunman seeking to add the notch to his gun that he had killed "Wild Bill" Hickok. Some called him "Hickok the Magnificent." Others called him "Duck Bill." In fact, calling him this dubious nickname cost a man his life.

Hickok, ever the storyteller, reportedly told the story of his first killings of the ruffians out to do him in, to Mrs. George A. Custer. The actual story was never confirmed. Ruffians went after plenty of characters in the Old West, some survived, some didn't. The following year, 1859, Bill signed on as a wagon and stage driver on the Sante Fe Trail, which took him to many scattered and desolate areas. On one of these runs he was attacked and mauled by a grizzly bear, and the company brought him back to Kansas City to recover. He next worked for a short time for the Pony Express, and was assigned to the Rock Creek Station in Nebraska Territory. His supervisor was one Dave McCanles.

McCanles owned the land on which the station stood, and he was an agent for the company. McCanles was reportedly a mean character and he didn't care for young Bill, and according to Bill himself, was especially mean to him. He made fun of Bill's large nose, calling him "Duck Bill." Bill did his work anyway. Then the company defaulted on property payments to McCanles, so McCanles resigned his post and then tried to collect the money owed him from the agent that replaced him, Horace Wellman. Bill Hickok had a thing for women and the femme fatale here was pretty Kate Shell. The lady took a liking to Bill, welcomed his affection, and turned down McCanles, who wanted her for himself. This only added to the disgust McCanles had for young Bill.

The date was July 21, 1861. An argument between McCanles and Bill ensued. Bill let go of all he had been swallowing for some time. The argument escalated and Bill shot McCanles, killing him as well as two of his men who ran up to see what was going on. This incident was well documented and even the encyclopedias highlight it. Bill decided to leave the company, going to Missouri next. By now, the story had been slightly exaggerated. Instead of the three men, the number Bill reportedly killed amounted to "six of the McCanles outlaws." Records later found in 1927 indicated the plea from Wild Bill and Wellman was self-defense.

In Independence, Missouri, a gang of badmen had been terrorizing the town. Nobody had the fortitude to rein them in and bring them to justice. Singlehandedly, with a pair of Colt six-guns, Bill tracked them down and brought them in—the entire group—to an admiring crowd, where one of them, reportedly a woman, yelled out "You did well there, Wild Bill," and the title stuck from then on. At least, that's how Wild Bill himself recalled it.

Wild Bill Hickok was an imposing figure. Just over six feet tall, he had a rather large prominent nose, a handsome face framed with long, light brown hair in locks that he wore shoulder length. He had a large, flowing moustache and steel-gray eyes. He wore buckskins and carried two guns, worn butt first on his wide belt, and he carried a large Bowie knife. People who were later interviewed that had either known Bill or had dealt with him indicated he was totally fearless, and was not above doing any of the single-handed acts to which his legends were made. But Bill's reputation was still to be made and that has been well documented.

The Civil War came along and he joined the Union as a teamster, a scout, and for a short time, a spy. He served in various posts in Missouri, Arkansas, and the Indian Territory. He served his officers well and did his duty. By the end of the war, he was last serving as a scout for General Hancock in Missouri, a job he continued to do until 1868, later transferring to Indian duty under General Penrose, and continuing to serve as scout, courier, and guide. During the war he met and became friends with fellow scout William F. Cody, better known as "Buffalo Bill," and Gen. George A. Custer.

July 12, 1865, found Bill in Springfield, Missouri, and involved with a local woman named Susanna Moore. The scenario was the same: Bill won over her affections while one Dave Tutt decided to test Bill's response with his sidearms. They had approached each other from the opposite end of town, a scene right out of *Gunsmoke*. At 40 yards, Dave Tutt drew, fired, and missed. Bill fired almost simultaneously, the first bullet hitting Tutt in the heart. Before Tutt hit the ground, Bill had whirled around, both guns in hand, carefully eyeing the crowd to be sure some of Tutt's friends didn't shoot him in the back.

This gunfight has been documented. Some recall that when Tutt was first hit, he stood perfectly still, then tried to raise his hand to fire again, but slumped to the ground. He had the first shot, and missed. Wild Bill's legend continued to grow.

In 1866, still in Army service at Fort Riley, Kansas, Bill was appointed deputy marshal, and he began his law enforcement career, so to speak. In August 1869, he was elected county sheriff and sent to Hays City, Kansas, a rip-roaring cowtown where Texas cattle drives came through up from the Chisholm Trail. Bill ruled the town with an iron fist, took no guff from anyone, and literally restored law and order to a town that had lost it long ago. Bill's reputation had spread far and wide by now, and leather-headed cowboys bent on showing off Texas "macho" were in for a surprise.

One of these was a character named Jack Strawhan, who challenged Bill to take his guns away "personally." Before Strawhan could unholster his gun, Bill killed him in a "draw" that people said was "lightning fast." Bill wore fancy frock coats with velvet borders, French shirts, and a wide sombrero-style hat, so he was an even more imposing figure to reckon with. The account was recorded by no less than Miguel Antonio Otero, a former governor of New Mexico in his memoirs, *My Life on The Frontier.* A coroner's jury had a round of drinks and issued the statement, "served him right, and so we declare." Not much fanfare in those days.

Bill also engaged in "trick shooting" to applauding crowds to further prove he was a "dead shot," and the legend says that cowboys soon steered away from Hays City and went to Abilene to give Hickok plenty of space. While in Hays City, Hickok carried both his six-guns, his Bowie knife, and a sawed-off shotgun when he had to stare down some rowdies. His appearing on the street was enough, some said, for cowboys bent on raising hell to leave quietly or be carried out.

In 1870, Capt. Tom Custer, of the 7th Cavalry, (yep, that's the general's brother), got drunk and rowdy in Hays City. Wild Bill arrested him and hauled him off to the cooler. The

Wild Bill Hickok ready for action— two guns butt first and a large Bowie knife. (Courtesy of Kansas State Historical Society)

Guy Madison, handsome actor who will always be remembered as TV's "Wild Bill Hickok." Note the double holster set with guns butt first, just like the real Hickok.

Guy Madison as "Wild Bill" with his sidekick, the lovable, raspy-voiced "Jingles," played by Andy Devine. (Courtesy of Old West Shop)

next day, Tom promised Hickok he'd return with his troopers to settle the score. Bill replied he'd be in the local saloon if he was stupid enough to return, brother or no brother to a general. Return they did, and Bill was in the local saloon. One trooper attempted to grab Bill from behind, another jumped him from the front. Bill killed both men, shooting so fast that witnesses in the saloon couldn't follow the action. Bill would have spared Tom Custer his destiny at Little Big Horn had not other troopers calmed him down and got him out of the saloon. On the advice of local politicians, Bill was told he couldn't buck the cavalry, and he decided to leave Hays City.

Next stop? Abilene, Kansas, where the cowboys had all been drawn to. Hickok was offered the job as marshal of Abilene at $150 a month, plus half of all the fines he collected. He had replaced the former great marshal, Tom "Bear River" Smith, who had been killed only a few months before. News accounts of the day confirm that Hickok did his job well, was well respected, and ruled the town the same as he had in Hays City. He was quiet, reserved. He walked about town like a cougar, always moving, always expecting, always keeping his own back covered, and always sitting with his back to the wall in local establishments. He did his job well, one man with two guns and one deputy, keeping some 5,000 hell-raising cowhands in check.

The Bull's Head Saloon in Abilene was owned by Phil Coe and Ben Thompson, two Texans. Thompson was already a well-known gunfighter and former ex-con who had served time for murder and assault. Coe was an old buddy from Austin, and the two Texans soon shared mutual hatred of Wild Bill Hickok, and often sided with the cowboys from their home state. There is some question over what started the feud. At least one story indicates that Hickok didn't like the sign for the Bull's Head Saloon that the two men put up because it showed too much of the bull's genitals. Another story has a mysterious female playing a part in the feud. But Ben Thompson knew enough not to cross Hickok, and for the most part, they stayed clear of each other. Coe wasn't as smart as Thompson and he proved it one day in early October 1871.

Thompson had gone to Kansas City to meet up with his wife. Coe got himself tanked up and began whooping it up with a bunch of cowboys from Texas just in town from a drive. Bill was in the Alamo Saloon at the time when he first heard the shots being fired outside. Leaping to his feet, guns in hand, he went outside, only to face Coe, who was waving a gun, and told Hickok he had just "shot a dog." The gang of Texans watched as Bill relaxed, started to holster his guns, and tell Coe to go cool off, when Coe fired a shot at Bill, missing, in his drunken stupor. Bill fired back, mortally wounding Coe. Just as Bill shot Coe, his deputy, Mike Williams, came running up behind Bill to see what the trouble was. Without even looking, or even thinking, Bill whirled around and shot Williams, killing his own deputy instantly.

This was the real frontier, pardners. How can you stop and ask questions when you are facing a gang of drunken cowboys, you've just shot their leader, they're itching to take revenge, and someone's running up behind you? Coe died a few hours later. Bill was devastated at the death of his deputy. It was later reported that as Bill looked over the body of Deputy Williams, the scene was reported this way: "Tears are the safety valves of a woman's soul. Without them, she could not survive. Sometimes they aid strong men also. Jesus wept, declared the Gospel, and so did Wild Bill." Only a month later, in November 1871, he headed out, leaving Abilene for good.

At the urging of his old friend, William F. Cody, he joined Buffalo Bill Cody's stage act, *The Scout of The Plains.* The show was a tremendous hit, but Bill was no actor. It was said that the "act" of stupid heroics bothered a real gunfighter like Bill, and he decided to leave the show.Hickok headed out to Colorado, then Wyoming. It was about this time that he is reported to have met Martha "Calamity Jane" Cannary, and it has never been really documented as to whether they shared just whiskey or each other.

Historians have woven all kinds of romance between two of the West's most notable characters, even that they had a daughter together. But the truth is that Hickok met and fell in love with Agnes Lake, a widowed actress, while touring with Cody in New York. Older than Wild Bill, she evidently left a mark on him, and he proposed to her twice. Finally, meeting for a third time in Cheyenne, Wyoming, she agreed, and they married in March 1876. Bill took Agnes to Cincinnati, and after a short honeymoon, he left for the gold rush in the Black Hills, organizing a gold expedition in St. Louis.

One very important point of history was found quite by accident by famed author Mari Sandoz, who wrote *Crazy Horse and Cheyenne Autumn*. While doing her research at the National Archives, she came across war records that indicated the post surgeon at Camp Carlin,Wyoming, had noted an office visit with Wild Bill Hickok. The surgeon had examined Bill's eyes and apparently discovered that Hickok was at an advanced stage of glaucoma, and would go blind in a very short time. Bill reportedly told the surgeon he had decided to see an Army surgeon in order to keep his many enemies from knowing how he was nearly blind.

He wrote letters back to his wife, telling her of his great love for her, and that he would always have her in his heart and his mind even unto death. Along with his friend, "Colorado Charley" Utter, Bill arrived in Deadwood, Dakota Territory, in June 1876. Hickok wanted to do some mining, nothing else, but his reputation would not let it be. His arrival in Deadwood caused a news blitz of the time, and the reaction was both positive and negative. The Black Hills attracted all sorts of characters, as any gold rush did in those days. Deadwood was no different. Gunslingers migrated there and the gamblers filled the saloons, and ladies in cheap costumes, and even cheaper perfume, kept the men happy. Hickok was both a celebrity and a target. He did, however, stay away from trouble, and he and his friend worked several claims after their arrival.

Jeff Bridges played Wild Bill Hickok in the 1995 MGM movie **Wild Bill**. *He certainly looked the part of the famous lawman-gunfighter. (Courtesy of Old West Shop)*

The talk of the town among the lawless element was obvious: Wild Bill Hickok had been sent to become Marshal, and the gamblers and cowboys weren't going to stand for it. Hickok let it be known that he was there to do some serious mining and wanted to be left alone. No doubt his failing eyesight must have rested heavily on his mind. But the remarks and the stories about what these badmen were going to do to "Hickok the Magnificent" kept filtering back to Bill, and he decided it was time to settle this once and for all.

Hickok walked slowly into a jam-packed saloon. His presence brought immediate silence to the place. After eyeing everyone, slowly and methodically, Hickok started to speak. He stated he was in Deadwood for mining purposes and wanted to be left alone, and he repeated, "If I am not going to be left alone, this town's going to have a lot of cheap funerals in a very short time." It was typical Wild Bill Hickok at his best. Then he walked up briskly to a group of about six of the loudmouths and disarmed all six of them. He then turned and walked out of the saloon.

His mining companion, Charley Utter, recalled later in interviews that Wild Bill Hickok had a strong premonition that he would not leave Deadwood alive. This feeling of doom was reflected in the endearing love letters to his wife. The premonition proved prophetic. A cross-eyed, loud mouthed, whiskey-sodden ex-buffalo hunter named Jack McCall was pumped up by the locals into thinking he'd be a "big man" if he killed Hickok, and McCall agreed do it. But like Bob Ford, who didn't have the guts to face Jesse James, McCall couldn't face Hickok.

On August 2, 1876, it was mid-afternoon as Bill arrived at Carl Mann's Number Ten Saloon to sit down and play some poker. It was a warm Wednesday. Bill greeted his friends, Charlie Rich, Captain Massey, and the owner Carl Mann, who all agreed to sit down for the hand. Everyone was in great spirits. Bill's seat allowed him to see the front door, but a rear door was also wide open due to the warm day, and when Bill complained about his usual spot with his back to the wall, his friends jokingly laughed him out of changing places. It was Wild Bill Hickok's unprecedented moment of carelessness. The game was on and nobody really noticed Jack McCall when he strode in the back door. He was a drunk anyway.

McCall casually walked up behind Bill, pulled out a .45, and shot Wild Bill Hickok in the back of the head at close range. The bullet came out of Bill's cheek and struck Captain Massey in the arm. Bill fell over the table, then slumped to the floor, still clutching his cards. McCall ran out the same way he came in before anyone could believe what had happened, and hid in a local butcher shop until Calamity Jane had the daring to go in and drag him out by his coat tails. At the time of his cowardly murder, Wild Bill Hickok was holding a pair of aces and a pair of eights, and it soon became known as "the dead man's hand."

Ironically, the bullet that killed Hickok was the only bullet in McCall's gun that would fire. Hickok was buried in Deadwood initially, but three years later, he was re-buried under a

Leslie-Henry small frame Wild Bill Hickok, nickel with checkered horse head grips. This model came in both nickel and gold variety.

Leslie-Henry 9-inch nickel plated Wild Bill Hickok with superb butterscotch horse head grips. Also came in long-barreled variety as well a gold-finish model.

Leslie-Henry 9-inch Wild Bill Hickok with copper steerhead grips with full title of "Marshal Wild Bill Hickok" on the grips.

beautiful stone monument erected by his friend Charley Utter, complete with a moving inscription that read: "WILD BILL" JB Hickok, killed by the assassin, Jack McCall, Deadwood, Black Hills, Aug. 2, 1876. Pard, we will meet again, in the Happy Hunting Grounds, to part no more."

Like the other coward, Bob Ford, Jack McCall found no peace, but justice found him. Initially acquitted in Deadwood on the grounds that he was avenging the death of a brother supposedly killed by Hickok, McCall left Deadwood soon after, another scorned and hated man, and not the "hero" he was pumped up to believe he was going to be for his act. Moving on to Custer City, he got drunk and bragged that he had fooled the courts and boasted of the killing. It appears some qualities of criminals never change. Early in October 1876, he was arrested by a U.S. Marshal and put on trial again for Hickok's murder. He was convicted in one day. On March 1, 1877, he swung into eternity. The papers didn't scream that the state "killed" McCall; instead the headlines beamed that justice was served for the murder of a fearless lawman.

It was said that Calamity Jane always loved Wild Bill Hickok. A wild, hard-drinking, tobacco-chewing, vile, cursing woman who hid her sex to join General Crook's Sioux campaign as a scout (until she was found out when she went skinny dipping with the troopers), Calamity Jane wore buckskins, carried a six-gun she wasn't afraid to use, herded mules, worked as a laborer, and after drifting all over the Midwest, returned to Deadwood. As she lay dying on August 2, 1903, she asked "what day is it?" When told the date, she whispered "It's the twenty-seventh anniversary of Bill's death. Bury me next to Bill." Her funeral was one of the largest in the history of Deadwood. The chapters were closed on two of the Wild West's most controversial characters.

THE TV SHOW

The Adventures of Wild Bill Hickok sought to introduce Wild Bill Hickok to the young audiences of 1951 as the western legend and fearless crime-fighter that he also was. Cast as Hickok was one of Hollywood's most handsome matinee idols of the time, actor Guy Madison. Tall, rugged, athletic, with natural riding and acting ability, Guy Madison was a native Californian. Serving in the Coast Guard in World War II, he was on a pass in Hollywood when an agent for David Selznick spotted him and brought him to Selznick's office.

Seeing major heart-swooning material in the young, blonde, handsome sailor, he immediately wrote him into the film, *Since You Went Away*, which was still in production. Cast as a sailor in a scene with Jennifer Jones, his real name, Robert Moseley, was changed to conceal the role from the military. Fan mail poured in, and upon his release from the service, Madison had found a new career.

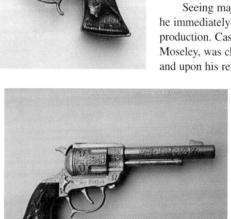

Large frame 10-inch Leslie-Henry Wild Bill Hickok with pop-up cap box and copper Marshal steerhead grips.

Seldom seen and very desirable Leslie-Henry long barrel model with copper grips showing the steerhead and "Marshal" markings.

Cast in starring roles with Dorothy McGuire in *Till the End of Time* in 1946, it was followed by *Honeymoon* with Shirley Temple in 1947. Some of Guy Madison's films in his long career before, during, and after *Wild Bill Hickok* were *The Command, Bullwhip, The Hard Man, Five Against the House, The Charge at Feather River,* and *Drums in the Deep South.* During the 1960s, Guy Madison, like many other western stars of the 1950s, went to Europe and did a string of "spaghetti westerns" in Italy and Spain. He returned in the 1970s, and was miscast in *Won Ton Ton, the Dog that Saved Hollywood.* In 1988, he was cast in the TV remake of *Red River.* But Guy Madison will always be remembered for his role as TV's *Wild Bill Hickok.*

Cast as his rotund, raspy, shrill-voiced sidekick, Jingles P. Jones, was veteran character actor Andy Devine. Andy Devine started in silent films, and when the talkies came in the 1920s, it looked as if his career was dead when his crackley, but high-pitched voice, was first heard. After winning a part in The *Spirit of Notre Dame* due to his own background in college football, his performance won critical acclaim, and in 1931, he landed a contract with Universal. In 25 years, Devine acted in a staggering 300 films. Never complaining that he was given second banana roles, Devine was usually cast as bumbling sidekicks, misery loving hobos, even dim-witted jolly men. Filmmakers fed him non-stop, and in the 1940s, he was doing as many as six films a year.

Born in Arizona, Devine suffered a fall as a youngster while he had a stick in his mouth, and permanently injured his vocal chords and roof of his mouth. It was his athletic ability and his huge frame at Santa Clara University playing both baseball and football that caught an agent's eye, and he was cast in the silent serial *The Collegians.* He married Dorothy House in January 1939, whom he had met on a movie lot, and they raised two sons. For all of his 300-plus films, Devine was proud to say that it was his role as "Jingles" on the *Wild Bill Hickok* series that made him a popular actor with both youngsters and adults. He never regretted his role, and later told interviewers, "I loved every minute of playing Jingles." So did we.

As Wild Bill Hickok and Jingles, the duo would begin a confrontation with Guy Madison introducing himself in a no-nonsense manner, "James Butler Hickok, mister," whereupon his jovial 300-pound sidekick would pick up with his shrill, gravelly voice, "That's Wild Bill Hickok mister! The bravest, strongest, fightin'est U.S. Marshal in the whole West!" A bit corny? The audiences loved it! Of course, the real Wild Bill didn't look like Guy Madison, and he never had such a loyal partner like Jingles. Despite that huge girth on his 300-pound frame, Jingles was no slouch when it came to backing up Wild Bill, and he was great with various disguises on the show as well. Two items were kept from the real Wild Bill Hickok—Guy Madison wore fringed buckskins, and he was the only TV western character that wore his guns butt first. The long hair, big nose, and drooping moustache, however, had to go.

The Adventures of Wild Bill Hickok lasted seven years and 113 episodes. Guy Madison and Andy Devine also did the radio version on Mutual Radio from 1951 to 1956. After the run of *Wild Bill Hickok,* both actors continued to make major films as they had been doing all through the weekly grind of the show. Both actors shunned the Hollywood glitz and stayed out of the scandals and limelight. Andy Devine was a devoted family man who raised his sons in the very typical 1950s America we love. In 1957, he told a reporter that, "I made a deal with my boys years ago. If they'd do nothing to embarrass me, I'd do nothing to embarrass them; it's worked out just fine." Guy Madison raised three daughters and a son.

Large Leslie-Henry 11-inch Wild Bill Hickok 44 with revolving cylinder and horse head grips. Note Oval "H" logo on grips. Also came in gold variety.

Schmidt small-frame Wild Bill Hickok and Jingles unique C-K Deputy possible prototype made to go with C-K Corkale Manufacturing Company that also marketed spurs and other western accessories. Left side has "Wild Bill Hickok" within floral grips.

Right side of Schmidt C-K Deputy which has "Kwik-Draw" on right side of frame below cylinder. Gun in opened position. (Courtesy of Bob Skaggs)

Leslie-Henry 10-inch Wild Bill Hickok with front lever, pop-up cap box, and black horse head grips. Note square hole screws usually denoting Canadian manufacturer.

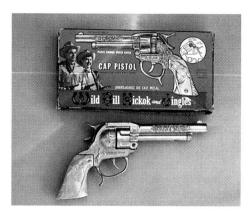

Leslie-Henry 9-inch Wild Bill Hickok with original box. Note Jingles on box with Wild Bill. Note butterscotch grips. (Courtesy of Ron Doub)

Leslie-Henry 10-inch Wild Bill Hickok with original box. Note color variation of boxes. Gun has transparent amber grips with white cameo insert. Seldom seen. (Courtesy of Ron Doub)

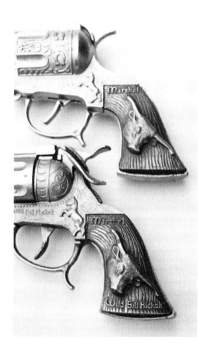

Close-up of details confirming that two varieties of copper steerhead grips were used. Top is Marshal while Marshal Wild Bill Hickok is below. Note that the first letter of each word made up of entwined horse shoes like Wild Bill's name.

In 1986, he was presented with the Golden Boot Award for Excellence in Western Entertainment. Andy Devine Boulevard was named for him in Kingman, Arizona, a few years before he passed away in February 1977, at the age of 71. Guy Madison passed away in 1996 at the age of 74. How can we simply say that these were "just actors" and "just cowboys" of the 1950s, when the public adulation paid them homage in such immortal ways? More than just characters, they were great role models!

The popularity of *Wild Bill Hickok* was strong and far reaching. The first actor to play him was William S. Hart. In addition to the dozens of Hickok movies on the big screen, many TV westerns couldn't help including Hickok as a character on whatever western was on the air. The last movie about Wild Bill Hickok starred Jeff Bridges in the title role in the 1995 MGM/United Artists release *Wild Bill* which also starred Ellen Barkin as "Calamity Jane." Bridges certainly looked every bit like the real Wild Bill. For most of us, however, there will only be one Wild Bill Hickok, and that's the role that was immortalized by Guy Madison on the small screen for seven years.

CAP GUN COLLECTIBLES

Besides the movies, of course, Wild Bill Hickok books, comics, coloring books, puzzles and games soon sported Wild Bill and Jingles everywhere. Lunch boxes, thermos bottles, marshal and deputy star badges all became and remain great collectibles. Both Guy Madison and Andy Devine graced the boxes of Kellogg's Sugar Pops cereals, with guns drawn, of course.

Wild Bill Hickok cap guns were very popular, and Leslie-Henry made five models in several patterns. Additionally, between boxed guns and boxed holster sets, both single and double, we can be assured that collecting the cap guns and holsters of Wild Bill Hickok and Jingles will keep us hunting for a good long time.

Leslie-Henry carried one main characteristic of the Wild Bill Hickok line of guns on all the models, and that is the name itself, with the first letters—W, B, and H—made up of two horseshoes entwined. This is a characteristic of the Wild Bill Hickok line that was carried also to the boxed guns, the labels, and the holster sets. The same holds true for the "J" in Jingles.

The smallest of the Wild Bill guns was Leslie-Henry's 7-inch model in the Buzz Henry style. It is also one of the most difficult to find. This came in both nickel and gold patterns and was extensively engraved overall, with the name raised on both sides of the frame. The lever to break open the gun is located just below the hammer on the left side. The grips are white with both checkering and the upraised horse head design. The small rearing horse has the lasso around its neck, which then forms a border around the name.

The most common Wild Bill model is the standard 9-inch Leslie-Henry. Nickel-plated and gold-plated models exist with the larger rearing horse on the frame without the lasso around its neck. It has scrolling on the barrel and frame. Grips in plastic with the large full horse head design came in white, black, amber, cameo, butterscotch, root beer, and copper. The copper grips have the heavily sculptured and raised steer head design, grained background, but also came with two grip variations. One style has "Marshal" at the top of the grip, over the steer head. The other style has both "Marshal" at the top and "Wild Bill Hickok" across the bottom of the grips.

We know that gun companies slapped on whatever they may have had on hand to fill orders. We know the Marshal grip was used on other Leslie-Henry guns as well as by Schmidt on its Wyatt Earp model. However, the much-harder-to-find copper grip with the full title was used only by Leslie-Henry on its Wild Bill models. Look closely at the "Marshal" on the copper grips. The model made for the Wild Bill Hickok also has the "M" in entwined horse shoes, while the "Marshal" lettering used for Gunsmoke goes back to a standard "M."

Leslie-Henry made the beautiful 10-inch larger model with the pop-up cap box with the front frame lever for opening with extensive scrollwork and engraving throughout. This model can be found in both nickel and gold, with white, black, and copper grips. It is believed the models containing the screw with the square inset hole were Canadian-made at the M.A. Henry plant in Ontario. However, this attractive model comes with and without the Canadian features.

Leslie-Henry made its long barrel model of the 9-inch pattern, as it did with almost all of its character guns such as Bonanza, Gunsmoke, Wyatt Earp, and Wagon Train. The long-barrel model is 10 inches in length, adding the one-and-a-half inches to the barrel. The grips were the usual horse head models in the several colors already described.

Leslie-Henry made the Wild Bill Hickok in its long barrel, "44" model with the left side gate and the revolving cylinder. At 11 inches, this is the largest of the five Leslie-Henry models. Extensively engraved, this model opens the side gate with the frame lever on the left side, has "Wild Bill Hickok" on the rocker panel behind the cylinder on the frame, and came with white, black, amber, and stag grips. The grips have the Oval "H" logo. While this was one of the most popular Leslie-Henry models, which as we have seen, came in nickel, gold, and the bronze finish, your scribe has yet to see a bronze Wild Bill Hickok model. We know that the "44" was made for Bonanza, Wagon Train, Gene Autry, U.S. Marshal, and others.

Leslie-Henry gunslinger single holster Wild Bill Hickok with 44 model pistol. Note low-slung style. Wild Bill Hickok on horse depicted on belt. Lots of studs! Sometimes two of these sets were worn criss-crossed as a pair.

While Leslie-Henry appears to have made the only Wild Bill Hickok line of guns, at least one seldom seen George Schmidt special model was made, perhaps as a prototype, or to match the C-Bar-K Corkale Manufacturing's line of spurs of the same name. This Schmidt is the 7-inch model that they made for its deputy in the Buck 'n Bronc series. This nifty little gun came with copper notch pattern grips, which have "Wild Bill Hickok" across the grips on the right side and "Jingles" on the left side. The entwined horseshoes were used in the lettering. The left side of the frame has "C-K Deputy" raised above the same notch pattern design of the frame, and the right side reads "Kwik Draw."

Corkale Manufacturing of California made several spurs and one cannot escape the connection, which leads to a good conclusion that this gun may have been either a Schmidt prototype, or was specially made and sold with C-Bar-K spurs. The gun is not marked "Geo. Schmidt." Its left side lever breaks open from the top for cap loading, the same as the Schmidt Deputy model.

Identical model, except this variety is marked both "Wild Bill" and "Jingles," and comes with turquoise-enhanced conchos and turquoise bullet loops. Color scheme suggests usage by both cowboys or cowgirls.

Leslie-Henry went to town with a great variety of Wild Bill Hickok and Jingles holsters. One very special feature was its gunfighter model, sold both separately or in pairs so that the youngster could strap on both single holsters with the buckle on each side of the hip. This super set hangs low for real gunfighter action. This pattern came in top grain tooled leather in several colors, but is usually found in black and brown, accented with numerous studs, conchos, jewels, and with 12 bullets, six on each side of the holster. The belt has a large round section with "Wild Bill Hickok" well tooled, along with Wild Bill on his rearing horse, Buckshot. This large holster came with, and takes, both the long barrel and "44" models perfectly.

An identical gunfighter-style holster is found with Wild Bill Hickok and Jingles on the round leather belt section. Identical to the gunfighter model described, this Jingles pattern came in black and white tooled leather, silver conchos with turquoise jewels on the belt and holster pocket, with blue bullet holders and red bullets, and it could have easily been marketed for a cowgirl or cowboy bent on being "Wild Bill" or "Wild Belle" in the neighborhood. It is a beautiful rig and holds the long barrels and the "44" models perfectly.

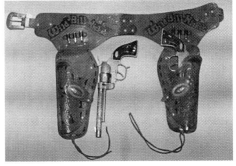

Leslie-Henry double holster set with Wild Bill Hickok 44's nickel-plated with transparent root beer grips. Complete coverage of tooled foliage and "Wild Bill Hickok's" name over both holster pockets. Note same lettering as on gun frames. (Courtesy of J. Schleyer)

Leslie-Henry double holster sets also came with and without "Jingles" added to the tooling, and all were ornate, large, impressive-quality sets. The official use of the entwined horseshoes for the lettering confirms they were specifically made for the Wild Bill Hickok line of guns. No guns marked "Jingles" made by Leslie-Henry are known to exist. No rifles or shotguns marked to either Wild Bill Hickok and/or Jingles have surfaced to date. All the separately boxed Wild Bill Hickok guns came in boxes with images of both Guy Madison and Andy Devine on the cover with both guns drawn and in vibrant colors.

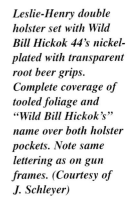

Above: Never before seen Canadian made (M.R. Henry, Ontario) Buzz-Henry pair of Wild Bill Hickok cap shooters with inset grips. Note the "square" screw on the left side of the frame on the lower gun, which usually indicates the Canadian made models. Super rare nickel models with cream grips!

We are fortunate that Hollywood brought Wild Bill Hickok back. It was good for the youngsters, western buffs, and certainly a bonanza for cap gun collectors since Wild Bill Hickok is well represented in the quality line of guns made by Leslie-Henry. James Butler Hickok may have had the premonition of his untimely end, but he could have never imagined that youngsters would be playing with guns with his real name on them some 80 years after his death!

THE LIFE AND LEGEND OF WYATT EARP

The man who epitomizes all that the Wild West stood for—probably America's most admired, talked about, debated, and recognized lawman—was Wyatt Earp. He has withstood the test of time. More biographies, conspiracies, documentaries, movies, and television programs have been about him, his life, his times, his legends, his gunfight at the O.K. Corral, and the impact he left on Tombstone, Arizona. Wyatt Earp outlived his contemporaries—Bat Masterson, Wild Bill Hickok, Pat Garrett, Texas John Slaughter, Bill Tilghman, even all of the Earp brothers, four of whom were lawmen themselves. He continues to represent the American frontier marshal, a man of courage and tenacity against the lawless element of the Old West.

Movies on Wyatt Earp have been produced through more than 50 years. Dozens of actors, both newcomers and world famous have all portrayed Wyatt Earp, from Burt Lancaster to Henry Fonda, from Kurt Russell to Kevin Costner. Yet, as memorable as some of these great movies may be, the image of Wyatt Earp falls on actor Hugh O'Brien, who starred as Wyatt in the highly popular television western, *The Life and Legend of Wyatt Earp,* which was based on Earp's official biography by Stuart N. Lake. For some reason, efforts to portray Earp as he really was in these movies fall short of the superbly dressed, clean-shaven lawman portrayed by Hugh O'Brien. We will get back to all of Hollywood's "Wyatt Earps" later on in this section.

It is difficult to do the real Wyatt Earp justice, if you will, in a few pages, but it is a story that cannot be ignored. No matter how it is told, no matter how it is slanted, amateur or historian, the fact remains that Earp was, indeed, an accredited U.S. marshal, with prominent government officials backing him up. His remarkable long life also typifies the last of a special breed that spanned the old and new frontier. It made him the subject of the movies and the TV western we so fondly recall, and like Wild Bill Hickok, his name and persona remain immortal on the large quantity of cap pistols and Buntline cap guns that we so avidly collect. Allow me, then, as a long standing "Earpaphile" to do my best to honor his memory.

The real Wyatt Earp, circa 1886. America's most recognized lawman. (Courtesy of Western History Collection, University of Oklahoma)

THE REAL WYATT EARP

Wyatt Berry Stapp Earp was born on the *Feast of St. Joseph,* March 19, 1848, in Monmouth, Illinois. His father, Nicholas Earp, was a Mexican War veteran, and the family could be traced back to the French and Indian Wars and the American Revolution. He was of Scotch descent. It was a large family, which consisted of, in order, James, Martha, Virgil, Wyatt, Morgan, Warren, and Adelia. There was also a half-brother, Newton. There was certainly an exceptionally strong resemblance in all the brothers. His father named him in honor of his commanding officer in the Mexican War, Wyatt Berry Stapp of the Illinois Mounted Volunteers.

In 1850, the family moved to Pella, Iowa. When the Civil War began, James, Virgil, and even the veteran father, all enlisted in the Union army. The father resigned in 1863 when Lincoln's Emancipation Proclamation Act was made public. James was severely wounded during the war and was sent home; Virgil served the entire time. The family moved again, to San Bernardino, California, in 1864. Already an experienced rider and good shot, Wyatt did the hunting for the wagon train en route to California. In California, only age 17, Wyatt got his first job as a stage driver for the Banning Line, running between San Bernardino and Los Angeles. He did a good job, and also was given routes to Prescott, Arizona, and Salt Lake. Soon thereafter, in mid-1865, his older brother Virgil, just out of the army, joined the same company.

In 1868, the family moved back to Illinois. On the way, both Virgil and Wyatt worked for Union Pacific Railroad construction crews. At age 20, Wyatt bought his own wagons, hired them out to the railroads, and made some decent money. While visiting his grandfather back in Illinois, he married a child bride, Urilla Southerland, in 1870. His wife died during childbirth. The family moved to Lamar, Missouri, where Wyatt, running against his brother Newton, was elected constable. His young wife's death deeply affected Wyatt and he took off, drifting for awhile through the Indian Territory and ending up in Kansas. He hired out as a guard and hunter for a group of engineers going through Indian Territory. By the spring of 1871, he turned to buffalo hunting, and met Bat Masterson in 1872. They remained friends for life. Wyatt hunted buffalo between 1871 and 1873.

Wyatt Earp neither drank nor smoked. He had a reputation for deadly accuracy in pistol matches and was a good gambler. He was also a good bare-knuckle fighter. Earp was not a braggart, but rather quiet, but when he spoke, he meant what he said. He was strongly attached to his brothers and they were to him. He dressed well, was a handsome man, with dark brown hair, flowing handle-bar moustache, grey eyes, and stood 6'1". He was well mannered and strongly loyal to the friends he made. Earp dressed in black, as did his brothers, with the only distinction being a white shirt. He preferred the three-quarter-length frock coat and black brimmed hat. He was an imposing figure wherever he went.

The summer of 1873 brought Wyatt to Ellsworth, Kansas. Ellsworth was a typical cow town, temporary shelter to thousands of cowboys that came up from the Chisholm Trail, herding beef to Northern markets. Parched, lonely, ornery, and itching for a good time, these cowboys let loose in these towns all over the Midwest. Two very feared Texans were notorious brothers Ben and Billy Thompson. Checking their guns at the Grand Central Hotel, the brothers sat down to a poker game. An argument ensued and one Jack Sterling accused Bill Thompson of cheating, and slapped him around. The brothers got up and got their guns. Someone went to call Sheriff Chauncey Whitney, and before Sheriff Whitney could get the Thompsons to cool down, Bill fired two shotgun blasts into Whitney, killing him. Bill got on a horse and took off, leaving Ben and a gang of Texans to face the furious citizens of Ellsworth. Watching all this was young Wyatt Earp, then 25 years old, standing by Beebe's Store and Brennan's Saloon.

Mayor Jim Miller ordered Marshal Jack Norton and his two deputies, Charles Brown and Ed Crawford, into action, but they hesitated, trying to figure out a way to get around Ben Thompson and his shotgun, with his Texan buddies behind him. Wyatt then made the following statement that was to launch his law enforcement career: "It's none of my business, but if it was me, I'd get a gun and arrest Ben Thompson or kill him." The mayor tore the badge off Norton's shirt and said "I'll make it your business. I order you to arrest Ben Thompson." Wyatt picked up two guns and a gunbelt at Beebe's Store, strapped them on, and walked towards Ben Thompson. Seeing the young newly-appointed marshal walking fearlessly towards him, the following exchange took place:

The real Virgil Earp. Wyatt's older brother, also took part in the O.K. Corral Gunfight. He was later ambushed and crippled for life. (Courtesy of Ben Traywick)

Thompson:	"What do you want?"
Wyatt:	"I want you, Ben."
Thompson:	"You have me all surrounded. . . .I'd rather talk than fight."
Wyatt:	"I'll get you either way, Ben." *Earp never stopped walking towards Thompson.*
Thompson:	"Wait a minute! What do you want me to do?"
Wyatt:	"Throw your shotgun in the road, put up your hands, and tell your friends to stay out of this play."
Thompson:	"Will you stop walking and let me talk to you?" *Earp stopped walking.* "What are you going to do with me?"
Wyatt:	"Kill you or take you to jail."
Thompson:	"I see Brown over there (referring to Deputy Charles Brown) by the depot with a rifle. The minute I give up my guns, he'll cut loose at me."
Wyatt:	"If he does, I'll give you back your guns and we'll shoot it out with him. As long as you're my prisoner, the man that gets you will have to get me."
Thompson:	"You win." *Thompson threw down the shotgun and Earp took him in.*

A procession of angry Texans followed Earp, his celebrated prisoner, and the mayor, all to Judge Osborne's Court. Thompson was fined $25 for disturbing the peace and was allowed to leave to rejoin his killer brother, long gone from Ellsworth. But Wyatt's almost incredible show of courage, tenacity, and principle—that he was willing to shoot it out with Thompson if Thompson was harmed while his prisoner—had made its point. The mayor offered him a job at $125 a month, but Wyatt turned it down, saying he was on his way to Wichita where the railroad had finally reached, and he wanted to go into the cattle business. Ben Thompson, who was later killed in a shootout in 1884, reportedly told Bat Masterson that he had a hunch Wyatt Earp would kill him if he tried to shoot it out, and he didn't feel like "dying that day."

Wyatt's reputation got to Wichita before he did the following year, 1874. No sooner did he arrive when Mayor James Hope asked "You that fellar that run in Ben Thompson?" And as

The real Morgan Earp. Wyatt's younger brother, also took part in the O.K. Corral Gunfight. He was later ambushed and killed. (Courtesy of Ben Traywick)

The Dodge City Peace Commission brought together Wyatt Earp *(sitting, second from left); Bat Masterson (standing, far right); Luke Short (standing center); and other great lawmen of the time. (Courtesy of Kansas City Historical Society)*

Hugh O'Brien, who starred in television's **Life and Legend of Wyatt Earp.**

Wyatt nodded and started to reply, the mayor pinned a deputy marshal's badge on his robust chest. Wyatt took the job this time. Wichita was full of cowboys, including Ben Thompson, the Clements brothers and other assorted malcontents. Wyatt forbid the wearing of guns within city limits and strictly enforced it. During this time, he corralled noted Texan "Shanghai" Pierce, and 40 of his men.

In a showdown with Manning Clements, who brought 50 men gunning for Wyatt, he faced them alone on Douglas Avenue, telling them to put up their guns or leave; they left. Wyatt Earp strictly enforced his existing town ordinance of not wearing guns in Wichita. Only one known blast of gunfire took place, when the Texans put up an 18-year-old tough guy to try and make a name for himself by shooting Wyatt Earp. The kid got the drop on Wyatt from behind, but in a fraction of a second, Wyatt turned and fired, nicking him in the arm. The kid ran. Within a year, Wichita was tamed down, and Wyatt Earp moved on to Dodge City.

Between 1876 and 1877, Wyatt worked as chief deputy marshal under Larry Deger, and was also a member of the celebrated Dodge City Peace Commission, which consisted of noted lawmen of the day—Bat and Jim Masterson, Luke Short, Charlie Bassett, M.C. Clark, Neal Brown, W.C. Harris, and Joe Mason. Great peace officer Bill Tilghman was sheriff of Ford County and a good friend of Wyatt Earp. There is no question that Dodge City, later to be the same town where the fictitious "Marshal Matt Dillon" ruled in TV's *Gunsmoke*, was the "Queen of the Cowtowns."

It had a reputation also known as "Gomorrah of the Plains" and "the wickedest Babylon of the frontier." Here a real cowboy could get liquored up real good, grab a lady of the night from Kate Fisher's palace of beauties, lose all his money at the Alhambra's games of chance, and then fire his six-guns at the first man who crossed him on the street. Death was often swift, either at the hands of another hot-head, or, with the blessing of the courts, the gallows were always in vogue to see that justice was done.

Nearby was the celebrated cemetery, Boot Hill, since most of the hapless souls that went there for permanent residence died with their boots on. The *Hays City Sentinel* reported that Dodge City was "full of prostitutes and brothels." The editor reported after inspecting Dodge that "no restriction is placed on licentiousness." A cowpuncher once remarked, "All they raise in Dodge is cattle, dust, and hell." The newspapers reported that cowboys walked around "armed with cannons" but in reality, there were no more than an average of 25 deaths a year. This pales with even Hartford, Connecticut, where over 100 years later, in a so-called civilized society far removed from the "Wild West," that number is surpassed within six months of a given year.

Dime novelists of the time, the most famous being Ned Buntline, came to Dodge City, and it was at this time, that he presented Wyatt Earp, Bat Masterson, Bill Tilghman, and Neal Brown with his famous Buntline Special that he had especially made for them. It was a single action Colt .45 with a 12-inch barrel and an overall length of 18 inches. Wyatt reportedly cherished this Buntline and carried it with him most of the time. He became amazingly proficient with it, and was said to have been able to unholster it with amazing speed and shoot a coyote at 400 feet. "Colonel" Ned Buntline was such a colorful character, scoundrel, rogue, and novelist that he was probably most responsible for making the West wilder than it was, and bringing it east. In order to do him some justice, since his name was lent to Buntline Specials that were so unique that even the toy gun companies copied them, we will highlight Colonel Ned Buntline at the end of this chapter.

A long line of tough law and order types tried to tame Dodge before Wyatt got there, none that had any effect. William Brooks, Jack Allen, and others were all run out of town by the rough bands of Texan cattle drivers. It was after Wyatt had made an even bigger name for himself in Wichita, that Mayor George Hoover sent for him, offering him the chief deputy's job at $250 a month, and he added a bonus of $2.50 for every arrest in efforts to clean up the western jezebel of a town. Wyatt, and his three trusted deputies, Bat and Jim Masterson and Joe Mason, did a fine job, and between Wyatt's "crowning" the heads of cowboys bent on testing his resolve with his Buntline, and Bat's use of his moniker, they cleaned up Dodge in no time.

Wyatt Earp later recalled that "a thoroughly buffaloed prisoner (the official western name of getting crowned with a gun barrel on your noggin') heaved into the calaboose put a quick dent into cowboy conceit." The emphasis was on changing your attitude, giving you a chance to respect the law, or get out of town. While lawmen of the day had more backup than any police force of today, they did not engage in wholesale slaughter of bad men. But if a man "needed killing," then so be it; there was an ample supply of both sides of the law to test it. Wyatt was more into "buffaloing" unruly cowboys, not killing them.

In late 1877, Wyatt and his brother Morgan headed for the gold rush in the Black Hills, ending up in Deadwood, South Dakota. Wild Bill Hickok had been killed the year before. Wyatt and Morgan ended up making big money buying wagons and hauling lumber to the tune of about $5,000 in just six months. Dodge City's new mayor, James H. "Dog" Kelley, soon wired Wyatt, telling him that his town ordinance was in shambles and that cowboys were again thrashing the town and its good citizens. In July 1877, Wyatt returned to Dodge.

His Honor, Mayor Kelley was no slouch. He owned pieces of both the Alhambra Saloon and Gambling Parlor, as well as The Dodge City Opera House, which was actually a dance hall. He also wanted a law-abiding town and he didn't care much for "tapping the wrist" of hot-headed and overheated cowboys. "I'll back up any move you make" he told Wyatt Earp. Wyatt Earp went to work again.

In July of 1878, a Texan named George Hoyt came up to try to collect the $1,000 bounty on Wyatt's head. Wyatt was outside the Comique Theater, reduced to standing room only as Eddie Foy did his act. Hoyt shot at Wyatt while on horseback, emptying his six-gun and missed every shot. Turning his bucking horse around, he galloped out of town. Pulling out his celebrated rifle-gun, the Buntline Special, Wyatt went into a kneeling position and blasted Hoyt out of his saddle at several hundred feet. Hoyt died a month later making a dying confession that he had been paid to try and kill Earp. For all of the alleged gunplay and shootings attributed to Wyatt Earp, Hoyt was the only man he killed in Dodge City's "clean-up campaign." The message was clear and the cowboys tamed down real fast.

During his Dodge City tenure, Wyatt also had the famous encounter with Clay Allison, one of the West's worst killers. Tennessean by birth, but working in the New Mexico Territory as a cowman, Allison was a vicious, quick-tempered, hair-trigger alcoholic killer. It was said the Texans sent for him to "take care of Marshal Earp." Allison had about 21 notches to his credit, two of which were lawmen, the marshals of Las Animas and Cimarron, New Mexico. He had a penchant for riding buck naked through towns shooting wildly at anyone who looked. Every Christmas and Fourth of July, he'd do the same in Las Animas, with his brother John, in what was called "hurrahing" the towns. He once agreed to fight a duel with Bowie knives, and he and his opponent got into a freshly dug grave and cut each other up until Clay emerged, and he ended filling up the grave of his unlucky victim. He once rode a horse right into a court-room in Canadian, Texas, clearing everyone out as he fired while drunk on his horse. But Allison met his match in Wyatt Earp.

Arriving in Dodge, Allison met up with Wyatt by the Long Branch Saloon. As they talked, he edged closer to Wyatt. Suddenly, he went for his gun. Before he had unholstered it, he felt Wyatt's Buntline Special stick him in the ribs. Allison lowered his gun, backed off, and got on his horse to leave, but then turned around to take one last charge at Wyatt. Wyatt stood in the middle of the street and took dead aim. That was too much for Allison, and he rode off without any further trouble. Sometime later, he had to return to Dodge on cattle business; he wrote a note to Wyatt, asking for his permission to come to town. There was also an unconfirmed legend that he was also faced down by Bat Masterson. A year later, roaring drunk and violently driving his wagon back to his ranch, it hit a hole, throwing him out of the buckboard. The rear wheel rolled over and broke his neck. Clay Allison was dead at age 37.

It was during his time in Dodge that Wyatt Earp spent considerable time with a man that was to remain a life-long friend, the deadly dentist, Doc Holliday. They met briefly in November 1877, while Wyatt traveled to Fort Griffin, Texas, but it was in Dodge City that Doc Holliday became forever loyal to Wyatt Earp. No movie or television program about Wyatt Earp was complete without the inclusion of Doc Holliday.

DOC HOLLIDAY

Born John Henry Holliday in Griffin, Georgia, in 1851, he was brought up in the gentleman-ly ways of the old South. His father, Henry Holliday, had been a Confederate army major and a prior veteran of the Indian and Mexican wars. His mother, Alice, died when young John was only 15 in 1866. His father remarried, and the family moved to Valdosta, Georgia. Although the family sunk into poverty after the war, they scraped together enough money to send John Henry Holliday to study dentistry; first in Baltimore, later in Pennsylvania. A thorough and intelligent student, John Henry wrote his thesis on the "Diseases of the Teeth." On March 1, 1872, he was one of 26 students graduating from the Pennsylvania College of Dental Surgery.

He first worked in a dental office in Atlanta. His professional career was soon cut short when he was found to be consumptive and given only three years to live. He was advised to go

The real John Henry Holliday, the deadly dentist known as "Doc." (Courtesy of Ben Traywick)

west to a drier climate. He did practice dentistry for a short time in Dallas, and it was said he enjoyed his work, but his hacking cough as the tuberculosis progressed turned away his clients, and he started to drink heavily and gamble. He was soon a proficient poker and faro player, and it became his main line of support.

He was also said to be able to down three quarts of whisky a day, but was as steady and steel-eyed as anyone else. Doc Holliday, in spite of his illness, got himself a pair of pistols and practiced with them daily until he became a very proficient pistoleer. He once told Wyatt Earp that there were only two instances when he wasn't nervous—working on somebody's teeth or in a gunfight. Legends about Doc Holliday are just as vivid as they were about Wild Bill Hickok and Wyatt Earp. In fact, it's often difficult to separate reality from the legend.

Some stories claim that Doc Holliday had shot some Negroes that he found swimming near his home, but this has never been confirmed. His first killing involved a man over a card game in 1875, and he left Dallas, moving on to Jacksboro. It was said that by the time he reached there, he was already being called the "deadly dentist" for having allegedly killed some gamblers who didn't take losing easily, and later still, killing a soldier. He moved on to Denver, Colorado. Some say he was involved in a fight where he slashed the throat of a man named Budd Ryan. It was later recalled by both Wyatt Earp and Bat Masterson that Doc pulled his knife and slashed Ryan because Ryan went for his gun. Doc moved on to Wyoming, drinking and gambling, and by now it was said he would constantly cough up blood into a handkerchief.

By the end of 1877, Doc went back to Texas, to Fort Griffin. By chance, there he met Wyatt Earp, who was chasing an outlaw named Dave Rudabaugh. Doc had few friends. He was well known as a sarcastic, if not witty, cynical, and generally unpleasant man. But Doc quickly saw a serious man in Wyatt Earp, admired him and gave him information that Rudabaugh was in Fort Davis, which proved to be correct. The two parted company but remained friends.

While in Fort Griffin, Doc Holliday met Kate Elder, also known as "Big Nose Kate." Her real name was Mary Katherine Harony. She was born in Hungary. A sometimes lady of the night and dance hall floozy, she would become Doc's love-hate interest the rest of his life. She was also devoted to Doc, and when he was jailed for the killing of a gambler named Bailey, Kate, who was just as tough, fearless, and stubborn as Doc, started a fire to divert attention away from Doc and freed her lover. They fought constantly, but were devoted to each other in a strange way. She tried to play the Southern lady role as Mrs. John H. Holliday, but tired of it, and returned to being a prostitute and dance hall girl, which infuriated Doc.

Doc and Kate got to Dodge City by 1878. Doc tried to re-start his dentistry office for a short time. He and Kate quarreled, especially when she took off, and the venture fizzled. Kate left for parts unknown and Doc went back to gambling and drinking even more than he did before. While in Dodge, however, he came to Wyatt Earp's aid when a group of Texans tried to shoot him. Doc jumped in, pulled out his two pistols, and shot one of the men. In the diversion, Wyatt was able to regain his own gun and together, they disarmed and collected some 50 guns from the Texas cowhands. Wyatt never forgot Doc's gesture and felt he had saved his life, further strengthening the bond between them.

When Wyatt Earp left Dodge City with his brother James and his family, Doc joined them along the way. They ended up in Tombstone, Arizona, where Wyatt's other brothers, Virgil and Morgan, also joined them. Doc's time in Tombstone was not without controversy. He got back with Big Nose Kate, had confrontations with outlaws such as Johnny Ringo, and Curly Bill Brocius, and made enemies real fast. Between Doc's drinking and gambling and Kate's drinking binges and saloon activities, he had enough one day and threw her out. She was furious with Doc and went on a real binge.

As fate would have it, a holdup of the Kinnear Stage Line in 1881 by unknown robbers caused the death of two employees. The cowboys in town blamed it on Doc Holliday. Sheriff Johnny Behan, who sympathized with the Clantons and McLowerys, didn't care much for Doc or the Earps. Behan found Kate on her drunken binge and fed her even more whiskey, sympathized with her and suggested he could help her "get back" at Doc for throwing her out. She signed a prepared affidavit implicating Doc in the holdup and the two murders. Justice Wells Spicer issued a warrant for Doc on the contents of Kate's affidavit.

When Kate sobered up and realized what she had done, she insisted she had been forced to sign the affidavit while binging. Along with the testimony of witnesses to Doc's location at the time of the holdup, the plot failed, and the district attorney threw out Doc's charges. That was the last straw for Doc. He allegedly gave her a thousand dollars, put her on a stage coach, and never saw her again. Kate went on to an interesting life of her own, married a man named Cummings, and died in 1940 in a rest home in Arizona at the age of 90.

Doc and the Earps, along with other lawmen, took part in border skirmishes with the Mexicans and rustlers that erupted in gunfire as posses went after the rustlers, trying to stop a full scale border war between Mexico, Arizona, and New Mexico. Doc was briefly wounded in one of the skirmishes and ended up walking with a cane for a time. Warren Earp, the youngest of the Earp brothers, was also wounded, and while recovering from wounds, missed the most famous gun-fight of the Old West. But Doc Holliday, cane and all, did not.

Doc came to the aid of the Earp brothers at the famous gunfight at the O.K. Corral. He was slightly wounded, but managed to kill both Frank and Tom McLowery during the exchange of gunfire. After the crippling of Virgil Earp and the murder of Morgan Earp, Doc's devotion to Wyatt continued as Wyatt and others went on a posse to avenge his brother's death. Doc stayed with the posse, at one point, heroically pulling posse member Texas Jack out of the line of fire after his horse had been shot from under him when the posse was ambushed by the men they were after. Doc stayed with Wyatt as he completed what he had set out to do, to avenge the death of Morgan Earp, and the crippling of Virgil Earp. They got as far as Trinidad, Colorado, and Doc and Wyatt said goodbye for the last time.

Doc went on to Denver, and with the tuberculosis ravaging his body that should have finished him off a dozen years before, he opted to head for Glenwood Springs, where it was said that guests at the Hotel Glenwood could enjoy some relief from the Yampah Hot Springs. There was even talk that some people were "healed." But by May 1887, Doc's consumption had nearly consumed him totally. He spent his last 57 days in bed. On November 8, 1887, he woke up, asked for a glass of whiskey, sent it down, looked down at his feet, and said "Well, I'll be damned. . .this is funny." He always said he'd die with his boots on, that's what was funny to him at the end. He was barefoot. He died, peacefully, in bed. Doc Holliday, survivor of many gunfights, one of Wyatt Earp's most loyal friends, and certainly one of the Old West's most colorful characters, was only 36 years old. His grave, in Linwood Cemetery in Colorado, even has "He died in bed" inscribed into the monument.

Several fine actors have portrayed the hard drinking, incessant coughing "deadly dentist." Kirk Douglas played him opposite Burt Lancaster in *Gunfight at the O.K. Corral.* Cesar Romero (*The Cisco Kid*) played Doc Holiday in 1939. Victor Mature, Kent Taylor (*The Rough Riders),* Arthur Kennedy, Jason Robards, and Stacey Keach have all starred as Doc Holliday. In the same way as TV western shows have had old western characters such as Wild Bill Hickok, Wyatt Earp, and Buffalo Bill come in contact with the characters of the show itself, Doc Holliday appeared on episodes of *Colt. 45, Maverick, Bonanza, High Chaparral, Lawman,* and *Wells Fargo,* played by a host of TV western character actors including Peter Breck *(Black Saddle, The Big Valley),* Adam West (TV's *Batman),* Jack Kelly *(Bart Maverick)* Martin Landau *(Mission Impossible)* and several others.

In 1993, Val Kilmer played Doc in the movie *Tombstone* followed in 1994 by Dennis Quaid, who played Doc in *Wyatt Earp* with Kevin Costner in the title role. On *The Life and Legend of Wyatt Earp,* with Hugh O'Brien, Doc Holliday was played by veteran character actor, Douglas Fowley, who captured Doc's known characteristics quite well, from 1956 to 1961. The part of "Big Kate" was played by actress Carol Stone.

There is no question that Doc Holliday, who once said he wanted to "forget himself" is far from being forgotten. There is even the Doc Holliday Tavern in Glenwood Springs, Colorado, a place that Doc himself would have approved.

WYATT EARP AND THE GUNFIGHT AT THE O.K. CORRAL

In April 1878, Bat Masterson's older brother, Ed, was killed by a drunken cowboy. In May, Wyatt was hired as assistant marshal of Dodge City. He had just returned from Texas and was now married a second time, to Celia Ann Blaylock, who he called "Mattie." By June of 1878, the Dodge City Globe reported that "Wyatt Earp is doing his duty as Ass't Marshal in a very credible way—adding new laurels to his splendid record every day." Both Bat and his other brother, Jim Masterson, worked as deputies along with Wyatt.

By May 1879, Wyatt had just about enough of Dodge City. His older brother Virgil was already in Arizona, and wired Wyatt that Tombstone was a new "booming" town. Virgil had been hired as a deputy sheriff in Tombstone. Wyatt decided to move the entire Earp clan, which includes his brothers James and Morgan, and families, and Doc Holliday tagged along as well. Wyatt and his family arrived in Tombstone by November and he took a job as deputy sheriff of Pima County in May 1880. Meanwhile, his brother Virgil was commissioned as a U.S. deputy marshal.

Between May 1879 and June 1880, Tombstone went from 250 to 3,000 residents. It's also obvious that it had the lawless element in the form of Old Man Clanton and his sons, Billy, Finn, and Ike. Rounding the local desperadoes were Johnny Ringo, Curly Bill Brocius, Tom and Frank McLowery (also spelled McLaury), Billy Claiborne, Buckskin Frank Leslie, and

Warren Earp, Wyatt's youngest brother, killed in 1900 in New Mexico. He had accompanied Wyatt on the search for Morgan's killers. (Courtesy of Glenn Boyer)

others. Soon, however, lawmen Bat Masterson, Morgan and Warren Earp, Crawley Dake, Fred White, Luke Short, and others drew the line between the good and the bad, as well as the very ugly. Doc Holliday cast his lot with the Earps. Sheriff Johnny Behan seemed to lean towards the Clantons and the McLowerys. Sheriff Behan's new girlfriend from San Francisco, Josephine "Sadie" Marcus, took a liking to Wyatt Earp, and he to her, adding fuel to the fire between the two lawmen.

The cowboys, rustlers, and assorted outlaws kept Wyatt, his brothers and the other lawmen busy on constant posses. It is obvious that Sheriff Behan protected the Clantons and McLowerys from the Earps. Then on October 25, 1881, the fued exploded. Word came to the Earps that the Clantons and the McLowerys and Billy Claiborne were waiting for them at the O.K. Corral. As the Earps begin their walk into history, they are joined by Doc Holliday. Sheriff Behan tried to stop the Earps by telling them he had already disarmed the cowboys, which was not true.

They ignored Behan and kept walking towards the Corral. Virgil Earp, as Tombstone's marshal, then orders the cowboys to give up their guns as they were under arrest. The Clantons and the McLowerys responded by cocking their guns. At 2:47 p.m., Wyatt utters the words, "You sons of bitches have been looking for a fight and now you can have it." The shooting began and lasted for just about 30 seconds, at which time some thirty shots were fired.

When the smoke cleared, the most famous gunfight in America's history left the following victims: Tom and Frank McLowery and Billy Clanton dead; Virgil and Morgan Earp were both wounded, as was Doc Holliday. Only Wyatt Earp came out unscathed. Ike Clanton and Billy Claiborne chickened out, running into Fly's Photography Studio. Sheriff Behan tried to arrest the Earps, but Wyatt replied "I won't be arrested, Johnny. You threw us." A coroner's jury was convened; the Earps and Holliday were briefly jailed. Ike Clanton had sworn out a warrant for the Earps. On November 29, 1881, Justice Spicer finishes hearing testimony and his decision is final. The Earps and Holliday are exonerated. The outlaws swear revenge.

In December 1881, Virgil Earp, barely recovered from his O.K. Corral wounds, was ambushed. Shotgun blasts ring out by midnight as he walked home, and crippled him for good. On March 18, 1882, after attending a play at the Schieffelin Theater with Mayor John Clum, Wyatt and Morgan Earp headed for Hatch's Saloon for a game of pool. Two shots ring out. One just narrowly missed Wyatt's head; the second shot strikes Morgan Earp in the back, shattering his spine. He died in Wyatt's arms. The Earp families were in deep mourning.

The next day, Wyatt's birthday, Morgan's body lay in state, after which Wyatt shipped it to California, where the rest of the Earp family lived. Virgil and James Earp and their families were accompanied to the train station for the trip back to California. Wyatt and his youngest brother Warren swear out revenge to find and settle the score for the death of Morgan and the crippling of Virgil. Doc Holliday, Texas Jack Vermillion, Sherm McMasters, and Turkey Creek Johnson joined the Earps in search of the cowardly killers. Wyatt Earp said "vengeance is mine" and dropped his Christian ethics.

Armed with warrants and a cache of weapons, Wyatt and his posse began the manhunt for the killers and anyone even remotely involved in the Earp shootings. He killed Frank Stilwell first, one of Morgan's killers, followed by Indian Charlie, who confessed to Wyatt that he had been paid $25 to watch the horses when the others killed Morgan. His body, like all the others, was found riddled with bullets. Wyatt next came upon Curly Bill Brocius and killed him with a shot-gun blast. Meanwhile, Sheriff Johnny Behan organized a posse to go after the Earp party. By April 1882, Wyatt Earp had left Arizona for the last time. Although it has never been fully confirmed, some historians believe that Wyatt Earp also found and killed Johnny Ringo, and made it look like a suicide. Although evidence exists that it was anything but a suicide, the official cause of death according to a coroner's report, was a suicide after a drinking binge.

Upon reaching Trinidad, Colorado, Wyatt and Doc Holliday parted for the last time. Wyatt and his brother, Warren, went on to rejoin the family in Colton, California. By this time, Wyatt had left his second wife, Mattie, and had been living with Josephine Marcus. In 1888, Mattie Earp died of an apparent suicide. Wyatt and Josephine lived in San Francisco for several years, then in San Diego. On December 2, 1896, Wyatt Earp refereed the famous Bob Fitzsimmons and Tom Sharkey key fight in San Francisco.

In March 1897, both Wyatt Earp and Bat Masterson were reunited as bouncers at the Bob Fitzsimmons and James Corbett fight in Carson City, Nevada. The same year, word reached San Francisco of the gold rush in Alaska, and Wyatt and his wife headed north. He started the Dexter Saloon and within two years, his profits exceeded $80,000. Some historians also report that

Wyatt's famous Buntline Special was lost in the Yukon, on the trip to Alaska, when he lent it to a friend who dropped it overboard. Others indicate that it is in a museum in California.

In 1887, Wyatt learned that one of his most loyal friends, Doc Holliday had died in Colorado. On July 6, 1900, word reached Wyatt that his youngest brother, Warren Earp, working for a Cattleman's Association, in New Mexico, was killed by a Johnny Boyette, who was later acquitted of the shooting. By 1902, Wyatt was now in Nevada, to another booming bonanza camp called Goldfield. Even his brother Virgil went along. Wyatt ran the Northern Saloon with a friend named Martin. In 1905, Virgil Earp died of pneumonia in Goldfield, Nevada. His devoted wife, Allie, who had stood by Virgil's side for 32 years, never remarried and died at the age of 99 in1947.

In November 1907, Wyatt's father, Nicholas Earp, died at the Soldier's Home in Sawtelle, California. He had outlived three of his sons and was aware of the legend of his son, Wyatt. In October 1921, Wyatt received word that one of his best friends, Bat Masterson, had suffered a heart attack at the *Morning Telegraph* where he worked as sports writer. On January 25, 1926, Wyatt's brother James Earp, died in Los Angeles. Newton Earp, the half-brother and oldest of the six Earps, died in Sacramento in 1928.

By this time, Wyatt had made a good living running gold and copper mines in the Mojave mountains and in San Bernardino County. He was very successful in real estate, running horses, mining, and he was still a gambling man. Wyatt and Josephine were together for just about 50 years. On January 13, 1929, the Old West's most famous marshal, Wyatt Earp, died in bed, two months before his 81st birthday. He had outlived them all. Josephine Marcus Earp died in 1944. Wyatt Earp never had any children.

Ironically, two of the honor pallbearers at Wyatt's funeral were William S. Hart and Tom Mix, two of Hollywood's earliest cowboy stars. Stuart N. Lake was Wyatt's official biographer, but Wyatt did not live to see the book on his famous life, *Wyatt Earp: Frontier Marshal*, which was published in 1931. Many more books on Wyatt Earp were yet to come, mostly positive, but some negative. There is no question he left a memorable impact that will be debated for years to come. Wyatt Earp was a real man of his time—courageous and principled, yet he had to learn to live by frontier rules.

Stuart Lake's book, of course, led to Wyatt's life and legend being portrayed in more than 20 movies. The first actor to portray Wyatt Earp was Richard Dix. Others who have portrayed Wyatt are Henry Fonda, Burt Lancaster, Randolph Scott, Johnny Mack Brown, Walter Houston and even James Garner *(Maverick)*. Interestingly enough, Guy Madison, TV's "Wild Bill Hickok," starred as Wyatt Earp in one of the spaghetti westerns he made overseas in the 1960s. The latest portrayals were Kurt Russell as Wyatt in *Tombstone*, and Kevin Costner in the title role. Additional books have been written about Wyatt Earp, but once again, to us collectors and TV western amateur historians, "Wyatt Earp" will always be remembered by the TV version as portrayed by Hugh O'Brien, in *The Life and Legend of Wyatt Earp,* the first adult western to come to television.

THE TV SHOW

The Life and Legend of Wyatt Earp came to television on September 6, 1955. The theme song went like this: "Wyatt Earp, Wyatt Earp, brave, courageous, and bold; long live his fame and long live his glory, and long may his story be told."

It came to ABC starring a handsome and relatively unknown young actor named Hugh O'Brien. Between 1950 and 1955, the former Marine acted in almost 30 movies. Some of these were: *Buckaroo Sheriff of Texas; The Return of Jesse James; Cave of Outlaws; The Cimarron Kid; Battle at Apache Pass; The Man from The Alamo; The Stand at Apache River; Broken Lance; and Drums Across The River.* Yet, even with these movies under his belt, O'Brien's career went from relative obscurity to one of the most popular and coveted roles on television. *The Life and Legend of Wyatt Earp* ran for seven straight years.

To its credit, this TV western cast several characters based on the real men of Wyatt Earp's time and now that the reader has read the story of the real Wyatt Earp, here is the amazing list of the characters and the actors who portrayed them:

Val Kilmer (left), as "Doc Holliday" and Kurt Russell, as "Wyatt Earp" in the 1994 movie Tombstone. *Both actors shared a strong resemblance to the real Doc and Wyatt. (Courtesy of Old West Shop)*

- Wyatt Earp—*Hugh O'Brien*
- Virgil Earp—*John Anderson*
- Morgan Earp—*Dirk London*
- Doc Holliday—*Douglas Fowley*
- Big Nose Kate Holliday—*Carol Stone*
- Ned Buntline—*Lloyd Corrigan*
- Bat Masterson—*Mason Alan Dinehart, III*
- Ben Thompson—*Denver Pyle*
    (The Dukes of Hazzard)
- Bill Thompson—*Hal Baylor*
- Mayor Jim "Dog" Kelly—*Paul Brinegar*
- Judge Wells Spicer—*James Seay*

- Mayor Hoover—*Selmer Jackson*
- Sheriff Johnny Behan—*Lash LaRue* in the
    1958 season
- Sheriff Johnny Behan—*Steve Brodie,* in the
    1959-1961 season
- Mayor John Clum—*Stacey Harris*
- Old Man Clanton—*Trevor Bardette*
- Nellie Cashman—*Randy Stuart*
- Curly Bill Brocius—*William Phipps*
- Johnny Ringo—*Britt Lomond* ("Captain
    Monastario" from Zorro).
- Shotgun Gibbs—*Morgan Woodward*

The only fictitious character written into the show was "Shotgun Gibbs," in the 1958-1961 time period. The others, of course, were main characters based on Stuart N. Lake's biography of Wyatt Earp. To its credit, this TV western tried to at least remain within the scope of historical information, even though it was obviously glamorized in typical Hollywood style.

The opening episode, for example, dealt with Wyatt's becoming a marshal in Ellsworth, Kansas. Ned Buntline came along to present Wyatt with the Buntline Special. Instead of showing Wyatt staring down killer Clay Allison, for some reason, it was changed to another Texas killer named John Wesley Hardin, with whom the real Wyatt never tangled.

Once the show was a hit, the producers continued to introduce the real life characters in Wyatt's life, including Bat Masterson and Doc Holliday. His brothers, Virgil and Morgan, also had recurring roles in the series. When the show moved from Dodge City to Tombstone, Wyatt was given a love interest, Nellie Cashman, the owner of the Birdcage Saloon. As the series neared the end of its seven-year run, the famous showdown at the O.K. Corral was dramatized over a five-part story, and Wyatt Earp went back into history, as far as television was concerned, after a whopping 266 episodes, ending its run on September 26, 1961. After the end of this series, Hugh O'Brien starred in an adventure series called *Search* in the 1972-1973 season,

The real Ned Buntline, writer and rogue, as he appeared on Buffalo Bill's Wild West Show. (William Tell Images)

and later went back to the big screen, and turned in a super performance with John Wayne in *The Shootist.* He last starred in *Twins* with Danny DeVito and Arnold Schwarzenegger. Hugh O'Brien is still with us.

The success of *The Life and Legend of Wyatt Earp* didn't just make Hugh O'Brien a wealthy man. Hugh O'Brien and the life of the real Wyatt Earp were chronicled in three issues of *TV Guide, TV Western* magazine, and it brought renewed interest in the venerable lawman. The show was sponsored by General Mills and Proctor & Gamble. I mention these two products for two very interesting reasons. The boxes of Cheerios featured Hugh O'Brien as "Wyatt Earp" on the front, and the back of the box gave you instructions on how to make up your own cardboard play gun and target game. But as a sponsor for Proctor and Gamble's Gleem toothpaste, you could send for your own Buntline Special, an identical replica plastic clicker gun, the same size, length, and complete with Wyatt's signature.

Before we get into the multitude of Wyatt Earp cap guns and Buntline Special cap pistols, as previously stated, it is important to include some biographical data on Ned Buntline, whose "pen name," shall we say, has been immortalized on the famous Buntline Special—first on the real ones, and then on the toy cap pistols of the same name. He was quite a character.

NED BUNTLINE

His real name was Edward Zane Carroll Judson, and he was born on March 20, 1823, in Stamford, New York. His father, Levi Judson, was a frustrated writer, and didn't get along with his son. At age 14, young Judson ran away to sea. He developed a thirst for adventure, and writing of the things he observed in flowing and glamorized, if not totally fictional, form—but with just the right touch of reality to make it believable. Only five-feet tall, he served four years in the Navy. But his short fuse of a temper, legendary drinking habits, and brawls with just about everyone, both sailor and civilian, eventually convinced the U.S. Navy they would be better off without this short brawler, and he was summarily discharged. Some say he rose to rank of midshipman, and left in 1844 to "serve in the Seminole War" and travel west. This has never been confirmed, and it may have been his own version of why he left the Navy.

The same year, he took the pen name "Ned Buntline" and established the short lived *Ned Buntline* magazine in Cincinnati, Ohio. He also contributed stories to the *Knickerbocker* magazine. Moving to Nashville, he started a newspaper called *Ned Buntline's Own*. But Ned Buntline had a passion for four things in life—writing, drinking, brawling, and women. Buntline got involved with a man named Hines from Cincinnati, who had a few dollars to invest, but who had a reputation for manipulating loans, devising questionable money-raising schemes, and handling overdrafts to keep the failing literary enterprise going. At the same time, the portly, mustachioed little man had an insatiable appetite for women. Nobody ever knew how many times he married, but if he had to marry a girl to seduce her, or be forced to marry one after he seduced her, a quick ceremony was performed by the local Justice of the Peace. It didn't matter if the girl was now his bride; when Buntline tired of her, he left without even the formality of a divorce, and simply went after another. It didn't matter if the lady was married or single.

Hugh O'Brien as Wyatt gets ready to level his Buntline Special.

All these numerous wives and lovers failed to satisfy Buntline's lust for the opposite sex. His outrageous affairs with married women kept his partner Hines paying off irate husbands and pacifying furious fathers-of-the-brides. In March 1846, Buntline found himself in Nashville and involved with a woman named Mary Porterfield, the wife of a prominent businessman. Seducing the woman in a graveyard, the act was witnessed by the local preacher. Shocked, the man of the cloth quickly reported the incident to Mr. Porterfield. Grabbing his pistols, the outraged husband went after Buntline. Himself armed, Buntline exchanged fire with Mr. Porterfield, killing him. Taken in custody, the local mob burst into jail, and taking the little Romeo to the nearest tree, strung him up pronto, leaving him dangling in the air as the mob marched away. It was never revealed how Buntline was saved, but when the mob returned later, they found the rope had been cut and Buntline long gone. Leaving Hines to handle the mess, Buntline took off and headed for Boston.

In Boston, broke and hungry, Buntline's wild imagination turned to writing dime novels, and he wrote *The Last Days of Galilee* and *The Doomed City of Sin,* no doubt fueled by his own adventures of the flesh. These turned out to be hair-rasing, flamboyant, erotic and deadly. The little writer was said to be able to write 60,000 words of sex, blood, and gore in two days, and soon he was putting out two novels a week. His fame and fortune grew beyond his wildest dreams. He moved to New York and resurrected *Ned Buntline's Own* now that his name was a household word, but he changed the format and himself. He found God and morality, and the former roaring drunk and insatiable seducer turned the magazine into a call for morality, prohibition, and the Lord. He even refused to take ads for liquor, gave new lectures on the sins of the world, and organized temperance societies. He did not charge a fee for his lectures and, soon, his reluctance to publish sex and liquor ads began to empty the magazine's treasury.

Depressed, Buntline went to the nearest whorehouse, got himself drunk, and spent the night with two girls. Seeing a prominent official in the same brothel, he seized the chance to become a spy, and a few days later, approached the hapless man with the news that as a newspaperman, he'd have to print what he had observed in the brothel. A fat check silenced Buntline. He soon saw that blackmail paid off. He harbored a hatred of foreigners, especially the British and the Irish Catholics, and with some political ambitions, formed the Know-Nothing Party in New York. Leading a riot against the English actor William Charles McCready, due to play in *Macbeth* in 1849, at the Astor Palace Theater, Buntline led the brawl dressed in the uniform of an American Revolutionary Minute Man, swinging a cutlass. The brawl, known as the "Astor Palace Riot," left four dead and 134 people wounded and landed Buntline in prison. He was eventually freed, but Buntline's party failed, and he was saved by the tumultuous start of the Civil War.

Buntline enlisted in the Union Army, rose to the rank of corporal, but was soon demoted, and eventually discharged in 1864 for drunkenness. But the former corporal purchased a colonel's uniform, had the famous Matthew Brady take his photograph in it, and soon there-after, he was known as "Colonel Ned Buntline." Back in New York, he lost everything and his friends all deserted him. He decided to go west, to California.

On the way, he heard about the Major Frank North killing of Tall Bull, a renegade Sioux chief, and since it also involved a white woman with the Indians, it fueled his imagination again, and he went to Fort McPherson to meet Major North and get permission to write a dime

Hugh O'Brien wearing the special holster set that carried the Buntline on his right and his standard six-gun on the left, gets ready to "shoot it out" as Wyatt Earp.

Leslie-Henry small-frame Wyatt Earp with amber grips.

Leslie-Henry Wyatt Earp 9-inch model, with cameo grips.

Leslie-Henry Wyatt Earp, long barrel and standard model.

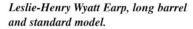

Above: Leslie-Henry Canadian-made Wyatt Earp with long barrel.

Close-up of detail showing the longhorn cameo insert of the Canadian-made Wyatt Earp long barrel model. Seldom seen.

novel about him as the hero, killing the renegade chief with a white woman. Major North refused, but he suggested that Buntline meet William F. Cody, known as "Buffalo Bill," one of his scouts. Buntline met Cody, fed his ever-turning wheels of imagination and returned East to write his first *Wild West Dime Novel.* It was August 1869.

By December 1869, Buntline got the New York Weekly to publish the first of his serial stories called *Buffalo Bill, King of the Border Men,* along with the subtitle "The Wildest and Truest Story I Ever Wrote." When the copies reached Fort McPherson in Nebraska, even Cody himself was surprised that he had become the "greatest Indian fighter of the West." The Buntline serial continued for weeks, with the *New York Weekly* running off more than 200,000 dime novels a week and the Buffalo Bill story of the killing of Tall Bull sold more than a million copies. It wasn't until three years later that Buntline met Cody again and along with Cody's partner, a fellow scout and guide named Texas Jack, organized the play *Scout of The Plains.* Panned by the critics, the audiences went wild; it played to full houses and soon went on to St. Louis. Cody proved to be a natural actor and his ability to ad lib, his colorful outfits, and stage presence made him one of the greatest American showmen of all time.

In 1876, Col. Ned Buntline attended the Philadelphia Centennial and first laid his eyes on the Colt 12-inch barreled .45. Colt reportedly made 30 of these, which came with an adjustable stock and a special holster. Buntline saw they retailed for $26, and ever the eccentric rogue, bought five of them. He reportedly kept one for himself. The other four he then presented, with considerable fanfare, to four prominent frontier lawmen—Neal Brown, Bill Tilghman, Bat Masterson, and Wyatt Earp, all in Dodge City. Not all the lawmen cared for this very strange gun, heavy and cumbersome. After the flamboyant little colonel left, Bill Tilghman and Bat Masterson reportedly cut the barrels down to eight inches. Wyatt kept his intact. It came in a black Colt factory finish, had a 12-inch barrel and reportedly had a brass shield with "NED" on one side of the walnut grip, and the recipient's name on the left side of the grip.

Ned Buntline had more heroes to write about after spending a week in Dodge City with all the illustrious lawmen. It is believed that Wyatt's Buntline was lost in the Yukon when a friend dropped it overboard. Bat Masterson's and Bill Tilghman's Buntline are believed to be in the hands of collectors who obtained them after their deaths. No information was found on what happened to Neal Brown's Buntline Special.

Col. Ned Buntline continued to write novels, stories, hymns, and serials, and retired back to his home in Stamford, New York. On July 16, 1886, this bombastic rogue, raconteur, and drunken Casanova, who gave us the most distorted picture of the Wild West, died of a heart attack. In 1952, a book on his life was published called *The Great Rascal* by James Monaghan. And now, you see, the Buntline Special takes on a whole new meaning for us collectors!

CAP GUN COLLECTIBLES

The toy gun companies began to churn out Wyatt Earp cap pistols by the millions, and for us collectors of today, there is no shortage of toy gun companies and Wyatt Earp guns in many sizes and shapes, with both long and short barrels, as well as the Buntline models, since no less than ten companies all made the Wyatt Earp cap guns, and more if you count the plastic clickers. One could

Schmidt Wyatt Earp in engraved nickel with copper Marshal steerhead grips. Note raised name-style on frame. Seldom-seen cap shooter.

Hubley's two Wyatt Earp models—the Buntline long barrel model (top) and the standard 9 inch model (below), both with purple swirl grips.

simply amass a large and worthwhile collection of just Wyatt Earp cap pistols. When you also add all the patterns of each manufacturer, the number swells to over 20 models. By far, the Wyatt Earp was the most popular mass-produced cap pistol in terms of quantity by manufaturers, and by patterns and models.

Let's start with the Leslie-Henry models. They made the 7-inch models with the extensive engraving, raised name within the lasso around the rearing pony's neck, and with the checkered section horse head grips in off white, amber, and black. The opening lever is on the right side of the hammer and breaks from the top for cap loading.

Leslie-Henry also made the standard 9-inch model. Nickel plated with a variety of grips, we have the standard horse head type in various colors as well as the popular cameo insert models. "Wyatt Earp" is raised on the frame without the lasso around the larger rearing horse. The lever is the large type of the left side.

Leslie-Henry made the 9-inch model with the long barrel, for a total of 10 inches. Identical in design to the 9-inch model, this model was nickel plated. The grips came in white horse head as well as the cameo insert models. There is also the Canadian manufactured ones which have, in contrast to the American-made cameo ones, a long-horn on both sides of the cameo insert. The American cameo models all seem to have the four leaf clover, entwined horseshoes, and the six-point star variations. The Canadian ones also have the special inset screw. Thus, in total, this gives a minimum of three Leslie-Henry models of the Wyatt Earp, and this is not counting variation grips.

George Schmidt made two patterns of the Wyatt Earp, both being the 10-inch size. The first is in high-polished nickel with ribbed barrel and checkered copper grips. "Wyatt Earp" is raised on the rather plain frame with the roped border. The opening lever is on the left side of the hammer. The other pattern is richly engraved on barrel, frame, and cylinder and comes with the usually seen Leslie-Henry-style copper grips with the raised steerhead and "Marshal" title. It's certainly possible Schmidt made these for the Canadian market, since they were carried in the 1959-1960 Nerlich & Company Christmas catalogs. Both models have the ribbed barrel, and break open from the top, with the lever on the left side of the hammer. Both are rather scarce and seldom seen. No small models of the Schmidt Wyatt Earp have surfaced to date. Thus, Schmidt gives us two distinct models of the Wyatt Earp.

Hubley made two models of the Wyatt Earp. The first is the 9-inch, nickel-plated model, which is the same pattern as Hubley's popular Western model. This has a plain frame and breaks open by friction, from the top. "Wyatt Earp" is raised within a roped oval frame on both sides of the frame

Hubley Wyatt Earp single holster set with Buntline with turquoise grips. Note Hubley pony medallion and "Wyatt Earp" across holster pocket strap.

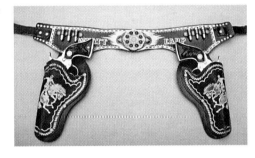

Hubley Wyatt Earp double holster set with 9-inch cap guns. Name on belt.

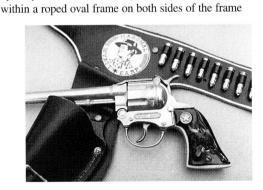

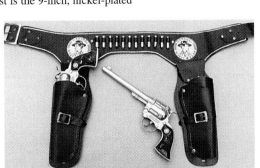

Left: Close-up of details showing Hugh O'Brien's image as "Marshal Wyatt Earp" on gunbelt and spectacular purple swirl grips on the cap pistol.

Hubley Wyatt Earp double holster set with Buntline cap shooters on black gunslinger-type holsters. Note graphics on belt and 12 bullets! Super!

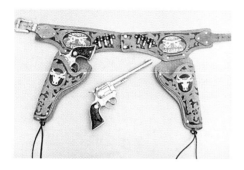

A super colorful Wyatt Earp double holster set with Hubley Buntlines. Note the basket weave underlay of the holster pockets, steerhead logo, and name on belt.

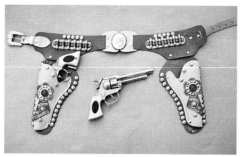

Leslie-Henry double holster set with 9-inch cap shooters. Note the exceptional amount of studs on this Wyatt Earp set, marked on the holster pockets.

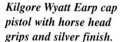

Kilgore Wyatt Earp cap pistol with horse head grips and silver finish.

Kilgore super Wyatt Earp double holster set with Kilgore guns, wrist cuffs, and spurs. White pockets and details. Possibly intended for a cowgirl. Seldom seen.

Above: Esquire-Actoy Wyatt Earp models—Buntline Special, simulated stag grips (top left); large frame model with simulated stag grips (top right); large frame model with federal grips (center); small frame model with simulated stag grips (bottom).

Right: Esquire-Actoy Wyatt Earp models—top shows both Buntline Specials in nickle and bronze; lower shows the large-frame model with federal grips, and the small-frame model with white simulated stag grips. A collection all by themselves!

under the cylinder. The grips came in a beautiful purple swirl and have the raised steerhead design. The Hubley star logo is on the grips. The second model is the Hubley Wyatt Earp Buntline Special model, which was basically the same 9-inch model, but with a 5-inch barrel, for a total length of 10 inches. Also nickel plated, this model has been found with the purple swirl grips and turquoise grips, possibly for a cowgirl. Thus, we have two Hubley models of the Wyatt Earp. The Hubley Buntline is not marked "Buntline Special."

Service Manufacturing of Yonkers, New York, and the Long Island Die Casting Company both made Wyatt Earp guns in both the short and Buntline patterns. These two models are nearly identical to the Hubley Wyatt Earp, and were made under contract. The Service Manufacturing model is marked to Service Manufacturing and is identical to the Hubley, except for a slightly smaller hammer. It even has the Hubley star logo on the same steerhead grips, usually found in white, turquoise, or brown.

The Long Island Die Casting model comes with a highly-scrolled barrel, and is identical to the Long Island Texas model. Like the Service Manufacturing model, it is also 9 inches long and nickel plated, and comes with the same spear head grips in white, brown, and turquoise. The logo is a large "T" on the grips. Both guns open by friction pressure on the barrel. The back of the cap box is marked to the "Long Island Die Casting, Inc.," giving its full address in Inwood, L.I., N.Y. The Long Island Wyatt Earp model is the only one with a scrolled barrel. This gives us at least three more Wyatt Earp cap guns.

Kilgore made one Wyatt Earp cap pistol in its 9-inch pattern, using the Roy Rogers model cap gun. With the same upside down horse head design, the Kilgore has "Wyatt Earp" raised only on the left side of the frame, and the right side has the Circle "K" logo. Cleverly, Kilgore carefully filled in and blotted out the "RR" and "DE" branding iron markings found on the highly decorative barrel of the Roy Rogers model. No doubt they realized the popularity of Wyatt Earp and decided to cash in on it. The Kilgore Wyatt Earp came in both the nickel and gold flash finishes, and with the off-white light swirl grips. The gun breaks open by friction pressure on the barrel. The Circle "K" is also found on the barrel. The Kilgore Wyatt Earp is seldom seen. Thus, Kilgore made one model of the Wyatt Earp.

Esquire-Actoy of New Jersey made the highest number of the Wyatt Earp. Beginning with its 8-inch model, it was nickel plated, with simulated stag grips, lanyard ring, and Actoy pony medallion on the grips. It has "Wyatt Earp" raised on both sides of the frame, breaks open from the top for cap loading, and has barrel scrolling and light frame and cylinder designs. The same model was used for the Esquire Rin Tin Tin, Johnny Ringo, and others.

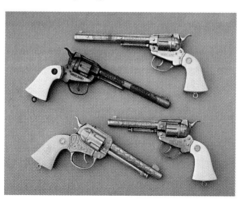

Esquire made the large-frame Wyatt Earp, which has the deeply-engraved frame, extensive barrel scrollwork, and is the 9-inch model. As we know, Esquire used this model for the large Restless Gun and Lone Ranger character guns. Esquire made three sets of grips for this large-frame model. These are the white simulated stag, the dark stag, and the so-called federal grips, with its checkered design, the raised shield, and border made up of stars. This is the scarcest of the three grip variations. All three came with the lanyard ring under the gun butt.

Esquire made the "Buntline Special" in two patterns. Both are 11 inches long, and both came with the simulated stag grips and the lanyard ring. Deeply engraved into the barrel design in raised marking is "Buntline Special" on both sides of the barrel, and "Wyatt Earp" on both sides of the frame. This big gun came in both nickel and antique bronze finish. The grips are found in both black stag and white simulated stag. Thus, Esquire made three Wyatt Earp cap pistols, which includes the Buntline Special, and they made them in finish and grip variations totaling eight guns.

The Young Premium Company of California made the Wyatt Earp Buntline Special model that Proctor & Gamble used in its Gleem toothpaste promotion. Ironically, this Buntline Special is almost an identical replica of the real Buntline Special. At 18 inches, in black plastic clicker-style, it has the "signature" of Wyatt Earp on the right side of the grips, and "Buntline Special" on the left side of the grips. The molded engraving of the frame and the grips are identical to the Buntline Special that Colt made for Ned Buntline. Young Premium also made a black vinyl plastic holster for this long toy gun. This is the longest of all the Buntline Specials.

The Haig Manufacturing Company of Alhambra, California, made a Buntline Special that it called "The New Western Haig Pistol." At 13 inches, this extremely well-made, all-plastic gun came with a target, lead pellets, and a complete instruction manual on how to become an expert "pistol shooter," with instructions on the position of your feet, legs, arms, body, and head. It also gave you tips of breathing, squeezing the trigger, and of course, aiming. It also was very strict about gun safety.

Although the Western Haig is not marked "Buntline Special," its size and almost accurate copy of the Colt Buntline is unmistakable. While both the Young Premium Buntline and the Haig Buntline are fragile guns, no collector of Wyatt Earp and Buntline Specials should be without them as good representative pieces. The Haig sold for just $3, and for another $1, they would send you 1,500 lead "bullets" and single caps. The #6 "chilled shot" lead pellet could be "used over and over again. A great gun you can really use for target shooting and learning how to become a "fast draw" gunfighter!"

Louis Marx made a Wyatt Earp Special prototype plastic and metal die works which is very attractive. It is 11 inches long, with a black plastic barrel and frame. The orange grips have the raised and beautifully sculptured steer head on the left side, and the horse head on the right side. The logo on the grips, in black, has "Marx" on it. The right side of the barrel has "Wyatt Earp Special" in white lettering calligraphy. The hammer and trigger are in gray die-cast metal. This was made at the Erie, Pennsylvania, plant and is quite scarce.

And now we go overseas, since Wyatt Earp was extremely popular in England, and all three of the most prestigious toy gun companies rolled out cap guns honoring Wyatt Earp and the Buntline Special. Once again, several models exist. Thus, even collecting just the British models can make a substantial collection all its own.

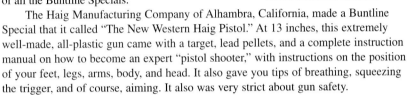

Esquire's Wyatt Earp Buntline Specials in bronze and nickel finish.

Left: Close-up showing details on Buntline barrel and name on frame.

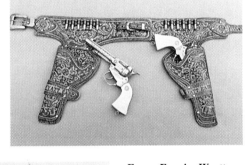

Fancy Esquire Wyatt Earp double holster set with 8-inch model cap guns. Note superior tooling on the entire holster set and waist tightening belt on back of gunbelt.

Super Wyatt Earp gunfighter set by Esquire with extension-laced holsters to accomodate the Buntline and standard model cap guns, just like what Hugh O'Brien wore on the show. Note these two particular Actoy models are full stag grips!

Left: Young Premium Gleem promotional Buntline Special, the longest of them all.

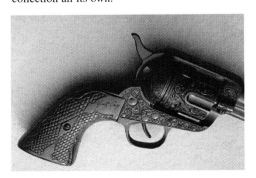

Left: Close-up of details showing Wyatt's signature on grips. Almost identical gun to the real Buntline Special. What a toy!

Right: Marx Wyatt Earp Special long barrel prototype with calligraphy name on barrel, and beautifully molded horse head grips. Die-cast parts. Very scarce.

Haig's Western Buntline Special complete with original shipping box, target, lead pellets, and instruction booklet. Seldom-seen all complete.

British Crescent Toys Buntline Special with original box. Note details and reference to Wyatt Earp's time frame in Dodge City. Seldom seen.

Close-up of details showing name on frame and galloping rider on grips.

Crescent Toys came out with its Buntline Special in an unusual style. It is a 9-inch, small-framed gun, yet it has a 5-inch barrel. It came in both nickel and black factory finishes. It breaks open from the top for cap loading by friction, which they labeled "auto-snap," marked right on the top of the frame. The barrel is plain, but the frame is highly engraved, and has "Buntline Special" raised on both sides. The grips came in white and red, with a rope design border and with a cowboy riding off on a galloping horse on both sides. Strangely, where the logo is normally located, the black circle has "38" in it.

The box has "Buntline Special" and "Wyatt Earp 1876-1879" on it, along with "Dodge City Marshal." Obviously, they were noting his time in Dodge City. The box has black and orange graphics and shows a young-looking "Wyatt" dressed in the typical Hugh O'Brien duds, drawing his Buntline at a masked outlaw holding a money bag and a six-gun. Both the box and the back of the cap box are marked "Crescent Toys" with the England address. This is a well-made gun with an attractive box.

Lone Star made two models of the Buntline Special. The first model is 10 inches long, with a beautifully-scrolled barrel and frame. The opening lever is on the right side of the hammer. At first glance, this beautifully-nickeled gun resembles a Leslie-Henry, but the horse head raised on the frame and the raised "Bunt-Line" on both sides of the frame quickly confirm it is a Lone Star. The grips are the brown and white stag and have the "notch bar"-raised portion, and close scrutiny confirms the same pattern was used for the Lone Star Maverick, Bat Masterson, and Cowpoke models, all of which were marketed through Carnell Roundup of New York. This gun is beautifully made, of excellent quality, and a great piece of Wyatt Earp memorabilia.

The second Lone Star model is larger and longer than the above 10-inch pattern. This second model is 13 inches long, and came in both factory black and nickel plate. This model has a 9-inch barrel, while the above model has a 5-inch barrel. The barrel is plain but the frame is highly engraved. This model has "Buntline" on both sides of the frame as opposed to "Bunt- Line" of the above pattern. This model also carries "Lone Star" on a rocker panel just behind the cylinder on both sides. This model came with beautiful horse head grips which are highly sculptured, and are found in white, red, and brown. The horse head looks downward, with excellent detail of the teeth. The five-pointed star logo is on the grips in black. The sights are the same on both models, as are the ejector rods. The side lever is also the same.

The box for this model has exceptional color graphics, showing Wyatt Earp on horseback blasting away at three outlaws. The box on this model is marked "Wyatt Earp U.S. Marshal Buntline Special" and "100 shot repeater cap gun." It also sports "extra long barrel," which would indicate this was the "new" second model, longer and more up to date, with the correct spelling of "Buntline." The inside of the cap box is stamped "A Lone Star product, Made in England." The box carries the Lone Star address of Palmers Green, London, and D.C.M.T. for "Die Cast Metal Toys." This is a beautifully made, quality Buntline Special.

The final Buntline Special highlighted here is one of the finest cap guns ever made. This is the British Cast Metals (BCM) model. At just under 14 inches long, it is the largest and longest of all the Buntline Specials, except for the 18-inch "Young Premium" plastic model. As a cap firing repeater, however, this is the longest, and like its Lone Star cousin, it is a quality piece. This model is also the only known Buntline

Lone Star Buntline Special with notch bar grips in brown and white stag. Note on this model, the Brits spelled it "Bunt-Line." Note horse head logo on frame.

Lone Star second model Buntline Special with its original box with super color graphics marked to both Wyatt Earp and Buntline Special. Seldom seen complete.

with a revolving cylinder. It has the opening for the side gate on the left side, up on the barrel, and opens similarly, but not identical, to the Leslie-Henry "44" models. The factory black finish comes on a plain barrel and frame. The left side of the frame, because of the side gate assembly, has "Buntline" to the front of the frame, and "Special" just behind the cylinder. The right side has "Buntline Special" beginning on a rocker panel from the back of the cylinder and ending up under the cylinder itself on the frame. The logo of the BCM appears to be an Indian-style "thunderbird." The most astounding feature of this Buntline are the grips. They sport a highly sculptured Indian chief with a full headdress, and the detail of the feathering beats anything your scribe has ever seen on American guns.

Equally interesting is the box for this Buntline. An off-white plain box with red lettering, it has "The Outlaw" and "The Buntline Special." On the sides it has, "A Replica of the famous gun used by U.S. Marshal Wyatt Earp." Leave it to the Brits to have such strange and interesting descriptions. The flaps of the box are marked to "BCM." This is one Wyatt Earp Buntline Special no collector should be without! While all of the Lone Star Wyatt Earps and Buntline Specials are fairly scarce, the "hunt" for these models makes it all worthwhile. After all, it's the "hunt" that fuels a collector's passion and satisfaction.

The holsters for the Wyatt Earp cap pistols and Buntline models are just as numerous in both quantity and style as are the Roy Rogers and Gene Autry models. Hubley made Wyatt Earp holsters in single and double sets, for boys and girls. Carnell Roundup made single and double holsters for the Lone Star Buntline models. Esquire, Halco, and Hubley made a variety of sets that carried graphics of Hugh O'Brien as "Wyatt Earp," as well as all types of Wyatt Earp titles in tooling, silk screen, on the holster straps, belt itself, pockets, vertical as well as horizontal, and in a never-ending array of studs, conchos, jewels, buckles, horse heads, and fringe. Sets came with and without wrist cuffs, spurs, and U.S. Marshal star badges for the youngster to emulate his hero. One set made by Esquire came with one Buntline model and one standard 9-inch model, and with adjustments on the holsters themselves, so that both models could be raised or lowered for the kid's arm length.

On some of the episodes, Hugh O'Brien wore a special holster when he would carry both the Buntline and his standard six-shooter, and thus Esquire used that to market its set of both model guns in adjustable holsters. The Wyatt Earp holsters, for both boys and girls are practically infinite, and some of the most attractive and most popular are represented here. Boxed sets also carried colorful images of Hugh O'Brien as "Wyatt Earp." For some reason, even with the immense popularity of Wyatt Earp, no rifles or shotguns have surfaced with "Wyatt Earp" markings. It's obvious our frontier marshal was a two-gun man! No guns marked "Doc Holliday" or "Shotgun Gibbs" have ever surfaced. Other than "Johnny Ringo" and "Billy the Kid"-marked guns, none of the other well-known outlaws that roamed our American West have surfaced to date.

There is little doubt that *The Life and Legend of Wyatt Earp* will continue for years to come. The impact that Wyatt Earp made on our western history cannot be ignored. Hero or rogue, he'll be honored by western buffs and much maligned by revisionists. Let's put him back to rest with the words of Attorney William J. Hunsaker, Dean of the Los Angeles Bar, and one of the pallbearer's at Wyatt Earp's funeral in 1928:

"He was a quiet, but absolutely fearless man; as a peace officer, above reproach. He usually went about in his shirt sleeves and wore no weapons. He was cool and never excited, but very determined and courageous. He never stirred up trouble, but he never ran away from it or shirked responsibility. He was an ideal peace officer and a fine citizen." Amen.

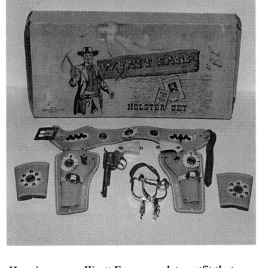

Here is a super Wyatt Earp complete outfit that includes double holsters with Actoy large frame guns with federal grips, with matching cuffs and spurs. The box cover confirms that Service Merchandising Company of New York used Actoy guns in these sets. "Wyatt Earp" is stamped vertically on the sides of the holster pockets in white details. A fabulous outfit for any youngster! (Courtesy of Terry Graham)

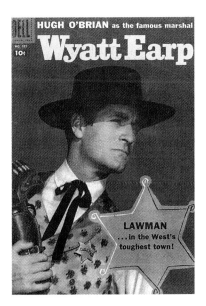

One of several Dell Comics issued for Wyatt Earp.

Left: BCM-British Cast Metal's The Outlaw Buntline Special with its original box, also named to "Wyatt Earp." One of the finest cap guns made, seldom seen.

Left: Close-up of superb Indian chief with full headdress on grips, name on frame, and BCM "thunderbird" logo on grip. This variation has a red and white marbelized grip.

ZORRO

Guy Williams as "Zorro"—the best-loved and most-remembered of all the big screen and television actors who portrayed the masked crusader.

Advertisement for **The Ghost of Zorro** Republic picture serials starring another future masked man, Clayton Moore. Ironically, actor George J. Lewis was cast as "Don Diego's" father in the TV series of **Zorro** several years later.

As we come to the final section of this book, I hope the reader trusts me enough to do the following: Tell your wife, kids, significant other, to be quiet; stop banging pots and pans. Shut off the boob tube, there's not much worth watching anyway. Tell everyone that you don't want to be disturbed. Put the dog and the cat out. Throw a cover over the canary and turn off the filter on the fish tank. Shut off the phones, faxes, and answering machines. Retire to your room and get on your bed. Lie on your back. Turn off all the lights. Go to the memory file in your brain and bring yourself back to October 10, 1957. Relax. Ready?

> "Out of the night, when the full moon is bright,
> comes the horseman known as Zorro;
> This bold renegade carves a "Z" with his blade;
> a "Z" that stands for "Zorro."
> Zorro, the fox so cunning and free; Zorro,
> who makes the sign of the "Z"
> Zorro! Zorro! Zorro! Zorro!"

And this brings a smile to your lips, as you fondly recall the memories of your youth, sitting down every Thursday evening, from 8:00 to 8:30 p.m., as you watch your masked and caped hero on his thundering black stallion, "Tornado," crusade against injustice in old California. "Zorro" wears a mask, but more importantly, he leaves a special mark to serve as a reminder that he will return every time power and tyranny reign against the poor people, the innocent people, and the hard working peasants in 1820s California. He leaves a "Z," which stands for his name—Zorro!

But Zorro, like "The Lone Ranger," that other masked man fighting for justice, goes back much further than 1957. Zorro captured the attention of America, and soon, the rest of the world. It was inevitable that Hollywood would take notice, because movies, serials, and no less than three television programs were telecast on Zorro. Zorro came into the 1990s just as strong as ever. We'll get back to the current phenomenon of Zorro a bit later.

Zorro was created in 1919 by a writer named Johnston McCully for his novel, which was a series entitled *The Curse of Capistrano.* This was the first installment in a series that peaked to 65 very popular episodes of the swashbuckling hero fighting for the downtrodden of early Los Angeles, Monterey, and other areas of old California. Some film historians claim that George Trendle, the creator of "The Lone Ranger," was such an avid fan of Zorro, that he loosely based his own creation on him, but of course, placed him in the Old West, proving that not much had changed in the fight for injustice from 1820 to 1870.

The following year, 1920, an adaptation of *The Curse of Capistrano* was made into the first movie about our hero titled *The Mark of Zorro* starring Douglas Fairbanks, which remains to this day, one of the all-time classics of the silent screen. Douglas Fairbanks returned as Zorro in "Don Q., Son of Zorro" also a silent film in 1925. When Johnson McCully wrote his book, *The Mark of Zorro,* based on his serial, *The Curse of Capistrano,* he dedicated his book to none other than Douglas Fairbanks, who brought Zorro to life on the screen.

In 1940, Tyrone Power starred, along with Basil Rathbone, in a remake of *The Mark of Zorro* complete with sound and fury, and it became one of Tyrone Power's finest screen roles for which he is still remembered. His fencing master was Fred Cavens, who had also trained Fairbanks in the silent Zorro films. Both Fairbanks and Power became avid fencers.

In 1937, Republic Pictures' first color film brought Zorro to the big screen in *The Bold Caballero,* starring Robert Livingston, who ironically, later starred as the "Lone Ranger." This turned out to be a 12 chapter serial as *Zorro Rides Again,* with the role going to actor John Carroll. The serial was so popular that Republic ordered eight more Zorro serials that lasted another five years, well into 1942, even as the Tyrone Power classic was released.

In 1939, actor Reed Hadley (Radio's "Red Ryder") starred in *Zorro's Fighting Legion.* This was followed by the a short serial in 1944 with Linda Sterling as *Zorro's Black Whip.* In 1949, Clayton Moore starred as "Zorro" in *The Ghost of Zorro.* There is no escaping the connection between "Zorro" and "The Long Ranger." No doubt that seeing Clayton Moore in his Zorro outfit left a serious impression on George Trendle. The movie, *The Ghost of Zorro,* which initially had been a serial venture, returned as a feature film in 1959 starring Clayton Moore. Zorro quickly became very popular in Europe.

In 1957, Walt Disney took on the task of finding an actor to portray Zorro for his television series. It was Thursday, April 18, 1957, when Guy Williams, probably one of the most handsome actors ever to don the mask and cape, arrived at Disney's Burbank studios for a screen test. It was certainly Guy Williams' luckiest day, as he was signed on to an exclusive contract to star as "Zorro" to betelecast on ABC-TV. It was soon to be a challenge for the young Williams, trying to step into the black boots already worn by two of Hollywood's greatest actors, Douglas Fairbanks and Tyrone Power.

Guy Williams was truly an unknown actor in 1952. The son of Italian immigrants, his real name was Armando Catalano. Born and raised in New York City, Catalano was a 6'3" Italian-American with drop-dead good looks. He attended George Washington High School and later went on to the Peekskill Military Academy. He soon landed modeling roles, even though his father, an insurance broker, wanted him to go into the brokerage business. Catalano met model Janice Cooper and they soon married.

Interviewed by Hollywood coach Sophie Rosenstein, he was already acting in New York's Neighborhood Theater, and also on early television's *Studio One* in small roles. Changing his name to Guy Williams, he went out to the West Coast and did a few relatively obscure movies, such as *Bonzo Goes to College* in 1952, and *Mississippi Gambler* in 1953, followed by *Last Frontier* in 1955. That same year, he starred in *Seven Angry Men* and *Sincerely Yours*. He also had a part in *I Was a Teenage Werewolf* in 1957.

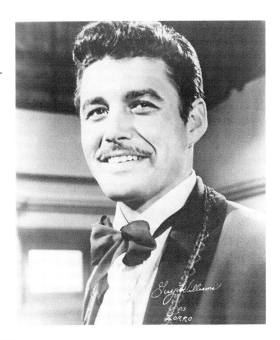

Zorro unmasked? No, it's Guy Williams as "Don Diego de la Vega," known only to his faithful servant, "Bernardo" that he is one and the same. . .Zorro!

Left: Zorro rides on his white horse "Phantom" to help the downtrodden. Look at that killer smile!

Director Norman Foster, who had already achieved fame in directing Fess Parker in *Disney's Davy Crockett,* saw Williams was bound for instant stardom and he was right. He was, in no understatement, an overnight success as the foppish "Don Diego de la Vega" by day and "Zorro" by night. Williams plunged into the role, learning to play the guitar from Vincente Gomez, who had tutored dozens of stars on the romantic instrument. Fred Cavens, the Belgian-born fencing master who had already trained the two previous Zorros, Douglas Fairbanks and Tyrone Power, was called in to train Williams. But his father had already been an avid fencer in Italy and he had interested his son in the sport, so fencing soon came easily to Williams. With riding lessons and the romantic Latin look, complete with sideburns and a thin

moustache, Williams became the best remembered Zorro of all time, then and now.

Walt Disney's *Zorro* was a huge hit, with youngsters and adults alike, almost immediately. In the television *Zorro,* the series was set in Spanish California. It was set in the 1820s. "Don Alejandro de la Vega," played by veteran actor George J. Lewis, is a wealthy landowner. His son is "Don Diego de la Vega," who has been sent to Spain to be royally educated. In the meantime, "Capitano Monastario," a ruthless army officer, becomes the Commandante of the Fortress de Los Angeles, imposing martial law, over-taxing the landowners, and brutalizing the peasants.

The part of Capitano Monastario went to another handsome actor, Britt Lomond, himself a very good fencer. Rounding out his soldiers was the bumbling and portly "Sergeant Garcia," played by character actor Henry Calvin, with a grizzled unshaven face and drooping moustache. His assistant was "Corporal Reyes," played by Don Diamond, who had previously been "El Toro," the sidekick to Bill Williams, in the *Kit Carson* series.

Unable to deal with Capitan Monastario, Don Alejandro sends for his son to return to California from Spain, hoping that young blood will be able to organize an uprising to wrench control from the evil Commandante. Diego returns, of course, and with him comes his faithful mute man-servant, Bernardo, played by character actor Gene Sheldon, who added moments of both humor and serious business as he follows his master's orders to the letter with total loyalty.

Don Diego soon analyzes the situation and pretends to be a lazy, foolish, aristocrat who is more interested in music and poetry. He appears to be generally

The cast of Zorro, *from left to right, Juan Botta; Duncan Regehr as "Zorro," Henry Darrow, James Victor; sitting is Patrice Cambi and Michael Tylo, 1990-1993. (Courtesy of Old West Shop)*

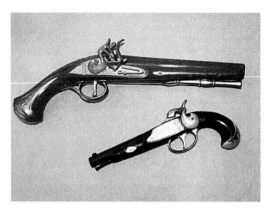

Marx flintlock cap shooter and percussion cap shooter, plastic and die-cast works, marketed on Zorro cards numbered #131Z and #133Z.

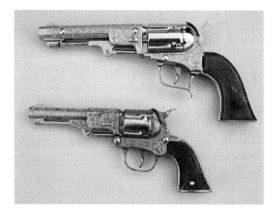

Hubley Pioneer (top), and Hubley Coyote, (below), both sold with Zorro sets marketed by Daisy as well as Hubley.

Daisy Zorro holster set with Hubley Coyote cap pistol, all-metal, nickel-plated cap repeater. Note the Walt Disney official trademark on belt and wrist cuff.

unconcerned with the plight of the people and he certainly doesn't want to have a confrontation with Capitano Monastario. But the young and clever Diego reveals to his faithful servant, Bernardo, that he has devised a plan to battle the ruthless Commandante and his men. By day, he will continue his act as Don Diego, much to his father's dismay and disappointment at seeing his son appear so cowardly—more interested in books than fighting like a man.

By night, however, he will become the swashbuckling, black-caped, black-garbed, and black-masked champion of justice. He tells Bernardo that only he will know his secret and he must never let anyone catch on, not even his father. With his choice of weapons to include a gleaming rapier-type sword, bullwhip, and a flintlock mounted on his horse, Don Diego takes the name of "Zorro"—the "fox" in Spanish. This will remain his secret identity. He shows Bernardo an underground cavern where he will keep his two horses, a black steed named "Tornado" and a white steed named "Phantom." Bernardo will take care of both of them and move them, when needed, to various locations to keep the already bewildered soldiers at the garrison in an even more state of confusion.

Don Diego also instructs Bernardo that in order for him to aid in eavesdropping for his master, he will pretend he is deaf as well as mute, and Bernardo agrees, of course. Only Don Diego will know this additional secret, which is also kept from Don Alejandro. At times, it actually pains Diego that his father seems to be totally frustrated and exasperated with his son's almost cowardly actions, especially when Monastario confronts Don Alejandro and other landowners, and this makes the father ashamed of what his son has become.

At night, however, with his sword gleaming, and on his magnificent Tornado, or Phantom, the champion of the oppressed, with a handsome smile and cool daring antics, soon proves that he is more than a match for Monastario and his entire command, aided by the fact, of course, that most of the soldiers are incompetent. Zorro begins to foil all the schemes that Monastario comes up with, and in so doing, at the end of each episode, he leaves his unmistakable mark—a "Z" which he carves where convenient at the moment—the side of an adobe wall, the fortress gates, even across fumbling Sergeant Garcia's uniform, snapping the buttons, or tearing the trousers across his fat belly. Zorro never kills anyone; rather he disarms them, shames them, and wins every sword fight, leaving his mark as he escapes into the night, ready to return for another show of his clever, fox-like acts of daring. It was pure adventure, thrills, humor, and romance.

The *Zorro* series was such a hit with youngsters that Zorro products, costumes, hats, masks, bullwhips, and plastic swords were the rage for two years. The weekly episodes at times ran almost like a serial, much like the original intent of *Zorro.* The episode ended with Zorro riding on his horse at thundering speed, coming up to a huge cliff or canyon and turning back to see his group of followers, he makes a mad dash, clears the cliff, as he rears his horse, waves at his astounded enemies, and rides off, only to be continued the following week. Zorro's distinct smile became almost too much to bear for the women, and several beautiful actresses were cast as available love interests, but Don Diego and Zorro remained free and cunning, dedicated only to righting wrongs and removing the yoke of oppression from the poor people of the Pueblo de Los Angeles.

Many guest stars graced the episodes of *Zorro,* including Annette Funicello, Gloria Talbot, Lisa Gay, veteran character actor Gilbert Roland (no slouch himself when it came to romantic scenes or sword fighting), Ross Martin (*Wild Wild West),* John Dehner *(The Westerner),* Richard Anderson, and Eduard Franz. The theme song of Zorro became a hit parade favorite in 1958. Ironically, it was first recorded by Henry Calvin, the fat Sergeant Garcia. The hit version was sung by a pop group, the Chordettes. *Zorro* was last telecast on September 24, 1959, after a total of 117 episodes.

After the television run of *Zorro,* Guy Williams portrayed Zorro in two movies, *The Sign of Zorro* in 1960, and *Zorro the Avenger* in 1961. Guy Williams went on to star in *Lost in Space* from 1965 to 1968, along with Mark Goddard *(Johnny Ringo)* and June Lockhart, who had previously starred in *Lassie.* Although this proved to be a popular science fiction show, Guy Williams will always be remembered as Zorro. Guy Williams also made another movie for Disney in 1962 titled *Damon and Pythias,* and in 1963 he starred in *Captain Sinbad,* another swashbuckling role. Sadly, Guy Williams passed away in May 1989, at the relatively young age of 65, while in Argentina. Gene Sheldon, who played Bernardo, died in 1982.

But Zorro did not die so quickly, any more than he has since the 1920s. Ever popular in Italy, Spain, and France, a number of Zorro movies were made in joint Italian-French ventures. Several American and European actors took on the role. Sean Flynn, the son of Errol Flynn played Zorro in the 1962 movie *The Sign of Zorro. The Shadow of Zorro,* also in 1962, cast Frank Latimer in the role. In 1963, it was Pierre Brice in *Zorro Versus Maciste,* a French-Italian production. George Ardisson portrayed Zorro in the 1963 movie, *Zorro at the Court of Spain.* Gordon Scott, who starred in Tarzan movies, played Zorro in the Italian-French movie, *Zorro and the Three Musketeers* in 1963.

The 1970s brought Zorro to the screen in the most notable film in Europe under the same title, *Zorro,* starring Alain Delon. In 1974, actor Frank Langella portrayed the masked hero in *The Mark of Zorro* for U.S. television.

The 1980s brought us the animated series, *The New Adventures of Zorro,* on CBS Saturday mornings from 1981 to 1983. In 1981, suave George Hamilton was cast in a spoof of Zorro in the feature film *Zorro, the Gay Blade,* in which he played a dual role. This led to another spoof of Zorro on television in the series *Zorro and Son,* starring Henry Darrow ("Manuelito" from *The High Chaparral)* in the title role. This aired from April to June of 1983, being canceled after only nine episodes. Comedian Bill Dana *(The Steve Allen Show)* played "Bernardo," and "Comandante Paco Pico" was played by Gregory Sierra (one of *Barney Miller's* detectives).

Zorro and Son was full of poor jokes and plays on words. In it, the original Zorro, now 25 years older, was injured trying to do his brave antics. Bernardo sends for his son, Don Carlos, from Spain to come and aid his father, but he was a swinger who refused to give up gambling, wine, women, and song. The young son was played by Paul Regina. Ironically, this *Zorro and Son* series was a Disney venture, shot on the same lot as the Guy Williams series, but this did not go over well with the viewers, who no doubt recalled the 1957-1959 *Zorro* with great fondness and nostalgia.

Zorro returned with a vengeance on the Family Channel in Zorro, starring Duncan Regehr in the title role. Filmed in Spain, this was a joint U.S.-French-Italian production released by New World TV, Ellipse of France, and RAI of Italy. Zorro returned to its more serious format. It is shown in more than 50 countries. Cast as Zorro's aging father, "Don Alejandro," initially was Efrem Zimbalist, Jr. *(FBI)* but was soon replaced by Henry Darrow, who had played the aging Zorro in the *Zorro and Son* spoof. This new Zorro premiered on January 5, 1990, and ran to 1993 for a total of 88 episodes. The deaf-mute man servant in this series is "Felipe," played by Juan Britto. The current dictator is the "Alcalde," played by Michael Tylo. At 6'5", the handsome Duncan Regehr is the tallest of the "Zorros," and he handled a sword quite well, but it's difficult to fill the boots of Guy Williams.

Disney decided to ride Zorro's cape once again, by using state-of-the-art computer colorization of its classic *Zorro* series with Guy Williams, and it is currently being shown on the Disney Channel all over the United States and scores of foreign countries. What keeps Zorro alive? How does he survive each decade? This question spurred a program on the Arts & Entertainment channel that was an interesting, comprehensive, hour-long *History of Zorro* that premiered in June 1996 and is still being shown repeatedly. Zorro is ageless.

Zorro seems to fit into the pantheon of heroes, a multi-dimensional character who is brave, cunning, good-looking, romantic, a master swordsman, a champion of liberty, and defender of the oppressed. As such, he will always be welcome! Zorro also has appeal to youngsters, adults, males, and females. In 1998, *The Mask of Zorro* starring Antonio Banderas in the title role, was released. It will be most interesting to see if the fifth generation of viewers will embrace this new Zorro as it did Guy Williams and the phenomenon that followed.

CAP GUN COLLECTIBLES

The appeal of Zorro was phenomenal, almost another Davy Crockett bonanza, as the image of Guy Williams in both Zorro and Don Diego costumes became instant collectibles. Scores of children's books by Whitman, Big and Little Golden Books, Dell Comics, and Gold Key Comics featured Zorro. Games, coloring books, fencing sets, and school supplies all featured Zorro.

It spread to costumes, lunch boxes, and thermos bottles, and of course, puppets, figures, and figurines in plastic, china, and hard rubber. It seemed that Zorro products never ceased. It was only inevitable that it would soon include cap guns, swords, holsters, bullwhips, even rifles, all of which, of course, came with and without Zorro's mask.

Marx marketed its Davy Crockett and Daniel Boone derringer and flintlock cap guns on Zorro cards. The derringer was the 8-inch black plastic and die-cast works

Hubley single holster set marked to "Zorro" with Hubley Coyote. Note the western-style conchos used on the belt. Hubley Pioneer cap pistol was also used.

Hubley western-style Zorro double holster set with Texan Jr.'s cap pistols. Note "Z" on belt with western buckle, and "Zorro" on holster pockets with fancy fringe. (Courtesy of Jim Lefante)

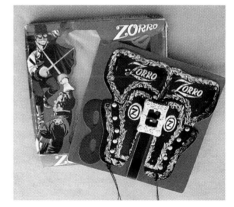

Italian-made Zorro double holster set in western style with fancy gold designs, and mask. Note colorful graphics of Zorro sword fighting on box. Note details on Italian Zorro holster set. Fancy! Note line across "Z." (Courtesy of Mike Cherry)

Extremely rare Daisy Model #961 metal and wooden stock Zorro rifle, which was a well-made "bang and smoke" rifle. The Zorro image on the stock also has the Walt Disney copyright. This is a heavy and well-made rifle. It also carries the 1957 address of Daisy at Plymouth, Michigan. Note the pierced barrel extension and sights. The metal is gun-blue with black-painted stock and silver decal. It is 25 inches in length.

Right: Close-up of the Daisy #961 Zorro rifle in its open and cocked position. The rifle is cocked by firmly pulling downward on the stock. It makes a lound "bang" sound and smoke pours out of the barrel. There is a side hole in the barrel to add oil for the smoke. A super-rare rifle.

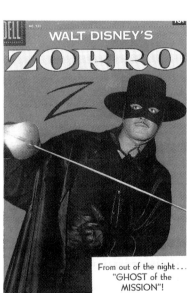

One of several Zorro comics issued by Dell featuring Guy Williams.

percussion-style model that was already carded to both Daniel Boone and Davy Crockett characters. This was followed by its 12-inch plastic and die-cast metal flint-lock pistol, proper for Zorro's time frame, of course, and nearly identical to the one he would occasionally use on the series. Both the derringer and the flintlock are cap firing. Neither is marked "Zorro" on the gun; only the card is marked "Zorro" and shows a black image of the masked hero. It carries the Walt Disney copyright, making it an official Disney product, and a "Z" was added to the Marx inventory order number, #133Z.

Marx also re-introduced its flintlock rifle, which had already been marketed for its Davy Crockett line on a Zorro card that measured a whopping 9 inches by 45 inches, since the flintlock rifle itself, molded plastic with die-cast works, is 35 inches long. It was labeled "Zorro Flintlock Rifle" by Marx. The Marx flintlock rifle is one of the most beautiful cap-firing rifles made, shown in the Davy Crockett section.

Daisy marketed Zorro sets, which included Hubley cap pistols in the early dragoon styles, the Coyote, the 8-inch, all-metal cap repeater, and the Pioneer. The Coyote is extensively engraved, and comes with black, all-metal checkered grips. The bullet ejector is non-functional on the Coyote, but it is perfectly made, identical to an original gun. The Coyote breaks from the top by friction and is marked Hubley on the cap box.

Besides the Daisy boxed sets, Hubley also made both single and double sets for Zorro, with official "Walt Disney" copyright markings on the holsters, which were of quality leather in black-and-white details, with Zorro on his rearing horse, sword in hand. "Zorro" is shown in black and white as it crosses the image of Zorro on his horse. The Zorro holsters have Hubley studs and rivets. The Coyote came only in nickel plating.

It is very interesting that Hubley chose to use the Coyote for its Zorro sets. The coyote, as we know, is a cousin to the fox, and the word "coyote" is spelled and pronounced the same in both Spanish as well as English, and means the same—a small, cunning, western prairie wolf.

Hubley also marketed larger Zorro holster sets, both single and double, using its magnificent Pioneer dragoon model cap pistol. The Pioneer was also extensively engraved, with beautiful caramel swirl grips, and a functioning bullet ejector rod. The Pioneer came in nickel plate only, and is 9 inches in length. This was marketed both by Hubley and in Daisy sets that included a metal rifle, wrist cuffs, and holsters by Hubley. The metal rifle has the Disney copyright along with the Zorro image on the stock, which is made of black wood.

The largest double holster sets marked "Zorro" on western-style belt and pockets came with that reliable standby, Hubley Texan Jr's. All the Zorro holsters sets were mainly black with white details. Some have Western-style conchos, studs, and colored jewels, but the colors are usually black with white or gold details. The belts show very fancy scrollwork around the "Z," and "Zorro" is on the holster pockets vertically. The official Walt Disney models carry the copyright and Guy Williams as either Don Diego or Zorro. The pirated copies, just like the Davy Crockett products, do not.

Several foreign holsters were marketed for Zorro, most notably from Italy, in both single and double sets. These came with and without a Zorro mask. The boxes show great graphics of Zorro, but not the Guy Williams photo images. The foreign Zorro sets do not have Walt Disney trademarks. Additionally, a foreign Zorro set, even if not marked on the box "Made in Italy" or "Fabricado en Espana" will have the typical European "Z" with a line through the center.

It was probably a great loss for other toy cap gun companies such as Leslie-Henry, Schmidt, or Nichols to not come out with a Zorro cap gun or put the name "Zorro" on one of their western guns as they did with the Davy Crockett series. As we know and have seen in the "Davy Crockett" chapter, while Davy was not a western character, most of the cap pistol and cap rifle companies jumped on the financial bandwagon of the highly marketable frontiersman. Even Hubley could have easily added Zorro to its quality line of flintlocks, both single and double barrels, in the large and Flintlock Jr. sizes, but it didn't—and it certainly was their loss then, and a loss now, for us Zorro lovers. It just makes the scarce Zorro guns and holsters that much more desirable.

And now, as Zorro gallops away back into your memory bank, get up, turn on the lights and get back to reality. It was all such a wonderful dream, the memories of growing up in the 1950s. Adios, amigos!

THE MISSING CAP GUNS

As I have stated repeatedly through this book, we can only wonder, 50 years later, why certain TV westerns that were very popular have no guns and why other shows that didn't last very long did. It's strange to look back at the following list of some wonderful TV westerns for which there are no cap guns, or at least, none that have surfaced during the research for this book. Yet, as we have seen through the vivid descriptions throughout this book, some relatively short-lived TV westerns spawned several guns and collectibles. While the list below is not every western show ever telecast, I tried to include those that lasted at least a year, and where perhaps, a toy gun manufacturer would have looked twice at it. Herewith, then, old buckaroos, are some TV westerns you may remember, that unfortunately, have left us no cap guns, rifles, or shotguns to "play with." The "missing cap guns," if you will:

The Alaskans, starring Roger Moore, Jeff York, Dorothy Provine, 1959-1960
Alias Smith & Jones, starring Peter Deuel and Ben Murphy, 1971-1973
The Big Valley, starring Barbara Stanwyck, Peter Breck, Lee Majors, Richard Long, 1965-1969
Boots and Saddles, starring Pat McVey, John Pickard, Gardner McKay, 1957-1959
Branded, starring Chuck Connors, 1965-1966
Brave Eagle, starring Keith Larson, 1955-1956
Broken Arrow, starring John Lupton and Michael Ansara, 1956-1960
Buckskin, starring Tommy Nolan, Mike Road and Sallie Brophy, 1958-1959
Cade's Country, starring Glenn Ford, Edgar Buchanan, and Peter Ford, 1971-1972
The Californians, starring Richard Coogan and Adam Kennedy, 1957-1959
Casey Jones, staring Alan Hale and Dub Taylor, 1957-1959
Cimarron City, starring George Montgomery, John Smith, Dan Blocker, 1958-1959
Cimarron Strip, starring Stuart Whitman, 1967-1968
Custer, starring Wayne Maunder, Slim Pickens, Michael Dante, 1967
Death Valley Days, with narrators Stanley Andrews, Ronald Reagan, Robert Taylor, 1955-1975
Empire, starring Richard Egan, Ryan O'Neal, Anne Seymour, 1962-1964
F Troop, starring Forrest Tucker, Larry Storch, Ken Berry, 1965-1967
Frontier Doctor, starring Rex Allen, 1957-1959
Gabby Hayes Show, starring George "Gabby" Hayes, 1950-1956
Guns of Will Sonnet, starring Walter Brennan and Dack Rambo, 1967-1969
Gunslinger, starring Tony Young, 1961
Hawkeye and the Last of the Mohicans, starring John Hart and Lon Chaney, Jr., 1956-1957
Hec Ramsey, starring Richard Boone, 1972-1974
Hondo, staring Ralph Taeger and Noah Berry, Jr., 1967
Iron Horse, starring Dale Robertson and Gary Collins, 1966-1968

Jefferson Drum, starring Jeff Richards, 1958-1959
Kung Fu, starring David Carradine and Keye Luke, 1972-1975
Lancer, starring Andrew Duggan, James Stacy, Paul Brinegar, 1968-1970
Lash of the West, starring Lash LaRue, 1953
The Loner, starring Lloyd Bridges, 1965-1966
MacKenzie's Raiders, starring Richard Carlson, Jack Ging, 1958-1959
Man Called Shenandoah, starring Robert Horton, 1965-1966
Man from Blackhawk, starring Robert Rockwell, 1959-1960
Man Without A Gun, starring Rex Reason and Mort Mills, 1958-1959
Marshal of Gunfight Pass, starring Russell Hayden, 1950
Nichols, starring James Garner, 1971-1972
Outcasts, starring Don Murray and Otis Young, 1968-1969
Outlaws, starring Barton MacLane, Bruce Yarnell, Slim Pickens, 1960-1962
Riverboat, starring Darren McGavin and Burt Reynolds, 1959-1961
Saga of Andy Burnett, starring Jerome Courtland, Jeff York, Andrew Duggan, 1957-1958
Sky King, starring Kirby Grant, 1951-1952
Stagecoach West, starring Wayne Rogers and Robert Bray, 1960-1961
Steve Donovan-Western Marshal, starring Douglas Kennedy and Eddy Waller, 1958-1959
Stoney Burke, starring Jack Lord, 1962-1963
Swamp Fox, starring Leslie Nielsen, 1959-1961
Tate, starring David McLean, 1960
Temple Houston, starring Jeffrey Hunter and Jack Elam, 1963-1964
Twenty-Six Men (26 Men), starring Tris Coffin and Kelo Henderson, 1957-1959
Union Pacific, starring Jeff Morrow, 1958-1959
The Virginian, starring James Drury, Lee J. Cobb, Doug McClure, Clu Gulager, 1962-1970
Whiplash, starring Peter Graves, 1960-1961
Wichita Town, starring Joel McCrea and Jody McCrea, 1959-1960
Whispering Smith, starring Audie Murphy and Guy Mitchell, 1961
Wild Wild West, starring Robert Conrad and Ross Martin, 1965-1970
Yancy Derringer, starring Jock Mahoney and X. Brands, 1958-1959

Well, buckaroos, are you surprised that *The Virginian,* one of TV's longest-running westerns, didn't spawn a cap gun? How about *Custer? Broken Arrow? Yancy Derringer?* And let's not forget the real early ones— *Gabby Hayes, Audie Murphy,* and *Lash LaRue.* Like I said, it's all so strange, but whatever motivated the toy gun companies on some shows and characters and not on others will always remain a mystery. Perhaps it was copyrights, perhaps marketing. Then again, maybe they are "out there" somewhere! No book is ever "complete." It is my hope that readers will contact your scribe in the celebrated event that a TV western character cap gun or TV western show cap gun or rifle surfaces. Perhaps one is hidden away somewhere in a Wells Fargo strongbox! Now, wouldn't that be a "find." If nothing else, I sure hope this list of the *pistole non facit* brings back a few memories of some great TV westerns! **HAPPY MEMORIES!**

VALUE GUIDE

At the request of the publisher, I am including a value guide for the items depicted in this book. As any collector knows, this is no easy task. No matter how this is done, I am not about to please everyone. Many factors have gone into this value guide. I have tried to provide a range in the value system based mainly on condition and contents. I have tried to stay away from words like "very rare," "rare," as well as "scarce" and "common" because as I have stated, this has been covered in great detail and in many ways and in many other books. I have tried to provide a guide for the new enthusiasts as well as the advanced collector. The ranges I have provided are the coming together of several experienced collectors in many categories. I have also exercised much research into the prices that have been generated at antique shows, flea markets, auctions and toy gun shows as well as the buying and selling of collections that have come on the market.

It would be virtually impossible to list every single cap gun and holster set available on the market, especially since even the most advanced collectors haven't seen them all! New varieties, never-before-seen characters, and other models are constantly being uncovered! The following represents the guns described and associated with the TV western characters in this book. The range I have used is only a guide and it refers to a piece in good condition versus a mint, unused, never-fired specimen, often in its original box.

Generally, any holster that is appealing to the collector's eye is more desirable and thus, has a higher value. Some collectors like the rather plain "gunfighter" styles that came along with the "adult westerns." However, the large amount of studs, conchos, graphics, jewels, fringe, belt adornments, bullets, show titles, and character names that are usually associated with the earlier westerns such as *The Cisco Kid*, *Roy Rogers*, *Gene Autry*, *Hopalong Cassidy*, and *The Lone Ranger* are very much sought after by collectors. Even the amount and the size of bullets can have an effect on the values of some holster sets. There was, and is, no shortage of the wide variety of colorful holster sets!

Remember that in the final analysis, it's what the seller asks and what you are finally willing to pay for that item that sets a personal "price guide". . .therefore, YOU set the price! The final decision is YOURS— when you pay the asking price, decide to negotiate, or you decide to pass. . .Good luck in your quest!

WESTERN CHARACTER ITEM *Name, Size, Special Features*	GOOD CONDITION *Operable w/no damage*	EXCELLENT, UNFIRED, UNUSED *w/box, holsters, outfits, etc.*	WESTERN CHARACTER ITEM *Name, Size, Special Features*	GOOD CONDITION *Operable w/no damage*	EXCELLENT, UNFIRED, UNUSED *w/box, holsters, outfits, etc.*
Alan Ladd, Schmidt, 10 inch	$200	$400 w/box	•Bat Masterson, Classy, Fancy Dan Set	$350	$450 w/ accouterments
•Alan Ladd Shane Holster	200	400	•Billy The Kid, Stevens, 7 inch	150	250 box, gold, et
•Alan Ladd, Schmidt double holsters	200	300 w/ accouterments	•Black Saddle Double Holster Set	250	400 w/guns
•Annie Oakley, L-H, 7 inch	150	250	•Bonanza, L-H, 9 inch	150	300 w/cameo, et
•Annie Oakley, L-H, 9 inch	250	350	•Bonanza, L-H, 10 inch, long barrel	200	300 w/cameo, et
•Annie Oakley, Daisy Holsters	350	500 w/box, etc	•Bonanza, L-H, 11 inch, RC	250	350 special grip colors
•Annie Oakley, Hubley Western Set	350	600 w/guns, etc	•Bonanza, L-H, 45 model, RC	350	500 w/holsters
•Annie Oakley, Daisy rifle	250	400 w/box, sling, etc	•Bonanza, Halco, 9-1/2 inch model	250	450 w/holsters
Bat Masterson, Lone Star, 1st pattern 250	250	350	•Bonanza, Marx, Pistol, Hoss model	75	150 w/card
•Bat Masterson, Lone Star, 2nd pattern	200	300	•Bonanza, Marx, Ranch Outfit	250	350 w/ accouterments
•Bat Masterson, Carnell, RC	500	750 w/ box, bullets	•Bonanza, Pilen, cap pisto	125	200 w/box
•Bat Masterson, Carnell, boxed outfit	400	600 box, cane, vest, etc	•Bonanza, L-H, 45 model, RC	350	500 w/ holsters

WESTERN CHARACTER ITEM *Name, Size, Special Features*	GOOD CONDITION *Operable w/no damage*	EXCELLENT, UNFIRED, UNUSED *w/box, holsters, outfits, etc.*	WESTERN CHARACTER ITEM *Name, Size, Special Features*	GOOD CONDITION *Operable w/no damage*	EXCELLENT, UNFIRED, UNUSED *w/box, holsters, outfits, etc.*
•Bonanza, Halco, 9-1/2 inch model	$250	$450 w/holsters	•Cisco Kid, Lone Star, 10 large frame	$350	$450 w/holster
•Bonanza, Marx, Pistol, Hoss model	75	150 w/card	•Cisco Kid, American Holster Set	400	950 w/guns, cuffs, box
•Bonanza, Marx, Ranch Outfit	250	350 w/ accouterments	•Colt 45, Hubley, 13 inch, RC	150	300 w/box, bullets, etc.
•Bonanza, Pilen, cap pisto	125	200 w/box	•Colt 44, Hubley, 13 inch, RC	175	350 w/box, bullets, etc.
•Bonanza, L-H, cap rifle	200	300	•Colt 45, Hubley, single holster	125	275 w/gun, bullets
•Bronco, Kilgore, 7 inch, RC	100	200 w/box	•Colt 45, Hubley, double holsters	200	500 w/guns, bullets
•Bronco, Kilgore, 8 inch, RC	150	250 w/box	•Cowboy G-Men, Lone Star pistol	125	250 w/holster, star
•Bronco, L-H, 7 inch	125	175 w/box	•Cowboy in Africa, Mattel, Fanner	100	250 w/box, black, bronze
•Buffalo Bill, Stevens, nickel	125	300 w/holsters	•Cowboy in Africa, Mattel holster set	150	350 w/ both guns
•Buffalo Bill, Stevens, gold model	150	350 w/holsters	•Cowboy in Africa, Rifle w/drum	150	200 mint
•Buffalo Bill, L-H, nickel, amber grips	150	200 w/box			
•Buffalo Bill, Lone Star Cody 45	75	150 w/box	Dale Evans, Buzz-Henry, 7 inch	250	400 w/box
•Buffalo Bill, Young, L-H, 7 inch	75	100 w/box	•Dale Evans, Schmidt, 10 inch	350	700 w/box
•Buffalo Bill, Young, L-H, 9 inch	150	250 w/box	•Dale Evans, Schmidt, 8 inch	400	700 w/box
•Buffalo Bill, Young, L-H, Canadian	100	150 w/box, holster, belt	•Dale Evans, Double Holster Sets	400	1000 & above w/guns
•Buffalo Bill, L-H, rifle	100	150 w/box, scope, sling	•Daniel Boone, Marx, Derringer, 8 inch	75	125 on card
Champion, L-H, 9 inch	125	200 w/box, gold	•Daniel Boone, Marx, Flintlock, 12 inch	125	200 on card
•Champion, Kilgore, 10 inch	125	200 w/box, timer	•Daniel Boone, Marx Flintlock Rifle	100	150 w/box
•Cheyenne, Hamilton, 9-1/2 inch	150	250 w/box	•Daniel Boone, Japanese, Litho Tin	75	100 w/box
•Cheyenne, Kilgore, 9 inch	150	250 w/box, holster	•Davy Crockett, L-H, 7 inch, SS	100	150 w/ holster, belt
•Cheyenne, Daisy, w/ Nichols Stallion	250	400 w/box, etc	•Davy Crockett, L-H, 7 inch, repeater	150	250 w/box, holster, belt
•Cheyenne, Daisy Outfit	250	500 w/ accouterments	•Davy Crockett, L-H, 9 inch	250	350 w/box, holster
•Cheyenne, Daisy, Saddle Carbine	100	200 w/box	•Davy Crockett, L-H, Double Holster	300	650 w/guns, 9 inch
•Cisco Kid, Lone Star, 8 inch, frame logo	100	175 on card	•Davy Crockett, Hubley, Flintlock	100	250 w/box, holster
•Cisco Kid, Lone Star, Holster Sets	100	350 w/guns			
•Cisco Kid, Lone Star, name on barrel	150	200 on card w/holster			

WESTERN CHARACTER ITEM Name, Size, Special Features	GOOD CONDITION Operable w/no damage	EXCELLENT, UNFIRED, UNUSED w/box, holsters, outfits, etc.	WESTERN CHARACTER ITEM Name, Size, Special Features	GOOD CONDITION Operable w/no damage	EXCELLENT, UNFIRED, UNUSED w/box, holsters, outfits, etc.
•Davy Crockett, Hubley, Flintlock, Knife	$150	$350 w/ holsters, guns	Frontier, Kilgore, 8 inch repeater, RC	$150	$200 w/box
•Davy Crockett, Multiple Products, Gun/Knife	75	100 on card, mint	•Fury, Italian, MAM, 11 inch w/RC	150	200 w/box, disc caps
•Davy Crockett, Schmidt, 7-1/2 inch, nickel	250	350	Gene Autry, Buzz-Henry, 7 inch	200	300 w/box
•Davy Crockett, Schmidt, 10 inch, cursive	250	350 copper grips	•Gene Autry, L-H, nickel, gold, 7 inch	250	300-350 gold model
•Davy Crockett, Schmidt, 12 inch Pathfinder	500	800+ w/ compass, box	•Gene Autry, L-H, 9 inch, nickel, bronze, gold	250	350 gold, box, etc
•Davy Crockett, Marx, Flintlock, 11 inch	125	250 w/box marked	•Gene Autry, L-H, 10 inch long barrel	300-350	400-450 w/box
•Davy Crockett, Marx, Flintlock, 16 inch	150	275 w/box marked	•Gene Autry, L-H, 9-1/2 inch, pop-up box	300	350 gold
•Davy Crockett, Marx, Flintlock Rifle	150	200 w/box	•Gene Autry, L-H, 11 inch, 44 model, RC	250	350 gold, box, bullets
•Davy Crockett, Marx, Winchester Rifle	200	225 w/box	•Gene Autry, L-H, 11 inch, 44 model, bronze	300	350 w/box, bullets
•Davy Crockett, L-H, Winchester Rifle	150	250 w/box	•Gene Autry, single holsters	250	Increase w/ gun, box, cuffs
•Davy Crockett, Hubley, Flintlock, Buffalo	150	250 w/box, marked	•Gene Autry, double holsters	350	Increase w/ guns, box, spurs
•Davy Crockett, Daisy, Rifle, 35 inch	150	250 w/box, marked	•Gene Autry, L-H, Western Ranch rifle	200	250-300 w/box
			•Gene Autry, L-II, 26 inch rifle, red model	100	200 w/box

With any Davy Crockett holsters and combination outfits, the value is higher depending on holster markings, studs, jewels, conchos, buckles, fringe, single holster, double holsters, with knives, powder horn, other assorted collectibles and boxes with lid images of Davy Crockett.

With any Gene Autry holsters, the value is higher depending on holster markings, conchos, studs, jewels, markings, bullets, buckles, fringe, box and lid images of Gene and/or Champion.

WESTERN CHARACTER ITEM	GOOD CONDITION	EXCELLENT, UNFIRED, UNUSED	WESTERN CHARACTER ITEM	GOOD CONDITION	EXCELLENT, UNFIRED, UNUSED
•Deputy, Hubley, nickel w/cameo	150	250 w/box, badge, etc	•Gray Ghost, Lone Star, 9 inch	350	650 w/outfit, bullets
•Deputy, Kilgore, 7 inch, repeater	100	150	•Gray Ghost, Hubley Pioneer	150	400 w/cavalry outfit
•Deputy, Schmidt, 8 inch repeater, nickel	125	250 w/holster, card	•Gray Ghost, Lone Star Boxed Outfit	600	750 complete, mint
•Deputy, Halco, single holster	125	250 w/box, gun	•Grizzly, Kilgore, nickel, w/RC	200	250 w/box
•Deputy, Halco, double holster set, deluxe	250	400 w/box, guns	•Grizzly, Kilgore, gold, w/RC	300-350	350-400 **w/box**
Elfego Baca, Daisy, w/ Kilgore Pinto	100	200 w/holster	•Gunsmoke, L-H, 9 inch, nickel	150	300 w/box, holster
•Elfego Baca, Daisy, Law & Order Outfit	250	350 w/ accouterments	•Gunsmoke L-H, 9 inch, copper grips w/name	250	350 w/box, holster
			•Gunsmoke, L-H, 10 inch w/pop-up box	250	300 w/box, gold

WESTERN CHARACTER ITEM *Name, Size, Special Features*	GOOD CONDITION *Operable w/no damage*	EXCELLENT, UNFIRED, UNUSED *w/box, holsters, outfits, etc.*	WESTERN CHARACTER ITEM *Name, Size, Special Features*	GOOD CONDITION *Operable w/no damage*	EXCELLENT, UNFIRED, UNUSED *w/box, holsters, outfits, etc.*
•Gunsmoke, L-H, long barrel model	$250	$300 w/box, grips, etc	•Hopalong Cassidy, Schmidt, gold, black grips	$500	$850 w/.box
•Gunsmoke-Matt Dillon, Halco 45 model w/RC	300	400 w/box, bullets	•Hopalong Cassidy, Schmidt, black grip, white bust	450	500-600 mint
•Gunsmoke Single Holster sets	150	300 w/box, gun	•Hopalong Cassidy, Schmidt, white grip, black bust	500	500-600 mint
•Gunsmoke, Double Holster sets	200	500 w/box, guns, etc	•Hopalong Cassidy, Schmidt, plain grips, jewel, etc	350	400-500 mint

With any Gunsmoke holster sets, values and desireability increase if the holsters carry the name and graphics associated with the show title and with those of marshal "Matt Dillon."

Have Gun Will Travel, L-H, 9 inch w/cameo	300	500 w holsters	•Hopalong Cassidy, Wyandotte, 7 inch, nickel, SS	300	350 mint
•Have Gun Will Travel, L-H, 11 inch .45 w/RC	350	450 w/ bullets, etc	•Hopalong Cassidy, Wyandotte, 7 inch, gold, SS	350	450 mint
•Have Gun Will Travel, Halco, 8 inch	200	350 w/box, holster	•Hopalong Cassidy, Wyandotte, 8 inch, nickel	400	500 w/good graphics
•Have Gun Will Travel, Halco 10 inch, cursive	350	450 w/box, holster	•Hopalong Cassidy, Wyandotte, 8 inch, gold	450	550 w/good graphics
•Have Gun Will Travel, w/Schmidt Patrol	200	500 w/box, guns	•Hopalong Cassidy, M.A. Henry, 6-1/3 inch metal	400	500 mint, w/box
•Have Gun Will Travel, single holster set	150	450 w/ gun, markings	•Hopalong Cassidy, L-H, 9 inch w/horse head grip	600-700	800-850 gold, box
•Have Gun Will Travel, double holsters set	300	800 w/box, guns, card	•Hopalong Cassidy, single holster set	250	400-600 w/gun/box
•Have Gun Will Travel, w/Halco Derringer	50	65 w/special holster	•Hopalong Cassidy, double holster sets	400-600	900-1300 w/guns/box
•Have Gun Will Travel, holsters w/generic guns	200	350 w/ generic guns			
•Have Gun Will Travel, small tan double set w/metal guns	100	150 mint/ unused w/card			

With any Hopalong Cassidy holsters, the value is higher depending on holster markings, conchos, studs, jewels, markings, bullets, buckles, fringe, box, foreign, and lid images of Hoppy and/or Topper.

With any "Have Gun Will Travel" and "Paladin"-marked holsters, the value is higher depending on holster markings to show title and/or character name, conchos, jewels, graphics, bullets, buckles, sizes, if with Derringer and Paladin's calling card, and the box lid images of Paladin.

			•Hotel de Paree/ Sundance Carnell Holster Set	300-350	400-500 w/ box, guns, mint
•High Chaparral, Daisy holsters w/Hubley guns	250	350 w/ Hubley guns	•How The West Was Won, Nichols-Kusan	200-250	300 w/box, guns
•High Chaparral, Redondo, nickel, black	150	300 w/box badge	Jesse James, Hubley, Remington .36 w/bullets	100-150	250-300 w/box poster, gun
•High Chaparral, Daisy Rifle, Winchester	150	200 w/box, leather	•Jim Bowie, Marx, 8 inch Derringer	75	100-125 on card
•High Chaparral, Daisy Outfit	300	400 w/box, guns, etc	•Jim Bowie, Marx, Flintlock cap pistol	125	150-200 on card
			•Jim Bowie, Elvin, 9 and 10 inch knives	45-65	75-85 on card graphics
•Hopalong Cassidy, Schmidt, Buck-n-Bronc	350	450 w/bust on grips	•John Wayne, Chancy Co, w/generic guns	400-500	750-850 w/ box, guns
			•Johnny Ringo, Marx, dragoon style, nickel	200-250	300-350 w/ box, holster
			•Johnny Ringo, Marx, dragoon, factory black	200-250	350 w/ holster on card

WESTERN CHARACTER ITEM *Name, Size, Special Features*	GOOD CONDITION *Operable w/no damage*	EXCELLENT, UNFIRED, UNUSED *w/box, holsters, outfits, etc.*	WESTERN CHARACTER ITEM *Name, Size, Special Features*	GOOD CONDITION *Operable w/no damage*	EXCELLENT, UNFIRED, UNUSED *w/box, holsters, outfits, etc.*
•Johnny Ringo, Actoy, nickel, 9 inch	$200-250	$350-400 w/ holsters	•Lone Ranger, Marx, 10 inch clicker model	$125-175	$225 w/box
•Johnny Ringo, Actoy, double holster set	250	400-500 w/ both guns	•Lone Ranger, Marx, Thundergun Model 12 inch	250-300	350 w/box
•Johnny Ringo, Actoy, single holster, small	75-125	200 w/ small gun	•Lone Ranger, Marx, 26 inch rifle	150-200	225-250 w/ box
•Judge Roy Bean, Law West of the Pecos gun	400-500	650-750 w/ 1936 holster	•Lone Ranger, Marx, 23 inch Winchester rifle	150-225	225-250 w/ box
•Kit Carson, Kilgore, 8-1/4 inch, cap shooter	75-125	150-200 w/ box, gold	•Lone Ranger, Mattel, Shootin Shell Models	150-200	250-300 w/ box, metal plate
•Kit Carson, Kilgore, 9 inch, cap shooter	125-175	250 w/ box, gold	•Lone Ranger and Tonto, Esquire, Indian Outfit	250-350	500 w/all accouterments
•Kit Carson, Carnell holster sets w/generic guns	250	350 w/box, both guns	•Lone Ranger and Tonto, Stevens, Big Chief	100-150	250 w/ Tonto holster
•Klondike, Nichols, .44 model, 9 inch, blued	300-350	500 w/box, holster	•Lone Ranger and Tonto, Hubley Chief, 5 inch	25-50	100-150 w/ Tonto holster
•Laramie, L-H, 8-1/4 inch, nickel, cap shooter	150	250 w/ holster, single			

With any Lone Ranger holsters, the value is higher depending on holster markings, conchos, studs, jewels, buckles, fringe, box, bullets, images and if marked to both Lone Ranger and/or Tonto.

WESTERN CHARACTER ITEM	GOOD CONDITION	EXCELLENT, UNFIRED, UNUSED
•Laramie, L-H, 9 inch, w/horse head grips	200-250	350-400 w/ box, holsters
•Laramie, Jr, Kilgore, 7 inch, nickel w/stag	75-100	200 w/box, holster
•Laredo, Kilgore, 7 inch, nickel w/stag	75-100	250-300 w/ holsters
•Laredo, Double Holster sets, marked	200-250	350-400 w/ both guns, shells
•Lasso 'em Bill, Schmidt, nickel, white stag	100-200	250 w/box
•Lasso 'em Bill, Kenton, boxed sets	200-250	300 w/box, gun, cuffs
•Lawman, Double Holsters w/Hubley Marshals	200	350 w/guns
•Lone Ranger, Actoy, .32, metal flowered grips	150-250	250-300 w/ box or holster
•Lone Ranger, Actoy, 9 inch, bronze	200-250	300 w/ holster, single
•Lone Ranger, Actoy, 9 inch, nickel	225-275	350-500 w/ holsters & guns
•Lone Ranger, Actoy, 4-in-1 rifle gun	400-500	750-800 w/ all parts, mint
•Lone Ranger, Mattel, Fanner 50 model	150-200	400 w/ holsters
•Lone Ranger, Marx, 9 inch, black	125-150	200 w/box

WESTERN CHARACTER ITEM	GOOD CONDITION	EXCELLENT, UNFIRED, UNUSED
•Maverick, L-H, 9 inch nickel, cap shooter	150-200	250 w/ cameo, amber, etc
•Maverick, L-H, 8 inch, Buzz-Henry style, stag	100-150	200 w/box, holster
•Maverick, L-H, 10 inch, pop-up box, large frame	250-300	350-400 w/ holsters
•Maverick, L-H, 10 inch long barrel, assorted grips	250-300	350-400 w/ holsters
•Maverick, L-H Halco, 11 inch .45 w/RC	300-350	400-500 w/ holster
•Maverick, Halco, Derringer, colored grips	50	65-75 on card or w/holster
•Maverick, Carnell, notch grips, 9 inch cap shooter	175-225	250-350 w/ holsters
•Maverick, Carnell, notch grips, 10 inch long barrel	250-300	350-450 w/ holsters
•Maverick, Carnell Rifle, die cast works	100-150	150-200 w/ box, items
•Maverick, Schmidt, 10 inch, engraved, copper grip	300-400	450-500 w/ box, holster
•Maverick, Marx, Saddle Ring rifle	$150-200	$250-300 w/box

With any Maverick holsters and holster sets, the value is higher depending on holster graphics, studs, jewels, bullets, buckles, fringe, conchos, box, foreign or American, and Maverick images.

WESTERN CHARACTER ITEM *Name, Size, Special Features*	GOOD CONDITION *Operable w/no damage*	EXCELLENT, UNFIRED, UNUSED *w/box, holsters, outfits, etc.*
•McCloud, Pilen, 9 inch w/RC, nickel	$100-150	$200 w/box, graphics
Overland Trail, Hubley, Flip, 9 3/4 inch gun	150-200	300-600 w/ box, holsters
•Overland Trail, Hubley, Kelly's Rifle	200-250	300-350 w/box
•Overland Trail, Hubley, Holster Sets	200-250	400-600 w/guns
Pecos Bill, Italian, Mondial, 8 and 12 inch w/RC	100-125	150-200 w/ box, size, discs
•Plainsman, National, Dodge-Melton, 10 inch w/RCw/	150-200	200-250, w/ box,engraved
•Pancho Villa, Italian, MAM/Strauss 23 inch rifle	75	100-150 w/box, graphics
Range Rider, Schmidt, 10 inch, copper grips	150	200-250 w/ single holster
•Range Rider, L-H, Boxed holster set	250-300	300-350 w/ gun, derringer
•Range Rider, Halco Derringer, assorted color grips	50	75 w/special holster
•Range Rider, Lone Star, Mark II, gold, 11 inch	400-500	600 w/box, holster
•Rango, Mattel, Fanner 50, nickel	75-150	250-350 w/box, 1 or 2 holsters
•Rawhide, Carnell, Cowpoke, notch grips, 9 inch	100-150	250 w/holster
•Rawhide, Carnell, Cowpoke Jr, metal, 8 inch	75-100	150 w/holster
•Rawhide, Carnell, rifle, die cast works	100-150	250 w/box
•Rawhide, Carnell, Trail Boss Outfit	250-300	350 box, rifle, gun, canteen
•Rawhide, L-H, Longhorn, 10 inch pop-up box	200-250	250-350 w/ card, holster
•Rawhide, Hubley, Cowpoke, 8 inch, gold	75-125	200 w/holsters
•Rawhide, Lone Star, Ramrod, 8 inch	75-125	200 w/box
•Rawhide, Daisy, Trail Boss, Winchester rifle	$100-125	$150 w/box
•Rebel, Lone Star, 10-1/2 inch dragoon, w/RC	250-300	300-350 w/box, black, nickel
•Rebel, Kilgore, 10-1/2 inch, cap shooter	250-300	300 w/box
•Rebel, Harvel-Kilgore, Southerner set	150-200	250 on card w/flap holster
•Rebel, Classy, Scattergun, 21 inch w/box, holster	350-450	600-800
•Rebel, Marx, Johnny Yuma, Scattergun, 22 inch	400-500	600 w/shells, mint
•Rebel, Hubley, Coyote, w/Nick Adams holster	200-300	350 w/full gunbelt
•Rebel, Classy holsters, black, gray, flap style	200-250	400-500 w/ gun, holster rig, cap
•Red Ryder, #111 Carbine, Model 40	200-250	300 w/box
•Red Ryder, Cork Rifle, Model 65, 13-1/2 inch	50-75	100 w/box
•Red Ryder, Little Beaver Buffalo Rifle, wood stock	200-250	250-300 w/ box, mint
•Red Ryder, Daisy, Holster Sets	200-250	300-350 w/ Hubley Texans
•Restless Gun, Esquire, 9-1/2 inch, nickel	150-200	300-450 w/ holsters
•Restless Gun, Esquire, w/secret compartment	200-250	250-350, gold, holster
•Restless Gun, Esquire, 4-1 rifle-gun, extension	400-500	600-750 w/ special holster rig

With any Restless Gun holsters and holster outfits, the value is higher depending on single, double, 4-1 holster rig, markings, character or show name, studs, jewels, bullets, box and images.

WESTERN CHARACTER ITEM	GOOD CONDITION	EXCELLENT, UNFIRED, UNUSED
•Ric-O-Shay, Hubley, Jr. nickel model, 9 inch	100-150	250 w/box or single holster
•Ric-O-Shay, Hubley, 13 inch .45 w/ ricochet sound	150-200	250 w//frame box, or holster
•Rifleman, Hubley, Flip Special Ring rifle	200-250	350 w/box
•Rifleman, Marx, Flip Rifle, Wild West	125-175	200-250 w/ box
•Rifleman, Halco holsters exist, but seldom seen	250-300	350-450 w/ guns, bullets
•Rin-Tin-Tin, Esquire, 9 inch bronze cap shooter	150-200	250 mint
•Rin-Tin-Tin, Esquire, nickel model, cap shooter	250	350-400 w/ western holsters
•Rin-Tin-Tin, Esquire, Cavalry Outfit	350-450	500 w/all components
•Rin-Tin-Tin, Marx, Winchester style rifle, 33 inch	200	250 w/box

WESTERN CHARACTER ITEM *Name, Size,* *Special Features*	GOOD CONDITION *Operable* *w/no damage*	EXCELLENT, UNFIRED, UNUSED *w/box, holsters,* *outfits, etc.*	WESTERN CHARACTER ITEM *Name, Size,* *Special Features*	GOOD CONDITION *Operable* *w/no damage*	EXCELLENT, UNFIRED, UNUSED *w/box, holsters,* *outfits, etc.*
•Rough Riders, Latco, Ruf Rider, 10-1/4 inch	**$150-200**	**. . . . . .$250** w/copper floral grips	**S**hotgun Slade, Esquire, Rifle-Shotgun combo	**$350-500**	**. . . .$600** w/ special holster
•Rough Riders, Latco, Double Holster Set	**200-250**	**. . . . .350-500** w/ both guns	•Smoky Joe, Hubley, 8 inch, nickel, steerhead grip	**75-125**	**. . . . . . .150** w/box holster
•Roy Rogers, Kilgore, 8-1/2 inch, nickel	**250**	**. . . . . .250-300** w/box	•Smoky Joe, L-H, 9 inch w/ variation grips	**125-175**	**. . . . .200** w/box, holster
•Roy Rogers, Kilgore, 10-1/4 inch, w/RC	**400-600**	**. . . . . .750** w/box	•Smoky Joe, L-H, 9 inch gold, w/copper grips	**150-200**	**. . . . . .250** w/box, or holsters
•Roy Rogers, Buzz-Henry, 7-1/2 inch, inset grips	**250-350**	**. . . . .350-400** w/box, gold	•Smoky Joe, Stevens, antique bronze, black grips	**125-175**	**. . . . .200** w/box, or holster
•Roy Rogers, L-H, 9 inch, heavy frame model	**350-400**	**. . . . .450-500** w/box, gold	•Sugarfoot, Daisy, Bullseye 50, blued, holster sets	**150-200**	**. . . . .250-350** w/ box, single, double
•Roy Rogers, Schmidt, 9 inch, copper grips	**300-350**	**. . . . .400** w/box	**T**all Man, Hubley, holster set w/ Western Guns	**250**	**. . . . . .350-450** w/ box, both guns
•Roy Rogers, Schmidt, 10-1/2 inch, variation grips	**350-450**	**. . . . .400-500** w/box	•Tombstone Territory, Harvel-Kilgore, Classy	**200-250**	**. . . . .350-500** w/ box, guns
•Roy Rogers, Schmidt, early, stag, checkering	**250-350**	**. . . . .350-450** w/box, various jewels	•Tombstone Territory, Classy, w/Kilgore guns	**250-300**	**. . . . .350-500** w/ box, holster
•Roy Rogers, Classy, R-90 model, copper grips	**250-300**	**. . . . .350-400** w/box, gold	•Texan, Hubley, 9 inch, nickel, gold, variation grips	**125-200**	**. . . . .250-350,** w/ box, gold, etc
•Roy Rogers, Classy, 10-1/2 inch, floral grips	**350-450**	**. . . . .500-750,** gold model	•Texan, Hubley, 8-1/2 inch, Texan Jr models	**75-1501**	**. . . . . .50-300** w box, gold, etc
•Roy Rogers, Classy, Pee-wee, Model R-30	**75-100**	**. . . . . . .150** w/holster, card	•Texan, Model 38, w/RC, variation grips	**150-200**	**. . . . . .250-300** w/ box, turquoise
•Roy Rogers, BCM, 10-1/2 inch, w/RC, Indian grips	**500-600**	**. . . . .750** w/box, bullets	•Texan, Holster Sets, single and double	**250-300**	**. . . . .350-450** w/ box, both guns
•Roy Rogers, Balantyne, RR & Trigger grips, w/RC	**200-300**	**. . . . .350** w/box, card	•Texas John Slaughter, Daisy, w/Kilgore Pinto	**100**	**. . . . . .250** w/ marked holsters
•Roy Rogers, Stevens, Trigger, 8-1/2 inch	**100-150**	**. . . . .200** w/box	•Texas John Slaughter, Daisy, Repeating Cap Rifle	**150**	**. . . . . .200** w/box
•Roy Rogers, Lone Star, 9 inch, w/RC, lanyard Ringo	**300-400**	**. . . . . .450** w/box	•Texas John Slaughter, Daisy, Law & Order Outfit	**250**	**. . . . . . . .350** w/all components
•Roy Rogers, Marx, Winchester Rifle, silver	**200-300**	**. . . . .350** w/box	•Texas Rangers, L-H, 8-1/2 inch, 1st model	**100-125**	**. . . . . .150-200** w/ box
•Roy Rogers, Marx, Winchester Deluxe Model rifle	**300-350**	**. . . . . .400** w/box	•Texas Rangers, L-H, 9 inch, nickel, gold, variations	**125-175**	**. . . . .200-250** w/ box, holster
•Roy Rogers, single, double holster sets	**250-600**	**. . . . . . . .600-1500** w/ guns	•Texas Rangers, L-H, 11 inch, Cavalry style, bronze	**200-250**	**. . . . . .300** w/ holster
			•Texas Rangers, L-H, 11 inch, 44 Model w/RC	**200-250**	**. . . . . .300-350** w/box,
			•Texas Rangers, L-H, Buzz-Henry style, 8 inch	**75-100**	**. . . . . . .150-200** w/ box, holster

With any Roy Rogers holsters, the value is higher depending on RR markings, conchos, studs, jewels, buckles, bullets, fringe, boxes, foreign or American, lid images of Roy and/or Trigger, Bullet.

WESTERN CHARACTER ITEM Name, Size, Special Features	GOOD CONDITION Operable w/no damage	EXCELLENT, UNFIRED, UNUSED w/box, holsters, outfits, etc.	WESTERN CHARACTER ITEM Name, Size, Special Features	GOOD CONDITION Operable w/no damage	EXCELLENT, UNFIRED, UNUSED w/box, holsters, outfits, etc.
•Texas Rangers, L-H, Law & Order outfit	$200-250	$350-450 w/box, all components	•Wagon Train, L-H, Flint McCullough holster set	$200-250	$400 w/gun, 44 Model
•Texas Rangers, L-H, 10 inch, "Texas" long barrel	200	250 w/cameo, box	•Wagon Train, L-H, Flint, Winchester Scout Rifle	150-200	250 w/box
•Texas Rangers, L-H, saddle gun rifle	100-150	200 w/box	*With any Wagon Train holster sets, the values are higher depending on holster markings to show title or character name, single, doubles, conchos, jewels, buckles, bullets, studs, and box lid images.*		
•Texas Rangers, L-H, 5-in-1 rifle gun, extension	250-350	500-600 w/box, all parts	•Wanted: Dead or Alive, Esquire, Mare's Laig Riflegun	200-250	300-400 w/ special holster rig
With any Texas Rangers holsters and combination outfits, the values are higher depending on single, double holsters, studs, markings, jewels, bullets, fringe, buckles, with rifle, guns, can teens, cuffs, spurs.			•Wanted: Dead or Alive, Marx, Mare's Laig, 13 inch	100-125	150 w/holste rig
•Trackdown/Hoby Gilman, L-H Texas Ranger dragoon	200-2503	50-400 w/ holster	•Wanted: Dead or Alive, Marx, Mare's Laig, 17-1/2 inch	150-200	250 w/card, holster
•Trackdown/Hoby Gilman, Classy Double Holsters	250-300	300-400 w/ guns	•Wanted: Dead or Alive, Marx, Mare's Laig, 19 inch	275-325	350 w/holster rig, box
U.S. Marshal, L-H, 8-1/2 inch Marshal	50-75	125 w/holster or box	•Wanted: Dead or Alive, Rayline, "Pursuer," 16 inch	150-200	250 w/box, special bullets
•U.S. Marshal, L-H, Marshal, w/cameo grips	150-200	250 w/box	•Wells Fargo, Esquire, 7-1/2 inch Buckaroo w/holster	100-150	200 w/card, graphics
•U.S. Marshal, L-H, .44 Model, 11 inch w/RC	200-250	300 w/box holster	•Wells Fargo, Esquire, 8 inch Special, w/holsters	125-150	250 w/holsters, guns
•U.S. Marshal, Halco, Marshal, 6-7 Shooter	350-400	450 w/box, holster	•Wells Fargo, Esquire, 11 inch Buntline model	200-250	300-350 w/ holsters
•U.S. Marshal, Hubley, Marshal, 10 inch, stag	75-125	200 w/box, holster	•Wells Fargo, Pony Express, w/11 inch Buntline guns	200	400-450 w / holsters, guns
•U.S. Marshal, Schmidt, BB Marshal, copper stag	150-200	200-250 w/box	•Wells Fargo, Lone Star, w/ Gunfighter cap shooter	150	200-250 card, holster, belt
•U.S. Marshal, Shoulder Holster w/L-H Marshall	150	250 w/gun	•Wells Fargo, Marx, Double Barrel Shotgun	275-325	350-400 w/box, graphics
Wagon Train, L-H, 9 inch w/horse head grips	150-200	250-350 w/box, gold, holster	*With any Wells Fargo holsters and holster sets, the values are higher depending on holster markings, graphics, conchos, studs, jewels, special gunfighter holsters, and if with Dale Robertson graphics).*		
•Wagon Train, L-H, 9-1/2 inch w/pop-up box	200-250	250-300 w/box, holster	•Westerner, Hamilton, 9-1/2 inch, black grips	100-150	150-200 w/ box
•Wagon Train, L-H, 10 inch long barrel model	250-300	300-350 w/box, holster	•Wild Bill Hickok, L-H, 7-1/2 inch, nickel, gold	250-300	300-350 w/ box, holster
•Wagon Train, L-H, 11 inch, 44 model w/RC	250-300	350 w/box, ricochet zing	•Wild Bill Hickok, L-H, 9 inch, assorted grips	200-250	300-400 w/ box, holster
•Wagon Train, Halco, 45 with stag and RC	350-400	400-450 w/box single holster	•Wild Bill Hickok, L-H, 10 inch, pop-up box, large frame	225-275	300-350 w/ box, holster
•Wagon Train, Halco, 8 inch Buzz Henry style	100-150	200 w/holster or box	•Wild Bill Hickok, L-H, 10-1/2 inch, long barrel model	250-300	300-400 w/ box, holster
•Wagon Train, L-H, 5-in-1 Rifle Gun Outfit	500-600	750-800 w/box,			

WESTERN CHARACTER ITEM Name, Size, Special Features	GOOD CONDITION Operable w/no damage	EXCELLENT, UNFIRED, UNUSED w/box, holsters, outfits, etc.
•Wild Bill Hickok, L-H, 11 inch, 44 model w/RC	$250-300	$350-400 w/ box, gold, rig
•Wild Bill Hickok, Schmidt, CK Deputy, both names	200-250	250-300 w/ box, cuffs, spurs
•Wild Bill Hickok, Gunfighter gun, 44 model	200-250	400-450 w holster rig
•Wild Bill Hickok, Gunfighter rig, named to Jingles 44 model	250-300	400-450 w gun

With any Wild Bill Hickok holsters and holster rigs, the values are higher depending on size of the guns, also conchos, studs, jewels, leather tooling, gunfighter styles, box and lid images of both Wild Bill and/or Jingles, or both. The same applies to names on holsters.

•Wyatt Earp, L-H, 7-1/2 inch cap gun, assorted grips	125-175	200 w/box, holster
•Wyatt Earp, L-H, 9 inch, standard, assorted grips	150-200	200-250 w/ box, holster
•Wyatt Earp, L-H, 10-1/2 inch, Long Barrel model	200-250	250-300 w/ box, holster
•Wyatt Earp, L-H, 9-10 inch, Canadian models	250-300	300-350 w/ box, holster
•Wyatt Earp, Esquire, 8 inch, white stag, lanyard Ringo	125-175	200-250 w/ box, holster
•Wyatt Earp, Esquire, 9 inch, stag grip, large frames	150-200	200-250 w/ box, holste
•Wyatt Earp, Esquire, 9 inch, Federal grips, large frame	175-225	250-300 w/ box, holster
•Wyatt Earp, Esquire, 11 inch Buntline Special	200-250	275-350, w/ box, bronze, rig
•Wyatt Earp, Hubley, 9 inch, nickel, steerhead grips	125-175	175-250 w/ box, holster
•Wyatt Earp, Hubley, 10-1/2 inch Buntline Special model	150-200	250-350 w/ holsters, box
•Wyatt Earp, Service Manufacturing, Long Island, models	150-200	200-250 w/ holsters, box
•Wyatt Earp, Kilgore, 9 inch, horse head grips	125-175	175-250 w/ gold, box, rig
•Wyatt Earp, Schmidt, 10 inch, nickel, copper grip	250-300	300-350 w/ box, gold, rig
•Wyatt Earp, Schmidt, 10 inch, engraved model, stag grip	350-450	450-600 w/ box or holster
•Wyatt Earp, Young Premium Buntline Special	100-50	200 w/ special holster
•Wyatt Earp, Haig,	$125-175	$200 w/box,

WESTERN CHARACTER ITEM Name, Size, Special Features	GOOD CONDITION Operable w/no damage	EXCELLENT, UNFIRED, UNUSED w/box, holsters, outfits, etc.
Buntline Special		pellets, target
•Wyatt Earp, Marx, 11-1/2 inch "Special" Prototype	150-200	250 w/box
•Wyatt Earp, Crescent Toys, 9 inch Buntline Special	150-200	250 w/box
•Wyatt Earp, Lone Star, 10-1/2 inch Bunt-Line Special	150-200	250-350 w/ holster, box
•Wyatt Earp, Lone Star, 13-1/2 inch Buntline Special	250-300	300-350 box, graphics, rig
•Wyatt Earp, BCM, Buntline Special, Indian Chief grips	350-400	450-500 w/ box, holster, rig

With any Wyatt Earp holsters and holster sets, the values are higher depending on size, single, double, conchos, studs, fringe, bullets, buckles, gunfighter styles, graphics that show title, Hugh O'Brien, combination standard holster and Buntline holster sets, spurs, cuffs, box lid title and character images.

Zorro, Hubley, Coyote, dragoon, 8-1/2 inch, engraved	100-150	150-200 w/ box or holster
•Zorro, Hubley, Pioneer, dragoon, 9-1/2 inch, caramel	150-175	200-250 w/ box or holster
•Zorro, Marx, 8 inch, derringer, die cast works	75-100	150 on Zorro card
•Zorro, Marx, 12-1/2 inch flintlock, die cast works	100-125	200 on Zorro Card
•Zorro, Hubley, double holsters, marked Zorro	100-150	200-250 w/ Hubley guns
•Zorro, Hubley, single holster set, marked Zorro	100-150	150-200 w/ Hubley gun
•Zorro, Daisy, Model #961 Rifle, stock graphics	200-250	250-300 w/ box
•Zorro, Daisy, Official Shooting Outfit	200-250	350-450 w all components
•Zorro, Italian, double holster set w/mask	150-200	250-300 w/ Hubley guns

With any Zorro outfits, the holsters marked "Zorro" and with Walt Disney markings are the most valuable. No "official" Zorro marked gun is known, however the "Daisy"-marked Zorro rifle along with Hubley "Zorro"-marked holsters came with Hubley Coyote, Pioneer and Texan Jr.'s, as well as the wrist cuffs, bullwhips, lariats, mask, and assorted Zorro memorabilia. Values are higher that show Zorro images, as well as Guy Williams as both Zorro and Don Diego on boxes and lid graphics.

BIBLIOGRAPHY AND SELECTED READING

If there is one thing I've learned in almost 30 years of working as a private detective, 13 years in the army, both active and reserves, and my 35 year fascination with America's Old West, it's that the more you read, the more you learn. Biographies, conspiracies, sensationalism, newspapers that ran the actions of the day, and the Hollywood slant all have to be thoroughly read. The reader must match the contents with other books and other author's accounts in order to draw a more concise conclusion to what actually happened and then separate fact from fiction. Investigative research is an art that takes many years to develop. The alternative, in my opinion, would be the same as watching the movie The Ten Commandments starring Charlton Heston and then saying you read the Bible. Notice that most of the books say "Life and Legend of. . ." and so it is incumbent upon the reader to read as many books on the subjects, from many diverse periods of time, since information seems to surface all the time which adds or takes away from the "life and the legend of". . . our favorite characters. Whenever I have been able to carry on correspondence with relatives and early authors of some of the actual historical figures, it also provided me with a more personal look at the character, even if it came without total objectivity. But then, what is "total objectivity?" For any writer to pick a certain subject over another begins to lean towards the opposite end of objectivity. Since I prefer the western over science fiction, for example, as much as I want to be "totally objective," I must confess that with me, the American West wins every time! I encourage the readers, especially the young readers who were not fortunate enough to have come along before the turbulent 1960s, to obtain, seek out, and read as many of these books and periodicals so that you can also come up with your own conclusion on these characters. It was, without any doubt, the movie and television westerns that spearheaded my drive to learn more about the real characters of the Old West. I sure worked hard and saved all my paper route money and bought many of the following books from the 1950s which I still own; however, all of them are easily available from your public libraries, and book search companies for the older and out of print books. Enjoy!

THE REAL WEST

Bakeless, John. *Daniel Boone, Master of the Wilderness.* New York: W. Morrow, 1939.

Baugh, Virgil E. *Rendezvous at the Alamo.* New York: Pageant Press, Inc., 1960.

Ball, Larry. *Elfego Baca in Life and Legend.* Texas Western Press, 1992.

Bartholomew, Ed. *Wild Bill Longley, a Texas Hard Case.* Houston: Frontier Press, 1953.

Bartholomew, Ed. *Biography of Western Gunfighters.* Frontier Book Company, 1958.

Bell, Bob Boze. *The Illustrated Life & Times of Wyatt Earp.* Boze Books, 1993.

Bell, Bob Boze. *The Illustrated Life & Times of Doc Holliday.* Tri-Star-Boze Books, 1993.

Beller, S. *Mosby and His Rangers.* Ingram Company, 1992.

Boyer, Glenn G. *Wyatt Earp's Tombstone Vendetta.* Thorndike, Maine: G.K. Hall, 1993.

Boyer, Glenn G. *Suppressed Murder of Wyatt Earp.* San Antonio: Naylor Company, 1967.

Breihan, Carl F. *The Complete and Authentic Life of Jesse James.* F. Fell Publishing, 1973.

Breihan, Carl F. *The Day Jesse James Was Killed.* F. Fell Publishing, 1961.

Burns, Walter Noble. *Tombstone, an Iliad of the Southwest.* Doubleday, Doran & Co., 1927.

Cody, William F. *The Life and Adventures of Buffalo Bill.* John R. Stanton & Co, 1917.

Cox, Mike. *Texas Ranger Tales: Stories that need Telling.* Republic of Texas Press, 1997.

Crichton, Kyle. *Law and Order: Elfego Baca.* Arno Press, 1974.

Dearment, Robert K. *Bat Masterson, The Life and The Legend.* University of Oklahoma Press, 1979.

Derr, Mark. *The Frontiersman: The Real Life and Many Legends of Davy Crockett.* William Morrow & Company, 1993.

Dillon, Richard. *The Legend of Grizzly Adams.* Coward-McCann Publishers, 1966.

Earp, Josephine Sarah Marcus. *I Married Wyatt Earp.* University of Arizona Press, 1976.

Erwin, Allen. *The Southwest of John H. Slaughter.* California: A.H. Clark Co., 1965.

Flynn, Jean. *Jim Bowie, a Texas Legend.* Sunbelt Media, 1980.

Garrett, Pat F. *The Authentic Life of Billy the Kid.* MacMillan & Company, 1927.

Hall, Holbrook Stuart. *Wild Bill Hickok Tames the West.* New York: Random House, 1952.

Harris, Larry A. *Pancho Villa: Strongman of the Revolution.* New Mexico: Hi Lonesome Books, 1996.

Havighurst, Walter. *Annie Oakley of the Wild West.* New York: MacMillan Company, 1954.

Hogan, Ray. *The Life and Death of Clay Allison.* Signet Books, 1961.

Horan, James D. *The Wild Bunch*. New York: New American Library, 1958.

Hunt, Frazier. *The Tragic Days of Billy the Kid*. Hastings House Publishers, 1956.

Jahns, Pat. *Frontier World of Doc Holliday*. University of Nebraska Press, 1979.

Jennewei, Leonard J. *Calamity Jane of the Western Trails*. Huron, South Dakota: Dakota Books, 1953.

Lake, Stuart N. *Wyatt Earp; Frontier Marshal*. Boston: Houghton Mifflin Company, 1931.

Lawliss, Chuck. *Civil War Sourcebook*. New York: Random House, 1991.

Lloyd, Everett. *Law West of The Pecos: The Story of Roy Bean*. Gaunt Publishers, 1996

Mackfaragher, John. *Daniel Boone: Life and Legend of an American Pioneer*. New York: Henry Holt and Company, 1992.

McCaffrey, Terry. Project Manager. *Legends of the West*, U.S. Postal Service, 1993.

Michelson, Charles. *Mankillers at Close Range*. Houston: Frontier Press, 1958.

Monaghan, Jay. *The Great Rascal, Ned Buntline*. Little, Brown & Company, 1952.

Mosby, John S. *The Gray Ghost: Memoirs of Col. John S. Mosby*. Indiana University Press, 1959.

Myers, John. *Doc Holliday*. Lincoln, Nebraska: University of Nebraska Press, 1955.

O'Brien, Steven. *Pancho Villa, Mexican Revolutionary*. Chelsea House Press, 1994.

Otero, Miguel. *Life on The Frontier*. Denver: Press of The Pioneers, 1935.

Reader's Digest Association. *American Folklore and Legend*. Pleasantville, N.Y., 1985.

Scanland, John Milton. *Life of Pat Garrett*. El Paso: Carleton F. Hodge, 1952.

Sell, Henry Blackman and Victor Weybright. *Buffalo Bill and the Wild West*. Signet, 1959.

Spinner, Stephanie. *Little Sure Shot; The Story of Annie Oakley*. Random Books, 1993.

Stanley, F. *Desperadoes of New Mexico*. Denver: The World Press, 1953.

Tilghman, Zoe A. *Marshal of the Last Frontier*. California: Arthur H. Clark Company, 1949.

Vestal, Stanley. *Dodge City: Queen of the Cowtowns*. Harper & Brothers, 1952.

Waters, William. *A Gallery of Western Gunfighters*. Kentucky: Americana Publications, 1954.

Wilstach, Frank J. *Wild Bill Hickok: Prince of the Pistoleers*. Garden City Publishing, 1926.

Winders, Gertrude Hecker. *Jim Bowie, Boy with a Hunting Knife*. Indianapolis: Bobbs-Merrill Co., 1961.

HOLLYWOOD AND THE "REEL" WEST:

Brooks, Tim and Earle Marsh. *The Complete Directory to Prime Time Network and Cable TV Show, 1946 to Present*, Sixth Edition. Ballantine Books Division of Random House, 1995.

Buscombe, Edward. *Companion to The Western*. DeCapo Press, 1988.

Hardy, Phil. The Western: *The Film Encyclopedia*. New York: William Morrow & Co., 1983.

Hofstede, David. *Hollywood Heroes: 30 Screen Legends*. Madison Books, 1994.

Jackson, Ronald. *Classic TV Westerns*. Citadel Press, Carol Publishing Group, 1994.

Jarvis, Everett G. *Final Curtain: Deaths of Noted Movie & TV Personalities*. Secaucus, New Jersey: Citadel Press, Carol Publishing Group, 1992.

Ketchum, Richard M. *Will Rogers, His Life and Times*. American Heritage Publishing, 1973.

McCully, Johnston. *The Mark of Zorro*. New York: Grosset & Dunlap Publishers, 1924.

Miller, Lee O. *The Great Cowboy Stars of Movies & Television*. Westport, Connecticut Arlington House Publishers.

Moore, Clayton with Frank Thompson. *I Was That Masked Man!*, Taylor Publishing Co., 1996.

Summers, Neil. *The Official TV Western Book*, 4 Volumes, 1987 to 1992, Old West Shop Publishing, Vienna, West Virginia

The Overlook Guide to Westerns: Silent Era to 1990s, by Overlook Press, 1994.

CAP GUNS AND WESTERN COLLECTIBLES:

Ball, Robert W.D. and Ed Vebell. *Cowboy Collectibles and Western Memorabilia*. Atglen, Pennsylvania: Schiffer Publishing, 1991.

Caro, Joe. *Hopalong Cassidy Collectibles*. California: Cowboy Collector Publications, California, 1997.

Hake, Ted and Robert D. Cauler. *Six-Gun Heroes*. Pennsylvania: Wallace-Homestead Book Company, 1976.

Hake, Ted. *Hake's Guide to Cowboy Character Collectibles*. Pennsylvania: Wallace-Homestead Books, 1996.

Logan, Samuel H. *Cast Iron Toy Guns & Capshooters*. Davis, California: Charles W. Best.

Nichols, Talley. *A Brief History of Nichols Industries (Toy Guns)*. Jacksonville, Texas, 1991.

O'Brien, Richard. *Collecting Toys, 7th Edition.* Florence, Alabama: Books Americana, 1995.

Overstreet, Robert M. *Comic Book Price Guide, 11th Edition.* New York: Harmony Books, 1982.

Phillips, Robert. *Roy Rogers: A Biography.* McFarland & Company, 1995.

Rinker, Harry L. *Hopalong Cassidy, King of the Cowboy Merchandisers.* Atglen, Pennsylvania: Schiffer Publishing Ltd, 1995.

Schleyer, Jim. *Backyard Buckaroos-Collecting Western Toy Guns.* Iola, Wisconsin: Krause Publications, 1996.

MAGAZINES, PERIODICALS, AND NEWSLETTERS:

Cowboy Collectors Network, Joe Caro, Quarterly Newsletter, Long Beach, California.

Frontier Times, 1956 to 1960, Western Publications, Austin, Texas.

Miller, Nyle H., Kansas State Historical Society Director. *Some Widely Publicized Western Police Officers,* 1958, written for the Nebraska Historical Society; Contains news articles of the Kansas cowtowns where Wyatt Earp, Bat Masterson, and Wild Bill Hickok lived and served as peace officers, attesting to their service records and actions performed.

Real West magazine, 4 Volumes, 1958 to 1961, Charlton Publications, Derby, Connecticut.

Time magazine, Volume LXXIII, No. 13, March 30, 1959.

Toy Gun Purveyor, by Jim Schleyer, 16 Volumes, 1989 to 1993, Burke, Virginia.

Toy Gun Collectors Association, Jim Buskirk, Quarterly Newsletter, San Mateo, California.

True West magazine, 1954 to 1960, Western Publications, Austin, Texas.

True Western Adventures, 1957 to 1959, Fawcett Publications, Greenwich, Connecticut.

TV and Movie Western magazine, 1958 to 1960, 2 Volumes, Monarch Magazines, New York.

TV Western Roundup, 1958, Skyline Features Syndicate, New York.

West, The, 1964, Western Periodicals, Inc., New York, New York.

PERSONAL CORRESPONDENCE:

Boyer, Glenn, Author and Wyatt Earp historian, New Mexico, 2 letters.

Breihan, Carl H. Writer and historian, author of Jesse James books, St. Louis, Missouri, 32 letters.

Buffalo, Chief Moses. Sioux chief, descendant of Sioux that fought in Custer's Last Stand, Sissiton, South Dakota, 3 letters.

James III, Jesse Lee. Grandson of Jesse James, Manitou Springs, Colorado, 9 letters.

Mack, Richard Lee Western writer and historian, Jesse James expert, Narka, Kansas, 39 letters.

Mills, Jack. Western writer, journalist, historian, Albuquerque, New Mexico, 7 letters.

Tilghman, Zoe A. Oklahoma City, Oklahoma, widow of famous marshal Bill Tilghman, friend of Wyatt Earp, Bat Masterson, and member of the Dodge City Peace Commission, 10 letters.

Waters, William. Writer and historian, author of Gallery of Western Badmen, Cleveland Heights, Ohio, 5 letters.

THE HOLLYWOOD CONNECTION:

Personal Letters, postcards and photographs from the following TV stars of the 1950-1965 era, both living and those that have passed away:

Ward Bond, Robert Horton, Clint Walker, Hugh O'Brien, Jock Mahoney, Richard Boone, Jeff York, Dale Robertson, Tom Tryon, Robert Loggia, William Boyd, Duncan Renaldo, Leo Carillo, Clayton Moore, Jay Silverheels, Henry Fonda, Dick West, Kent Taylor, James Garner, Jack Kelly, Fess Parker, Scott Forbes, Wayde Preston, Clint Eastwood, Eric Fleming, Gail Davis, Steve McQueen, Dennis Weaver, Gene Barry, John Russell, Jim L. Brown and Lee Aacker with Rin Tin Tin, James Arness, Michael Ansara, Mason Alan Dinehart III, John Payne, Pat Conway, Allen "Rocky" Lane, Gene Autry, George "Gabby" Hayes, Bill Williams, Tod Andrews, Lorne Greene, Pernell Roberts, Dan Blocker, Michael Landon, Guy Williams, and Roy Rogers.

Just saying "thanks, pardners" seems so redundant. To those on whom the "final curtain" has come down, I can only look back with fondness at the wonderful memories you have left with me through your work, and to those that are still with us, I wish you all the best for good health and many more years of memories.

INDEX

ABOUT THE AUTHOR

Rudy A. D'Angelo was born in Pratola Peligna, in the Abbruzzo region of Italy, in 1944 and came to the United States with his mother and younger brother in 1952. His father had already left Italy in 1947 to look for work and had come to the United States by way of Venezuela in 1950. The family settled in Hartford, Connecticut, where Rudy and his brother (and later, two sisters) attended public and parochial schools.

Rudy's love of history began early in life, and by the time he graduated Hartford Public High School, he had sailed throught five courses of it. A history and art major, he became interested in our nation's western history as he was exposed to growing up with the TV westerns in the 1950s and early 1960s, and playing with the very same cap guns that are the subject of this study. After service in the army, he returned to Connecticut, where he works as a private detective, his profession for the past 30 years. Always a collector of antique weapons and militaria, it was finding one of the many cap guns that he used to play with some 15 years ago, that sparked the wide-eyed youngster from within to start actively collecting, studying, and researching the cap guns and rifles.

"My parents gave me values, guidance, discipline, love, and plenty of cap guns to play with," recalled D'Angelo. "We were poor by today's standards, but I never knew it."

His love of TV westerns got him to write to the western stars of the 1950s and early 1960s, who sent him autographed photos, letters, and short film biographies, all of which Rudy cataloged, and painstakingly saved for the past 40 years. This book and the memories of his youth, his family, and the cap guns that are passionately collected today by many "kids" of the 1950s and 1960s is the culmination of a love affair and a dream he had harbored for decades. Rudy has one of the best and most complete collections of TV western character cap pistols and rifles in the country, but he is always looking for that elusive western character that has yet to surface.

As a military historian and writer, Mr. D'Angelo has collaborated on 23 books, and has written over 90 articles on military history, weapons, and militaria. He also writes on family, social issues, and the highs and lows of his profession as a free-lance writer for several papers and magazines. Mr. D'Angelo continues to reside in Connecticut.

1954 - HANDS UP!

Rudy, with his Roy Rogers cap gun, disarms Louy, who drops his Gene Autry cap gun (Note blur!!)

1960

Anna Maria, getting the drop on her brothers with the Fanner 50.

1956

Diana blasting away at her brothers with her Dale Evans cap pistol.

Antique Trader Books

we write the books on collectibles

{all kinds of collectibles}

Here are some of the books published by Antique Trader Books. For a complete list, please call 1-800-334-7165 and ask for a free catalog.

Star Wars Collectibles Price Guide • Stuart W. Wells III • AT5978 ....$26.95
Film & TV Animal Star Collectibles • Dana Cain • AT5986 ....$26.95
Signatures Of The Stars: Guide For Autograph Collectors, Dealers, and Enthusiasts • Kevin Martin • AT5935 ....$16.95
The Monkees Collectibles Price Guide • Marty Eck • AT5188 ....$21.95
The Beatles Memorabilia Price Guide, Third Edition • Jeff Augsburger, Marty Eck & Rick Rann • AT5684 ....$24.95
America's Standard Gauge Electric Trains • Peter H. Riddle • AT5226 ....$26.95
The Die Cast Price Guide, Post War: 1946 To Present • Douglas R. Kelly • AT5277 ....$26.95
Kiddie Meal Collectibles • Robert J. Sodaro and Alex G. Malloy • AT5161 ....$19.95
Comics Values Annual 1999 • Alex G. Malloy • AT5153...$16.95
Tuff Stuff's Baseball Memorabilia Price Guide • The Editors of Tuff Stuff • AT5242 ....$18.95
Mickey Mantle, The Yankee Years: The Classic Photography of Ozzie Sweet • AT5218............................$39.95
Antique Trader's Antiques & Collectibles Price Guide 1999 • Kyle Husfloen, Editor • AT1999..................$15.95
Petretti's Coca-Cola Collectibles Price Guide, 10th Edition • Allan Petretti • AT5765.............................$42.95
Classic Coca-Cola Serving Trays • Allan Petretti And Chris Beyer • AT2596..$32.95
Petretti's Soda Pop Collectibles Price Guide • Allan Petretti • AT5250 ....$26.95
The Matchcover Collector's Price Guide, 2nd Edition • Bill Retskin • AT5773 ....$21.95
The Bean Family Pocket Guide 1999, Values & Trends • Shawn Brecka • AT5560 ....$9.95
Composition & Wood Dolls And Toys: A Collector's Reference Guide • Michele Karl • AT5927 ....$29.95
Crissy® Doll and Her Friends • Beth Gunther • AT5714...$24.95
Contemporary Barbie® Dolls: 1980 And Beyond, 1998 Edition • Jane Sarasohn-Kahn • AT5846 ....$26.95
Modern Doll Rarities • Carla Marie Cross • AT5676 ....$24.95
Marionettes And String Puppets: Collector's Reference Guide • AT5943...$24.95
Maloney's Antiques & Collectibles Resource Directory, 4th Edition • David J. Maloney, Jr. • AT5870 ......$28.95
50 Years of Collectible Glass, 1920-1970: Easy Identification And Price Guide • Tom & Neila Bredehoft • AT2579 $26.95
Springfield Armory Shoulder Weapons, 1795-1968 • Robert W. D. Ball • AT5749 ....$34.95
American Military Collectibles Price Guide • Ron Manion • AT5471 ....$16.95
Japanese & Other Foreign Military Collectibles Price Guide • Ron Manion • AT5439 ....$16.95
German Military Collectibles Price Guide • Ron Manion • AT5447 ....$16.95

Published by Antique Trader Books

P.O. Box 1050 • Dubuque, IA • 52004-1050 • Credit Card Orders Call 1-800-334-7165
www.collect.com/atbooks
Sales Tax and Shipping and Handling Charges Apply